SOUTH-WESTERN
CENGAGE Learning™

PROMO
2011 Edition

Thomas C. O'Guinn, Chris T. Allen, and Richard J. Semenik

Executive Vice President and Publisher, Business & Computers: Jonathan Hulbert

Vice President of Editorial, Business: Jack W. Calhoun

Editor-in-Chief: Melissa S. Acuña

Director, 4LTR Press: Neil Marquardt

Executive Editor: Mike Roche

Developmental Editor: Julie Klooster

Project Manager, 4LTR Press: Steve Joos

Executive Brand Marketing Manager, 4LTR Press: Robin Lucas

Vice President of Marketing, Business & Computers: Bill Hendee

Marketing Coordinator: Shanna Shelton

Sr. Marketing Communications Manager: Sarah Greber

Content Project Manager: Darrell E. Frye

Media Editor: John Rich

Print Buyer: Miranda Klapper

Editorial Assistant: Kayti Purkiss

Production House: Integra Software Services Pvt. Ltd.

Sr. Art Director: Stacy Jenkins Shirley

Internal & Cover Designer: KeDesign, Mason, OH

Cover Image: ©Getty Images/FoodPix and iStock Photo

Sr. Image Acquisition Specialist: Deanna Ettinger

Photo Researcher: Susan Van Etten-Lawson.

Sr. Rights Acquisitions Specialist: Mardell Glinski Schultz

Text Permissions Researcher: Sue C. Howard

Library of Congress Control Number: 2010928243

Student Edition package ISBN-13: 978-0-538-47327-9
Student Edition package ISBN-10: 0-538-47327-4
Student Edition ISBN-13: 978-0-538-47328-6
Student Edition ISBN-10: 0-538-47328-2

South-Western Cengage Learning
5191 Natorp Boulevard
Mason, OH 45040
USA

Cengage Learning products are represented in Canada by Nelson Education, Ltd.

For your course and learning solutions, visit **www.cengage.com.**

Purchase any of our products at your local college store or at our preferred online store **www.cengagebrain.com.**

Printed in the United States of America
1 2 3 4 5 6 7 14 13 12 11 10

PROMO

| Brief Contents

Contents

Photo Courtesy, OmniTerra Images.

PART 1
THE PROCESS OF BRAND PROMOTION IN MARKETING

© EdBockStock/Shutterstock.

© Yuri Arcurs/Shutterstock.

© Andrew Lever/Shutterstock.

PART 2
UNDERSTANDING THE MARKET AND ENVIRONMENT FOR PROMOTING BRANDS

© Fotocrisis/Shutterstock.

5 Understanding Buyer Behavior and the Communication Process 86

© Monkey Business Images/Shutterstock.

6 The Regulatory and Ethical Environment of Promotions 112

© michaeljung/Shutterstock.

7 The International Market Environment for Brand Promotion 138

Courtesy, Sears Roebuck Company.

© Haywiremedia/Shutterstock.

© Sean Prior/Shutterstock.

© Gilian McGregor/Shutterstock.

© ifoto/Shutterstock.

© Rafael Ramirez Lee/Shutterstock.

© R. Gino Santa Maria/Shutterstock.

© Sean Prior/Shutterstock.

© Ronen/Shutterstock.

CHAPTER 1

The World of Integrated Marketing Communication

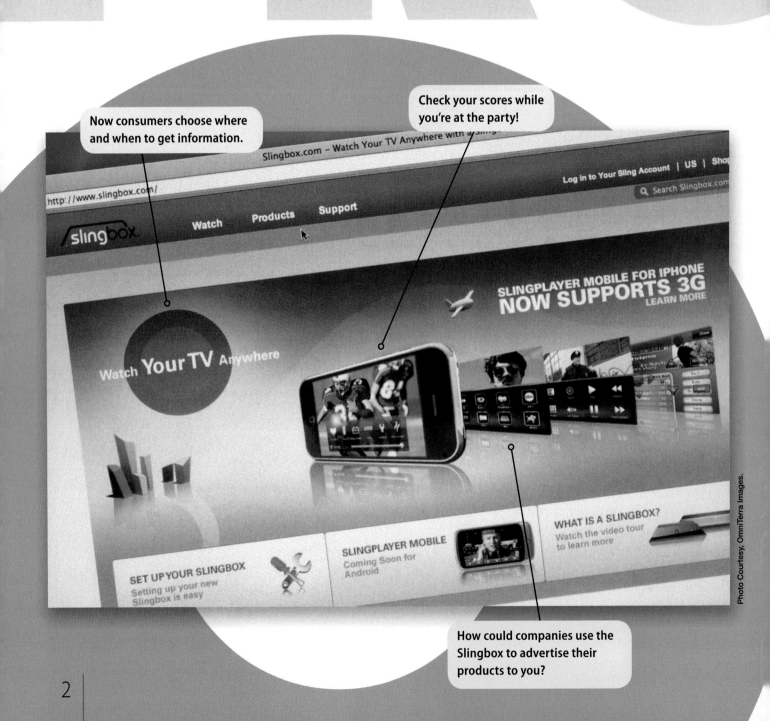

Photo Courtesy, OmniTerra Images.

> "Customers must recognize that you stand for something."
>
> —Howard Schultz

Sound Familiar?

It's a Friday night, and you just battled your way through an online quiz in Anthropology that had to be submitted by 11 PM, and you beat the deadline by a couple of hours. Feeling pretty good about the quiz (and suddenly having a little free time on Friday night), you check Facebook to see who's attending what parties and concerts that night. You notice that some friends you haven't seen for a while are having a party, so you text two of your buddies to ask if they want to hit the party. Then you click to the Ticketmaster website (www.ticketmaster.com) because the Red Hot Chili Peppers are coming to the big arena on campus (you signed up for the Ticketmaster "performer alert" service and got an email this afternoon) and you want to snag a couple of tickets as soon as possible. Your buddies text back and say they are up for the party and will be at your place in half an hour. Before they arrive, you have just enough time to download the new Deftones CD from Amazon (www.amazon.com) and set your Slingbox (www.slingmedia.com) so that you can check the NBA scores on SportsCenter from the Internet on your cell phone while you're at the party. (A Slingbox is a device that lets you access your television or TiVo from your computer or cell phone. Check out their ad on the opposite page.)

Does this scenario sound familiar? If you're into keeping up with your friends and your interests, then it probably does. And you and your friends represent a huge challenge for companies that want to reach you with their promotional messages. For the last 50 years, firms have primarily been using television, radio, newspapers, magazines, and other traditional media to send messages to consumers about the companies' brands. However, the imaginary "you" in this scenario encountered little, if *any*, mass media advertising, even though you bought concert

What do you think?

I'm in control when I see or hear advertising.

1   2   3   4   5   6   7
STRONGLY DISAGREE   STRONGLY AGREE

tickets and a CD and accessed television programming on the Internet. Instead, a whole series of individually controlled information sources let you access all the information *you* wanted to see—not just information some company wanted you to see or hear.[1]

So, what are companies going to do to reach you with messages about their products and brands? They will still try to reach you and every other consumer around the globe who is acquiring information in new ways. But rather than relying as much on the old style of mass media, companies are turning to a wide range of new promotional techniques that complement their mass media advertising.[2]

The New World of Integrated Marketing Communication

As the world of promotion undergoes enormous change, companies are trying to keep up with how and where consumers want to receive information about brands. While they have not abandoned mass media, marketers are supplementing and supporting traditional communication channels with new ways to reach consumers. Consumer preferences and new technology are reshaping the communication environment. The lines between information, entertainment, and commercial messages are blurring. As one analyst put it, "The line of demarcation was obliterated years ago, when they started naming ballparks after brands."[3] Companies are turning to branded entertainment, the Internet, influencer marketing, and other communication techniques to reach consumers and get their brand messages across. *Advertising Age* calls this new world of advertising "Madison and Vine," as Madison Avenue advertising agencies attempt to use Hollywood entertainment-industry techniques to communicate about their brands.[4]

But no matter how much technology changes or how many new media are available for delivering messages, it's still all about the brand. As consumers, we know what we like and want, and advertising—regardless of the method—helps expose us to brands that can meet our needs. Even Heinz ketchup—which, according to chief marketing officer Brian Hansberry, is "in every household" with "higher household penetration than salt and pepper"—has to remind consumers why they value it. Conversely, a brand that does *not* meet our needs will not succeed—no matter how much is spent on advertising or brand communication. That's a painful lesson U.S. automakers have learned over more than two decades of declining market share.

LO 1 Promotion via Integrated Marketing Communication

You see advertising every day, even if you try to avoid most of it. It's just about everywhere because it serves so many purposes. To the CEO of a multinational corporation, like Pepsi, advertising is an essential marketing tool that helps create brand awareness and brand loyalty. To the owner of a small retail shop, advertising is an invitation that brings people into the store. To a website manager, it's a tool to drive traffic to the URL.

While companies believe in and rely heavily on advertising, it is only a single technique in a bigger process, the marketing activity known as promotion. As a business process, promotion is relied on by companies big and small to build their brands—the central theme of this book. As we will show, successful marketers do more than pay for advertising and other promotional activities; they plan how to com-

CONSUMER PREFERENCES AND NEW TECHNOLOGY ARE RESHAPING THE COMMUNICATION ENVIRONMENT.

bine them to strengthen their brands. These efforts at promotion and integrated marketing communication are keys to building awareness and preference for brands.

Promotion

As described later in this chapter, marketing encompasses activities such as designing products, setting a price, making the products available to customers, and promoting them, the topic of this book. **Promotion** is the communications process in marketing that is used to create a favorable predisposition toward a brand of product or service, an idea, or even a person. Most often, it involves promotion for a brand of product or service.

Promotion includes planning and carrying out a variety of activities, selected from a wide range of possibilities. Together these activities for a brand form its **promotional mix**, a blend of communications tools used by a firm to carry out the promotion process and to communicate directly with audiences. Here is a list of the most prominent tools:

- Advertising in mass media (television, radio, newspapers, magazines, billboards)
- Sales promotions (coupons, premiums, discounts, gift cards, contests, samples, trial offers, rebates, frequent-user programs, trade shows)
- Point of purchase (in-store) advertising
- Direct marketing (catalogs, telemarketing, email offers, infomercials)
- Personal selling
- Internet advertising (banners, pop-ups/pop-unders, websites)
- Social media
- Blogs
- Podcasting
- Event sponsorships
- Branded entertainment (product placement in television programming, webcasts, video games, and films), also referred to as "advertainment"
- Outdoor signage
- Billboard, transit, and aerial advertising
- Public relations
- Influencer marketing (peer-to-peer persuasion)
- Corporate advertising

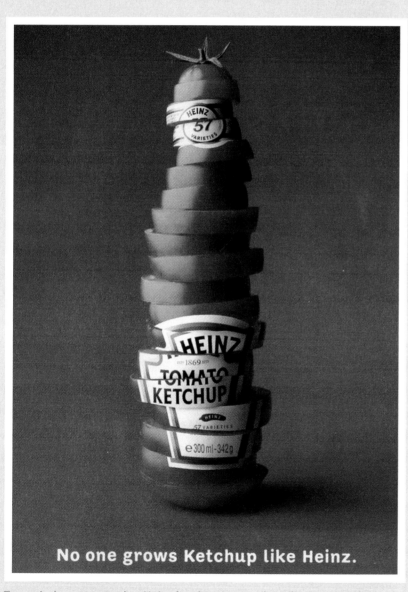

Courtesy, Advertising Archives.

No one grows Ketchup like Heinz.

To remind consumers that Heinz ketchup is a product the company has "cared for from seed to plate," the company's advertising combines the "No one grows Ketchup like Heinz" slogan with images of fresh tomatoes.[5]

advertising a paid, mass-mediated attempt to persuade

client or **sponsor** the organization that pays for advertising

Notice that this list includes various types of advertising, one of the most widely used promotional tools. Simply defined, **advertising** is a paid, mass-mediated attempt to persuade. This definition is loaded with distinctions.

First, advertising is *paid* communication by a company or organization that wants its information disseminated (see Exhibit 1.1). In advertising language, the company or organization that pays for advertising is called the **client** or **sponsor**. If a communication is *not paid for*, it's not advertising. *Publicity* is not advertising because it is not paid for. For the same reason, public service announcements (PSAs) are not advertising either, even though they look and sound like ads.

Second, advertising is *mass mediated*. This means it is delivered through a communication medium designed to reach more than one person, typically a large number—or mass—of people. Advertising is widely disseminated through traditional and new media:

- Television
- Radio
- Newspapers
- Magazines
- Direct mail
- Billboards
- Websites
- Podcasts

The mass-mediated nature of advertising creates a communication environment where the message is not delivered face to face. This distinguishes advertising from *personal selling* as a form of communication.

Third, all advertising includes an *attempt to persuade*. Put bluntly, ads are designed to get someone to do something. The ad informs the consumer for some purpose and that purpose is to get the consumer to like the brand and, because of that liking, to eventually buy the brand.

Integrated Marketing Communication

Imagine how much more impact a promotional effort can have if ads, salespeople, point-of-purchase signs, and other communications send a consistent message, rather than work independently. Beginning in about 1990, many marketers embraced the concept of *integrated marketing communication (IMC)*. IMC attempts to coordinate promotional efforts so that messages are synergistic. But the reality of promotional strategies in the 21st century demands that the emphasis on *communication* give way to an emphasis on the *brand*. Recent research and publications on IMC are recognizing that, in effective marketing communications, the brand plays a central role.[6]

Exhibit 1.1
Is It an Ad?

What You See	Advertisement?
Will Smith appears on the *Late Show with David Letterman* to promote his newest movie.	**No**, it's publicity. The producer or film studio did not pay the *Late Show with David Letterman* for airtime. Rather, the show gets an interesting and popular guest, the guest star gets exposure, and the film gets plugged.
A film studio produces and runs ads on television and in newspapers for the newest Will Smith movie.	**Yes**. This communication is paid for by the studio and placed in media to reach consumers.
Trojan pays for print media to run a message that tells readers to "Get Real" and use a condom.	**Yes**. Trojan paid the print media to run an ad intended to increase demand for condoms, including Trojan condoms.
The United Kingdom's Health Education Authority prepares a message that urges readers to wear a condom; print media run the message.	**No**, it's a public service announcement. It is not paid for by an advertiser but offered in the public interest.

As a result, marketers have begun using a brand-oriented approach: **integrated marketing communication (IMC)**, defined as the process of using a wide range of promotional tools working together to create widespread brand exposure. IMC retains the goal of coordination and synergy of communication, but the emphasis is on the brand, not just the communication. With a focus on building brand awareness, identity, and ultimately preference, the IMC perspective recognizes that coordinated promotional messages need to have brand-building effects in addition to their communication effects.

Just as the definition of promotion was loaded with meaning, so too is the definition of integrated marketing communication. First, IMC is a *process*. It has to be. It is complicated and needs to be managed in an integrated fashion.

Second, IMC uses a *wide range of promotional tools* that have to be evaluated and scheduled. These communications tools, listed in the description of the promotional mix, include advertising, direct marketing, sales promotion, event sponsorships, point-of-purchase displays, public relations, and personal selling. In IMC, all of these varied and wide-ranging tools allow a marketer to reach target customers in different ways with different kinds of messages to achieve broad exposure for a brand.

Third, the definition of IMC highlights that all of these tools need to *work together*. That is, they need to be integrated to create a consistent and compelling impression of the brand. Having mass media advertising send one message and create one image and then having personal selling deliver another message will confuse consumers about the brand's meaning and relevance.

Finally, the definition of IMC specifies that all of the promotional efforts undertaken by a firm are designed to create *widespread exposure for a brand*. Unless consumers are reached by these various forms of messages, they will have a difficult time understanding the brand and deciding whether to use it regularly.

Advertising in IMC

As we noted, advertising is the most-used tool in the promotion mix, so IMC often relies heavily on advertising. An advertising plan combines advertisements in an advertising campaign. An **advertisement** refers to a specific message that someone or some organization has placed to persuade an audience. An **advertising campaign** is a series of coordinated advertisements that communicate a reasonably cohesive and integrated theme. The theme may be made up of several claims or points but should advance an essentially singular theme. Successful advertising campaigns can be developed around a single advertisement placed in multiple media, or, like the ads for Altoids shown on the next page, they can be made up of several different advertisements with a similar look, feel, and message. Advertising campaigns can run for a few weeks or for many years.

The advertising campaign is, in many ways, the most challenging aspect of advertising execution. It requires a keen sense of the complex environments within which a company must communicate to different audiences. One factor is that audience members have been accumulating knowledge from previous ads for a particular brand. Consumers interpret new ads through their experiences with a brand and previous ads for the brand. Even ads for a new brand or a new product are situated within audiences' broader knowledge of products, brands, and advertising. After years of viewing ads and buying brands, audiences bring a rich history and knowledge base to every communications encounter.

When marketers combine advertising campaigns with other promotional tools such as contests, a website, event sponsorship, and point-of-purchase displays, all aimed at building and maintaining brand awareness, they are using integrated marketing communication. BMW did just that when the firm (re)introduced the Mini Cooper automobile to the U.S. market. The IMC campaign used billboards, print ads, an interactive website, and "guerrilla" marketing (a Mini was mounted on top of a Chevy Suburban and driven around New York City). Each part of the campaign was coordinated with all the others.[7] Without coordination among these various promotional efforts, the consumer will merely encounter a series of unrelated (and often confusing) communications about a brand.

As consumers encounter a daily blitz of commercial messages and appeals, brands and brand identity offer them a way to cope with the overload of information. Brands and the images they project allow consumers to quickly identify and evaluate the relevance of a brand to their lives and value systems. The marketer who does not use IMC as a way to build brand exposure and meaning for consumers will, frankly, be ignored.

integrated marketing communication (IMC) the use of a wide range of promotional tools working together to create widespread brand exposure

advertisement a specific message that an organization has placed to persuade an audience

advertising campaign a series of coordinated promotional efforts, including advertisements, that communicate a single theme or idea

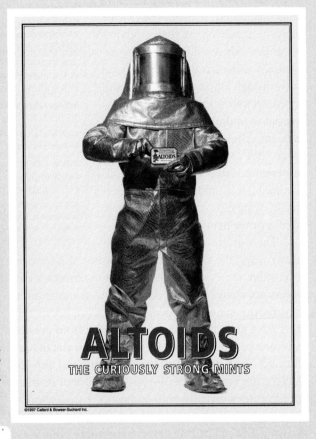

Notice the similar look and feel in this well-connected and well-executed advertising campaign.

LO 2 Mass-Mediated Communication

Promotion occurs through various forms of communication, and advertising is a particular type: mass-mediated communication (meaning it occurs not face to face but through a medium, such as magazines or the Internet). Therefore, to understand promotion, you must understand something about communication in general and about mass communication in particular. To help with gaining this understanding, let's consider a contemporary model of mass communication.

While there are many valuable models, Exhibit 1.2 presents a contemporary model of mass-mediated communication. This model shows mass communication as a process where people, institutions, and messages interact. It has two major components, each representing quasi-independent processes: *production* and *reception*. Between these are the mediating (interpretation) processes of *accommodation* and *negotiation*.

Production of the Content

Moving from left to right in the model, the first element is the process of communication production, where the content of any mass communication is produced. An advertisement, like other forms of mass communication, is the product of institutions (such as networks, corporations, advertising agencies, and governments) interacting to produce content (for example, what you watch on television or read in a magazine). The creation of the advertisement is a complex interaction of several variables:

- The company's message

- The company's expectations about the target audience's desire for information

- The company's assumptions about how the audience will interpret the words and images in an ad

- The rules and regulations of the medium that transmits the message

Advertising is rarely (if ever) the product of any one individual. Rather, it is a collaborative (social) product between people receiving a message and the institutions (companies and media companies) that send them that message.

Accommodation, Negotiation, and Reception

Continuing to the right in the model, the mediating processes of accommodation and negotiation lie between the production and reception phases. Accommodation and negotiation are the ways in which consumers interpret ads. Audience members have some ideas about how the company wants them to interpret the ad (we all know the rules of advertising—somebody is trying to persuade us to buy something). And consumers also have their own needs, agendas, and preferred interpretations. They also know about the way other consumers think about this product and this message because brands have personalities and send social signals. Given all this, consumers who see an ad arrive at an interpretation of the ad that makes sense to them, serves their needs, and fits their personal history with a product category and a brand.

This whole progression of consumer receipt and interpretation of a communication is usually wholly incompatible with the way the company wants consumers to see an ad! In other words, the receivers of the communication must *accommodate* these competing forces, meanings, and agendas and then *negotiate* a meaning, or an interpretation, of the ad. That's what makes communication an inherently *social* process: What a message means to any given consumer is a function not of an isolated solitary thinker but of an inherently social being responding to what he or she knows about the producers of the message (the companies), other receivers of it (peer groups, for example), and the social world in which the brand and the message about it resides. This interpretation happens very fast and without much contemplation, but it does happen. The level of conscious interpretation might be minimal (mere recognition) or it might be extensive (thoughtful, elaborate processing of an ad), but there is *always* interpretation.

Limits of Mass-Mediated Communication

The processes of production and reception are partially independent. Although the producers of a message can control the placement of a message in a medium, they cannot control or even closely monitor the circumstances that surround reception and interpretation of the ad. Audience members are exposed to advertising outside the direct observation of the company and are capable of interpreting advertising any way they want. (Of course, most audience interpretations are not completely off the wall, either.) Likewise, audience members have little control over or input into the actual production of the message—the company developed a message that audience members are *supposed* to like. As a result, producers and receivers are "imagined," in the sense that the two don't have significant direct contact with each other but have a general sense of what the other is like.

Exhibit 1.2
Mass-Mediated Communication

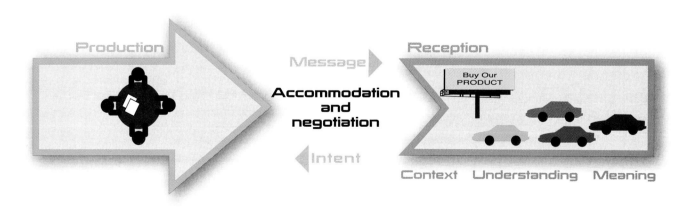

audience a group of individuals who may receive and interpret promotional messages

target audience a particular group of consumers singled out for an advertising or promotion campaign

household consumers the most conspicuous audience for advertising

members of business organizations advertising audience that buys business and industrial goods and services

members of a trade channel advertising audience that includes retailers, wholesalers, and distributors

professionals advertising audience that includes workers with special training or certification

The communication model in Exhibit 1.2 underscores a critical point: No ad contains a single meaning for all audience members. An ad for a pair of women's shoes means something different for women than it does for men. Nevertheless, although individual audience members' interpretations will differ to some extent, they may be close enough to the company's intent to make the ad effective. When members of an audience are similar in their background, social standing, and goals, they generally yield similar enough meaning from an ad for it to accomplish its goals.

LO 3 Audiences for Promotion

In the language of promotion, an **audience** is a group of individuals who receive and interpret advertisements and other promotional messages sent from companies. The audience could be made up of household consumers, college students, or businesspeople. Any large group of people can be an audience.

A **target audience** is a particular group of consumers singled out by an organization for an advertising campaign or promotion strategy. These target audiences are singled out because the firm has discovered that audience members like or might like the product category. Target audiences are always *potential* audiences because a company can never be sure that the message will actually get through to them as intended.

Audience Categories

While companies can identify dozens of different target audiences, five broad audience categories are commonly described:

- **Household consumers** are the most conspicuous audience in that most mass media advertising is directed at them. McDonald's and State Farm have products

and services designed for the consumer market, so their advertising targets household consumers. In the approximately 111 million U.S. households, there are about 300 million household consumers.[8] Total yearly retail spending by these households is about $5 trillion in the United States.[9] This huge audience is typically where the action is in advertising. Under the very broad heading of "consumer advertising," companies can make very fine audience distinctions—for example, men aged 25 to 45, living in metropolitan areas, with incomes greater than $50,000 per year.

- **Members of business organizations** are the focus of advertising for firms that produce business and industrial goods and services, such as office equipment and data storage. While products and services targeted to this audience often require personal selling, advertising is used to create awareness and a favorable attitude among potential buyers. Not-for-profit organizations such as universities, some research laboratories, philanthropic groups, and cultural organizations represent an important and separate business audience for advertising.

- **Members of a trade channel** include retailers (like Best Buy for consumer electronics), wholesalers (like Castle Wholesalers for construction tools), and distributors (like Sysco Food Services for restaurant supplies). They are a target audience for producers of both household and business goods and services. In the case of household goods, for example, Microsoft needs adequate retail and wholesale distribution through trade channels for the Xbox or else the brand will not reach target customers. The promotional tool used most often to communicate with this group is personal selling because this target audience represents a relatively small, easily identifiable group. When advertising also is directed at this target audience, it can serve an extremely useful purpose, as we will see later in the section on IMC as a business process.

- **Professionals** form a special target audience defined as doctors, lawyers, accountants, teachers, or any other professional group that has special training or certification. This audience warrants a separate classification because its members have specialized needs and interests. Promotional efforts directed to professionals typically highlight products and services uniquely designed to serve their more narrowly defined needs. The language and images used in promoting to this target audience often rely on esoteric terminology and unique circumstances that members of professions readily recognize. Advertising to professionals is predominantly carried out through trade publications. **Trade journals** are magazines published specifically for members of a trade and carry highly technical articles.

- **Government officials and employees** constitute an audience in themselves due to the large dollar volume of buying that federal, state, and local governments do. Government organizations from universities to road maintenance operations buy huge amounts of various types of products. Producers of items such as office furniture, construction materials, and business services all target government organizations. Promotion to this target audience is dominated by direct mail, catalogs, and web advertising.

Audience Geography

Audiences for promotional messages also can be broken down by geographic location. Because of cultural differences that often accompany geographic location, very few messages can be effective for all consumers worldwide, and many are directed to one of the more limited geographic areas:

- **Global promotion** involves messages used worldwide with only minor changes. The few messages that can use global promotion are typically for brands that are considered citizens of the world and whose manner of use does not vary tremendously by culture. Using a Sony television or taking a trip on Singapore Airlines doesn't change much from culture to culture or from geographic location to geographic location. Firms that market brands with global appeal try to develop and place messages with a common theme and presentation in all markets around the world where the firm's brands are sold. Thus, global placement is possible only when a brand and the messages about that brand have a common appeal across cultures.

- **International promotion** occurs when firms prepare and place different messages in different national markets outside their home market. Often, each international market requires unique or original promotion due to product adaptations or message appeals tailored specifically for that market. Unilever prepares different

trade journals
magazines that publish technical articles for members of a trade

government officials and employees advertising audience that includes employees of government organizations at the federal, state, and local levels

global promotion
developing and placing messages with a common theme and presentation in all markets around the world where the brand is sold

international promotion preparation and placement of messages in different national and cultural markets

© Zurijeta/Shutterstock.

GLOBAL WHERE A WORD IS WORTH A THOUSAND PICTURES

When Chase Design Group agreed to develop advertising for a store selling women's lingerie, it accepted a huge challenge. The store, Al Mashat, is located in Saudi Arabia, where the law prohibits showing photographs of women. Chase Design found a creative solution. Its ad campaign relied on "language that was rich, textured, layered, and sensual," printed in a specially designed font. Along with print and radio ads, the promotional effort included a direct-mail piece featuring bags imprinted with the store logo and filled with potpourri and an invitation printed on iridescent pearl-colored paper. In Al Mashat's first year, revenues topped $3.2 million.

Source: Arundhati Parmar, "Out from Under," *Marketing News*, July 21, 2003.

versions of messages for its laundry products for nearly every international market because consumers in different cultures approach the laundry task differently. Consumers in the United States use large and powerful washers and dryers and a lot of hot water. Households in Brazil use very little hot water and hang clothes out to dry.

- **National promotion** reaches all geographic areas of one nation. It is the kind of promotion we see most often in the mass media in the U.S. market. As the box highlights, national promotion is appropriate where a product category or promotional effort must be tailored to the unique situation of a particular culture. Organizations that promote their brand in several nations may combine different national-promotion efforts to engage in international promotion.

- **Regional promotion** is carried out by producers, wholesalers, distributors, and retailers that concentrate their efforts in a relatively large, but not national, geographic region. Albertson's, a regional grocery chain, has stores in 31 Western, Northwestern, Midwestern, and Southern states. Because of the nature of the firm's markets, it places messages only in regions where it has stores.

- **Local promotion**, much like regional promotion, is directed at an audience in a single trading area, either a city or state. For example, Daffy's is a discount clothing retailer with stores in the New York/New Jersey metropolitan area, and it uses local promotion to reach that market. Retailers like Daffy's use all types of local media to reach customers.

- **Cooperative promotion** (or **co-op promotion**) is a team approach to promotion in which national companies share promotion expenses in a market with local dealers to achieve specific objectives. For example, TUMI luggage and one of its retailers, Shapiro, have run co-op promotions that describe the benefits of TUMI's Safecase briefcase for carrying a laptop computer and also indicate that this product is available at Shapiro stores. If consumers respond by visiting Shapiro to buy the Safecase, then both promoters benefit.

LO 4 IMC as a Business Process

Besides being a communication process, promotion—especially in the context of integrated marketing communication (IMC)—is very much a business process, too. For multinational organizations like Microsoft, as well as for small local retailers, promotion within the framework of IMC is a basic business tool that is essential to retaining current customers and attracting new customers.

IMC in Marketing

Every organization *must* make marketing decisions. There simply is no escaping the need to develop brands, price them, distribute them, and advertise and promote them to a target audience. As organizations carry out these activities, IMC helps them do so in a way that achieves profitability and other goals.

Daffy's, a clothing retailer with several shops in the New York/New Jersey metropolitan area, services a local geographic market, so it communicates through local advertising.

WHEN A CLOTHING STORE HAS A SALE ON SELECTED MERCHANDISE, WHY IS IT ALWAYS MERCHANDISE YOU'D NEVER SELECT?

At Daffy's you'll find 40-70% off all our clothes, every day. 5th Ave. & 18th St., Madison Ave. & 44th St.

DAFFY'S
CLOTHES THAT WILL MAKE YOU, NOT BREAK YOU.™

Courtesy of Daffy's.

Exhibit 1.3
The Marketing Mix

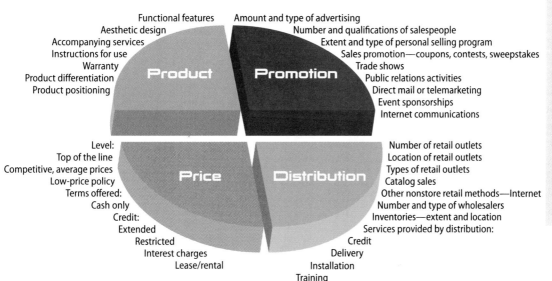

Product
- Functional features
- Aesthetic design
- Accompanying services
- Instructions for use
- Warranty
- Product differentiation
- Product positioning

Promotion
- Amount and type of advertising
- Number and qualifications of salespeople
- Extent and type of personal selling program
- Sales promotion—coupons, contests, sweepstakes
- Trade shows
- Public relations activities
- Direct mail or telemarketing
- Event sponsorships
- Internet communications

Price
- Level:
- Top of the line
- Competitive, average prices
- Low-price policy
- Terms offered:
- Cash only
- Credit:
- Extended
- Restricted
- Interest charges
- Lease/rental

Distribution
- Number of retail outlets
- Location of retail outlets
- Types of retail outlets
- Catalog sales
- Other nonstore retail methods—Internet
- Number and type of wholesalers
- Inventories—extent and location
- Services provided by distribution:
- Credit
- Delivery
- Installation
- Training

marketing the process of conceiving, pricing, promoting, and distributing ideas, goods, and services to create exchanges that benefit customers and companies

marketing mix the blend of the four responsibilities of marketing (conception, pricing, promotion, and distribution) used for a particular idea, product, or service

brand a name, term, sign, symbol, or any other feature that identifies one seller's good or service as distinct from those of other sellers

Promotion in the Marketing Mix

A formal definition of marketing reveals that promotion is one of the primary marketing tools available to any organization: "**Marketing** is the process of planning and executing the conception, pricing, promotion, and distribution of ideas, goods, and services to create exchanges that satisfy individual and organizational objectives."[10]

Marketing people assume a wide range of responsibilities in an organization related to conceiving, pricing, promoting, and distributing goods, services, and even ideas. These four areas of responsibility and decision making in marketing are referred to as the **marketing mix**. The word *mix* is used to describe the blend of strategic emphasis on the product versus its price versus its promotion versus its distribution when a brand is marketed to consumers. This blend, or mix, results in the overall marketing program for a brand.

Exhibit 1.3 identifies factors typically considered in each area of the marketing mix. Decisions under each of the marketing mix areas can directly affect promotional messages. Thus, a firm's promotional effort must be consistent with and complement the overall marketing mix strategy. As we saw earlier, IMC is a process that helps companies meet that objective, with an eye toward strengthening their brands.

Looking specifically at promotional tools such as advertising, the role of IMC in the marketing mix is to communicate to a target audience the *value* a brand has to offer. Value consists of more than simply the tangible aspects of the brand itself. Indeed, consumers look for value in the brand, but they also demand such benefits as convenient location, credit terms, warranties and guarantees, and delivery. In addition, consumers may look for brands that satisfy a wide range of emotional values such as security, belonging, affiliation, excitement, and prestige. Think about the fact that a $14,000 Ford Focus can get you from one place to another in pretty much the same way as a $120,000 BMW M5. Emotionally, however, driving the BMW would deliver something extra—more thrill and style. People look for more than function in a brand; they often buy the emotional kick that a brand and its features provide.

Because consumers search for such diverse values, marketers must determine which marketing mix ingredients to emphasize and how to blend the mix elements in just the right way to attract customers. These marketing mix decisions play a significant role in determining the message content and media placement of advertising and other brand-related messages.

Supporting Brand Management

When embedded in IMC, promotion plays a critical role in brand development and management. To appreciate its role, we need a formal understanding of what a brand is. A **brand** is a name, term, sign, symbol, or any other feature that identifies one seller's good or service as distinct from those of other sellers.[11] A brand is in many ways the most precious business

brand extension an adaptation of an existing brand to a new product area

asset owned by a firm. It allows a firm to communicate consistently and efficiently with the market.

Business Week magazine in conjunction with Interbrand, a marketing analysis and consulting firm, has attached a dollar value to brand names based on a combination of sales, earnings, future sales potential, and intangibles other than the brand that drive sales. Often, the brand name is worth much more than the annual sales of the brand. In a recent year, Coca-Cola was identified as the most valuable brand in the world, with an estimated worth of about $65 billion, even though sales of branded Coca-Cola products were only about $20 billion that year.[12]

Lack of effective marketing communication can leave a brand at a serious competitive disadvantage. Staples, the office supply retailer, was struggling with an outdated advertising campaign featuring the tagline "Yeah, we've got that." Customers were complaining that items were out of stock and sales staff didn't care. So the company's vice president of marketing, Shira Goodman, determined that shoppers wanted an "easier" shopping experience with well-stocked shelves and helpful staff. Once those operational changes were made, Staples introduced the "Staples: That Was Easy" campaign, featuring big red "Easy" buttons that were available for sale at the stores. Clear, straightforward ads and customers spreading the word (called "viral" marketing) by wearing their "Easy" buttons in offices all over the country helped make Staples the runaway leader in office retail.[13]

For every organization, promotion supports brand development and management in five important ways:

1. **Information and persuasion**. Target audiences learn about a brand's features and benefits through the message content of advertising and, to a lesser extent,

THE CREST BRAND WAS ORIGINALLY ASSOCIATED WITH TOOTHPASTE; ADVERTISING HELPED THE COMPANY EXTEND THE BRAND TO THIS LINE OF TOOTHBRUSHES. HOW DID THE CREST NAME HELP WITH BRAND EXTENSION?

other promotional tools used in the IMC effort. Advertising has the best capability to inform or persuade target audiences about the values a brand has to offer. No other variable in the marketing mix is designed to accomplish this communication. Branding is crucial to the multibillion-dollar cell phone market as Verizon, Sprint Nextel, T-Mobile, and AT&T compete for 250 million wireless subscribers.[14] Marketing a cellular-service brand helps consumers distinguish why they should choose a particular service provider when the decision is complex and several providers offer essentially the same product.

2. **Introduction of new brands or brand extensions**. Advertising is absolutely critical when organizations introduce a new brand or extensions of existing brands to the market. A **brand extension** is an adaptation of an existing brand to a new product area. For example, the Snickers Ice Cream Bar is a brand extension of the original Snickers candy bar. When brand extensions are brought to market, advertising attracts attention to the brand—so much so that researchers now suggest that "managers should favor the brand extension with a greater allocation of the ad budget."[15] In IMC, the advertising campaign works in conjunction with other promotional activities such as sales promotions and

A BRAND IS IN MANY WAYS THE MOST PRECIOUS BUSINESS ASSET OWNED BY A FIRM.

point-of-purchase displays. Mars (famous for candy) invested heavily in advertising when it extended the Uncle Ben's Rice brand into ready-to-eat microwave Rice Bowls of all varieties, including Italian, Mexican, and Chinese.[16]

3. **Building and maintaining brand loyalty**. One of the most important assets a firm can have is **brand loyalty**, which occurs when a consumer repeatedly purchases the same brand to the exclusion of competitors' brands. This loyalty can result because of habit, the prominence of a brand in the consumer's memory, barely conscious associations with brand images, or the attachment of some fairly deep meanings to a brand. The most important influence on building and maintaining brand loyalty is a brand's features, but promotion also plays a key role in the process by reminding consumers of the brand's values—tangible and intangible. Promotions such as frequent-buyer programs can give customers an extra incentive to remain brand loyal. When a firm creates and maintains positive associations with the brand in the minds of consumers, the firm has developed **brand equity**.[17] While development of brand equity occurs over long periods of time, short-term advertising activities are key to long-term success.[18] For example, Kraft defended its Miracle Whip brand against a new campaign by competitor Unilever for Imperial Whip by investing heavily in television advertising just before Unilever lowered prices on the Imperial Whip brand.[19]

4. **Creating an image and meaning for a brand**. Because advertising can communicate how a brand addresses certain needs and desires, it plays an important role in attracting customers to brands that appear to be useful and satisfying. But advertising can go further. It can help link a brand's image and meaning to a consumer's social environment and to the larger culture, and in this way, it actually delivers a sense of personal connection for the consumer. To advertise its prenatal vitamins, Schiff communicates with ads whose message is about love, not just the health advantages of using a nutritional supplement during pregnancy.

5. **Building and maintaining brand loyalty in the trade**. You might expect wholesalers, retailers, distributors, and brokers to be too practical to be brand loyal, but they will favor one brand over others given the proper support from a manufacturer. Advertising, particularly when integrated with other brand promotions, is an area where support is welcome. Marketers can provide the trade with sales training programs, collateral advertising materials, point-of-purchase advertising displays, premiums (giveaways like key chains or caps), and traffic-building special events. These promotional efforts are important because trade buyers can be a key to the success of new brands or brand extensions. To introduce a brand, marketers depend on cooperation among wholesalers and retailers in the trade channel. Research also shows that retailer acceptance of a brand extension is key to the success of the new product.[20] IMC is essential because the trade is less responsive to advertising messages than to other forms of promotion, such as displays, contests, and personal selling.

Implementing Market Segmentation, Differentiation, and Positioning

The third role for IMC in marketing is helping the firm implement market segmentation, differentiation, and positioning. **Market segmentation** is the process of breaking down a large, widely varied (heterogeneous) market into submarkets, or segments, that are more similar (homogeneous) than dissimilar in

brand loyalty
decision-making mode in which consumers repeatedly buy the same brand to fulfill a specific need

brand equity positive associations with a brand in the minds of consumers

market segmentation
breaking down a large, heterogeneous market into submarkets that are more homogeneous

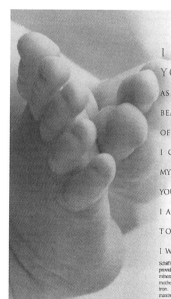

I HAVE LOVED YOU ALWAYS.
AS AN IDEA, A HEARTBEAT, A FUZZY IMAGE OF TEN PERFECT TOES. I CARRY YOU UNDER MY HEART. I WILL TEACH YOU ALL THAT I KNOW. I AM STRONG ENOUGH TO FEED US BOTH. I WILL LEARN LULLABIES.

Schiff's New Beginning Prenatal Multivitamin provides 100% of 12 essential vitamins and minerals needed by expectant and lactating mothers, including folic acid, calcium and iron. Its balanced formula delivers the maximum benefits to you and your baby.

Benefits Beyond Your Daily Requirements.

Weider Nutrition International Copyright © 1995.

The message mines associations related to love and caring for an unborn or recently born child. Even the slogan for the brand, "Benefits Beyond Your Daily Requirements," plays on the notion that a vitamin is more than a vehicle for dosing up on folic acid. What meanings do you find in this message?

terms of what the consumer is looking for. Underlying the strategy of market segmentation are two variables: consumers differ in their wants and the wants of one person can differ under various circumstances. Thus, the market for automobiles can be divided into submarkets for different types of automobiles based on the needs and desires of various groups of buyers. Identifying those groups, or segments, of the population who want and will buy large or small, luxury or economy models is an important part of basic marketing strategy. In addition to needs, markets are often segmented on characteristics of consumers such as age, marital status, gender, and income. For example, Bayer has four different versions of its basic aspirin brand: regular Bayer for headache relief; Bayer Enteric Safety Coated 81 mg aspirin for people with cholesterol and heart concerns; Women's Bayer, which includes a calcium supplement; and Children's Bayer, which is lower dose and chewable. The role of IMC in market segmentation is to develop messages that appeal to the wants and desires of different segments and then to transmit those messages via appropriate media.

Differentiation is the process of creating a perceived difference, in the mind of the consumer, between an organization's brand and the competition's. This definition emphasizes that brand differentiation is based on *consumer perception*. Perceived differences can be tangible features or related to image or style. A $20 Timex and a $12,000 Fendi watch tell you the same time of day, but the consumers who pay extra for a Fendi are looking for a different degree of style and the experience of making a fashion statement or impressing a gift recipient with a prestigious brand. The differentiation works only if consumers *perceive* a difference between brands. Differentiation is one of the most critical of all marketing strategies. Perceiving a firm's brand as distinctive and attractive gives consumers a reason to choose that brand over a competitor or to pay more for the "better" or "more meaningful" brand. Advertising can help create

a difference in the mind of the consumer between an organization's brand and its competitors' brands. To do this, the ad may emphasize performance features or create a distinctive image for the brand. Either way, the goal is to develop a message that is different and unmistakably linked to the organization's brand.

Positioning is the process of designing a brand so that it can occupy a distinct and valued place in the target consumer's mind relative to other brands and then communicating this distinctiveness through advertising. Positioning, like differentiation, depends on a perceived image of tangible or intangible features. Consumers create a *perceptual space* in their minds for all the brands they might consider purchasing. A perceptual space describes how one brand is seen on any number of dimensions—such as quality, taste, price, or social display value—in relation to those same dimensions for other brands.

There are two positioning decisions for a brand:

1. **External position**—the niche the brand will pursue relative to all the competitive brands on the market.

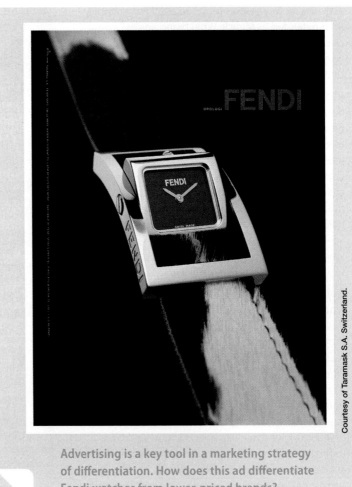

Courtesy of Taramask S.A. Switzerland.

Advertising is a key tool in a marketing strategy of differentiation. How does this ad differentiate Fendi watches from lower-priced brands?

2. **Internal position**—the niche the brand will occupy with regard to the other similar brands within the firm.

With the external-positioning decision, a firm tries to create a distinctive *competitive* position based on design features, pricing, distribution, or promotion or advertising strategy. For example, BMW's 550i is priced around $100,000, while the Chevrolet Cobalt aims for the budget-conscious consumer with a base price of about $15,000. Effective internal positioning involves either developing vastly different products within the firm's own product line or creating advertising messages that appeal to different consumer needs and desires. Procter & Gamble does both to position its many laundry detergent brands. One P&G brand is advertised as being effective on kids' dirty clothes, while another brand is portrayed as effective for preventing colors from running.

The methods and strategic options available to an organization with respect to market segmentation, product differentiation, and positioning will be fully discussed in Chapter 4.

Enhancing Revenues and Profits

Many people believe that the fundamental purpose of marketing can be stated quite simply: to generate revenue. Marketing is the only part of an organization that has revenue generation as its primary purpose. In the words of highly regarded management consultant and scholar Peter Drucker, "Marketing and innovation produce results: all the rest are 'costs.'"[21] The "results" Drucker refers to are revenues. The marketing process is designed to generate sales and therefore revenues for the firm.

Creating sales as part of the revenue-generating process is where promotion plays a significant role. As we have seen, the promotional mix communicates persuasive information to audiences based on the values created in the marketing mix related to the product, its price, or its distribution. This communication highlights brand features—price, emotion, or availability—and attracts a target market. In this way, promotional messages make a direct contribution to the marketing goal of revenue generation. Although promotion *contributes* to the process of creating sales and revenue, it cannot be solely responsible for creating sales and revenue—it's not that powerful. Some organizations mistakenly see advertising or promotion as a panacea—the salvation for an ambiguous or ineffective overall marketing strategy. However, sales occur when a brand has a well-conceived and complete marketing mix.

The effect of promotion on profits comes about when it gives an organization greater flexibility in the price it charges for a product or service. Advertising can help create pricing flexibility in two ways:

1. Contributing to economies of scale
2. Helping create inelasticity of demand

When an organization creates large-scale demand for its brand, the quantity of product produced increases, and **economies of scale** lead to lower unit production costs. Cost of production decreases because fixed costs (such as rent and equipment costs) are spread over a greater number of units produced. Promotion contributes to demand stimulation by communicating to the market about the features and availability of a brand. By stimulating demand, advertising then contributes to the creation of economies of scale, which ultimately translates into higher profits per unit.

Brand loyalty, discussed earlier, brings about the other important source of pricing flexibility, **inelasticity of demand**, a situation in which consumers are relatively insensitive to price increases for the brand. When consumers are less price sensitive, firms have the flexibility to raise prices and increase profit margins. For example, Louis Vuitton, the maker of luxury handbags ($1,000 per bag or more) and other luxury items, enjoys an operating margin of 45 percent.[22] Advertising contributes directly to brand loyalty, and thus to inelasticity of demand, by persuading and reminding consumers of the satisfactions and values related to a brand. This business benefit of advertising was recently supported by a large research study in which companies that built strong brands and raised prices were more profitable than companies that cut costs as a way to increase profits—by nearly twice the profit percentage.

Promotion Objectives

An important set of decisions in IMC involves what the promotional objectives are supposed to achieve. For example, should the message increase demand for an entire product category or just a particular brand? Do you want the audience to act immediately or develop positive associations that will shape future decisions? In an integrated strategy, answering such questions will shape the kinds of messages you create and the elements you choose to include in the promotional mix.

internal position niche a brand occupies with regard to the company's other, similar brands

economies of scale lower per-unit production costs resulting from larger volume

inelasticity of demand low sensitivity to price increases; may result from brand loyalty

Primary versus Selective Demand Stimulation

Promotional messages may stimulate either primary or selective demand. In **primary demand stimulation**, a company is trying to create demand for an entire product *category*. Primary demand stimulation is challenging and costly, and research evidence suggests that it is likely to have an impact only for products that are totally new, not for brand extensions or mature product categories. An example of effective primary demand stimulation was the introduction of the VCR to the consumer market in the 1970s. With a product that is totally new to the market, consumers need to be convinced that the product category itself is valuable and that it is, indeed, available for sale. When the VCR was first introduced in the United States, RCA, Panasonic, and Quasar ran primary demand stimulation advertising to explain to household consumers the value and convenience of taping television programs with this new product—something no one had ever done before at home.

For organizations that have tried to stimulate primary demand in mature product categories, typically trade associations, the results have been dismal. The National Fluid Milk Processor Promotion Board has tried using advertising to stimulate primary demand for the product category of milk. While the multibillion-dollar "mustache" campaign is popular and wins awards, milk consumption has *declined* every year during the time of this campaign.[23] Even if the attempts at primary demand have reduced the overall decline in milk consumption (which can't be determined), this result is still not very impressive. This should come as no surprise, though. Research over decades has clearly indicated that attempts at primary demand stimulation in mature product categories (orange juice, beef, pork, and almonds have also been tried) have never been successful.[24]

While some corporations have tried primary demand stimulation, the true power of advertising is shown when it functions to stimulate demand for a particular company's brand. In this approach, known as **selective demand stimulation**, the objective of the promotion is to point out a brand's unique benefits compared with the competition. For example, advertising for Tropicana orange juice notes that the brand offers a calcium-fortified option that can help keep bones strong.

Direct- versus Delayed-Response Promotion

Another promotion decision involves how quickly we want consumers to respond. **Direct-response promotion** asks consumers to act immediately. Examples include ads that direct you to "call this toll-free number" or "mail your $19.95 before midnight tonight." In many cases, direct-response promotion is used for products that consumers are familiar with, that do not require inspection at the point of purchase, and that are relatively low cost. However, the proliferation of toll-free numbers, websites that provide detailed information, and the widespread use of credit cards have been a boon to direct response for higher-priced products, such as exercise equipment.

Delayed-response promotion relies on imagery and message themes that emphasize the brand's benefits and satisfying characteristics. Rather than trying to stimulate an immediate action from an audience, delayed-response promotion attempts to develop awareness and preference for a brand over time. In

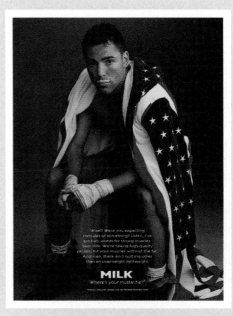

The National Fluid Milk Processor Promotion Board uses the famous milk mustache ads in an effort to build primary demand for milk, not for a particular brand.

general, delayed-response promotion attempts to create brand awareness, reinforce the benefits of using a brand, develop a general liking for the brand, and create an image for a brand. When a consumer enters the purchase process, the information from delayed-response promotion comes into play. Most advertisements we see on television and in magazines are of the delayed-response type. When McDonald's runs television ads during prime time, the company doesn't expect you to leap from your chair to go out and buy a Big Mac, but the company does hope you'll remember the brand the next time you're hungry.

© Valentyn Volkov/Shutterstock.

Promoting the Company or the Brand

Promotional messages can be developed to build a favorable attitude toward either a brand or the image of the company itself. **Brand advertising**, as we have seen throughout this chapter, communicates the specific features, values, and benefits of a particular brand offered for sale by a particular organization.

Corporate advertising is meant to create a favorable attitude toward a company as a whole. Prominent users of corporate advertising include Microsoft and General Electric. Similarly, Philips, the Dutch electronics and medical device conglomerate, turned to corporate advertising to unify the image of its brand name across a wide range of superior technologies.[25] Corporate campaigns have been designed to generate favorable public opinion toward the corporation as a whole, which can also affect the company's shareholders. When they see good corporate advertising, it instills confidence and, ultimately, long-term commitment to the firm and its stock. We'll consider this type of advertising in detail in Chapter 13.

Another form of corporate advertising is carried out by members of a trade channel, mostly retailers. When corporate advertising takes place in a trade channel, it is referred to as *institutional advertising*. Retailers such as Nordstrom and Walmart advertise to persuade consumers to shop at their stores. While these retailers may occasionally feature a particular manufacturer's brand in the advertising, the main purpose of the advertising is to get the audience to shop at their stores.

Economic Impact of Promotion

Promotion not only has an important impact on the individual business organizations that pay for it, but [it] also has effects across a country's entire economic system. These effects may seem far removed from marketing decisions, but they help shape public attitudes toward businesses and marketers.

Impact on Gross Domestic Product

The **gross domestic product (GDP)** is the measure of the total value of goods and services produced within an economic system. As a part of the marketing mix, promotion increases GDP indirectly by working with product, pricing, and distribution decisions to stimulate sales. When sales of products such as DVDs or alternative energy sources grow, producers have to make more of these products. In addition, the greater demand helps to fuel housing starts and corporate-investment in finished goods and capital equipment. Consequently, GDP is affected by promotion, especially when it involves sales of products in new, innovative product categories.[26]

Impact on Business Cycles

Promotion can have a stabilizing effect on downturns in business activity. There is evidence that many firms increase advertising during times of recession in an effort to spend their way out of a business downturn.

Impact on Competition

Promotion is alleged to stimulate competition and therefore motivate firms to strive for better products, better production methods, and other competitive advantages that ultimately benefit the economy as a whole. Additionally, when promotion serves as a way to enter new markets, it fosters competition across the economic system.

Promotion is not universally hailed as a stimulant to competition. Critics point out that the amount of advertising dollars needed to compete effectively in many industries is often prohibitive. This requirement makes advertising a barrier to entry into an industry; that is, a firm may be able to compete in an industry in every way except spending enough on the advertising needed to compete. If this occurs, promotion can actually decrease the overall amount of competition in an economy.[27]

Impact on Prices

One of the widely debated effects of promotion has to do with its effect on the prices consumers pay for products and services. Some say that the millions or even billions of dollars spent on advertising are added to the prices for the products and services advertised. However, this relationship is not necessarily true.

First, across all industries, advertising costs incurred by firms range from about 2 percent of sales in the automobile and retail industries up to 30 percent of sales in the personal care and luxury products businesses.[28] Exhibit 1.4 shows the ratio of advertising to sales for three firms in different industries. Notice that there is no consistent and predictable relationship between advertising spending and sales. Different products and different market conditions demand that firms spend different amounts of money on advertising. These same conditions make it difficult to identify a predictable relationship between advertising and sales.

It is true that the cost of advertising is built into product costs, which are ultimately passed on to consumers. But this effect on price must be judged against a couple of cost savings that lower the price. First, there is the reduced time and effort a consumer has to spend in searching for a product or service. Second, economies of scale, discussed earlier, have a direct impact on cost and then on prices. When economies of scale lower the unit cost of production by spreading fixed costs over a large number of units produced, the cost reduction can be passed on to consumers in terms of lower prices, as firms search for competitive advantage with lower prices. Nowhere is this effect more dramatic than the price and performance of personal computers. In the early 1980s, an Apple IIe computer that ran at about 1 MHz and had 64K of total memory cost more than $3,000. Today, you can get a computer that is several hundred times faster with vastly increased memory and storage for less than $600, even though companies like HP and Dell are spending more on advertising (even on an inflation-adjusted basis) today than Apple did back in the 1980s.

Exhibit 1.4
Ad Spending as a Percent of Sales

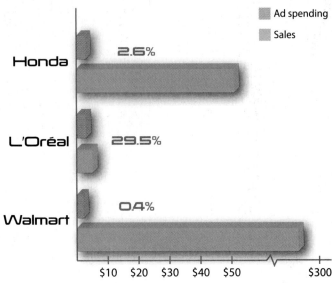

Impact on Value

The password for successful marketing is *value*. In modern marketing and advertising, **value** refers to consumers' perception that a brand provides satisfaction beyond the cost incurred to obtain that brand. The value perspective of the modern consumer is based on wanting every purchase to be a "good deal." Promotion can add value to the consumption experience. Consider the effect of branding on bottled water. Promotion helps create enough value in the minds of consumers that they (we) will *pay* for water that comes free out of the tap.

Promotion also affects a consumer's perception of value by contributing to the symbolic value and social meaning of a brand. **Symbolic value** refers to what a product or service means to consumers in a nonliteral way. For example, branded clothing such as Guess? jeans or Doc Martens shoes can symbolize self-concept for some consumers. In reality, all branded products rely, to some extent, on symbolic value; otherwise, they would not be brands but just unmarked commodities (like potatoes).

Social meaning refers to what a product or service means in a societal context. For example, social class is marked by various products that are used and displayed to signify class membership. An example is United Airlines' Connoisseur Class aimed at international business travelers. Often, the product's connection to a social class addresses a need within consumers to move up in class.

© Andre Blais/Shutterstock.

Researchers from various disciplines have long argued that objects (brands included) are never just objects. They take on meaning from culture, society, and consumers.[29] It is important to remember that these meanings often become just as much a part of the brand as the product's physical features. Because the image of a brand is developed through promotion, it contributes directly to consumers' perception of the value of the brand. The more value consumers see in a brand, the more they are willing to pay to acquire the brand. If consumers value the image of a Nissan coupe or a Four Seasons hotel stay, then they will pay a premium to acquire that value.

CONCLUSION: PROMOTION MATTERS

When you get involved with brand promotion, you're not just selling goods that you hope consumers need. You're helping to make consumption experiences more valuable. You're contributing to the efficiency of trade, potentially making products more affordable. You're keeping competitors on their toes, so everyone gets better at serving customers. And especially when promotion is part of a careful IMC effort, you're helping your company or clients achieve strategic goals. The remaining chapters in this part and Part 2 will prepare you for this role by introducing you to how the promotion industry works and how buyers make decisions. Then the chapters in Part 3 explore how a variety of promotional tools can be used in a complete, effective IMC campaign. For the creative thinker, the possibilities are endless. And changes such as the ones described at the beginning of this chapter are making the industry more exciting than it ever has been. Welcome to the world of brand promotion!

STUDY TOOLS CHAPTER 1

Located at back of the textbook
- **Rip out Chapter in Review Card.**

Located at www.cengagebrain.com
- **Review Key Terms Flashcards (Print or Online).**
- **Complete the Practice Quiz to prepare for tests.**
- **Play "Beat the Clock" and "Quizbowl" to master concepts.**
- **Complete "Crossword Puzzle" to review key terms.**
- **Watch videos on IBM and McDonald's for real company examples.**
- **You will find additional examples that support integrated marketing communication in the online examples. Examples include: Cadillac, Victoria's Secret, Exide, and Colgate.**

When you see a Coke cup on the judges' desk, does it make you want to drink a Coke?

Coca-Cola and *American Idol* team up to target consumers.

© AP Images/MichaelBecker/PictureGroup.

Learning Outcomes

After studying this chapter, you should be able to:

LO 1 Discuss important trends transforming the promotion industry.

LO 2 Describe the promotion industry's size, structure, and participants.

LO 3 Summarize what advertising and promotion agencies do and how they are compensated.

LO 4 Identify experts who help plan and execute integrated marketing communication campaigns.

LO 5 Discuss the role played by media organizations in IMC campaigns.

> "Any damn fool can put on a deal, but it takes genius, faith, and perseverance to create a brand."
>
> —David Ogilvy

AFTER YOU FINISH THIS CHAPTER GO TO PAGE 43 FOR STUDY TOOLS

Welcome to the Power Struggle

There have always been power struggles in the promotion industry: brand versus brand; one agency versus another; agency versus media company; big advertiser with lots of money versus big retailer with lots of money. But those old-style power struggles were child's play compared with the 21st-century power struggle. Consumers, who on average encounter between 1,000 and 5,000 advertising messages every day,[1] are tired of the barrage of ads and try to avoid most of them. So today's power struggle is about how the promotion industry can adapt to the new technologies consumers are using to gain more control over their information environment.

From Facebook to YouTube to millions of blogs, consumers are seeking out information environments where *they* control their exposure to information rather than an advertiser or media company being in control. They are insisting on the convenience and appeal of their PC, iPod, and TiVo or Slingbox (as we saw in Chapter 1). Recognizing their success, *Advertising Age* (the main advertising-industry trade publication) named "the consumer" as its "Best Advertising Agency for 2006."[2] This so-called mass collaboration by consumers is such a dramatic change from traditional information flow techniques that marketers, advertising and promotion agencies, and media companies are struggling to reinvent themselves.[3] Coca-Cola and American Idol are teaming up to do just that.

The traditional approach to promotion was for a marketer, like Nike or American Express, to work with an advertising agency, like Leo Burnett or J. Walter Thompson, which would develop television, radio, newspaper, magazine, or billboard ads. Then the marketer and its agency would buy media time or space to place the ads so that consumers would see and hear them. This still happens—a lot. Major media rake in about $600 billion worldwide in a year, and individual

What do you think?

Featuring a brand in a TV show can be as creative as a great TV commercial.

| 1 | 2 | 3 | 4 | 5 | 6 | 7 |

STRONGLY DISAGREE   STRONGLY AGREE

Find out what others think at CourseMate for PROMO.

media companies like Hearst Corp. generate several billion dollars in annual revenue.[4] But even as marketers, agencies, and media companies try to reach control-seeking consumers, some very smart people think the industry is on the cusp of even more dramatic changes.[5]

While the traditional structure of the promotion industry may be changing, the *goal* has not changed: The brand still needs to be highlighted. The change in consumer orientation will make product branding *more* important as consumers choose what persuasive messages they want to receive and where they want to receive them.

As marketers, agencies, and their media partners struggle with how to meet enduring goals in this new environment, some think the answer is to go with the flow and invite consumers to contribute to brand content (for example, by sponsoring competitions for the best consumer-created ad).[6] Others, like Coca-Cola, respond to consumers' impatience with advertisements by using subtler and seemingly more natural ways to make brands part of consumers' daily lives. Part of Coke's approach: pay $20 million to have Coke cups

on the judges' desks during Fox Network's *American Idol* program.[7] Other marketers are paying video game developers to insert their branded products into their games, reaching millions or tens of millions of players.[8]

Big media companies are adapting, too. NBC Universal, often referenced as the "classic" big media company with the deepest roots in the old media structure, is wooing advertisers by offering to help prepare advertising with the network's vast digital studio resources.[9] MTV Networks is offering new-media distribution like broadband channel MotherLoad, which is associated with Comedy Central programming.[10]

With much of the consumer control exerted online, spending for advertising on the Internet (through pop-ups, opt-in email, banner ads, paid search, and other options) now exceeds $20 billion.[11] Although that is less than 10 percent of worldwide expenditures in traditional advertising media, some analysts believe the Internet will ultimately become the primary form of message delivery.[12]

If you consider changes in technology, economic conditions, culture, lifestyles, and business philosophies, one or more of these broad business and soci-

© Alex Staroseltsev/Shutterstock.

GLOBAL RICH SOIL FOR AGENCY GROWTH

- Hispanic agencies in the United States that develop campaigns for Spanish-speaking consumers have been enjoying double-digit growth. As Hispanic online spending has risen above $150 million a year, more of these agencies are starting interactive units.

- China is struggling to keep up with the need for advertising and promotional materials fueled by that country's dramatic economic growth. For some agencies in China, finding enough talent to hire is a "crisis."

- In Europe, Amsterdam has emerged as a hot agency market. Why? The city itself is artistic, easily attracts creative talent, and features broad diversity.

Sources: Laurel Wentz, "Look at Them Grow: U.S. Hispanic Agencies Thrive," *Advertising Age*, December 4, 2006, 31; Laurel Wentz and Normandy Madden, "China's Ad World: A New Crisis Every Day," *Advertising Age*, December 11, 2006, 6; and Jack Ewing, "Amsterdam's Red-Hot Ad Shops," *BusinessWeek*, December 18, 2006, 52.

etal forces are always affecting the effort to promote brands and communicate messages about what the brands stand for. Change in the promotion industry is nothing new, but the pace and complexity of the change are more challenging than the industry has ever faced. As you read about the structure of the industry, notice how the players are being shaped by—but also shaping—this change.

LO 1 Promotion Industry Trends

Often advertisers struggle with whether to use traditional mass media, like television and radio, which have wide reach, or to use newer, highly targeted media like personalized emails and social networking. But in the end, what is important is not the technology itself but rather the need to focus on the brand, its image, and a persuasive, integrated presentation of that brand to the target market. The choice of the Web or television should be based on which medium is likely to achieve the right persuasive impact.

Nevertheless, to understand the promotion industry, we need to know what is happening in it today.

Limits of Consolidation

The advertising industry went through a period of extreme consolidation from 1999 through 2002. Full-service agencies acquired and merged with other full-service agencies and interactive shops. One such merger sequence began when Leo Burnett (the long-standing Chicago-based full-service agency) merged with the MacManus Group to create the $1.7 billion-a-year Bcom3 Group, with 500 operating units in 90 countries and 16,000 employees. Adding globalization to that merger, the Japanese agency Dentsu took a partnership position in the agreement as well. Then, two years later, the Paris-based global agency Publicis bought up the whole Bcom3 setup and by 2007 was a $5.1 billion global conglomerate of agencies.[13] Another global agency, Interpublic Group, acquired more than 300 agencies from 1998 through 2002 at a cost of more than $5 billion. Since then, Leo Burnett has reemerged as an independent agency, and most of the mergers from the 1998 to 2002 period of consolidation have been undone.

The consolidation and globalization provided an enormous array of services to clients, but it created

problems as well. First, not all clients were impressed with the giant agencies. In a survey of nearly 300 major companies, only 43 percent said it was "very important" to have a single agency offer fully integrated services. They felt they would be missing out on the creativity that small shops can offer through specialization.[14] And giant agencies inevitably run into conflicts of interest when trying to go after new business because the potential new client is often in the same business as an existing client. Also, bigger has not always meant better or more profitable. Interpublic's buying binge did not increase its net income appreciably, yet it created crushing debt and made the agency unwieldy. Analysts now say these big agencies need to consolidate, get rid of money-losing operations, and turn what's left "loose to pursue their own clients."

It is unlikely that the giant agencies will dismantle all they have created. Some advertising clients are pleased to be able to consolidate all their integrated marketing communication (IMC) needs with one shop. But the burden of debt, potential conflict of interest, and migration of ad dollars to nontraditional media are enough to make some "unconsolidation" possible.

Narrower Media Control

Consolidation has also been taking place at another level of the industry, that of the media. As a result, control over media outlets is in fewer hands. Historically, there has been a legal limit on how much control any one media company could seize. But in 2003, the Federal Communications Commission (FCC) relaxed a decades-old rule that restricted media ownership. Now a single company can own television stations that reach up to 45 percent of U.S. households—up from the 35 percent specified in the old rule. In addition, the FCC voted to lift all "cross-ownership" restrictions, ending a ban on one company owning both a newspaper and broadcast station in a city.[15]

The consolidation is not restricted to television. Media companies of all types tend to pursue more and

Not to be outdone, the Web has its own media conglomerates. InterActiveCorp (IAC) has amassed a media empire of Internet sites that include Ask.com, Match.com, Evite, and Dictionary.com. Together, these sites generate about $7 billion in revenue, which makes IAC nearly as big as better-known Internet merchants, but much more diversified.

more "properties" if they are allowed to, thus creating what are now referred to as "multiplatform" media organizations.[16] Consider the evolution of media giant News Corp. and its holdings, which include television networks (Fox), newspapers (more than 20 worldwide, including the *Wall Street Journal*), in-store and at-home promotional materials (News America Marketing Group), satellite (Sky Italia), cable systems (Fox News), and MySpace in the peer-to-peer media world. News Corp.'s worldwide media holdings generate more than $40 billion in revenue and reach every corner of the earth. As big as News Corp. is, the ultimate multiplatform may be Disney, which owns the ABC broadcasting network and the ESPN cable network group, plus 10 other cable stations, 15 radio stations, two dozen websites, eight podcasting operations, video on demand, books, and magazines.

Media Clutter

Even though media companies and advertising agencies have been consolidating into fewer large firms, the number of media options has grown, giving marketers more ways to *try* to reach consumers than ever before. In television alone, the options have multiplied. In 1994, the consumer had access to about 27 television channels. Today, the average U.S. household has access to well over 100 channels. That means consumers are harder to find. In 1995, it took three well-placed TV spots to reach 80 percent of women television viewers. By 2003, it took 97 spots to reach them.[17]

The types of media also have proliferated with the introduction of cable television channels, direct-marketing technology, Web options, and alternative new media (podcasting, for example). New and increased media options have resulted in so much clutter that the probability of any one message breaking through and making a real difference continues to diminish.

As marketers struggle to stand out amid the clutter, they are losing faith in advertising alone. Promotion options such as online communication, brand placement in film and television, point-of-purchase displays, and sponsorships are more attractive to advertisers. For example, advertisers on the Super Bowl, notorious for its clutter and outrageous ad prices (about $2.5 million to $3 million for a 30-second spot), have begun emphasizing promotional tie-ins to enhance the effect of the advertising. To combat the clutter and expense at one Super Bowl, Miller Brewing Company distributed thousands of inflatable Miller Lite chairs by game day. The chairs were a tie-in with a national advertising campaign that began during the regular season before the Super Bowl.[18]

As marketers focus on integrating more tools within the overall promotional effort in an attempt to reach more consumers in different ways, traditional media expenditures are falling. Consider the decisions by Johnson & Johnson. In 2007, J&J announced that it had shifted $250 million in spending from traditional media—television, magazines, and newspapers—to "digital media," including the Internet and blogs.[19]

Advertisers are shifting spending out of traditional media because they are looking to the full complement of promotional opportunities in sales promotions (like the Miller chairs), event sponsorships, new-media options, and public relations as means to support and enhance the primary advertising effort for brands. Some advertisers are enlisting the help of Hollywood talent agencies in an effort to get their brands featured in television programs and films. The payoff for strategic placement in a film or television show can be huge. Getting Coca-Cola placed on *American Idol*, as we talked about earlier, is estimated to be worth up to $20 million in tra-

ditional media advertising.[20] This topic also is covered in Chapter 12, where we consider branded entertainment in detail.

blog personal journal on a website that is frequently updated and intended for public access

Consumer Control

Historically, advertisers controlled information and the flow of information as a one-way mode of communication through mass media. But today's consumers are in greater control of the information they receive about product categories and the brands within those categories. The simplest and most obvious example is when consumers visit Internet sites *they* choose to visit for either information or shopping. But it gets a lot more complicated from there. **Blogs**—or websites frequented by individuals with common interests where they can post facts, opinions, and personal experiences—are emerging as new and sophisticated sources of product and brand information. Once criticized as the "ephemeral scribble" of 13-year-old girls and the babble of techno-geeks, blogs are gaining greater sophistication and organization. Web-based service firms like Blogdrive, Feedster, and Blogger are making blogs easier to use and accessible to the masses.

Another way in which consumers exert control over the messages they receive is by using digital video recorders (DVRs) like TiVo and controllers like Slingbox. Analysts expect that the use of DVRs will reduce ad viewership by as much as 30 percent. That translates to taking approximately $20 billion out of U.S. advertising industry revenue. Marketers and their agencies can expect that, by 2010, approximately 39 percent of all U.S. television households will have "ad-skipping" capability.[21]

Marketers and marketing professionals must adapt to consumers' control over the information they choose to receive. One adaptation is to be

MARKETERS AND MARKETING PROFESSIONALS MUST ADAPT TO CONSUMERS' CONTROL OVER THE INFORMATION THEY CHOOSE TO RECEIVE.

more creative with messages. The more entertaining and informative an ad is, the more likely consumers will want to watch the ad. Another technique—less creative but certainly effective—is to run advertising messages along the bottom of the programming. Finally, TiVo is rolling out a service that sounds crazy: ads on demand.[22] The premise is that consumers about to buy expensive items like cars or resort vacations may want to watch information about alternative brands.

WEB 2.0

Recently, consumer control has moved to a whole new level of collaboration via Web 2.0. A phrase coined by O'Reilly Media in 2004, *Web 2.0* refers to a second generation of Web-based use and services—such as social networking sites and wikis—that emphasize online collaboration and sharing among users. O'Reilly Media used the phrase as a title for a series of conferences, and it has since become widely adopted.

Because networking activity (e.g., Facebook) and informational services (e.g., Wikipedia) have been available from the beginning of the World Wide Web, some analysts challenge whether Web 2.0 is really new or different at all. But those who champion the concept of Web 2.0 argue that the change in how people are using that technology is so significant that it needs to be recognized as a distinct element of the Web world. When you consider that 70,000 videos are uploaded to YouTube every day by people all over the world, it is hard to argue that this sort of application of Web technology does not deserve its own designation.[23] Consider further that Google believes enough in this particular application of Web technology to have spent $1.65 billion to buy YouTube and that IBM, the icon of old corporate America, is exploring corporate applications for blogs, wikis, podcasts, social networking, and RSS (Really Simple Syndication).[24] While there are doubters of Web 2.0, it represents another element of the communication landscape to consider in the application of promotion tools.

For years to come, these trends and the changes they bring about will force advertisers to think differently about the promotional mix and IMC. Similarly, advertising agencies will need to think about the way they serve their clients and the way communications are delivered to audiences. Big clients such as Procter & Gamble and Miller Brewing Company are already demanding new and innovative programs to enhance the impact of their advertising and promotional dollars.

LO 2 Industry Scope and Structure

The promotion industry plays a significant role in the economy. More than $300 billion is spent in the United States alone on various categories of advertising, with nearly $600 billion spent worldwide. Spending on all forms of promotion including advertising exceeds a trillion dollars.[25]

Promotional efforts are a significant expense for many individual firms. The top U.S. advertisers spend billions of dollars a year on advertising alone. To keep this in perspective, however, these amounts need to be measured against revenues. Procter & Gamble spent about $4.9 billion on advertising in 2006, but this amount represented just under 7 percent of its sales.[26]

Overall, the 100 leading advertisers in the United States spent just over $105 billion on advertising in 2006, which was a healthy 3.1 percent increase over 2005.[27] While this is good news for ad agencies, there is no doubt that this rapidly increasing spending is related to increased clutter. Advertising may be quickly becoming its own worst enemy.

Who is spending all these ad dollars, and where are they spending that money? The structure of the industry tells us *who* does *what, in what order*, during the brand promotion process. The promotion industry is actually a collection of a wide range of talented people, all of whom have special expertise and perform a wide variety of tasks in planning, preparing, and placing promotional messages. Exhibit 2.1 shows the structure of the promotion industry by identifying the participants in the process.

Exhibit 2.1 demonstrates that *marketers* (such as Kellogg) can employ the services of *advertising and promotion agencies* (such as Grey Global Group) that may or may not contract for specialized services with various *external facilitators* (such as Simmons Market Research Bureau), which results in advertising and other promotional messages being transmitted with the help of various *media organizations* (such as the TBS cable network) to one or more *target audiences* (like you).

Note the options available in Exhibit 2.1. Marketers do not always need to employ the services of advertising agencies, nor do agencies always seek the services of external facilitators. Some marketers deal directly with media organizations for placement of their advertisements or implementation of their promotions. In the case of traditional advertising, this happens either when a marketer has its own internal advertising/promotions department that prepares all the materials for the process or when media organizations (especially radio, television, and newspapers) provide technical assistance in the preparation of materials. Also, interactive media formats provide advertisers the opportunity to work directly with entertainment programming firms, such as Walt Disney and SFX Entertainment, to provide integrated programming that features brand placements in films and television programs or at entertainment events. And, as you will see, many of the new-media agencies provide the creative and technical assistance advertisers need to implement campaigns through new media.

Marketers

The first participants in the promotion industry are the marketers. From the local pet store to multinational corporations, organizations of all types and sizes seek to benefit from the effects of advertising and other elements of the promotional mix. **Marketers** are business, not-for-profit, and government organizations that use advertising and other promotional techniques to communicate with target markets and to stimulate awareness and demand for their brands. Marketers are also referred to as **clients** by their advertising and promotion agency partners. Different types of marketers use advertising somewhat differently, depending on the type of product or service they market.

Manufacturers and Service Firms

The most prominent users of promotion are large national manufacturers of consumer products and services, which often spend hundreds of millions of dollars annually. Procter & Gamble and Merrill Lynch have national or global markets for their products and services. The use of advertising, particularly mass media advertising, by these firms is essential to creating

> **marketer** business, not-for-profit, or government organization that uses advertising and other promotional techniques to communicate with target markets to stimulate awareness of and demand for its brands
>
> **client** organization that pays for advertising

Exhibit 2.1
Structure of the Promotion Industry

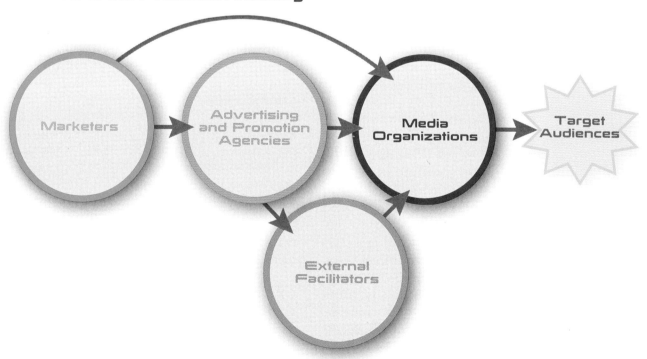

awareness and preference for their brands.

But advertising is useful not just to national or multinational firms; regional and local producers of household goods and services also rely heavily on advertising. For example, regional dairy companies typically sell milk, cheese, and other dairy products in several states. These firms often use ads placed in newspapers and regional editions of magazines. Further, couponing and sampling are ways to communicate with target markets with IMCs that are well suited to regional application. Local producers of products are relatively rare, but local service organizations are common. Medical facilities, auto dealers, and arts organizations are examples of local service providers that use advertising to create awareness and stimulate demand. What car dealer in America has not advertised a holiday event or used a remote local radio broadcast to attract attention?

Firms that produce both business goods and services also may promote their products on global, national, regional, and local levels. IBM (computer and business services) and Deloitte (accounting and consulting services) are examples of global companies that produce business goods and services. At the national and regional levels, firms that supply agricultural and mining equipment and repair services are common users of promotion, as are consulting and research firms. At the local level, firms that supply janitorial, linen, and bookkeeping services use advertising to companies in their area.

Trade Resellers

The term **trade reseller** is simply a general description for all organizations in the marketing channel of distribution that buy products to resell to customers. Resellers can be retailers, wholesalers, or distributors. Their customers may include household consumers and business buyers at all geographic market levels.

The most visible reseller advertisers are retailers that sell in national or global markets. Walmart and McDonald's are examples of global retail companies that use various forms of promotion to communicate with customers. Regional retail chains, typically grocery chains such as Albertson's or department stores such as Dillard's, serve multistate markets and use advertising suited to their regional customers. At the local level, small retail shops of all sorts rely on newspaper, radio, television, and billboard advertising and special promotional events to reach a relatively small geographic area.

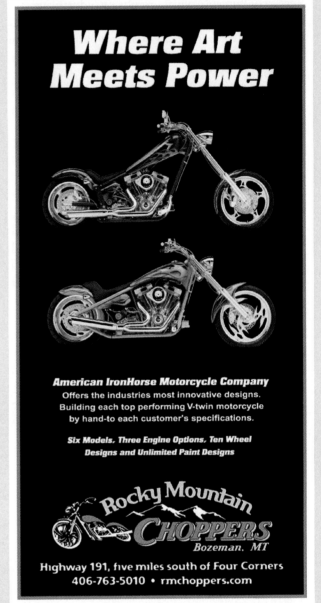

Advertising is not reserved for manufacturers like Ford and giant retail chains like Target. Here, Rocky Mountain Choppers offers customized motorcycles to bikers in Montana.

Wholesalers and distributors, such as Ideal Supply (a company that supplies contractors with blasting and surveying equipment), are a completely different breed of reseller. Technically, these types of companies deal only with business customers because their position in the distribution channel dictates that they sell products either to producers (who buy goods to produce other goods) or to retailers (who resell goods to household consumers). Occasionally, an organization will call itself a wholesaler and sell to the public. Such an organization is actually operating as a retail outlet.

Wholesalers and distributors have little need for mass media advertising over media such as television and radio. Rather, they use trade publications, directory advertising such as the Yellow Pages and trade directories, direct mail, and their websites as their main advertising media.

Federal, State, and Local Governments

Government bodies may not seem to need advertising, but various agencies invest millions of dollars in advertising annually. The U.S. government often ranks as one of the 50 largest spenders on advertising in the United States, with expenditures typically exceeding $1 billion annually.[28] If you add in other IMC expenses, including brochures, recruiting fairs, and the personal selling expense of recruiting offices, the U.S. government easily spends well over $2 billion annually. The federal government's spending on advertising and promotion is concentrated in two areas: armed-forces recruiting and social issues. The U.S. government's broad-based advertising for military recruiting includes the U.S. Army's "Army Strong" campaign, which uses television, magazines, newspapers, and interactive games (America's Army) hosted at the Army recruiting website (www.goarmy.com).[29]

Social and Not-for-Profit Organizations

Advertising by social organizations at the national, state, and local levels is common. The Nature Conservancy, United Way, American Red Cross, and art organizations use advertising to raise awareness of their organizations, seek donations, and attempt to shape behavior (deter drug use or encourage breast self-examinations, for example). Organizations such as these use both the mass media and direct mail to promote their causes and services. Unique organizations such as historical societies and charities serve every state. Social organizations in local communities represent a variety of special interests, from computer clubs to food banks. The advertising used by social organizations has the same fundamental purpose as the advertising carried out by major multinational corporations: to stimulate demand and disseminate information. While big multinationals might use national or even global advertising, local organizations rely on advertising through local media to reach local audiences.

If these categories of marketers sound familiar, it's because, in Chapter 1, we identified the same groups as distinct audiences for promotional messages. Firms are targets for marketing as well as marketers themselves.

The Marketer's Role in IMC

Very few of the marketers just discussed have the employees or financial resources to strategically plan and then totally prepare effective advertising or IMC programs. Most turn to advertising and promotion agencies, which play an important role in the promotion industry. But the marketer does play an important role before enlisting the services of an agency. For the agency to do its job effectively, marketers have to be prepared for their interaction with an agency. Marketers must:

- Fully understand and describe the value that the firm's brand provides to users.

- Fully understand and describe the brand's position in the market relative to competitive brands.

- Describe the firm's objectives for the brand in the near term and long term (e.g., brand extensions, international market launches).

- Identify the target markets that are most likely to respond favorably to the brand.

- Identify and manage the supply chain/distribution system that will most effectively reach the target markets.

- Be committed to using advertising and other promotional tools as part of the organization's overall marketing strategy to grow the brand.

Once a marketer has fulfilled these six responsibilities, then and *only* then is it time to enlist the services of an agency for help in effectively and creatively developing the market for the brand. While an agency can work with a marketer to help define and refine these factors, it is a mistake for a marketer to enter a relationship with an agency (of any type) without first preparing for a productive partnership.

LO 3 Advertising and Promotion Agencies

When you need to devise an advertisement or fully integrated marketing communication, no source will be more valuable than the advertising or promotion agency you work with. Advertising and promotion agencies are a critical link in the IMC process and give it the essential creative firepower. Marketers are fortunate to have a full complement of agencies that specialize in every detail of advertising and promotion.

Advertising Agencies

Most marketers choose to enlist the services of an advertising agency. An **advertising agency** is an organization of professionals who provide creative and business services to clients in planning, preparing, and placing advertisements. The reason so many firms rely on advertising agencies is that agencies house a collection of professionals with specialized talent, experience, and expertise that simply cannot be matched by in-house talent.

Advertising agencies are located in most big cities and small towns in the United States. Many agencies are global businesses. In a recent year, the biggest firms globally were Dentsu, based in Tokyo, Japan, and several New York City–based firms: BBDO Worldwide, McCann-Erickson Worldwide, JWT, and DDB Worldwide.[30]

Many types of agency professionals help advertisers in the planning, preparation, and placement of advertising and other promotional activities. Exhibit 2.2 lists some of the most widespread agency positions. As this list suggests, some advertising agencies can provide advertisers with a host of services, from campaign planning through creative concepts to e-strategies to measuring effectiveness. Also, because an agency is a business, agencies have CEOs, CFOs, and CTOs. Salaries in the positions listed range from about several million a year for a big agency chief executive officer to about $50,000 a year for a media planner.[31] Of course, those salaries change depending on whether you're in a big urban market or a small regional market.

It is up to the marketer to dig deep into an agency's background and determine which agency or set of multiple agencies will fulfill the company's marketing needs. Several different types of agencies are available, offering varying degrees of expertise and services:

- A **full-service agency** typically includes an array of advertising professionals to meet all the promotional needs of their clients. Often, such an agency will also offer global contacts. Giant full-service agencies like Omnicom Group and Dentsu employ hundreds or even thousands of people. Smaller shops can be full service with just a few dozen employees and serve big clients. Crispin Porter + Bogusky, a highly creative shop in Miami, has produced full-service, highly creative campaigns for Burger King and Mini USA.[32] Likewise, you don't have to be a big corporation with an ad budget in the hundreds of millions to hire a full-service agency. Cramer-Krasselt, a midsize agency, has built a stable of international clients one small to medium account at a time.[33]

- A **creative boutique** typically emphasizes creative concept development, copywriting, and artistic services. A marketer can employ this alternative for the strict purpose of infusing greater creativity into the message theme or individual advertisement. As one advertising expert put it, "If all clients want are ideas, lots of them, from which they can pick and mix to their hearts' delight, they won't want conventional, full-service agencies. They all want fast, flashy, fee-based idea factories."[34] Creative boutiques are these idea factories. Some large global agencies such as McCann-Erickson Worldwide and Leo Burnett have set up creative-only project shops that mimic the services provided by creative boutiques, with mixed results. The creative boutique's greatest advantage, niche expertise, may be its greatest liability as well. As firms search for IMC programs and make a commitment to IMC campaigns, the creative boutique may be an extra expense that they feel they cannot afford. Still, the creative effort is so essential to effective brand building that creativity will rise to prominence in the process, and creative boutiques are well positioned to deliver that value.

- **Interactive agencies** help advertisers prepare communications for new media such as the Internet, podcasting, interactive kiosks, CDs, and interactive television. These

ADVERTISING AND PROMOTION AGENCIES ARE A **CRITICAL LINK** IN THE IMC PROCESS AND GIVE IT THE **ESSENTIAL CREATIVE FIREPOWER.**

Interactive-advertising agencies specialize in developing banner ads and corporate websites. An example is Bluestreak, whose goal is to provide the infrastructure so that marketers and their agencies can create online campaigns that meet goals for consumers to click on links and then make purchases.

agencies focus on ways to use Web-based solutions for direct marketing and target market communications. Interactive agencies do work for Oracle, Nintendo, and the U.S. Army. But when the big shake-out occurred among dot-coms in 1999, many interactive agencies folded up shop; others were acquired by large agencies. Today, even a midsize full-service agency will offer interactive services to clients. This being the case, many firms have consolidated all their IMC needs, including interactive media, with their main full-service agency. The future for interactive agencies may be the *virtual agency*—a website where users who pay a flat fee can make their own TV, print, radio, and interactive ads (for example, see www.pick-n-click.com). The idea is being brought "mainstream" by Zimmerman agency (part of the Omnicom Group) as a way for multiunit businesses, like franchises and car dealers, to respond quickly and specifically to varying geographic or competitive needs.[35]

- An **in-house agency** is often referred to as the advertising department in a firm and takes responsibility for the planning and preparation of advertising materials. This option has the advantage of greater coordination and control in all phases of the advertising and promotion process. Some prominent marketers that do most of their work in-house are Calvin Klein and Revlon. The marketer's own personnel have control over and knowledge of marketing activities, such as product development and distribution tactics. Another advantage is that the firm can essentially keep for itself any commissions an external agency would have earned. While the advantages of doing advertising work in-house are attractive, there may be a lack of objectivity, which could constrain the execution of all phases of the advertising process.

in-house agency
advertising department of a marketer's own firm

Exhibit 2.2
Advertising Agency Positions

Account planners	Creative directors
Marketing specialists	Sales promotion and event planners
Account executives	Copywriters
Media buyers	Direct marketing specialists
Art directors	Radio and television producers
Lead account planners	Web developers
Chief executive officers (CEOs)	Researchers
Chief financial officers (CFOs)	Interactive media planners
Chief technology officers (CTOs)	Artists
Public relations specialists	Technical staff—printers, film editors, and so forth

media specialist organization that specializes in buying media time and space and that offers media strategy consulting to agencies and advertisers

promotion agency specialized agency that handles promotional efforts

direct-marketing agency or **direct-response agency** agency that maintains large databases of mailing lists and may design direct-marketing campaigns

database agency agency that helps customers construct databases of target customers, merge databases, develop promotional materials, and execute direct-marketing campaigns

fulfillment center operation that ensures consumers receive products ordered in response to direct marketing

infomercial long advertisement that resembles a talk show or product demonstration

e-commerce agency agency that handles planning and execution of activities related to promotions using electronic commerce

consumer sales promotion sales promotion that is aimed at consumers and focuses on price-off deals, coupons, sampling, rebates, and premiums

trade-market sales promotion sales promotion that is designed to motivate distributors, wholesalers, and retailers to stock and feature a firm's brand in their merchandising programs

Also, an in-house agency could not match the breadth and depth of talent available in an external agency.

- While not technically agencies, **media specialists** are organizations that specialize in buying media time and space and that offer media strategy consulting to advertising agencies and advertisers. Although media-buying services have been a part of the advertising industry structure for many years, media planning is a recent addition to these specialists' services. An example is Starcom MediaVest Group (**www.smvgroup.com**), a subsidiary of Paris-based Publicis Groupe. Starcom encompasses an integrated network of nearly 3,800 contact architects specializing in media management, Internet and digital communications, response media, entertainment marketing, sports sponsorships, event marketing, and multicultural media. Strategic coordination of media and promotional efforts has become more complex because of the proliferation of media options and extensive use of promotional tools beyond advertising. Marketers are finding that a firm that buys space can provide keen insights into the media strategy as well. Also, because media specialists buy media in large quantities, they often can negotiate a much lower cost than an agency or marketer could. Furthermore, media specialists often have time and space in inventory and can offer last-minute placement of advertisements.

Promotion Agencies

While advertisers often rely on an advertising agency as a steering organization for their promotional efforts, many specialized agencies, known as **promotion agencies**, also enter the process. This is because advertising agencies, even full-service agencies, will concentrate more on the advertising and often provide only a few key ancillary services for other promotional efforts. This is particularly true in

the current era, in which new media are offering many different ways to communicate to target markets. Promotion agencies can handle everything from sampling to event promotions to in-school promotional tie-ins.

- **Direct-marketing agencies** (sometimes also called **direct-response agencies**) provide a variety of direct-marketing services. Direct-marketing agencies and **database agencies** maintain and manage large databases of mailing lists. They also can design direct-marketing campaigns that use mail or telemarketing or direct-response campaigns that use all forms of media. These agencies help advertisers construct databases of target customers, merge databases, develop promotional materials, and then execute the campaigns. In many cases, the agencies maintain **fulfillment centers**, which ensure that customers receive the product ordered through direct mail. Many of these agencies are set up to provide creative and production services to clients. These firms will design and help execute direct-response advertising campaigns using traditional media such as radio, television, magazines, and newspapers. Some firms can prepare **infomercials**: 5- to 60-minute information programs that promote a brand and offer direct purchase to viewers.

- **E-commerce agencies** handle a variety of planning and execution activities related to promotions using electronic commerce. These agencies differ from the interactive agencies discussed earlier. Rather than creating websites or banner ads, they help firms conduct all forms of promotion through electronic media, particularly the Internet. They can run sweepstakes, issue coupons, help in sampling, and do direct-response campaigns. A firm like 24/7 Real Media (**www.247media.com**) offers advertisers the option of providing consumers with online coupons, contests, and loyalty programs. Another of these new-media e-commerce organizations is DoubleClick, which provides services related to Internet advertising, targeting technology, complete advertising management software solutions, direct-response Internet advertising, and Internet advertising developed for regional and local businesses.

- *Sales promotion agencies* design and then operate contests, sweepstakes, special displays, or coupon campaigns for advertisers. When these agencies specialize in **consumer sales promotions**, they focus on price-off deals, coupons, sampling, rebates, and premiums. Other firms specialize in **trade-market sales promotions** designed to help advertisers use promotions aimed at wholesalers, retailers, vendors, and trade resellers. These agencies are experts in designing incentive programs, trade shows, sales force contests, in-store merchandising, and point-of-purchase materials.

- **Event-planning agencies** and organizers are experts in finding locations, securing dates, and putting together a team of people to pull off a promotional event: audiovisual people, caterers, security experts, entertainers, celebrity participants, or whoever is necessary to make the event come about. The event-planning organization often takes over advertising the event and making sure the press provides coverage (publicity) of the event. When an advertiser sponsors an entire event, such as a PGA golf tournament, managers will work closely with the event-planning agencies. If a marketer is just one of several sponsors of an event, such as a NASCAR race, then it has less control over planning. Like sales promotion, event sponsorship can be targeted to household consumers or the trade market.

- *Design firms* provide experts who do not get nearly enough credit in the advertising and promotion process: designers and graphics specialists. If you take a job in advertising or promotion, your designer will be one of your first and most important partners. While **designers** are rarely involved in strategy planning, they are intimately involved in the execution of the advertising or IMC effort. Most basically, they help a firm create a **logo**—the graphic mark that identifies a company—and other visual representations that promote an identity for a firm. This mark will appear on everything from advertising to packaging to the company stationery, business cards, and signage. Beyond the logo, graphic designers will design most of the materials used in supportive communications such as the package design, coupons, in-store displays, brochures, outdoor banners for events, newsletters, and direct-mail pieces. One of the largest consumer package goods firms recently increased its commitment to design across all aspects of its marketing and promotion, claiming that design was critical to "winning customers in the store."[36]

- **Public relations firms** manage an organization's relationships with the media, the local community, competitors, industry associations, and government organizations. Their tools include press releases, feature stories, lobbying, spokespersons, and company newsletters. Some of these firms, including PR Newswire (**www.prnewswire.com**), will handle putting all of a firm's news releases online. Most marketers prefer not to handle their own public relations tasks. One reason is that public relations requires highly specialized skills and talent not normally found in an advertising firm. Also, because managers are so close to public relations problems, they may not be capable of handling a situation, particularly a negative one, with measured public responses. For these reasons, marketers and advertising agencies turn to public relations firms. In a search of more and distinctive visibility, marketers have been turning to public relations firms to achieve film and television placements.[37] William Morris, originally a talent agency and now a public relations firm, served client Anheuser-Busch by getting Budweiser accepted as the first beer advertiser on the Academy Awards.

HOW MANY BRANDS CAN YOU RECOGNIZE JUST FROM THEIR LOGOS? WHICH LOGOS DO YOU EXPECT TO FIND WHEN YOU SEE A PRO GOLFER?

© Carlos E. Santa Maria/Shutterstock.

Agency Services

As suggested by the many types of firms, advertising and promotion agencies offer a wide range of services. Therefore, before hiring any agency, marketers need to identify the particular services they need and then negotiate with the agency to reach an agreement on the services to be provided. Exhibit 2.3 shows where to find each of the main types of services in a typical full-service advertising agency that also provides a significant number of IMC services.

Account Services

Account services entail identifying the benefits a brand offers, the brand's target audiences, and the best competitive positioning, and then developing a complete promotion plan. These services are offered by managers who have titles such as account executive, account supervisor, or account manager and who work with clients to determine how the brand can benefit most from promotion. In some cases, account services in an agency can provide basic marketing and consumer behavior research, but, in general, the client should bring this information to the table. Knowing the target segment, the brand's values, and the positioning strategy is really the marketer's responsibility (more on this in Chapters 4 and 5).

Account services managers also work with the client in translating cultural and consumer values into advertising and promotional messages through the creative services in the agency. Finally, they work with media services to develop an effective media strategy for determining the best vehicles for reaching the targeted audiences. One of the primary tasks in account services is to keep the various agency teams' creative, production, and media on schedule and within budget.

Marketing Research Services

Research conducted by an agency for a client usually consists of the agency locating studies (conducted by commercial research organizations) that have bear-

Exhibit 2.3
Structure of a Full-Service Ad Agency

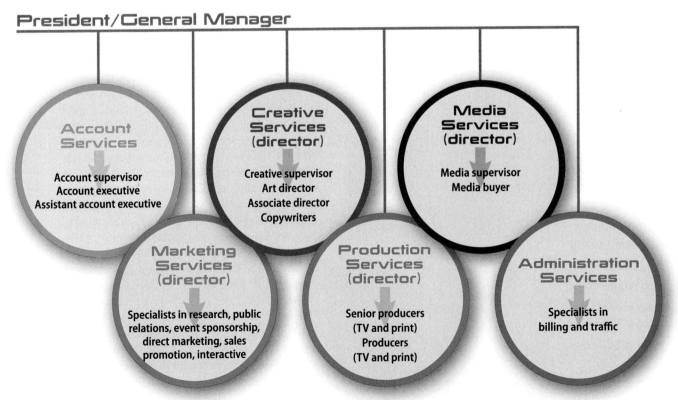

President/General Manager

Account Services
Account supervisor
Account executive
Assistant account executive

Creative Services (director)
Creative supervisor
Art director
Associate director
Copywriters

Media Services (director)
Media supervisor
Media buyer

Marketing Services (director)
Specialists in research, public relations, event sponsorship, direct marketing, sales promotion, interactive

Production Services (director)
Senior producers (TV and print)
Producers (TV and print)

Administration Services
Specialists in billing and traffic

Advertising agencies' greatest contribution to the promotion process may be their creative prowess. Here, FJCandN, a regional agency, implores marketers to "aim higher" (by working with its creative people, of course).

account planner
person in an advertising agency who synthesizes all relevant consumer research and uses it to design an advertising strategy

creative services
group in an advertising agency that develops the message to be delivered through advertising, sales promotion, direct marketing, event sponsorship, or public relations

ing on a client's market or advertising and promotion objectives. The research group will help the client interpret the research and communicate these interpretations to the creative and media people. If existing studies are not sufficient, research may be conducted by the agency itself. As mentioned in the account services discussion, some agencies can assemble consumers from the target audience to evaluate different versions of proposed advertising and determine whether messages are being communicated effectively.

Many agencies have established the position of **account planner** to coordinate the research effort. An account planner's stature in the organization is on par with that of an account executive. The account planner is assigned to clients to ensure that research input is included at each stage of development of campaign materials. Some agency leaders, like Jay Chiat of Chiat/ Day, think account planning has been the best new business tool ever invented.[38] Others are a bit more

measured in their assessment. Either way, agencies understand that research, signaled by the appointment of an account planner, is the key to successful promotional campaigns.

Creative Services

The **creative services** group in an agency comes up with the concepts that express the value of a company's brand in interesting and memorable ways. In simple terms, the creative services group develops the message that will be delivered though advertising, sales promotion, direct marketing, event sponsorship, or public relations.

Clients will push their agencies hard to come up with interesting and expressive ways to represent the brand. Geoffrey Frost, vice president of consumer communications for Motorola's Personal Communications Sector, expressed his company's approach to demanding creative excellence by saying, "What we've challenged the agencies to do was to help us to figure out how to position Motorola as the company that has really figured out the future."[39] That statement beautifully captures the kind of creative services advertisers seek from their agencies.

The creative group in an agency will typically include a creative director, art director, illustrators or designers, and copywriters. In specialized promotion agencies, event planners, contest experts, and interactive media specialists will join the core group.

Production Services

Production services include producers (and sometimes directors) who take creative ideas and turn them into advertisements, direct-mail pieces, or events materials. Producers generally manage and oversee the endless details of production of the finished advertisement or other promotion material. Advertising agencies maintain the largest and most sophisticated creative and production staffs.

Media Planning and Buying Services

The service of media planning and buying was described earlier as being available from a specialized agency. Full-service advertising agencies also provide **media planning and buying services** similar to those of the specialized agencies. The central challenge is to determine how a client's message can most effectively and efficiently reach the target audience. Media planners and buyers examine an enormous number of options to put together an effective media plan within the client's budget. But media planning and buying is much more than simply buying ad space, timing a coupon distribution, or scheduling an event. A wide range of media strategies can be implemented to enhance the impact of the message. Agencies are helping clients sort through the blizzard of new media options such as CDs, DVDs, interactive media, and the Internet. Most large agencies, such as Omnicom, Chiat/Day, and Fallon McElligott, set up their own interactive-media groups years ago in response to client demands that the Internet media option be included in nearly every IMC plan.

The three positions typically found in the media area are media planner, media buyer, and media researcher. These people are critically important because they provide services where most of the client's money is spent.

Administrative Services

Like other businesses, agencies have to manage their business affairs. Agencies have personnel departments, accounting and billing departments, and sales staffs that go out and sell the agency to clients. Most important to clients is the traffic department, which is responsible for monitoring projects to be sure that deadlines are met. Traffic managers make sure the creative group and media services are coordinated so that deadlines for getting promotional materials to printers and media organizations are met. The job requires tremendous organizational skills and is critical to delivering the other services to clients.

As marketers use more different forms of promotion and enlist the help of multiple agencies, one of the most difficult tasks is coordinating what all the agencies are doing and how they get paid. A key to effective IMC is integrated agency communication. When all of a marketer's agencies work together and coordinate their efforts, not only are promotional efforts well integrated, but relations between agencies are improved.[40]

Agency Compensation

The way agencies get paid is somewhat different from the way other professional organizations are compensated. While accountants, doctors, lawyers, and consultants often work on a fee basis, advertising agencies often base compensation on a commission or markup system. Promotion agencies occasionally work on a commission basis, but more often they work on a fee or contract basis.

Commissions

The traditional method of agency compensation is the **commission system**, which is based on the amount of money the advertiser spends on media. Under this method, an agreed-upon percent of the total amount billed by a media organization is retained by the advertising or promotion agency as compensation for all costs in creating advertising/promotion for the advertiser. (The percentage has

© Lopall/Shutterstock.

Exhibit 2.4
Agency Commissions: An Example

Marketer's cost of airtime = $1,000,000

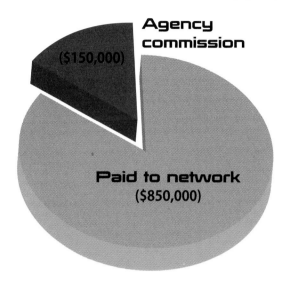

Agency commission ($150,000)

Paid to network ($850,000)

traditionally been 15 percent, but in practice, many agencies today charge different amounts.) For outdoor media, the rate typically changes to 16.67 percent. As shown in Exhibit 2.4, there are three basic steps to calculate an agency's compensation in the commission system:

1. The agency bills the client for the media time or space—in this case, $1 million for television airtime.

2. The agency pays the media 85 percent ($850,000 in the example).

3. The agency keeps a 15 percent commission ($150,000).

In recent years, advertisers and agencies themselves have questioned the wisdom of the commission system. As the chairman of a large full-service agency put it long ago, "It's incenting us to do the wrong thing, to recommend network TV and national magazines and radio when other forms of communication like direct marketing or public relations might do the job better."[41] Still, about half of all advertisers compensate their agencies using a commission system based on media cost.

Markup Charges

Another method of agency compensation is to add a percentage **markup charge** to a variety of services the agency purchases from outside suppliers. In many cases, an agency will turn to outside contractors for art, illustration, photography, printing, research,

and production. The agency then, in agreement with the client, adds a markup charge to these services.

The reason markup charges became prevalent in the industry is that many promotion agencies were providing services that did not use traditional media. Because the traditional commission method was based on media charges, there was no way for these agencies to receive payment for their work. A typical markup on outside services is 17.65 to 20 percent.

Fee Systems

A **fee system** is much like that used by consultants or attorneys, whereby the advertiser and the agency agree on an hourly rate for different services provided. The hourly rate can be based on average salaries within departments or on some agreed-upon hourly rate across all services. This is the most common basis for promotion agency compensation.

Another version of the fee system is a fixed fee, or contract, set for a project between the client and the agency. It is imperative that the agency and the marketer agree on precisely what services will be provided, by what departments in the agency, and over what specified period of time. In addition, the parties must agree on which supplies, materials, travel costs, and other expenses will be reimbursed beyond the fixed fee. Fixed-fee systems have the potential for causing serious rifts in the client-agency relationship because out-of-scope work can easily spiral out of control when so many variables are at play. When such controversies arise, the client-agency relationship is damaged and trust suffers.

Most agencies are vigorously opposed to the fee system. They argue that creative impact cannot be measured in "work hours" but rather must be measured in "the value of the materials the agency is creating for the client."[42]

Pay-for-Results

Recently, many marketers and agencies have been working on compensation programs called **pay-for-results**; these base the agency's fee on the achievement of agreed-upon results. Historically, agencies have not agreed to be evaluated on results because results have often been narrowly defined as sales volume, which is

markup charge method of agency compensation based on adding a percentage charge to a variety of services the agency purchases from outside suppliers

fee system method of agency compensation whereby the advertiser and agency agree on an hourly rate for services provided

pay-for-results compensation plan based on an agreement in which fee amounts are tied to a set of results criteria mainly related to factors outside the agency's control (product features, pricing strategy, and distribution programs—that is, the overall marketing mix, not just advertising or IMC). An agency may agree to be compensated based on achievement of sales levels, but more often (and more appropriately), the main results criteria are communications objectives such as the target audience's brand awareness, brand identification, or knowledge of brand features.

LO 4 External Facilitators

While agencies offer clients many services and are adding more, marketers often need to rely on specialized external facilitators in planning, preparing, and executing promotional campaigns. **External facilitators** are organizations or individuals that provide specialized services to marketers and agencies.

eTHICS TRUST—BUT VERIFY

When marketers and their agencies had long histories together, they sealed deals with a handshake. Today, marketers are quick to change partners, so they need a new basis for trust in the client–agency relationship. Enter the auditor. Auditing firms scrutinize all aspects of agency work, from creative services to billing practices. In one assignment, an international ad-agency auditing firm called Firm Decisions found that an agency staffer had billed an average of 17 hours a day, including weekends, for an entire month. One day, she even logged 26 hours. That's not the norm for agency behavior, but it sure does make the auditors look like a wise investment.

Sources: Claire Atkinson, "GM Ad Boss Takes Agencies to Task," *Advertising Age*, June 30, 2003, 1, 26; Erin White, "Making Sure the Work Fits the Bill," *Wall Street Journal*, February 5, 2004, B8.

Marketing and Advertising Research Firms

Many firms rely on outside assistance during the planning phase of advertising. Research firms such as Burke and Simmons can perform original research for marketers, using focus groups, surveys, or experiments to assist in understanding the potential market or consumer perceptions of a product or services. Other research firms, such as SRI International, routinely collect data (from grocery store scanners, for example) and have these data available for a fee.

Advertisers and their agencies also seek measures of promotional program effectiveness after a campaign has run. After an advertisement or promotion has been running for some reasonable amount of time, firms such as Starch INRA Hooper will run recognition tests on print advertisements. Other firms such as Burke offer day-after recall tests of broadcast advertisements. Some firms specialize in message testing to determine whether consumers find advertising messages appealing and understandable.

Consultants

A variety of **consultants** specialize in areas related to the promotional process. Marketers can seek out marketing consultants for assistance in the planning stage. Creative and communications consultants provide insight on issues related to message strategy and message themes. Consultants in event planning and sponsorships offer their expertise to marketers and their agencies. Public relations consultants often work with top management. Media experts can help a marketer determine the proper media mix and efficient media placement.

Three new types of consultants have emerged in recent years:

1. A database consultant works with marketers and agencies to help them identify and then manage databases that allow for the development of IMC programs. Organizations such as Shepard Associates can merge or cross-reference diverse databases from research sources discussed earlier.

2. Consultants specializing in website development and management typically have the creative skills to develop websites and corporate home pages and the technical skills to advise marketers on managing the technical aspects of the user interface.

3. Other consultants work with a firm to integrate information across a wide variety of customer contacts and to organize all this information to achieve customer relationship management (CRM).

consultant individual who specializes in areas related to the promotional process

production facilitator organization that offers essential services during and after the production process

In addition, traditional management consultants, such as Accenture and McKinsey, have started to work with agencies on structure and business strategy.[43] These sorts of consultants also can advise on image strategy, market research procedure, and process and account planning. But the combination of traditional consulting and advertising has not always produced compelling results; the typical role of consultants—focusing on marketing, creative, or technical issues—is the more likely role for consultants in the future.

Production Facilitators

External **production facilitators** offer essential services during and after the production process. Production is the area where advertisers and their agencies rely most heavily on external facilitators. All forms of media advertising require special expertise that even the largest full-service agency, much less a marketer, typically does not retain on staff. In broadcast production, directors, production managers, songwriters, camera operators, audio and lighting technicians, and performers are all essential to preparing a professional, high-quality radio or television ad. Production houses can provide the physical facilities, including sets, stages, equipment, and crews, needed for broadcast

© Yuri Arcurs/Shutterstock.

production. Similarly, in preparing print advertising, brochures, and direct-mail pieces, graphic artists, photographers, models, directors, and producers may be hired. In-store promotions is another area where designing and producing materials require the skills of a specialty organization.

Software Firms

An interesting and complex new category of facilitator in advertising and promotion is that of software firms. The technology in the industry, particularly new media technology, has expanded so rapidly that a variety of software firms facilitate the process. Some of these firms are well established and well known, including Microsoft and Oracle. These firms provide software that gathers and analyzes data on the behavior of Web

Software firms like Hyperion are providing marketers with help in audience analysis and broadband communications. As detailed in its ad, Hyperion specializes in gathering customer data from website visits.

surfers, streams audio and video files, and manages relationships with trade partners. The expertise provided by these firms is so esoteric that even the most advanced full-service or e-commerce agency must seek their assistance.

LO 5 Media Organizations

At the next level in the industry structure are media organizations, which own and manage the media access to consumers. Exhibit 2.5 shows the basic categories of media providers available to marketers:

- *Broadcast media* include television (networks, independent stations, cable, and broadband) and radio (networks and local stations, as well as satellite programming).

- *Print media* include magazines, newspapers, direct mail, and specialty publications such as handbills and theater programs.

- *Interactive media* include online computer services, home-shopping broadcasts, interactive broadcast entertainment, kiosks, CDs, Internet, podcasts, and cell phones.

- *Support media* include all those places that advertisers want to put their messages other than mainstream traditional or interactive media. Often referred to as *out-of-home media*, support media include outdoor (billboards, transit ads, and posters); directories such as print and online Yellow Pages; premiums (for example, logos or messages on key chains, calendars, clothing, and pens); point-of-purchase displays; event sponsorship; and placement of the brand in films, video games, and television programs.

- *Media conglomerates* bring together most or all of these media under one corporate roof. For example, Time Warner, which has been ranked as the world's largest media conglomerate, offers broadcasting, cable, music, film, print publishing, and an Internet presence.[44]

In traditional media, major television networks such as NBC and Fox, as well as national magazines such as *U.S. News & World Report* and *People*, provide advertisers with time and space for their messages at considerable cost. Other media options are more useful for reaching narrowly defined target audiences. Specialty programming on cable television, tightly focused direct-mail pieces, and a well-designed

**Exhibit 2.5
Types of Media Organizations**

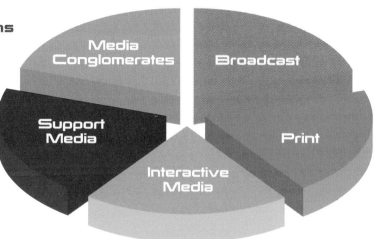

Internet campaign may be better ways to reach a specific audience. One of the new-media options, broadband, lets advertisers target very specific audiences. Internet users can customize their programming by requesting specific broadcasts from various providers. For example, Kit Digital (formerly The FeedRoom) (www.kit-digital.com) is an interactive broadband television news network that allows Web users to customize what news broadcasts they receive.

Target Audiences

The structure of the promotion industry (Exhibit 2.1) and the flow of communication would obviously be incomplete without an audience: If there's no audience, there's no communication. One interesting thing about the audiences for promotional communications is that, with the exception of household consumers, they are also the marketers that use advertising and IMC.

We all are familiar with the type of advertising directed at us in our role as consumers: ads for tooth-paste, sport-utility vehicles, insurance, and on and on. But business and government audiences are keys to the success of many, many firms that sell only to business and government buyers. While many of these firms rely heavily on personal selling in their promotional mix, many also use a variety of IMC tools. For example, KPMG Consulting uses high-profile television and magazine advertising and sponsors events. Many business and trade sellers regularly need public relations, and most use direct mail to communicate with potential customers as a prelude to a personal selling call.

Located at back of the textbook

- **Rip out Chapter in Review Card.**

Located at www.cengagebrain.com

- **Review Key Terms Flashcards (Print or Online).**
- **Complete the Practice Quiz to prepare for tests.**
- **Play "Beat the Clock" and "Quizbowl" to master concepts.**
- **Complete "Crossword Puzzle" to review key terms.**
- **Watch videos on Microsoft for real company examples.**
- **For additional examples, go online to learn about the Web's media conglomerates such as IAC, or read more about the Hispanic, Chinese, and Dutch agencies growing abroad.**

The Evolution of Promoting Brands

Then

Now

Brand promotion evolves to show consumers that they understand the contemporary social scene.

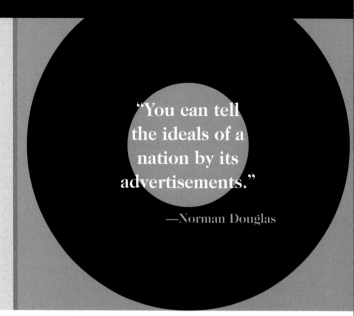

"You can tell the ideals of a nation by its advertisements."

—Norman Douglas

AFTER YOU
FINISH THIS
CHAPTER
GO TO
PAGE 64
FOR STUDY
TOOLS

When Soap Saved Marriage

The 1935 Lux advertisement shown on the first page of this chapter is undoubtedly curious to contemporary audiences. It is, however, typical of its time and probably made perfect sense to its original audience. In the 1930s, in the middle of the Great Depression, anxiety about losing one's husband—and thus one's economic well-being—to divorce was not unfounded. These ads were targeted to a new generation of stay-at-home housewives potentially insecure about their exclusion from the modern world of their husbands, geographically separated from their usually agrarian parents, and living in a fast-paced and unsure urban environment. These ads went out to women at a time when losing one's source of income (husband) could mean poverty and shame. They were read by women in a society where daily bathing was still relatively new but where self-doubt about personal hygiene was on the rise. Such an ad pushed (maybe even created) just the right buttons. If Lux can "remove perspiration odor from underthings," it might save more than colors and fabrics. It might save affection; it might save marriages. If Bob's romantic indifference continues, Sally soon may be back home with Mom or even on the street. But with Lux on the scene, Bob goes home for dinner.

Although some ads today use the same general strategy to sell deodorants, soaps, and feminine-hygiene products, this ad is not read today as it was in 1935. Ads and other promotional messages are part of their times. To really understand marketing, you must understand that successful advertisements, like all types of brand promotion, convey a perceptive understanding of the contemporary social scene. The makers of this 1930s ad understood, helped create, and used the pressures bearing down on the young married women of that time. Society was changing, and these changes affected Sally and a lot of young women like her. This social change and

What do you think?

The Lux ad shown here is timeless.

1   2   3   4   5   6   7
STRONGLY DISAGREE   STRONGLY AGREE

the associated feelings, including uncertainty and anxiety, gave advertisers a chance to offer new products and services to address these very fears and to leverage society's upheaval to their branded benefit.

There is a valuable lesson here from history: When the sands of culture and society shift beneath consumers' feet, marketing opportunities usually present themselves. Today, Sally likely would have a job and be far less economically vulnerable and socially isolated—not to mention that Sally and Bob would both be bathing more often. So we see the 1930s in this ad in the same way that students of the future will view ads of our time: as interesting, revealing, but still somewhat distorted reflections of daily life in the early 21st century. But ads look enough like life to work, at least sometimes. Good promotion is in touch with its time and constantly looks for social and cultural changes that open up marketing opportunities.

Throughout the decades, marketers have tried many different strategies and approaches, and you can learn a lot from their successes and failures. Just about every strategy used today came about decades ago; only the specifics have changed. Studying advertisements and other promotional efforts will teach you when a given technique is really something new, and when and why it worked. You can see how it leveraged the social forces of its time. Besides being inter-

esting, history is very practical. Hint: When you are interviewing for a job in a marketing position, explain how that marketer's best brand promotions worked.

LO 1 The Rise of Advertising

Before there was brand promotion, there was advertising. In many histories of advertising, the process is portrayed as having originated in ancient times, with even primitive peoples practicing some form of advertising. This is substantively incorrect. Whatever those ancients were doing, they weren't advertising. Although the Romans and others communicated with one another with persuasive intent in buying and selling, they were not using advertising. Advertising is a product of modern times and modern media. It came into being as a result of at least four major factors (see Exhibit 3.1):

1. The rise of capitalism
2. The Industrial Revolution
3. Branding as a way for manufacturers to assert power in distribution channels
4. The rise of modern mass media

Exhibit 3.1
A Foundation for Advertising

Photo: © Jason Titzer/iStockphoto.

Rise of Capitalism

In capitalism, organizations compete for resources, called *capital*, in a free-market environment. Part of the competition for resources involves stimulating demand for the seller's goods or services. When an organization successfully stimulates demand, it attracts capital to the organization in the form of money (or other goods) as payment. One of the tools used to stimulate demand is advertising. So, as the Western world turned to capitalism, it was laying a foundation for advertising to become a prominent part of the business environment.

Industrial Revolution

Another economic force that yielded the need for advertising was the **Industrial Revolution**, a rapid shift from an agricultural to an industrial economy. Beginning around 1750 in England, the revolution spread to North America, where it progressed slowly until the early 1800s, when the War of 1812 in the United States boosted domestic production. The emergence of the principle of interchangeable parts and the perfection of the sewing machine, both in 1850, coupled with the American Civil War a decade later, set the scene for widespread industrialization. In the 1840s, the **principle of limited liability**, which caps an investor's risk in a business venture at only his or her shares in a corporation, rather than all personal assets, gained acceptance and resulted in the accumulation of large amounts of capital to finance the Industrial Revolution.

Several changes associated with the Industrial Revolution made advertising attractive and important. Western societies shifted away from fulfilling material needs through household self-sufficiency and became more dependent on a marketplace as a way of life. The mass-production of goods increased rapidly, so manufacturers needed to stimulate demand, something that advertising can do well.

Other developments that were part of the broad Industrial Revolution contributed to the growth and concentration of populations, providing the marketplaces essential to the widespread use of advertising. A revolution in transportation, most dramatically symbolized by the East–West connection of the United States in 1869 by the railroad, represented the beginnings of the distribution network needed to move mass quantities of goods. Finally, rapid population growth and urbanization began in the 1800s. From 1830 to 1860, the population of the United States nearly tripled, from 12.8 million to 31.4 million. During the same period, the number of cities with more than 20,000 inhabitants grew to 43. Historically, there is a strong relationship between per capita outlays for advertising and an increase in the size of cities.[1] As the potential grew for goods to be produced, delivered, and introduced to large numbers of people residing in concentrated areas, the stage was set for advertising to emerge and flourish.

LO 2 Power in Distribution Channels

Another force behind the emergence and growth of advertising relates to manufacturers' pursuit of power in their channel of distribution. If a manufacturer can persuade shoppers to demand its products, wholesalers and retailers will need to sell those products to comply with their customers' desires. A manufacturer that enjoys this level of power in the channel of distribution not only can force other participants in the channel to stock its products, but it is also in a position to command a higher price. In contrast, retail giants like Walmart and Costco recently have grown so large they can dictate what will be carried in their stores and at what price.

In the 1800s, some manufacturers discovered that they could increase their power in distribution channels by using a strategy of **branding** products. These manufacturers developed brand names so that consumers could focus their attention on a clearly identified item. Manufacturers began branding previously unmarked commodities, such as work clothes and packaged goods. Some of the first branded goods to show up on shopkeepers shelves were Ivory soap (1882) and Maxwell House coffee (1892). Once a product had a brand mark and name that consumers could identify, marketers gained power. Of course, an essential tool in stimulating demand for a brand was advertising.

Today, when Procter & Gamble and Kraft spend billions of dollars each year to stimulate demand for such popular brands as Crest and Velveeta, wholesalers and retailers carry these brands because integrated marketing communication has stimulated demand and brought consumers into the store to find those brands. This sort of pursuit of power by manufacturers is argued to have caused the widespread use of advertising.[2]

Modern Mass Media

Advertising also is inextricably tied to the rise of mass communication. The invention of the telegraph in 1844 set in motion a communication revolution. The telegraph not only allowed nations to benefit from the inherent efficiencies of rapid communication, but it also did a great deal to engender a sense of national identity. People began to know and care about people and things going on thousands of miles away. This changed commerce and society.[3]

During the same period, publishers launched many new magazines designed for larger and less socially privileged audiences. They made magazines both a viable mass advertising medium and a democratizing influence on society.[4] Advertising in these mass-circulation magazines projected national brands into national consciousness. National magazines made national advertising possible; national advertising made national brands possible.

For the most part, mass media are supported by advertising. Television networks, radio stations, newspapers, magazines, and websites produce shows, articles, films, programs, and Web content, not for the ultimate goal of entertaining or informing, but to make a healthy profit from selling brands through advertising and branded entertainment. Media vehicles sell audiences to make money.

LO 3 Evolution of Promotion

In the years following the emergence of the first published advertisements, promotion has evolved toward today's focus on brands and an integrated effort at marketing and brand communication. Until recently, most of the developments involved changes in the content and methods of advertising. By looking at this evolution in terms of several periods of history (see Exhibit 3.2), we gain insights into the marketing process and the importance of brands.

Preindustrialization (before 1800)

In the 17th century, printed advertisements appeared in newsbooks (the precursor to newspapers).[5] The messages were informational and appeared on the last pages of the tabloid. In America, the first newspaper advertisement is said to have appeared in 1704 in the *Boston News Letter*. Two notices printed under the heading "Advertising" offered rewards for the return of merchandise stolen from an apparel shop and a wharf.[6]

Advertising grew in popularity during the 18th century in Britain and the American colonies. The *Pennsylvania Gazette* was the first newspaper to separate ads with blank lines, which made the ads easier to read and more prominent.[7] As far as we know, the *Gazette* was also the first newspaper to use illustrations in advertisements.

Advertising changed little over the next 70 years. The early 1800s saw the advent of the penny newspa-

Exhibit 3.2
Periods of Promotion

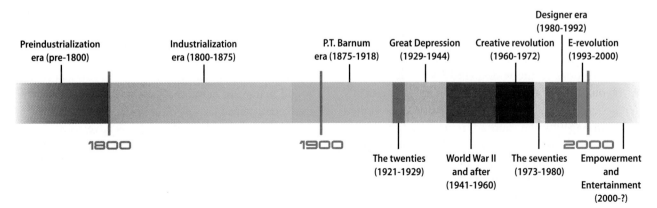

per, which resulted in widespread distribution of the news media. However, advertisements in penny newspapers were dominated by simple announcements by skilled laborers. As one historian notes, "Advertising was closer to the classified notices in newspapers than to product promotions in our media today."[8]

Industrialization (1800–1875)

In practice, marketers in the mid- to late 1800s were trying to cultivate markets for growing production in the context of an increasing urban population. A middle class, spawned by the economic windfall of regular wages from factory jobs, was beginning to emerge. This newly developing populace with economic means was concentrated geographically in cities more than ever before.

By 1850, circulation of the **dailies**, as newspapers were then called, was estimated at 1 million copies per day. The first advertising agent—thought to be Volney Palmer, who opened shop in Philadelphia—basically worked for the newspapers by soliciting orders for advertising and collecting payment from advertisers.[9] Merchants readily embraced this new opportunity to reach consumers, and at least one newspaper doubled

its advertising volume from 1849 to 1850.[10]

With the expansion of newspaper circulation fostered by the railroads, a new era of opportunity emerged for advertising. The practice of advertising was not universally hailed as honorable, however. Without any formal regulation, advertising was considered an embarrassment by many segments of society, including some parts of the business community. At one point, firms that used advertising even risked their credit ratings; banks considered the practice a sign of financial weakness. The negative image wasn't helped much by ads for patent medicines, the first products heavily advertised on a national scale. These advertisements promised cures for every ailment from rheumatism to cancer.

P. T. Barnum Era (1875–1918)

Only when America was well on its way to being an urban, industrialized nation did advertising become a vital and integral part of the social landscape. Shortly after the Civil War in the United States, marketers began using modern advertising—ads that we would recognize as advertising. From about 1875 to 1918, advertising ushered in what has come to be known as **consumer culture**, a way of life centered on consumption.

Advertising became a full-fledged industry in this period. It was the time of advertising legends: Albert Lasker, head of Lord and Thomas in Chicago, possibly the most influential agency of its day; Francis W. Ayer, founder of N. W. Ayer; John E. Powers, the most important copywriter of the period; Earnest Elmo Calkins, champion of advertising design; Claude Hopkins, influential in promoting ads as "dramatic salesmanship"; and John E. Kennedy, creator of "reason why" advertising.[11] These were the founders, visionaries, and artists who played principal roles in the establishment of the advertising business. An interesting side note: Several of the founders of this industry had fathers who shared the very same occupation: minister. These young men would have been exposed to public speaking and the passionate selling of ideas as well as to the new "religion" of modernity: city life, science, progress, unapologetic fun, and public consumption.

By 1900, total sales of patent medicines in the United States had reached $75 million—an early

As newspaper circulation grew, so did the use of advertising. Unfortunately, ads like this one—for a patent medicine that supposedly could cure all liver ailments, including cancer—did not help the image of advertising.

demonstration of the power of advertising.[12] The stage was set for advertising's modern form. During this period, the first advertising agencies were founded, and the practice of branding products became the norm. Advertising was motivated by the need to sell the vastly increased supply of goods brought on by mass production and by the demands of an increasingly urban population seeking social identity through (among other things) branded products. In earlier times, when shoppers went to the general store and bought soap sliced from a large, locally produced cake, advertising had no place. But with advertising's ability to create meaningful differences between near-identical soaps, advertising suddenly held a very prominent place in early consumer culture. Advertising made unmarked commodities into social symbols and identity markers, which allowed marketers to charge far more money for them. This is the power of brands.

Advertising was completely unregulated in the United States until 1906. In that year, Congress passed the **Pure Food and Drug Act**, which required manufacturers to list the active ingredients of their products on their labels. You still could put some pretty amazing things in products; you just had to tell the consumer. The direct effect of this federal act on advertising was minimal; advertisers could continue to say just about anything—and usually did. But the law probably started to slow some of the more outrageous offenders of truth and ethics. Many advertisements still took on the style of a sales pitch for "snake oil." The tone and spirit of advertising owed more to P. T. Barnum—"There's a sucker born every minute"—than to any other influence. And as Barnum was the famous showman and circus entrepreneur (Barnum and Bailey Circus) of his day, ads of this period were bold, carnivalesque, garish, and often full of dense copy that hurled incredible claims.

Ads of this era have some notable qualities:

- A lot of copy (words)
- Prominence of the product itself and relative lack of real-world context (visuals) in which the advertised product was to be consumed
- Small size
- Little color, few photographs
- Plenty of hyperbole

Ads from the P. T. Barnum era were often packed with fantastic promises, like this claim you could raise ducks profitably anywhere.

During this period, despite some variation and steady evolution, ads generally remained this way until World War I.

Consider the world in which these ads existed. It was a period of rapid urbanization, massive immigration, labor unrest, and significant concerns about the abuses of capitalism. Some of capitalism's excesses and abuses, including deceptive and misleading advertising, were the targets of early reformers. It also was the age of suffrage, the progressive movement, motion pictures, and mass culture. The world was changing rapidly, which was disruptive and unsettling, but advertising was there to offer solutions to the stresses of modern life, no matter how real, imagined, or suggested. Remember, social and cultural change often opens up opportunities for marketers.

The Twenties (1918–1929)

In many ways, the Roaring Twenties began a couple of years early. After World War I, advertising found respectability, fame, and glamour. It was the most modern of all professions and, short of starring in the movies, the most fashionable. According to popular perception, it was where the young, smart, and sophisticated worked and played. During the 1920s, it also was a place where institutional freedom rang. The prewar movement to reform and regulate advertising was pretty much dissipated by the distractions of the war and advertising's role in the war effort. During World War I, the advertising industry learned a valuable lesson: Donating time and personnel to the common good is not only good civics but smart business.

The 1920s were prosperous times. Most (but not all) enjoyed a previously unequaled standard of living. It was an age of considerable hedonism; the pleasure principle was practiced and appreciated, openly and often. The Victorian Age was over, and a great social experiment in the joys of consumption was under way. Victorian repression and modesty gave way to a more open sexuality and a love affair with modernity. Advertising was made for this burgeoning sensuality; advertising gave people permission to enjoy. Ads of the era exhorted consumers to have a good time and instructed them in how to do it. Consumption not only was respectable but expected. Being a consumer became synonymous with being a citizen—a *good* citizen.

During these good economic times, advertising taught consumers how to be thoroughly modern and how to avoid the pitfalls of this new age. Consumers learned of halitosis from Listerine advertising and about body odor from Lifebuoy advertising. There happened to be a product with a cure for just about any social anxiety and personal failing, many of which had supposedly been brought on as side effects of modernity. This was perfect for the growth and entrenchment of advertising as an institution: Modern times bring on many wonderful new things, but the new way of life has side effects that, in turn, have to be fixed by even more modern goods and services. For example, modern canned food replaced fresh fruit and vegetables, thus "weakening the gums," causing dental problems— which could be cured by a modern toothbrush. The result was a seemingly endless consumption chain: Needs lead to products, new needs are created by new products, newer products solve newer needs, and so on. This chain of needs is essential to a capitalist economy, which must continue to expand in order to survive. It also makes a necessity of advertising.

Other ads from the 1920s emphasized other modernity themes, such as the division between public workspace, the male domain of the office and the private, "feminine" space of the home. Two separate consumption domains were created, with women placed in charge of the latter, more economically important one. Advertisers figured out that women were responsible for as much as 80 percent of household

These ads from the 1920s show widely divergent roles for men and women. The business world was a male space, and the home was where women's work was done.

Advertising during the 1920s chronicled the state of technology and styles for clothing, furniture, and social functions. Advertising specified social relationships between people and products by depicting the social settings and circumstances into which people and products fit. Consider this ad for Standard Sanitary bathroom fixtures showing a carefully constructed snapshot of domestic life. Note the attention to the social setting into which plumbing fixtures were to fit. Is the ad really about plumbing? Yes, in a very important way, because it demonstrates plumbing in a social context that works for both advertiser and consumer. Modern consumers, consumers who really care about the best for their family, use modern plumbing.

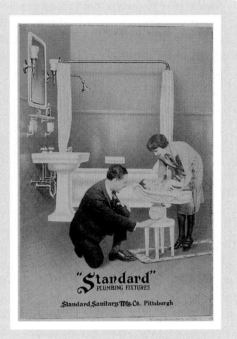

purchases. While 1920s men were out in the "jungle" of the work world, women made most purchase decisions. From this time forward, women became the primary target of brand promotion.

Another important aspect of advertising in the 1920s and beyond was the role played by science and technology. Science and technology were in many ways the new religions of the modern era. Consumers saw ads appealing to the popularity of science in virtually all product categories during this period. Sonatron said its radio tubes were "bombarded with energy," and Pet evaporated milk announced that it was "approved by" the new field of "domestic science."

The style of 1920s ads was more visual than ads of earlier eras. Twenties ads showed slices of life—carefully constructed "snapshots" of social life with the product. In these ads, the relative position, background, and dress of the people using or needing the advertised product were crafted carefully, as they are today. These visual lessons generally were about how to fit in with the "smart" crowd, how to be urbane and modern by using the newest conveniences, and how not to fall victim to the perils and pressures of the new fast-paced modern world.

The J. Walter Thompson advertising agency was the dominant agency of the period. Stanley Resor, Helen Resor, and James Webb Young brought this agency to a leadership position through intelligent management, vision, and great advertising. Helen Resor, the first prominent female advertising executive, was instrumental in J. Walter Thompson's success. Still, the most famous ad person of the era was a man named Bruce Barton. Not only the leader of BBDO, Barton also was a best-selling author, most notably of a 1924 book called *The Man Nobody Knows*,[13] which portrayed Jesus as the archetypal ad man. This blending of Christian and capitalist principles was enormously attractive to a people struggling to reconcile traditional religious thought, which preached against excess, and the new religion of consumption, which preached just the opposite.

Great Depression (1929–1941)

If you weren't there, it's hard to imagine how bad the **Great Depression** was:

By 1932, a quarter of American workers were unemployed. But matters were worse than this suggests, for three quarters of those who had jobs were working part-time—either working short hours, or faced with chronic and repeated layoffs. . . . Millions actually went hungry, not once, but again and again. Millions knew what it was like to eat bread and water for supper, sometimes for days at a stretch. A million people were drifting around the country begging, among them thousands of children, including numbers of girls disguised as boys.[14]

The Depression was brutal, crushing, and mean. It killed people; it broke lives. And it forever changed the way people thought about a great many things: their government, business, money, spending, saving, credit, and, not coincidentally, advertising.

Just as sure as advertising was glamorous in the 1920s, it was villainous in the 1930s. It was part of big business, and big business, big greed, and big lust had gotten America into the great economic depression beginning in 1929—or so the story goes. The public began to see advertising as something that had tempted and seduced them into the excesses for which they were being punished.

Advertisers responded to this feeling by adopting a tough, no-nonsense advertising style. The stylish and highly aesthetic ads of the 1920s gave way to harsher and more cluttered ads. As one historian said, "The new hard-boiled advertising mystique brought a proliferation of 'ugly,' attention-grabbing, picture-dominated copy in the style of the tabloid newspaper."[15] Clients wanted their money's worth, and agencies responded by cramming every bit of copy and image they could into their ads or using obviously inappropriate sex appeals. This type of advertising persisted, quite likely making the relationship between the public and the institution of advertising even worse. (Regrettably, it remains an industry impulse in bad economic times today.) The themes in advertisements traded on the anxieties of the day—losing one's job, being a bad provider, and lack of sex appeal.

Another notable event during these years was the emergence of radio as a significant advertising medium. During the 1930s, the number of radio stations rose from a handful to 814 by the end of the decade, and the number of radio sets in use more than quadrupled to 51 million, just over one radio set per household. Radio was in its heyday as a news and entertainment medium, and it would remain so until the 1950s, when television emerged. Radio offered the ability to create a sense of community in which people thousands of miles apart listened to and became involved with their favorite radio soap opera, so named in reference to the soap sponsors of these shows.

Advertising, like the rest of the country, suffered dark days during this period. Agencies cut salaries and forced staff to work four-day weeks, without pay for the mandatory extra day off. Clients demanded frequent review of work, and agencies were compelled to provide more and more free services to keep accounts. Advertising would emerge from this depression, just as the economy itself did, during World War II. However, the advertising industry never again would reach its pre-Depression status. It became the subject of a well-organized and angry consumerism movement. The U.S. Congress passed real reform in this period. In 1938, the Wheeler-Lea Amendments to the Federal Trade Commission Act declared "deceptive acts of commerce" to be against the law; this was interpreted to include advertising. Between 1938 and 1940, the FTC issued 18 injunctions against advertisers; one of these forced Fleischmann's Yeast "to stop claiming that it cured crooked teeth, bad skin, constipation, and halitosis."[16]

World War II and After (1941–1960)

Many people mark the end of the Depression with the start of America's involvement in World War II in December 1941. During the war, advertising often made direct reference to the war effort, linking the product with patriotism and helping to rehabilitate the tarnished image of advertising. Marketers sold war bonds and encouraged conservation. Of all companies, Coca-Cola probably both contributed to and benefited the most from the company's amazingly successful efforts to get Coca-Cola to the front lines. When the war was over, Coke had bottling plants all over the globe, and returning American GIs were loyal to Coke over competitors such as Pepsi by 4:1.[17]

He had to fight himself so hard...
he didn't put it over

YES, he was his own worst enemy. His appearance was against him and he knew it. Oh why had he neglected the bath that morning, the shave, the change of linen? Under the other fellow's gaze it was hard to forget that cheap feeling. There's self-respect in soap and water. The clean-cut chap can look any man in the face and tell him the facts—for when you're clean, your appearance fights for you.

There's self-respect in SOAP & WATER

PUBLISHED BY THE ASSOCIATION OF AMERICAN SOAP AND GLYCERINE PRODUCERS, INC. TO AID THE WORK OF CLEANLINESS INSTITUTE

Advertising during the 1930s traded on the anxieties of the day.

The war got women to join the workforce in what were non-traditional roles, as seen in the so-called Rosie the Riveter ads. After the war ended in 1945, many women left their jobs (both voluntarily and involuntarily). In her recollections of the 1950s, Wini Breines notes the return to traditional roles:

> *Almost one-half of all women married while they were still teenagers. Two out of three white women in college dropped out before they graduated.*[18]

Following World War II, the economy continued (with a few starts and stops) to improve, and the consumption spree was on again. The first shopping malls were built. This time, however, public sentiment toward advertising was fundamentally different from what it had been following WWI. This time, there was widespread belief that America's successful propaganda experts at the War Department had simply moved over to Madison Avenue and started manipulating consumer minds. Perhaps because there was also great concern about the rise of communism and its use of "mind control," it was natural to believe that advertising was involved in the same type of pursuit, only aimed at purchasing instead of politics. The United States was filled with suspicion on a variety of topics—McCarthyism, the bomb, repressed sexual thoughts (a resurgence of Freudian thought), and even aliens from outer space. Otherwise-normal people were building bomb shelters in their backyards, wondering whether their neighbors were communists and whether listening to rock 'n' roll would make their daughters less virtuous.

In this environment of mass fear, stories began circulating that advertising agencies were doing motivation research and using the "psychological sell," which served only to fuel an underlying suspicion of advertising. Similarly, Americans began to fear they were being seduced by **subliminal advertising** (subconscious advertising) to buy all sorts of things they didn't really want or need. As their homes and garages filled up with their purchases, some consumers blamed advertising—and so a great excuse for lack of self-control was born. A best-selling 1957 book, *The Hidden Persuaders*, bolstered that view by maintaining that slick advertising works on the subconscious.[19] Suspicions about slick advertising persist and are a big business for the "aren't consumers dumb?/aren't

Advertisers often used America's involvement in World War II as a way to link their products with patriotism. That link gave advertising a much-needed image boost.

advertisers evil?" propagandists. Selling fears about advertising always has been good business.

The most incredible story of the period involved a man named James Vicary. According to historian Stuart Rogers, in 1957, Vicary convinced the marketing world, and most of the U.S. population, that he had successfully demonstrated a technique to get consumers to do exactly what advertisers wanted. He claimed to have placed subliminal messages in a motion picture, brought in audiences, and recorded the results. He claimed that the embedded messages of "Eat Popcorn" and "Drink Coca-Cola" had increased sales of popcorn by 57.5 percent and Coca-Cola by 18.1 percent. He held press conferences and took retainer fees from advertising agencies. According to later research, he then skipped town, just ahead of reporters who had figured out that none of his claims was true. He disappeared, leaving no bank accounts and no forwarding address, with about $4.5 million (around $28 million in today's dollars) paid to him by advertising agencies and clients.[20] Vicary probably pulled off the greatest scam in advertising history. Unfortunately, a lot of people still believe in the hype he was selling and that advertisers can actually manipulate unsuspecting people.

Besides fears, the 1950s were about sex, youth culture, rock 'n' roll, and television. In terms of sex, volumes could be written about the paradoxical '50s. This was the time of neo-Freudian pop psychology and *Beach Blanket Bingo*, with sexual innuendo everywhere; at the same time, very conservative pronouncements about sexual mores were giving young people, particularly women, contradictory messages. What's more, young people were advertised to with a singular focus and force never seen before, becoming, as a result, the first "kid" and then "teen" markets. Because of their sheer numbers, they ultimately would constitute an unstoppable youth culture, one that everyone else had to deal with and try to please—the baby boomers. They would, over their parents' objections, buy rock 'n' roll records in numbers large enough to revolutionize the music industry. Now they buy SUVs, mutual funds, and $8,000 bicycles.

And then there was TV. Nothing like it had happened before. Its rise from pre–World War II science experiment to 90 percent penetration in U.S. households occurred during this period. At first, advertisers didn't know what to do with it and did two- and three-minute commercials, typically demonstrations. Of course, they soon began to learn TV's look and language.

This era also saw growth in the U.S. economy and in household incomes. The suburbs emerged, and along with them, there was an explosion of consumption. Technological change was relentless and was a national obsession. Along with the television, the telephone and automatic washer and dryer became common to the American lifestyle. Advertisements of this era were characterized by scenes of modern life, social promises, and reliance on science and technology.

Into all of this, 1950s advertising projected a confused, often harsh, at other times, sappy presence. It rarely is remembered as advertising's golden age. Two of the most significant advertising personalities of the period were Rosser Reeves of the Ted Bates agency, who is best remembered for his ultra-hard-sell style, and consultant Ernest Dichter, best remembered for his motivational research, which focused on the subconscious and symbolic elements of consumer desire.

Typical advertisements from this contradictory and jumbled period in American advertising show mythic nuclear families, well-behaved children, our "buddy" the atom, the last days of unquestioned faith in science, and rigid (but about to break loose) gender roles, while the rumblings of the sexual revolution of the 1960s were just audible. In a few short years, the atom no longer would be our friend; we would question science; youth would rebel and become a hugely important market; women and African Americans would demand inclusion and fairness; and bullet bras would be replaced with no bras.

Creative Revolution (1960–1972)

The cultural revolution in the 1960s affected just about everything—including advertising. Ads started to take on the themes, the language, and the look of the 1960s. But as an institution, advertising in the United States during the 1960s was actually slow to respond to the massive social revolution going on all around it. While the nation was struggling with civil rights, the Vietnam War, and the sexual revolution, advertising often still was portraying women and other minorities in subservient roles. Advertising agencies remained one of the whitest industries in America, despite images in the ads. In fact, much of the sexual revolution just made women into boy toys in ads. Gays and lesbians, as far as advertising was concerned, didn't exist.

In the 1950s, society's view of sex was paradoxical: titillating but innocent. (It's just underwear, and she's alone, just getting dressed.)

The only thing truly revolutionary about 1960s advertising was the **creative revolution**. This revolution was characterized by the "creatives" (art directors and copywriters) having a bigger say in the management of their agencies and the look and voice of the ads. The emphasis in advertising turned "from ancillary services to the creative product; from science and research to art, inspiration, and intuition."[21]

At first, the look of this revolutionary advertising was clean and minimalist, with simple copy and a sense of self-effacing humor. Later (around 1968 or so), it became self-aware and unabashedly latched itself onto social revolution—including, irony of all ironies, the antimaterialist movement. Advertising admitted being advertising (and even poked fun at itself). More than anything, the creative revolution was about self-awareness, saying, "OK, here's an ad, you know it's an ad—and so do we."

The 1960s was also a time when advertising began to understand that it was all about hip, cool, youth, and rebellion. Whatever became cool, ads had to incorporate into their messages. The '60s cultural revolution soon became ad copy. Everything became rebellion; even an unhip brand like Dodge traded successfully on the "Dodge Rebellion."[22] Even hip anti-advertising sentiment could be used to help sell stuff through advertising. Marketers learned that people (particularly youth) play out their revolutionary phase *through* consumption—you've got to have the right look, the right clothes, the right revolutionary garb. Once advertising learned that it successfully could attach itself to youth, hipness, and revolution, it never went back:

> *Every few years, it seems, the cycles of the sixties repeat themselves on a smaller scale, with new rebel youth cultures bubbling their way to a happy replenishing of the various culture industries' depleted arsenal of cool. . . . As adman Merle Steir wrote back in 1967, "Youth has won. Youth must always win. The new naturally replaces the old." And we will have new generations of youth rebellion as certainly as we will have generations of mufflers or toothpaste or footwear.*[23]

The creative revolution, and the look it produced, most often is associated with four famous advertising agencies: Leo Burnett in Chicago, Ogilvy & Mather in New York (a little less so), Doyle Dane Bernbach

$1.02 a pound.

Volkswagen of Ameica, Inc.

Through innovative advertising, Volkswagen refuels its original message that cars aren't expensive luxuries. At $1.02 a pound, this Beetle is cheaper than ground round.

in New York (the most), and Wells Rich and Green in New York (deserving of more credit than they get). They were led in this revolution by agency heads Leo Burnett, David Ogilvy, Bill Bernbach, and Mary Wells.

Of course, it would be wrong to characterize the entire period as a creative revolution. Many ads in the 1960s still reflected traditional values and relied on relatively uncreative executions. Typical of the more traditional ads during the era is a message from Goodyear featuring a helpless and anxious young woman gazing at a flat tire on her car next to the headline "When there's no man around, Goodyear should be."

In the era from 1960 to 1972, advertisers became generally aware of their industry's role in consumer culture: Advertising was an icon of a culture fascinated with consumption. Besides playing a role in encouraging consumption, advertising had become a symbol of consumption itself. The creative revolution did not last long, but advertising was changed forever. After the 1960s, it never again would be quite as naive about its own place in society; it since has become much more self-conscious. In a very significant way, advertising learned how to dodge the criticism of capitalism forever: Hide in plain sight.

The Seventies (1973–1980)

The reelection of Richard Nixon in 1972 marked the real start of the 1970s. America had just suffered through its first lost war, the memory of four student protesters shot and killed by the National Guard at Kent State University in the spring of 1970 was still vivid, Mideast nations appeared to be dictating the energy policy of the United States, and we were, as President Jimmy Carter suggested late in this period, in a national malaise. In this environment, advertising again retreated into the tried-and-true but hackneyed styles of decades before. The creative revolution of the 1960s gave way to a slowing economy and a return to the hard sell.

This period also marked the beginning of the second wave of the American feminist movement. In the 1970s, advertisers actually started to present women in "new" roles and to include people of color. Twenty years later, they would admit gays and lesbians exist.

The '70s were the end of "the '60s" and the end of whatever revolution one wished to speak of. Accounts of this period describe it as a time of excess and self-induced numbness. This was the age of polyester, disco, blow, and driving 55, the era of self-help and self-ishness. "Me" became the biggest word in the 1970s. What a great environment for advertising. All of society was telling people that it not only was okay to be selfish, but it was the right thing to do. Selfishness was said to be natural and good. A refrain similar to "Hey, babe, I can't be good to you if I'm not good to me," became a '70s mantra. Of course, being good to oneself often meant buying stuff.

Paradoxically, the '70s also resulted in added regulation and the protection of special audiences.

© Andrew Lever/Shutterstock.

ETHICS DISCOVERING GAY CONSUMERS

One of the first gay-friendly commercials aired by a major corporation showed a couple shopping for a dining room table at IKEA. The 1994 ad, in which the couple debating furniture styles and finishing each other's sentences were two men, broke down a long-standing cultural barrier. It generated controversy but eventually became a touchstone for marketers considering how to appeal to gay and lesbian consumers.

In 2006, IKEA prominently featured a gay couple in another ad, this time with a young child and a golden retriever. The ad for living room furniture closes with the line "Why shouldn't sofas come in flavors, just like families?" Why shouldn't advertisements as well?

Sources: Aparna Kumar, "Commercials: Out of the Closet," *Wired*, May 8, 2001, http://www.wired.com; Stuart Elliott, "Hey, Gay Spender, Marketers Spending Time with You," *New York Times*, June 26, 2006, C8.

Advertising encountered a new round of challenges on several fronts. First, there was growing concern over what effect $200 million a year in advertising had on children. A group of women in Boston formed **Action for Children's Television**, which lobbied the government to limit the amount and content of advertising directed at children. Established regulatory bodies, in particular the **Federal Trade Commission (FTC)** and the industry's **National Advertising Review Board**, demanded higher standards of honesty and disclosure from the advertising industry. Several firms were subjected to legislative mandates and fines because their advertising was judged to be misleading. Most notable among these firms were Warner-Lambert (for advertising that Listerine mouthwash could cure and prevent colds), Campbell's (for putting marbles in the bottom of a soup bowl to bolster its look in ads), and Anacin (for advertising that its aspirin could help relieve tension).

Even as the process of advertising was being restricted by consumer and governmental regulatory challenges, technological advances posed unprecedented opportunities. It was also the birth of what were essentially program-length commercials, particularly in children's television. Product/show blends for toys like Strawberry Shortcake made regulation more difficult: If it's a show about a product, then it's not really an ad (and can't be regulated as an ad)—or is it? This drove regulators crazy, but program-length commercials were incredibly smart marketing.[24] They generally were treated by regulators as shows and opened the door for countless numbers of imitators. The "new" branded entertainment had its real start here, not 30 years later.

While advertising during this period featured more African Americans and women, the effort to adequately represent and serve these consumers was fairly minimal; advertising agency hiring and promotion practices with respect to minorities were formally challenged in the courts. Despite this, two important agencies owned and managed by African Americans emerged and thrived: Thomas J. Burrell founded Burrell Advertising, and Byron Lewis founded Uniworld. Burrell perhaps is best known for ads that rely on the principle of "positive realism." Positive realism is the use of black actors "in authentic, optimistic settings" in which it is evident that "the products are intended for them, not just the general [white] market."[25] (Go to www.littleafrica.com/resources/advertising.htm for a current list of major African-American advertising agencies and resources.)

Another very important person in opening up the promotion industry to minorities was John H. Johnson, founder of *Ebony* magazine. He was in many ways the man who made possible the black American experience in publishing, marketing, and advertising. He opened up enormous opportunities for black entrepreneurs, advertisers, and artists.

The 1970s also signaled a period of growth in communications technology. Consumers began to surround themselves with devices related to communication. The VCR, cable television, and the laserdisc player were all developed during the 1970s. Cable TV claimed 20 million subscribers by the end of the decade. Similarly, cable programming grew in quality, with viewing options such as ESPN and Nickelodeon. As cable subscribers and their viewing options increased, marketers learned how to reach more specific audiences through the diversity of programming on cable systems.

This era saw the beginning of the merger mania that swept the industry throughout the end of the decade and into the next. Most of the major agencies merged with one another and with non-U.S. agencies as well.

In all of this, the look of advertising was about as interesting as it was in the 1950s. Often, advertisements focused on the product itself, rather than on creative technique. At ad agencies, management took control. Among employees used to creative control, the idea of "bottom-liners" struck deep at the soul. But the cultural revolution of the 1960s and 1970s (and the creative revolution) was over. By the end of the 1970s, American culture was really very different, so the ad business changed as well. The youth undercurrent of revolution and rebellion was more cynical and ambivalent about consumption and advertising. These youth were the first generation to grow up on TV advertising.

Photos: top, © Zoltan Pataki/Shutterstock; bottom, © PiotrMaciejewski/Shutterstock.

Designer Era (1980–1992)

Consumers had a lot of income to spend in the 1980s. By one account, "In 1980, the average American had twice as much real income as his parents had had at the end of WWII."[26] The political, social, business, and advertising landscapes changed in 1980 with the election of Ronald Reagan. The country made a right, and conservative politics were the order of the day. There was, of course, some backlash and many countercurrents, but the conservatives were in the mainstream. Greed was good, stuff was good, and advertising was good.

Many ads from the Republican era are particularly social-class conscious and values conscious. They openly promote consumption but in a conservative way, all wrapped up in "traditional American values." The quintessential 1980s ad may be the 1984 television ad for President Ronald Reagan's reelection campaign, "Morning in America." Other advertisers quickly followed with ads that looked similar to "Morning in America."

At the same time, several new trends in communication technology were emerging, and these led to more creative, bold, and provocative advertising. Television advertising of this period was influenced by the rapid-cut editing style of music videos shown on MTV. George Lois, himself of the 1960s creative revolution, was hired by MTV to save the fledgling

SOME CIRCLES SHALL REMAIN EXCLUSIVE.

The ultimate recognition from your banker: A gold MasterCard card.

Courtesy of MasterCard.

This MasterCard ad demonstrates the social-class and designer consciousness of the 1980s.

network after a dismal first year. After calling a lot of people who were unwilling to take the chance, he got Mick Jagger to proclaim, "I want my MTV." The network turned around, and music television surged into popular consciousness. Most importantly for us, television ads in the 1980s started looking like MTV videos: rapid cuts with a very self-conscious character.

> **infomercial** long advertisement that looks like a talk show or product demonstration

This was also the age of the **infomercial**, a long advertisement that looks like a talk show or a half-hour product demonstration. If you watch late-night cable television, you've probably seen some guy lighting his car on fire as part of a demonstration for car wax. These very long ads initially aired in late-night television time slots, when audiences were small and airtime was relatively inexpensive. Infomercials have since spread to other off-peak time slots, including those with somewhat larger audiences, and they have gained respect along the way. The Psychic Friends Network, Bowflex, and a wide assortment of weight loss and hair care products are all examples of products and services recently promoted on infomercials. You might check out www.as-on-tv-ads.com for more examples.

The advertising of the 1980s had a few other changes. One was the growth and creative impact of British agencies, particularly Saatchi and Saatchi. One lesson Saatchi and Saatchi realized earlier than most was that politics, culture, and products all resonate together. The Saatchi and Saatchi ads of this period were often sophisticated and politically non-neutral. They worked and began to be copied (at least the sensibility) in other places, including the United States.

The late 1970s and into the 1980s was the "golden" age of punk and alternative. The idealism of the 1960s was fading, and cynicism was on the rise. Youth's power as a market and as style arbiters continued to grow. If an overall attitude toward commerce can be characterized, it was one of deep ambivalence: People didn't trust commerce—it somehow had helped kill whatever was "authentic"—but they also knew it wasn't going to go away. So, just as author Thomas Frank (author of *Conquest of Cool*) would have predicted, punk, alternative, and anti-1960s cynicism started showing up as the basis for hip ads of this era.

E-Revolution (1993–2000)

As modern advertising entered its second century, it had become more self-conscious than ever. In the 1990s, self-parody was the inside joke of the day, except everyone was "inside." Winks and nods to the media-savvy audience were becoming pretty common. Advertising was fast, and it was everywhere. Nineties ads were generally more visually oriented and much more self-aware. They said "this is an ad" in their look and feel. They had a young and ironic flavor. Some call them "postmodern."

Some said advertising in the 1990s was "dead," killed by the World Wide Web and other new media, but that turned out to be an exaggeration. By the end of the decade, ads were still ads, and they were very much alive. Still, it was phase 1 of the Web revolution in advertising. It ended with mixed results, after a couple of scary moments:

- *The setting*: American Association of Advertising Agencies (4As) annual conference, May 1994. *The speaker*: Edwin L. Artzt, then chairman and CEO of Procter & Gamble, the then $40 billion-a-year marketer of consumer packaged goods. *The news*: Artzt dropped a bomb on the advertising industry when he warned that agencies must confront a "new media" future that wouldn't be driven by traditional advertising. Although P&G was spending about $1 billion a year on television advertising, Artzt told the 4As audience, "From where we stand today, we can't be sure that ad-supported TV programming will have a future in the world being created—a world of video-on-demand, pay-per-view, and subscription TV. These are designed to carry no advertising at all."[27] An icy chill filled the room.

- *The setting*: The 4As annual conference, one year later. *The speaker*: William T. Esrey, chairman and CEO of Sprint. *The news*: Esrey gave advertisers another jolt with a point that was somewhat different but equally challenging. He said clients would "hold ad agencies more closely accountable for results than ever before." Again, the challenge would come from technology: "It's . . . because we know the technology is there to measure advertising impact more precisely than you have done in the past."[28]

Esrey's point was that **Interactive media** would allow direct measurement of ad exposure and impact, quickly revealing which advertisements or other brand messages perform well and which do not, and marketers would hold their agencies accountable for results. Exhibit 3.3 shows how this was supposed to work with direct-response advertising online. Well, the precise measurement didn't really work out, but accountability still became the order of the day. As a result, ad agencies are operating with fewer staff and smaller

margins than before. Clients became more tight-fisted and at least tried to demand accountability. Also, there was more competition for the money: The new media wanted it, but so did the old.

Unsure of what could be delivered and what could be counted, Procter & Gamble hosted an August 1998 Internet "summit" to investigate "the difficulties confronted by marketers using online media to pitch products."[29] Some of these problems were technological: incompatible technical standards, limited bandwidth, and disappointing measurement of audience size and return on investment. Others were the result of naïveté. Marketers such as P&G want to know what they are getting and what it costs when they place an Internet ad. Does anyone notice these ads, or do people click right past them? What would "exposure" in this environment really mean? Is "exposure" really even a meaningful term in the new media ad world? How do you use these new media to build brand relationships? At the end of this summit, P&G reaffirmed its commitment to the Internet.

But history again showed that measurement of bang for buck (return on investment, ROI) in advertising (Internet or not) is very elusive. While better than TV, the Internet fundamentally was unable to

Advertising of the 1990s was highly visual and self-aware. This shoe ad parodies advertising formats with a dog for a model and the statement "Bull terrier wears shoes from Pussyfoot."

Exhibit 3.3
Better Data Online?

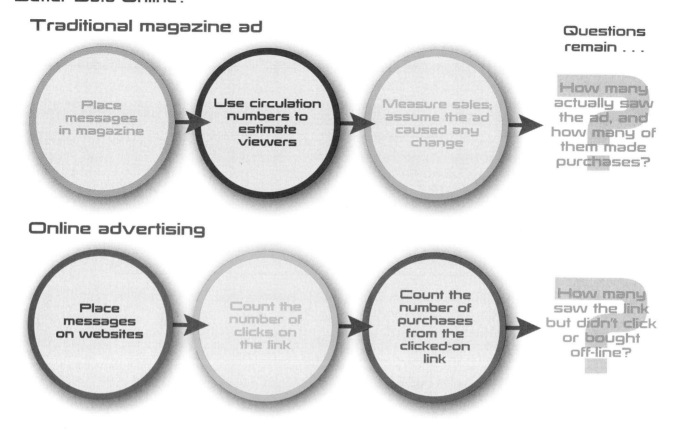

Traditional magazine ad

Place messages in magazine → Use circulation numbers to estimate viewers → Measure sales; assume the ad caused any change → Questions remain . . . How many actually saw the ad, and how many of them made purchases?

Online advertising

Place messages on websites → Count the number of clicks on the link → Count the number of purchases from the clicked-on link → How many saw the link but didn't click or bought off-line?

yield precise measurements of return on investment in advertisement. Too many variables, too much noise in the system, too many lagged (delayed) effects, and too many uncertainties about who is really online abound.

That's not a big surprise for those who pay attention to history: Advertising's impact is always tough to measure. Even with all this technology, it still is. Which bump in sales comes from where is still elusive.

Another change in the world of promotion was a challenge to New York's claim as the center of advertising activity. In the United States, the center moved west, with the ascendancy of agencies in California, Minnesota, Oregon, and Washington. In the 1990s, these agencies tended to be more creatively oriented and less interested in numbers-oriented research than those in New York. Other hot or nearly hot ad-shop markets include Minneapolis, Austin, Atlanta, Houston, and Dallas. Outside the United States, London emerged as the key player, with Singapore and Seoul as close seconds.

LO 4 Consumer Empowerment (2000-Present)

In 2000, the dot-com bubble burst as Internet companies that had burned cash like kindling without turning a profit died off. Part of the problem was the lack of a good revenue model for brand promotion on the Web. Pop-ups and easy-to-avoid Internet ads had just not generated enough advertising revenue. Online buying continued to grow, but online advertising couldn't catch up until companies became more sophisticated at using alternative media to generate calculable and attributable real sales.

Since 2001 or so, this has really begun to happen. Phase 2 of the e-promotion revolution (Web 2.0) has been much more successful. Agencies like StarCom were truly revolutionary and brilliant in their ability to figure how to make real money in this new environment.

Besides delivering more sophisticated brand messages, Web 2.0 made consumers more in charge than ever. It is widely admitted in industry circles that the day of the marketer's heavy hand is pretty much over. Consumers can communicate with each other, actually talk back to the marketer with one voice or millions, and even make their own ads and distribute them on media such as YouTube. The promotion industry is accepting the fact that consumers now can do many of the very same things that only big studios, agencies, and distributors could do a decade ago. Consumers now co-create brands. The reactions of consumers (particularly young people) are fused with agency "professional" creative to make ads that are one step from homemade, or in some cases completely homemade—what is typically called **consumer-generated content (CGC)**. This has turned the industry upside down. The industry bible, *Advertising Age*, has declared this era the "post-advertising age." Still, even with these amazing and fundamental changes, it would be an exaggeration to say that advertising is dead or that advertisers have absolutely no power.

Ads of this period are diverse, as they are in any period, but generally continue to be self-aware—to proclaim "This is an ad" and to do so proudly. They portray a newfound consumer awareness, that is, an awareness of a savvy, connected, and easily turned-off consumer. Everyone is in on the purpose of the message. Today's ads are often visual, young, and stylish, but straightforward traditional ads are still a big part of the mix.

In 2007, consumer-created advertising went mainstream, with four consumer-created ads aired during the Super Bowl. Among them was one of 280 entries submitted when Mozilla Corporation invited users of its Firefox open-source Web browser to submit ads in a competition for the glory of being aired on TV. The winning entry featured a teenage girl who says, "I love things fast," talks about surfing, and then declares, "My other browser is a surfboard."[30]

© Alfgar/Shutterstock.

A growing share of promotion on the Web is undertaken in support of e-business. **E-business** is promotion in which companies selling to business customers (rather than to household consumers) rely on the Internet to send messages and close sales (we'll cover this in detail in Chapter 9).

Web advertising growth will be fostered by three aspects of technology: interactive, wireless, and broadband. Because of advances in technology, firms like Procter & Gamble continue to invest heavily in these means of sending messages and reaching target customers. P&G has developed and maintains dozens of websites for the company's approximately 300 brands to serve and interact with customers.[31] P&G also has gone beyond just product-oriented sites and has launched "relationship building" sites like Beinggirl, a teen community site. With such a site, the firm can gather data, test new product ideas,

THE DAY OF THE MARKETER'S HEAVY HAND IS PRETTY MUCH OVER.

and experiment with interactivity. For example, if a website visitor wants to know what nail polish will match the lipstick she just saw in a commercial, she can get an immediate answer. Thus, target audiences do not have to be broadly defined by age or geographic groups—individual households can be targeted through direct interaction with the audience member. Also, P&G can reach a global audience through beinggirl.com without the cost and time-consuming effort of placing traditional media ads in dozens of markets. Furthermore, the consumer comes willingly to the advertiser, not the other way around, as in the case of the more intrusive traditional media. Social networking sites such as Facebook and YouTube have made brand communities and personal identity projects the stuff of e-commerce.

Branded Entertainment

No aspect of the evolution of promotion is more significant than the emergence of "branded entertainment." **Branded entertainment** is the blending of integrated marketing communication with entertainment, primarily film, music, and television programming. A subset of branded entertainment is *product placement*, the significant placement of brands within films or television programs. When James Bond switched to the BMW Z8 from his beloved Aston Martin (by the way, he has switched back) and when the cast of *Friends* drank Pepsi, audiences took notice. Branded entertainment takes product placement a quantum leap forward. With branded entertainment, a brand is not just a bit player; it is the star of the program. An early participant in branded entertainment and still a leader in using the technique is BMW. Similarly, along with videos, the U.S. Army offers Web-based computer games at its recruiting site (www.goarmy.com).

Branded entertainment offers the marketer many advantages—among them, not running into the consumer's well-trained resistance mechanisms to ads. Many consumers have turned to solutions like **TiVo** to avoid traditional advertising. With TiVo, consumers can skip commercials, and 63 percent of TiVo users report that they do just that.[32]

Another advantage is greater freedom. With branded entertainment, marketers are not subject to all the ad regulations. In an ad, BMW has to use a disclaimer ("closed track, professional driver") when it shows its cars tearing around, but in movies, like *The Italian Job*, no such disclaimer is required. Also, movies have been seen by the courts as artistic speech, not as the less protected "commercial speech." Branded entertainment, therefore, gets more First Amendment protection than ordinary advertising does. This is an important distinction because regulation and legal fights surrounding ads represent a large cost of doing business.

This merger of advertising with music, film, television, and other telecom arenas (such as cell phones) often is referred to as Madison & Vine, a nod to New York's Madison Avenue, the traditional home

branded entertainment embedding brands or brand icons as part of an entertainment property in an effort to connect with consumers in a unique and compelling way

TiVo service that automatically records a consumer's selected television shows when they air and allows consumers to skip commercials

The ultimate in branded entertainment, the BMW Web videos entertain viewers by featuring their cars in short features made by well-known movie directors, including Wong Kar-Wai, Ang Lee, John Frankenheimer, Guy Ritchie, and Alejandro González Iñárritu. The videos have attracted millions of viewers, who watch for more than 15 minutes at a time.

© Hugo Philpott/Reuters/Landov.

of the advertising industry, and the famous Hollywood intersection of Hollywood and Vine. Whatever you call it, branded entertainment has opened up enormous real possibilities for what has become a much cluttered and a bit beat-up traditional advertising industry.

As you can imagine, marketers love the exposure and freedom of using branded entertainment. But not all consumers are wildly enthusiastic about the blurring line between marketing and entertainment. One survey showed that 52 percent of respondents were worried about advertisers influencing entertainment content. But in which real world are no brands visible and being used? We doubt that today's consumers find branded entertainment particularly distracting, particularly if it's done well.

LO 5 Does History Matter?

As intrigued as we are by new technology like Wi-Fi and new media like Web films, we shouldn't jump to the conclusion that everything about promotion will change. So far, it hasn't. Advertising still will be a paid attempt to persuade, and it still will be one of the primary tools in the promotional mix that contribute to revenues and profits by stimulating demand and nurturing brand loyalty. Even though executives at P&G believe there is a whole new world of communication and have developed dozens of websites to take advantage of this new world, the firm still spends about $3.5 billion a year on traditional advertising through traditional media.[33]

It also is safe to argue that consumers still will be highly involved in some product decisions and not so involved in others. That means some messages will be particularly relevant, but others will be completely irrelevant to forming and maintaining beliefs and feelings about brands. To this date, technology (particularly e-commerce) has changed the way people shop, gather information, and make purchases. And while the advance in online advertising continues, net TV revenues are still attractive. Where else are you going to get such an enormous audience with sight and sound?

History is very, very relevant and practiced. You don't have to make the same mistakes over and over. Learn from the past what works and what doesn't. It's a smart thing to do.

STUDY TOOLS
CHAPTER 3

Located at back of the textbook
- **Rip out Chapter in Review Card.**

Located at www.cengagebrain.com
- **Review Key Terms Flashcards (Print or Online).**
- **Complete the Practice Quiz to prepare for tests.**
- **Play "Beat the Clock" and "Quizbowl" to master concepts.**
- **Complete "Crossword Puzzle" to review key terms.**
- **Watch videos on Samsung and Patrick Jean Pixels for real company examples.**
- **For additional examples, go online to learn about the creative revolution (1960–1972), the iPod mini ads, and consumer-generated advertising.**

SPEAK UP! SHE DID

PROMO was built on a simple principle: to create a new teaching and learning solution that reflects the way today's faculty teach and the way you learn.

Through conversations, focus groups, surveys, and interviews, we collected data that drove the creation of the current version of PROMO that you are using today. But it doesn't stop there—in order to make PROMO an even better learning experience, we'd like you to SPEAK UP and tell us how PROMO worked for you.

What did you like about it? What would you change? Are there additional ideas you have that would help us build a better product for next semester's students?

At **www.cengagebrain.com** you'll find all of the resources you need to succeed—**videos, flashcards, interactive quizzes** and more!

Speak Up! Go to **www.cengagebrain.com**.

CHAPTER 4

Understanding the Marketing Environment:

Segmentation, Targeting, and Positioning

This short movie, produced to promote Folgers, hopes to grab your attention.

Folgers promises to defend you when those annoying "morning people" try to talk to you before you've had your coffee.

> "The more you engage with customers the clearer things become and the easier it is to determine what you should be doing."
>
> —John Russell

AFTER YOU FINISH THIS CHAPTER GO TO PAGE 85 FOR STUDY TOOLS

How Well Do You "Tolerate Mornings"?

You know by now that advertising, in its many forms, always is sponsored for a reason. Generally that reason has something to do with winning new customers or reinforcing the habits of existing customers.[1] However, advertising has no chance of producing a desired result if we are unclear about whom we want to reach. We need a target audience. Folgers targeted net-savvy young adults with the Yellow People movie seen opposite.

One special problem that most companies face is reaching potential customers just as they are experimenting in a product category for the first time. This is a pivotal time when the marketer wants the consumer to have a great experience with the brand. So, for example, if we are Gillette and seek to market anything and everything associated with shaving, we will want one of our shavers in the hands of the consumer the first time he or she shaves. First-time users are not heavy users, but they represent the future. If we don't keep winning these beginners, eventually, we go out of business. Developing advertising campaigns to win with first-time users often is referred to as point-of-entry marketing. More on that later . . .

Folgers does a huge business in the coffee category but can take nothing for granted when it comes to new users. Thus, the marketers of Folgers must launch campaigns to appeal specifically to the next generation of coffee drinkers: young people just learning the coffee habit. Attracted by coffee titans like Starbucks and Dunkin' Donuts, many people get to know coffee in their teens. But when it's time to start brewing coffee at home, Folgers sees its big chance to get in your cupboard.

The Folgers brand team launched an advertising initiative aimed to attract just-graduated 20-somethings. When young adults move into the "real world" and take

What do you think?

Before you can sell anything, you have to know what your customer wants.

1	2	3	4	5	6	7
STRONGLY DISAGREE				STRONGLY AGREE		

Problem: Morning invades my rest. Solution? Folgers coffee.

that first job with a new apartment in a strange city, they are primed to develop the coffee habit. Folgers aspires to be the brand of choice for this target as they potentially commit to a morning brew-it-yourself coffee ritual. Mornings are tough, so Folgers realistically aims to make them tolerable. But how does Folgers, your grandparents' brand, connect with a new generation of coffee drinkers? Tried-and-true slogans ("The best part of waking up is Folgers in your cup") and 30-second TV spots just won't do.

Working with its ad agency Saatchi & Saatchi, the Folgers brand team started with the premise that mornings are hard, filled with emails and bosses making demands and those darn "morning people" (who, for some bizarre reason, seem to love sunrises). Folgers exists to help a person tolerate mornings, particularly to tolerate those morning people. A short film was produced to show Folgers as your first line of defense when the fanatical Yellow People try to invade your space first thing in the morning. The film also was designed to generate traffic to toleratemornings.com, which offered other tools (boss-tracker, auto emails, wake-up calls, screensaver) for making mornings better. The campaign

also included print ads code-named "Dreamscapes," reflecting that frightful moment just before dawn when the creepy Yellow People are planning their attack.

To distribute the Yellow People film, Folgers spent zero dollars. Rather, the spot was submitted to three websites (Adcritic, Bestadsontv.com, and Boards), where 20-somethings had their way with it. Chatter quickly spread across the blogosphere, website hits increased, and the film soon was posted on YouTube (receiving 4 out of 5 stars and more than 300,000 viewings). This little sample of YouTube comments suggests that the Folgers team was on the right track in their effort to engage new users:

"I now watch this every morning to wake up, cause it's just so damn funny and awesome that it wakes me right up. If I ever get rich, I'm going to hire a bunch of people to dress like happy yellow people and come wake me up with that song every morning."

"I am without speech at the sheer brilliance. If commercials were like this . . . I wouldn't skip them on the DVR."

(COMPANIES) MUST **BE CLEAR** ABOUT WHOM THEY ARE TRYING TO REACH AND ABOUT WHAT THEY CAN SAY THAT WILL **RESONATE WITH CONSUMERS.**

Many companies share the problem we see embedded in the Folgers example: They must be clear about whom they are trying to reach and about what they can say that will resonate with consumers. Companies address this challenge through a process referred to as STP marketing. From their standpoint, the process is critical because it leads to decisions about *whom* they need to advertise to, *what* value proposition they want to present to them, and *how* they plan to reach them with their message.

LO 1 STP Marketing

The Folgers example illustrates the process that marketers use to decide whom to advertise to and what to say. The Folgers brand team started with the diverse market of all possible coffee drinkers and then broke the market down by age segments. The team then selected *just-graduated 20-somethings* as its target segment. The **target segment** is the subgroup (of the larger market) chosen as the focal point for the marketing program and advertising campaign.

Markets are segmented; products are positioned. To pursue the target segment, a firm organizes its marketing and advertising efforts around a coherent positioning strategy. **Positioning** is the process of designing and representing one's product or service so that

it will occupy a distinct and valued place in the target customer's mind. **Positioning strategy** involves the selection of key themes or concepts that the organization will feature when communicating this distinctiveness to the target segment. In Folgers's case, the positioning concept is "Tolerate Mornings," expressed in a way that positions Folgers so that just-graduated 20-somethings can relate. Folks on the Folgers team assumed they would not convert this segment with an old-fashioned slogan like "The best part of waking up is Folgers in your cup." Instead, they used a skillful, low-cost approach to getting the message in front of the target: Let YouTube do it!

Planning the Folgers marketing strategy followed the specific sequence illustrated in Exhibit 4.1: *segmenting, targeting,* and *positioning*. This sequence of activities, often referred to as **STP marketing**, represents a sound basis for generating effective advertising.[2] While no formulas or models guarantee success, the STP approach is strongly recommended for markets in which customers' needs and preferences are diverse. In markets with any significant degree of diversity, it is impossible to design one product that would appeal

> **target segment** the subgroup (of the larger market) chosen as the focal point for a marketing program and advertising campaign
>
> **positioning** the process of designing and representing a product or service to occupy a distinct and valued place in the target customer's mind
>
> **positioning strategy** the key themes or concepts that an organization features when communicating a product's or service's distinctiveness to a target segment
>
> **STP marketing** developing a strategy through segmenting, targeting, and positioning

Exhibit 4.1
STP Marketing

to everyone or one advertising campaign that would communicate with everyone. Organizations that lose sight of this simple premise run into trouble.

In most product categories, different consumers are looking for different things, and the only way for a company to take advantage of the sales potential represented by different customer segments is to develop and market a different brand for each segment. No company has done this better than cosmetics juggernaut Estée Lauder.[3] Lauder has more than a dozen cosmetic brands, each developed for a different target segment.[4] Exhibit 4.2 shows just some of the cosmetics brands that Estée Lauder has marketed to appeal to diverse target segments. Check out the company's current brand lineup at http://www.elcompanies.com.

We offer the Estée Lauder example to make two key points before moving on. First, STP marketing is a lot more complicated than the Folgers case; it involves far more than deciding to target a particular age group. Second, as in the descriptions of the groups served by Estée Lauder, many factors beyond demographics can come into play when marketers identify target segments. Considerations such as attitudes, lifestyles, and basic values all may play a role in describing customer segments.

Compare the ad for the Marines with the ad for Hard Candy lip gloss. Both ran in *Seventeen* magazine, so it is safe to say that both advertisers were trying to reach adolescent girls. But it should be obvious that the advertisers were trying to reach out to very different segments of adolescent females.

Exhibit 4.2
Something for Everyone
from Estée Lauder

Estée Lauder	For women with conservative values and upscale tastes
Clinique	A no-nonsense brand that represents functional grooming for Middle America
Bobbi Brown	For the working mom who skillfully manages a career and her family and manages to look good in the process
M.A.C.	For those who want to make a bolder statement (as represented by such spokespersons as Boy George, Missy Elliott, Linda Evangelista, and RuPaul)
Prescriptives	For a hip, urban, multiethnic target segment
Origins	For those who appreciate the connection between Mother Nature and human nature, signaled by earthy packaging and natural ingredients

Beyond STP Marketing

Even when STP marketing yields profitable outcomes, one must presume that success will not last indefinitely. Indeed, an important feature of marketing and advertising—a feature that can make these professions both terribly interesting and terribly frustrating—is their dynamic nature. To paraphrase a pop-

Photo Courtesy, Susan Van Etten.

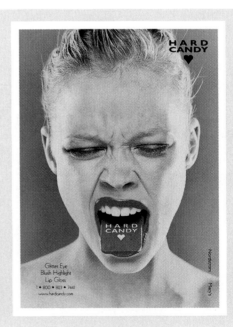

Courtesy, Hard Candy.

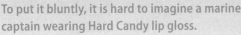

To put it bluntly, it is hard to imagine a marine captain wearing Hard Candy lip gloss.

ular saying, shifts happen. Consumer preferences shift, competitors improve their marketing strategies, and technology changes, making a popular product obsolete. Successful marketing strategies need to be modified or even reinvented as shifts occur in the organization's competitive environment.

To maintain the vitality and profitability of its products or services, an organization has two options. The first is to reassess the segmentation strategy. Reassessment may come through a more detailed examination of the current target segment to develop new and better ways of meeting its needs, or the organization may have to adopt new targets and position new brands for them, as Estée Lauder often does.

The second option is to pursue a product differentiation strategy. As defined in Chapter 1, product differentiation focuses the firm's efforts on emphasizing or even creating differences for its brands to distinguish them from competitors' offerings. Advertising plays a critical role as part of the product differentiation strategy because often the consumer will have to be convinced that the intended difference is meaningful. For example, Schick's response to Gillette's Mach3 Turbo was the Schick Quattro with four blades instead of three. But does that fourth blade really deliver a better shave? Following a product differentiation strategy, the role of Schick's advertising is to convince men that that fourth blade is essential for a close shave. But next up is Gillette's Fusion, with five blades to shave you closer than close. And so it goes.

The message is that marketing strategies and the advertising that supports them are never really final. Successes realized through proper application of STP marketing can be short lived in highly competitive markets, where any successful innovation is almost sure to be copied or one-upped by competitors.

Thus, the value-creation process for marketers and advertisers is continuous; STP marketing must be pursued over and over again and may be supplemented with product differentiation strategies.

LO 2 Identifying Target Segments

The first step in STP marketing involves breaking down large, heterogeneous markets into more manageable submarkets or customer segments. This activity is known as **market segmentation**. It can be accomplished in many ways, but, whatever the method, each segment should have common characteristics that will lead the members of that segment to respond distinctively to a marketing program. For a segment to be really useful, advertisers also must be able to reach that segment with information about the product. Typically, this means that advertisers must be able to identify the media that will allow them to get a message to the segment. For example, teenage males can be reached through product placements in video games and on selected rap, contemporary rock, or country radio stations.

Segmenting by Usage and Commitment

One of the most common ways to segment markets is by consumers' usage patterns or commitment levels. With respect to usage patterns, it is important to recognize that, for most products and services, some users will purchase much more frequently than others. It is common to find that **heavy users** in a category account for the majority of a product's sales and thus become the preferred or primary target segment.[5]

To illustrate, Coffee-mate executives launched a program to get to know their customers better by returning calls to those who had left a complaint or suggestion using the toll-free number printed on the product packaging.[6] As a result, they met Paula Baumgartner, a 44-year-old who consumes four jars of Coffee-mate's mocha-flavored creamer every week (more than 200 jars a year!). Conventional marketing thought holds that it is in Coffee-mate's best interest to get to know heavy users like Paula in great depth and to make them a focal point of the company's marketing strategy.

nonusers a market segment made up of consumers who do not use a particular product or service

brand-loyal users a market segment made up of consumers who repeatedly buy the same brand of a product

switchers or **variety seekers** a market segment made up of consumers who often buy what is on sale or choose brands that offer price incentives

emergent consumers a market segment made up of the gradual but constant influx of first-time buyers

point-of-entry marketing advertising strategy designed to win the loyalty of consumers whose brand preferences are under development

demographic segmentation market segmentation that divides consumers according to basic descriptors such as age, gender, race, marital status, income, education, and occupation

In spite of its obvious appeal, the heavy-user focus has some potential downsides. For one, devoted users may need no encouragement at all to keep consuming. A heavy-user focus could take attention and resources away from those who do need encouragement to purchase the marketer's brand. Perhaps most important, heavy users may differ significantly from average or infrequent users in terms of their motivations to consume, their approach to the brand, or their image of the brand.

Another segmentation option combines prior usage patterns with commitment levels to identify four fundamental segment types:[7]

- **Nonusers** offer the lowest level of opportunity relative to the other three groups.

- **Brand-loyal users** are a tremendous asset if they are the advertiser's customers, but they are difficult to convert if they are loyal to a competitor.

- **Switchers** or **variety seekers** often buy what is on sale or choose brands that offer discount coupons or other price incentives. Whether they are pursued through price incentives, high-profile advertising campaigns, or both, switchers are a costly target segment. Marketers can spend heavily to get their business, merely to have it disappear quickly when these customers move on.

- **Emergent consumers** are motivated by many different factors, but they share one notable characteristic: Their brand preferences are still under development. In most product categories, there is a gradual but constant influx of first-time buyers. Reasons for this influx include purchase triggers such as college graduation or a new job. Immigration also can be a source of new customers in many product categories.

Each segment represents a unique opportunity for the advertiser. For example, targeting emergents with messages that fit their age or social circumstances may produce only modest effects in the short run, but it eventually may yield a brand loyalty that pays handsome rewards for the discerning organization. Developing advertising campaigns to win with first-time users often is referred to as **point-of-entry marketing**. This was exactly Folgers' rationale in targeting *just-*

Wells Fargo Bank targets students at the University of Arizona with this ad. Why do you think these emergent consumers present a long-term opportunity for Wells Fargo?

graduated 20-somethings. Similarly, banks actively recruit college students, who have limited financial resources in the short term but offer excellent potential as long-term customers.

Segmenting by Demographics

A widely used method for selecting target segments is **demographic segmentation**, which divides consumers according to basic descriptors such as age, gender, race, marital status, income, education, and occupation (see the array of possibilities at http://www.factfinder.census.gov). Demographic information has special value in market segmentation because, if an advertiser knows the demographic characteristics of the target segment, choosing media to efficiently reach that segment is easier.

Demographic information has two specific applications. First, demographics are commonly used to describe or profile segments that have been identified with some other variable. If an organization first had segmented its market in terms of product usage rates, the next step would be to describe or profile its heavy users in terms of demographic characteristics such as age or income. In fact, one of the most common approaches for identifying target segments is to combine information about usage patterns with demographics.

Mobil Oil Corporation used such an approach in segmenting the market for gasoline buyers and identified five basic segments: Road Warriors, True Blues, Generation F3, Homebodies, and Price Shoppers.[8] Extensive research on more than 2,000 motorists revealed considerable insight about these five segments. At one extreme, Road Warriors spend at least $1,200 per year at gas stations; they buy premium gasoline and snacks and beverages and sometimes opt for a car wash. Road Warriors are generally more affluent, middle-aged males who drive 25,000 to 50,000 miles per year. (Note how Mobil combined information about usage patterns with demographics to provide a detailed picture of the segment.) In contrast, Price Shoppers spend no more than $700 annually at gas stations, are generally less affluent, rarely buy premium, and show no loyalty to particular brands or stations. In terms of relative segment sizes, there are about 25 percent more Price Shoppers on the highways than Road Warriors. If you were the marketing vice president at Mobil, which of these two segments would you target? Second, demographic categories are used frequently as the starting point in market segmentation. This was true in the Folgers example, where young people who recently had graduated from college turned out to be the segment of interest. Demographics also will be a major consideration for targeting by the tourism industry; often, families with young children are the marketer's primary focus. For instance, the Bahamian government launched a program to attract families to its island paradise. But instead of reaching out to mom and dad, Bahamian officials made their appeal to kids by targeting the 2- to 11-year-old viewing audience of Nickelodeon's cable television channel.[9] Marketing to and through children is always complex—and often controversial as well.

Another demographic group that is receiving renewed attention from advertisers is the "woopies,"

or well-off older people. In the United States, consumers over 50 years old control two-thirds of the country's wealth, around $28 trillion. The median net worth of households headed by persons 55 to 64 is 15 times larger than the net worth for households headed by a person under age 35. Put in simple terms, for most 20-year-olds, $100 is a lot of money. For woopies, $100 is change back from the purchase of a $10,000 home theater system. Marketers such as Sony and Virgin Entertainment Group have reconsidered their product offerings with woopies in mind.[10] By 2025, the number of people over 50 will grow by 80 percent to become a third of the U.S. population. Growth in the woopie segment also will be dramatic in other countries, such as Japan and the nations of Western Europe. Still, like any other age segment, older consumers are a diverse group, and the temptation to stereotype must be resisted. Some marketers advocate partitioning older consumers into groups aged 50–64, 65–74, 75–84, and 85 or older, as a means of reflecting important differences in needs. That's a good start, but again, age alone will not tell the whole story.

Segmenting by Geography

Geographic segmentation needs little explanation other than to emphasize how useful geography is in segmenting markets. Geographic segmentation may be conducted within a country by region (for example, the Pacific Northwest versus New England in the United States). Climate and topographical features yield dramatic differences in consumption by region for products such as snow tires and surfboards, but geography also can correlate with other differences that are not so obvious. Eating and food preparation habits, entertainment preferences, recreational activities, and other aspects of lifestyle have been shown to vary along geographic lines. As shown on the U.S. map, even a brand like Hostess Twinkies has its red and blue states.

The states in red have the highest consumption of Twinkies.

Simmons Market Research Bureau.

In recent years, skillful marketers have merged information on where people live with the U.S. Census Bureau's demographic data to produce a form of market segmentation known as geodemographic segmentation.[11] **Geodemographic segmentation** identifies neighborhoods (by ZIP codes) around the country that share common demographic characteristics. One such system, known as PRIZM (potential rating index by ZIP marketing), identifies 62 market segments that encompass all the ZIP codes in the United States. Each of these segments has similar lifestyle characteristics and can be found throughout the country. For example, the American Dreams segment is found in many metropolitan neighborhoods and comprises upwardly mobile ethnic minorities, many of whom were foreign-born. This segment's brand preferences differ from those of people belonging to the Rural Industrial segment, who are young families with one or both parents working at low-wage jobs in small-town America.

Systems such as PRIZM are very popular because of the depth of segment description they provide. Also, they can identify where the segment is located precisely (for more details, search for PRIZM at http://www.claritas.com).

Segmenting by Psychographics and Lifestyle

Psychographics is a term that advertisers created in the mid-1960s to refer to a form of research that emphasizes the understanding of consumers' activities, interests, and opinions (AIOs).[12] Many advertising agencies were using demographic variables for segmentation purposes, but they wanted insights into consumers' motivations, which demographic variables did not provide. Psychographics were created as a tool to supplement the use of demographic data. Because a focus on consumers' activities, interests, and opinions often produces insights into differences in the lifestyles of various segments, this approach usually results in **lifestyle segmentation**. Details about the lifestyle of a target segment can be valuable for creating advertising messages that ring true to the consumer.

Lifestyle or psychographic segmentation can be customized with a focus on the issues germane to a single product category, or it may be pursued so that the resulting segments have general applicability to many different product or service categories. An illustration of the former is research conducted for Pillsbury to segment the eating habits of American households.[13] Based on consumer interviews with more than 3,000 people, this study identified five population segments with distinct eating styles:

- **Chase and Grabbits,** at 26 percent of the population, are heavy users of all forms of fast food. These are people who can make a meal out of microwave popcorn; as long as the popcorn keeps hunger at bay and is convenient, this segment is happy with its meal.

- **Functional Feeders,** at 18 percent of the population, are a bit older than the Chase and Grabbits but no less convenience oriented. Because they are more likely to have families, their preferences for convenient foods involve frozen products that are prepared quickly at home. They constantly seek faster ways to prepare the traditional foods they grew up with.

- **Down-Home Stokers,** at 21 percent of the population, involve blue-collar households with modest incomes. They are very loyal to their regional diets, such as meat and potatoes in the Midwest and clam chowder in New England. Fried chicken, biscuits and gravy, and bacon and eggs make this segment the champion of cholesterol.

© Fotocrisis/Shutterstock.

- **Careful Cooks,** at 20 percent of the population, are more prevalent on the West Coast. They have replaced most of the red meat in their diet with pasta, fish, skinless chicken, and mounds of fresh fruit and vegetables. They believe they are knowledgeable about nutritional issues and are willing to experiment with foods that offer healthful options.

- **Happy Cookers,** the remaining 15 percent of the population, are a shrinking segment. These cooks are family oriented and take substantial satisfaction from preparing a complete homemade meal for the family. Young mothers in this segment are aware of nutritional issues but will bend the rules with homemade meat dishes, casseroles, pies, cakes, and cookies.

Even these abbreviated descriptions of Pillsbury's five psychographic segments should make it clear that very different marketing and advertising programs are called for to appeal to each group.

As noted, lifestyle segmentation studies also can be pursued with no particular product category as a focus, and the resulting segments could prove useful for many different marketers. A notable example of this approach is the VALS (originally for "values and lifestyles") system developed by SRI International and now owned and marketed by Strategic Business Insights, an SRI spinoff, of Menlo Park, California.[14] The VALS framework originally had nine potential segments, but in the late 1980s was revised to feature eight segments. The VALS system groups consumers by psychological characteristics and several key demographics instead of using social values as it originally did. As shown in Exhibit 4.3, the segments are organized in terms of resources (including age, income, and education) and primary motivation. For instance, experiencers are relatively affluent and expressive. This enthusiastic and risk-taking group

Exhibit 4.3
VALS™ Segments

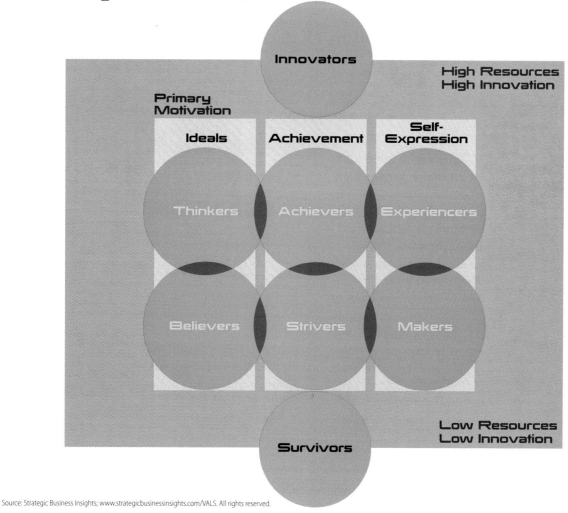

benefit segmentation market segmentation that identifies the various benefit packages consumers want from a product category

consumer markets the markets for products and services purchased by individuals or households to satisfy their specific needs

business markets the institutional buyers who purchase items to be used in other products and services or to be resold to other businesses or households

is highly social. Its members look to sports, recreation, exercise, and social activities as outlets for their abundant energies. Strategic Business Insights sells detailed information and marketing recommendations about the eight segments to corporations' new product development and marketing divisions.

Segmenting by Benefits

Another segmentation approach developed by advertising researchers and used extensively over the past 30 years is **benefit segmentation**. In benefit segmentation, target segments are delineated by the various benefit packages that different consumers want from competing products and brands. For instance, different people want different benefits from their automobiles. Some consumers want efficient and reliable transportation; others want speed, excitement, and glamour; and still others want luxury, comfort, and prestige. One product possibly could not serve such diverse benefit segments. Similarly, the two ads for hair care products promise different kinds of benefits to comparable consumers.

Segmenting Business Buyers

Thus far, our discussion of segmentation options has focused on ways to segment **consumer markets**. Consumer markets are the markets for products and services purchased by individuals or households to satisfy their specific needs. Consumer marketing often is compared and contrasted with business-to-business marketing. **Business markets** are the institutional buyers who purchase items to be used in other products and services or to be resold to other businesses or households. Although advertising is more prevalent in consumer markets, products and services such as consulting services and a wide array of business machines are promoted commonly to business customers around the world. Hence, segmentation strategies also are valuable for business-to-business marketers.

Business markets can be segmented using several of the options already discussed.[15] For example, business customers differ in their usage rates and geographic locations, so these variables may be productive bases for segmenting business markets. Additionally, one of the most common approaches uses the Stan-

Bed Head promises a "superstar" look, while Catwalk is all about care for curls: defrizz, define, detangle.

dard Industrial Classification (SIC) codes prepared by the U.S. Census Bureau. SIC information is helpful for identifying categories of businesses and then pinpointing the precise locations of these organizations.

Some of the more sophisticated segmentation methods used by firms that market to individual consumers do not translate well to business markets.[16] Rarely would there be a place for psychographic or lifestyle segmentation in the business-to-business setting. In business markets, advertisers fall back on simpler strategies that are easier to work with from the perspective of the sales force. Segmentation by a potential customer's stage in the purchase process is one such strategy. It turns out that first-time prospects, novices, and sophisticates want very different packages of benefits from their vendors, so they should be targeted separately in advertising and sales programs.

LO 3 Prioritizing Target Segments

Whether segmentation is done through usage patterns, demographic characteristics, geographic location, benefit packages, or any combination of options, it typically yields a mix of segments that vary in their attractiveness to the advertiser. In pursuing STP marketing, the advertiser must get beyond this potentially confusing mixture of segments to a selected subset that will become the target for its marketing and advertising programs. Recall the example of Mobil Oil Corporation and the segments of gasoline buyers it identified via usage patterns and demographic descriptors. What criteria should Mobil use to help decide between Road Warriors and Price Shoppers as possible targets?

Perhaps the most fundamental criterion in segment selection revolves around what the members of the segment want versus the organization's ability to provide it. Every organization has distinctive strengths and weaknesses that must be acknowledged when choosing its target segment. The organization may be particularly strong in some aspect of manufacturing. Or perhaps its strength lies in well-trained and loyal service personnel, like those at FedEx, who effectively can implement new service programs initiated for customers, such as next-day delivery "absolutely, positively by 10:30 AM." To serve a target segment, an organization may have to commit substantial resources to acquire or develop the capabilities to provide what that segment wants. If the price tag for these new capabilities is too high, the organization must find another segment.

Another major consideration in segment selection is the segments' size and growth potential. Segment size is a function of the number of people, households, or institutions in the segment, plus their willingness to spend in the product category. When assessing size, advertisers must keep in mind that the number of people in a segment of heavy users may be relatively small, but the extraordinary usage rates of these consumers can more than make up for their small numbers. In addition to looking for adequate size as of today, marketers often are most interested in devoting resources to segments projected for dramatic growth. As we have seen already, the purchasing power and growth projections for people age 50 and older have made this age segment one that many companies are targeting.

So does bigger always mean better when choosing target segments? The answer is a function of the third major criterion for segment selection. In choosing a target segment, an advertiser must also look at the **competitive field**—companies that compete for the segment's business—and then decide whether it has a particular expertise, or perhaps just a bigger budget, that would allow it to serve the segment more effectively.

Upon considering the competitive field, marketers often determine that smaller is better when selecting target segments. Almost by definition, large segments tend to be established segments already targeted by many companies. Trying to enter the competitive field in a mature segment isn't easy because established competitors (with their many brands) can be expected to respond aggressively with advertising campaigns or price promotions in an effort to repel any newcomer.

Alternatively, large segments simply may be poorly defined segments; that is, marketers may need to break down a large segment into smaller categories before they can understand consumers' needs well enough to serve them effectively. The segment of older consumers—age 50 and older—is huge, but in most instances, it would simply be too big to be valuable as a target. Too much diversity exists in the needs and preferences

competitive field the companies that compete for a segment's business

© Tony Mathews/Shutterstock.

market niche a
relatively small group of
consumers with a unique set
of needs and the willingness to
pay a premium price to a firm
that meets those needs

of this age group, so further segmentation based on other demographic or perhaps psychographic variables is called for before an appropriate target can be located.

The smaller-is-better principle has become so popular in choosing target segments that it now is referred to as niche marketing. A **market niche** is a relatively small group of consumers who have a unique set of needs and who typically are willing to pay a premium price to the firm that specializes in meeting those needs.[17] The small size of a market niche often means serving it would not be profitable for more than one organization. Thus, identifying and developing products for market niches reduces the threat of competitors developing imitative products.

Niche marketing will continue to grow in popularity as the mass media splinter into a more complex and narrowly defined array of specialized vehicles. Specialized cable programming—such as the History Channel or the 24-hour Golf Channel—attracts small and very distinctive groups of consumers, providing advertisers with an efficient way to communicate with market niches.[18] In addition, perhaps the ideal application of the Internet as a marketing tool is in identifying and accessing market niches.

Let's return to the question faced by Mobil Oil Corporation. Who should it target—Road Warriors or Price Shoppers? Road Warriors are a more attractive segment in terms of both segment size and growth potential. Although there are more Price Shoppers in terms of sheer numbers, Road Warriors spend more at the gas station, making them the larger segment from the standpoint of revenue generation. Road Warriors are also more prone to buy extras, such as a sandwich and a coffee, which could be extremely profitable. In contrast, it's hard to win in gasoline retailing by competing on price.

Mobil selected Road Warriors as its target segment and developed a positioning strategy it referred to as "Friendly Serve." Gas prices went up at Mobil stations, but Mobil also improved the gas-purchasing experience. Cleaner restrooms and better lighting yielded sales gains between 2 and 5 percent. Next, more attendants were hired to run between the pump and the snack bar to get Road Warriors in and out quickly—complete with their sandwich and beverage. Early results indicated that helpful attendants boosted station sales by another 15 to 20 percent.

Svetlana addresses this ad to a very small niche—those who prefer imported tubes for high-end tube stereo amplifiers. Expect to pay a little extra for such a specialized product.

Created in-house by Svetlana Electron Devices. Creative Director Jerri Batres; Photographer Jared Cassidy.

LO 4 Formulating the Positioning Strategy

If a firm has been careful in segmenting the market and selecting its targets, then a positioning strategy should occur naturally. In addition, as an aspect of positioning strategy, we entertain ideas about how a firm can communicate best to the target segment what it has to offer. This is where advertising plays its vital role. A positioning strategy will include particular ideas or themes that must be communicated effectively if the marketing program is to succeed.

Positioning Strategies

Any sound positioning strategy includes several essential elements. Effective positioning strategies are based on meaningful commitments of organizational resources to produce substantive value for the target segment. They also are consistent internally and over time, and they feature simple and distinctive themes. Each of these essential elements is described below.

Deliver on the Promise

For a positioning strategy to be effective and remain effective over time, the organization must be committed to creating substantive value for the customer. Take the example of Mobil Oil Corporation and its target segment, the Road Warriors. Road Warriors are willing to pay a little more for gas if it comes with extras such as prompt service or fresh coffee. So Mobil must create an ad campaign that depicts its employees as the brightest, friendliest, most helpful people you'd ever want to meet. The company asks its ad agency to come up with a catchy jingle that will remind people about the great services they can expect at a Mobil station. It spends millions of dollars running these ads over and over. Will it win the enduring loyalty of the Road Warriors? Certainly, a new ad campaign will have to be created to make Road Warriors aware of the new Mobil, but it all falls apart if they drive in with great expectations and the company's people do not live up to them.

Effective positioning begins with substance. In the case of Mobil's "Friendly Serve" strategy, this means keeping restrooms attractive and clean, adding better lighting to all areas of the station, and upgrading the quality of the snacks and beverages available in each station's convenience store. It also means hiring more attendants and training and motivating them to anticipate and fulfill the needs of the harried Road Warrior. Raising service levels at thousands of stations nationwide is expensive and time consuming, but without some substantive change, there can be no hope of retaining the Road Warrior's lucrative business.

There's Magic in Consistency

A positioning strategy also must be consistent internally and consistent over time. Regarding internal consistency, everything must work in combination to reinforce a distinct perception in the consumer's eyes about what a brand stands for. If we have chosen to position our airline as the one that will be known for on-time reliability, then we certainly would invest in things like extensive preventive maintenance and state-of-the-art baggage-handling facilities. There would be no need for exclusive airport lounges as part of this strategy. If our target segment wants reliable transportation, then this should be our obsession. This particular obsession has made Southwest Airlines a formidable competitor, even against much larger airlines, as it has expanded its routes to different regions of the United States.[19]

A strategy also needs consistency over time. Consumers have perceptual defenses that allow them to screen or ignore most of the ad messages they are exposed to. Breaking through the clutter and establishing what a brand stands for is a tremendous challenge, but it is a challenge made easier by consistent positioning. If year in and year out an advertiser communicates the same basic themes, then the message may get through and shape the way consumers perceive the brand. An example of a consistent approach is the long-running

FOR A POSITIONING STRATEGY TO **BE EFFECTIVE AND REMAIN EFFECTIVE** OVER TIME, THE ORGANIZATION MUST BE COMMITTED TO **CREATING SUBSTANTIVE VALUE** FOR THE CUSTOMER.

"Good Neighbor" ads of State Farm Insurance. While the specific copy changes, the thematic core of the campaign does not change.

Make It Different Simply

Simplicity and distinctiveness are essential to the advertising task. No matter how much substance has been built into a product, it will fail in the marketplace if the consumer doesn't perceive what the product can do. In a world of harried consumers who can be expected to ignore, distort, or forget most of the ads they are exposed to, complicated, imitative messages simply have no chance of getting through. The basic premise of a positioning strategy must be simple and distinctive if it is to be communicated effectively to the target segment.

Verizon is notable for its use of a simple message about the wireless network's reliability. The anonymous but amiable "Verizon test guy" who consistently pops up in the company's marketing materials reassures us that we can trust him to help us use a service that is mysterious but essential in modern times. His "Can you hear me now?" expresses in basic terms what it means for this high-tech service to perform optimally, and the "Good" that always follows that question promises us that Verizon works relentlessly to deliver on its promise.

Most important, the Verizon test guy is more than just an actor in an advertising campaign. He embodies a real job function performed by Verizon workers to deliver on the promise of reliable service. The company in fact hires scores of technicians to drive around service areas in vehicles loaded with computers, antennas, and GPS, testing for dead zones and weaknesses in the cellular network. Their objective is to keep dropped calls and blocked reception below 2 percent of calls.[20]

Positioning Themes

Positioning themes that are simple and distinctive help an organization make internal decisions that yield substantive value for customers, and they assist in the development of focused ad campaigns to break through the clutter of competitors' advertising. Choosing a viable positioning theme is one of the most important decisions that advertis-

ers face. In many ways, the raison d'être for STP marketing is to generate viable positioning themes.

Positioning themes take many forms, and they can benefit from creative breakthroughs. Yet while novelty and creativity are valued in developing positioning themes, some basic principles should be considered when selecting a theme. Whenever possible, it is helpful if the organization can settle on a single premise—such as "Tolerate Mornings"—to reflect its positioning strategy.[21] In addition, three fundamental options should be always considered in selecting a positioning theme: benefit positioning, user positioning, and competitive positioning.[22]

"Friendly Serve" is an example of **benefit positioning**. Notice that it expresses a distinctive customer benefit. This single-benefit focus is the first option that should be considered when formulating a positioning strategy. Consumers purchase products to derive functional, emotional, or self-expressive benefits, so an emphasis on the primary benefit they can expect to receive from a brand is fundamental. While it might seem that more compelling positioning themes would result from promising consumers a wide array of benefits, keep in mind that multiple-benefit strategies are hard to implement. Not only will they send mixed signals within an organization about what a brand stands for, but they also will place a great burden on advertising to deliver and validate multiple messages.

Functional benefits are the place to start in selecting a positioning theme, but in

© Rui Vale de Sousa/Shutterstock.

WHETHER OR NOT YOU GET HOW WIRELESS NETWORKS OPERATE, IT'S EASY TO SEE VERIZON'S TECHNICIANS ARE HARD AT WORK FOR YOU.

Courtesy, Colgate-Palmolive Company.

When the functional benefits of 24-hour protection and no white residue became commonplace, this deodorant advertiser thought of emotional benefits.

user positioning a positioning option that focuses on a specific profile of the target user

competitive positioning a positioning option that uses an explicit reference to an existing competitor to help define precisely what a brand can do

Kist has promoted dolphin-safe fishing practices. There's a meaningful trend here: In a survey of executives from 211 companies, 69 percent said their companies planned to increase participation in cause-related marketing as a way to build emotional bonds with their consumers.[24]

Self-expressive benefits also can be the bases for effective positioning strategies. With this approach, the purpose of an advertising campaign is to create distinctive images or personalities for brands and then to invite consumers into brand communities.[25] These brand images or personalities can be of value to individuals as they use the brands to make statements about themselves to other people. Feelings of status, pride, and prestige might be derived from the imagery associated with brands such as BMW, Rolex, and Gucci. Brand imagery also can be valued in gift-giving contexts. The woman who gives Calvin Klein's Euphoria for men is expressing something very different than the woman who gives Old Spice. Advertisers help brands acquire meaning and self-expressive benefits to distinguish them beyond their functional forms.

Besides benefit positioning, another fundamental option is **user positioning**. Instead of featuring a benefit or attribute of the brand, this option takes a specific profile of the target user as the focal point of the positioning strategy. In advertising for high-performance Pinarello bicycles, the camera gazes lovingly at the bike's components, attracting serious cyclists who are passionate about the technical features. An ad for novice riders or parents buying for their children might emphasize low price or deliver an emotional appeal.

The third option for a positioning theme is **competitive positioning**. This option sometimes is useful in well-established product categories with a crowded competitive field. The goal is to use an explicit reference to an existing competitor to help define precisely what the brand can do. Often, smaller brands use this approach to carve out a position relative to the market share leader in their category. For instance, many companies selling over-the-counter pain relievers have used market leader Tylenol as an explicit point of reference in their positioning strategies. Excedrin, for one, has attempted to position itself as the best option

many mature product categories, the functional benefits provided by the various brands in the competitive field are essentially the same. In these instances, the organization may turn to emotion in an effort to distinguish its brand. Emotional benefit positioning may involve a promise of exhilaration, like "Exciting Armpits," or may feature a way to avoid negative feelings, such as the embarrassment felt in social settings due to bad breath.

Another way to add an emotional benefit in one's positioning is by linking a brand with important causes that provoke intense feelings. Avon Products' former CEO James E. Preston insisted that tie-ins with high-profile social issues can cut through the clutter of rivals' marketing messages.[23] It's not surprising, then, that Avon has been a regular sponsor of important causes, such as the Avon Walk for Breast Cancer. Likewise, Star-to treat a simple headache, granting that Tylenol might be the better choice to treat the various symptoms of a cold or the flu.

Besides using any of the three fundamental options for creating a positioning strategy, an advertiser can combine these options to create a hybrid strategy in which two or more of them work together. A frequent hybrid is benefit-plus-user positioning. Whether strategies are used alone or in combination, the point is to arrive at a strategy that reflects substance, consistency, simplicity, and distinctiveness.

Repositioning

STP marketing is far from a precise science, so marketers do not always get it right the first time. Furthermore, markets are dynamic. Even when marketers get it right, competitors can react, or consumers' preferences may shift for any number of reasons. Then, what once was a viable positioning strategy must be altered if the brand is to survive. One of the best ways to revive an ailing brand or fix the lackluster performance of a new market entry is to redeploy the STP process to arrive at a revised positioning strategy. This type of effort commonly is referred to as **repositioning**.

Even though repositioning efforts are a fact of life for marketers and advertisers, they present a tremendous challenge. When brands that have been around for some time are forced to reposition, perceptions of the brand that have evolved over the years must be changed through advertising. This problem is common for brands that become popular with one generation but fade as that generation ages and emergent consumers come to view the brand as passé. So, for several years, the makers of Oldsmobile tried to breathe new life into their brand with catchy ad slogans such as "This is not your father's Oldsmobile," "Demand better," and "Defy convention." Ultimately, none of these efforts could save a brand that had become passé.[26]

In contrast, marketers of many other brands have persuaded consumers to take a fresh look. Mazda found itself in a funk in the '90s when it tried to go head-to-head with Toyota and Honda around dependability and good value. So Mazda's new CEO

What elements of this ad signal Xootr's user and competitive position?

decided to return the brand to its roots as a stylish and fun-to-drive vehicle, targeting the 25 percent of the car-buying market who consider themselves auto enthusiasts. The "Zoom Zoom" theme resulted, and with it the Mazda brand got its groove back.[27]

LO 5 Capturing Your Strategy in a Value Proposition

Marketers have to assess customer segments, target markets, and the competitive field to make decisions about various kinds of positioning themes that might be appropriate in guiding the creation of a campaign. Not only can these tasks get complicated, but as time passes, new people from both the client and agency sides will be brought in to work on the brand team. Before long, team members can lose sight of what the brand used to stand for in the eyes of the target segment. If the people who create the advertising for a brand get confused about the brand's desired identity, then the consumer is bound to get confused as well.

This is a recipe for disaster. We need a way to capture and keep a record of what our brand is supposed to stand for in the eyes of the target segment.

Although there are many ways to capture one's strategy on paper, we recommend doing it by articulating the brand's value proposition. The following definition of a **value proposition** is a natural extension of marketing concepts; it simply consolidates this chapter's emphasis on customer benefits:

> A brand's value proposition is a statement of the functional, emotional, and self-expressive benefits delivered by the brand that provide value to customers in the target segment. A balanced value proposition is the basis for brand choice and customer loyalty, and is critical to the ongoing success of a firm.[28]

If a company is crystal clear on what value it believes its brand offers to consumers, and everyone on the brand team shares that clarity, the foundation is in place for creating effective advertising and integrated brand promotion.

Exhibit 4.4 lists the value propositions for two global brands.[29] Notice from these two statements that, over time, many different aspects can be built into the value proposition for a brand. Brands like Nike may offer benefits in all three benefit categories; McDonald's from two of the three. Benefit complexity of this type is extremely valuable when the various benefits reinforce one another. In these examples, this cross-benefit reinforcement is especially strong for Nike, with all levels working together to deliver the desired state of performance excellence.

The job of advertising is to carry the message to the target segment about the value that is offered by the brand. For brands with complex value propositions such as McDonald's and Nike, no single ad could be expected to reflect all aspects of the brand's value. If any given ad is not communicating some selected aspects of the brand's purported value, then we have to ask, why run that ad?

One gains tremendous leverage from the process of STP marketing because it is all about anticipating and servicing customers' wants and needs. But targeting groups for focused advertising and promotion has a controversial side. This is especially true when children are in your target market.

value proposition
a statement of the functional, emotional, and self-expressive benefits that are delivered by the brand and provide value to customers in the target segment

Exhibit 4.4
Value Propositions for Two Popular Brands

McDonald's

Functional benefits	Good-tasting hamburgers, fries, and drinks served fast; extras such as playgrounds, prizes, premiums, and games.
Emotional benefits	Kids—fun via excitement at birthday parties; relationship with Ronald McDonald and other characters; a feeling of special family times. Adults—warmth via time spent enjoying a meal with the kids; admiration of McDonald's social involvement such as McDonald's Charities and Ronald McDonald Houses.

Nike

Functional benefits	High-technology shoe that will improve performance and provide comfort.
Emotional benefits	The exhilaration of athletic performance excellence, feeling engaged, active, and healthy; exhilaration from admiring professional and college athletes as they perform wearing "your brand"—when they win, you win too.
Self-expressive benefits	Using the brand endorsed by high-profile athletes lets your peers know your desire to compete and excel.

© Monkey Business Images/Shutterstock.

GLOBAL MICKEY MOUSE TAKES THE HIGH ROAD

Critics including the American Psychological Association and American Academy of Pediatrics have called for restrictions on advertising to children. One reason is concern that promotion of junk food has contributed to America's obesity crisis. Disney has tried a different route. It launched a companywide initiative to promote healthy eating and eliminate most foods with high fat and sugar content from its theme-park menus and co-promotions with corporate partners. Now most of the foods Disney promotes contain 0 grams of trans fats, and most of the children's meals at its theme parks are sold with healthier sides, such as apples and milk instead of fries and soft drinks.

Sources: Walt Disney Company, "Children and Family," *2008 Corporate Responsibility Report*, Disney corporate website, http://a.media.global.go.com/corporateresponsibility/pdf/ Disney_CR_Report_2008.pdf (accessed September 8, 2009), 16–20; and Merissa Marr and Janet Adamy, "Disney Pulls Characters from Junk Food," *Wall Street Journal*, October 17, 2006, D1, D6.

Putting It All Together

To pull together the concepts presented in this chapter, we can use a practical model: the strategic planning triangle proposed by advertising researchers Esther Thorson and Jeri Moore.[30] As shown in Exhibit 4.5, the corners of this triangle represent the segment(s) selected as targets for the campaign, the brand's value proposition, and the array of persuasion tools that will be deployed to achieve campaign goals.

The starting point of STP marketing is identifying who the customers or prospects are and what they want, so identification and specification of the target segment appear at the top of Thorson and Moore's model. For the campaign to succeed, the client and the agency must reach a consensus about which segments will be targeted. Compelling advertising begins with personal and precise insights about the target segment.

The second important apex in the planning triangle is specification of the brand's value proposition—a statement of the functional, emotional, and/or

ADVERTISING AND INTEGRATED BRAND PROMOTION ALWAYS ENTAILS FINDING THE RIGHT MIX TO DO THE JOB.

**Exhibit 4.5
Thorson and Moore's Strategic
Planning Triangle**

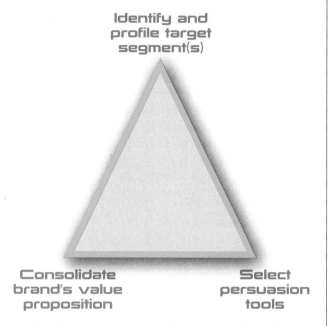

Identify and
profile target
segment(s)

Consolidate
brand's value
proposition

Select
persuasion
tools

Adapted from Esther Thorson and Jeri Moore, *Integrated Communication Synergy of Persuasive Voices*, Mahwah, NJ: Erlbaum, 1996.

self-expressive benefits delivered by the brand. In formulating the value proposition, one should consider both what a brand has stood for or communicated to consumers in the past and what new types of value or additional benefits one wants to claim for the brand. For mature, successful brands, reaffirming the existing value proposition may be the primary objective of any campaign. Launching a new brand provides an opportunity to start from scratch in establishing the value proposition.

The final apex of the planning triangle considers the various persuasion tools that may be deployed as part of the campaign. A description of these tools is yet to come. Chapter 9 looks at the Internet advertising option; Chapter 11 considers support media, sales promotions, and the exciting new arena of branded entertainment; Chapter 13 discusses the public relations function; and Chapter 14 fills out the tool box by providing a comprehensive look at direct marketing. The mix of tools used will depend on campaign goals. The point here is simply to reinforce our mantra that advertising and integrated brand promotion always entails finding the right mix to do the job: Knowing the target segment and the value proposition are essential to doing the job right.

STUDY TOOLS CHAPTER 4

Located at back of the textbook

- **Rip out Chapter in Review Card.**

Located at www.cengagebrain.com

- **Review Key Terms Flashcards (Print or Online).**
- **Complete the Practice Quiz to prepare for tests.**
- **Play "Beat the Clock" and "Quizbowl" to master concepts.**
- **Complete "Crossword Puzzle" to review key terms.**
- **Watch videos on Dagens Industri Zoo and John Smiths UK Diner for real company examples.**
- **For additional examples, go online to learn about taking special care promoting to kids, Estee Lauder brands of cosmetics, and more about Mickey Mouse and the "Disney Magic Selections" products.**

CHAPTER 5

Understanding Buyer Behavior and the Communication Process

Branding from *The Simpsons*, outside and inside the store.

Would *Simpsons* fans be more likely to shop at 7-Eleven with the store disguised as the show's Kwik-E-Mart?

Learning Outcomes

After studying this chapter, you should be able to:

LO 1 Describe the four stages of consumer decision making.

LO 2 Explain how consumers adapt their decision-making processes based on involvement and experience.

LO 3 Discuss how brand communication influences consumers' psychological states and behavior.

LO 4 Describe the interaction of culture and advertising.

LO 5 Explain how sociological factors affect consumer behavior.

LO 6 Discuss how advertising transmits sociocultural meaning in order to sell things.

"The one thing a brand can never be is just a box on the shelf."

—Martin Davidson[1]

AFTER YOU FINISH THIS CHAPTER GO TO PAGE 111 FOR STUDY TOOLS

Ay Caramba!

In the summer of 2007, 7-Eleven and *The Simpsons* teamed up for a contemporary piece of branded entertainment, cross-promotion, and buzz advertising.[2] In a project arranged by FreshWorks, an Omnicom Group virtual-agency network headed up by Tracy Locke of Dallas, twelve U.S. and Canadian 7-Eleven stores were remodeled, literally overnight, into Kwik-E-Marts from *The Simpsons* television show. The change was total: Professional set designers installed more than a thousand items from the show, including KrustyO's and Buzz Cola. (Duff Beer was not included because promoting beer would clash with the movie's PG rating.) Gracie Films, the production company for *The Simpsons*, failed to persuade 7-Eleven to carry one Kwik-E-Mart staple, month-old hot dogs, but the Squishee was accepted. The new look lasted one month, and then the stores reverted to 7-Elevens.

The goal was to promote the release of *The Simpsons Movie* and, for 7-Eleven, to attract a crop of new customers: die-hard *Simpson* fans. Some have called this promotion "reverse product placement." Tim Stock, of Scenario DNA, said, "It's pop culture commenting on pop culture commenting on itself." Welcome to 21st-century consumer culture and brand promotion.

Why would a consumer who generally doesn't buy Pepsi at 7-Eleven make a trip to Kwik-E-Mart for a Buzz Cola? How do moviegoers choose between *The Simpsons* and *Spider-Man 3*, another movie released the same summer? The answers are a function of psychological, economic, sociological, anthropological, historical, textual, and other forces. Marketers combine those perspectives to understand consumer behavior. Like all human behavior, the behavior of consumers is complicated, rich, and varied. However, marketers must make it their job to

What do you think?

If brand messages aren't fun, I'll just ignore them.

1	2	3	4	5	6	7
STRONGLY DISAGREE					STRONGLY AGREE	

understand consumers if they want to experience sustained success. Sometimes, this understanding comes from comprehensive research efforts. Other times, it comes from years of experience coupled with creative management.

This chapter summarizes the concepts and frameworks we believe are most helpful in understanding **consumer behavior**, using two major perspectives. The first portrays consumers as reasonably systematic decision makers who seek to maximize the benefits they derive from their purchases. The second views consumers as active interpreters of advertising, influenced by their membership in various cultures, societies, and communities. These two perspectives are different ways of looking at the exact same people and many of the exact same behaviors. Both perspectives are valuable to the marketer because no one perspective can adequately explain consumer behavior. Consumers are psychological, social, cultural, historical, and economic beings all at the same time, so understanding their behavior is complex but also exciting.

© Monkey Business Images/Shutterstock.

LO 1 Consumers as Decision Makers

One way to view consumer behavior is as a fairly predictable sequential process culminating with the individual's reaping a set of benefits from a product or service that satisfies the person's perceived needs. In this basic view, we can think of individuals as purposeful decision makers who either weigh and balance alternatives or (typically in complex situations with too much information) resort to simple decision rules of thumb to make the choice easier.

Basic Decision-Making Process

Often, but not always, consumers' decision-making process occurs in a straightforward sequence. Many consumption episodes then might be conceived as a sequence of four basic stages, shown in Exhibit 5.1. Understanding what typically happens at each stage gives the marketer a foundation for understanding consumers, and it also can illuminate opportunities for developing more powerful brand communication.

Need Recognition

A consumer's decision-making process begins when he or she perceives a need. A **need state** arises when one's desired state of affairs differs from one's actual state of affairs.

Exhibit 5.1
Consumer Decision Making

Need recognition → Information search and alternative evaluation → Purchase → Postpurchase use and evaluation

SOME DAY SOON, HE'LL
HAVE A SUPERHERO
SEAT ON
THE BUS, AND A NEW
BEST FRIEND

NOW, WHILE YOU CAN,
JOHNSON'S BABY HIM.

Johnson's Baby Bath: still the mildest baby bath you can buy. And now the number one choice of hospitals. Today, teach him the meaning of gentle, with Johnson's Baby Bath. The mildest you can buy, it's clinically proven as gentle to his eyes as pure water—yet cleans far better than water ever could. It's hypoallergenic and carefully pH-balanced, too. No wonder it's the number one choice of hospitals. He'll grow up soon enough. For now, just Johnson's Baby him.

PROTECT THEM.
SHELTER THEM.
JOHNSON'S BABY THEM.

Parents feel protective of their babies. This ad promises both functional benefits and emotional rewards for diligent parents.

Need states are accompanied by a mental discomfort or anxiety that motivates action; the severity of this discomfort can be widely variable, depending on the genesis of the need. For example, when you run out of toothpaste, your need state probably involves mild discomfort, but if you're driving on a dark and deserted highway in North Dakota in mid-February and your car breaks down, your need state might approach true desperation.

One way brand communication works is to point to and thereby activate needs that will motivate consumers to buy a company's product or service. For instance, in the fall in northern climates, marketers of snow blowers and boots roll out predictions for another severe winter and encourage consumers to prepare themselves before it's too late. Every change of season brings new needs, large and small, and advertisers are at the ready.

Many factors can influence consumers' need states. A popular model, Maslow's hierarchy of needs, says individuals try to satisfy basic survival needs before addressing "higher-level" needs such as status or a sense of accomplishment. Thus, because they have plenty to eat and a roof over their heads, more-

affluent consumers may fret over which new piece of Williams-Sonoma kitchen gadgetry or other accoutrement to place in their uptown condo, perhaps seeking to validate personal accomplishments and derive status and recognition through consumption and social display. Even though income clearly matters in this regard, it would be a mistake to believe that the poor have no aesthetic concerns. Rather, a variety of needs can be fulfilled through consumption.

One of the marketer's primary jobs is to make the connection between the consumer's need states and the benefits delivered by the marketer's products. Benefits come in different forms:

- Some benefits are "functional"—that is, they derive from the more objective performance characteristics of a product or service. Examples of such **functional benefits** are convenience, reliability, nutrition, durability, and energy efficiency.

- Products also may provide **emotional benefits**; these are not typically found in some tangible feature or objective characteristic of a product. Emotional benefits are more subjective and may be perceived differently from one consumer to the next. Products and services help consumers feel pride, avoid guilt, relieve fear, and experience pleasure. These are powerful consumption motives that advertisers often try to activate. Can you find the emotional benefits promised in the ad for Johnson's Baby Bath?

Some scholars believe *all* benefits are functional, even emotional ones; in other words, they believe all benefits serve a purpose. But distinguishing the benefit types can be helpful for crafting brand communication.

Marketers must develop a keen appreciation for the kinds of benefits that consumers derive from their brands. Even within the same product category, the benefits promised may vary widely. For instance, the makers of Ernst Benz watches promise that their product delivers precision measurements, whereas advertising for Duby & Schaldenbrand watches emphasizes the feelings of elegance and pride afforded the owner of a prestigious timepiece. To create advertising that resonates with your customers, you must know what benefits they are looking for—or might look for, if you suggest it.

Information Search and Alternative Evaluation

When a consumer has recognized a need, he or she may not be sure about the best way to satisfy that need. For example, if you have a fear of being trapped

functional benefits benefits that come from a product's objective performance characteristics

emotional benefits benefits not typically found in a product's tangible features or objective characteristics

in a blizzard in North Dakota, a condo on Miami Beach may be a much better solution than a Jeep or new snow tires. Need recognition simply sets in motion a process that may involve an extensive information search and careful evaluation of alternatives before purchase. Of course, during this search and evaluation, marketers have numerous opportunities to influence the final decision.

Once a need has been recognized, consumers acquire information:

- The consumer's first option for information is an **internal search**, which draws on personal experience and prior knowledge. When a consumer has considerable experience with the product type, attitudes about alternatives may be well established and could determine choice. An internal search also can tap into information that has accumulated in one's memory as a result of repeated advertising exposures, such as "Tide's In, Dirt's Out," or stored judgments, such as a belief that Apple computers are unlikely to crash. Marketers want internal searches to result in their brand being in the "evoked set"—the set of brands (usually two to five) that come to mind when a category is mentioned. The evoked set is usually highly related to the **consideration set**, the set of the brands the consumer

© Hallgerd/Shutterstock.

GLOBAL JOY IN JAPAN

The Japanese marketplace is tough, even for giants like Procter & Gamble. To find an opening for its dishwashing soap, P&G began investigating consumer behavior. Managers videotaped Japanese homemakers as they washed dishes and then talked to them about the chore. They learned that, as Japanese diets added more meat and fried foods, it had become harder to scrub grease stains out of plastic dishes and storage containers, and homemakers were using too much dish soap.

P&G began offering a highly concentrated Joy dish soap formulated for the Japanese market. A TV ad demonstrated how a squirt of Joy could dissolve the grease in a sink full of dirty dishes. Joy rapidly gained market share, largely thanks to the television ads.

Source: Reprinted with permission of *The Wall Street Journal*, Copyright © 1977 Dow Jones & Company, Inc. All Rights Reserved Worldwide.

will consider for purchase. If your brand is the first one recalled, you have achieved something even better: "top of mind." Many people believe that top-of-mind awareness predicts purchase of inexpensive and low-risk consumer packaged goods. As noted in Chapter 1, the purpose of delayed-response advertising is to generate recognition of and a favorable predisposition toward a brand so that, when consumers enter search mode, that brand will be one they immediately consider.

- If an internal search does not turn up enough information to yield a decision, the consumer proceeds with an **external search**. This search involves visiting retail stores to examine the alternatives, seeking input from friends and relatives about their experiences with the products in question, or perusing professional product evaluations from various sources such as *Consumer Reports* or *Car and Driver*. In addition, when consumers are in an active information-gathering mode, they may be receptive to detailed, informative advertisements delivered through any of the print media, or they may deploy a shopping agent or a search engine to scour the Internet for the best deal or for opinions of other users.

During an internal or external search, consumers are not merely gathering information for its own sake. They have a need that is propelling the process, and their goal is to make a decision that yields benefits for them. Consumers search for and simultaneously are forming attitudes about possible alternatives. This effort, alternative evaluation, is another key phase for the marketer to address.

Alternative evaluation is structured by two variables:

1. The *consideration set* is the subset of brands from a particular product category that becomes the focal point of the consumer's evaluation. Most product categories contain too many brands for all to be considered, so the consumer finds some way to focus the evaluation. For autos, a consumer might consider only cars priced less than $20,000, or only cars that have antilock brakes, or that are foreign-made, or that are sold at dealerships within a five-mile radius of home. Thus, advertising often aims to make consumers aware of the brand and to keep them aware so that the brand has a chance to be part of the consideration set.

2. Next, consumers form evaluations by applying **evaluative criteria**—product attributes or performance characteristics used to compare various brands. Evaluative criteria differ from one product category to the next. Examples include price, texture, warranty terms, service support, color, scent, and carb content.

Marketers need to have an understanding as complete as possible of the evaluative criteria that consumers use to make their buying decisions. They also must know how consumers rate their brand in comparison with others from the consideration set. This information furnishes a powerful starting point for any promotional campaign.

Purchase

At the third stage of consumers' decision making, a purchase occurs. The consumer has made a decision, and a sale is made. That might sound like the culmination of the decision-making process, but from the marketer's standpoint, it should be only one action in a longer-term relationship. In any product or service category, the consumer is likely to buy again in the future. Therefore, what happens after the sale is very important to marketers. The first purchase is in effect a trial; marketers then want conversion (repeat purchase). They want brand loyalty. Some want to create brand ambassadors—users who will become apostles for the brand, spreading its gospel. At the same time, competitors will be working to persuade consumers to give their brand a try.

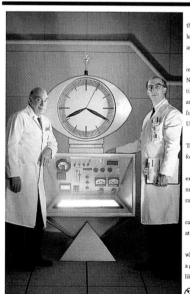

The evaluative criteria for an airline include on-time arrival.

customer satisfaction good feelings that come from a favorable postpurchase experience

cognitive dissonance anxiety or regret that lingers after a difficult decision

Postpurchase Use and Evaluation

The goal for marketers must not be simply to generate a sale; it must be to create satisfied and, ultimately, loyal customers. The data to support this position are astounding. Research shows that about 65 percent of the average company's business comes from its present satisfied customers, so they are essential to retain. In addition, 91 percent of dissatisfied customers again will never buy from the company that disappointed them, so disappointing a customer is a huge mistake.[3] For good or for ill, consumers' evaluations of products in use become a major determinant of which brands will be in the consideration set the next time around.

Customer satisfaction derives from a favorable postpurchase experience. It may develop after a single use, but more likely it will require sustained use. Brand communication can play an important role in inducing customer satisfaction by creating appropriate expectations for a brand's performance or by helping the consumer who already has bought the advertised brand to feel good about it.

Advertising plays an important role in alleviating the **cognitive dissonance** that can occur after a purchase. Cognitive dissonance is the anxiety or regret that lingers after a difficult decision, sometimes called "buyer's remorse." Often, rejected alternatives have attractive features that lead people to second-guess their own decisions. If the marketer's goal is to generate satisfied customers, this dissonance must be resolved in a way that leads consumers to conclude they made the right decision.

When dissonance is expected (it's most likely with high-cost items or products that have many competitors), marketers should reassure buyers by providing detailed information about their brands. Postpurchase reinforcement programs might involve direct mail, email, or other types of personalized contacts with the customer. Nowadays, consumers often search the Internet for other purchasers of the product to tell them they did the right thing. Some marketers sponsor or contribute to online discussion groups and user sites so that they can provide information aimed at converting buyers into satisfied customers. This postpurchase period represents a great opportunity because the consumer is likely to be attentive and willing to provide information and advice about product use that will increase customer satisfaction.

LO 2 Modes of Decision Making

The decision-making process we've been considering is deliberate and systematic, but as consumers ourselves, we know that some purchase decisions are hasty, impulsive, or even irrational. The time and effort that people put into their purchase decisions can vary dramatically for different types of products. Maybe you buy whatever toothpaste you usually use, agonize a little bit about picking out a Valentine's gift for someone special, and do some thoughtful research to choose a college or a car.

Our decision-making model takes this into account by defining four decision-making modes that help marketers appreciate the richness and complexity of consumer behavior. These four modes are determined by a consumer's degree of involvement and level of experience with the product or service in question (see Exhibit 5.2).

Exhibit 5.2
Modes of Decision Making

	Involvement	
	High	**Low**
Low (Experience)	Extended problem solving	Limited problem solving
High (Experience)	Brand loyalty	Habit or variety seeking

In this model, **involvement** refers to the degree of perceived relevance and personal importance accompanying the choice of a certain product or service within a particular context. Many factors have been identified as potential contributors to an individual's level of involvement with a consumption decision:[4]

- Interests and avocations, such as cooking and pet ownership, can enhance involvement levels in related product categories.

- Any time a great deal of risk is associated with a purchase—perhaps as a result of a high price or the need to live with the decision for a long time—involvement tends to be elevated.

- Products and brands that carry important symbolic meaning will generate high involvement. For example, this occurs when owning or using a product helps people reinforce some aspect of their self-image or makes a statement to other people who are important to them. In the case of choosing a Valentine's Day gift, the purchase may carry both great symbolic meaning and real consequences.

- Purchases that tap into deep emotional concerns or motives are associated with high involvement. Marketing messages that appeal to patriotism are aimed at generating or maintaining this kind of involvement.

Together with consumers' degree of experience, their level of involvement determines the way they will use or modify the decision-making process. As shown in Exhibit 5.2, consumers may engage in extended problem solving, limited problem solving, habit or variety seeking, or brand loyalty.

Extended Problem Solving

When consumers are inexperienced in a particular consumption setting yet find the setting highly involving, they are likely to engage in **extended problem solving**. In this mode, consumers go through a deliberate decision-making process that tracks the steps in Exhibit 5.1: explicit need recognition, careful internal and external search, alternative evaluation, purchase, and a lengthy postpurchase evaluation.

Consumers might engage in extended problem solving when choosing a home or a diamond ring. These products are expensive, are publicly evaluated, and can carry a considerable amount of risk in terms of making an uneducated decision. These purchases also tend to be infrequent. Extended problem solving is the exception, not the rule.

Limited Problem Solving

When experience and involvement are both low, consumers are more likely to use **limited problem solving**. In this mode, a consumer is less systematic in his or her decision making. The consumer has a new problem to solve, but the problem is not interesting or engaging, so the information search is limited to trying the first brand encountered. For example, let's say a young couple has just brought home a new baby, and suddenly the parents perceive a very real need for disposable diapers. At the hospital, they received complimentary trial packs of several products, including Pampers disposables. They try the Pampers, find them an acceptable solution to their messy new problem, and take the discount coupon

involvement degree of perceived relevance and personal importance accompanying the choice of a product or service in a particular context

extended problem solving decision-making mode in which inexperienced but highly involved consumers go through a deliberate decision-making process

limited problem solving decision-making mode in which relatively inexperienced and uninvolved consumers are not systematic about decisions

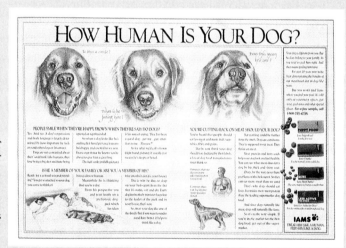

Courtesy, The IAMS Company.

Involvement levels vary not only among product categories but also among individuals for any given product category. People who think of their pets as human take the selection of pet food very seriously. For example, some pet owners will feed their pets only the expensive canned products that look and smell like people food. IAMS understands this and made a special premium dog food for consumers who think of their pets as close to humans. Many other pet owners, however, are perfectly happy with feeding Rover from a 50-pound, economy-size bag of dry dog food.

that came with the sample to their local grocery, where they buy several packages.

In the limited problem-solving mode, consumers often are simply seeking adequate solutions to mundane problems. Also, trying a brand or two may be the most efficient way of collecting information about one's options. Smart marketers realize that trial offers can be a preferred means of collecting information, and they facilitate trial of their brands through free samples, inexpensive "trial sizes," or discount coupons.

Habit or Variety Seeking

In settings where a decision isn't involving and an experienced consumer repurchases from the category over and over again, the mode of purchase is some combination of habit and variety seeking. **Habit** refers to buying a single brand repeatedly as a solution to a simple consumption problem. Habitual purchases are probably the most common decision-making mode. Consumers find a brand of laundry detergent that suits their needs, they run out of the product, and they buy it again. The cycle repeats itself many times per year in an almost mindless fashion. The habit of buying just one brand simplifies life and minimizes the time invested in "nuisance" purchases. A lot of consumption decisions are boring but necessary; habits help us minimize the inconvenience.

In some product categories where a buying habit would be expected, variety seeking may be observed instead. **Variety seeking** refers to the tendency of consumers to switch their selection among various brands in a given category in a seemingly random pattern. Habitual buying can be tedious, and some consumers use variety seeking to fight the boredom. This is not to say that a consumer will buy just any brand; he or she probably selects from two to five brands that provide similar levels of satisfaction. However, from one purchase occasion to the next, the individual will

switch brands from within this set, just for the sake of variety.

Variety seeking is most likely in frequently purchased categories where sensory experience, such as taste or smell, accompanies product use. In such categories, no amount of ad spending can overcome the consumer's basic desire for fresh sensory experience.[5] Satiation occurs after repeated use and leaves the consumer looking for a change of pace. Product categories such as soft drinks and alcoholic beverages, snack foods, breakfast cereals, and fast food are prone to variety seeking, so marketers in these categories constantly introduce new possibilities to feed the craving for variety.

Brand Loyalty

In situations typified by high involvement and rich prior experience, **brand loyalty** becomes a major consideration in the purchase decision. Consumers demonstrate brand loyalty when they repeatedly purchase a single brand as their choice to fulfill a specific need. In one sense, brand-loyal purchasers may look as if they have developed a simple buying habit; however, it is important to distinguish brand loyalty from simple habit. Brand loyalty is based on highly favorable attitudes toward the brand and a conscious commitment to find this brand each time the consumer purchases from this category. Conversely, habits are merely consumption simplifiers that are not based on deeply held convictions. Habits can be disrupted through a skillful combination of advertising and sales promotions. Spending advertising dollars to persuade truly brand-loyal consumers to try an alternative can be a great waste of resources.

Brands such as Starbucks and Apple have inspired very loyal consumers. Brand loyalty is something that any marketer aspires to have, but in a world filled with more-savvy consumers and endless product (and advertising) proliferation, it is becoming harder and harder to attain. What causes brand loyalty to emerge? Here are some answers:

- The consumer perceives that one brand simply outperforms all others in providing some critical functional benefit. Apple's computers are known for having little, if any, trouble with computer viruses, and its iPods caught on partly because users found it easy and fun to download music from iTunes.

- Perhaps even more important, brand loyalty can be due to the emotional benefits that accompany certain brands. In one of the strongest indicators for brand loyalty, some loyal consumers have tattooed their bodies with the insignia of their favorite brand. Supposedly, the worldwide leader in brand-name tattoos is Harley-Davidson. What accounts for Harley's fervent following? Do its motorcycles simply perform better? More likely, part of the loyalty comes from the association of the Harley brand with the deep emotional benefit of taking a big bike out on the open road and leaving civilization far behind, as well as feelings of pride, kinship, and community with other Harley riders. Owning a Harley—and perhaps the tattoo—makes a person feel different and special. Harley ads are designed to reaffirm the deep emotional appeal of this product.

Strong emotional benefits might be expected from consumption decisions that we classify as highly involving, and they are major determinants of brand loyalty. Indeed, with so many brands in the marketplace, it is becoming harder and harder to create loyalty for one's brand through functional benefits alone. To break free of this brand-parity problem and provide consumers with enduring reasons to become or stay loyal, marketers are investing more and more effort in communicating the emotional benefits that might be derived from brands in categories as diverse as greeting cards (Hallmark—"When you care enough to send the very best") and vacation hot spots (Las Vegas—"What happens in Vegas, stays in Vegas"). You might go to YouTube and check out one of those Vegas spots or some of the consumer-generated parodies. Many, probably most, companies are exploring ways to use the Internet to create dialogue, manage relations, and even create a community with their customers. To do this, one must look for means to connect with customers at an emotional level.

As we noted earlier in the chapter, a good deal of advertising is designed to ensure recognition and create favorable predispositions toward a brand so that, as consumers search for solutions to their problems, they will think of the brand immediately. The goal of any delayed-response ad is to affect some psychological state that subsequently will influence a purchase. This generally involves some combination of attitudes and beliefs, illustrated in Exhibit 5.3.

- **Attitude** is an overall evaluation of any object, person, or issue that varies along a continuum, such as favorable to unfavorable or positive to negative. Attitudes are learned, and if they are based on substantial experience with the object or issue in question, they can be held with great conviction. Attitudes simplify decision-making; when faced with a choice among several alternatives, we do not need to process new information or analyze the merits of the alternatives. We merely select the alternative we think is the most favorable. Marketers are most interested in one particular class of attitudes, **brand attitudes**, which are summary evaluations that reflect preferences for various products and services.

- **Beliefs** represent the knowledge and feelings a person has accumulated about an object or issue. They can be logical and factual, or biased and self-serving. A person might believe that the Mini Cooper is cute. That belief can serve as a basis for the person's attitude toward Minis. People have many beliefs about various features and attributes of products and brands. Typically, a small number of beliefs—on the order of five to

attitude overall evaluation of any object, person, or issue; varies along a continuum, such as favorable to unfavorable or positive to negative

brand attitudes summary evaluations that reflect preferences for various products or brands

beliefs a person's knowledge and feelings about an object or issue

LO 3 Key Psychological Processes

To complete our picture of the consumer as a fairly thoughtful decision maker, one key issue remains. We need to examine the explicit psychological consequences of brand communication. What do advertisements or other brand messages leave in the minds of consumers that ultimately may influence their behavior?

Exhibit 5.3
Beliefs Shape Attitudes

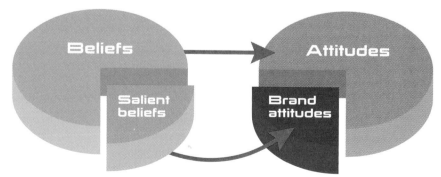

nine—underlie brand attitudes.[6] These beliefs are the critical determinants of an attitude and are referred to as **salient beliefs**.

If we know a person's beliefs, usually it is possible to infer attitude. Someone with many favorable beliefs about a product or brand is likely to have a favorable attitude toward it.

The number of salient beliefs varies between product categories. The loyal Harley owner who proudly displays a tattoo will have many more salient beliefs about his bike than he has about his brand of shaving cream. Also, salient beliefs can be modified, replaced, or extinguished. For example, Nicorette Stop Smoking Gum has advertised a new product, Fruit Chill Gum, that "tastes like a dream." One interpretation of this message is that many people held the belief that earlier versions didn't taste very good, and the ad was seeking to replace that belief and improve attitudes toward the product.

Because belief shaping and reinforcement can be one of the principal goals of brand communication, marketers make belief assessment a focal point in their attempts to understand consumer behavior.

Multi-Attribute Attitude Models (MAAMs)

Multi-attribute attitude models (MAAMs) provide a framework and a set of research procedures for collecting information from consumers to assess their salient beliefs and attitudes about competitive brands. Any MAAMs analysis will feature four fundamental components:

1. *Evaluative criteria* are the attributes or performance characteristics that consumers use in comparing competitive brands. In pursuing a MAAMs analysis, a marketer must identify all evaluative criteria relevant to its product category.

2. *Importance weights* reflect the priority that a particular evaluative criterion receives in the consumer's decision-making process. Importance weights can vary dramatically from one consumer to the next. Some people will merely want good taste from their bowl of cereal, while others will be more concerned about fat and fiber content.

3. The *consideration set* is the group of brands that represents the real focal point for the consumer's decision. For example, the potential buyer of a luxury sedan might be focusing on Acura and Lexus. These and comparable brands would be featured in a MAAMs analysis. If

© Losevsky Pavel/Shutterstock.

another automaker aspired to be part of this consideration set, it could conduct a MAAMs analysis featuring its brand and its major competitors.

4. *Beliefs* represent the consumers' knowledge and feelings about various brands. A MAAMs analysis assesses beliefs about each brand's performance on all relevant evaluative criteria. Beliefs can be matters of fact (a 12-ounce Pepsi has 150 calories) or highly subjective (the Cadillac XLR Roadster is the sleekest, sexiest car on the street). Beliefs may vary widely among consumers.

In conducting a MAAMs analysis, first we must specify the relevant evaluative criteria for our category as well as our direct competitors (see Exhibit 5.4). We then go to consumers and let them tell us what's important and how our brand fares against the competition on the various evaluative criteria. The information generated from this survey research will give us a better appreciation for the salient beliefs that underlie brand attitudes, and it may suggest important opportunities for changing our marketing or advertising to yield more favorable brand attitudes:

- If consumers do not accurately perceive the relative performance of a brand on an important evaluative criterion, brand communication may try to correct the misperception. For example, if Colgate marketers learn that consumers perceive Crest to be far and away the best brand of toothpaste for fighting cavities, when in fact all brands with a fluoride additive perform equally well on cavity prevention, they might try to correct this misperception.

- If a brand is perceived as the best performer on an evaluative criterion that most consumers view as unimportant, the task for brand communication would be to persuade consumers that the brand's benefits are more important than they had thought.

- If consumers don't have favorable attitudes toward a brand, marketers sometimes conclude that the only way to improve attitudes would be through the introduction of a new attribute, which then will be featured in promotional messages. Marketers may add the new attribute or feature to an existing product or develop a new or extended product line.

When marketers use the MAAMs approach, they can improve both brand attitudes and market share. When marketers carefully isolate key evaluative criteria, bring products to the marketplace that perform well on the focal criteria, and develop ads that effectively shape salient beliefs about the brand, the results can be dramatic.

Information Processing and Perceptual Defense

Brand promotion would be easy if consumers would just pay close attention to what marketers say and believe every message, and if competitors weren't so busy spreading their own messages. Of course, these things aren't going to happen. In real life, marketers

encounter resistance. One way to think about this problem is to portray the consumer as an information processor who must advance through a series of stages before a brand message can have its intended effect:

1. Pay attention to the message

2. Comprehend the message correctly

3. Accept the message exactly as it was intended

4. Retain the message until it is needed for a purchase decision

Unfortunately, problems can and do occur at any or all of these four stages, completely negating the effect of the brand communication.

The first major obstacle that marketers must overcome if their message is to have its intended effect is the **cognitive consistency** impetus, which stems from the individual consumer. A person tends to maintain a set of beliefs and attitudes over time. These consistent attitudes help him or her make efficient decisions that yield pleasing outcomes. When a consumer is satisfied with these outcomes, there is really no reason to alter the belief system that generated them. New information that challenges existing beliefs can be ignored or disparaged to prevent modification of the present cognitive system.

A second obstacle is **advertising clutter**, which derives from the context in which ads are processed. Even if a person wanted to, it would be impossible

cognitive consistency maintenance of a system of beliefs and attitudes over time

advertising clutter volume of similar ads for products or services that presents an obstacle to brand promotion

Exhibit 5.4
Using MAAMs Analysis

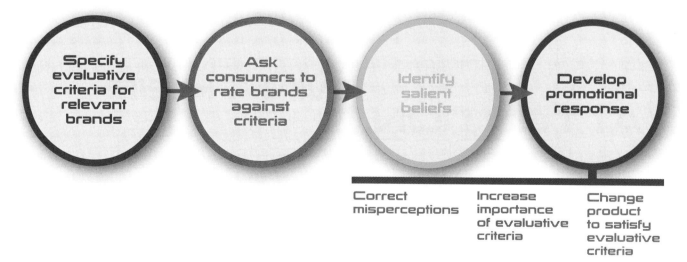

Specify evaluative criteria for relevant brands → Ask consumers to rate brands against criteria → Identify salient beliefs → Develop promotional response

Correct misperceptions | Increase importance of evaluative criteria | Change product to satisfy evaluative criteria

to process and integrate every marketing message that he or she is exposed to each day. If you pick up today's newspaper, you won't have time to study every ad and read the stories, too. The clutter problem is magnified further by competitive brands making very similar performance claims.[7] Was it Advil, Anacin, Aveda, Aleve, Avia, Aflexa, Aveya, Actonel, Motrin, Nuprin, or Tylenol Gelcaps that promised you 12 hours of relief from your headache? (Can you select the brands from this list that aren't headache remedies?) The simple fact is that each of us is exposed to hundreds, maybe thousands, of ads each day, and no one has the time or inclination to sort through them all. Some industry experts and researchers believe that the simple mass of advertising, the enormous number of ads, is now working very hard against the institution of advertising itself.

Consumers thus employ perceptual defenses to simplify and control their own processing of marketing messages. That means the consumer is in control, and the marketer must find some way to engage the consumer if a message is to have any impact. Of course, the best way to engage consumers is to offer information about a product or service that will address an active need state.

The advertiser's greatest challenge is **selective attention**. Consumers simply ignore most ads. They turn the page, change the station, mute the sound, head for the refrigerator, TiVo past the ad, or just daydream or doze off. Advertisers employ a variety of tactics to catch consumers' attention. Devices for combating selective attention include popular music, celebrity spokespersons, sexy models, rapid scene changes, and anything that is novel. In their never-ending battle for the attention of the consumer, marketers try so hard to be noticed that they often step over the line between novelty and annoyance. In addition, the provocative, attention-attracting devices used to engage consumers often become the focal point of consumers' ad processing. Viewers remember seeing an ad featuring 27 Elvis Presley impersonators, but they can't recall what brand was being advertised or what claims were being made about the brand. If advertisers must entertain consumers to win their attention, they also must be careful that the brand and message don't get lost in the shuffle.

Even when a brand-related message gets attention and the consumer comprehends the message, more resistance will follow if the message is asking the consumer to alter beliefs. At that point, the cognitive consistency impetus kicks in, and cognitive responses can be expected. **Cognitive responses** are the thoughts that occur to individuals at that exact moment when their beliefs and attitudes are being challenged by some form of persuasive communication. Most ads will not provoke enough mental engagement to yield any form of cognitive response, but when these responses occur, the valence of the responses is critical to the acceptance of one's message.

The final stage of information processing involves memory. Traditionally, marketers have tested consumers' memory of advertising messages asking them to recall brand names and points made in advertising copy. However, recent models of human memory provide strong evidence that memory is a much more fluid and interpretive system than we have thought in the past.[8] Human memory is not a mental VCR; it's more likely to combine, delete, add, and rewrite information. Still, it does stand to reason that if a consumer can remember most of your ad, it can benefit your brand.

IF ADVERTISERS MUST ENTERTAIN CONSUMERS TO **WIN THEIR ATTENTION,** THEY ALSO MUST BE CAREFUL THAT THE BRAND AND MESSAGE **DON'T GET LOST** IN THE SHUFFLE.

The Elaboration Likelihood Model (ELM)

Cognitive responses are one of the main components of an influential framework for understanding the impact of advertising: the **elaboration likelihood model (ELM)**. The ELM has been borrowed from social psychology; it gathers the concepts of involvement, information processing, cognitive responses, and attitude formation in a single, integrated framework, which can be applied to advertising settings.[9] It has limitations but applies to many advertising situations and has a certain intuitive appeal. The basic premise of the ELM is that, to understand how a persuasive message may affect a person's attitudes, we must consider his or her motivation and ability to elaborate on the message during processing. For most marketing contexts, motivation and ability will be a function of how involved the person is with the consumption decision in question. When involvement is high, consumers will engage in active mental elaboration during ad processing; when involvement is low, ad processing will be more passive.

As indicated in Exhibit 5.5, the ELM uses the involvement dichotomy to map two distinct routes to attitude change:

1. *Central route to persuasion:* When involvement is high, the consumer tends to draw on prior knowledge and experience and scrutinize or elaborate on the central arguments of the message. The nature of the individual's effortful thinking about the issues at hand can be judged from the cognitive responses to the message. These cognitive responses may be positive or negative, and they can be reactions to specific claims or any element of the ad. Responses are more likely to be positive when messages are designed to reinforce existing beliefs or shape beliefs for a brand that the consumer was unaware of. If the cognitive responses provoked by an ad are primarily negative, the ad has backfired: The consumer is maintaining cognitive consistency by disparaging the ad, and his or her negative thoughts are likely to foster negative evaluation of the brand. However, when the central route induces positive attitudes, they are based on careful thought, so they will come to mind quickly for use in product selection, resist the change efforts of other advertisers, persist in memory without repeated ad exposures, and be excellent predictors of behavior. These properties cannot be expected of attitudes that are formed in the peripheral route.

2. *Peripheral route to persuasion:* For low-involvement contexts, attitude formation tends to follow a more peripheral route, where peripheral cues become the focal point for judging the impact of a brand communication. **Peripheral cues** refer to features of a promotional message other than the actual arguments about the brand's performance. They include an attractive or comical spokesperson, novel imagery, humorous incidents, or a catchy jingle. (Critics of the ELM find this the weakest part of the model: We can all think of ads where the music and pictures are anything but peripheral. The

> **elaboration likelihood model (ELM)** social psychological model of the response to a persuasive communication, expressing the response in terms of motivation and ability
>
> **peripheral cues** features of an advertisement other than the actual arguments about the brand's performance

Exhibit 5.5
Routes to Attitude Change

model works better with traditional copy-heavy ads.) In the peripheral route, the consumer can still learn from the marketer's communication, but the learning is passive and typically must be achieved by frequent association of the peripheral cue (for example, the Eveready Energizer Bunny) with the brand in question. It even has been suggested that advertises might use classical conditioning principles to facilitate and accelerate this associative learning process.[10] As consumers learn to associate pleasant feelings and attractive images with a brand, their attitude toward the brand should become more positive. However, this is an expensive tactic because any gains made along the peripheral route are short lived and repetition of a message, coupled with a never-ending search for the freshest, most popular peripheral cues, demands huge budgets.

When all brands in a category offer similar benefits, the most fruitful avenue for advertising strategy is likely to be the peripheral route, where the advertiser merely tries to maintain positive or pleasant associations with the brand by constantly presenting it with appealing peripheral cues. Of course, peripheral cues can be more than merely cute, with the right ones adding an undeniable level of "hipness" to aging brands.[11] Selecting peripheral cues can be especially important for mature brands in low-involvement categories, where the challenge is to keep the customer from getting bored.[12] Marketing typical of the peripheral route includes advertising campaigns for high-profile, mature brands such as Budweiser and Doritos. They entertain in an effort to keep you interested.

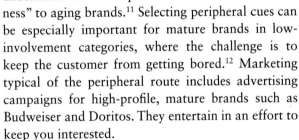
THEY ENTERTAIN IN AN EFFORT TO KEEP YOU INTERESTED.

Limits of Decision-Making Models

The view of the consumer as decision maker and information processor has been popular, but it is not without its limitations and critics. In fact, the critics are getting louder, particularly in the actual practice of integrated marketing communication. Although what goes on in consumers' minds is obviously important, it tells only part of the story of consumer behavior and brand promotion.

The decision-making perspective is reasonably good at explaining how consumers make decisions. For example, it tells us that, in general, consumers tend to use less as opposed to more information. Although

consumers *say* more information is best, they tend to *actually use* less. If you think about it, this makes perfect sense. Consumers store and retrieve previously made judgments (e.g., "Honda is the best value") to spare themselves from deciding all over again every time they make a purchase. If this were not true, a trip to the convenience store would take hours.

But in their effort to isolate psychological mechanisms, information-processing academic researchers typically take consumer behavior (and consumers) out of its (their) natural environment in favor of a laboratory. This makes a great deal of sense if your desire is experimental control, the elimination of other possible explanations for a certain effect, or evidence of a mental process. But few consumers actually watch ads and buy products in laboratories. In fact, some critics argue that, under such obviously unrealistic conditions, researchers no longer are studying marketing but only "stimulus material." According to this view, marketing messages really exist *only* in the real social world and natural environment. When removed from that environment, ads are no longer ads in any meaningful sense.

Apply that idea to your own experience: When you watch advertising on television, you usually see 10 ads in a commercial break. You may or may not be paying attention. You might be talking to friends or family, reading, or doing just about anything else. Chances are you are not watching an ad on a computer monitor for class credit. In the real world, where you might see 800 to 2,000 ads per day, many ads just become wallpaper, nothing you really focus on. But in a lab, the degree of focus typically is far greater. Subjects pay more attention; they watch the "ads" differently. More importantly, what the ad means often is completely lost in the quest for "information" being "processed."

The allure of science and its symbols (e.g., labs and their perceived certainty and infallibility of science) is one of the modern period's best-known seductions and comfortable mythologies. The trappings and appearance of science give people (including clients) feelings of certainty and truth, whether it is deserved or appropriate. And, to be fair, the aims of academic experimental research (to advance basic knowledge and theory) often are quite different from the aims of the advertising industry (to make ads that sell things).

Industry critics and more and more academic researchers believe that much of the psychological "information-processing" research (most popular in the industry in the 1950s) has significantly less to do with the promotion and consumption of real goods and services in the real world than with advancing psychological theory—a completely worthy goal for some college professors but not necessarily important to the actual practice of marketing. In the real world of advertising, what matters is real consumers and how they respond to real brand promotion in real environments.

Consumers as Social Beings

For quite some time, at least 40 years, marketers—particularly in the advertising industry—have been moving away from purely psychological approaches. This shift gathered enormous momentum in the 1980s. At that time, U.S. West Coast agencies began adopting what they called "British research," which was really just qualitative research as has been practiced by anthropologists, sociologists, and others for more than a century. It was called "British" because some very hot London agencies had been doing research this way all along. A good example comes from Judie Lannon, then–creative research director at J. Walter Thompson, London, who beautifully sums up this emphasis on meaning:

> And if Advertising contributes to the meaning of inanimate goods, then the study of these values and meanings are of prime importance . . . the perspective of research must be what people use advertising for.[13]

meaning what a brand message intends or conveys

This industry trend toward qualitative research and naturalistic methods resonated with a similar move in academic research toward more qualitative field work, and interpretive and textual approaches to the study of human behavior, including consumer behavior. Investigators began to see consumers as more than "information processors" and to see ads as more than socially isolated attempts at attitude manipulation. The truth is most major companies do a lot of qualitative research, often under the heading "consumer insights." In this approach, **meaning** becomes more important than attitudes. Consumers do "process" information, but they also do a whole lot more. Furthermore, "information" itself is a rich and complex textual product, bound by history, society, and culture, and it is interpreted in sophisticated ways by human beings. Brand promotion is not engineering or chemistry; ads are not atoms or molecules. This approach centers on knowing how to use brand promotion to connect with human beings around their consumption practices. That's why advertising agencies hire people who know about material culture (anthropology), demography and social process (sociology), the history of brands and consumption practices (history), memory (psychology), communication, text (literature), and art (what a lot of ads are). Humans and their creations (including ads and branded goods) are not just processors of information; they are that and much more.

© T. O'Guinn.

REAL CONSUMERS DO NOT CONSUME IN A LABORATORY. RATHER, THEY ARE CONNECTED TO ONE ANOTHER THROUGH SOCIAL IDENTITIES, FAMILIES, CULTURES, AND MORE.

Therefore, this second perspective on consumer behavior is concerned with social and cultural processes. It should be considered another part of the larger story of how advertising works, viewing the same consumers' behavior from a different vantage point.

LO 4 Consuming in the Real World

The lives of real consumers include several major components: culture, family, race and ethnicity, geopolitics, gender, and community.

Culture

If you are in the business of brand promotion, you are in the culture business. Culture infuses, works on, is part of, and generally lands on all consumption. **Culture** is what a people do, or "the total life ways of a people, the social legacy the individual acquires from his (her) group."[14] It is the way we eat, groom ourselves, celebrate, and mark our space and assert our position. It is the way things are done. Cultures often are thought of as large and national, but, in reality, cultures usually are smaller and not necessarily geographic, such as *urban hipster culture* or *teen tech-nerd culture.*

Usually it's easier to see and note culture when it's distant and unfamiliar, such as while traveling to another place. Members of a culture find the ways they do things to be perfectly natural. Culture thus is said to be invisible to those who are immersed in it. When everyone around us behaves in a similar fashion, we do not easily think about the existence of some large and powerful force acting on us all. But it's there; this constant background force is the force of culture. The sociocultural perspective offers the tools to help us see the culture that is all around us, as if we were visiting a strange land.

When marketers spend time and money studying why consumers consume certain goods or services, or why they consume them in a certain way, they are considering culture. Culture informs consumers' views about food, the body, gifts, possessions, a sense of self versus others, mating, courtship, death, religion, family, jobs, art, holidays, leisure, satisfaction, work—just about everything. It does this through several types of cultural expression:

- Values
- Rituals
- Stratification (social class), expressed through taste and cultural capital

Values are the defining expressions of culture. Values express in words and deeds what is important to a culture. For example, some cultures value propriety and restrained behavior, while others value open expression. Values are cultural bedrock; they cannot be changed quickly or easily. They thus are different from attitudes, which can be changed through a single advertising campaign or even a single ad. As shown in Exhibit 5.6, values are the foundation for attitudes and behavior. They influence attitudes, which then shape behavior. In this context, effective brand promotion is consistent with a culture's values. Marketers cannot expect to use advertising to change values in any substantive way. Rather, advertising influences values in the same way a persistent drip of water wears down a granite slab—very slowly and through cumulative impact, over years and years.

Typically, advertisers try to associate their product with a cultural value or criticize a competitor for being out of step with one. Advertisements that are out of step with the values of a people likely will be rejected. Many argue that the best (most effective) ads are those that best express and affirm core cultural values. For example, one core American value is said to be individualism, or the predisposition to value the individual over the group. To the extent that this is true, marketers in America can appeal to consumers' sense of individual style or their rugged individual-

IF YOU ARE IN THE BUSINESS OF BRAND PROMOTION, YOU ARE IN THE CULTURE BUSINESS.

Exhibit 5.6
Culture Shapes Consumer Behavior

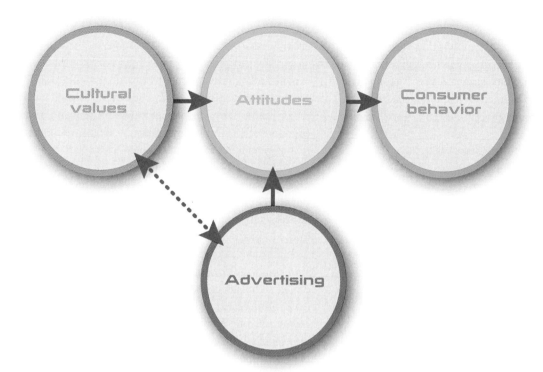

rituals repeated behaviors that affirm, express, and maintain cultural values

stratification (social class) individuals' relative standing in a social system as produced by systematic inequalities

ism. However, globalization makes the world more homogeneous in media and consumption. The trick for transnational companies is to understand how to adjust for both globalism and local values.

Cultures affirm, express, and maintain their values through rituals. **Rituals** are "often-repeated formalized behaviors involving symbols."[15] Through the practice of rituals, individuals are made part of the culture, and the culture constantly renews and perpetuates itself. For example, ritual-laden holidays such as Thanksgiving and the Fourth of July help perpetuate aspects of American culture through their repeated reenactment (tradition).

As a part of their cultures, consumers participate in rituals. In fact, rituals help intertwine culture and consumption practices in a very real way. For example, Jell-O may have attained the prominence of an "official" American holiday food because of its regular usage as part of the Thanksgiving dinner ritual.[16] If you are a consumer packaged-goods manufacturer, understanding these types of ritual is not a trivial concern at all. Likewise, when a married couple buys a new home, they do all sorts of "unnecessary" things to make it theirs. They clean the carpets even if they were just cleaned; they trim trees that don't need trimming—all to make the new possession theirs and remove any trace of the former owner. These behaviors are not

only important to anthropologists; they also are important to those making and trying to sell products such as rug shampoos or lawn and garden equipment.

Rituals don't have to be the biggest events of the year. There are everyday rituals, such as the way we eat, clean ourselves, and groom. Think about all the habitual things you do from the time you get up in the morning until you crawl into bed at night. These things are done in a certain way; they are not random.[17] Members of a common culture tend to do them one way, and members of other cultures do them other ways. Daily rituals seem inconsequential because they are habitual and routine, and thus "invisible." If, however, someone tried to get you to significantly alter how often you shower or the way you handle a fork, that person would quickly learn just how resistant to change these rituals are.

If a product or service cannot be incorporated into an already-existing ritual, marketers will find it difficult and expensive to affect a change. Conversely, when a marketer can incorporate the consumption of a good or service into an existing ritual, success is much more likely. Clearly, there are important opportunities for marketers who successfully can link their products to consumption rituals.

Stratification (social class) refers to a person's relative standing in a social system as produced by systematic inequalities in measures such as wealth, income, education, power, and status. For example, some members of society exist within a richer group (stratum), others within a less affluent stratum. Race and gender also are unequally distributed across these strata. For example, men generally have higher incomes than women. Thus, a cross-section, or slice, of American society would reveal many different

Photo courtesy of Target Stores, Minneapolis.

Target has been one of the most amazing brands, with amazing ads to match over the last few years. The company's ads are almost devoid of words (copy) and are stylish, hip, and self-aware. Throughout the years, Target has made the logo for its store mean more than the labels on many of its products. It is, in our view, the best branding communication of the past few years.

levels (or strata) of the population along these different dimensions. Contemporary consumer societies have a much more fluid sense of class, and strata themselves are in flux more and have more permeable boundaries than we once believed. Also, it is argued that the emergence of the *New Class*, a class of technologically skilled and highly educated individuals with great access to information and information technology, has changed the way we define social class: "Knowledge of, and access to, information may begin to challenge property as a determinant of social class."[18]

Income alone does not define "social class" very accurately. For example, successful plumbers often have higher incomes than unsuccessful lawyers, but their occupation tends to be seen as less prestigious, and the prestige of one's occupation also enters into what we call social class. Education also has something to do with social class, but a person with a little college experience and a lot of inherited wealth probably would rank higher than an insurance agent with an MBA. Bill Gates left Harvard without a degree, and he has pretty high social standing, not to mention wealth. Thus, income, education, and occupation are three important variables for indicating social class, but they must be viewed together. Further complicating the picture, rock stars, professional athletes, and successful actors have high incomes but are generally thought to be somewhat outside the social class system. This is another reason the term "social class" has been falling away.

Members of the same social strata tend to live in similar ways, have similar views and philosophies, and, most critically, tend to consume in somewhat similar ways. Markers of social class would include what one wears, where one lives, and how one speaks. In a consumer society, consumption marks or indicates stratification in a myriad of ways. Stratification-related consumption preferences reflect value differences and ways of seeing the world. Writer John Seabrook notes that we now know social class mostly by "the services you use, where you live, and the control they have over other people's labor."[19] In other words, other than housing, social stratification is marked through consumption by a consumer's ability to afford all sorts of services, particularly those such as housekeepers and personal trainers.

Social class affects consumption through tastes. **Taste** refers to a generalized set or orientation to consumer preferences. We think of upper classes preferring tennis to bowling and eating brie more than Velveeta. Tastes include media habits and, thus, exposure to various advertising media vehicles—for example, *RV Life* versus *Wine Spectator*. Today fashion and taste cycle faster than they once did, and consumers may be more playful in their use of class markers than they once were. We refer to this as the Targetization of style in the United States. Target combined low prices with designer labels in a way that attracted shoppers from various strata. Some have seen this retail success as a democratization of style and taste.

A concept related to taste is *cultural capital*, the value that cultures place on certain consumption practices and objects. For example, a certain consumption practice (say, snowboarding) has a certain capital or value (like money) for some segment of the population. If you own a snowboard (a certain amount of cultural capital), and actually can use it (more cultural capital), and look good while using it (even more capital), then this activity is like cultural currency or cultural money in the bank. You can "spend" it. It gets you things you want. Depending on your cultural group, you might get cultural capital from ordering the right pinot noir, flying first class, or knowing about the funniest new video on YouTube. The value of the cultural capital will depend on which consumer practices are favored within the culture. Advertisers try to figure out which ones are valued more, and why, and how to make their product sought after because it has higher cultural capital and can be sold at a higher price. Does an iPhone have more cultural capital than a BlackBerry? To whom? To what cultural group? To what market segment? Maybe the coolest people don't have any of those things; they are free of their electronic leash. Having good "taste" helps you know which things have high cultural capital.

© archetype/Shutterstock.

Family

Consumer behavior also takes place within the context of families. Advertisers not only want to discern the needs of different kinds of families but also to discover how decisions are made within families. The first is possible; the latter is much more difficult. For a while, consumer researchers tried to determine who in the traditional nuclear family (that is, Mom, Dad, and the kids) made various purchasing decisions. This was largely an exercise in futility. Due to errors in reporting and conflicting perceptions between partners, it became clear that the family purchasing process is anything but clear. While some types of purchases are handled by one family member, many decisions actually are diffuse nondecisions, arrived at through what consumer researcher C. W. Park aptly calls a "muddling-through" process.[20] These "decisions" just get made, and no one really is sure who made them, or even when. For an advertiser to influence such a diffuse and vague process indeed is a challenge.

The consumer behavior of the family is a complex and often subtle type of social negotiation. One person handles this, another one takes care of that. Sometimes specific purchases fall along gender lines, but sometimes they don't. While children may not be the buyers in many instances, they can play important roles as initiators, influencers, and users in many categories, such as cereals, clothing, vacation destinations, fast-food restaurants, and technology (like computers). Still, some advertisers capitalize on the flexibility of this social system by suggesting in their ads who *should* take charge of a given consumption task, and then arming that person with the appearance of expertise so that whoever wants the job can take it and defend his or her purchases.

Families have a lasting influence on the consumer preferences of family members. One of the best predictors of the brands adults use is the ones their parents used. This is true for cars, toothpaste, household cleansers, and many more products. Say you go off to college. You eventually have to do laundry, so you go to the store, and you buy Tide. Why Tide? Well, you're not sure, but you saw it around your house when you lived with your parents, and things seemed to have worked out okay for them, so you buy it for yourself. The habit sticks, and you keep buying it. This is called an **intergenerational effect**.

intergenerational effect choice of products based on what was used in the consumer's childhood household

Marketers often focus on the major or gross differences in types of families because different families have different needs, buy different things, and are reached by different media. *Family* is a very open concept these days. The old-fashioned norm of two parents and a few children is not today's norm. There are a lot of single parents and quite a few second and even third marriages. Many households include members of the extended family (nuclear family plus grandparents, cousins, and others). Also, there are gay and lesbian households with and without children. Even in traditional family structures, roles often change when both parents (or a single parent) take jobs outside the home. For instance, a teenage son or daughter may be given the role of initiator and buyer, while the parent or parents merely serve as influences.

Beyond the basic configuration, advertisers often are interested in knowing details such as the age of the youngest child, the size of the family, and the family income. The age of the youngest child living at home is called a **life stage** variable; it tells an advertiser where the family is in terms of its needs and obligations (that is, toys, investment instruments for college savings, clothing, and vacations). When the youngest child leaves home, the consumption patterns of a family radically change.

Celebrity is a unique sociological concept, and it matters a great deal to advertisers. Twenty-first-century society is all about celebrity. Current thinking is that, in a celebrity-based culture, celebrities help contemporary consumers with identity. Identity in a consumer culture becomes a "fashion accessory" prop for a day—head

banger, corporate slave at work in a screwbed (a term for being assigned to a cubicle rather than the preferred office), and so forth. The idea is that contemporary consumers are very good at putting on and taking off, trying on, switching, and trading various identities, in the same way that they have clicked through the channels since they could reach the remote. E-generation children have become who they are, in some part, through celebrity-inspired identities—the way they do their hair, the way they think about their bodies, their relationships, their aspirations, and certainly their styles. Of course, style often is purchased and accessorized. This means that celebrities and images of them are used moment to moment to help in a personal parade of identity. For this reason, the understanding of the celebrity is much more complex and vital than merely thinking in terms of similar attitudes and behaviors. It affects who we are to some degree, minute to minute, ad to ad, mall to mall, purchase to purchase. Further, with YouTube, MySpace, and Facebook, the line between mass media and daily contemporary life blurs more all the time. Advertisers generally think this is a good thing because rapid identity shifts are another kind of marketing opportunity.

Race and Ethnicity

Race and ethnicity provide other ways to think about important social groups. Answering the question of how race figures into consumer behavior is very difficult. Our discomfort stems from having, on the one hand, the desire to say, "Race doesn't matter, we're all the same," and on the other hand not wanting (or not being able) to deny the significance of race in terms of reaching ethnic cultures and influencing a wide variety

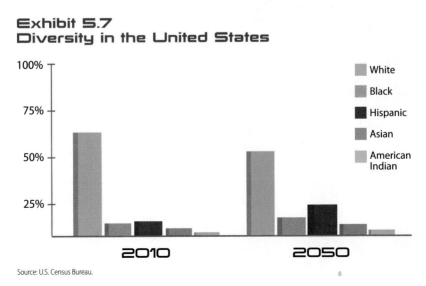

Exhibit 5.7
Diversity in the United States

White
Black
Hispanic
Asian
American Indian

2010   2050

Source: U.S. Census Bureau.

of behaviors, including consumer behavior. The truth is we are less and less sure what *race* is and what it means. Obviously, a person's pigmentation, in and of itself, has almost nothing to do with preferences for one type of product over another. But because race has mattered in culture, it does still matter in consumer behavior.

The United States, Europe, and much of the world is becoming an increasingly ethnically diverse culture, while at the same time becoming more homogeneous (important exceptions exist) in terms of consumer culture. Exhibit 5.7 compares current and projected racial diversity in the United States. By the middle of the 21st century, whites probably will be very close to only 50 percent of the U.S. population. This demographic reality is very important to advertisers and marketers. However, it wasn't until the mid- to late 1980s that most American corporations made a concerted effort to court African-American consumers, or even to recognize their existence.[21] Efforts to serve the Hispanic consumer have been intermittent and inconsistent.

There probably isn't an area in consumer behavior where research is more inadequate. This probably is because everyone is terrified to discuss it and because most of the findings we do have are suspect. What is attributed to race often is due to another factor that is itself associated with race. For example, consumer behavior textbooks commonly say something to the effect that African Americans and Hispanics are more brand loyal than their Anglo counterparts. Data on the frequency of brand switching is offered, and lo and behold, it does appear that white people switch brands more often. But why? Some ethnic minorities live in areas where there are fewer retail choices. When we statistically remove the effect of income disparities between white people and people of color, we see that the brand-switching effect often disappears. This suggests that brand loyalty is not a function of race but of disposable income and shopping options.

Still, race does inform one's social identity to varying degrees. One is not blind to one's own ethnicity. African Americans, Hispanics, and other ethnic groups have culturally related consumption preferences. Certain brands become associated with racial or ethnic groups. It is not enough, however, for advertisers to say one group is different from another group, or that people prefer one brand over another simply because they are members of a racial or ethnic category. If advertisers really want a good, long-term relationship with their customers, they must acquire,

through good consumer research, a deeper understanding of who their customers are and how this identity is affected by culture, felt ethnicity, and race. In short, advertisers must ask why groups of consumers are different or prefer different brands, and they must not settle for an easy answer.

Geopolitics

In spite of increasing globalization and general homogeneity at the level of accepting the basic ethos and trappings of consumer culture, there are some important countercurrents: brands for "us." There are many places in the world where religious-ethnic-political strife is abundant, and this gets played out in consumption domains. An example is Mecca Cola, created to appeal to consumers in parts of the world where the West is not admired. Current issues also have provided the impetus for "green" brands and brands associated with fair labor practices.

Quite a few advertisers are realizing the advantages of marketing to gay and lesbian communities. Here, American Express recognizes the special financial challenges faced by lesbian couples.

Gender

Gender is the social expression of sexual biology, sexual choice, or both. Obviously, gender matters in consumption. But are men and women really that different in any meaningful way in their consumption behavior, beyond the obvious? Again, to the extent that gender informs a "culture of gender," the answer is yes. As long as men and women are the products of differential socialization, then they will continue to be different in some significant ways. There is, however, no definitive list of gender differences in consumption because the expression of gender, just like anything else social, depends on the situation and the social circumstances. In the 1920s, advertisers openly referred to women as less logical, more emotional, and the cultural stewards of beauty.[22] (Some say that the same soft, irrational, emotional feminine persona still is invoked in advertising.) Advertising helps construct a social reality, with gender a predominant feature. Not only is it a matter of conscience and social responsibility to be aware of this, but it is good business as well. Advertisers must keep in mind, though, that it's hard to keep the business of people you patronize, insult, or ignore.

Obviously, gender's impact on consumer behavior is not limited to heterosexual men and women. Gay men and lesbians are large and significant markets. Of late, these markets have been targeted by corporate titans such as IBM and United Airlines.[23] Again, these are markets that desire to be acknowledged and served, but not stereotyped and patronized.

Just as marketers discovered working women in the late 1970s, African-American and Hispanic consumers in the 1980s, and then somewhat later Asian Americans, they recently have discovered gays and lesbians. Of course, these people weren't missing. They were there all along. These "discoveries" of forgotten and marginalized social groups create some interesting problems for advertisers. Members of these groups, quite reasonably, want to be served just like any other consumers. Consider what Wally Snyder of the American Advertising Federation said:

Advertising that addresses the realities of America's multicultural population must be created by qualified professionals who understand the nuances of the disparate cultures.

Otherwise, agencies and marketers run the risk of losing or, worse, alienating millions of consumers eager to buy their products or services. Building a business that "looks like" the nation's increasingly multicultural population is no longer simply a moral choice, it is a business imperative.[24]

Attention and representation without stereotyping from a medium and a genre that is known for stereotyping might be a lot to expect, but it's not that much.

Community

Consumers also are members of communities. **Community** is a powerful and traditional sociological concept with a meaning that extends well beyond the idea of a specific geographic place. Communities can be imagined or even virtual. Community members believe that they belong to a group of people who are similar to them in some important way and different from those not in the community. Members of communities often share rituals and traditions, and they feel some sort of responsibility to one another and the community.

Advertisers are becoming increasingly aware of the power of community. Products have social meanings, and community is the quintessential social domain, so consumption is inseparable from the notion of where we live (actually or virtually), and with whom we feel a kinship or a sense of belonging. Communities often exert a great deal of power. A community may be your neighborhood, or it may be people like you with whom you feel a kinship, such as members of social clubs, other consumers who collect the same things you do, or people who have, use, or admire the same brands you do.

Brand communities are groups of consumers who feel a commonality and a shared purpose attached to

a consumer good or service.[25] When owners of vintage Corvettes experience a sense of connectedness by virtue of their common ownership or usage, a brand community exists. When two perfect strangers stand in a parking lot and act like old friends simply because they both own Corvettes, a type of community is revealed.

Most of these communities exist online. Like many other companies, the online T-shirt business Threadless builds a community around its brand. But at Threadless, the community builds the brand, too. Threadless designs come not from big-name stylists but from customers. Anybody who wants to can submit a design; about 125 new submissions come in daily. Entries are posted online, where site visitors rate them on a zero-to-five scale. Each week, the company picks six of the most popular designs to print on T-shirts. Threadless also relies on its online community to be its primary marketing tool. Site visitors are encouraged to upload photos, leave comments, and refer friends. "The bigger and more active the community, the more sales go up," said creative director Jeffrey Kalmikoff. "It's hard to argue with that formula."[26]

The promise of community—not to be alone, to share appreciation and admiration of something or someone, no matter how odd or inappropriate others feel it to be—is fulfilled in online communities. The language looks much like that of people pleased that they discovered others with the same sexual orientation, the same health problems, or the same religion. It is a rewarding and embracing social collective centered on a brand. This should not surprise us too much, given how central consumption and branding have become in contemporary society. Brands matter socially, so brands matter.

LO 5 Advertising, Social Rift, and "Revolution"

Thomas Frank, Doug Holt, Heath and Potter, and others have noted that consumers sometimes use their consumption choices to stake out a position in a "revolution" of sorts. Frank traces this to the 1960s cultural revolution (discussed in Chapter 3) and sees it as an opportunity, particularly for youth markets, to provide the costumes and consumable accessories for these "revolutions": certain "looks," such as dressing all in black, that say "I'm part of this political-social group."

More generally, marketers should keep in mind that any time there is a great social movement or a time of rapid change, opportunities galore are opened up to the marketer. When the earth moves under our feet, we feel off balance and in need of reassurance. At those times, branded products often promise that reassurance.

LO 6 How Ads Transmit Meaning

Things always stand for other values; and the advertiser is merely making sure the translation is vivid and to the product's advantage.
—Michael Schudson

Advertising can be thought of as a text. It is "read" and interpreted by consumers. You can think of it as being like other texts, books, movies, posters, paintings, and so on. To "get" ads, you have to know something of the cultural code, or they would make no sense. To understand a movie fully, you have to know something about the culture that created it. When you see a foreign film (even in your native tongue), you might not get all the jokes and references because you don't possess the cultural knowledge necessary to "read" the text effectively. Like these other forms, advertisements are sociocultural texts. Ads try to turn already meaningful things into things with very special meaning—carefully projected and crafted meaning concentrated through the mass media with the purpose of selling.

Of course, consumers are free to accept, reject, or adjust that meaning to suit their taste. Marketers say the product they are selling is cool. The consumer might say, "No, it isn't," or "Yeah, it is," or "Well, yeah, but not in the way they think," or "Maybe for you, but not for me." While marketers try very hard to project just the right meaning, it is ultimately consumers who determine the meaning of ads and brands. Likewise, consumers determine what is or is not cool, what has cultural value (capital) to them, and how much.

In this regard, Martin Davidson aptly expressed the advertiser's challenge:

Start work in an ad agency and the first thing they teach you is the difference between a product and a brand. That is because it is advertising's job to turn one into another.[27]

Exhibit 5.8
The Movement of Meaning

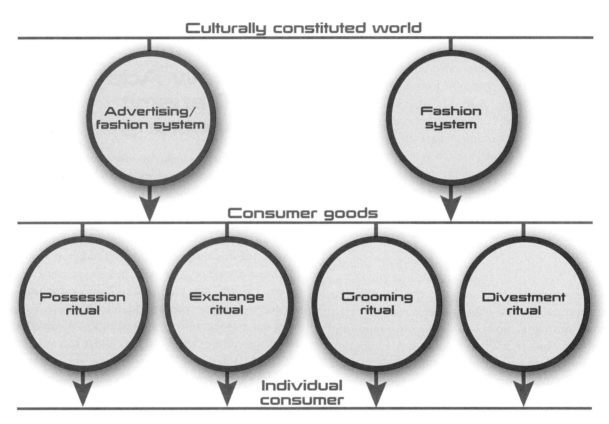

Yes, ads turn products into brands, and sometimes successful ones. They do this, in large part, by trying to wrap material objects or marketed services with a certain meaning—a meaning that comes from culture.

The key is the link between culture and advertising. Anthropologist Grant McCracken has offered the model in Exhibit 5.8 to explain how advertising (along with other cultural agents) functions in the transmission of meaning. To understand advertising as a mechanism of cultural meaning transfer is to understand a great deal about advertising. In fact, one legitimately could say that advertisers really are in the meaning transfer business. You take meaning that exists in the culture and massage it, shape it, and try to transfer it onto your brand.

Think about McCracken's model as you examine the ad for Johnston & Murphy. The product—in this case, shoes—exists "out there" in the culturally constituted world (the real social world), but it needs adver-

tising to link it to certain social scenes, certain slices of life. The advertiser places the advertised product and the slice of social life in an ad to get the two to rub off on each other, to intermingle, to become part of the same social scene. In other words, the product is given social meaning by being placed within an ad that represents an idealized context. This slice of life, of course, is the type of social setting in which potential customers might find, or desire to find, themselves. According to McCracken's model, meaning has moved from the world to the product (shoes) by virtue of its sharing space within the frame of the advertisement. When advertisers put things within the frame of an ad, they want the reader of the ad to put them together seamlessly, to take them together as part of each other. When a consumer purchases or otherwise incorporates that good or service into his or her own life, the meaning is transferred to the individual consumer. Meaning is thus moved from the world to the product (via advertising) to the individual. When the individual uses the product, that person conveys to others the meaning he or she and the advertisement have given it now. Their use incorporates various rituals that facilitate the movement of meaning from good to consumer. The rituals aren't central to this discussion, but they would be the kinds of activities we already discussed in the section on rituals, such as possession rituals that make a product feel like one's own.

Ads also become part of consumers' everyday landscape, language, and everyday reality. Characters, lines, and references all become part of conversations, thoughts, and—coming full circle—the culture. Children, coworkers, family members, and talk-show hosts all pick up phrases, ideas, slogans, and agendas from ads, and then they replay them, adapt them, and recirculate them as they do with similar elements from movies, books, and other texts. Ads, in many ways, don't exist just within the sociocultural context; they *are* the sociocultural context of our time. If you want to do well in the real world of brand promotion, it's a very good idea to understand that getting the contemporary culture and knowing how to move it into ads is worth its weight in gold.

A Johnston & Murphy shoe is not just any shoe. One goal of this advertisement is to create a special meaning for this brand.

STUDY TOOLS CHAPTER 5

Located at back of the textbook

- Rip out Chapter in Review Card.

Located at www.cengagebrain.com

- Review Key Terms Flashcards (Print or Online).
- Complete the Practice Quiz to prepare for tests.
- Play "Beat the Clock" and "Quizbowl" to master concepts.
- Complete "Crossword Puzzle" to review key terms.
- Watch videos on Old Spice and Chevrolet for real company examples.
- Additional examples can be found online for use.net groups, GM's promotion of Cadillac, and peripheral cues used in advertising campaigns.

CHAPTER **6** | # The Regulatory and Ethical Environment of Promotions

Some Things Are Still A Mystery.

Your Online Visitors Shouldn't Be One Of Them.

Your strategy hinges upon gaining an in-depth understanding of your visitors. Where do they come from? What do they do while they're on your site? Capturing, analyzing and reporting on visitor behavior is what Buystream is all about. We provide powerful analytics and reporting software with optional research and consulting services. That means you get clear, insightful analysis that is customized to your business strategy – intelligence that cuts through the data clutter to reveal visitor behavior and important trends.

For more information about our software and services that deliver actionable intelligence that is customized to your needs, visit **www.buystream.com** or call **1.800.261.1726.**

Buystream is a Safeguard Scientifics partner company.

buystream

Measure What Matters.

© Buystream, Inc.

> **Many firms provide information to advertisers to effectively deliver brand promotion messages to target audiences.**

> **The questions of ethics and privacy come into play when companies sell consumers' names and addresses to others for database marketing.**

Learning Outcomes

After studying this chapter, you should be able to:

LO 1 Discuss the impact of promotion on society's well-being.

LO 2 Summarize ethical considerations related to brand promotion campaigns.

LO 3 Describe aspects of advertising regulated by the U.S. government.

LO 4 Summarize the regulatory role of the Federal Trade Commission.

LO 5 Explain the meaning and importance of self-regulation by marketers.

LO 6 Discuss the regulation of direct marketing, sales promotion, and public relations.

"Never write an advertisement which you wouldn't want your own family to read."

—David Ogilvy

I Didn't Sign Up for This!

AFTER YOU FINISH THIS CHAPTER GO TO **PAGE 137** FOR **STUDY TOOLS**

When Anne Marie saw the Eddie Bauer edition of a Ford Explorer as a sweepstakes giveaway, she couldn't resist. It was her dream car, so she entered the sweepstakes. She wasn't surprised not to win, but she hadn't expected that submitting an entry would unleash a nightmare. "Every Jeep dealer in the galaxy was calling me after that," she says. "There was a span of about two weeks that a different car dealer called or mailed something [every day] about me coming in to test drive a car. I was furious."[1]

What happened to Anne Marie happens to millions of Americans every day. Marketers call it "database marketing." They use contests, sweepstakes, supermarket discount cards, and product warranty cards to gather information about customers and create a database to be used for integrated marketing communication (IMC) strategies. Big data "warehouse" companies such as Acxiom and R. L. Polk specialize in collecting massive amounts of consumer information. They sell the data—including names, addresses, phone numbers, and email addresses—to companies that use direct marketing, such as catalog publishers, Internet retailers, charities, credit card issuers, book clubs, and music clubs.

What marketers call database marketing, some consumer advocates call an invasion of privacy. And there is ample and growing evidence that consumers are getting aggravated with database-marketing efforts. Several years ago, a survey by Planetfeedback.com showed that 80 percent of respondents were "very annoyed" by pop-up ads and spam email; only about 10 to 15 percent reported being "very annoyed" by print or TV ads.[2]

How do marketers respond? Some database management companies avoid infringing on customer privacy; they collect multiple sources of data. For example,

What do you think?

On the whole, brand promotion is good for our society.

1	2	3	4	5	6	7
STRONGLY DISAGREE					STRONGLY AGREE	

Find out what others think at CourseMate for PROMO. 113

Omeda (http://www.omeda.com) combines the information it gathers from multiple sources into one database for its clients to use for their marketing needs. Other marketers defend database marketing, saying good marketing research (including database development) leads to greater efficiency and more value for customers. According to this argument, effective direct marketers know you better, so they can serve you better.[3]

Consumer advocates insist that even when offers are targeted, the avalanche of promotions is a nuisance. They prefer "permission marketing," in which marketers can direct advertising and promotions *only* to people who have expressly indicated that they "opt in" to receiving offers through the mail or email.[4]

The story of Anne Marie highlights that the social, ethical, and regulatory aspects of marketing are dynamic and controversial. What is socially responsible or irresponsible, ethically debatable, politically correct, or legal? The answers are changing constantly. As a society changes, so, too, do its perspectives. And marketing, like anything else with social roots and implications, will be affected by these changes.

Many criticisms of promotional campaigns are uninformed, naïve, and simplistic; they fail to consider the complex social and legal environment in which contemporary brand promotion operates. Especially as marketers, we need to distinguish valid critiques of overzealous promotion efforts from irrational criticism based only on intuition and emotion.

GET YOUR GAME FACE ON!

GET THE PAINT. GET PUMPED. GET A DESIGNATED DRIVER. THAT'S PREPARATION!!

85% OF COLLEGE STUDENTS WHO DRINK USE A DESIGNATED DRIVER.*

Advertising can be used to inform the public about important social issues. Here, Anheuser-Busch tells possible beer drinkers that they should pick a designated driver *before* they start celebrating.

LO 1 Social Impact of Brand Promotion

For those who feel that advertising is intrusive, manipulative, and wasteful, the impact of brand promotion on society usually fuels heated debate. From a balanced perspective, however, we can consider the effect of brand promotion on consumers' knowledge, standard of living, and feelings of happiness and well-being, and its potential effects on the mass media. Our approach is to offer the pros and cons on several issues that often arise in discussions of marketing's impact on society (see Exhibit 6.1). These are matters of opinion, with no clear right and wrong answers. As you draw your own conclusions, be analytical and thoughtful. Until you understand and contemplate these issues, you really haven't studied promotion at all.

Education or Intrusion?

Does brand promotion give consumers valuable information, or does it only confuse or entice them? Here's what experts on both sides have to say.

Promotion Informs

Supporters of brand promotion argue that it educates consumers, equipping them with information needed to make informed purchasing decisions. By regularly

Exhibit 6.1
Pros and Cons of Brand Promotion

Where would you rate brand promotion on each scale?

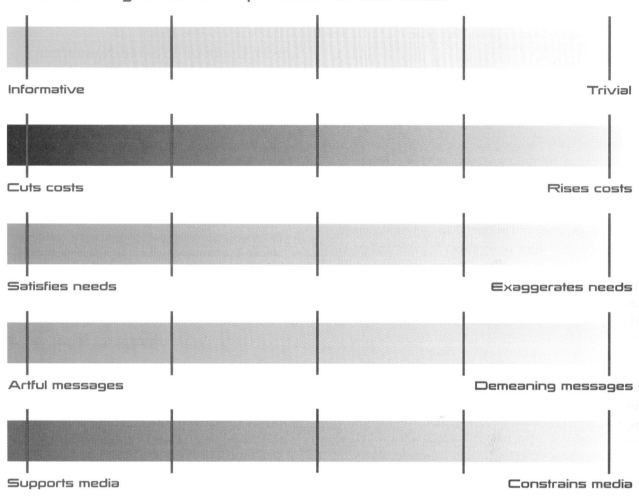

Informative				Trivial
Cuts costs				Rises costs
Satisfies needs				Exaggerates needs
Artful messages				Demeaning messages
Supports media				Constrains media

assessing the information in promotional messages, consumers become more educated about the features, benefits, functions, and value of products. Further, consumers can become more aware of their own tendencies to be persuaded by and rely on certain types of product information. Historically, the view has been that advertising is "clearly an immensely powerful instrument for the elimination of ignorance."[5] That might be a *little* bit overstated, but there's logic to the idea that better-educated consumers enhance their lifestyles and economic power through astute decision making.

A related argument is that brand promotion reduces the amount of time spent in searching for desired products and services. The large amount of information readily available through advertisements, websites, and other marketing communication helps consumers learn about the potential value of brands; they don't have to travel from store to store, trying to evaluate each one.

Advertising also informs the public about important social issues. Miller Brewing devotes millions of dollars a year to promoting responsible drinking through advertisements. Another brewer, Anheuser-Busch, has developed an integrated marketing campaign designed to combat drunken driving, underage drinking, and binge drinking. Anheuser-Busch has spent more than $500 million on efforts that include the website http://www.beeresponsible.com, which details company policies and programs and also offers statistics about the issue plus links to resources and information. Advertising messages have promoted the use of designated drivers and cab rides home, as well as encouraged parents to discuss responsible drinking with their children. The firm's "Responsibility Matters" campaign supports community-based programs that promote responsible behavior.[6]

Promotion Is Superficial and Intrusive

Critics argue that brand promotion does not provide good product information at all but only superficial ideas. Some would go so far as to say that advertising messages are biased, limited, and inherently deceptive. This argument is based on an attitude that promotional efforts should provide information related strictly to functional features and performance results—qualities that can be measured and tested brand by brand.

Marketers respond that, in many instances, consumers are interested in more than a physical, tangible material good with performance features and purely functional value. Emotional factors also play an important role in consumer's choices. Thus, critics often dismiss as unimportant or ignore the totality of brand benefits that consumers seek, including emotional, hedonic (pleasure-seeking), or aesthetic benefits. Marketers say they are trying to communicate relevant information for buyers who focus on these qualities.

Critics further contend that brand promotion is not merely unhelpful but so pervasive and intrusive that it is downright annoying. Similarly, consumers are frustrated with brands working their way into entertainment programming. In a different survey, 72 percent of consumers said product placement and integration with entertainment content were allowing advertising to become too pervasive.[7] Are marketers paying attention? Even as consumers say brand promotion is intruding on their lives, big advertisers like American Express are pushing to become more "relevant" to consumers than a mere 30-second advertising spot and to make their brands part of consumer lifestyles. The chief marketing officer at American Express said in a keynote speech to a large advertising audience, "We need to adapt to the new landscape by thinking not in day-parts [referring to television advertising schedules] but to mindparts."[8]

Marketers should pay attention to consumers' aggravation with the intrusiveness of promotional messages because clutter and intrusiveness reduce the effectiveness of those messages. According to one expert, "The ability of the average consumer to even remember advertising 24 hours later is at the lowest level in the history of our business."[9] But there is little evidence that marketers will reduce clutter. Another industry expert suggests, "New media have more potential to deliver even more saturation, clutter, and intrusiveness than traditional media, in which case the new media will only worsen marketing resistance."[10]

Lower Costs or Wasted Resources?

Another hotly debated issue is whether brand promotion raises or lowers costs. Opinions on this issue go right to the heart of whether promotional efforts are a good use or a waste of energy and resources.

Lower Product Costs

According to supporters of brand promotion, it helps lower the cost of products in four ways:

1. By stimulating demand, promotion results in economies of scale (as a company produces larger quantities, the cost of each unit falls). As a result, products cost less than if there was less promotion and hence less demand. Presumably, companies with lower production and administrative costs per unit will pass on the savings to consumers.

2. Promotion increases the probability that new products will succeed, so consumers have a greater variety of choices. They can more easily switch to a new offering, so marketers have an incentive to keep costs and prices low.

3. As brand promotion fuels the pressures of competition and the desire to have fresh, marketable brands, firms are motivated to produce improved products and brands and to introduce lower-priced brands.

4. The speed and reach of the marketing process aids in the diffusion of innovations. This means that new discoveries can be communicated to a large percentage of the marketplace very quickly. Innovations succeed when the promotional mix communicates their benefits.

All four of these factors can contribute positively to a society's standard of living and quality of life. Brand promotion may be instrumental in bringing about these effects because it serves an important role in demand stimulation and keeping customers informed.

Wasted Resources and Uneven Benefits

One of the traditional criticisms of marketing, especially advertising, is that it represents an inefficient, wasteful process that channels monetary and human resources in a society to the "shuffling of existing total demand," rather than to the expansion of total demand.[11] In this view, a society is no better off with

BRAND PROMOTION HELPS CREATE THE ECONOMIC CONDITIONS IN WHICH CONSUMERS HAVE AN ABUNDANCE OF CHOICES. DO YOU FIND SUCH CHOICES EXCITING OR OVERWHELMING?

advertising because ads do not stimulate demand—they only shift demand from one brand to another. Advertising thus brings about economic stagnation and a *lower* standard of living, not a higher standard of living.

Similarly, critics argue that brand differences are trivial, so the proliferation of brands does not offer a greater variety of choice but rather a meaningless waste of resources, with confusion and frustration for the consumer.

Some critics go so far as to argue that advertising is a tool of capitalism that only helps widen the gap between rich and poor, creating strife between social classes.

Greater Well-Being or More Dissatisfaction?

Critics and supporters of brand promotion differ significantly in their views about how it affects consumers' happiness and general well-being. This is a complex issue.

Need Creation

A common cry among critics is that brand promotion creates needs and makes people buy things they don't really need or even want. The argument is that consumers are relatively easy to seduce into wanting the next shiny bauble offered by marketers. Critics would say, for example, that any issue of *Seventeen* magazine seems to be intent on teaching young women to covet slim bodies and a glamorous complexion. Cosmetics giants like Estée Lauder and Revlon typically spend from 15 to 30 cents of every dollar of sales to promote their brands as the ultimate solution for those in search of the ideal complexion.

Need Satisfaction

Supporters of brand promotion take a broad understanding of human needs as their starting point. Abraham Maslow, a pioneer in the study of human motivation, conceived that human behavior is motivated by a hierarchy of need states:[12]

- *Physiological needs:* Biological needs that require the satisfaction of hunger, thirst, and basic bodily functions.

- *Safety needs:* The need to provide shelter and protection for the body and to maintain a comfortable existence.

- *Love and belonging needs:* The need for affiliation and affection. A person will strive for both the giving and receiving of love.

- *Esteem needs:* The need for recognition, status, and prestige. In addition to the respect of others, there is a need and desire for self-respect.

- *Self-actualization needs:* Maximum fulfillment of individual capabilities. This highest of the need states is achieved by only a small percentage of people, according to Maslow.

Recognizing that Maslow was describing *basic* human needs and motivations, not consumer needs and motivations, this model supports the idea that in the context of an affluent society, individuals will turn to goods and services to satisfy needs.

Many products directly address the requirements of one or more of Maslow's need states. Food and healthcare products, for example, relate to physiological needs. Home security systems and smoke detectors help address safety needs. Many personal care products promote feelings of self-esteem, confidence, glamour, and romance. In the pursuit of esteem, many consumers buy products they perceive to have status and prestige: expensive jewelry and homes are examples. Although it may be difficult to buy self-actualization, educational pursuits and high-intensity leisure activities (e.g., extreme sports) certainly can foster feelings of pride and accomplishment that contribute to self-actualization. But while marketing messages may be directed at many different forms of need fulfillment, that does not make it powerful enough to *create* basic human needs.

Promotion of Materialism

Critics also claim that brand promotion distorts individuals' wants and aspirations. The long-standing argument is that, in societies characterized by heavy advertising, people seek conformity and engage in status-seeking behavior, both of which are considered materialistic and superficial, because material goods are placed ahead of spiritual and intellectual pursuits.[13] Advertising, which portrays brands as symbols of status, success, and happiness, thus contributes to a society's materialism and superficiality. It creates wants and aspirations that are artificial and self-centered. As a result, societies overemphasize the production of private goods, to the detriment of public goods, such as highways, parks, schools, and infrastructure.[14]

Reflection of Society's Priorities

Although marketing messages undeniably promote the good life, defenders of brand promotion argue that it did not create the American emphasis on materialism. For example, in the United States, major holidays such as Christmas (gifts), Thanksgiving (food), and Easter (candy and clothing) have become festivals of consumption. This is the American way. Historian and social observer Stephen Fox concludes his treatise on the history of American advertising as follows:

> One may build a compelling case that American culture is—beyond redemption—money-mad, hedonistic, superficial, rushing heedlessly down a railroad track called Progress. Tocqueville and other observers of the young republic described America in these terms in the early 1800s, decades before the development of national advertising. To blame advertising now for these most basic tendencies in American history is to miss the point. . . . The people who have created modern advertising are not hidden persuaders pushing our buttons in the service of some malevolent purpose. They are just producing an especially visible manifestation, good and bad, of the American way of life.[15]

While we clearly live in the age of consumption, goods and possessions have been used by all cultures throughout history to mark special events, to play significant roles in rituals, and to serve as vessels of special meaning long before there was modern marketing. Still, it is worth asking whether marketing has taken it too far.

Demeaning or Artistic?

Marketers are always on the lookout for creative and novel ways to grab and hold the attention of their audience. Additionally, as we saw in Chapter 4, a marketer has a very specific profile of the target customer in mind when a promotional message is being created. Critics and defenders of marketing practices have reacted to the consequences of grabbing attention and appealing to social groups.

Perpetuating Stereotypes

Advertisements often portray people who look like members of their target audience. Marketers hope that, as a result, people who see the ad will be more prone to relate to it and attend to its message. Critics charge that advertisers trying to portray a target audience end up

© Simon Krzic/Shutterstock.

perpetuating stereotypes, especially in the portrayal of women, the elderly, and ethnic minorities. For example, many ads show women as homemakers or objects of desire, even though women really hold a wide variety of roles in society. The elderly often are shown as helpless or ill, even though many active seniors enjoy a rich lifestyle. Critics contend that advertisers' propensity to feature African-American or Latino athletes in ads is simply a more contemporary form of stereotyping.

Showing Sensitivity

Blatant stereotyping is becoming part of the past. Although advertisements from prior generations show a vivid stereotyping problem, today's images offer more variety. For example, Dove launched its "Campaign for Real Beauty" in September 2004 with advertisements featuring women whose appearances do not conform to the stereotypical and relatively narrow norms of beauty. The ads invited viewers to join in a discussion of beauty issues at http://www.campaignforrealbeauty.com.

Marketers are realizing that a diverse world requires diversity in the social reality that ads represent and help construct. However, many remain dissatisfied with the pace of change. Ads for women's beauty products that offer something other than the body of a supermodel as a valid point of reference are still the exception, not the rule.

Offending Sensibilities

Another criticism of brand promotion messages is that many of them are in poor taste, even offensive. Some would say the trend in American advertising is to be rude, crude, and sometimes lewd, as advertisers struggle to grab attention. Of course, taste is an inherently subjective evaluation. What offends one person is merely satiric to another. What should we call an ad prepared for the Australian market that shows the owner of an older Honda Accord admiring a newer model? The owner's admiration of the new car spurs the old version to lock its doors, rev its motor, and drive off a cliff—with the owner still inside. Critics decry the ad as trivializing suicide—an acute problem among young people, who also are the target market for this ad.[16]

But not all advertising deemed offensive has to be as extreme as this example. Many times, advertisers get caught in a firestorm of controversy because relatively small segments of the population are offended. Do you think the makers of Black Flag bug spray could have expected the reaction to their commercial? A war veterans' group objected to the playing of "Taps" over dead bugs.[17]

Maybe hypersensitivity to consumer reaction is unnecessary. GoDaddy.com is making a nice living running risqué ads on the Super Bowl every year. In 2006, broadcaster ABC rejected the Web firm's first

Do these advertisers portray women as objects to look at or as human beings? Would you call their messages affirming or offensive? Effective or ineffective?

Richard Avedon for Gianni Versace.

Extract used with kind permission of The Body Shop Int'l PLC UK.

13 ad submissions as "tasteless." The still-racy ad that finally ran during that year's Super Bowl created a 15-fold spike in traffic to the firm's website.[18]

In the end, we have to consider whether advertising is truly offensive or whether society is merely pushing the limits of what is appropriate for freedom of speech and expression. Standards for what is acceptable and what is offensive change over time in a culture.

Promising Liberation

Where some see stereotyping and poor taste, others see fulfillment and liberation. In fact, some argue that the consumption glorified by promotional campaigns is actually good for society. Most people sincerely appreciate modern conveniences that liberate us from the fouler facets of everyday life, such as body odor and close contact with dirty diapers. Some observers remind us that, when the Berlin Wall came down, those in East Germany did not immediately run to libraries and churches—they ran to department stores and shops.

Before the modern consumer age, the consumption of many goods was restricted by social class. Modern marketing has helped bring us a "democratization" of goods. In that sense, brand promotion and consumption offer a kind of liberation that should be appreciated and encouraged.

Deceiving with Subliminal Messages

Ever since a crackpot allegedly inserted the phrases "Eat Popcorn" and "Drink Coca-Cola" in a movie back in the 1950s, the world has been terrified that unscrupulous marketers will use subliminal messaging techniques to sell products. Much controversy—and almost a complete lack of understanding—persists about the issue of subliminal (below the threshold of consciousness) communication.[19] Despite rumors you may have heard, no one ever sold anything by putting images of breasts in ice cubes or the word *sex* in the background of an ad. Furthermore, no one at an advertising agency, except the very bored or the very eager to retire, has time to sit around dreaming up such things. Although it makes a great story, hiding pictures in other pictures doesn't get anyone to buy anything.

Recently, the issue has resurfaced as a research topic among neural scientists, but what they seem to be "rediscovering" is that you only can communicate commercial messages to people below the conscious threshold of awareness. People, indeed, can process information transmitted to them subliminally. However, these effects are very short lived and found only in laboratories. And the next effect never has been discovered: You cannot persuade people to act on the information they may have received this way. In other words, subliminal advertising doesn't work. The Svengali-type hocus-pocus that has become advertising mythology simply does not exist.[20] If the rumors are true that some advertisers actually are trying to use subliminal messages in their ads, the best research on the topic would conclude that they're wasting their money.[21]

Bringing Art to the Masses

Some argue that one of the best aspects of advertising is its artistic nature. The pop art movement of the late 1950s and 1960s, particularly in London and New York, was characterized by a fascination with commercial culture. Some of this art critiqued consumer culture and simultaneously celebrated it. Above all, Andy Warhol, himself a commercial illustrator, demonstrated that art was for the people and that the most accessible art was advertising. Art was not restricted to museum walls; it was on Campbell's soup cans, Life Savers candy rolls, and Brillo pads. Advertising is anti-elitist, pro-democratic art. As Warhol said about America, democracy, and Coke,

> *What's great about this country is that America started the tradition where the richest consumers buy essentially the same things as the poorest. . . . A Coke is a Coke and no amount of money can get you a better Coke than the one the bum on the corner is drinking. All the Cokes are the same and all the Cokes are good.*[22]

ADVERTISING GIVES PEOPLE **INVALUABLE EXPOSURE** TO SOCIAL AND POLITICAL ISSUES.

Enabling or Controlling Mass Media?

One final issue that advertisers and their critics debate is the matter of advertising's influence on the mass media. Here again, we find a wide range of viewpoints.

Support for Mass Media

Supporters of brand promotion describe advertising as the best thing that can happen to an informed democracy. Advertising expenditures support magazines, newspapers, and television and radio stations. In 2006, mass-media ad expenditures (counting mainly print and broadcast media) in the United States exceeded $300 billion.[23] If you include online advertising, the number approaches $400 billion. With this support of the media, citizens have access to a variety of information and entertainment sources at low cost. Without advertising support, network television and radio broadcasts would not be free, and newspapers and magazines likely would cost two to four times more.

Furthermore, advertising gives people invaluable exposure to social and political issues. When noncommercial organizations (like social service organizations) advertise, members of society receive information on important issues. For example, the U.S. government, working in conjunction with the Partnership for a Drug-Free America, launched a multimedia campaign to remind the American public of the ruinous power of drugs such as heroin.[24] Over five years, the campaign has spent nearly $1 billion and prepared almost 400 ads, including powerful messages about the ultimate consequence of drug abuse.

Influence over Programming

Critics argue that marketers who place ads in media have an unhealthy effect on the content of information in the media. The CEO of a firm headed for prosecution was accused of hiring a public relations firm to turn out a series of newspaper articles sympathetic to the CEO's firm.[25] Similarly, there have been several instances of "stealth sponsorship" of newspaper editorials: journalists were being paid by corporations that received favorable treatment in the editorials.[26]

Another type of influence comes indirectly when marketers purchase air time only on programs that draw large audiences. Critics argue that these mass market programs lower the quality of television because cultural and educational programs, which draw smaller and more selective markets, are dropped in favor of mass-market programs. Watch a few episodes of *Survivor* or *Lost*, and it's hard to argue against the proposition that shallow content indeed is winning out over culture and education.

Similarly, television programmers have difficulty attracting advertisers to shows that may be valuable yet are controversial. Programs about abortion, sexual abuse, or AIDS may have trouble drawing advertisers, who fear the consequences of any association with controversial issues, given the predictable public reaction.

> **ethics** moral standards and principles against which behavior is judged
>
> **deception** making false or misleading statements in a promotional message
>
> **puffery** use of superlatives like "number one" and "best in the world" in promotional messages

LO 2 Ethical Issues in Promotion

Where the social impact of brand promotion may be negative, ethical questions arise. **Ethics** are moral standards and principles against which behavior is judged. A broad definition of ethical behavior includes honesty, integrity, fairness, and sensitivity to others. In particular situations, however, determining what is ethical or unethical often comes down to personal judgment.

Telling the Truth

Truth in advertising is a legal issue with ethical dimensions. The most fundamental ethical issue has to do with **deception**—making false or misleading statements in a promotional message. The difficulty involves determining just what is deceptive. A manufacturer that claims a laundry product can remove grass stains is exposed to legal sanctions if the product cannot perform the task. In contrast, a manufacturer that claims to have "The Best Laundry Detergent in the World" is perfectly within its rights to employ superlatives. Just what constitutes "The Best" is a subjective determination; it cannot be proved or disproved. The use of superlatives such as "Number One" or "Best in the World" is called **puffery** and is considered legal. The courts have long held that consumers recognize and interpret superlatives as the exaggerated language of advertising.

Various promotional tools often are challenged as being deceptive. Consumers criticize the "small print" that spells out the details of contests or sweepstakes. Similarly, they get angry when the appeal of a "free" gift for listening to a pitch on a resort time-share leads them to a persistent hard sell. A consumer watchdog group is challenging brand placements in television shows as another kind of deception. The group Commercial Alert argues that television networks are deceiving consumers by not disclosing that they are taking money for highlighting brands within their programming.[27]

Another area of debate regarding truth in advertising relates to emotional appeals. It is likely impossible to legislate against emotional appeals such as those made about the beauty- or prestige-enhancing qualities of a brand because these claims are unquantifiable. Because these types of appeals are legal, the ethics of such appeals fall into a gray area. Beauty and prestige, it is argued, are in the eye of the beholder, and such appeals are neither illegal nor unethical. Your challenge is to develop ethical standards and values against which you will judge yourself and the actions of any organization for which you may work.

Targeting Children

The desire to restrict promotional messages aimed at children is based on a wide range of concerns, particularly because children between 2 and 11 years old see about 25,600 advertisements in a year. One concern is that brand promotion teaches superficiality and values founded in material goods and consumption, as we discussed earlier in the broader social context. Another is that children are inexperienced consumers and easy prey for marketers' sophisticated persuasions, so promotion influences children's demands for everything from toys to snack foods. These demands, in turn, create an environment of child-parent conflict. Parents have to say no over and over again to children whose desires are piqued by effective brand promotion. Child psychologists contend that advertising advocates violence, is responsible for child obesity, creates a breakdown in early learning skills, and results in a destruction of parental authority.[28]

A related contention is that many television shows aimed at children constitute program-length commercials. These programs feature commercial products, especially products aimed at children. A movement against this programming began in 1990, when critics counted 70 programs based on commercial products such as He-Man, the Smurfs, and the Muppets.[29] Special-interest groups have made several attempts to regulate this type of programming aimed at children, but, to date, the Federal Communications Commission permits it.

One of the earliest restrictions on advertising to children came in response to efforts of the special-interest group Action for Children's Television. Before the group disbanded in 1992, it helped get the Children's Television Act passed in 1990. This law restricts advertising on children's programming to 10.5 minutes per hour on weekends and 12 minutes per hour on weekdays.[30] More recently, in an attempt to head off government regulation, big food and beverage marketers—including Kraft and General Mills—signed the Children's Food and Beverage Advertising Initiative. The initiative is a voluntary commitment by firms to address obesity among children. Food and beverage marketers will devote half of their advertising dollars to ads directed to children to promote more healthful eating choices.[31]

© Anetta/Shutterstock.

DO CHILDREN HAVE ENOUGH JUDGMENT AND EXPERIENCE TO MAKE SAFE, HEALTHY PURCHASE DECISIONS? DO MARKETERS HAVE AN OBLIGATION TO PROTECT THEM?

Controversial Products

Some people question the wisdom of allowing the promotion of controversial goods and services, such as tobacco, alcoholic beverages, gambling and lotteries, and firearms. Critics charge that makers of tobacco and alcoholic beverages are targeting adolescents with promotional messages and are making dangerous and addictive products appealing.[32] This issue is complex.

Tobacco and Alcohol

Many medical journals have published survey research claiming that advertising "caused" cigarette smoking and alcohol consumption, particularly among teenagers.[33] However, these recent studies contradict research conducted since the 1950s carried out by marketing, communications, psychology, and economics researchers—including assessments of all the available research by the Federal Trade Commission.[34] The earlier studies (as well as several Gallup polls during the 1990s) found that family, friends, and peers—not advertising—are the primary influences on the use of tobacco and alcohol products. Studies published in the late 1990s and early in this decade have reaffirmed the findings of this earlier research.[35] While children at a very early age, indeed, can recognize tobacco advertising characters like Joe Camel, they also recognize as easily the Energizer Bunny (batteries), the Jolly Green Giant (canned vegetables), and Snoopy (life insurance)—all characters associated with adult products. Kids also are aware that cigarettes cause disease and know that these products are intended for adults. Research in Europe offers the same conclusion: "Every study on the subject [of advertising effects on the use of tobacco and alcohol] finds that children are more influenced by parents and playmates than by the mass media."[36]

Why doesn't advertising cause people to smoke and drink? The simple answer is that advertising just isn't that powerful. Eight out of 10 new products fail, and if advertising were so powerful, no new products would fail. The more detailed answer is that advertising cannot create primary demand in mature product categories. **Primary demand** is demand for an entire product category. With mature products—like milk and alcohol—advertising isn't powerful enough to have that effect. Research across several decades has demonstrated repeatedly that advertising does not create primary demand for tobacco or alcohol.[37]

Although smoking any amount or drinking to excess is certainly not good for you, these behaviors emerge in a complex social context. The vast weight of research evidence over 40 years suggests that advertising is not a significant causal influence on initiation behavior (e.g., smoking, drinking). Rather, advertising plays its most important role in consumers' choice of brands (e.g., Camel, Coors) after they have decided to use a product category (e.g., cigarettes, beer).

primary demand
demand for an entire product category

Gambling and Lotteries

Another controversial product area is that of gambling and state-run lotteries. What is the purpose of promoting these activities? Informing gamblers and lottery players of the choices available would be selective demand stimulation. Stimulation of demand for engaging in wagering behavior would be primary demand stimulation. Do you consider one more ethical than the other? Your answer might depend on your concern for compulsive gamblers. Some might argue that the state has an obligation to protect vulnerable citizens by restricting the placement or content of lottery advertising. In the late 1990s, as online gambling became widespread, it proved to be a fast and easy way for people to lose their life savings. Stories of out-of-control online gambling were widespread.[38] Even as online gaming revenues approached $1 billion, the federal government in October 2006 banned all online gambling in the United States.[39]

One way to think about vulnerable audiences is to consider the basis for this vulnerability—a consideration that can become complex and emotionally charged. Some might describe gamblers as an audience that is "information poor"—that is, people who tend not to seek out information from a wide range of sources. Others find descriptions of "information poverty" demeaning, patronizing, and paternalistic.

"Junk" Food

Reflecting on the complexity of sorting out the ethics of promoting controversial products, we wrote in a 2003 textbook:

> But consider this as you contemplate the role advertising plays in people's decisions regarding these types of products. Currently, one in three children in the United States is diagnosed as clinically obese. Will parents of these kids begin to sue McDonald's, Coca-Cola, Kellogg's, and General Mills because they advertise food products to children?

As a matter of fact, this is *exactly* what happened. McDonald's and other food companies had to prepare themselves for lawsuits from people claiming food providers "made them fat." The food industry has countered with the proposition that kids are obese because of unconcerned parents, underfunded school systems that have dropped physical activity programs, and sedentary entertainment like home video games.[40]

This issue is troublesome enough that the U.S. government passed legislation barring people from suing food companies for their obesity. In March 2004, the House of Representatives overwhelmingly approved legislation nicknamed the "cheeseburger bill" that would block lawsuits blaming the food industry for making people fat. During the debate on the bill, one of its sponsors said it was about "common sense and personal responsibility."[41]

Many marketers are worried about the intense focus on this global health problem. The chief creative officer of Coca-Cola Company called obesity concerns "our Achilles heel," adding, "It dilutes our marketing and works against us. It's a huge, huge issue."[42]

LO 3 Regulation of Advertising

Advertising is the promotional tool that tends to get the most scrutiny because of its global presence; therefore, much regulation of brand promotion focuses on advertising. Governments, industry groups, and advocacy organizations have identified several types of

Exhibit 6.2
Don't Go There . . .

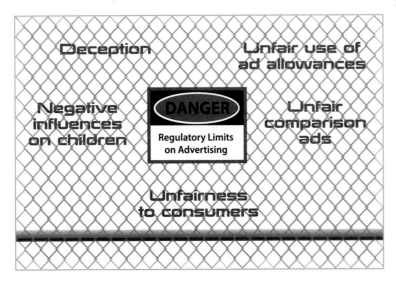

behavior that advertisers should avoid because they are illegal or socially unacceptable (see Exhibit 6.2).

Like the other topics in this chapter, regulation of advertising can be controversial, and opinions about what does and doesn't need to be regulated can be highly variable. However, while specific cases are in dispute, there is widespread agreement that deception, unfairness, anticompetitive behavior, and exploitation of children are unacceptable.

Deception and Unfairness

Deception in advertising is illegal, but determining whether a specific advertisement or promotional campaign is deceptive can be difficult. The authoritative source for defining deceptive advertising is a policy statement by the Federal Trade Commission (FTC). This policy statement specifies three elements as essential in declaring an ad deceptive:[43]

1. There must be a representation, omission, or practice that is likely to mislead the consumer.

2. This representation, omission, or practice must be judged from the perspective of a consumer acting reasonably in the circumstance.

3. The representation, omission, or practice must be a "material" one, meaning the act or the practice is likely to affect the consumer's conduct or decision with regard to the product or service, and consumer injury is likely as a result.

This definition of deception can lead to diverse interpretations when it is actually applied to advertisements in real life. Fortunately, the FTC offers practical advice for anticipating what can make an ad deceptive; this is available at the Advertising Guidance page of the FTC website (go to http://www.ftc.gov/bcp/guides/guides.htm, and under the Advertising section, click on "Frequently Asked Advertising Questions").

According to the FTC, both implied claims and *missing* information can be bases for deeming an ad deceptive. Obviously, the FTC expects any explicit claim made in an ad to be truthful, but it also is on the lookout for ads that deceive through allusion and innuendo or ads that deceive by not telling the whole story.

Many instances of deceptive advertising and packaging have resulted in formal government programs designed to regulate such practices. But there can be complications in regulating puffery. Conventional wisdom has argued that consumers don't actually believe extreme claims and realize advertisers are only trying to attract attention. Some people, however, disagree with this view of puffery and feel it actually represents "soft-core" deception because some consumers may believe exaggerated claims.[44]

In contrast to the definition of deception, the definition of unfairness in advertising has been left relatively vague. In 1994, Congress ended a long-running dispute in the courts and in the advertising industry by approving legislation that defines **unfair advertising** as "acts or practices that cause or are likely to cause substantial injury to consumers, which is not reasonably avoidable by consumers themselves, and not outweighed by the countervailing benefits to consumers or competition."[45] This definition obligates the FTC to assess both the benefits and costs of advertising, and rules out reckless acts on the part of consumers, before a judgment can be rendered that an advertiser has been unfair.

Competitive Issues

Because the large amounts spent on advertising may foster inequities that literally can destroy competition, several advertising practices relating to maintaining fair competition are regulated.

One of these practices is **vertical cooperative advertising**, an advertising technique whereby a manufacturer and dealer (either a wholesaler or retailer) share the expense of advertising. This technique is used commonly in regional or local markets where a manufacturer wants a brand to benefit from a special promotion run by local dealers (recall the co-op advertising example in Chapter 1). There is nothing illegal, per se, about this practice, and it is used regularly. The competitive threat arises when dealers (especially since the advent of first department store chains and now mega retailers like Walmart and Home Depot) are given bogus cooperative advertising allowances. These allowances require little or no effort or expenditure on the part of the dealer/retailer, so they really represent hidden price concessions. As such, they are a form of unfair competition and are deemed illegal. If an advertising allowance is granted to a dealer, that dealer must demonstrate that the funds are applied specifically to advertising.

Another area of unfair competition is to use comparison ads inappropriately. **Comparison advertisements** are those in which an advertiser makes a comparison between the firm's brand and competitors' brands. The comparison may or may not explicitly identify the competition. Again, comparison ads are completely legal and are used frequently by all sorts of organizations. But if an advertisement is carried out in such a way that the comparison is not fair, then there is an unfair competitive effect. For example, Duracell once ran ads that claimed its "Coppertop" battery outlasted Energizer's heavy-duty battery. While the claim was technically true, the Coppertop is an alkaline battery and was not being compared to Energizer's alkaline battery. The FTC may require a firm using comparisons to substantiate claims made in an advertisement and prove that the claims do not tend to deceive. It also may require that ads use a disclaimer to help consumers understand comparative product claims. Gillette, makers of Duracell, agreed to include a disclaimer in its Coppertop ads; it later pulled the campaign altogether.[46]

unfair advertising acts by advertisers that cause or are likely to cause substantial injury that is not reasonably avoidable or outweighed by other benefits

vertical cooperative advertising sharing of advertising expense by a manufacturer and dealer (wholesaler or retailer)

comparison advertisements ads that compare the advertiser's brand with competitors' brands

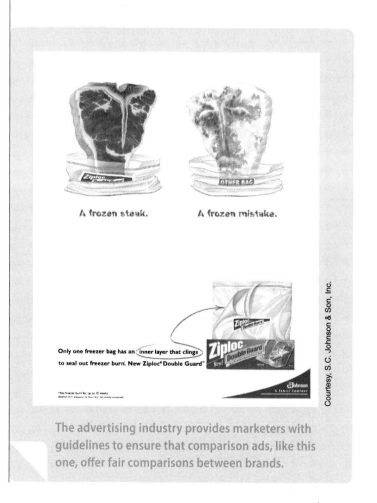

The advertising industry provides marketers with guidelines to ensure that comparison ads, like this one, offer fair comparisons between brands.

Some firms are so powerful in their use of advertising that **monopoly power** by virtue of their ad spending can become a problem. This issue normally arises in the context of mergers and acquisitions. As an example, the U.S. Supreme Court blocked the acquisition of Clorox by Procter & Gamble because the advertising power of the two firms combined would (in the opinion of the Court) make it nearly impossible for another firm to compete.

Advertising to Children

As we discussed in the area of ethics, critics argue that continually bombarding children with persuasive stimuli can alter their motivation and behavior. Even though government organizations such as the FTC have been active in trying to regulate advertising directed at children, industry and consumer groups have been more successful in securing restrictions. Recall that the group Action for Children's Television persuaded Congress to pass the Children's Television Act, which limits the amount of commercial airtime allowed during children's programs.

The Council of Better Business Bureaus established a Children's Advertising Review Unit and has issued a set of guidelines for advertising directed at children. These guidelines emphasize that advertisers should be sensitive to children's knowledge and sophistication as decision makers. The guidelines also urge advertisers to make a constructive contribution to children's social development by emphasizing positive social standards, such as friendship, kindness, honesty, and generosity. Similarly, the major television networks have set guidelines for advertising aimed at children. The guidelines restrict the use of celebri-

ties, prohibit exhortative language (such as "Go ask Dad"), and restrict the use of animation to one-third of the total time of the commercial.

The regulation of children's advertising seems to be having some direct effect. Children ages 2 to 11 see 25,600 television ads a year, constituting 10,700 minutes of promotional communications. More than 50 percent of these ads are viewed between 4 PM and midnight, and only 5 percent of the ads are viewed during Saturday-morning programming. The good news: Kids are actually seeing *fewer* ads than they were 20 years ago.[47]

Who Regulates Advertising?

As you would expect, much of the regulation of advertising involves government scrutiny and control of the advertising process. In addition, consumers themselves and several industry organizations exert regulatory power over advertising. Together, government, industry groups, and consumers shape and restrict the advertising process.

Given the multiple participants, the regulation of advertising turns out to be a highly complex activity. Additionally, although our discussion focuses on regulatory activities in the United States, advertising regulation can vary dramatically from country to country. Chapter 7 provides additional insights on advertising regulation around the world.

LO 4 Federal Government Regulation

Governments have a powerful tool available for regulating advertising: the threat of legal action. In the United States, several federal government agencies have been given the power and responsibility to regulate the advertising process. Six agencies are most directly involved in advertising regulation:

1. *Federal Trade Commission (FTC):* Controls unfair methods of competition, regulates deceptive advertising, and has various programs for controlling the advertising process.

2. *Federal Communications Commission (FCC):* Prohibits obscenity, fraud, and lotteries on radio and television.

3. *Food and Drug Administration (FDA):* Regulates the advertising of food, drug, cosmetic, and medical products; can

require special labeling for hazardous products; prohibits false labeling and packaging.

4. *Securities and Exchange Commission (SEC):* Regulates the advertising of securities and the disclosure of information in annual reports.

5. *U.S. Postal Service (USPS):* Regulates direct-mail advertising and prohibits lotteries, fraud, and misrepresentation; can regulate and impose fines for materials deemed to be obscene.

6. *Bureau of Alcohol, Tobacco, Firearms, and Explosives (ATF):* Regulates advertising for alcoholic beverages; can determine what constitutes misleading advertising in these product categories.

Several other agencies have minor powers in the regulation of advertising, such as the Civil Aeronautics Board (advertising by air carriers), the Patent Office (trademark infringement), and the Library of Congress (copyright protection).

Most active among these agencies is the Federal Trade Commission, which has the most power and is most directly involved in controlling the advertising process. The FTC has been granted legal power through legislative mandates and also has developed programs for regulating advertising.

FTC's Legislative Mandates

The Federal Trade Commission was created by the Federal Trade Commission Act in 1914. The original purpose of the agency was to prohibit unfair methods of competition. In 1916, the FTC concluded that false advertising was one way in which a firm could take unfair advantage of another, and advertising was established as a primary concern of the agency.

It was not until 1938 that the effects of deceptive advertising on consumers became a key issue for the FTC. Until the passage of the Wheeler-Lea Amendment (1938), the commission primarily was concerned with the direct effect of advertising on competition. The amendment broadened the FTC's powers to include regulation of advertising that was misleading to the public (regardless of the effect on competition). Through this amendment, the agency could order a firm to stop its deceptive practices. The amendment also granted the agency specific jurisdiction over drug, medical device, cosmetic, and food advertising.

Several other acts give the FTC legal powers over advertising. The Robinson-Patman Act (1936) prohibits firms from providing phantom cooperative-advertising allowances as a way to court important dealers. The Wool Products Labeling Act (1939), the Fur

Products Labeling Act (1951), and the Textile Fiber Products Identification Act (1958) provided the commission with regulatory power over labeling and advertising for specific products. Consumer protection legislation, which seeks to increase the ability of consumers to make more-informed product comparisons, includes the Fair Packaging and Labeling Act (1966), the Truth in Lending Act (1969), and the Fair Credit Reporting Act (1970). The FTC Improvement Act (1975) expanded the authority of the commission by giving it the power to issue trade regulation rules.

Recent legislation has expanded the FTC's role in monitoring and regulating product labeling and advertising. For example, the 1990 Nutrition Labeling and Education Act (NLEA) requires uniformity in the nutrition labeling of food products and establishes strict rules for claims about the nutritional attributes of food products. The standard "Nutrition Facts" label required by the NLEA appears on everything from breakfast cereals to barbecue sauce.

The Internet has drawn scrutiny from the FTC. Concern for children's privacy led to the Children's Online Privacy Protection Act of 1998, which makes it illegal for operators of websites directed at children—and any website operators who know they are getting information from children—to collect personal information from children.[48] Full disclosure of the website's information gathering (if any) must appear plainly on these websites.

FTC's Regulatory Programs and Remedies

The application of legislation has evolved as the FTC exercises its powers and expands its role as a regulatory agency. This evolution of the FTC has spawned several regulatory programs and remedies to help enforce legislative mandates in specific situations (see Exhibit 6.3). Not only does FTC enforcement cause advertisers to change advertising when it is found to violate the guidelines, but advertisers and their agencies also try to avoid violating FTC precepts as they plan the content of their ads.

The FTC's **advertising substantiation program** was initiated in 1971 with the intention of ensuring that advertisers make supporting evidence for their claims available to consumers. The program was strengthened in 1972 when the commission forwarded the

> **advertising substantiation program** FTC program that ensures advertisers make available to consumers supporting evidence for advertising claims

consent order FTC action asking an advertiser to stop running deceptive or unfair advertising without admitting guilt

cease-and-desist order FTC action requiring an advertiser to stop running an ad so that a hearing can be held to determine whether the ad is deceptive or unfair

affirmative disclosure FTC action requiring that important material determined to be absent from prior ads be included in future ads

corrective advertising FTC action requiring an advertiser to run additional ads to dispel false beliefs created by deceptive advertising

celebrity endorsements advertisements that use an expert or celebrity as spokesperson to endorse the use of a product or service

notion of "reasonable basis" for the substantiation of advertising. This extension suggests not only that advertisers should substantiate their claims, but also that the substantiation should provide a reasonable basis for believing the claims are true.[49] Simply put, before a company runs an ad, it must have documented evidence that supports the claim it wants to make in that ad. The kind of evidence required depends on the kind of claim being made. For example, health and safety claims require competent and reliable scientific evidence that has been examined and validated by experts in the field.

The most basic remedies used by the FTC to deal with deceptive or unfair advertising are the consent order and the cease-and-desist order. In a **consent order**, an advertiser accused of running deceptive or unfair advertising agrees to stop running the ads in question, without admitting guilt. For advertisers who do not comply voluntarily, the FTC can issue a **cease-and-desist order**, which generally requires that the advertising in question be stopped within 30 days so that a hearing can be held to determine whether the advertising is deceptive or unfair. For products that have a direct effect on consumers' health or safety (for example, foods), the FTC can issue an immediate cease-and-desist order.

If an advertisement is deemed deceptive because it fails to disclose important material facts about a product, the FTC may require another remedy, **affirmative disclosure**. This remedy requires that the important material absent from prior ads be included in subsequent advertisements.

The most extensive remedy for advertising determined to be misleading is **corrective advertising**.[50] If evidence suggests that consumers have developed incorrect beliefs about a brand based on deceptive or unfair advertising, the firm may be required to run corrective ads in an attempt to dispel those faulty beliefs. The commission can specify not only the message content for corrective ads but also the budgetary alloca-

Exhibit 6.3
Remedies Sought by the FTC

Advertising substantiation

Corrective advertising

Consent order

Affirmative disclosure

Cease-and-desist order

Federal Trade Commission

tion, the duration of transmission, and the placement of the advertising. The corrective-advertising remedy has been required of Listerine ads that claimed the mouthwash could "cure and prevent colds" (which it couldn't). Although corrective advertising is intended to rectify erroneous beliefs created by deceptive advertising, it hasn't always worked as intended.

Another area of FTC regulation and remedy involves **celebrity endorsements**. For advertisements in which the spokesperson for a product is an expert (someone whose experience or training allows a superior judgment of products), the FTC requires that the endorser's actual qualifications justify his or her status as an expert. In the case of celebrities (such as Sarah Jessica Parker as a spokesperson for Garnier Nutrisse), the celebrity must be an actual user of the product. When these requirements are not satisfied, the ad is considered deceptive.

State Regulation

When goods and services are marketed across state lines, any violation of fair practices or existing regulation is a federal government issue. The vast majority of companies are involved in interstate marketing, so state governments do not have extensive policing powers over the promotional activities of firms. However, they do exert control at times.

Typically, one state government organization, the attorney general's office, is responsible for investigating questionable promotional practices. In Texas, for example, the state attorney general's office claimed a demon-

Domino's Pizza CEO, Dave Brandon, delivers sweepstakes grand prize, pizza for a year, to Angela Waldrep of Killeen, Texas. The Big Taste Bailout promotion, which offers consumers three or more medium, one topping pizzas or oven baked sandwiches for just $5 each, kicked off earlier this month.

self-regulation the advertising industry's attempt to police itself

stration used by Volvo was misleading. In the ad, a monster truck with oversized tires was shown rolling over the roofs of a row of cars, crushing all of them except a Volvo. The problem was, the roof of the Volvo used in the test had been reinforced, while the other cars' roof supports had been weakened.[51]

In 1995, 13 states passed prize notification laws regarding sweepstakes and contests. The laws require marketers to make full disclosure of rules, odds, and retail value of prizes. The states were responding to what they felt was widespread fraud and deception. Some states aggressively prosecuted the sweepstakes companies in court.

Since the 1980s, the National Association of Attorneys General, whose members include the attorneys general from all 50 states, has been active as a group in monitoring advertising and sharing its findings. Overall, however, states will rely on the vigilance of federal agencies to monitor promotional practices and then act against firms with questionable activities.

LO 5 Industry Self-Regulation

The promotion industry has come far in terms of self-control and restraint. Some of this improvement is due to tougher government regulation and some to industry self-regulation. **Self-regulation** is the promotion industry's attempt to police itself. Depending on your viewpoint, you might think of self-regulation as a sign that government intervention is unnecessary or as a cynical attempt by marketers to head off further regulation

without necessarily behaving in a socially responsible manner. Most marketers would say that self-regulation is good and creates credibility for, and therefore enhances, promotion itself.

A review of all aspects of industry self-regulation suggests that many of these programs are effective. Those whose livelihoods depend on advertising are just as interested as consumers and legislators in maintaining high standards. If advertising deteriorates into an unethical and untrustworthy business activity, the economic vitality of many organizations will be compromised.

Self-regulation of advertising includes voluntary guidelines established by several industry and trade associations and public service organizations. Many organizations have taken on the task of regulating and monitoring promotional activities; here are a few examples, by type of organization:

- *Advertising associations:* American Advertising Federation, American Association of Advertising Agencies, Association of National Advertisers, and Business/Professional Advertising Association

- *Special industry groups:* Council of Better Business Bureaus, National Advertising Division of the National Advertising Review Board

- *Media associations:* American Business Press, Direct Marketing Association, National Association of Broadcasters

- *Trade associations:* Pharmaceutical Manufacturers Association, Bank Marketing Association, Motion Picture Association of America

Each of these organizations has established a code of standards.

MOST MARKETERS WOULD SAY THAT SELF-REGULATION IS **GOOD FOR THE PROMOTION COMMUNITY** AS A WHOLE.

The purpose of self-regulation by these organizations is to evaluate the content and quality of promotion specific to their industries. The effectiveness of such organizations depends on the cooperation of members and the policing mechanisms used. Each organization exerts an influence on the nature of promotion in its industry. Some are particularly noteworthy in their activities and warrant further discussion.

National Advertising Review Board

One important self-regulation organization is the National Advertising Review Board (NARB). The NARB is the operations arm of the National Advertising Division (NAD) of the Council of Better Business Bureaus. When the Better Business Bureau (BBB) receives complaints from consumers, competitors, or local branches, it forwards them to the NAD. Most such complaints come from competitors.

The NAD maintains a permanent professional staff that works to resolve complaints with the advertiser and its agency. After the NAD conducts a full review of the complaint, if no resolution is achieved, it may forward the issue to the NARB, where it is evaluated by a panel of three advertiser representatives, one agency representative, and one public representative. The panel holds hearings regarding the advertising in question. The advertiser is allowed to present its case. If the panel finds that the advertising is misleading, it will again request changes. If the advertiser does not comply, NARB publicly identifies the advertiser, the complaint against the advertiser, and the panel's findings. Then the case is forwarded to an appropriate government regulatory agency (usually the FTC). This procedure for dealing with complaints is summarized in Exhibit 6.4.

The NAD and NARB are not empowered to impose penalties on advertisers, but the threat of going before the board acts as a deterrent to deceptive and question-

Exhibit 6.4
Handling Complaints to the Better Business Bureau

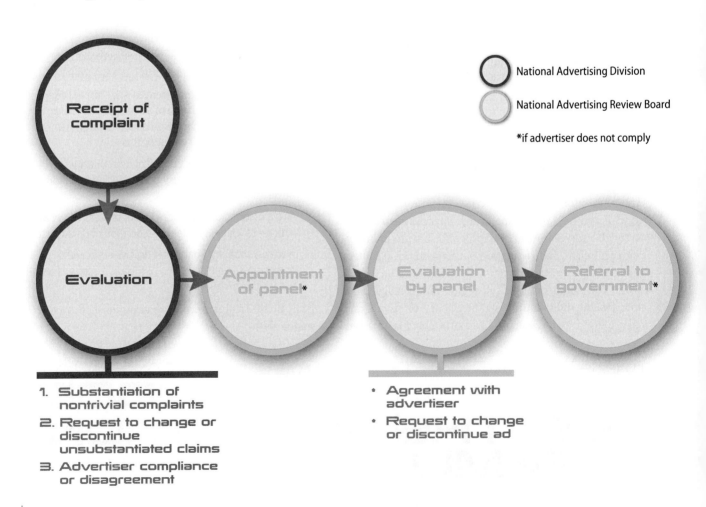

National Advertising Division

National Advertising Review Board

*if advertiser does not comply

Receipt of complaint

Evaluation

Appointment of panel*

Evaluation by panel

Referral to government*

1. Substantiation of nontrivial complaints
2. Request to change or discontinue unsubstantiated claims
3. Advertiser compliance or disagreement

- Agreement with advertiser
- Request to change or discontinue ad

able advertising practices. Further, the regulatory process of the NAD and the NARB probably is less costly and time consuming for all parties involved than if every complaint were handled by a government agency.

State and Local Better Business Bureaus

Aside from the national BBB, there are more than 140 separate local bureaus. Each local organization is supported by membership dues paid by area businesses. The three divisions of a local BBB—merchandise, financial, and solicitations—investigate the advertising and selling practices of firms in their areas. A local BBB has the power to forward a complaint to the NAD for evaluation.

Beyond its regulatory activities, the BBB tries to avert problems associated with advertising by counseling new businesses and providing information to advertisers and agencies regarding legislation, potential problem areas, and industry standards.

Advertising Agencies and Associations

It makes sense that advertising agencies and their industry associations would engage in self-regulation. An individual agency is legally responsible for the advertising it produces and is subject to reprisal for deceptive claims. The agency is in a difficult position in that it must monitor not only the activities of its own people but also the information that clients provide to the agency. Should a client direct an agency to use a product appeal that turns out to be untruthful, the agency is still responsible.

The American Association of Advertising Agencies (4As) has no legal or binding power over its agency members, but it can apply pressure when its board feels that industry standards are not being upheld. The 4As also publishes guidelines for its members regarding various aspects of advertising messages. One of the most widely recognized industry standards is the 4As' Creative Code. The code outlines the responsibilities and potential social impact of advertising and promotes high ethical standards of honesty

and decency. You can view the 4As' standards of practice, including the Creative Code, at http://www.aaaa.org.

Media Organizations

Individual media organizations evaluate the advertising they receive for broadcast and publication. The National Association of Broadcasters (NAB) has a policing arm known as the Code Authority, which implements and interprets separate radio and television codes. These codes deal with truth, fairness, and good taste in broadcast advertising. Newspapers historically have been rigorous in their screening of advertising. Many newspapers have internal departments to screen and censor ads believed to be in violation of the newspaper's advertising standards. The magazine industry does not have a formal code, but many individual publications have very high standards.

Direct mail may have a poor image among many consumers, but its industry association, the Direct Marketing Association (DMA), is active in promoting ethical behavior and standards among its members. It has published guidelines for ethical business practices. In 1971, the association established the Direct Mail Preference Service, which allows consumers to have their names removed from most direct-mail lists.

Internet Self-Regulation

Because few federal guidelines have been established for promotion on the Internet (with the exception of antispam legislation), the industry itself has been the governing body. So far, no industry-wide trade association has emerged to offer guidelines or standards. You will see later in this chapter that several special-interest groups are questioning the ethics of some Internet promotional practices. Some people are skeptical that the industry can regulate itself.

The Global Business Dialog on Electronic Commerce (GBDe) is trying to establish itself as a trade association for the online industry. But while it counts some big companies among its 200 members—Time Warner, Daimler AG, Toshiba—not one of the Internet heavyweights, like Amazon.com or Yahoo!, has joined the ranks. The GBDe has drawn up a proposal for dealing with harmful content (pornography), protecting personal information, enforcing copyrights, and handling disputes in e-commerce. But the organization's efforts have not created great enthusiasm. Lester Thurow, the prominent public policy professor from the Massachusetts Institute of Technology, may have pinpointed the problem: "Self-regulation can play a role if you have real regulation that will come piling in if you don't do it."[52]

Consumers as Regulators

Consumers themselves are motivated to act as regulatory agents based on a variety of interests, including product safety, reasonable choice, and the right to information. Advertising tends to be a focus of consumer regulatory activities because it is conspicuous. The primary vehicles for consumer regulatory efforts are consumerism and consumer organizations.

Consumerism, the actions of individual consumers or groups of consumers designed to exert power in the marketplace, is by no means a recent phenomenon. The earliest consumerism efforts can be traced to 17th-century England. In the United States, there have been recurring consumer movements throughout the 20th and into the 21st century. A recent example is the *Adbusters* magazine and website.

In general, these movements have focused on the same issue: Consumers want a greater voice in the whole process of product development, distribution, and information dissemination. Consumers commonly try to create pressures on firms by withholding patronage through boycotts. Some boycotts have been effective. Firms as powerful as Procter & Gamble, Kimberly-Clark, and General Mills all have historically responded to threats of boycotts by pulling advertising from programs consumers found offensive. Advertisers themselves have threatened to withhold advertising

dollars unless they can be assured of decency in programming by producers and networks.[53]

Consumers also seek to bring about regulation through established consumer organizations. The following three organizations are the most prominent:

1. *Consumer Federation of America (CFA;* http://www.consumerfed.org): This organization, founded in 1968, includes more than 200 national, state, and local consumer groups and labor unions as affiliate members. The CFA's goals are to encourage the creation of consumer organizations, provide services to consumer groups, and act as a clearinghouse for information exchange among consumer groups.

2. *Consumers Union* (http://www.consumersunion.org): This nonprofit consumer organization is best known for its publication of *Consumer Reports*. Established in 1936, Consumers Union has as its stated purpose "to provide consumers with information and advice on goods, services, health, and personal finance; and to initiate and cooperate with individual and group efforts to maintain and enhance the quality of life for consumers."[54] This organization supports itself through the sale of publications and accepts no funding, including advertising revenues, from any commercial organization.

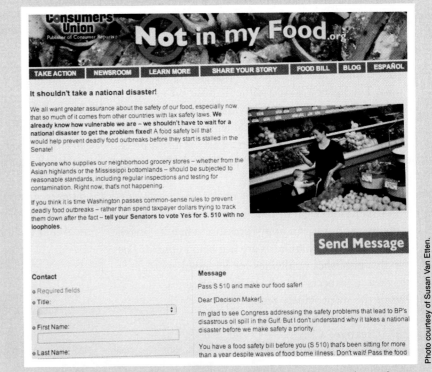

Photo courtesy of Susan Van Etten.

Consumer organizations, including Consumers Union, regulate advertising by influencing legislation and letting marketers know what they will and will not tolerate in products and promotional messages. This Consumers Union Web page is encouraging consumers to press for tougher food safety standards.

3. *Commercial Alert* (http://www.commercialalert.org): Commercial Alert is headed by Ralph Nader, a historic figure in consumer rights and protection. The organization's stated mission is to keep the commercial culture within its proper sphere and to prevent it from exploiting children and subverting the higher values of family, community, environmental integrity, and democracy.

These three consumer organizations are the most active and potent of the consumer groups, but there are hundreds of such groups organized by geographic location or product category.

Consumers have proven that, when faced with an organized effort, corporations can and will change their practices. In one of the most publicized events in recent times, after Coca-Cola tried modifying its formula, consumers applied pressure and, in part, were responsible for forcing the firm to re-market the original product (as Coca-Cola Classic). If consumers can exert such a powerful and nearly immediate influence on a firm such as Coca-Cola, what other changes might they affect in the market?

LO 6 Regulation of Direct Marketing and E-Commerce

The most pressing regulatory issue facing direct marketing and e-commerce is database development and the privacy debate that accompanies the practice. The crux of the privacy issue has to do with firms' emerging ability to merge offline databases with data about consumers' online search and shopping behavior.

Privacy

E-commerce privacy issues encompass a wide range, from database development to **cookies**, those online tracking markers that advertisers place on a Web surfer's hard drive to track that person's online behavior. The current environment is annoying and feels like a huge invasion of privacy. But it is nothing compared with the emerging possibilities. Currently, cookies do not reveal a person's name or address. But what is looming as a real possibility is merging the widely used offline databases that *do* include a consumer's name, address, phone number, credit card numbers, medical records, credit records, and Social Security number with online tracking data

from Web-browsing behavior.[55] With this combination of data, the following could happen easily: You are browsing a Web page on mutual funds, and, seconds later, you get a phone call from a telemarketer trying to sell you financial services.

This scenario may not be too far in the future, and the data/browsing merge already has occurred. The merger of DoubleClick with Abacus Direct created a database that contains transactional data from 1,700 cataloguers, retailers, and publishers—data that chronicles more than 3.6 *billion* transactions by 90 million U.S. households (out of 102 million total households in the United States). Double-Click, part of Google, offers a digital marketplace that connects ad agencies, marketers, and website publishers. As an example of its database activities, Double-Click has signed up more than 275 online retailers that contribute detailed transaction, geographic, and demographic information to a database.[56] Being in that database might feel like an invasion of privacy. Firms are searching for ways to guarantee to consumers that their privacy will be preserved.

In the meantime, the concern is great enough that Congress and the FTC are scrutinizing mergers of firms that would create such comprehensive online and offline databases, and privacy advocates are trying to alert people to the invasion.[57] But while this tracking of behavior seems pretty scary to some, many people seem not to care. In a recent survey that asked Web users whether they read a site's privacy policy before making a purchase, only 6 percent responded that they always do; 77 percent said they rarely or never do.

> **cookies** online tracking markers that advertisers place on a web surfer's hard drive to track that person's online behavior
>
> **spam** unsolicited commercial messages sent through email

Spam

Few of us would argue with the allegation that **spam**, unsolicited commercial messages sent through email, is the scourge of the Internet. To put the problem into perspective, an estimated 30 million spam emails are sent every *minute* worldwide—that comes out to about 50 billion messages a day.[58] Spam actually has shut down a company's entire operations.

To cope with the onslaught, individuals and companies use spam-filtering software to stem the flow and take back control of their email systems. Internet service providers have formed a coalition against spammers. In the spring of 2003, Yahoo!, AOL, and MSN announced a joint antispam offensive relying on technological and legal remedies. About the same time, the FTC convened a brainstorming session to determine what, if anything, could be done legally. In 2003, Congress passed the CAN SPAM Act. The act does not outlaw all unsolicited email but rather targets fraudulent, deceptive, and pornographic messages, estimated to make up about two-thirds of all commercial unsolic-

ited email.[59] The most severe prosecution to date has been notorious spammer Alan Soloway, operator of Newport Internet Marketing, which offered "broadcast email" software. Soloway is accused of facilitating the distribution of hundreds of millions of spam emails via hijacked networks.[60]

Spammers are challenging the legislation on legal grounds, claiming that it violates First Amendment free-speech rights. And they are doing what they do best—slamming their opponents with a barrage of emails. The concern, of course, is that legitimate marketers and advertisers who could use email in a reasonable way will be caught in this legislation.

© /Shutterstock.

eTHICS PAYING FOR PRAISE

"You can't believe anything you see or read." This cynical-sounding quote is from the founder of an interactive ad agency that pays bloggers to write nice things about corporate sponsors—without worrying much about whether the bloggers disclose the pay arrangement. In fact, some websites will connect marketers with bloggers, letting marketers post details about how they want bloggers to write about their brands. The bloggers then are paid for featuring the advertiser's brand. Even though the bloggers are paid for their comments, they still could give an honest opinion. But what do you expect when you read a magazine, newspaper, or blog? Many readers assume or at least hope advertisers are not directly involved in content decisions.

Sources: Jon Fine, "An Onslaught of Hidden Ads," *BusinessWeek*, June 27, 2005, 24; Associated Press, "GM Ends Boycott of LA Times," August 2, 2005, *Yahoo! News*, http://news.yahoo.com; Liz Moyer, "Managing Ads, Not News," *Forbes*, May 23, 2005, http://www.forbes.com.

Contests, Sweepstakes, Coupons

Another legal issue in the realm of direct marketing has to do with sweepstakes, contests, and coupons. Because of the success and widespread use of sweepstakes in direct marketing (such as the Publishers Clearing House sweepstakes), Congress has imposed limits on such promotions. The existing limits on direct-mail sweepstakes include the requirement that the phrases "No purchase is necessary to win" and "A purchase will not improve an individual's chance of winning" must be repeated three times in letters to consumers and again on the entry form. In addition, penalties can be imposed on marketers who do not promptly remove consumers' names from mailing lists at the consumers' request.[61]

The online version of sweepstakes and contests also has the attention of the U.S. Congress. Sweepstakes online are similar to traditional sweepstakes, lotteries, games, or contests. For example, visitors to the Lucky-Surf website merely need to register (providing name, home address, email address, and password), pick seven numbers, and then click on a four banner ad to activate an entry in a $1-million-a-day drawing. So far, these online games have avoided both lawsuits and regulation, but they have attracted the attention of policymakers.[62]

Coupons distributed through direct mail, newspapers, magazines, or the Internet require legal protection for the *marketer* more than anything else. Fraud abounds in the area of couponing, aggravated by the fact that approximately 76 percent of the U.S. population uses coupons, redeeming 2.6 billion coupons every year.[63] Phony coupons easily can be reproduced and redeemed well after the firm's promotional campaign ends. Starbucks ended up with a promotional nightmare by not enacting safeguards for a "Free Iced Beverage" coupon it intended for a small email distribution. The coupons were forwarded in huge numbers, and consumers throughout the United States tried to redeem them. Because of the unexpected nationwide demand, Starbucks had to cancel the offer before the coupons' expiration date, frustrating many customers.[64] Safeguards that reduce problems with contests, sweepstakes, and coupons include strict limitations on redemption, geographic limitations, and encrypted bar codes that can be scanned to detect fraud.[65]

Telemarketing

Direct marketing also has run into regulation of telemarketing practices. The first restriction on telemarketing was the Telephone Consumer Fraud and Abuse Prevention Act of 1994 (strengthened by the FTC

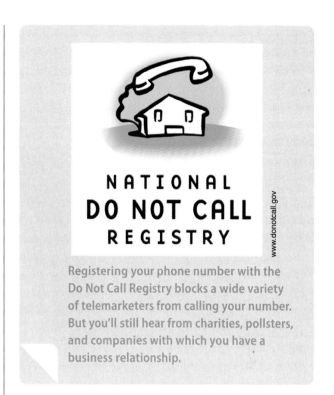

NATIONAL DO NOT CALL REGISTRY

www.donotcall.gov

Registering your phone number with the Do Not Call Registry blocks a wide variety of telemarketers from calling your number. But you'll still hear from charities, pollsters, and companies with which you have a business relationship.

in 1995), which requires telemarketers to state their name, the purpose of the call, and the company they work for. Telemarketers may not call before 8 AM or after 9 PM, nor may they call the same customer more than once every three months. In addition, they cannot use automatic dialing machines that contain recorded messages, and they must keep a list of consumers who do not want to be called.

Since the 1994 law, much stricter limits have been placed on telemarketers. At the center of new regulation is the Do Not Call Law, which allows consumers to sign up for a Do Not Call Registry (http://www.donotcall.gov). The Federal Trade Commission, the Federal Communications Commission, and states started to enforce the registry on October 1, 2003. When the program was launched, about 60 million phone numbers were registered by consumers as "do not call" numbers.

Under the Do Not Call Law, certain organizations still have rights to continue telemarketing efforts, so even if you have registered with the Do Not Call Registry, you still can get calls from:[66]

- Charities, politicians, pollsters, and market researchers
- Companies you do business with
- Companies that have sold you something or delivered something to you within the previous 18 months
- Businesses *you've* contacted in the past three months
- Companies that obtain your permission to call

Regulation of Sales Promotion

Regulatory issues in sales promotion focus on premium offers, trade allowances, and contests and sweepstakes.

Premium Offers

With respect to **premiums** (an item offered for "free" or at a greatly reduced price with the purchase of another item), the main area of regulation is a requirement that marketers state the fair retail value of the item offered as a premium.

© michaeljung/Shutterstock.

Trade Allowances

In the area of trade allowances, marketers need to be familiar with the guidelines set forth in the Robinson-Patman Act of 1936. The Robinson-Patman Act requires marketers to offer similar customers similar prices on similar merchandise. This means that a marketer cannot use special allowances as a way to discount the price to highly attractive customers. This issue was raised earlier in the context of vertical cooperative advertising.

Contests and Sweepstakes

In the previous discussion of e-commerce, we addressed regulation of sweepstakes and contests. Other issues arise as well. The FTC has specified four violations that marketers must avoid to meet regulations for sweepstakes and contests:

1. *Misrepresentations about the value of the prizes being offered:* For example, it is unlawful to state an inflated retail price.

2. *Failure to provide complete disclosure about the conditions necessary to win:* Are certain behaviors required on the part of the contestant?

3. *Failure to disclose the conditions necessary to obtain a prize:* Are certain behaviors required of the contestant after being designated a "winner"?

4. *Failure to ensure that a contest or sweepstakes is not classified as a lottery:* A contest or sweepstakes is a lottery if a prize is offered based on chance and the contestant has to give up something of value in order to play. A lottery is not permitted because it is considered a form of gambling.

Product/Brand Placement

The area of sales promotion receiving attention most recently in the regulatory arena is brand/product placement in television programs and films. In the view of consumer groups, unless television networks and film producers reveal that brands are placed into a program or film for a fee, consumers could be deceived into believing that the product use is natural and real. The industry makes this counterclaim: "There is a paranoia about our business that shouldn't be there. We don't control the storyline, or the brands that are included. The writers and producers do."[67] In reaction to criticism, Philip Morris has gone so far as to run print ads in *Variety* and the *Hollywood Reporter*, urging filmmakers not to put its products in films.[68]

Regulation of Public Relations

Public relations is not bound by the same sorts of laws as other elements of the promotional mix. Because public relations activities deal with public press and public figures, much of the regulation relates to these issues. A firm's public relations activities may place it on either side of legal issues with respect to privacy, copyright infringement, or defamation through slander and libel.

Privacy

The privacy problems facing a public relations firm center on the issue of appropriation. **Appropriation** is the use of pictures or images owned by someone else without permission. If a firm uses a model's photo or a photographer's work in an advertisement or company brochure without permission, then the work has been appropriated without the owner's permission. The same is true of public relations materials prepared for release to the news media or as part of a company's public relations kit.

Copyright Infringement

Copyright infringement can occur when a public relations effort uses written, recorded, or photographic material in public relations materials. Much as with appropriation, written permission must be obtained to use such works.

Defamation

When a communication occurs that damages the reputation of an individual because the information in the communication was untrue, this is called **defamation** (sometimes referred to as "defamation of character"). Defamation can occur in one of two ways:

1. **Slander** is oral defamation. In the context of promotion, it would occur during television or radio broadcast of an event involving a company and its employees.

2. **Libel** is defamation that occurs in print. It would occur in magazine, newspaper, direct mail, or Internet reports.

Public relations practitioners must protect clients from slanderous or libelous reports about a company's activities. Inflammatory TV "investigative" news programs often are sued for slander and are challenged to prove their allegations about a company and its personnel. The issues concern whether negative comments can be fully substantiated. Erroneous magazine or newspaper reports about a firm also can result in a defamation lawsuit. Less frequently, public relations experts need to defend a client accused of making defamatory remarks.

appropriation use of pictures or images owned by someone else without permission

defamation untrue communication that damages the reputation of an individual

slander oral defamation (for example, during a radio broadcast)

libel defamation that occurs in print (for example, in a magazine story)

STUDY TOOLS CHAPTER 6

Located at back of the textbook

- **Rip out Chapter in Review Card.**

Located at www.cengagebrain.com

- **Review Key Terms Flashcards (Print or Online).**
- **Complete the Practice Quiz to prepare for tests.**
- **Play "Beat the Clock" and "Quizbowl" to master concepts.**
- **Complete "Crossword Puzzle" to review key terms.**
- **Watch videos on Old Spice and Chevrolet for real company examples.**
- **Additional examples are available online including: supermarkets use of databases, ad choices that were not received as well as planned, and subliminal advertising.**

CHAPTER 7

The International Market Environment for Brand Promotion

Safeguard needed an engaging way to get their message across to families—that many infectious diseases are preventable through basic hygiene.

Commander Safeguard
Pakistan's First Super Hero

Commander Safeguard, the superhero, pitches hand washing to kids. Using a superhero, a popular idea in Pakistan, the brand comes across as the hero as well.

Website gets schools involved.

www.commandersafeguard.com

© Procter & Gamble. Used by permission.

Learning Outcomes

After studying this chapter, you should be able to:

LO 1 Identify types of audience research that contribute to understanding cultural barriers to effective communication.

LO 2 Describe challenges that complicate integrated marketing communication in international settings.

LO 3 Compare the basic types of agencies that can assist in brand promotion around the world.

LO 4 Discuss the advantages and disadvantages of globalized versus localized promotional campaigns.

"Any forward-thinking company needs to be thinking globally today."

—Barbara Turf,
Crate & Barrel[1]

AFTER YOU FINISH THIS CHAPTER GO TO PAGE 154 FOR STUDY TOOLS

Commander Safeguard Cleans Up

In 2003, the Safeguard soap brand was floundering in Pakistan. Amid strong competition from traditional favorites like Unilever's Lifebuoy, the antibacterial claim behind Safeguard's positioning was taking it nowhere. In Pakistan at that time, all antibacterial brands combined held only a skimpy 7 percent share of the bar soap market.

Pakistan had serious public health challenges that are common in less-developed economies. Significantly, 250,000 children were dying every year because of diarrhea. Many of these deaths were preventable through basic hygiene, like hand washing. But no one was getting this message out. A country struggling with poverty, terrorism threats, and a long-standing border war didn't have the resources to devote to public service announcements about hygiene. Dire situations like this one often hold great opportunity. For Safeguard, the challenge was to reach families with a message that many infectious diseases are preventable through basic hygiene; to make the message fun and engaging, especially for children; and to accomplish all this on a shoestring budget that would increase sales for Safeguard.

That sounds like a job for a superhero—someone on the order of Voltron, Captain Planet, or Spiderman, three popular cartoon characters in Pakistan. Inspired by these characters, the marketers of Safeguard launched one of their own: Commander Safeguard. Of course, for every superhero, there has to be a villain. Commander Safeguard's first foe would be Dirtoo, the germ king, whose evil mission was to stalk children at every turn to spoil their health.

Commander Safeguard was introduced to children via a 15-minute cartoon program code-named "Clean Sweep." This programming was delivered as part of

What do you think?

Brands can offer value even in nations with low incomes.

| 1 | 2 | 3 | 4 | 5 | 6 | 7 |
STRONGLY DISAGREE   STRONGLY AGREE

Find out what others think at CourseMate for PROMO.

a school edutainment program for kids. The aim from the beginning was to fuse entertainment with education to make the program high impact. Commander Safeguard storybooks also were provided for the kids to take home and share with their parents. This engaged both kids and parents around an idea that was fun and lifesaving.

Following an initial favorable response, Safeguard prepared a series of Commander Safeguard adventures for national TV and radio. New villains were invented, representing different infectious diseases, and Commander Safeguard defeated them all. Appealing to the local culture, these messages used Pakistani celebrities in the voiceovers for each episode. Plots included details that Pakistani kids could relate to; for instance, Dirtoo tried to spoil kids' enjoyment of a cricket match by making them all sick. This attention to details gave Commander Safeguard a unique status in Pakistan. He wasn't a borrowed superhero from some other country or culture; he was Pakistan's own superhero.

Safeguard also developed its brand relationship online and in schools. An art gallery hosted at http://www.commandersafeguard.com invited children to post drawings and poems created in school-sponsored Health Day contests to celebrate both good hygiene and Pakistan's first superhero. This popular program benefits from the ongoing support of the Safeguard brand, as well as the Pakistan Medical Association and the Infectious Diseases Society of Pakistan.

This integrated marketing communication (IMC) program helped Safeguard double its sales over the next two years and made Pakistan the fastest-growing Safeguard market in the world. Germ protection became the most important attribute influencing choice of a bar soap. Safeguard became the brand recommended by doctors and the brand associated with a movement to improve the health and hygiene of Pakistan. Eventually, the company began to export this promotion model to other countries, including China and the Philippines, where good hygiene and superheroes also were in short supply.

LO 1 Communicating across Cultures

The remarkable success of Safeguard's IMC effort in Pakistan has many intriguing elements. Some of these elements (superheroes) are familiar in U.S. culture; others (cricket matches) are less familiar. The unanticipated or underappreciated elements of a culture can trip up even the best marketers when they prepare to meet the needs of people in another culture or region. Just as Toyota goofed when it launched its Land Cruiser in China, even the most savvy companies must overcome hurdles as they take their products and brands to new markets.

International brand promotion is brand promotion that reaches across national and cultural boundaries. As with all the promotional efforts you've learned about thus far, it can take many forms, from Internet ads to superhero spokespersons to signage on the sides of buses. In the past, a great deal of international brand promotion was nothing more than translations of domestic advertising. Often these simple translations were ineffective, and sometimes they were even offensive. The day has passed—if there ever was such a day—when marketers based in industrialized nations can simply "do a foreign translation" of their ads. Today, international marketers have learned they must pay greater attention to local cultures. One reason the Safeguard campaign succeeded in Pakistan was that the managers who created it were in that country and totally immersed in the local culture.

As we said in Chapter 5, culture is a set of values, rituals, and behaviors that define a way of life. Culture is typically invisible to those who are immersed in it. Communicating *across* cultures is one of the most difficult of all communication tasks, largely because there is no such thing as culture-free communication. Brand communication is a cultural product; it means nothing outside of culture. Culture surrounds brand communication, informs it, and

© Shane White/Shutterstock.

GLOBAL STUMBLING INTO CHINA

With more than one billion people and a fast-growing economy, China is a key business opportunity. It also presents enormous challenges for marketers, including the use of seven major languages (with 80 spoken dialects) and vast differences in climate, income, and lifestyle. Toyota's launch of the Prado Land Cruiser in China illustrates the challenges. A print campaign showed a Prado driving past two large stone lions, which were bowing to the Prado, signifying the respect this vehicle should command. Chinese consumers saw it differently. The name Prado can be translated into Chinese as *badao*, meaning "rule by force" or "overbearing"; the bowing stone lions called to mind Japan's 1937 invasion of China. Toyota pulled the ads and issued an apology.

Sources: Geoffrey Fowler, "China's Cultural Fabric Is a Challenge to Marketers," *Wall Street Journal*, January 21, 2004, B7; Sameena Ahmad, "A Billion Three, but Not for Me," *The Economist*, March 20, 2004, 5, 6; Norihiko Shirouzu, "In Chinese Market, Toyota's Strategy Is Made in USA," *Wall Street Journal*, May 26, 2006, A1, A8; Laurel Wentz, "China's Ad World: A New Crisis Every Day," *Advertising Age*, December 11, 2006, 6; and Dexter Roberts, "Cautious Consumers," *BusinessWeek*, April 30, 2007, 32–34.

gives it meaning. To transport a marketing message across cultural borders, one must respect and understand the influence of culture.

For any kind of message, effective communication depends on shared meaning. The degree of shared meaning is significantly affected by cultural membership. When a marketer in culture A wants to communicate with consumers in culture B, culture B will surround the created message, form its cultural context, and significantly affect how it will be interpreted.

Nevertheless, some products and brands belong to a global consumer culture more than to any one national culture. Such brands travel well, as do their promotional messages, because there already is common cultural ground on which to build effective

Courtesy, LG Electronics, Inc.

Electronics is a product category that lends itself to global brands. For consumers who have the disposable income to afford these products, performance is performance, whether you watch, listen, or play in Montreal, Madrid, or Mexico City. If you're in the market for a plasma TV with a seven-foot screen and high-definition DVR, LG wants you to know it has the product for you, as it does for consumers in Asia, Europe, Latin America, and the rest of the world.

advertising. LG Electronics, headquartered in Seoul, South Korea, markets its products in dozens of countries around the world. Consumers who can afford high-performance electronics value the same performance measures everywhere. But brands like LG are more the exceptions than the rule, and, as "global" as they may be, they still are affected by local culture as to their use and, ultimately, their meaning.

Spotting Cultural Barriers

It's not hard to identify the companies that are making a major commitment to international brand promotion. Just follow the money. In a recent year, *Advertising Age* reported that Procter & Gamble spent more than $1 billion to advertise in China and $300 million in Germany.[2] Other companies with big international budgets include firms as diverse as Volkswagen and L'Oréal. In fact, most companies today consider their markets to extend beyond national boundaries and across cultures. Hence, marketers must come to terms with how they will overcome cultural barriers in trying to communicate with consumers around the world.

Cross-Cultural Blind Spots

Adopting an international perspective often is difficult for marketers. The experience gained over a career and a lifetime creates a cultural "comfort zone." One's own cultural values, experiences, and knowledge serve as a subconscious guide for decision making and behavior.

To succeed in international markets, marketers must overcome two related biases:

1. **Ethnocentrism** is the tendency to view and value things from the perspective of one's own culture.

2. A **self-reference criterion (SRC)** is the unconscious reference to one's own cultural values, experiences, and knowledge as a basis for decisions.

These two closely related biases are primary obstacles to success when conducting marketing and advertising planning that demand a cross-cultural perspective.

A decision maker's SRC and ethnocentrism can inhibit his or her ability to sense important cultural distinctions between markets. This, in turn, can blind advertisers to their own culture's "fingerprints" on the ads they've created. Sometimes these are offensive; at a minimum, they signal "outsider" influence.

Outsiders are sometimes welcome, but they may appear ignorant.

Consider humor, for example. Sense of humor is culturally bounded. For instance, while HBO's relationships-based *Sex in the City* TV show was popular in Germany, the ironic humor of *Seinfeld* was lost on Germans.[3] Marketers often use humor to engage their audiences, so differences in sense of humor can become a huge issue when trying to roll out promotional campaigns across cultures.

Apple ran into "humor problems" with its quirky campaign "Mac vs. PC," in which the character representing a nerdy PC keeps getting embarrassed by a hip Mac. Created in the United States, with droll *Daily Show* commentator John Hodgman personifying the bumbling PC and comic actor Justin Long as the Mac, the campaign had just the right amount of dry humor to tickle American funny bones. But in Japan, direct-comparison ads are viewed as rude and showing a lack of class, so the ads had to be completely revamped. Even in the United Kingdom, where Apple tried to re-create the exchanges using British comedians, the humor seemed to get lost along the way. A local polling firm found that Apple's reputation suffered after the ads started showing in British cinemas and on the Web.[4]

To counteract the confounding influence that ethnocentrism and SRC have on international brand communications, decision makers must be constantly sensitive to their existence and recognize that important differences among cultures are almost certain. Even with cross-cultural research, problems are likely. Without research, problems are inevitable.

Cross-Cultural Audience Research

Analyzing audiences in international markets can be a humbling task. For firms with worldwide product distribution networks, like Nestlé and Unilever, international audience research will require dozens of separate analyses. There really is no way to avoid the task of specific audience analysis. This typically involves research in each country, generally from a local research supplier.

In addition, good secondary resources provide broad-based information about international markets:

- The International Trade Administration (ITA), a division of the U.S. Department of Commerce, helps companies based in the United States develop foreign market opportunities for their products and services. The ITA publishes specialized reports that provide economic and regulatory information about most of the major markets in the world (see http://www.ita.doc.gov).

- The United Nations' *Statistical Yearbook* (http://unstats.un.org/unsd), updated annually, provides general economic and population data for more than 200 countries.

An international audience analysis also will involve evaluation of economic conditions, demographic characteristics, values, customs and rituals, and product use and preferences.

Economic Conditions

From nation to nation, consumers' access to resources varies enormously. As shown by the examples in Exhibit 7.1, gross domestic product (GDP) per capita varies widely. Another way to think about the economic conditions of a potential international audience is to break the world's markets into three broad classes of economic development:

1. **Less-developed countries** represent nearly 75 percent of the world's population. Some of these countries are plagued by drought and civil war, and their economies lack almost all the resources necessary for development: capital, infrastructure, political stability, and trained workers. Many of the products sold in these economies are business products used for building infrastructure (such as heavy construction equipment) or agricultural equipment.

less-developed countries countries whose economies lack most resources necessary for development: capital, infrastructure, political stability, and trained workers

DECISION MAKERS **MUST . . . RECOGNIZE** THAT IMPORTANT DIFFERENCES AMONG CULTURES ARE ALMOST CERTAIN.

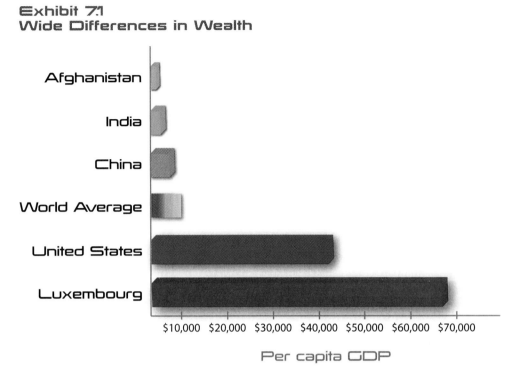

Exhibit 7.1
Wide Differences in Wealth

Afghanistan
India
China
World Average
United States
Luxembourg

$10,000 $20,000 $30,000 $40,000 $50,000 $60,000 $70,000

Per capita GDP

Source: Central Intelligence Agency, *The World Factbook*, https://www.cia.gov/library/publications/the-world-factbook, accessed January 27, 2010.

newly industrialized countries countries where traditional ways of life are changing into modern consumer cultures

highly industrialized countries countries with a high GDP and a high standard of living

2. **Newly industrialized countries** have economies defined by change: traditional ways of life that endured for centuries are changing, and modern consumer cultures are emerging. This change creates problems for the outside marketer trying to hit a moving target. But many marketers see low-income consumers as an opportunity deserving more attention, partly because some of these countries—Brazil, India, and China—include billions of consumers. When Nestlé Brazil appealed to low-income consumers by shrinking the package size for Bono cookies from 200 to 140 grams and lowering its price, sales jumped 40 percent.[5] But communicating with low-income consumers is an ongoing challenge for the big, multinational firms, in part because their employees and those of their ad agencies are well educated and highly affluent. Understanding the wants and needs of a person in different economic circumstances is difficult.

3. The **highly industrialized countries** of the world have mature economies and high levels of affluence, as indicated by data such as GDP per capita. These countries also have invested heavily over many years in infrastructure—roads, hospitals, airports, power-generating plants, educational institutions, and the Internet. Within this broad grouping, an audience assessment will focus on more-detailed analyses of the market, including the nature and extent of competition, marketing trade channels, lifestyle trends, and market potential. This is the usual method of market analysis in the United States. Brand promotion in these countries often varies based on unique cultural and lifestyle factors, and consumers are accustomed to seeing a full range of creative appeals for goods and services.

These categories provide a basic understanding of the economic capability of the average consumer in a market and thus help place consumption in the context of economic realities.

Demographic Characteristics

Advertisers must be sensitive to demographic similarities and differences in international markets, along with key trends. Demographics, including size of population, age distribution, income distribution, education levels, occupations, literacy rates, and household size, can dramatically affect the promotional mix prepared for a market. Also, marketing expenditures flow to where the purchasing power resides. Big marketers generally place a higher priority on wealthy nations with their high levels of purchasing power per household, but the sheer number of households in countries like India and China is changing the dynamics of marketing spending.

The world's wealthy nations are, for the most part, getting older,[6] and this also creates the potential for wealth redistribution around the world.[7] It could work this way: While the United States, Japan, and Western

Europe will struggle in the future with pension plan shortfalls and rising health care costs, countries like Brazil and Mexico have an opportunity to surge ahead economically because of something referred to as the **demographic dividend**. In these developing nations, falling labor costs, a younger and healthier population, and the entry of millions of women into the workforce produce a favorable climate for economic expansion. The experts say these developing nations have about a 30-year window to capitalize on their demographic dividend. Better education for more of their populations will be an essential element in realizing this dividend.

Increases and decreases in the proportion of the population in specific age groups also are closely related to the demand for particular products and services. As populations continue to increase in developing countries, new market opportunities emerge for products and services for teens and young families. Similarly, as advanced-age groups continue to increase in countries with stable population rates, the demand for consumer services such as health care, travel, and retirement planning will increase. Thus, knowing the age segment you want to target is critical for developing effective international marketing.

Information on nations' demographic characteristics is generally available. Both the U.S. Department of Commerce and the United Nations publish annual studies of population for hundreds of countries.

demographic dividend favorable climate for economic expansion in developing nations as a result of falling labor costs, a younger and healthier population, and entry of women into the workforce

Values

Cultural values are enduring beliefs about what is important to the members of a culture. They are the defining bedrock of a culture and an outgrowth of the culture's history and collective experience. (Even though there are many cultures within any given nation, many believe that there still are enough shared values to constitute a meaningful national culture, such as "American culture.") For example, the value of individualism enjoys a long and prominent place in American history and is considered by many to be a core American value. Other cultures seem to value the group or collective more. Even though a "collectivist" country like Japan may be becoming more individualistic, there still is a Japanese tradition that favors the needs of the group over those of the individual. In Japan, organizational loyalty and social interdependence are values that promote a group mentality. Japanese consumers thus are thought to be more sensitive to appeals that feature stability, longevity, and reliability, and they find appeals using competitive comparisons to be rude and inappropriate.[8] Some researchers believe this continuum from individualism to collectivism to be a stable and dependably observed difference among the people of the world, or at least stable enough to serve as a basis for crafting different ads for different cultures.[9]

Customs and Rituals

Among other things, rituals perpetuate a culture's connections to its core values. They seem perfectly natural to members of a culture, and they often can be performed without much thought (in some cases, none at all) regarding their deeper meaning. Rituals are involved in many consumer behaviors, such as grooming, gift giving, or food preparation. Effective cross-cultural advertising not only appreciates the rituals of other cultures but also understands them. This requires in-depth and extended research efforts, explaining the growing popularity of ethnographic studies.[10] Quick marketing surveys rarely do anything in this context except invite disaster.

Heineken's distinctive red star is a logo known around the world. Here Heineken challenges partygoers in France to choose the bottle opener over the corkscrew for their next celebration.

Something as simple as preparing a meal can entail different rituals from one culture to another. In many European countries, a common morning ritual is to create a homemade batch of cereal from natural grains and fresh fruit. In this ad from Switzerland's Mövenpick, the marketer is attempting to align the convenient packaging of its new product with the homemade tradition. The headline reads, "At the end, you'll even think that you made it yourself."

Religion is an obvious expression of values in a culture. In countries adhering to the precepts of the Islamic religion (including most Arab nations), traditional religious beliefs restrict several products, such as alcohol and pork, from being advertised at all. These countries also may forbid advertisements from showing women and may restrict the manner in which children can be portrayed in advertisements. Each market must be evaluated for the extent to which prevalent customs or values translate into product choice and other consumer behaviors.

One of the most devastating mistakes an advertiser can make is to presume that consumers in one culture have the same rituals as those in another. But understanding values and rituals can represent a special challenge (or opportunity) when economic development in a country or region creates tensions between the old and the new. The classic example is marketing in communities where more wives are leaving the home for outside employment, creating tensions in the home about who should do the housework. This tension over traditional gender assignments in household chores has been particularly acute in Asia, and marketers have tried to respond by featuring husbands as homemakers. For example, an ad for vacuum cleaners made by LG Electronics showed a woman lying on the floor exercising and giving herself a facial with slices of cucumbers, while her husband cleaned around her. The ad received mixed reviews from women in Hong Kong and South Korea: Younger women approved, but their mothers disapproved.[11] The marketer's dilemma in situations like these is how to make ads that reflect real changes in a culture without alienating important segments of consumers by appearing to push the changes.

Product Use and Preferences

Information about product use and preferences is available for many markets. The major markets of North America, Europe, and the Pacific Rim typically are relatively heavily researched. In recent years, A. C. Nielsen has developed an international database on consumer product use in 26 countries. Also, Roper Starch Worldwide has conducted "global" studies on product preferences, brand loyalty, and price sensitivity in 40 countries.

Studies by firms such as Nielsen and Roper document how consumers around the world display different product use characteristics and preferences. One area of great variation is personal-care products. There is no market in the world like the United States, where consumers are preoccupied with the use of personal-care products such as toothpaste, shampoo, deodorant, and mouthwash. Procter & Gamble, maker of brands such as Crest, Head & Shoulders, Secret, and Scope, among others, learned the hard way in Russia with its Wash & Go shampoo. Wash & Go was a shampoo and conditioner designed for the consumer who prefers the ease, convenience, and speed of one-step washing and conditioning. Russian consumers, accustomed to washing their hair with bar soap, didn't understand the concept of a hair

conditioner and didn't perceive a need to make shampooing any more convenient.

Other examples of unique and culture-specific product uses and preferences come from Brazil and France. In Brazil, many women still wash clothes by hand in metal tubs, using cold water. Because of this behavior, Unilever must specially formulate its Umo laundry powder and tout its effectiveness under these washing conditions. In France, men commonly use cosmetics like those used by women in the United States. Advertising, therefore, must be specifically prepared for men and placed in media to reach them with specific male-oriented appeals.

Such tales remind us that communicating with consumers around the world is a challenge, only in terms of the obvious issue of language.

picturing creating representations of things

Less obvious is the role of **picturing** in cross-cultural communication. There is a widely held belief that pictures are less culturally bound than words are and that pictures can speak to many cultures at once. International marketers are increasingly using ads that feature few words and rely on visuals to communicate. This is, as you might expect, a bit more complicated than it sounds. A few human expressions, such as a smile, are widely accepted to mean a

LO 2 Challenges of International Brand Promotion

Cross-cultural audience research on basic economic, social, and cultural conditions is an essential starting point for planning international promotion. But even with excellent audience analysis, marketers face formidable and unique challenges.

Creative Challenge

Written or spoken language is a basic barrier to cross-cultural communication. Ads written in Japanese are typically difficult for those who speak only Spanish—this much is obvious. But language issues always will be a formidable challenge. We've all heard stories of how some literal translation of an ad said something very different from what was intended. International blunders are a rich part of advertising lore:[12]

- The name *Coca-Cola* in China was first rendered as "Ke-kou-ke-la." Unfortunately, Coke did not discover until after thousands of signs had been printed that the phrase means "bite the wax tadpole" or "female horse stuffed with wax," depending on the dialect. Coke then researched 40,000 Chinese characters and found a close phonetic equivalent, "ko-kou-ko-le," which can be loosely translated as "happiness in the mouth."

- Scandinavian vacuum manufacturer Electrolux used the following in an American ad campaign: "Nothing sucks like an Electrolux."

Courtesy, Sears Roebuck Company.

¿Cuál será el afortunado?
☑ Vestidos formales para el "PROM"
☑ Zapatos y accesorios de fiesta
☑ ¿Pedro, Juan o Luis?

Sears combina una gran variedad de estilos y accesorios para el "PROM" en un solo lugar. Ojalá elegir tu pareja fuese tan fácil.
SEARS Todo para ti

In this ad, Sears tells girls that its stores have everything they need to be shining stars at their high school prom. The ad ran in Spanish-speaking countries throughout South America, but the high school prom is a more common ritual in North America. Can a teen in Santiago spark to the offer of a formal prom dress when she has no cultural context for interpreting the meaning of "prom"? Not likely.

positive feeling. Such expressions and their representations, even though culturally connected, have widespread commonality. But cultureless picture meanings are rare.

As a general rule, picturing *is* culturally bound. Photographic two-dimensional representations are not even recognizable as pictures to those who have not learned to interpret such representations. Even in cultures that use such images, different cultures use different conventions or rules to create representations (or pictures). Like words, pictures must be "read" or interpreted, and the "rules" for doing this vary from culture to culture. Assuming that everyone knows what a certain picture means is an example of ethnocentrism. Symbolic representations that seem absolute, common, and harmless in one culture can have varied, unusual, and even threatening meaning in another.

Cross-cultural commonalities are more likely in representations that are part of a far-flung culture of commerce and thus have taken on similar meanings in many (but certainly not all) nations. With sports playing an ever-larger role in international commerce, the sports hero often is used to symbolize common meaning across the world. What do you think? In what markets would Serena Williams be an effective spokesperson? Similarly, other types of celebrities add their star power in marketing campaigns around the world. But few will have common, desirable meaning across all cultures.

Media Challenge

Of all the challenges faced by marketers in international markets, the greatest may be the media challenge. Assumptions about media availability are likely to be faulty in other cultures.

Media Availability and Coverage

Some international markets simply have too few media options. Even in markets where diverse media are available, governments may place severe restrictions on the type of advertising that can be done or the way in which advertising is organized in a certain medium.

The presence of a particular medium in a country does not necessarily make it useful for advertisers if there are restrictions on accepting advertising. A prominent example is the BBC networks in the United Kingdom, where advertising still is not accepted. While the United Kingdom does have commercial networks in both radio and television, the BBC stations are widely popular. Or consider television advertising in the Netherlands. There, television advertising cannot constitute more than 5 percent of total programming time, and most time slots must be purchased nearly a year in advance. Similar circumstances exist in many markets around the world.

Many countries have dozens of subcultures and language dialects within their borders, each with its own newspapers and radio stations. This complicates the problem of deciding which combination of newspapers or radio stations will achieve the desired coverage of the market. Newspapers actually are the most localized medium worldwide, and they require the greatest amount of local market knowledge to be used correctly as an advertising option. Turkey, for example, has hundreds of daily newspapers; the Netherlands has only a handful. Further, many newspapers (particularly regional papers) are positioned in the market based on a particular political philosophy. Advertisers must be aware of this, making certain that their brand's position with the target audience does not conflict with the politics of the medium.

The best news for marketers from the standpoint of media availability and coverage is the emergence of several global television networks made possible by cable and satellite technology. Viacom bills its combined MTV Networks (MTVN) as the largest TV network in the world, with a capability to reach more than 300 million households worldwide. MTVN also offers expertise in developing special promotions to

OF ALL THE CHALLENGES FACED BY MARKETERS IN INTERNATIONAL MARKETS, THE GREATEST MAY BE THE MEDIA CHALLENGE.

Generations X, Y, and Z around the world. MTVN has facilitated international campaigns for global brands such as Pepsi and Swatch. Additionally, MTV has proven expertise in producing programs for specific country markets, including *Mochilao*, a backpack travel show hosted by a popular Brazilian model, as well as programming designed to appeal to its key demographic across cultures.[13] If there is such a thing as "global consumers," MTVN offers an efficient means for reaching them.

Another development affecting Europe and Asia is direct broadcast by satellite (DBS), via systems like SkyPort. DBS transmissions are received through the small, low-cost receiving dishes that have become a familiar sight on rooftops around the world. STAR, which stands for Satellite Televisions Asian Region, sends BBC, U.S., Bollywood, and local programming to 300 million households in 53 countries across Asia.[14] With literally billions of people in its viewing area, STAR has the potential to become one of the world's most influential broadcasting systems.

Media Costs and Pricing

Confounding the media challenge is the issue of media costs and pricing. As discussed with regard to media availability, some markets have literally hundreds of media options. Whenever the marketer chooses a different medium, separate payment and placement must be made. Additionally, in many markets, media prices are subject to negotiation, no matter what the official rate cards say. The time needed to negotiate these rates is a tremendous cost in and of itself.

Global coverage is an expensive proposition, and both ad rates and the demand for ad space are rising. In some markets, advertising time and space are in such short supply that, regardless of the published rate, a bidding system is used to escalate the prices. Media costs represent the majority of costs in an advertising budget. With the seemingly chaotic buying practices in some international markets, media costs indeed are a great challenge in executing cost-effective marketing campaigns.

Regulatory Challenge

The regulatory restrictions on international advertising are many and varied, reflecting diverse cultural values, market by market. The range and specificity of regulation can be aggravatingly complex. Tobacco and liquor advertising are restricted (typically banned from television) in many countries,

Courtesy, SkyPort T.V. of Japan.

Direct broadcast by satellite allows households to receive television transmission via a small, low-cost receiving dish. This is an ad for Skyport TV, one of the early DBS services to serve Japan.

including India, where the beer market has been slow to develop in part because there is no beer advertising.[15] With respect to advertising to children, Austria, Canada, Germany, and the United States have specific regulations. Other products and topics monitored or restricted throughout the world are drugs (Austria, Switzerland, Germany, Greece, and the Netherlands), gambling (United Kingdom, Italy, and Portugal), and religion (Germany, United Kingdom, and the Netherlands).

This regulatory complexity continues to grow. For instance, the European Union, the world's largest trading bloc, has strict regulations protecting citizens' privacy, which limit marketers' access to kinds of data readily available in North America. To cope with these regulations, many global companies have dozens of employees in Europe whose job is to keep their companies in compliance with various regulations.[16]

© Monkey Business Images/Shutterstock.

ETHICS ENDING OBESITY BY LIMITING ADS

As in the United States, debate is raging across Europe about who is to blame for increases in childhood obesity and, more importantly, how to reverse the trend. In 2007, U.K. regulator Ofcam announced a sweeping ban on TV ads for foods high in fat, salt, and sugar that are targeted to children under age 16. Britain's health minister, Caroline Flint, announced that the ban would apply to all print, poster, online, and cinema ads. Ofcam developed a nutrient-profiling system to decide which foods are subject to the restrictions. Ads for low-fat cheese, butter, and dark chocolate, among other things, were banned.

Sources: Emma Hall, "Brit Ban on Junk-Food Ads to Cost TV Titans $75 Mil," *Advertising Age*, November 27, 2006, 18; and Emma Hall, "In Europe, the Clash over Junk-Food Ads Heats Up," *Advertising Age*, March 5, 2007, 32.

Generally, marketers must be sensitive to the fact that advertising regulations, depending on the international market, can impose limitations in the following areas:

- Types of products that can be advertised
- Kinds of data that can be collected from consumers
- Types of message appeals that can be used
- Times during which ads for certain products can appear on television
- Advertisements that target children
- Use of foreign languages (and talent) in advertisements
- Use of national symbols, such as flags and government seals, in advertisements
- Taxes levied against advertising expenditures

In short, just about every aspect of advertising can be regulated, and every country has some peculiarities with respect to ad regulation.

LO 3 Ad Agencies for International Marketing

An experienced and astute advertising agency can help a marketer deal with the creative, media, and regulatory challenges of international promotion. In Brazil, using a local agency is essential to getting the creative style and tone just right. In Australia, Australian nationals must be involved in certain parts of the production process. And in China, trying to work through the government and media bureaucracy is nearly impossible without the assistance of a local agency. There are nearly 80,000 to choose from in China.[17]

Marketers looking for an agency to help them prepare and place advertising in other countries have the three basic alternatives shown in Exhibit 7.2. They can use a global agency, an international affiliate, or a local agency.

Global Agencies

The consolidation and mergers taking place in the advertising industry are creating more and more **global agencies**, or worldwide advertising groups.

Among the giants are Omnicom Group, WPP Group, Interpublic Group of Companies, Publicis Groupe, and Dentsu. These multibillion-dollar businesses have assembled a network of diverse service providers to deliver integrated marketing communication for clients who demand global reach.

When a marketer uses a global agency for its domestic and international brand promotion, the great advantage of this type of organization is that the global agency will know the marketer's products and current advertising programs before it plans campaigns for other countries. With this knowledge, the agency either can adapt domestic campaigns for international markets or launch entirely new campaigns. Another advantage is that the marketer may select a global agency whose headquarters is nearby or at least in the same country, which can often facilitate planning and preparation of ads. The size of a global agency can be a benefit in terms of economies of scale and political leverage.

Global agencies' greatest disadvantage stems from their distance from the local culture(s). Exporting meaning is never easy. However, most advertising experts recognize this and have procedures for acquiring local knowledge.

global agencies
advertising agencies with a worldwide presence

**Exhibit 7.2
Take Your Pick**

International Affiliates

Many agencies do not own and operate worldwide offices but rather have established foreign-market **international affiliates** to handle clients' international advertising needs. Many times, these agencies join a network of foreign agencies or take minority ownership positions in several foreign agencies. The benefit of this arrangement is that the marketer typically has access to a large number of international agencies that can provide local market expertise. These international agencies usually are well established and managed by foreign nationals, giving the marketer a local presence in its international markets while avoiding any resistance to foreign ownership.

The risk of these arrangements is that, while an international affiliate will know the local market, it may be less knowledgeable about the marketer's brands and competitive strategy. The threat is that the real value and relevance of the brand will not be incorporated into the foreign campaign.

Local Agencies

The final option is for an advertiser to choose a **local agency** in every foreign market where brand promotion will be carried out. Local agencies have the same advantages as the affiliate agencies just discussed: They will be knowledgeable about the culture and local market conditions. Such agencies tend to have well-established contacts for market information, production, and media buys.

On the downside, a marketer that chooses this option is open to administrative problems. There is less opportunity for standardization of the creative effort; each agency in each market will feel compelled to provide a unique creative execution. This lack of standardization can be expensive and potentially disastrous for brand imagery when the local agency seeks to make its own creative statement without a good working knowledge of a brand's heritage. Finally,

working with local agencies can create internal communication problems, which increases the risk of delays and errors in execution.

LO 4 Globalized versus Localized Campaigns

Planning for brand promotion in international markets also involves the extent to which a campaign will be standardized across markets versus localized for each market. In discussions of this issue, the question often is posed in terms of two options:

1. **Globalized campaigns** use the same message and creative execution across all (or most) international markets. The "Got Milk?" campaign promoting milk consumption looks essentially the same in the United States and in the Spanish-speaking countries of South America. Only the language and choice of models are adjusted for the different locations.

2. **Localized campaigns** involve preparing specific messages and/or creative executions for a particular market.

To decide the degree to which a campaign should be globalized, the marketer must examine both the brand and its overall marketing strategy. The marketer first must consider the extent to which the brand can be standardized across markets and then the extent to which the promotional campaign can be globalized across markets.

The degree to which advertising in international markets can use a common appeal has been a widely debated issue.[18] Those who favor the globalized campaign assume that similarities as well as differences between markets can be taken into account. They argue that standardization of messages should occur whenever possible, adapting the message only when absolutely necessary. For example, Mars's U.S. advertisements for Pedigree dog food have used golden retrievers, while poodles were deemed more effective for the brand's positioning and image in Asia. Otherwise, the advertising campaigns were identical in terms of basic message appeal. Those

© Yuriy Chaban/Shutterstock.

who argue for the localized approach see each country or region as a unique communication context and claim that the only way to achieve advertising success is to develop separate campaigns for each market.

The two most fundamental arguments for globalized campaigns are based on potential cost savings and creative advantages. Just as organizations seek to gain economies of scale in production, they also look for opportunities to streamline the communication process. Having one standard theme to communicate allows an advertiser to focus on a uniform brand or corporate image worldwide, develop plans more quickly, and make maximum use of good ideas. Thus, while Gillette sells hundreds of different products in more than 200 countries around the world, its corporate philosophy of globalization is expressed in its tagline, "Gillette—The Best a Man Can Get," which has been repeated again and again all over the world.

Several trends in the global marketplace are working in combination to create conditions that are supportive of globalized campaigns because they facilitate the creation of a global consumer:

- **Global communications.** Thanks to worldwide cable and satellite networks, television is becoming a truly global communications medium. Almost all of MTVN's 200 European advertisers run English-language-only campaigns in the station's 28-nation broadcast area. These standardized messages themselves homogenize the viewers within these market areas. Similarly, common experience and exposure on the Internet reinforces shared values around the world, especially among young people.

- **Global youth.** Young people around the world have a lot in common. Global communications, global travel, and the demise of communism are argued to have created common norms and values among teenagers around the world.[19] And it's not just teenagers. Toymakers like Mattel, Hasbro, and Lego once worked under the assumption that children around the world would value toys that carried some local flavor. No more. The large toymakers now

You don't need to speak Czech to appreciate the intent of this ad. As with any Nokio product, it's all about "connecting people" (especially young people).

Nokia Mobile Phones, Prague, Czech Republic.

create and launch standardized products for children worldwide.[20]

- **Common demographic and lifestyle trends.** Demographic and related lifestyle trends that emerged in the 1980s in the United States are manifesting themselves in other countries. More working women, more single-person households, increasing divorce rates, and fewer children per household are widespread demographic phenomena that are affecting common lifestyles worldwide, with marketers sure to follow. For instance, the rising number of working women in Japan caused Ford Motor Company to prepare ads specifically targeted to this audience.

- **The Americanization of consumption values.** Another advantage for U.S. advertisers has been the Americanization of consumption values around the world. American icons have gained popularity worldwide, especially due to the exportation of pop culture fueled by the U.S. entertainment industry. Adulation of Hollywood, high fashion, and celebrities transcends the United States. However, some countries have seen a backlash against American brands in reaction to some high-profile events such as failure to ratify the Kyoto treaty on greenhouse gas emissions, as well as the wars in Afghanistan and Iraq.

Arguments against globalization tend to center on issues relating to local market requirements and cultural constraints within markets. For a globalized campaign to be effective, the target audiences in different countries must understand and place the same level of importance on brand features or attributes. In practice, however, people in different markets value different features at different levels of intensity, making a common message inappropriate. Also, if a globalized campaign defies local customs, values, and regulations, or if it ignores the efforts of local competition, then it is unlikely to succeed.

Furthermore, local managers do not always appreciate the value of globalized campaigns. Because they did not help create the campaign, they may drag their feet in implementing it. Without the support of local managers, no globalized campaign can ever achieve its potential.

Developing global brands through standardized campaigns can succeed only when advertisers can find similar needs, feelings, or emotions as a basis for communication across cultures. Take McDonald's as a case in point. The fast-food chain has roughly 30,000 restaurants in more than 100 countries. To accommodate local interests, the company uses Olympic champions as spokespersons in China and excludes beef products from its menu in India. But everywhere it operates, McDonald's stands for being family friendly. That premise resonates from Moscow to Memphis, making McDonald's a legitimate global brand.[21]

Finally, when using a global approach to brand promotion, marketers need to distinguish between strategy and execution. The basic need identified may well be universal, but communication about the product or service that offers satisfaction of the need may be strongly influenced by cultural values in different markets, which may work against globalization.

STUDY TOOLS **CHAPTER 7**

Located at back of the textbook

- **Rip out Chapter in Review Card.**

Located at www.cengagebrain.com

- **Review Key Terms Flashcards (Print or Online).**
- **Complete the Practice Quiz to prepare for tests.**
- **Play "Beat the Clock" and "Quizbowl" to master concepts.**
- **Complete "Crossword Puzzle" to review key terms.**
- **Watch videos on Coca-Cola and Eastpack for real company examples.**
- **Additional examples can be found online including: perfume as a global product category, the importance of exploring how your ad will translate in a different language, and the Williams sisters try to revive the Avon brand.**

CHAPTER 8

Messaging and Media Strategies

You're creative if you can make "creepy" an asset.

By defining their target segment, CP+B unleashed a series of offbeat characters to engage these consumers.

HAVE IT YOUR WAY®

Use the sliders to have BK.com just the way you want it.

Fun   Food   King

WHOPPER® BAR
SOUTH BEACH
NOW OPEN

WHOPPER® Bar South Beach

WHOPPER® Bar

BK™ Flame · TV & Video · BK® Breakfast Value Menu · Cheeseburger · Funnel Cake Sticks

Made By You · Subservient Chicken · Original Chicken... · Steakhouse XT™ Burger · A.1.® Steakhouse XT™ Burger

WHOPPER® Freakout · WHOPPER® Virgins · Cavalcade of Comedy · Simpsonize Me · WHOPPER® · Buck Double · $1¹ WHOPPER JR.®

FUTBOL KINGDOMS M · Late Night · BK® Chicken Fries · BK® Kids · Company Info · Menu & Nutrition · Restaurant Locator

You're creative if you get customers to pay to play with your brand.

Photo Courtesy, Susan Van Etten.

Learning Outcomes

After studying this chapter, you should be able to:

LO 1   Describe characteristics of great creative minds.

LO 2   Contrast the roles of an agency's creative department and its business managers/account executives.

LO 3   Discuss how teams manage tensions and promote creativity in integrated marketing communication.

LO 4   Evaluate your own passion for creativity.

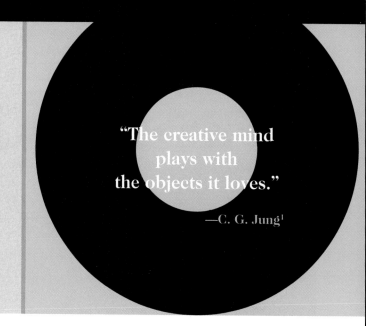

"The creative mind
plays with
the objects it loves."

—C. G. Jung[1]

AFTER YOU
FINISH THIS
CHAPTER
GO TO
PAGE 173
FOR STUDY
TOOLS

Creativity Begets a Creepy King

A few years ago, Crispin Porter + Bogusky (CP+B) was the hot little underdog agency working on low-budget but high-buzz campaigns for clients like Mini and IKEA. The business press had fallen in love with CP+B as the so-called prototype of ad agency fused with PR firm.[2] The agency's chief creative force, Alex Bogusky, was seen as the ad industry guru who had figured out how to thrive in a world where 30-second TV ads appeared on everybody's death watch.[3]

In contrast to CP+B, Burger King was in pretty rough shape. Customer traffic was steadily declining, and the product line was in need of some serious excitement. As promotion efforts failed to bring improvement, Burger King hired and fired four ad agencies in the course of four years. Many ad agencies would want to avoid being the unhappy fifth agency—but not feisty CP+B. When it took on the Burger King account, skeptics predicted doom and gloom, especially because CP+B had yet to prove itself with a major mass-market client. Some predicted that CP+B's culture of creativity would be stifled by a client that expected to communicate with customers through 30-second TV spots.[4]

But right from the start, CP+B showed its dexterity with creativity that befuddled the skeptics and maxed out the buzz factor. Success was grounded in an unequivocal focus on the one target segment that everyone agreed Burger King had to win: 18- to 35-year-old males, who are among the heaviest users of fast foods of all kinds. With the target defined, CP+B unleashed a series of offbeat characters to engage these consumers. First came "Subservient Chicken" a viral, online campaign hyping the new TenderCrisp chicken sandwich. Next up was "Blingo," an over-the-top rapper who mocked diet-crazed consumers and pushed the Angus steak burger as the antidote to politically correct fast food. And of course, CP+B would resurrect

What do you think?

I consider myself to be a creative person.

1   2   3   4   5   6   7
STRONGLY DISAGREE   STRONGLY AGREE

ETHICS CP+B'S RECIPE FOR "HOOPLA"

© Foto Factory/Shutterstock.

Many have tried to decode the CP+B model to understand how the agency achieves creative breakthroughs. In a recent book, CP+B's principals say it's just a matter of emulating P. T. Barnum and focusing on the Hoopla:

- *Mutation:* Look for the established rules, and then find a way to violate them.

- *Invention:* Consumers constantly crave new things, so CP+B's Alex Bogusky advises, "Do the opposite of what everybody else does."

- *Candor:* Don't overlook your flaws and limitations; do talk about them—they make the product unique.

- *Mischief:* Pranks and playfully naughty behavior keep people interested and engaged with your message.

- *Connection:* To really connect, stop shouting and get into a conversation. Use interactive media.

- *Pragmatism:* Find little ways to make the product and promotional mix more useful to consumers.

- *Momentum:* Get people—from celebrities to reporters to consumers—talking about your brand.

Sources: Warren Berger, "Dare-Devils," *Business 2.0*, April 2004, 111–116; David Kiley, "The Craziest Ad Guys in America," *BusinessWeek*, May 22, 2006, 73–80; and Crispin Porter + Bogusky with Warren Berger, *Hoopla*, New York: powerHouse Books, 2006.

The King, with a new and very strange persona. The King's first job would be to revive the breakfast menu, but ultimately he introduced us to a whole new dimension for evaluating corporate icons: No one does *creepy* better than The King.

The offbeat and out-of-the-box characters made a difference. Unlike its predecessors, CP+B did not get fired after one year. More importantly, it really did help turn around the fast-food business for Burger King. Three years into the relationship, Burger King was cel-ebrating 12 consecutive quarters of revenue growth.[5] The brand was relevant again and had entered the everyday conversations of men 18 to 35.

That Creepy King clearly is on a roll, driven by the genius of CP+B. His holiday promo with Xbox for adver-games like Pocketbike Racer and Big Bumpin set sales records.[6] Not only did more than 2 million people pay $3.99 for a video game; they also took home with them a stealth advertisement for Burger King. Every time they play the game, they see one more subtle plug for Burger King. And who's playing? Of course, it's young-adult males, who don't watch much TV but spend some 20 hours a week playing video games. Gone are the concerns about CP+B's ability to survive a relationship with a hard-to-please, mass-market client.

So in a matter of just a few years, CP+B went from underdog to big dog. It's noteworthy that CP+B also is an agency that the professional critics love to hate.[7] But this is exactly what we should expect. Creative people and creative organizations have to be risk takers. They shake things up. They step on some people's toes. They commonly are boastful, which of course irks their critics even more. They do things differently.

In a discussion of creativity, we should expect stories about great successes and also stories about great failures. But there can be absolutely no doubt that creativity is the secret ingredient in great brand promotion.

LO 1 Why Promotion Needs Creativity

What is it about creativity that makes it such a big deal in the promotion business? Why do big, successful marketing firms like Procter & Gamble send their employees on expensive junkets to the Cannes Lions International Advertising Festival to make connections with the best creative minds in the ad business?

Creativity contributes in numerous ways, but let's start with the pervasive problem of advertising clutter. Everyone hates ad clutter. To try to break through the clutter, advertisers generate more ads, which typically only increase the clutter.[8] If you want your message heard, you'll need a way to stand out from the crowd, and that will require creativity. Research shows that a primary benefit of award-winning, creative ads is that they break through the clutter and get remembered.[9] Part of the challenge is to make sure that the brand gets remembered along with the creativity.

But getting the consumer's attention and being memorable are hardly enough. Going back to Burger King's issues, the problem wasn't that consumers were unaware of Burger King or didn't know they served Whoppers. Rather, Burger King was boring—a syndrome one could expect with many mature brands.[10] The brand needed to become relevant again with its core customers, to get back in their everyday conversations. That's what Subservient Chicken and the creepy King did for Burger King.

Great brands use creativity to make emotional connections with consumers. Brands make emotional connections when they engage consumers through complex sensory experiences and deep emotional episodes.[11] Integrated marketing communication (IMC) in its many forms helps create these experiences, but great creative execution brings it all to life. For instance, Apple's iPod wasn't the first MP3 player. Creative Technology had a good one on the market almost two years before Apple.[12] But iPod was the first MP3

Apple's iPod advertising worked because of the simple creative genius of the silhouettes. They were everywhere, and we couldn't stop watching them. They showed us what to do if we wanted to become cool. Buy an iPod, obviously.

iPod

Welcome to the digital music revolution. 10,000 songs in your pocket, including your favorites from the iTunes Music Store. Mac or PC.

Courtesy, Apple Computer, Inc.; Ad Agency: TBWA Chiat Day, LA; Photographer: Matthew Welch; Model: Emory Livers/LA Models.

player to be brought to the market with great advertising—advertising that made iPod synonymous with hip and cool, that made the brand relevant in a social context.

Creative Minds

Creativity, in its essence, is the same no matter what the domain. People who create, create, whether they write novels, take photographs, ponder the particle physics that drives the universe, craft poetry, write songs, play a musical instrument, dance, make films, design buildings, paint, or make ads.

Creativity is the ability to consider and hold together seemingly inconsistent elements and forces, making a new connection. This ability to step outside of everyday logic, to free oneself of thinking in terms of "the way things are" or "the way things have to be," apparently allows creative people to put things together in a way that, once we see it, makes sense, is interesting, and is creative. To see love and hate as the same entity, to see "round squares," or to imagine time bending like molten steel is to have this ability. Ideas born of creativity reveal their own logic, and then we all say, "Oh, I see."

Creativity sometimes is seen as a gift—a special way of seeing the world. Throughout the ages, creative people have been seen as special, revered and reviled, loved and hated. They have served as power-

ful political instruments (for good and evil), and they have been ostracized, imprisoned, and killed for their art. Socrates associated creativity with various forms of madness:

> *Madness, provided it comes as the gift of heaven, is the channel by which we receive the greatest blessings. . . . [T]he men of old who gave their names saw no disgrace or reproach in madness; otherwise they would not have connected it with the name of the noblest of all arts, the art of discerning the future, and called by our ancestors, madness is a nobler thing than sober sense. . . . [M]adness comes from God, whereas sober sense is merely human.*[13]

Extraordinary Examples

Creativity reflects early childhood experiences, social circumstances, and cognitive styles. In one of the best books ever written on creativity, *Creating Minds,* Howard Gardner examines the lives and works of seven of the greatest creative minds of the 20th century: Sigmund Freud, Albert Einstein, Pablo Picasso, Igor Stravinsky, T.S. Eliot, Martha Graham, and Mahatma Gandhi (see Exhibit 8.1).[14] He uncovers fascinating similarities among great creators. All seven of these individuals were "self confident, alert, unconventional, hardworking, and committed obsessively to their work. Social life or hobbies are almost immaterial, represent-

Exhibit 8.1
Seven Creative Geniuses

ing at most a fringe on the creator's work time."[15]

Apparently, total commitment to one's craft is the rule. This commitment has a downside: "The self confidence merges with egotism, egocentrism, and narcissism: highly absorbed, not only wholly involved in his or her own projects, but likely to pursue them at costs of other individuals."[16] In other words, don't stand between a great creator and his or her work. It's not safe; you'll have tracks down your back.

Not coincidentally, these great creative minds had troubled personal lives and simply did not have time for ordinary people (such as their families). According to Gardner, they generally were not very good to those around them.

All seven of these great creative geniuses also were great self-promoters. Well-recognized creative people typically are not shy about seeking exposure for their work. Apparently, fame in the creative realm rarely comes to the self-effacing and timid.

All seven of these creators were able to see things as a child does. Einstein spent much of his career revolutionizing physics by pursuing in no small way an idea he produced as a child: What would it be like to move along with a strand of pure light? Picasso commented that ultimately much of his greatness came from his ability to paint like a child (along with amazingly superior technical skills). Freud's obsession with and interpretation of his childhood dreams had a significant role in what is one of his most significant works, *The Interpretation of Dreams*.[17] T.S. Eliot's poetry demonstrated imaginative abilities that typically disappear past childhood. The same is true of Martha Graham's modern dance. Even Gandhi's particular form of social action was formulated with a very simple and childlike logic at its base. These artists and creative thinkers never lost the ability to see the ordinary as extraordinary and to maintain their particular form of imagination despite the process of "growing up."

These individuals also behaved as children throughout most of their lives. Their social behavior was egocentric and selfish. They expected those around them to be willing to sacrifice at the altar of their gift.

¡Yo Quiero Taco Bell!

AP/Topic Gallery.

This ad for Taco Bell is among the famous themes created under Lee Clow's leadership.

Gardner put it this way: "[T]he carnage around a great creator is not a pretty sight, and this destructiveness occurs whether the individual is engaged in solitary pursuit or ostensibly working for the betterment of humankind."[18] They, however, could be extraordinarily charming when it suited their ambitions.

Apparently, the creative mind also desires marginality.[19] Gardner found that his subjects reveled in being outsiders. This marginality seems to have been absolutely necessary to these people and provided them with some requisite energy.

Emotional stability did not mark these creative lives either. All but Gandhi had a major mental breakdown at some point in their lives, and Gandhi suffered from at least two periods of severe depression. Extreme creativity, as the popular myth suggests, seems to come at a psychological price.

Creativity in the Ad Business

While their influence may be more mundane than Gandhi's or Freud's, some individuals who worked in the advertising business have been praised for remarkable careers that revealed sparks of creative genius. One example is Lee Clow, who at the time of this writing was in his sixties and still the main creative force with TBWA/Chiat/Day. His portfolio includes such familiar messages as the Energizer Bunny, billboards for Nike, "Dogs Rule" for Pedigree, the "1984" spot that launched Apple's Mac, and the iPod silhouettes.

Lee Clow is one of the great creative maestros of the modern advertising business. *Ad Age* referred to him simply as "The Dude Who Thought Different."[20] But those who have worked at his side say his real gift is as the synthesizer. Sorting through a wall full of creative ideas in the form of rough sketches, Lee is the guy who knows how to pick a winner: the one simplest marketing idea that is most likely to resonate with consumers, as in "Shift" for Nissan. Some say he is fervent about great creativity; others say he is prone to fits of temper and can be mean to those who don't see things his way.[21] Doesn't that sound a lot like the seven great creators studied by Gardner?

Creativity in Corporations

If determining who or what is creative in the artistic world is difficult, that difficulty is at least as great in the business world. Certainly, no matter how this trait is defined, creativity is viewed in the business world as a positive quality for employees to have. It's been said that creative individuals assume almost mythical status in the corporate world. Everybody needs them, but no one is sure who or what they are. Furthermore, business types often expect that working with creative people will not be easy. Often, they are right.

In any organization, creativity is not tied to a particular job. Someone in a "creative" job in a marketing department or ad agency isn't necessarily a creative thinker. Conversely, someone on the account or business side of a marketing project (a.k.a. "a suit") isn't necessarily uninspired. As the folks at CP+B will tell you, good ideas can come from anyone, anywhere.[22] Tension and conflict (often between the suits and the creatives) occur regularly during the development of marketing campaigns. To get good outcomes, you have to anticipate and manage this conflict in positive ways.

Inherited or Learned?

Can people learn to be creative? This is an important question. The popular answer in a democratic society would be to say that anyone, with enough effort, can be a creative genius. But in the end, the genius of a Picasso or an Einstein is a standard that few of us will be able to achieve. And given some of the costs associated with intense creativity, maybe that's good.

An accurate answer to this question depends on what we mean by *creativity*. Is a person creative because he or she can produce a creative result or because of the way he or she thinks? While there

Doing Business: The Art of David Ross, p.10 Andrews and McMeel. A Universal Press Syndicate Co. 4520 Main St., Kansas City, MO 64111. Library of Congress #96-83993 TCRN: 0-8362-2178-8.

ARTIST DAVID ROSS'S "SWIMMING SUITS" SUGGESTS A VIEW OF CORPORATE INDIVIDUALITY AND CREATIVITY THAT OFTEN IS HELD BY ART DIRECTORS AND COPYWRITERS.

are numerous elusive elements on the path to being creative, we can learn how to improve our own level of creativity. We all start from a different baseline, but we can learn to be more creative and contribute to the creativity process in developing brand communication. While few of us are destined to become the next Pablo Picasso or even Lee Clow, we need to keep coming back to the point that in the business of brand promotion, we can't do without creative ideas.

LO 2 Agencies, Clients, and the Creative Process

Day to day, many creative pursuits boil down to spending a lot of time trying to get an idea, or the right idea. You turn things over and over in your head, trying to see the light. You try to find that one way of seeing it that makes it all fall into place. Copywriter and author Luke Sullivan says about one-fourth of his job looks like sitting and staring:

> The ad is due in two days. The media space has been bought and paid for. The pressure's building. And your muse is sleeping off a drunk behind a dumpster somewhere. Your pen lies useless. So you talk movies.
>
> That's when the traffic person comes by. Traffic people stay on top of a job as it moves through the agency; which means they also stay on top of you. They'll come by to remind you of the horrid things that happen to snail-assed creative people who don't come through with the goods on time . . .
>
> So you try to get your pen moving. And you begin to work; and working in this business means staring at your partner's shoes.[23]

Sometimes you get lucky and skip that part. A great idea just comes to you, as if by magic.

Every creative pursuit involves this sort of thing. However, the creation of brand promotion, like all creative pursuits, is unique in some respects. The creative personnel in an ad agency are trying to solve a problem, always under time pressure, given to them by a businessperson. Often the problem is poorly defined, and there are competing agendas. The clients may seem not to be creative at all, and they may seem to be preventing the agency from being creative. Even the agency practice of using a "creative department" makes it seem as if the executives keep all the creativity in some sort of warehouse, so they can find it when they need it, and so it won't get away.

Conflict between Creatives and Management

Brand promotion is produced through a social process. As a social process, it's marked daily by struggles for control and power within departments, between departments, and between agencies and their clients. From the creative side, advertising great William Bernbach is hardly tepid or diplomatic in his observations about management and creativity:

> The majority of businessmen are incapable of original thinking, because they are unable to escape from the tyranny of reason. Their imaginations are blocked.[24]

Most research concerning the contentious environment in advertising agencies places the creative department in a central position within these conflicts. One explanation for the central role of creative departments in conflict is the uncertain nature of that department's product. What do an agency's creative people do? From the outside, they appear to be having a lot of fun while everyone else has to dress formally and focus on how much they can sell.

Creatives versus Clients

Regardless of its participation in conflict, the creative department is an essential part of any agency's success. Creative talent is a primary consideration of potential clients when they select advertising agencies.[25] Creativity is crucial to a positive client–advertiser relationship. Interestingly, clients see creativity as an overall agency trait, whereas agency people place the responsibility for it on the shoulders of the creative department.[26]

However, many clients don't recognize their role in killing the very same breakthrough ideas they claim to be looking for. Anyone who has worked in the creative department of an advertising agency for any length of time has a full quiver of client stories— like the one about the client who wanted to produce a single 30-second spot for his ice cream novelty company. The creative team went to work and brought in a single spot that everyone agreed delivered the strategy perfectly, set up further possible spots in the same campaign, and, in the words of the copywriter, was just damn funny. It was the kind of commercial that you actually look forward to seeing on television. During the storyboard presentation, the client laughed in all the right places and admitted the spot was on strategy.

The client said the agency was trying to force him into a corner where he had to approve the spot, because they didn't show him any alternatives. The agency went back to work. Thirty-seven alternatives were presented during the next six months. Thirty-seven alternatives were killed. Finally, the client approved the first spot from half a year earlier. There was much rejoicing. One week later, he canceled the production, saying he wanted to put the money behind a national coupon drop instead. Then he took the account executive out to lunch and asked why none of the creatives liked him.

It's easy and sometimes fun to blame clients for all of the anxieties and frustrations of the creatives, especially if you've worked in a creative department. You can criticize the clients all you want, and because they aren't in the office next to you, they can't hear you. But, despite the obvious stake that creative departments have in generating superior advertising, no creative ever put $10 million of his or her own money behind a campaign.

Creatives versus Account Services

Indeed, you can't always blame the client. Sometimes the conflicts and problems that preclude wonderful creative work occur within the walls of the advertising agency itself. To say there can be conflict between the creative department and other departments within an agency is a bit like saying there will be conflict when Jerry Springer walks into the studio. In advertising, the conflict often centers on the creative department versus account services.

Conflict arises between the creative department and account services department because the departments do not always share the same ultimate goals for campaigns. Individuals in the creative department see an ad as a vehicle to communicate a personal creative ideology that will further their careers. The account manager, serving as liaison between client and agency, sees the goal of the communication as achieving some predetermined objective in the marketplace.[27]

Another source of conflict is that members of creative groups and members of account services teams have different perspectives due to differing background knowledge. Account managers must be generalists with broad knowledge. Creatives are specialists with great expertise in a single area.[28]

The difficulty of assessing the effectiveness of an advertisement also can create antagonism between the creative department and the research department.[29] Vaughn states that the tumultuous social environment between creative departments and ad testers represents the "historical conflict between art and science."[30] In the world of advertising, people in research departments are put in the unenviable position of judging the creatives—again, "science" judges art. Creatives don't like this, particularly when it's bad science or not science at all. Of course, researchers sometimes are creative themselves and don't typically enjoy being a constraint on those in the creative department.

So why doesn't everybody pull together and love each other within an agency? When a client is unhappy, it fires the agency. Billings and revenue drop. Budgets are cut. And pink slips fly. It's no wonder that conflict occurs. When someone is looking out for his or her job, it's tough not to get involved in struggles over control of the creative product.

Conflict with Account Executives

Account executives (AEs) are the liaison between the agency and the client. Their primary responsibility is to

MANY CLIENTS DON'T RECOGNIZE THEIR ROLE IN KILLING THE VERY SAME **BREAKTHROUGH IDEAS** THEY CLAIM TO BE LOOKING FOR.

WE'D LIKE TO TELL ALL OF TONIGHT'S AWARD HUNGRY, SMART ASS, HOLIER-THAN-THOU ADDY WINNERS EXACTLY WHERE THEY CAN GO.

Foote, Cone & Belding used a bit of sassy tongue-in-cheekiness to signal that résumés were wanted.

make sure that the client is happy. Because clients hold the final power of approval over creative output, the members of the account team see an advertisement as a product they must control before the client sees it.[31] Members of the account team perceive the creatives as experts in the written word or in visual expression. However, they believe that creatives don't understand advertising strategy or business dealings. Members of the creative department resent that.

For AEs to rise in their career, they must excel in the care and feeding of clients. It's a job of negotiation, gentle prodding, and ambassadorship. For creatives to rise, their work must challenge. It must arrest attention. It must provoke. At times, it must shock. Yet, as we indicated earlier, this kind of effectiveness makes clients nervous. And that is an account executive's nightmare.

This nightmare situation for the AEs produces the kind of ads that win awards for the creatives. People who win awards are recognized: Their work gets published in *The One Show* and *Communication Arts* and appears on the Clios. They are in demand and are wined and dined by rival agencies. They become famous and, yes, rich by advertising standards. So the trick is how to get creatives to want to pursue cool ads that also sell.

So is there any way around the tension and conflict inherent in the people-intensive business of creating integrated marketing communication? John Sweeney, a true expert on advertising creativity, emphasizes that, when creativity is the goal, agency management should establish a clear "vision of advertising and a code of behavior."[32] Managers should reward ideas consistent with that vision but allow flexibility for the creative process and creative ideas to unfold. They should insist that promotional communications be limited to one dominant message but should expect creative staff to try genuinely new ideas, rather than cutting and pasting ideas from other campaigns or other agencies. Whether an agency's work is good or bad is more a matter of structure than talent alone. Given a pool of talented people, managers have to provide some structure that allows them to produce their best work.

LO 3 Coordination, Collaboration, and Creativity

The execution of an IMC campaign is very much like the performance of a symphony orchestra. To produce glorious music, many individuals must make their unique contributions to the performance, but it sounds right only if the maestro brings it all together at the critical moment. Attend a symphony, and get there early so that you can hear each musician warming up. Reflect on the many years of dedicated practice that this individual put in to master that instrument and his or her specific part for tonight's performance. As each musician warms up independently, the sound becomes a collection of hoots and clangs. Mercifully, the maestro finally steps to the podium to quell the cacophony. All is quiet for a moment. Finally, the maestro calls the orchestra into action. As a team, with each person executing a specific assignment defined by the composer, under the direction of the maestro, they make beautiful music.

So it goes in the world of brand promotion. Preparing and executing breakthrough IMC campaigns is a people-intensive business. Many different kinds of expertise will be needed to pull it off, so people must be enlisted to play a variety of roles. But some order must be imposed on the collection of players. Frequently, a maestro will need to step in to give these players a common theme or direction for their work. Lee Clow of TBWA Worldwide once received a conductor's baton as a gift. About the role of maestro, he has said: "I was a pretty good soloist when I joined the orchestra, but I think I'm a much better conductor than I was a soloist. If we can make beautiful music together, that makes me happy. . . . And different people end up getting to do the solos and get the standing ovations."[33]

Coordination and collaboration will be required for executing any kind of promotional effort. Moreover, the creative essence of the campaign can be aided and elevated by skillful

use of teams. Teams can generate a synergy that allows them to rise above the talents of their individual members on many kinds of tasks. Even without an Igor Stravinsky, Pablo Picasso, or Martha Graham, a group of diverse and motivated people can be expected to generate big ideas and also put them into action.

Because great brand promotion and great teamwork go hand in hand, we don't just want to hope for a good team; we need to make it happen. Teamwork must be planned for and facilitated. People who lead brand promotion efforts therefore need to understand how winning teams operate.

What We Know about Teams

More and more instructors in all sorts of classes are incorporating teamwork as part of their courses because they know that interpersonal skills are highly valued in the real world of work. In fact, an impressive body of research indicates that teams have become essential to the effectiveness of modern organizations. In their book *The Wisdom of Teams*, consultants Jon Katzenbach and Douglas Smith review many valuable insights about the importance of teams. Here we summarize several of their key conclusions.[34]

- *Teams rule!* There can be little doubt that, in a variety of organizations, teams have become the primary means for getting things done. The growing number of performance challenges faced by most businesses—as a result of more-demanding customers, technological

© Losevsky Pavel/Shutterstock.

changes, government regulation, and intensifying competition—demand speed and quality in work products that simply are beyond the scope of what an individual can offer. Teams often are the only valid option for getting things done.

- *It's all about performance.* Research shows that teams are effective in organizations where the leadership makes it perfectly clear that teams will be held accountable for performance. Teams are expected to produce results that satisfy the client and yield financial gains.

- *Synergy through teams.* Modern organizations require many kinds of expertise to get the work done. The only reliable way to mix people with different expertise to generate solutions where the whole is greater than the sum of the parts is through team discipline. Research shows that blending expertise from diverse disciplines often produces the most innovative solutions to many different types of business problems.[35] The "blending" must be done through teams.

- *The demise of individualism?* Rugged individualism is the American way. But does a growing reliance on teams in the workplace mean a devaluation of the individual and a greater emphasis on conformity to what the group thinks? Not at all. Left unchecked, an "always look out for number one" mentality can destroy teams. But teams are not incompatible with individual excellence. Effective teams let each individual bring his or her unique contributions to the forefront. When an individual does not have a personal contribution to make, then one can question that person's value to the team.

- *Teams promote personal growth.* Teamwork promotes learning for each individual team member. In a team, people learn about their own work styles and observe the work styles of others. This learning makes them more effective team players in their next assignment. Once team principles take hold in an organization, momentum builds.

Leadership of Teams

A critical element in the equation for successful teams is leadership. Leaders do many things for their teams to help them succeed.[36] Teams ultimately must reach a goal to justify their standing, and here is where the leader's job starts. The leader's first job is to help team members build consensus about the goals they hope to achieve and the approach they will take to reach those goals. Without a clear sense of purpose, the team is doomed. Once goals and purpose are agreed upon, then the leader plays a role in ensuring that the work of the team is consistent with the strategy or plan. This is a particularly important role in the context of creating IMC campaigns.

Finally, team leaders must help do the real work of the team. Here the team leader must be careful to contribute ideas without dominating the team. There also are two key things that team leaders should never do: They should not blame or allow specific individuals to fail, and they should never excuse away shortfalls in team performance.[37] Mutual accountability must be emphasized over individual performance.

Applying these principles to brand promotion, think of an agency's **account team** as a bicycle wheel, with the team leader as the hub of the wheel. Spokes of the wheel reach out to the diverse disciplinary expertise needed in today's world of IMC. The spokes represent team members from direct marketing, public relations, broadcast media, graphic design, interactive, creative, accounting, and so on. The hub connects the spokes and ensures that all of them work in tandem to make the wheel roll smoothly.

To illustrate the multilayered nature of the team approach to IMC, we also can think of each account team member as a hub in his or her very own wheel. For example, the direct-marketing member on the account team is team leader for her own set of specialists charged with preparing direct-marketing materials. Through this type of multilevel "hub-and-spokes" design, agencies can achieve the coordination and collaboration essential for effective IMC campaigns.

Fostering Collaboration: The Creative Brief

The **creative brief** is a little document with a huge role in promoting good teamwork and fostering the creative process. It sets up the goal for any promotional

account team group of people comprising different facets of the promotion industry who work together under a team leader

creative brief document that outlines and channels an essential creative idea and objective

TEAMS OFTEN ARE THE ONLY VALID OPTION FOR GETTING THINGS DONE.

effort in a way that gets everyone moving in the same direction, but it should never force or mandate a particular solution. It provides basic guidelines with plenty of room for the creatives to be creative.

Preparation of the creative brief is a joint activity involving the client lead and the AE. Carefully and fully preparing the creative brief prevents many potential conflicts. An efficient template for the creative brief is featured in Exhibit 8.2. To prepare the brief effectively, write the answers in the language of the consumer, not business jargon. Write simply and concisely, trying to create evocative ideas. A well-prepared brief will make creative staff excited about executing the plan.

Exhibit 8.2
A Creative Brief

⬅ **Previous page**

PRODUCTS   **FORMS**

CLIENT [ ]   **DATE** [ ]   **JOB NO.** [ ]

Prepared by [ ]

What is the product or service?

Simple description or name of product or service.

Who/what is the competition?

Provide a snapshot of the brand situation including current position in the category, brand challenges, competitive threats, and future goals.

Who are we talking to?

Clear definition of who the target is both demographically and psychographically. Be as specific as possible in defining the target so the creative can connect target and brand in the most compelling way.

What consumer need or problem do we address?

Describe the unmet consumer need that this product or service fills or how this product addresses a need in a way that's unique.

What does the consumer currently think about us?

Uncover target insights to get at attitudes and behaviors related to broader context as well as specific category and brand. Determine whether insights currently exist or whether new research needs to be conducted.

What one thing do we want them to believe?

Be as single-minded as possible. Write in benefit (functional, emotional, or self-expressive) language. Should differentiate us . . . no other brand in the category can or is currently saying it.

What can we tell them that will make them believe this?

Not a laundry list of available support but the few things that clearly support the "one thing we want them to believe."

What is the tonality of the advertising?

A few adjectives or phrase that captures the tonality and personality of the advertising.

NEXT

Based on Northlich, http://www.northlich.com.

Teams Liberate Decision Making

With the right combination of expertise assembled on the account team, a carefully crafted creative brief, and a leader that has the team working well as a unit, what appears to be casual or spur-of-the-moment decision making can turn out to be breakthrough decision making. This is one of the huge benefits of good teamwork. Teams composed of members who trust one another are liberated to be more creative because no one is worried about having his or her best ideas stolen. No one is worried about trying to look good for the boss. What counts is the team. This type of "safe" team environment allows everyone to contribute and lets the whole be greater than the sum of the parts.

Researchers in many fields have tackled the issue of how to foster creativity in the workplace. Teresa Amabile, a researcher at Harvard, has identified what she refers to as the six keys to creativity in any organization (see Exhibit 8.3).[38] According to Amabile, the foundation for creativity is setting up people with just the right amount of challenge and then giving them the freedom to choose a path for meeting it. In the world of brand promotion, the creative brief typically lays out the challenge for a team in a simple framework that should not restrict or dictate solutions in any way.

Resources include time and money. Here again, it is a matter of finding just the right balance. For exam-

ple, setting deadlines is extremely important, and it's fine to make people stretch themselves, but fabricated deadlines or impossibly short time frames will kill the team's motivation and stifle creativity.

Exhibit 8.3
Keys to Creativity

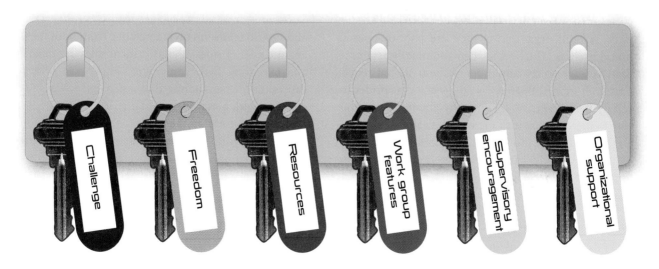

Challenge   Freedom   Resources   Work group features   Supervisory encouragement   Organizational support

© Pete Saloutos/Shutterstock.

Next is a theme you'll see over and over again in any literature about creativity: Pay careful attention to the design of your teams. Homogeneous teams get tasks done quickly and without a lot of conflict or problems, but they produce ordinary solutions. If you want creative solutions, you need to assemble teams characterized by diversity of thought and expertise. Such teams will make more waves but will produce more creative solutions.

The team leader must communicate that new ideas are valued and must prevent the critics from destroying momentum around new ideas. Finally, no one person or no one team will produce creative solutions if the overall organization they are part of doesn't brand itself as creative and then continually reinforce that message to its employees. As you should recall, Crispin Porter + Bogusky is an agency that prides itself on being creative. It is not shy about making this claim or promoting it to the world. Leaders at all levels of an organization must reinforce the creativity mantra if individual employees in those organizations are to take it seriously.

Along with using these basic tools for promoting creativity, leaders can have some fun bringing out their team members' creative side. In particular, many ad agencies do special things to let their employees know that creativity is job one. Notable perks offered by agencies include on-site yoga and game rooms, espresso bars, celebrity chefs, Halloween parties, movie nights, tai chi classes, and concierge services. The goal is to attract and retain interesting people and keep them happy about their jobs. As one agency leader put it: "We sell ideas, and if your employees are unhappy, you are not going to get a lot of good ideas."[39] Maybe it's as simple as that.

Igniting Creativity in Teams

Account teams, sub-specialist teams, creative teams, and hybrid teams involving persons from both the client and agency sides all play critical roles in preparing and executing IMC campaigns. Impressive evidence shows that, when managed in a proactive way, teams come up with better ideas—that is, ideas that are both creative and useful in the process of building brands.[40] Good teamwork may be serious stuff, but it doesn't have to be complicated, and it certainly will get rowdy at times. The requirements are building teams with the right expertise and diversity of thought, pushing individuals in those teams to challenge and build on each others' ideas, and creating just the right amount of tension to get the sparks flying.

Cognitive Styles

According to the stereotype, business types favor left-brain thinking, and advertising types favor right-brain thinking. Business types like to talk about testing and data and return on investment, while advertising types like to talk about movies and the Cannes Film Festival.[41] While such stereotypes misrepresent individual differences, the old left-brain/right-brain metaphor reminds us that people approach problem solving with different styles; they prefer to think in their own style.

The unique preferences of each person for thinking about and solving a problem are a reflection of **cognitive style**. For instance, some people prefer logical and analytical thinking; others prefer intuitive and nonlinear thinking. Numerous categorization schemes have been developed for classifying people based on their cognitive styles. Psychologist Carl Jung was a pioneer among cognitive stylists. He proposed essential differences among individuals along three dimensions of cognitive style: sensing versus intuiting, thinking versus feeling, and extraverted versus introverted.

These differences affect creativity of teams. The more homogeneous a team is in terms of cognitive styles, the more limited the range of its solutions to a problem will be. Simply stated, diversity of thought nourishes creativity.

Creative Abrasion

Teamwork is not a picnic in the park. That's why it's called team*work*. When teams bring together people with diverse cognitive styles and they truly get engaged in the task, there will be friction. Friction can be both good and bad:[42]

- We can have **creative abrasion**, which is the clash of *ideas*. This can produce new ideas and breakthroughs.

- We can have **interpersonal abrasion**, which is the clash of *people*. This causes communication to shut down and slaughters new ideas.

As we pointed out earlier, teams must have leadership that creates a safe environment, allowing creative abrasion to flourish. At the same time, leaders must be vigilant about defusing interpersonal abrasion. It's a fine line, but getting it right means the difference between creativity and chaos.

Brainstorming and Alien Visitors

A common complaint about meetings is that they bring together people who sit in a conference room and shoot the breeze for an hour, and when it is all over, they discover they just wasted another hour. Groups can waste a lot of time if not managed.

One of the key means for getting groups or teams to generate novel solutions is through the use of a process called brainstorming. **Brainstorming** is an organized approach to idea generation in groups. As suggested by Exhibit 8.4, there is a right way and a

cognitive style an individual's preference for thinking about and solving a problem

creative abrasion clash of ideas, abstracted from the people who propose them, from which new ideas can evolve

interpersonal abrasion clash of people, often resulting from an inability to regard idea feedback as separate from personal feedback, causing communication to shut down

brainstorming organized approach to idea generation in groups

Exhibit 8.4
Eight Rules for Brainstorming

1. Build off each other.	Don't just generate ideas; build off them.
2. Fear drives out creativity.	Be sure no one is teased or embarrassed.
3. Prime individuals before and after.	Give everyone a chance to prepare and learn.
4. Make it happen.	Put ideas into action.
5. It's a skill.	Use a skilled facilitator.
6. Embrace creative abrasion.	Welcome conflicting ideas and viewpoints.
7. Listen and learn.	Focus on learning and building trust.
8. Follow the rules.	If you don't, you're not really brainstorming.

Source: Based on Robert L. Sutton, "The Truth about Brainstorming," *Inside Business Week*, September 25, 2006, 17–21.

wrong way to brainstorm. Follow the rules laid out in Exhibit 8.4, and you can call it brainstorming. Otherwise, you're just shooting the breeze—and probably wasting time.

Adding more diversity to the group fosters creative abrasion; moreover, well-established teams can get stale and stuck in a rut. To ramp up the creative abrasion, you may need a visit from an alien. If you can get one from Pluto or Mars, that's fine, but more likely, this alien will be someone from outside the normal network, either from elsewhere in your organization or from outside the organization entirely. Perhaps the team will need to take a field trip to visit some aliens. Teams that insulate themselves from outside influences run the risk of eventually losing their spark.[43] Tranquility and sameness can be enemies of creativity.

Leadership from the Creative Director

The trust and open communication of effective teams can foster creativity in the preparation of an IMC campaign. Nevertheless, the creativity required for breakthrough campaigns also comes from personal work products generated by individuals laboring on their own. Thus, both personal and team creativity are critical in the preparation of IMC campaigns. The daunting task of facilitating both usually falls in the lap of an agency's creative director.

The position of creative director is very special because, much like the maestro of the symphony orchestra, the creative director must encourage personal excellence but at the same time demand team accountability. We interviewed veteran creative directors to get more insights into the challenge of channeling the creative energies of their teams. All acknowledge that creativity has an intensely personal element, often motivated by the desire to satisfy one's own ego or sense of self. But despite this interpersonal element, team unity has to be a priority. In orchestrating creative teams, these are some good principles to follow:

- Take great care in assigning individuals to a team in the first place. Be sensitive to existing workloads and the proper mix of expertise required to do the job for the client.

- Get to know the cognitive style of each individual. Listen carefully. Because creativity can be an intensely personal matter, one has to know when it is best to leave people alone, versus when one needs to support them in working through the inevitable rejection.

- Make teams responsible to the client. Individuals and teams are empowered when they have sole responsibility for performance outcomes.

- Beware of adversarial and competitive relationships between individuals and between teams. They quickly can lead to mistrust that destroys camaraderie and synergy.

- If the same set of individuals will work on multiple teams over time, rotate team assignments to foster fresh thinking, or bring in some aliens.

Here we see once again that the fundamentals of effective teams—communication, trust, complementary expertise, and leadership—produce the desired performance outcome. There's simply no alternative. Advertising is a team sport.

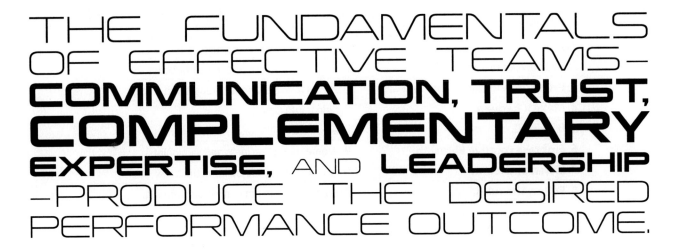

THE FUNDAMENTALS OF EFFECTIVE TEAMS— COMMUNICATION, TRUST, COMPLEMENTARY EXPERTISE, AND LEADERSHIP —PRODUCE THE DESIRED PERFORMANCE OUTCOME.

LO 4 Your Commitment to Creativity

Most of us are not going to model our lives after creative geniuses like Pablo Picasso or Martha Graham. While it's great to have role models to inspire us, it's unrealistic for most of us to aspire to be the next Gandhi or Einstein. But we all can take stock of our own special skills and abilities, and we candidly should assess our own strengths and weaknesses.

For example, we can complete assessments that reveal our own cognitive styles and then compare ourselves to others. And if you want to calibrate your level of creativity, you can search the Internet for "creativity tests" or "creativity assessments," and a host of options will present themselves. Get to know yourself, and think about your skills and abilities.

In addition, if you have any interest in a career in advertising, it would be a good thing to decide right now to make yourself more creative. Although we all may start in different places, becoming more creative is a worthy goal. Yale psychologist Robert Sternberg, who has devoted his professional career to the study of intelligence and creativity, advises his students as follows:

To make yourself more creative, decide now to:

Redefine problems to see them differently from other people;

Be the first to analyze and critique your own ideas, since we all have good ones and bad ones;

Be prepared for opposition whenever you have a really creative idea;

Recognize that it is impossible to be creative without adequate knowledge;

Recognize that too much knowledge can stifle creativity;

Find the standard, safe solution and then decide when you want to take a risk by defying it;

Keep growing and experiencing, and challenging your own comfort zone;

Believe in yourself, especially when surrounded by doubters;

Learn to cherish ambiguity, because from it comes the new ideas;

Remember that research has shown that people are most likely to be creative when doing something they love.[44]

It's good advice.

STUDY TOOLS CHAPTER 8

Located at back of the textbook

- **Rip out Chapter in Review Card.**

Located at www.cengagebrain.com

- **Review Key Terms Flashcards (Print or Online).**
- **Complete the Practice Quiz to prepare for tests.**
- **Play "Beat the Clock" and "Quizbowl" to master concepts.**
- **Complete "Crossword Puzzle" to review key terms.**
- **Watch videos on Ford and John Lewis Always a woman for real company examples.**
- **An additional example is available online that explains the outstanding creative work required of an Account Executive in an agency.**

Brand messages on YouTube, MySpace, or Flickr are believed to communicate in a more "social" way, seeming to be more part of "life" and less like corporate commercial-speak.

Marketers combine Web content with traditional media because it is more likely to stick for the Web generation.

Photo Courtesy, OmniTerra Images.

YouTube – AXE's Channel

Google

CHECK US OUT ON

http://www.youtube.com/axe

AXE

AXE Lounge

AXE HAIR Hair Action

AXE UNDIE RUN CHALLENGE

WAKE UP AND STAY ALERT

AXE AXE's Channel Subscribe

All Uploads Playlists

Double Pits to Chesty
1 day ago
more info

Wake Up and Stay Alert
20 hours ago
more info

Hair Action
18 hours ago
more info

AXE Undie Run Challenge
1 week ago
more info

Links to YouTube videos are a fun way to engage with the brand.

"The best way to predict the future is to create it."

—Peter Drucker

AFTER YOU
FINISH THIS
CHAPTER
GO TO
PAGE 197
FOR STUDY
TOOLS

Axe Goes Where the Boys Are

When Unilever, one of the world's largest consumer products companies (http://www.unilever.com), wanted a fresh and powerful promotional campaign for its Axe spray deodorant brand for men, the firm turned to London-based advertising agency Bartle Bogle Hegarty (BBH). Unilever wanted a global brand message that would work in all 75 countries where it sold Axe. BBH (http://www.bbh.co.uk) delivered a new phrase that guys would come to know and love as an expression of female attraction for any guy wearing Axe: BomChickaWahWah.[1]

Unilever's brand managers and BBH's creatives released a wave of BomChicka-WahWahs around the world through videos of an all-female band singing the phrase (which would show up on YouTube), online games, live performances by the band, and television ads also destined to end up on social-networking sites. Interested guys could learn about, replay, and interact with these messages by visiting Axe's brand-building website at http://www.theaxeeffect.com. The campaign attracted widespread attention, meeting its goal to make the phrase stick in the mind of millions of young guys around the globe.

Marketers combine Web content with traditional media because they expect the Web generation to seek out messages online and attend to those messages more readily than messages sent through magazines or television. Brand messages on YouTube, MySpace, or Flickr are believed to communicate in a more "social" way, seeming to be more part of "life" and less like corporate commercial-speak. When a message catches on and spreads through the networks, it reaches global target markets nearly instantaneously.

What do you think?

If a Web link looks interesting, I'll click on it.

1   2   3   4   5   6   7
STRONGLY DISAGREE   STRONGLY AGREE

Find out what others think at CourseMate for PROMO.   175

So how does this story end? Did BomChickaWah-Wah work? Axe has grabbed significant market share in the men's deodorant market around the world, including 8.9 percent in Germany, 13.5 percent in the United States, 17.6 percent in Australia, and 28.6 percent in India.[2]

What's more important in terms of understanding brand promotion is that this story *hasn't* ended. Axe is maintaining its online connection to young men, just varying the message enough to keep the target market interested. More recent visitors to http://www .theaxeeffect.com could go to the Skin Contact page not only for details about that line of skin products but also to pursue their interest in the purpose of those products (soft skin that invites some literal skin contact with the object of one's affection). Tips for getting along with girls are balanced with humorous offerings that keep the tone guy-friendly. Humor also is a feature of Axe's "Double Pits to Chesty" theme, which uses terms from skateboarding to instruct young men that they should apply Axe spray not only to their armpits but also to their chest for a full aromatic impact. That theme offers plenty of material for brand-related action videos (featuring skater and reality TV star Ryan Sheckler) on YouTube. Unilever is keeping a sharp edge on the Axe brand.

LO 1 The Internet's Role in Brand Promotion

The Internet has taken businesses on a wild ride ever since a boom in the 1990s became an investment bubble that burst at the beginning of this century. Despite terrorism, recession, and skepticism, use of the Internet continues to grow. Networked business-to-business Internet transactions exceed $10 trillion annually. Consumer e-commerce also exceeds $10 trillion annually, including more than $6 trillion spent by consumers on services such as music downloads and information subscriptions.[3]

The Web has become the brand promotion medium it was expected to be. As we talked about in Chapter 2, marketers are incorporating Web promotional messages into their integrated marketing communication (IMC) and channeling money once spent on traditional media over to the Web. Expenditures on Web advertising exceed $20 billion annually.[4]

What to Expect

As the Internet has developed as an option for marketers, many firms like Pepsi (http://www.pepsiworld .com) and BMW (http://www.bmw.com) have been highly successful in folding the Internet into their brand promotion strategies. A trip to these websites shows that they deliver a lot of information and promotion. But the Internet is more than corporate websites. What is the role of the Internet in brand promotion? A few "truths" have made themselves evident.

First, the Internet will *not* replace all other forms of advertising. Nor is it likely that the biggest spenders on promotion will use the Internet as the *main* method of communicating with their target audiences. Rather, marketers are using the Internet as a key component of IMC. Music distributors like Arista, which represents Pink and Sarah McLachlan, use the Internet to deliver digital music streams and generate exposure. In fact, for the music industry, the Web has become a primary method of promoting new artists and new singles.[5]

Second, all aspects of the Internet are still changing dramatically. In recent years, auction sites like eBay have provided huge opportunities for small business all over the world. Web 2.0, with its emphasis on social networking, provides a whole new way of delivering promotional messages.

Therefore, for marketers today, it's essential to understand the structure of the Internet and its potential as a promotional medium. That understanding prepares marketers to use the Internet as part of effective IMC.

THE WEB HAS BECOME THE **BRAND PROMOTION MEDIUM** IT WAS EXPECTED TO BE.

© U.P. images_photo/Shutterstock.

boasted 12 advertisers, including AT&T and Club Med; each paid $30,000 for a 12-week run of online ads, with no guarantee of the number or profile of the viewers.

Now the Internet is being accessed worldwide by well over a billion users.[6] Spending for advertising on the Internet was estimated at about $12 billion in 2005 and is forecast to grow to more than $36 billion by 2011.[7] The medium is used by all forms of companies—large, small, bricks and mortar, virtual, e-commerce, not-for-profit, you name it. Further, the medium is home to millions of websites, and the value of the Internet to individual consumers is growing daily.

Cyberspace: An Overview

The **Internet** is a global collection of computer networks linking both public and private computer systems. It originally was designed by the U.S. military to be a decentralized, highly redundant, and thus reliable communications system in the event of a national emergency. Even if some of the military's computers crashed, the Internet would continue to perform. Today, the Internet comprises computers from government, educational, military, and commercial sources.

In the beginning, the number of computers connected to the Internet roughly doubled every year, from 2 million in 1994 to 5 million in 1995 to about 10 million in 1996. But beginning in 1998, Internet use accelerated, with around 90 million people connected in the United States and Canada, and 155 million people worldwide. Exhibit 9.1 shows that Internet use has become a global phenomenon. The Internet users in these top 10 countries on four continents represent less than half of the estimated worldwide Internet population, which now exceeds 1.8 billion.[8]

The numbers in Exhibit 9.1 mask the potential for further growth, especially in developing nations. Although China is estimated to have the most users, its vast population means it could—and probably will—have far more. The percentage of China's population using the Internet is only 19 percent, and only about 7 percent of India's population uses the Internet. In contrast, almost three out of every four people in the United States and South Korea go online. In Europe, the share of Internet users typically is about one-half to two-thirds of the total population.

How It Started

Technology has the potential to change everything. And *communications* technology (including the Internet) can change fundamental aspects of human existence. By connecting people in real time, the Internet has the potential to deliver not only information but also community, empowerment, and even liberation.

Even though the Internet has experienced some growing pains, it can be truly revolutionary for marketers in terms of its ability to alter the basic nature of communication within a commercial channel. To see this, consider the short history of communication in this channel.

In 1994, marketers began working with Prodigy and CompuServe, the first Internet service providers (ISPs). These marketers hoped to send television commercials online, but the technology at that time made this idea impossible. Still, as more users went online, joining fast-growing ISPs such as America Online and EarthLink, the technology continued to develop. Newer Web browsers, such as Netscape (which replaced the first browser, Mosaic), seemed worth exploring as a way to send commercial messages. The first ads began appearing in *HotWired* magazine (the online version of *Wired* magazine) in October 1994. *HotWired*

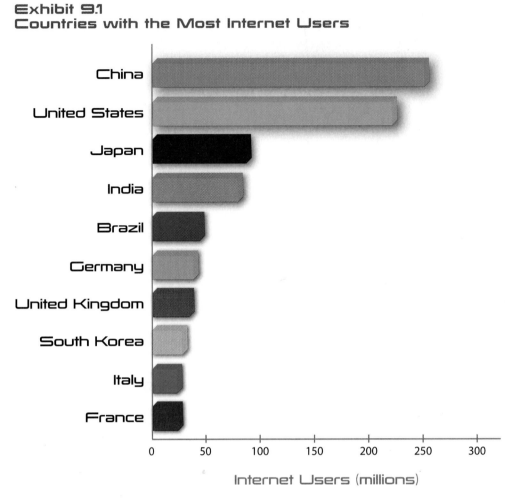

Exhibit 9.1
Countries with the Most Internet Users

Internet Users (millions)

Source: Data from "Stats—Web Worldwide," *ClickZ*, http://www.clickz.com/stats/web_worldwide, accessed December 1, 2009.

LO 2 Internet Media

Internet media for marketing consist of email (including electronic mailing lists), Usenet, and the World Wide Web.

Email

Marketers often use email to reach potential and existing customers. A variety of companies collect email addresses and profiles that allow marketers to direct email to a specific group. Widespread, targeted email advertising is facilitated by organizations like Advertising.com (http://www.advertising.com). These organizations target, prepare, and deliver emails to highly specific audiences for advertisers.

Marketers are addressing consumer resistance to email marketing by limiting who receives their messages. **Opt-in email** is commercial email that is sent with the recipient's consent, such as when website visitors give their permission to receive commercial email about topics and products that interest them. Typically, when customers purchase a product online, the order page includes a box for them to check if they want to receive future information about the company and its products. Service providers help OfficeMax, Exxon, and other companies manage their opt-in email promotions. Other firms, including L-Soft (http://www.lsoft.com), offer software for managing electronic mailing lists.

An ethical/social issue we discussed in Chapter 4 is sending uninvited commercial messages to electronic mailing lists, Usenet groups, or some other compilation of email addresses. These messages are called **spam,** and the practice, called spamming, is notorious. Various estimates suggest 120 *billion* spam emails are sent every day worldwide.[9] Few promotional techniques have drawn as much wrath from consumers and regulators. But as annoying as spam seems to be, it also appears to be effective. Those mass emailings can get a 5 to 7 percent response, compared with 1 to 3 percent for offline direct-marketing efforts.[10] Before we write off mass emails, we had better consider the results, not just the public reaction.

Usenet

Usenet is a collection of discussion groups in cyberspace. People can read messages pertaining to a given topic, post new messages, and answer messages. Users read and post email-like messages (called "articles" or "posts") to one or more of a number of categories, called newsgroups. Usenet resembles bulletin board systems (BBS) in most respects. One crucial difference from a BBS is that with Usenet, there is no central server or central system owner. Usenet is distributed among a large, constantly changing conglomeration of servers that store and forward messages to one another. These servers are loosely connected in a variable mesh. Individual users usually read from and post messages to a local server operated by their ISP, university, employer, or some other local organization. Then the servers exchange the messages among one another.

World Wide Web

The **World Wide Web (WWW)** is a "web" of information available to most Internet users, and its graphical environment makes navigation simple and exciting. For some people, spending time on the Web is replacing time once devoted to other media, such as print, radio, and television.

Of all the options available for Internet marketers, the Web provides the greatest breadth and depth of opportunity. It allows for detailed and full-color graphics, audio transmission, customized messages, 24-hour availability, and two-way information exchanges between the marketer and customer. There is one great difference between the Web and other cyber-advertising vehicles: The consumer actively searches for the marketer's home page. Of course, Web marketers are attempting to make their pages much easier to find—and harder to avoid.

Surfing the Web

About 70 percent of Americans use the Web.[11] Exhibit 9.2 shows what they're doing. In many cases, the desire for information, entertainment, and personal services leads to **surfing**—gliding from one Web page to another. Users can seek and find sites in a variety of ways: through search engines, through direct links with other sites, and by word-of-mouth.

Surfing is made fast and efficient by search engine technology. A **search engine** allows an Internet user to surf by typing in a few keywords; the search engine then finds all sites that contain the keywords. Search engines all have the same basic user interface but differ in how they perform the search and in the amount of the Web accessed. The big Internet sites like Yahoo!

Usenet collection of more than 13,000 discussion groups on the Internet

World Wide Web (WWW) database of information available online in a graphical environment that simplifies navigation

surfing gliding from website to website, guided by hyperlinks, a search engine, or word-of-mouth

search engine software tool for finding websites by entering keywords

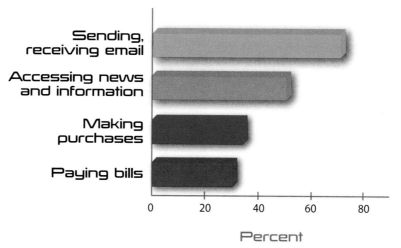

Exhibit 9.2
What Americans Are Doing Online

Source: Based on Digital Marketing & Media Fact Pack, *Advertising Age*, April 23, 2007, 32.

portal website that serves as a starting point for Web access and search

website collection of Web pages, images, videos, and other content hosted on a Web server

mash-up combination of websites into a single site for analyzing or comparing information

blog personal journal that is published on a website, frequently updated, and intended for public access

blogger author of a blog

and Google use search engine technology to optimize results, so they direct surfers to sites most likely to be of interest. Search engines also can provide convenience and speed for shoppers by using "bots," which visit store websites to check and report a specified product's availability and prices.

Portals and Websites

An Internet **portal** is a starting point for Web access and search. Portals can be general, like Yahoo!; vertical (serving a specialized market or industries, such as Jobster, http://www.jobster.com, for employment opportunities); horizontal (providing access and links across industries, such as MSN, http://www.msn.com, with access to a wide area of topics); or community based (such as Latina Online, http://www.latina.com). Portals designed for specific groups are intended to make surfing and searching a bit easier.[12]

In addition to the portals, the Web is dominated by individual company or brand websites. Formally defined, a **website** is a collection of Web pages, images, videos, and other digital content hosted on a Web server. Typically, an Internet user starts out at a portal and then navigates around a series of websites.

A variation of the standard website is the **mash-up** —a combination of one or more websites into a single site. An example is EveryBlock's Chicago crime section (http://chicago.everyblock.com/crime/), where local crime statistics are overlaid on Google Maps so you can see what crimes have been committed in particular neighborhoods.[13]

Personal Websites and Blogs

Many people have created their own Web pages that list their favorite sites. This is a fabulous way of finding new and interesting sites (as well as feeding a person's narcissism).

Although most people find Web pages via Internet resources (more than 80 percent of respondents in one survey found Web pages through search engines or other Web pages), sites also can be discovered through traditional word-of-mouth communications. Internet enthusiasts tend to share their experiences on the Web through discussions in coffeehouses, by reading and writing articles, and via other non-Web venues. There also are mega-search engines, like Dogpile (http://www.dogpile.com), that combine several search engines at once.

Another popular personal use of the Web is the **blog**, a short form for Weblog, referring to a personal journal that frequently is updated and intended for public access. Blogs generally represent the personality of the author (the **blogger**) or the website and its purpose. Topics include brief philosophical musings, favorite hobbies and music, political leanings, commentary on Internet and other social issues, and links to other sites the author favors. The essential characteristics of the blog are its journal form, typically a new entry each day, and its informal style.

Blogs get a lot of publicity, and about 57 million people reported using blogs. However, only about 12 percent of those blog users visit a blog once a week or more frequently—meaning 88 percent of Internet users seldom or never read blogs.[14] Still, big corporations like Procter & Gamble are finding that some of their brands are featured on customer blogs. Marketers in general feel this aspect of the Web holds great potential for peer-to-peer communication, which can be a powerful advocate for brands.[15]

Community portals like Latina Online offer a site that matches surfers' interests in information on a variety of topics from politics to culture to entertainment.

LO 3 Promotion on the Internet

Brand promotion via the Internet is growing dramatically. Marketers spent $54.7 million for Internet ads in 1995, and just over $8 billion in 2000. After a dip when the economy softened, ad revenues rebounded, reaching somewhere in the range of $20 billion in 2008.[16] The financial crisis that year triggered another economic slowdown, which took a bite out of all ad spending, but industry observers expect growth in online promotion to resume at a brisk pace.[17]

Advantages of Online Promotion

Marketers use more and more Internet advertising not only because the Web represents a new and different technological option. Several unique characteristics of the Internet offer advantages over traditional media options.

Target Market Selectivity

The Web gives marketers a precise way to target market segments. Not only are the segments precisely defined—you can place an ad on the numismatist (coin collecting) society page, for example—but the Internet allows forms of targeting that truly enhance traditional segmentation schemes such as demographics, geographics, and psychographics. Besides focusing on specific interest areas, marketers also can target based on geographic regions (including global), time of day, computer platform, or browser. American Airlines enlisted the help of TM Advertising to track the Web behavior of the readers of *Wall Street Journal* online travel columns and then "followed" those surfers around with American Airlines ads at various other sections. Response to the online advertising increased 115 percent.[18]

Tracking

The Internet allows advertisers to track how users interact with their brands and learn what interests current and potential customers. Display or banner ads and websites also provide the opportunity to measure the response to an ad by means of hits, a measure that is unattainable in traditional media. We'll discuss tracking and measurement in more detail later in the chapter.

Courtesy of Advertising.com.

Various firms, including Advertising.com, help marketers place highly targeted email messages online, delivering messages to select groups most likely to be interested. This level of selectivity is one of the chief attractions of Internet promotion.

Deliverability, Flexibility, and Reach

Online advertising and website content are delivered 24 hours a day, seven days a week, at the convenience of the receiver. Whenever receivers are logged on and active, ads are there. Just as important, a campaign can be tracked on a daily basis and updated, changed, or replaced almost immediately. This is a dramatic difference from traditional media, where changing a campaign might be delayed for weeks, given media schedules and the time needed to produce ads. The Maui Jim sunglasses website (http://www.mauijim.com) is a perfect example of this kind of deliverability and flexibility. It allows consumers to visit the site at any time to dig for information and check out new products. And with wireless options, there will be even more flexibility and deliverability.

Also, behind television and radio, no medium has the reach (use of a medium by audiences) of the Internet. As mentioned earlier, almost three-quarters of U.S. households have Internet access. In addition, the Internet is a global medium unlike any traditional media option.

Interactivity

A lofty and often unattainable goal for a marketer is to engage a prospective customer with the brand and the firm. This can be done with Internet advertising in a way that just cannot be accomplished in traditional media. A consumer can go to a company website or click through from a display or banner ad and take a tour of the brand's features and values. A **click-through** is a measure of the number of page elements (hyperlinks) that actually have been requested (that is, "clicked through" from the display or banner ad to the link).

Software is a perfect example of this sort of advantage. Let's say you are looking for software to do your taxes. If you log on to H&R Block tax consulting (http://www .hrblock.com), you will find the software, tax forms, and online information you need to prepare your taxes. Then you actually can file your taxes with the IRS and your state tax agency.

The click-through is an important component of Web advertising for another important reason. If advertisers can attract surfers to the company or brand website, then they have a chance to convert that surfer to a buyer if the site is set up for e-commerce. Researchers are discovering that design components of various Internet ad formats can have an important effect on click-through and, therefore, sales potential.[19]

Integration

Web advertising is the most easily integrated and coordinated with other forms of promotion. In the most basic sense, all traditional media advertising being used by a marketer can carry the website URL (uniform resource locator; basically, the website's address). Web display or banner ads can highlight themes and images from television or print campaigns. Special events or contests can be featured in display or banner ads and on websites. Overall, the integration of Web activities with other components

of the marketing mix is one of the easiest integration tasks in IMC, thanks to the flexibility and deliverability of Web advertising.

A great example of integrating consumer Web behavior with another part of the promotional process, personal selling, is the strategy used by Mazda Corp. Mazda's salespeople used to hate the Web because shoppers would come to the showrooms armed with "cost" data on every vehicle, obtained from various websites. Rather than battle consumers, Mazda embraced the fact that car shoppers use the Web to search for pricing information. The company installed Internet kiosks in its showrooms so that customers could look up information right there. One dealership owner found that the Internet access doesn't interfere with selling but rather "helps build trust and close sales faster."[20]

Cost of Online Promotion

Preparing an ad and placing it on a website once cost a few thousand dollars. But given the huge audiences that now can be reached on the Web and the availability of technology that tracks the number of people who visit a website and click on an ad, the cost has skyrocketed. A banner ad on a leading portal like Yahoo! now costs about $500,000 per day—about the same as a 30-second television spot on *CSI*. Granted, the ad runs all day versus one 30-second insertion, but that's still a huge cost increase.[21]

Measured in terms of **cost per thousand (CPM)**, however, the cost of Web ads for the most part compares favorably with ads placed in traditional media. Most agencies price banner ads on a CPM basis, while a smaller number base their prices on click-throughs.[22]

The real attraction of Internet promotion is not found in raw numbers and CPMs but rather in the expectation of reaching highly desirable, highly segmentable, and highly motivated audiences. The Internet enables niche marketing—that is, reaching only the consumers most likely to buy what the marketer is selling. Marketers can identify segments and deliver

© Monkey Business Images/Shutterstock.

almost-customized (or in the case of email, actually customized) messages directly to those customers, one by one.

Types of Internet Promotion

There are several ways for marketers to place their messages on the Web. The most prominent is paid search, and the best known is banner advertising, but many more options exist.

Paid Search

The biggest share of spending on Internet advertising is for **paid search**, the practice of paying websites and portals to place ads in or near relevant search results based on keywords. For example, if you search for "running shoes," links to ShopAdidas.com and Zappos.com will be displayed next to the search results as sources for purchasing running shoes. Paid search has grown astronomically and represents about 40 percent of the online ad spending by marketers.[23] The catalyst for growth in paid search is the success of Google, which pushed the concept from its beginning. Paid-search technology can fine-tune a Web user's search to more relevant and specific websites. For example, if an astronomy buff enters the word "saturn" in a search, paid search results would be returned for the planet, not the car company.

Paid search is extremely valued by firms as they try to improve the effectiveness and efficiency of their online promotion. Paid search is not particularly cheap—about 58 cents per verified click for second-tier search sites to about $1.61 on Google.[24] But 80 percent of advertisers using paid search report that it increased the traffic to their websites.[25]

An important principle for using paid search is that Web users are most likely to read and click on links that appear near the top of their results. To obtain those valued positions, marketers use **search engine optimization (SEO)**. SEO is a process whereby the volume and quality of traffic to a website from search engines is improved based on surfers' profiles.

Display or Banner Ads

When most people think of Internet advertising, they think of **display or banner ads**. These are paid placements of advertising on websites that contain editorial material. Not only do consumers see the ad, but they also can make a quick trip to the marketer's home page by clicking on the ad (the "click-through" defined earlier). Thus, the dual challenge of creating and placing display or banner ads is first to catch people's attention and then to entice them to visit the marketer's website and stay for a while. Research indicates that the ability to create curiosity and provide resolution to that curiosity can have an important impact on learning and brand attitude.[26]

A more targeted option is to place banner ads on sites that attract specific market niches. For example, a banner ad for running shoes would be placed on a site that offers information related to running. This option enables marketers to focus more closely on their target audiences. Niche users have particular interests that may represent important opportunities for the right marketer.

Display or banner ads such as this one generally invite the viewer to click on a link to expand the ad, learn more about the product, or place an order. Offering something of value, such as a coupon, for clicking can increase the chance of a response.

Photo Courtesy, OmniTerra Images.

A pricing evaluation service for these types of ads is offered by Interactive Traffic. The I-Traffic Index computes a site's advertising value based on traffic, placement and size of ads, ad rates, and evaluations of the site's quality. Firms such as Forrester Research assess the costs of display or banner ads on a variety of sites and provide marketers with an estimate of the audience delivered.

Sponsorship

Marketers can pay to maintain a section of a website, a type of brand promotion known as **sponsorship**. Along with the sponsorship, the marketer also may provide content for a site. On Yahoo!'s home page (http://m.www.yahoo.com), the Yahoo! Movies section and Yahoo! Marketplace section are almost always "sponsored by" a marketer. The Weather Channel website (http://www.weather.com) is another site that attracts sponsors. Public service or not-for-profit websites often try to recruit local sponsors.

In the context of more animated display or banner ads and paid search, it appears that sponsorships are becoming less and less popular. Marketers are spending about $500 million annually on sponsorship.[27]

Pop-Up and Pop-Under Ads

From the Web surfer's perspective, some of the most-hated ads are pop-up Internet ads. The idea is borrowed from TV. A **pop-up ad** is an Internet advertisement that opens in a separate window while a Web page is loading. The more times people click on these ads, the more money can be charged for the privilege of advertising. In a recent study, nearly 80 percent of surfers said pop-ups are annoying, and about 65 percent said display or banner ads were annoying.[28] But like spam, pop-ups are relatively effective, with 2 percent of Web visitors clicking on the pop-up—nearly double the click-through rate for display and banner ads.[29] Many Internet service providers provide pop-up blocking software that greatly reduces an advertiser's ability to get a pop-up onto a user's screen.

A subcategory of pop-up ads is the **interstitial**, also called "splash screen." These appear on a site after a page has been requested but before it has loaded, and they stay onscreen long enough for the message to be registered. So a surfer who wants to go to a certain site must see an ad page first, just as a television viewer must watch a commercial before seeing a favorite show. Interstitials often invite the viewer to link to another, related site.

Pop-under ads are ads that are present "under" the Web user's active window so that they are visible only when the surfer closes that window. Like pop-ups, pop-unders are seen as a nuisance by computer users. Regardless, if the click-through rate is not identifiable or if paid search comes to dominate online advertising (as it may), then pop-up and pop-under ads may become a bit of odd Internet history.

Email Communication

As mentioned earlier, email communication may be the Internet's most advantageous promotional application because it makes the Internet the only mass medium capable of customizing a message for thousands or even millions of receivers. The messages are delivered in a unique way, one at a time. The United States alone has about 170 million email users, and marketers are spending more than $1.6 billion annually on newsletters, direct messaging, and email list rental.

Email from organizations is most effective when Web users have agreed to receive it; this is called opt-in email, as discussed earlier, or **permission marketing**. Some Web firms, such as InetGiant, specialize in developing opt-in lists of Web users who have agreed to accept commercial emails. The data on permission-based emailing versus spamming are compelling. Sixty-six percent of Web users who give their permission to have email sent to them indicate that they either are eager or curious to read the email. This compares with only 15 percent of Web users who receive email through spamming.

Email marketers are turning to some traditional message strategies such as humor to make their messages more palatable and interesting. BitMagic, an Amsterdam-based Web advertising specialty firm, has Web users download software containing a joke, cartoon, or game along with the email message.[30]

Through email and electronic mailing lists, advertisers can encourage viral marketing. **Viral marketing** is the process of consumers marketing to consumers over the Internet through word-of-mouth transmitted through emails and electronic mailing lists. Hotmail (http://www.hotmail.com) is the king of viral mar-

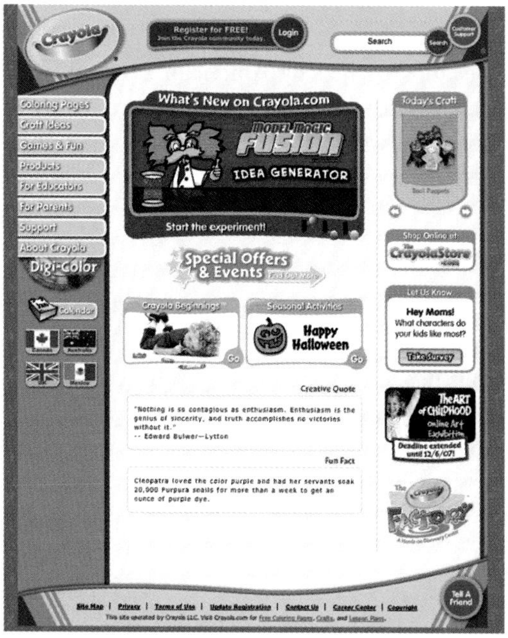

Permission granted by Binney & Smith.

In contrast to purely informational or business sites, the Crayola website offers parents, teachers, and kids a variety of educational and entertainment options.

keting. Every email from every Hotmail subscriber used to conclude with the tagline "Get your private, free email at www.hotmail.com." That viral marketing program helped the company sign up 12 million subscribers.[31]

Rich Media, Video, and Audio

Online marketers also are making their ads more engaging through the use of **rich media, video, and audio**—advanced technology like streaming video or audio that interacts with the user when the user's mouse passes over the ad. For example, if you go to the Yahoo! main page, you may see an ad for a new movie about to be released. As you pass your mouse over the ad, it launches a video clip from the film. Firms such as RealNetworks, NetRadio, and MusicVision insert streaming video into ads for advertisers. The future of such ads will depend on consumer access to high-speed Internet connections.

Besides simply making online ads more interesting, streaming audio and video can realize click-through rates of 3.5 percent—hundreds of times greater than click-throughs for display or banner ads. Academic literature supports the proposition that adding animation to Internet ads increases click-through rates, recall, and favorable attitudes toward Web ads.[32] When Adidas launched an online version of its television ad "Impossible Is Nothing," which featured a fantasy bout between Muhammad Ali and his daughter Laila, the two-week Net placement attracted 5 million streams, or viewings. Much of that audience consisted of 12- to 24-year-old consumers, who are highly prized by sports shoe sellers.

rich media, video, and audio use of streaming video and audio that plays when the user's mouse passes over an Internet ad

corporate home page website that focuses on a corporation and its products

virtual mall gateway to a group of Internet storefronts where the user gains access to a retailer by clicking on a storefront

Requiring the audience to click on or hover the mouse over the ad also lets marketers track consumer involvement with the message. New Balance recently used rich media in ads for its ZIP shoes. A message at the bottom of a display ad said, "Hover for video"; users who clicked on or hovered over the ad opened a video with information including a map of stores selling the shoes. To run the ad, New Balance paid a "cost per engagement" fee based on the number of videos opened.[33]

Corporate Home Pages

A **corporate home page** simply is the website where a business provides current and potential customers with information about the firm and usually its brands in great detail. The best corporate home pages not only provide corporate and brand information but also offer other content of interest to site visitors. The Crayola site doesn't have to explain details about its already-famous product. Instead, the website addresses the creative needs of the parents of children who use Crayola crayons. Visitors get craft ideas as they plan parties, look up family travel ideas, download coloring pages and projects, and, of course, create art with computerized Crayolas.

Virtual Malls

A variation on the corporate website is a website placed inside a virtual mall. A **virtual mall** is a gateway to a group of Internet storefronts that provide access to mall sites by simply clicking on a category of store, as shown on the Mall Internet site (http://www.mall-internet.com). This site is set up to lead shoppers to product categories. When a click is made to a product category, Mall Internet offers "featured store" click-throughs that lead to corporate websites and home pages. This additional presence gives stores such as the Sharper Image and Target more exposure.

Widgets

A new piece of technology with potential as an advertising option is a **widget**—a module of software that people can drag and drop onto their personal Web page of their social network (e.g., Facebook) or onto a blog. Widgets look like a website window but carry the power of a full website. Advertisers can create widgets that feature their brands or that direct the widget clicker to an e-commerce site. The advertiser will pay a fee each time a user installs the widget. Reebok offers a widget where users can create a customized virtual "fighting" sport shoe and place it on their Web page to "fight" other people's sneakers.[34]

Second Life and Virtual Worlds

Marketers can interact with consumers within virtual worlds. The most prominent of the virtual worlds is **Second Life**, an online virtual world where participants log into a space and then use their mouse and keyboard to roam landscapes, chat, create virtual homes, or conduct real business. Participants "exist" in Second Life (http://www.secondlife.com) as avatars, or onscreen graphical characters.

The growth of participation in Second Life has attracted the attention of advertisers for three reasons:

1. There are about 2 million active participants in Second Life, and that number is growing.[35]

2. Because participants in Second Life can "own" the objects they create, real commerce is taking place.

3. The landscapes and cityscapes created in Second Life offer an ideal environment for brand promotion. Along with paid search at the Second Life site, you will find merchants with offerings to outfit your "second life."

Real-world marketers can create billboards and branded product use, and avatars can wear branded apparel or use branded items. Several automobile firms have committed to Second Life as a good brand promotion opportunity. Pontiac and Toyota have established virtual dealerships and "sell" some of their most popular youth-oriented brands.[36]

But despite the excitement about brand promotion in virtual worlds, the ultimate potential of this venue as a promotional medium is still in question. One analyst described Second Life as "so popular, no one goes there anymore."[37] This analyst counted "actual" visitors and then repeat visitors to Second Life and found only about 100,000 Americans per week available for targeting by U.S. marketers—and "nobody" visiting virtual islands owned by American Apparel, Reebok, and Scion.[38] Virtual worlds may offer Internet users another social networking venue, but they may not offer marketers a very good message-communication venue.

Video Games

Marketers especially are interested in video games as a way to reach the elusive 18- to 34-year-old male segment that has abandoned many traditional media for digital media. For example, *Need for Speed: Carbon*, an auto-racing game from Electronic Arts, is full of ads. Advertising spending within video games, primarily through embedded billboards and posters, is expected to reach more than $700 million by 2010.

A question remains for marketers to address: Do players notice their brands? Even though the games are full of ads, there is some evidence that players focusing on the game pay almost no attention to those ads.[39]

LO 4 Establishing a Website

It's fairly easy to set up a website but setting up a commercially viable one is a lot harder and a lot more expensive. The top commercial sites can cost $1 million to develop, about $4.9 million for the initial launch, and about $500,000 to more than $1 million a year to maintain.[40] Setting up an attractive site costs so much because of the need for specialized designers to create the site and, most important, to update it constantly. The basic hardware for a site can be a personal computer, and the software to run the site ranges from free to several thousand dollars, depending on the number of extras needed. A site anticipating considerable traffic will need to plan for higher-capacity connections—and hence, a bigger phone bill.

Still, even small companies that want a Web presence can employ some inexpensive ways of setting up a site and finding hosts to maintain it. Companies like 1&1 Internet (http://www.1and1.com) offer small businesses a wide range of services, including hosting at extremely low cost, maintenance of domain names, website connectivity, email accounts, and some limited e-commerce applications for as little as $9.99 per month. One company that successfully set up and maintains an inexpensive site is Backcountry.com (http://www.backcountry.com). The two founders, former ski bums, started in 2000 with $2,000 and now run the second-largest online outdoor-gear organization, behind REI.[41]

In addition, use of the Web as a key component of a brand building is not reserved for consumer brands. Marketers of business products—from large firms like Caterpillar to small firms like PrintingForLess.com—are discovering the power of the Web in providing customer service and brand building. Plus, the Web is that fastest and most efficient way to reach a global market. The instant you establish a website, any computer user from any part of the globe can access your site and navigate through all the features and information opportunities you care to provide.

sticky site website that attracts visitors again and again and keeps them for a long time

Luring Surfers Back

Once a site is set up, a primary concern is getting those who spend considerable time on the Internet to spend time at the site and to come back often. A site that attracts visitors over and over again and keeps them for a long time is said to be a **sticky site** or to have features that are sticky.

© Bartlomiej Magierowski/Shutterstock.

GLOBAL THE NEXT NET WAVE

With more than 250 million users, China is the Internet's biggest population. And even though it's already number one, China represents a huge opportunity for future growth: Only one out of five Chinese people are using the Internet. Here are a few firms already surfing this massive Net wave:

- Sina, the most popular portal in the country, has links to online gaming and Yahoo! Auctions.
- NetEase operates a portal called 163.com, earning revenue through online ads, text messages, and games.
- Shanda is China's first indigenous online gaming company.
- TOM Online focuses on mobile Internet services.

Source: Bruce Einhorn, "The Net's Second Superpower," *BusinessWeek*, March 15, 2004, 54–56; "Stats—Web Worldwide," *ClickZ*, http://www.clickz.com/stats/web_worldwide, accessed December 1, 2009.

What makes a site sticky? Certainly not pages and pages of nothing but product photos and specifications, especially when product descriptions simply mimic printed brochures. Although such websites might satisfy the needs of consumers searching for specific product information, they are unlikely to attract and capture the interest of surfers long enough to entice them back. Research indicates that a home page that is moderately complex with respect to the number of links, graphics, and overall home page length influences consumer attention, attitudes, and purchase intent.[42] Service firms such as Ingenux (http://www.ingenux.com) will provide marketers with the tools and expertise needed to develop a sticky site.

To make a site sticky, a marketer should incorporate engaging, interactive features into the site. In an effort to break into the world of portals, iWon (http://www.iwon.com) offers all sorts of links to current information—as well as the chance to win $10,000 a day or $1 million each month for using the site—pretty much an all-out assault on trying to get surfers to come back. For home pages or websites, entertaining features such as online games or videos can increase the frequency and length of visits. One site that does a good job of using devices such as these is the U.S. Army. More than 1 million people have registered to play the Army's Web-based computer games at http://www.goarmy.com.[43]

Sticky sites deliver substance, ease of use, and entertainment value. Web users are discriminating. Even though pretty pictures are interesting, sites that have high user loyalty offer something more—for example, brand information and ongoing technical support, general news about a brand category, original writing, or the latest information about just about anything. For the major hosting sites and portals, recurring information such as the weather, late-breaking news, sports scores, and stock quotes attract visitors daily or even several times a day. The King Arthur Flour company website not only sells premium flour and baking products, but it also serves its target market of enthusiastic bakers with an online community called Baking Circle (http://www.bakingcircle.com). Customers who register for the Baking Circle swap recipes, post messages, and upload pictures of their delicious creations. The 100,000 or so online members of the Baking Circle may not sound like a lot, but they are enthusiastic repeat customers.[44]

The interactivity of a site has important consequences, not only for loyalty to a site, but also for intention to purchase items from the site. Research shows that when consumers engage in more human-message (an interactive message) or human-human interaction (like a chat room), there is a more positive attitude toward the site and a higher purchase intention.[45]

Developing a Domain Name

A **domain name** is a company's unique identity on the Internet, such as www.yourcompany.com. Companies like VeriSign help companies identify, register, and manage Internet names and keywords in both domestic and global markets.

If you are the Gap (http://www.gap.com) or Sony (http://www.sony.com), your domain name is your corporate name, and consumers know how to search for your location. But for thousands of Web startups that provide specialized products and services, selection of a domain name is a dilemma. The name should be descriptive but unique, and intuitive but distinctive. Consultant Dennis Scheyer once recommended that GoToTix.com, a ticketing and entertainment site, stick with its original name because it was intuitive and easy to remember. But the firm insisted on running a consumer contest to rename the company. It eventually chose Acteva.com (and the domain name http://www.acteva.com) because "Act conveys activity. E signifies E-commerce and 'va' has that international flavor." The company has expanded beyond selling tickets and provides online registration and tracking for all sorts of events from fundraisers to corporate meetings.[46]

The suffix of a website name is called the **top-level domain (TLD)**. Until late 2000, there were only five TLDs in the United States: .com, .edu, .org, .gov, and .net. Recently, the Internet Corporation for Assigned Names and Numbers (ICANN), a nonprofit formed in 1998 to coordinate technical management of the domain name system, issued new top-level domains. You can visit ICANN's website at http://www.icann.org to learn about the new TLD extensions available, as well as country-specific TLDs (e.g., .us and .uk). The purpose of releasing new TLDs, such as .tv and .us, is to relieve the pressure on the original top-level domains. But pairing an existing name with a new suffix could create confusion among consumers.

If you have an idea, be sure to register the URL for your company ASAP with a provider like Register.com. The cost can be less than $20 per year, and that price often includes email. Why hurry? Domain names are big business, and folks called "domainers" register every name they can think of, hoping they can resell the right to the name for a tidy sum. The domain http://www.cellphones.com was resold for $4.2 million.[47] An estimated 90,000 domain names are purchased each day, and Internet domain purchasing could become a $10 billion per year industry by 2010.[48]

Promoting Websites

After building a website, the next step is promoting it. Several agencies, including Wieden & Kennedy and OgilvyOne, specialize in promoting websites. Several methods are available:

- Feature the website address in traditional media advertising. Most print ads and many radio and TV ads feature the marketer's Web address.
- Notify Usenet groups; this is fast and costs little.
- Register the site with search engines such as Yahoo! and Ask.com. With Yahoo!, because it is a hierarchical search engine, pick keywords that commonly are chosen yet describe and differentiate the site.
- Register with the growing Yellow Pages on the Internet—for example, SuperPages, (http://www.bigyellow.com)—and with appropriate electronic mailing lists.
- Send press releases to Internet news sites.
- Use email as a form of direct mail.

> **top-level domain (TLD)** suffix that follows a website name

Security and Privacy Issues

Any Web user can download text, images, and graphics from the Web. Although marketers place trademark and copyright disclaimers in their online messages, trademarks and logos easily can be copied without authorization. Currently, there is no viable policing of this practice. Marketers have taken legal action only against users who have taken proprietary materials and blatantly used them in a fashion that is detrimental to the brand or infringes on the exclusivity of the marketer's own site. This may change.

In Chapter 6, we discussed privacy as an ethical and regulatory issue. It also is a matter of strategic management. Discussions at the highest levels focus on the extent to which regulations should be mandated for gathering and disseminating information about Web use. The concern among marketers is not only regulation but also sensitivity to consumers' concerns about their privacy being violated online.

Privacy is a legitimate concern for Internet users and will likely continue to be one for civil libertarians and regulators as well. But it is not clear that consumers themselves (as opposed to critics or watchdog groups) really care much about privacy. In a survey of U.S. consumers, only 6 percent said they always read a site's privacy policy, and another 15 percent said they sometimes read the policy.[49] Some interesting research has discovered that, for people from countries with "weak rule of law," privacy and security issues affect the perceived value of a website, whereas for people from countries that are high on

WE DISCUSSED **PRIVACY** AS AN ETHICAL AND REGULATORY ISSUE. IT IS ALSO A MATTER OF **STRATEGIC MANAGEMENT.**

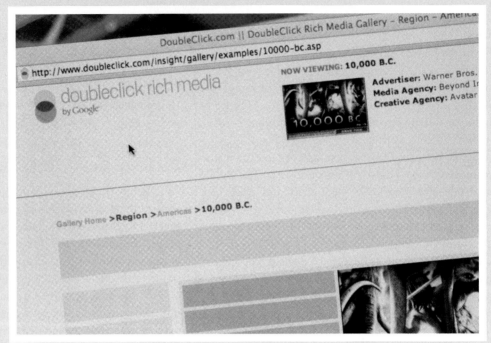

Warner Brothers used this widget ad to promote the release of its movie *10,000 B.C.* Because it's a widget, viewers not only can click to watch a video or see photos, but they also can grab it and share it with their friends. DoubleClick provides tracking technology so that marketers can find out how many times each tool is clicked, as well as where the ad is being shared.

national identity, privacy and security is less important than the cultural congruity between the site and themselves.[50]

Nevertheless, technology is changing rapidly, and a whole new level of concern and controversy could find its way into the privacy discussions. More consumers are accessing the Internet through wireless technology, which is more readily subject to monitoring. Hacking an in-home or in-firm wireless system without the proper security hardware is as easy as sitting in a car with a laptop with an antenna.

Measuring Effectiveness of Online Promotion

To measure the effectiveness of their online promotion, marketers want information about how many people visit a particular website and, if possible, details about who those people are. At a minimum, when a user connects with a website, the basic information that can be collected includes the IP ad-

dress of the computer requesting the page, the page requested, and the time of the request. For an opt-in site that requires registration, the marketer can obtain additional information provided by the user, such as email address, ZIP code, gender, age, and household income. Consumers tend to resist attempts to learn about them via registration. Still, plenty of service providers, described later in this section, are available to guide marketers through Web measurement options.

What Gets Counted

Several terms are used in Web audience measurement. The following are the most meaningful of these measurement factors:

- **Hits** are the number of elements requested from a given page. The number of hits provides almost no indication of actual Web traffic. For instance, a user's request for a page with four graphical images counts as five hits. By including many images, a site quickly can pull up its hit count. Thus, the *Seventeen* magazine site (http://www.seventeen.com) might get 3 million hits a day, placing it among the top websites, but this 3 million hits translates into perhaps only 80,000 visitors daily.

- Another measure of a site's advertising effectiveness is the extent to which visitors click through and request information from an ad, as we have discussed before. Most analysts consider the *click-through* number (and percentage) to be the best measure of Web advertising's effectiveness. An ad that motivates a visitor to click on it and follow the link to more information presumably was viewed and was motivating (more on this later).

- **Page views** are the pages (actually, the number of HTML—hypertext markup language—files) sent to the requesting user's computer. If a downloaded page occupies several screens, there is no indication whether the user examined the entire page. The page-view count also doesn't tell you how many visitors the page actually has: 100,000 page views in a week could be 10 people reading 10,000 pages, 100,000 people reading one page, or any variation in between.

- **Visits** are the number of occasions on which user X interacted with site Y after time Z has elapsed. Usually Z is set to some standard time, such as 30 minutes. If the user interacts with a site and then interacts again more than 30 minutes later, the second interaction would be counted as a new visit.

- **Unique visitors** are the number of different "people" visiting a site (a new user is determined from the user's registration with the site) during a specified period of time. Besides the address, page, and time, a website can find out the referring link address. This allows a website to discover what links are directing people to the site. This can be extremely helpful in Internet advertising planning. The problem is that what is really counted are unique IP numbers. Many Internet service providers use a dynamic IP number, which changes every time a given user logs in through the service, so you might show up as 30 different unique visitors to a site you visited daily for a month.

To obtain these statistics, marketers use Web analytic software. **Web analytic software** is measurement software that not only provides information on hits, pages, visits, and users but also lets a website track audience traffic within the site. The publisher of the site could determine which pages are popular and expand on them. It also is possible to track people's behavior as they go through the site, thus providing ideas about what people find appealing and unappealing. An example of Web analytic software is MaxInfo's WebC, which lets marketers track what information is viewed, when it is viewed, how often it is viewed, and where users go within a site. A

marketer then can modify the content and structure it accordingly. It also can help marketers understand how buyers make purchase decisions in general. But although it is possible to know a lot about users' behavior at sites, it still isn't possible to know what people actually do with website information.[51]

Despite all of these options, there is no industry standard for measuring the effectiveness of one interactive ad placement over another. There also is no standard for comparing Internet with traditional media placements. Moreover, demographic information on who is using the Web is severely limited to consumers who have signed up for opt-in programs and, for example, allow targeted emails to be sent to them. Until these limitations are overcome, many marketers will remain hesitant about spending substantial dollars for advertising on the Web.

Measurement Help

Plenty of companies offer measurement services for interactive media. Exhibit 9.3 lists only some of the companies providing measurement and evaluation services.

With Internet tracking services, an advertiser used to only be able to know how many people see an ad and how many respond to it with a click. But new

page views record of the pages that have been sent to a user's computer; multiscreen pages are counted as one page

visits number of occasions on which a particular user looks up a particular website during a given time period

unique visitors number of people (identified using registration information) who visit a site during a given time period

Web analytic software software that measures hits, pages, visits, and users, and allows a website to track audience traffic on the site

technologies now allow tracking of mouse movement on Web pages and grouping of shoppers by age, ZIP code, and reading habits. Double-Click, which places 200 billion ads a month for customers, can provide 50 different types of metrics for an Internet campaign. With mouse tracking, advertisers can know which parts of a banner ad appear to be of interest to visitors and how long they spend on different parts of an ad. With new control monitors, referred to as "dashboards," advertising strategists can check the performance of their online ads in real time. There is so much data available that agencies are hiring teams of analytic people, including PhDs in statistics, to make sense of the data.

The next step is to get inside users' heads. One agency, Tacoda Systems, announced plans to wire a group of Web surfers with brain scanners to see which ads register in their minds.[52] And academics are deep into the evaluation process, researching the effect of animation speed on attention, memory, and impression formation.[53]

Click Fraud

To measure effectiveness, you need to know that measures and data are valid. Unfortunately, sometimes they aren't. One big problem is **click fraud**—clicking on Internet advertising solely to generate illegitimate revenue for the website carrying the ad.[54] Click fraud

Exhibit 9.3
Measurement and Evaluation Services

Arbitron (http://www.arbitron.com)	One of the oldest advertising measurement firms; better known for traditional media (especially radio and television) measures but also specializes in providing data on Internet radio broadcasts.
Audit Bureau of Circulations (http://www.accessabc.com)	For many years, the main print circulation auditing organization; recently established ABC Interactive (ABCI), which offers independent measurement of online activity to ensure that website traffic and ad delivery metrics are reported accurately.
eMarketer (http://www.emarketer.com)	One of the newer entrants in the advertising measurement area; accumulates data from various research sources and provides summary statistics.
Experian Simmons (http://www.smrb.com)	Measures media and purchase behaviors of consumers; offers data on more than 8,000 brands across more than 460 product categories; creates 600 lifestyle profiles linked to every media genre, including information on Web use and product purchase.
Forrester Research (http://www.forrester.com)	Provides a wide range of data analysis, research, and advice for firms using the Internet for promotion and e-commerce.
Lyris HQ (http://www.lyris.com/solutions/lyris-hq/web-analytics/)	Web analytics program that makes it easy for marketers to compile website navigation patterns by users and compute return on investment (ROI) for Web advertising.
Nielsen NetRatings (http://en-us.nielsen.com/tab/product_families/nielsen_netratings)	Probably the highest profile of the data providers, ruling the ratings game for many years; relies on its traditional method of finding consumers who are willing to have their media behavior (in this case, Internet use) monitored by a device attached to their computers.
Ranking.com (http://www.ranking.com)	Performs market research on a statistically, geographically, and demographically significant number of Internet surfers; records these surfers' website visits and calculates rankings for the most-visited websites; one of the very few free sources of Web data research.

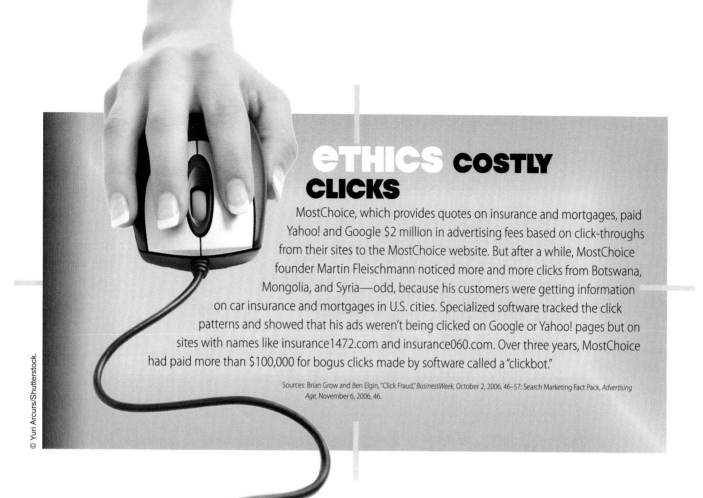

eTHICS COSTLY CLICKS

MostChoice, which provides quotes on insurance and mortgages, paid Yahoo! and Google $2 million in advertising fees based on click-throughs from their sites to the MostChoice website. But after a while, MostChoice founder Martin Fleischmann noticed more and more clicks from Botswana, Mongolia, and Syria—odd, because his customers were getting information on car insurance and mortgages in U.S. cities. Specialized software tracked the click patterns and showed that his ads weren't being clicked on Google or Yahoo! pages but on sites with names like insurance1472.com and insurance060.com. Over three years, MostChoice had paid more than $100,000 for bogus clicks made by software called a "clickbot."

Sources: Brian Grow and Ben Elgin, "Click Fraud," *BusinessWeek*, October 2, 2006, 46–57; Search Marketing Fact Pack, *Advertising Age*, November 6, 2006, 46.

takes place when a person is paid to visit websites, or when a computer program roams the Web and imitates a legitimate Web user by "clicking" on ads. Click fraud thus generates a charge per click without there having been actual interest in the ad's link.

Click fraud is a crime and occurs when an advertiser has a pay-per-click agreement with a website. There have been arrests related to click fraud with regard to malicious clicking in order to deplete a competitor's advertising budget. And this is no small problem. Forty percent of Web advertisers claim they have been victims of click fraud.

Google and Yahoo!, prime targets for click scammers, are working to stop click fraud by monitoring Web traffic for repeated clicks or unusual visit patterns from anonymous servers.[55] Yahoo! has named a senior executive to lead the company's effort to combat click fraud in its advertising business. The company also discards as invalid or inferior quality about 12 to 15 percent of clicks on advertisements; in the case of invalid clicks, it will not charge the advertiser. In a similar move, Google said its computers automatically reject up to 10 percent of potential advertising billings resulting from invalid clicks.

Managing the Brand in an E-Community

The Internet, besides giving marketers a medium for communicating with consumers, also gives consumers a new and efficient way to communicate with one another. In fact, the social aspect of the Internet is one of the most important reasons for its success. Via Usenet newsgroups, email, blogs, and social-networking Web pages, consumers have a way to interact and form communities. For marketers, this is yet another opportunity: the chance to communicate with consumers in a brand community or e-community.

Communities formed online among users of a particular brand behave much like a community in the traditional sense, such as a small town or ethnic neighborhood. They have their own cultures, rituals, and traditions. Members create detailed Web pages devoted to the brand. Members even feel a sense of duty or moral responsibility to other members of the community. For example, among many Volkswagen drivers, it is a common courtesy to pull over to help another VW broken down on the side of the road. Harley-Davidson riders feel a similar sense of affinity and desire to help others who use the same brand when they are in trouble.

© AP Photo/Peter Cosgrove.

Building a loyal e-community is a natural step for Harley-Davidson, whose enthusiastic customers look forward to company-sponsored motorcycle events.

In addition, the affinity to social-networking sites cannot be underestimated—or ignored. Sites like MySpace and Facebook attract 20 to 50 million unique visitors per month.[56] It seems clear that the credibility of these sites appeals to consumers who are weary of the blatant promotional intent of traditional media and commerce-oriented websites.

Because the Internet makes it easier for members of these communities to interact, brand communities are likely to continue to proliferate in coming years. Dealing effectively with these communities will be one of the challenges facing marketers. One approach is to encourage community-building on the brand's own website. Harley-Davidson's site (http://www.harley-davidson.com) tries to accomplish e-community interaction. Events around the country, promoted on the site, are a highlight for riders. Another technique for creating a community around the brand is to draw community members to the website by using features like those of Web portals, such as lifestyle and entertainment information.

LO 5 The Future of Online Promotion

When it comes to the Internet, the future seems to arrive with every new issue of *Business Week* or *Business 2.0*. But we are reasonably confident to say that the future of promotion on the Internet will be linked to two influences: technology and strategic IMC. And the two technologies expected to have the most impact on promotion are wireless communication and Web-launched video.

Wireless Technology

WiFi, which became widely popular in 2004, allows Internet-access connections that reach out about 300 feet. That meant people on the go—whether coffee drinkers at Starbucks or emergency workers at disaster sites—could have wireless access to information through their laptops. But WiFi is only the beginning. In the coming years, WiFi will likely yield to three innovative technologies that will push wireless networking into every facet of life from cars to homes to offices to the beach:

1. **WiMax** (Worldwide Interoperability for Microwave Access), like WiFi, creates "hot spots" around a central antenna within which people wirelessly can tap into the Net. But while WiFi creates a hot spot of 300 feet, WiMax has a potential range of 25 to 30 miles. Telecom industry scientists say the technology could be used in place of cable or DSL to deliver the "last mile" (final leg) of wireless broadband to the customer. WiMax won't replace DSL and cable modems in cities but is suited to rural areas.

2. **Mobile-Fi** is similar to WiMax in that it has multi-mile access, but it adds the capability of accessing the Net while the user is moving in a car or a train.

3. **Ultrabroadband** will allow people to move extremely large files quickly over short distances. On the road, a driver could download a large file from an on-board PC to a handheld computer. Or, at home, you could do a wireless upload of your favorite concert from your PC to your TV.

WiMax wireless Internet technology capable of a range of 25 to 30 miles

Mobile-Fi wireless Internet technology with multi-mile access and ability to access the Internet while the user is moving in a car or train

ultrabroadband wireless Internet technology allowing users to move extremely large files quickly over short distances

© Serg Salivon/Shutterstock.

GLOBAL TO RUSSIA WITH WIMAX

Alcatel-Lucent, developers of WiMax technology, recently landed a deal to build a nationwide rural WiMax access network in Russia, the world's most rural country. Alcatel-Lucent will work with Russian telecommunications company Synterra to build the WiMax infrastructure in towns with populations smaller than 100,000. The project is enormous, providing Internet access to more than 40 million Russians without a DSL or cable modem connection to the Internet. This, in turn, will give marketers a vast new market of Russian consumers.

Sources: Dan O'Shea, "Study: WiMax, MobileFi No Threat to DSL," *TelephonyOnline*, June 8, 2004, http://www.telephonyonline.com; Kevin Fitchard, "Alcatel-Lucent to Build WiMax in Russia," *TelephonyOnline*, July 6, 2007, http://www.telephonyonline.com.

Scientists at Intel, Alcatel-Lucent, and Motorola are working on these technologies primarily as modes of communication for the high-speed transmission of data. But in their practical application, these technologies will allow advertisers to communicate with audiences as they access the Internet through WiMax or Mobile-Fi. We are all just now getting accustomed to WiFi and the convenience it provides.

Another trend in wireless technology is the increasing use of cell phones to access the Web. Spending on mobile phone advertising is approaching $3 billion a year.[57] Placing messages on cell phones offers the opportunity to tailor a message to the user's location—for example, promoting a nearby restaurant or offering a deal at a store around the corner. Along with placing ads in online content accessed by cell phone, marketers are getting their brand onto phones by creating downloadable apps for the iPhone. Zippo created a "virtual lighter," which displays an image of a flame when the user flicks his or her wrist and sways when the user moves the phone. Millions of people downloaded the free application.[58]

Of course, this next step in the evolution of the Internet and its potential as an advertising alternative depends on consumer's willingness to allow mobile wireless communication to occur. Consumers are showing resistance, but it may be softening slowly. In a survey a few years ago, 51 percent of mobile phone users said they were "not willing at all" to receive promotional messages over their cell phones. In a more recent survey of U.S. Internet users, only a minority (38 percent) said they "don't want to see any ads" on their phones.[59]

Video on the Web

Marketers and advertising agencies are preparing for new opportunities with "broadcast Web." As more Web users have access to broadband (more than 60 percent of users in the United States now do), more complex data, including video files, can be streamed to them.[60] The possibilities are attracting all the big players—Microsoft, ABC, and CBS, to name just a few. They all see video streaming as another piece of the Web broadcast puzzle.[61] Does this mean that in the near future every television ad really is a Web ad? Well, maybe it won't be that extreme, but the technology is available to provide direct links to websites for information and purchasing through television ads—a huge opportunity and potential for marketers.

Strategic Online Communication

Early on, media and Internet companies already were thinking strategically about the Internet's role in brand promotion. The AOL/Time Warner merger in 2001 brought together movie studio properties, an emerging Internet movie business, digital delivery of Warner Bros. movies, and AOL's then-popular online services, including the Netscape browser and Instant Messenger. Later, as we saw in Chapter 2, interactive media giant IAC/InterActiveCorp assembled a conglomerate of Internet companies that can promote and sell each other's products.

More recent acquisitions have been aimed at amassing better online data to help track consumer interests and intentions: Google spent $3.1 billion to buy DoubleClick, and Yahoo! paid $680 million to assume ownership of Right Media.[62] Both Google and Yahoo! used those acquisitions to create a new way to buy and sell ads: advertising exchanges. With either the DoubleClick or the Right Media ad exchange, online media companies such as portals or Web publishers offer ad space to the highest bidder. Marketers provide information about their required target market and the price they're willing to pay. Much as eBay arranges deals between consumers, the ad exchanges match the available space with the highest bidder, who gets to place a highly targeted ad online.[63]

On the marketers' side, we are seeing some clever and effective applications of IMC to the Web. For example, when Mazda wanted to reposition its brand and appeal more broadly to a younger market, its marketers needed to understand the Web behavior of 24- to 36-year-old males—and not merely that this target segment was savvy about using Web tools in car-buying decisions. Mazda's dealerships and salespeople had to adopt a new role in the selling process. Mazda launched an integrated strategy that included using Web promotion to drive customers to the dealership, redesigning the dealerships' physical appearance (coffee shops and hip waiting rooms) and training salespeople to be as Web-savvy as the shoppers. The results of combining promotional tools have been impressive: Sales at Web-savvy Mazda dealerships rose 32 percent, and profits rose 50 percent.[64]

In the future, integrated efforts are likely to make more use of new tools, such as Second Life and widgets, as technological venues for brand communication on the Web. These new options offer wide-ranging possibilities that marketers only now are starting to understand and employ.

"WOULD YOU LIKE A CUP OF COFFEE?"

ONCE MAZDA REALIZED ITS CUSTOMERS WERE WEB-SAVVY AND REDESIGNED DEALERSHIPS TO INCLUDE COFFEE SHOPS AND HIP WAITING AREAS, THEY SAW SALES AND PROFITS RISE.

© Yuri Arcurs/Shutterstock.

As marketers try to engage consumers in brand messages, the Internet is likely to play a growing role. Will Internet brand promotion become the lead tool in most IMC campaigns? Not likely. But expect that, as technology advances and consumers become accustomed to accessing information in nontraditional ways, the Internet will be a more valuable tool.

STUDY TOOLS
CHAPTER 9

Located at back of the textbook

- Rip out Chapter in Review Card.

Located at www.cengagebrain.com

- Review Key Terms Flashcards (Print or Online).
- Complete the Practice Quiz to prepare for tests.
- Play "Beat the Clock" and "Quizbowl" to master concepts.
- Complete "Crossword Puzzle" to review key terms.
- Watch videos on **IKEA** and **iPad** for real company examples.
- For additional examples, go online to learn about Web-based contests, music stars getting their start online, and American Express Webisodes.

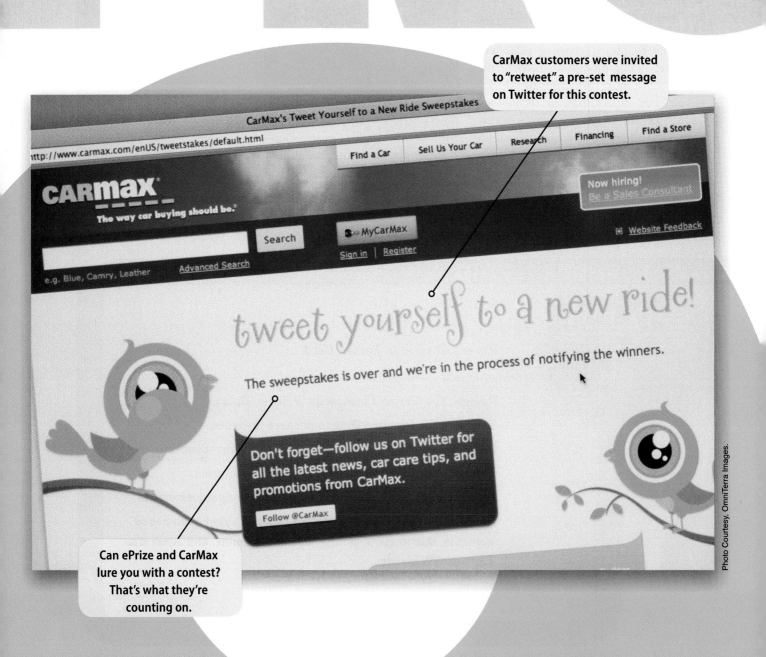

Learning Outcomes

After studying this chapter, you should be able to:

LO 1   Identify purposes served by direct marketing.

LO 2   Explain the popularity of direct marketing.

LO 3   Distinguish a mailing list from a marketing database, and review the applications of each.

LO 4   Describe the media used by direct marketers in delivering messages to consumers.

> "Fun without sell gets nowhere but sell without fun tends to become obnoxious."
>
> —Leo Burnett

AFTER YOU FINISH THIS CHAPTER GO TO PAGE 216 FOR STUDY TOOLS

Luring Consumers with ePrizes

When Josh Linkler was young, he bought a lot of Cracker Jack boxes in hopes of finding decoder rings as his sticky surprise. As an adult still intrigued by the decoder mystique, he used it as the big idea for a marketing service. His company, ePrize, has used decoder contests to drive curious customers to the Web, where they can play games online and, in the process, provide information about themselves and their interests.

One of ePrize's recent projects involved CarMax's "Tweet Yourself to a New Ride" sweepstakes. Customers were invited to "retweet" a message on Twitter that was pre-set by the contest rules. If their retweet was selected at the end of the eight week sweepstakes, the winner would receive $25,000 toward the purchase of any used car at CarMax. In addition, each week they awarded one winner with a $250 gas card. ePrize again played the key role of running the sweepstakes and collecting consumer information.[1]

In one application, Linkler worked with the Michigan International Speedway to build a database to unlock the secrets of NASCAR fans.[2] It started with mass distribution of e-decoder game pieces through ticket-order envelopes, movie theaters, and Pepsi retailers. The game pieces encouraged NASCAR fans to go online in the hopes of winning prizes like a $10,000 garage makeover from Gladiator Garage Works. First-time players registered by giving their name, address, email, age, and gender. With each return visit, they answered more questions so that they could go deeper into the game. Ultimately, the database was enriched with answers to around 150 demographic and lifestyle questions. There also were questions concerning leisure-time pursuits like camping and fishing, and specific questions like "Do you shop at Cabela's?"

What do you think?

Because I'm on mailing lists, I get information I value.

1   2   3   4   5   6   7

STRONGLY DISAGREE   STRONGLY AGREE

Find out what others think at CourseMate for PROMO.

Details about NASCAR fans help marketers connect with them via personalized offers that are timely and relevant. For example, Cabela's, a huge outdoor-sports retailer, can target offers to hunters or campers or boaters in the ePrize database. Why are NASCAR fans willing to divulge personal information? Well, some aren't, but Josh Linkler sees it as an issue of value: "If you want consumers to speak to you and provide information, you have to give them something to get them to react."[3]

The same principle has lured consumers to websites for other brand promotion and list-building efforts in which ePrize has played a role. For example, through mailings to local residents coupled with print and radio ads, Fifth Third Bank invited consumers to visit its bank branches and ask a teller for a game piece to enter its "Unlock Your Dreams" sweepstakes.[4] Consumers would go online and enter a code on their game piece to register for the sweepstakes with a grand prize of $250,000 plus smaller prizes. Of course, when they registered, they also provided information about themselves. Similarly, packages of Jelly Belly jelly beans invited candy lovers to go online to an ePrize-run site and enter a contest to choose a new flavor.[5] The winner received not only a cash prize but also fame and a chance to taste the new flavor, acai berry. Of course, Jelly Belly was a winner, too, because it drew 200,000 contestants and many more voters to its website and got them excited about the brand.

Evolution of Direct Marketing

When marketers speak of *direct marketing*, they generally are referring to something like the definition provided by the Direct Marketing Association (DMA): "**Direct marketing** is an interactive system of marketing, which uses one or more advertising media to affect a measurable response and/or transaction at any location."[6] Examined piece by piece, this definition furnishes an excellent basis for understanding the scope of direct marketing:[7]

*   *Interactive:* Direct marketing is interactive in that the marketer is attempting to develop an ongoing dialogue with the customer. Direct-marketing programs

How about a new moose rug or carved loon for your grandparents' cottage up north? You could find them at the Adirondack Country Store in upstate New York, call 1-800-LOON-ADK to request a catalog, or shop online at http://www.adirondackcountrystore.com.

commonly are planned with the notion that one contact will lead to another and then another so that the marketer's message can become more focused and refined with each interaction.

*   *Multiple media:* The use of multiple media in direct-marketing programs is an important point for two reasons. First, there is more to direct marketing than direct mail. Second, as we have noted before, a combination of media is likely to be more effective than any one medium alone.

*   *Immediate, measurable response:* Another key aspect of direct-marketing programs is that they almost always are designed to produce some form of immediate, measurable response, especially an immediate sale. The customer might be asked to return an order form with check or money order for $189 to get a stylish Klaus Kobec Couture Sports Watch, or to call an 800 number with credit card handy to get 22 timeless hits on a CD called *The Very Best of Tony Bennett*. This emphasis on immediate response enables direct marketers to judge the effectiveness of a particular program.

- *Any location:* When the DMA's definition notes that a direct-marketing transaction can take place "at any location," it means customers do not have to make a trip to a retail store for a direct-marketing program to work. Follow-ups can be made by mail, over the telephone, or on the Internet. At one time, the Internet was expected to provide so much convenience for shoppers that traditional retail stores would fall by the wayside. However, it now seems clear that consumers like the option of contacting companies in many ways.[8] Smart retailers make themselves available in both the physical and virtual worlds.[9] Customers are free then to choose where and how they want to shop.

A Look Back

From Johannes Gutenberg and Benjamin Franklin to Montgomery Ward and Lillian Vernon, the evolution of direct marketing has involved some of the great pioneers in business. The practice of direct marketing today is shaped by the successes of many notable mail-order companies and catalog merchandisers, such as those identified in Exhibit 10.1.[10] Among them, none is more exemplary than L. L. Bean, who founded his company in 1912 on his integrity and $400. His first product was a unique hunting shoe made from a leather top and rubber bottom sewn together. Other outdoor clothing and equipment soon followed in the Bean catalog.

A look at the L.L.Bean catalog of 1917 (black and white, only 12 pages) reveals the fundamental strategy underlying Bean's success. It featured the Maine Hunting Shoe and other outdoor clothing with descriptive copy that was informative, factual, and low key. On the front page was Bean's commitment to quality:

> *Maine Hunting Shoe—guarantee. We guarantee this pair of shoes to give perfect satisfaction in every way. If the rubber breaks or the tops grow hard, return them together with this guarantee tag and we will replace them, free of charge. Signed, L. L. Bean.*[11]

Bean realized that long-term relationships with customers must be based on trust, and his guarantee policy was aimed at developing and sustaining that trust.

As an astute direct marketer, Bean also showed a keen appreciation for the importance of building a good mailing list. For many years, he used his profits to promote his free catalog via advertisements in hunting and fishing magazines. Those replying to the ads received a rapid response and typically became Bean customers. Bean's obsession with building mailing lists is nicely captured by this quote from his friend, Maine native John Gould: "If you drop in just to shake his hand, you get home to find his catalog in your mailbox."[12]

Today, L.L.Bean still is a family-operated business that emphasizes the basic philosophies of its founder, thoughtfully summarized at http://www.llbean.com. Quality products, understated advertising, and sophisticated customer contact and distribution systems sustain the business. Additionally, L.L.Bean's 100 percent satisfaction guarantee still can be found in every Bean catalog. It remains at the heart of the relationship between Bean and its customers.

Exhibit 10.1
Some Direct-Marketing Milestones

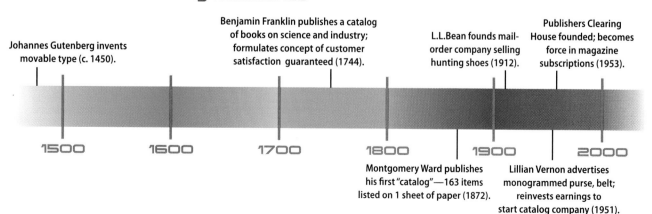

Johannes Gutenberg invents movable type (c. 1450).

Benjamin Franklin publishes a catalog of books on science and industry; formulates concept of customer satisfaction guaranteed (1744).

L.L.Bean founds mail-order company selling hunting shoes (1912).

Publishers Clearing House founded; becomes force in magazine subscriptions (1953).

Montgomery Ward publishes his first "catalog"—163 items listed on 1 sheet of paper (1872).

Lillian Vernon advertises monogrammed purse, belt; reinvests earnings to start catalog company (1951).

1500 1600 1700 1800 1900 2000

Source: Based on Direct Marketing Association, "Grassroots Advocacy Guide for Direct Marketers" (1993).

LO 1 Direct Marketing Today

Direct marketing today is rooted in the legacy of mail-order giants and catalog merchandisers such as L.L. Bean and Publishers Clearing House. Today, however, direct marketing has broken free from its mail-order heritage to become a tool used by all types of organizations throughout the world. Although many types of businesses and not-for-profit organizations are using direct marketing, it is common to find that such direct-marketing programs are not carefully integrated with an organization's other advertising efforts. Integration should be the goal for advertising and direct marketing. Again and again, the evidence supports our thesis that integrated programs are more effective than the sum of their parts.[13]

Because the label "direct marketing" now encompasses many different types of activities, it is important to remember the defining characteristics spelled out in the DMA's definition. Direct marketing involves an attempt to interact or create a dialogue with the customer; multiple media often are employed in the process, and a measurable response is immediately available for assessing a program's impact. With these defining features in mind, we can see that direct-marketing programs are commonly used for three primary purposes:

1. *Close sales:* The most common use of direct marketing is as a tool to close the sale with a customer. This can be done as a stand-alone program, or it can be coordinated with a firm's other promotional efforts. Telecommunications giants such as AT&T and Verizon make extensive use of the advertising and direct-marketing combination. High-profile mass media campaigns build awareness for their latest offer, followed by systematic direct-marketing follow-ups to close the sale.

2. *Cultivate prospects:* Direct-marketing programs also may aim to identify prospects for future contacts and, at the same time, provide in-depth information to selected customers. Any time you as a consumer respond to an offer for more information or for a free sample, you've identified yourself as a prospect and can expect follow-up sales pitches from a direct marketer. StairMaster uses advertising to initiate a dialogue with prospective customers. Ordering the free catalog and video, whether through the 800 number or at the website, begins a process of interactive marketing ultimately designed to produce the sale of another Free-Climber 4600.

3. *Engage customers with the brand:* Direct-marketing programs also are initiated as a means to engage customers, seek their advice, furnish helpful information about using a product, reward customers for using a brand, and in general foster brand loyalty. For instance, the manufacturer of Valvoline motor oil seeks to build loyalty for its brand by encouraging young car owners to join the Valvoline Performance Team.[14] To join the team, young drivers just fill out a questionnaire that enters them into the Valvoline database. Team members receive posters, special offers on racing-team apparel, news about racing events that Valvoline has sponsored, and promotional reminders at regular intervals that reinforce the virtues of Valvoline for the driver's next oil change.

Courtesy of Stairmaster Co., Kirkland, WA.

Most people won't buy a major piece of exercise equipment based on a magazine ad. The marketers at StairMaster know this, and their ad simply aims to start the purchase process by persuading consumers to order a free video.

LO 2 Growing Popularity

With the increasing concern about fragmenting markets and the diminishing effectiveness of traditional media in reaching those markets, we can expect that more and more promotion dollars will be moved into options besides advertising.[15] Direct-marketing programs are capturing some of that spending and growing in popularity for several reasons. Some of these have to do with changes in consumer lifestyles and technological developments that, in effect, create a climate more conducive to the practice of direct marketing. In addition, direct-marketing programs offer unique advantages vis-à-vis conventional mass media advertising.

From the consumer's standpoint, direct marketing's growing popularity might be summarized in a single word: *convenience*. Dramatic growth in the number of dual-income and single-person households has reduced the time people have to visit stores. Direct marketers give consumers access to a growing range of products and services in their homes, thus saving many households' most precious resource: time.

More liberal attitudes about the use of credit and the accumulation of debt also have contributed to the growth of direct marketing. Credit cards are the primary means of payment in most direct-marketing transactions. The widespread availability of credit cards makes it ever more convenient to shop from the comfort of one's home.

Developments in telecommunications also have facilitated the direct-marketing transaction. After getting off to a slow start in the late 1960s, toll-free telephone numbers have exploded in popularity to the point where one can hardly find a product or a catalog that does not include an 800 or 888 number for interacting with the seller. Whether consumers are requesting the StairMaster video or planning an adventure in Wyoming, the preferred mode of access for many consumers has been the 800 number.

Another obvious development having a huge impact on the growth of direct marketing is the computer. The diffusion of computer technology sweeping through all modern societies has been a tremendous boon to direct marketers. The computer allows firms to track, keep records on, and interact with millions of customers with relative ease. As we will see in an upcoming discussion, the computer power now available for modest dollar amounts is fueling the growth of direct marketing's most potent tool: the marketing database.

And just as the computer has given marketers the tool they need to handle massive databases of customer information, it too has provided convenience-oriented consumers with the tool they need to comparison shop with the point and click of a mouse. What could be more convenient than logging on to the Internet and pulling up a shopping agent like PriceScan.com or MySimon to check prices on everything from toaster ovens to snowboards? Why leave home?

© zentilia/Shutterstock.

Direct-marketing programs also offer some unique advantages that make them more appealing than what might be described as conventional mass marketing. A general manager of marketing communications with AT&T's consumer services unit put it this way: "We want to segment our market more; we want to learn more about individual customers; we want to really serve our customers by giving them very specific products and services. Direct marketing is probably the most effective way in which we can reach customers and establish a relationship with them."[16] As you might expect, AT&T is one of the organizations that has shifted more and more of its marketing dollars into direct-marketing programs.

The appeal of direct marketing is enhanced further by the persistent emphasis on producing measurable effects. For instance, in direct marketing, it is common for calculations such as **cost per inquiry (CPI)** or **cost per order (CPO)** to be featured in program evaluation. These calculations simply divide the number of responses to a program by that program's cost. When calculated for every program an organization conducts over time, CPI and CPO data tell an organization what works and what doesn't work in its competitive arena.

This emphasis on producing and monitoring measurable effects is realized most effectively through an approach called *database marketing*.[17] Working with a database, direct marketers can target specific customers, track their actual purchase behavior over time, and experiment with different programs for affecting the purchasing patterns of these customers. The programs that produce the best outcomes become the candidates for increased funding in the future.

Finding that waterfall in Wyoming will take some planning, and Wyoming's Office of Travel & Tourism is happy to help. The adventure begins with a request for a vacation packet. This ad provides two options: calling a toll-free number or visiting the tourism office's website.

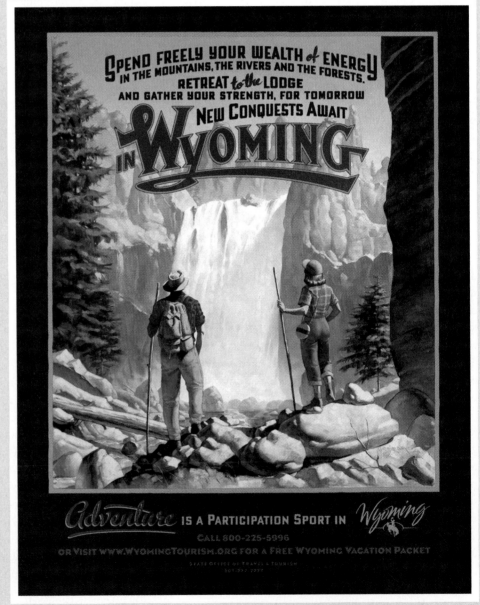

Courtesy, Wyoming Travel & Tourism.

LO 3 Database Marketing

If any ambiguity remains about what makes direct marketing different from marketing in general, that ambiguity can be erased by the database. The one characteristic of direct marketing that distinguishes it from marketing more generally is its emphasis on database development. Knowing who the best customers are along with what and how often they buy is a direct marketer's secret weapon.[18] This knowledge accumulates in the form of a marketing database.

Databases used as the centerpieces of direct-marketing campaigns take many forms and can contain many different layers of information about customers. At one extreme is the simple mailing list that contains nothing more than the names and addresses of possible customers; at the other extreme is the customized marketing database that augments names and addresses with various additional information about customers' characteristics, past purchases, and product preferences. Understanding this distinction between mailing lists and marketing databases is important for appreciating the scope of database marketing.

Mailing Lists

A **mailing list** simply is a file of names and addresses that an organization might use for contacting prospective or prior customers. Mailing lists are plentiful, easy to access, and inexpensive. For example, CD-ROM phone directories available for a few hundred dollars provide a cheap and easy way to generate mailing lists. More-targeted mailing lists are available from a variety of suppliers. The range of possibilities is mind-boggling, including groupings like the 238,737 subscribers to *Mickey Mouse Magazine*; 102,961 kindergarten teachers; 4,145,194 physical fitness enthusiasts; 117,758 Lord & Taylor credit card purchasers; and a whopping 269 archaeologists.[19]

Each time you subscribe to a magazine, order from a catalog, register your automobile, fill out a warranty card, redeem a rebate offer, apply for credit, join a professional society, or log on to a website, the information you provided about yourself goes on another mailing list. These lists are freely bought and sold through many means, including over the Internet. Sites such as Worldata, HDML, and InfoUSA allow marketers to buy names and addresses, or email address lists, for as little as 10 cents per record. What's out there is truly remarkable—go have a look.

Lists fall into two broad categories:

1. **Internal lists** simply are an organization's records of its own customers, subscribers, donors, and inquirers.

2. **External lists** are purchased from a list compiler or rented from a list broker.

At the most basic level, internal and external lists facilitate the two fundamental activities of the direct marketer: Internal lists are the starting point for developing better relationships with current customers, whereas external lists help an organization cultivate new business.

List Enhancement

Name-and-address files, no matter what their source, are merely the starting point for database marketing. The next step in the evolution of a database is mailing-list enhancement. Typically this involves augmenting an internal list by combining it with other, externally

mailing list file of names and addresses used for contacting prospects or customers

internal lists organization's records of its customers and inquirers; used for developing better customer relationships

external lists mailing lists purchased from a list compiler or rented from a list broker; used for cultivating new business

KNOWING WHO THE BEST CUSTOMERS ARE ALONG WITH WHAT AND HOW OFTEN THEY BUY IS A DIRECT MARKETER'S SECRET WEAPON.

supplied lists or databases. External lists can be appended or merged with a house list.

One of the most straightforward list enhancements entails simply adding or appending more names and addresses to an internal list. Proprietary name-and-address files may be purchased from other companies that operate in noncompetitive businesses. With today's computer capabilities, adding these additional households to an existing mailing list is simple. Many well-known companies such as Sharper Image and Hertz sell or rent their customer lists for this purpose.

A second type of list enhancement involves incorporating information from external databases into a house list. Here the number of names and addresses remains the same, but an organization ends up with a more complete description of who its customers are. Typically, this kind of enhancement includes any of four categories of information:

1. *Demographic data:* the basic descriptors of individuals and households available from the U.S. Census Bureau.

2. *Geodemographic data:* information that reveals the characteristics of the neighborhood in which a person resides.

3. *Psychographic data:* data that allow for a more qualitative assessment of a customer's general lifestyle, interests, and opinions.

4. *Behavioral data:* information about other products and services a customer has purchased. Knowledge about prior purchases can suggest a customer's preferences.

List enhancements that entail merging existing records with new information rely on software that allows the database manager to match records based on some piece of information the two lists share. For example, matches might be achieved by sorting on ZIP codes and street addresses. Many suppliers gather and maintain databases that can be used for list enhancement. One of the biggest is InfoUSA of Papillion, Nebraska (see http://www.infousa.com). With more than 210 million people in its database, and literally dozens of

pieces of information about each person, InfoUSA offers exceptional capabilities for list enhancement. Because of the massive size of the InfoUSA database, it has a high match rate (60 to 80 percent) when it is merged with clients' internal lists. A more common match rate between internal and external lists is around 50 percent.

Marketing Databases

Mailing lists come in all shapes and sizes, and when used to enhance internal lists, they can become rich sources of information about customers. But for a mailing list to qualify as a marketing database, it must include one important additional type of information.

Although a **marketing database** can be viewed as a natural extension of an internal mailing list, it also includes information collected directly from individual customers (see Exhibit 10.2). Developing a marketing database involves pursuing dialogues with customers and learning about their individual preferences and behavioral patterns. This can be potent information for hatching marketing programs that will hit the mark with consumers.

Aided by the dramatic escalation in processing power that comes from every new generation of computer chip, marketers see the chance to gather and manage more information about every individual who buys, or could buy, from them. Their goal might be portrayed as an attempt to cultivate a kind of cybernetic intimacy with the customer. A marketing database represents an organization's collective memory, which allows the organization to make the kind of personalized offer that once was characteristic of the corner grocer in small-town America. For example, working in conjunction with the Ohio State University Alumni Association, Lands' End created a special autumn promotion to offer OSU football fans all of their favorite gear just in time for the upcoming session. Print ads in the September issue of the OSU alumni magazine set the stage for a special catalog of merchandise mailed to Buckeye faithful. Of course, Lands' End had similar arrangements with other major universities to tap into fall football frenzy.

© Pete Saloutos/Shutterstock.

Database marketing at its best delivers consumers an offer that is both relevant and timely. That's cybernetic intimacy.

Database marketing also can yield important efficiencies that contribute to the marketer's bottom line. Cabela's, like many other multichannel retailers, finds it useful to create many targeted versions of its base or master catalogs, with seasonal points of emphasis. Why? The gender- or age-specific versions run about 100 pages, versus more than 1,000 pages for some of its master catalogs. A customer or household receives the targeted versions based on its profile in Cabela's database and the time of year. These streamlined catalogs are a great way to make timely offerings to targeted households in a cost-effective manner. In a nutshell, that's what database marketing is all about.

To summarize the information used by direct marketers, the crucial distinction between a mailing list and a marketing database is that the latter includes direct input from customers. Building a marketing database entails pursuing an ongoing dialogue with customers and continually updating records with new information. Thus, while mailing lists can be rich sources of information for program development, a marketing database has a dynamic quality that sets it apart.

Marketing Database Applications

Many different types of customer communication programs are driven by marketing databases. One of the greatest benefits of a database is that it allows an organization to quantify how much business the organization is actually doing with its current best customers. A useful way to isolate the best customers is with a recency, frequency, and monetary (RFM) analysis. An **RFM analysis** asks how recently and how often a specific customer is buying from a company, and how much money he or she is spending per order and over time. With this transaction data, it is a simple matter to calculate the value of every customer to the

Exhibit 10.2
What Makes a Marketing Database

frequency-marketing programs direct-marketing programs that provide concrete rewards to frequent customers

organization and identify customers that have given the organization the most business in the past. Past behavior is an excellent predictor of future behavior, so yesterday's best customers are likely to be an organization's primary source of future business.

A marketing database can be a powerful tool for organizations that seek to create a genuine relationship with their best customers. The makers of Ben & Jerry's ice cream have used their database in two ways: to find out how customers react to potential new flavors and product ideas, and to involve their customers in social causes.[20] In one program, their goal was to find 100,000 people in their marketing database who would volunteer to work with Ben & Jerry's to support the Children's Defense Fund. Jerry Greenfield, cofounder of Ben & Jerry's, justified the program as follows: "We are not some nameless conglomerate that only looks at how much money we make every year. I think the opportunity to use our business and particularly the power of our business as a force for progressive social change is exciting."[21]

Of course, when customers feel genuine involvement with a brand like Ben & Jerry's, they also turn out to be very loyal customers.

Reinforcing and recognizing your best customers is an essential application of the marketing database. This application may be nothing more than a simple follow-up letter that thanks customers for their business or reminds them of the positive features of the brand to reassure them that they made the right choice. Reinforcement also can include discounts and coupons mailed or emailed to regular customers.

To recognize and reinforce the behaviors of preferred customers, marketers in many fields are offering frequency-marketing programs that provide concrete rewards to frequent customers. **Frequency-marketing programs** have three basic elements:

1. A *database*, which is the collective memory for the program

2. A *benefit package*, which is designed to attract and retain customers

3. A *communication strategy*, which emphasizes a regular dialogue with the organization's best customers

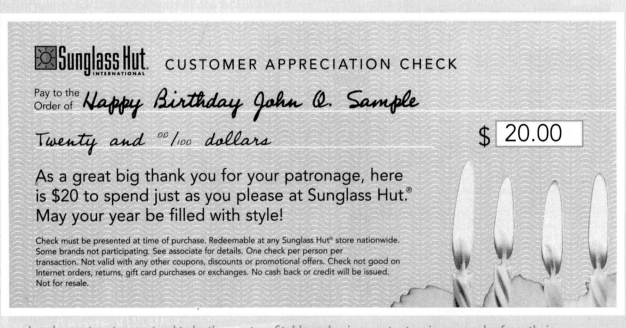

Courtesy, Sunglass Hut International.

Loyal repeat customers tend to be the most profitable, so businesses try to win more sales from their frequent customers. Date of birth is a common piece of information in a marketing database, so customers' birthdays are a great time to contact them. Sunglass Hut International uses a birthday card mailing to stay in a dialogue with its best customers. Of course, everyone likes a birthday present, so Sunglass Hut encloses a Customer Appreciation Check for $20, good at any Sunglass Hut store. According to the company's executives, this promotion, targeted to customers identified from its marketing database, is one of its best investments in advertising.

The casino industry is renowned for its application of frequency-marketing principles, and Harrah's Entertainment has set the standard for program innovation.[22] Harrah's "Total Rewards" program started out as a way for its 27 million members to accumulate points that could be cashed in for free meals and other casino amenities. This simple approach was quickly copied by the competition. Harrah's subsequently upgraded its program on a number of dimensions. One involved the benefit package: Harrah's upped the ante, allowing points to be used for Sony televisions and shopping sprees at Macy's. Harrah's also recognized that it needed separate reward packages for men and women, especially because women make up the majority of its customers. For the men, there are Big Bertha golf clubs and tickets to boxing matches; for the ladies, spa treatments and an evening with Chippendale dancers.

Another common application for the marketing database is **cross-selling**. Because most organizations today have many different products or services they hope to sell, one of the best ways to build business is to identify customers who already purchase some of a firm's products and to create marketing programs aimed at these customers but featuring other products. If they have a checking account with us, can we interest them in a credit card? If customers dine in our restaurants on Fridays and Saturdays, with the proper incentives perhaps we can get them to dine with us midweek, when we really need the extra business. A marketing database can provide a myriad of opportunities for cross-selling.

A final application for the marketing database is a natural extension of cross-selling. Once an organization gets to know who its current customers are and what they like about various products, it is in a much stronger position to go out and seek new customers. Knowledge about current customers is especially valuable when an organization is considering purchasing external mailing lists to append to its marketing database. If a firm knows the demographic characteristics of current customers—knows what they like about products, knows where they live,

and has insights about their lifestyles and general interests—then the selection of external lists will be much more efficient. The basic premise here simply is to try to find prospects who share many of the same characteristics and interests with current customers. And what's the best vehicle for coming to know the current, best customers? Marketing-database development.

Protecting Privacy

One very large dark cloud looms on the horizon for database marketers: consumers' concerns about invasion of privacy. It is easy for marketers to gather extensive information about consumers, and this is making the general public nervous. Many consumers are uneasy about the way their personal information is gathered and exchanged by businesses and the government without their knowledge, participation, or consent. Of course, the Internet only amplifies these concerns because the Web makes it easier for all kinds of people and organizations to get access to personal information.

In response to public opinion, state and federal lawmakers have proposed and sometimes passed legislation to limit businesses' access to personal information. Additionally, consumers' desire for privacy clearly was the motivation for the launch of the Federal Trade Commission's Do Not Call Registry. The registry has proved to be a very popular idea with consumers, but it has many opponents in business, including the Direct Marketing Association.[23] The DMA has estimated that the list could cost telemarketers on the order of $50 billion in lost sales. What the "do not call" list ultimately will mean for both sides remains to be seen. If you are one of those people who would like to do more to protect the privacy of your personal information, you can start with a visit to http://www.ftc.gov/privacy/protect.shtm.

Many in business are keenly aware of consumers' concerns about the privacy of their personal

cross-selling
marketing programs aimed at selling additional products to existing customers

zerøknowledge
Internet privacy solutions

I AM **NOT** A PIECE OF YOUR INVENTORY.

I am not a pair of eyeballs to
be captured or a consumer
profile to be sold.

I am an individual and you
will respect my privacy.

I will not be bartered,
traded or sold.

On the Net I am in control.

WWW.**ZEROKNOWLEDGE**.COM

This ad paints a dark picture of a future in which database marketers go unchecked. The ease of information sharing on the Internet has heightened concern about who is in control of personal information.

information. Companies can address customers' concerns about privacy if they remember two fundamental premises of database marketing. First, a primary goal for developing a marketing database is to get to know customers in such a way that an organization can offer them products and services that better meet their needs. The whole point of a marketing database is to keep junk mail to a minimum by targeting only exciting and relevant programs to customers. If customers are offered something of value, they will welcome being in the database.

The second premise is that developing a marketing database is about creating meaningful, long-term relationships with customers. If you want people's trust and loyalty, would you collect personal information from them and then sell it to a third party behind their back? We hope not! When collecting information from customers, an organization must help them understand why it wants the information and how it will use what it learns. If the organization is planning to sell this information to a third party, it must get customers' permission. If the organization pledges that the information will remain confidential, it must honor that pledge. Integrity is fundamental to all meaningful relationships, including those involving direct marketers and their customers. Recall that it was his integrity as much as anything else that enabled L. L. Bean to launch his successful career as a direct marketer. It will work for you, too.

LO 4 Media Used in Direct Marketing

Although mailing lists and marketing databases are the focal point for originating most direct-marketing programs, marketers implementing these programs must communicate information and arguments to consumers. As we saw in the definition of direct marketing, the message can be communicated through multiple media, typically with the overriding goal of achieving an immediate, measurable response. The desired response may be an order for services or merchandise, a request for more information, or the acceptance of a free trial offer. Because advertising conducted in direct-marketing campaigns emphasizes an immediate response, it commonly is referred to as **direct-response advertising**.

The direct marketer's prime media are **direct mail** and **telemarketing**. However, all conventional media, including magazines, radio, and television, can be used to deliver direct-response advertising, and many companies are deploying email as an economical means of interacting with customers. In addition, a dramatic transformation of the television commercial—the infomercial—has become especially popular.

Direct Mail

Direct mail has some notable faults as an advertising medium, not the least of which is cost. Reaching a person with a direct-mail piece can cost 15 to 20 times more than reaching that person with a television commercial or newspaper advertisement.[24] Additionally, in a society where people are constantly on the move, mailing lists commonly are plagued by bad addresses. Each bad address represents advertising dollars wasted. And direct-mail delivery dates, especially for bulk, third-class mailings, can be unpredictable. When precise timing of an advertising message is critical to its success, direct mail can be the wrong choice.

Despite these drawbacks, direct mail is the right choice in some situations. Direct mail's advantages stem from the selectivity of the medium. When an advertiser begins with a database of prospects, direct mail can be the perfect vehicle for reaching those prospects with little waste. Also, direct mail is a flexible medium that allows message adaptations literally on a household-by-household basis. For example, through surveys conducted with its 15 million U.S. subscribers, *Reader's Digest* amassed a huge marketing database detailing the health problems of specific subscribers.[25] In the database were 771,000 people with arthritis, 679,000 people with high blood pressure, 206,000 people with osteoporosis, 460,000 smokers, and so on. Using this information, *Reader's Digest* sent its subscribers disease-specific booklets containing advice on coping with their afflictions. The book-

lets also contained advertisements from drug companies that had tailored messages they wanted to communicate to those with a particular problem. This kind of precise targeting of tailored messages is the hallmark of direct marketing.

Direct mail as a medium also lends itself to testing and experimentation. With direct mail, it is common to test two or more different appeal letters using a modest budget and a small sample of households. The goal is to establish which version yields the largest response. When a winner is decided, that form of the letter is backed by big-budget dollars in launching the organization's primary campaign.

Additionally, direct mail allows marketers to use a substantial array of formats. Marketers can mail large, expensive brochures, CDs, or DVDs. They can use pop-ups, foldouts, scratch-and-sniff strips, or a simple, attractive postcard. If a product can be described in a limited space with minimal graphics, there really is no need to get fancy

direct-response advertising advertising that asks the receiver of the message to act immediately

direct mail direct-marketing medium that uses the postal service to deliver marketing materials

telemarketing direct-marketing medium that involves using the telephone to deliver a spoken appeal

© Gilian McGregor/Shutterstock.

with the direct-mail piece. The double postcard (DPC) format has an established track record of outperforming more expensive and elaborate direct-mail packages.[26]

Moreover, if an organization follows U.S. Postal Service guidelines carefully in mailing DPCs, the pieces can go out as first-class mail for reasonable rates. Because the Postal Service supplies address corrections on all first-class mail, using DPCs usually turns out to be a winner on either CPI or CPO measures, and DPCs can be an effective tool for cleaning up the bad addresses in a mailing list.

This postcard for Fleece & Flannel announces the grand opening of a store in Livingston, Montana. In that part of the country, it's perfectly natural to select a fly-fishing guide and guru to serve as your spokeswoman.

Telemarketing

As with direct mail, telemarketing contacts can be targeted selectively, the impact of programs is easy to track, and experimentation with different scripts and delivery formats is simple and practical. Because telemarketing involves live, person-to-person dialogue, no medium produces better response rates.

Telemarketing also shares many of direct mail's limitations. It is very expensive on a cost-per-contact basis, and just as names and addresses go bad as people move, so do phone numbers. Furthermore, telemarketing lacks direct mail's flexibility in terms of delivery options. When you reach people in their home or workplace, you have a limited amount of time to convey information and request some form of response.

The biggest concern with telemarketing is that it probably is the direct marketer's most invasive tool. Because telemarketing is powerful and highly intrusive, it must be used with discretion. High-pressure telephone calls at inconvenient times can alienate customers. Telemarketing will give the best results over the long run if it is used to maintain constructive dialogues with existing customers and qualified prospects.

Email

Perhaps the most controversial tool deployed of late by direct marketers has been unsolicited or "bulk" email. Commonly referred to as spam, this junk email can get you in big trouble with consumers. In a worst-case scenario, careless use of the email tool

BECAUSE TELEMARKETING IS POWERFUL AND HIGHLY INTRUSIVE, IT MUST BE USED WITH DISCRETION.

can earn one's company the label of a "spammer," and because of the community-oriented character of the Internet, this then can be a continuing source of negative buzz.

But is this drawback discouraging companies from deploying this tool? Hardly. In 2006, 70 percent of the 180 billion emails sent daily was spam.[27] Better filtering tools are helping computer users control this epidemic, but still it is estimated that by 2010, active email users will receive on average 1,600 spam messages annually.[28] It does make you wonder, with so much spam out there, and with so many who hate it, why does anyone do it? The ethics box tackles this weighty question.

One school of thought says some consumers are not averse to receiving targeted email advertisements, and as the Internet continues to evolve as an increasingly commercial medium, companies that observe proper etiquette on the Net will be rewarded through customer loyalty.[29] The key is to get the consumer's permission to send information about specific products or services; as discussed in Chapter 9, they must opt in. Consequently, many e-marketing service providers claim to have constructed email lists of consumers who have opted in for all manner of products and services. Others now promise large lists of consumers who have agreed to receive commercial emails; for two examples, visit http://www.infousa.com and http://www.yesmail.com. The

© Ivan Ponomarev/Shutterstock.

ETHICS MEET A FORMER SPAM QUEEN

Everybody hates spam—even Laura Betterly, and she once referred to herself as the "spam queen" (she meant it ironically, she explained later). Betterly used to make her living by delivering bulk email; her company, Data Resources Consulting (DRC), reportedly sent out as many as 60 million email messages a month. DRC also sold email addresses to other bulk emailers. At least for a time, the business was profitable. Betterly said DRC could make money when as few as 100 people responded to a mailing of 10 million. (For direct mail, marketers typically look for a response of 2 percent or better.) Betterly has acknowledged that commercial email messages aren't always welcome but insists that DRC aimed to stay on the right side of the law.

Sources: Mylene Mangalindan, "Web Vigilantes Give Spammers a Big Dose of Their Medicine," *Wall Street Journal*, May 19, 2003, A1, A13; Mylene Mangalindan, "For Bulk E-Mailer, Pestering Millions Offers a Path to Profit," *Wall Street Journal*, November 13, 2002, A1, A17; Laura Betterly, "It's 2006—E-mail Is Dead," *Laura Betterly Official Blog: Rants of a Marketing Executive*, September 22, 2005, http://laurabetterly.blogspot.com.

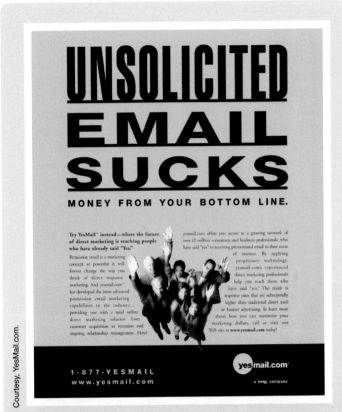

Courtesy, YesMail.com.

Purveyors of permission email have sprung up like mushrooms in the forest after a rain. This ad for yesmail.com points out that writing to people who think of you as just a spammer is a waste of promotion dollars. Yesmail.com is an example of the firms that have worked diligently to make email marketing a workable alternative for conscientious advertisers.

Courtesy, Oreck Corporation.

This magazine ad for Oreck floor vacuums, which ran in *Bon Appetit,* delivers the basics of direct marketing: an introduction to the product plus three ways to respond: a toll-free number, website address, and coupon with a mailing address. Throwing in a free iron gives consumers an extra incentive to act.

future of direct marketing may be in reaching people who already have said yes.

Our advice is to stay away from the low-cost temptations of bulk email. The quickest way to get flamed and damage your brand name is to start sending out bulk emails to people who do not want to hear from you. Instead, through database development, ask your customers for permission to contact them via email. Honor their requests. Don't abuse the privilege by selling their email addresses to other companies, and when you do contact them, have something important to say. Seth Godin, whose 1999 book *Permission Marketing* really launched the opt-in mindset, puts it this way: "The best way to make your [customer] list worthless is to sell it. The future is, this list is mine and it's a secret."[30] Perhaps you can imagine L. L. Bean feeling exactly the same way about his customer list 95 years ago.

Other Media

As direct marketers try to convey their appeals for a customer response, they have experimented with many other methods. In magazines, a popular device for executing a direct marketer's agenda is the bind-in insert card. If you thumb through a copy of any magazine, you will see how effective these light-cardboard inserts are at stopping the reader and calling attention to themselves. Insert cards not only promote their product, but they also provide tempting offers like $25 off your next order at Coldwater Creek or a free sample of Skoal smokeless tobacco.

When AT&T introduced the first 800 number in 1967, it simply could not have known how important this service would become to direct marketing. Newspaper ads from the *Wall Street Journal* provide toll-free numbers for requesting everything from really cheap online trading services (800-619-SAVE) to leasing a Learjet 40 (800-FLEXJET). If you watch late-night TV, you may know the 800 number to call to order the Grammy-winning CD by Walter Ostanek and his polka band. Finally, magazine ads are commonly used to provide an 800 number to initiate contact with customers. As these diverse examples indicate, toll-free numbers make it possible to use nearly any medium for direct-response purposes.

Infomercials

The infomercial is a novel form of direct-response advertising that merits special mention. An **infomercial** fundamentally is just a long television advertisement made possible by the lower cost of ad space on many cable and satellite channels. Infomercials range in length from 2 to 60 minutes, but the common length is 30 minutes. Although producing an infomercial is more like producing a television program than it is like producing a 30-second commercial, infomercials are all about selling.

There appear to be several keys to successful use of this unique vehicle (see Exhibit 10.3).[31] A critical

infomercial long advertisement that looks like a talk show or product demonstration

Exhibit 10.3
Elements of a Successful Infomercial

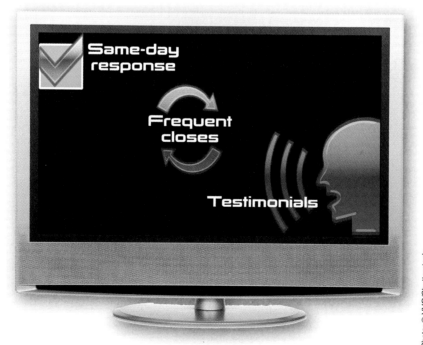

Photo: © VVO/Shutterstock.

element is testimonials from satisfied users. Celebrity testimonials can help catch a viewer as he or she is channel surfing past the program, but celebrities aren't necessary—and, of course, they add to the production costs. Whether testimonials are from celebrities or from folks just like us, without them, your chances of producing a profitable infomercial diminish hugely.

Another requirement for successful infomercials arises from the fact that viewers are not likely to stay tuned for the full 30 minutes. An infomercial is a 30-minute direct-response sales pitch, not a classic episode of *South Park* or *The Simpsons*. Therefore, the call to action should not come just at the end of the infomercial; most of the audience could be long gone by minute 28 into the show. For a 30-minute infomercial, a good rule of thumb is to divide the program into three 10-minute increments, with a close at the end of each segment. Each closing should feature the 800 number or Web address that allows the viewer to order the product or request more information.

Finally, an organization should not offer information to the customer unless it can deliver speedy follow-up. The goal in pursuing leads generated by an infomercial should be a same-day response.

Many different types of products and services have been marketed using infomercials via Internet extensions such as http://www.iqvc.com. Self-help videos, home exercise equipment, kitchen appliances, and Annette Funicello Collectible Bears all have had success with the infomercial. Although it is easy to associate the infomercial with gadgets such as the Ronco Showtime Rotisserie & BBQ (yours for just four easy payments of $39.95!), many familiar brands have experimented with this medium. Brand marketers such as Quaker State, Disney, and even Mercedes-Benz have used infomercials to help inform consumers about their offerings.[32]

How can we explain the growing appeal of the infomercial for all manner of marketers? Data generated by TiVo's StopWatch service are revealing.[33] They show that bare-bones, direct-response ads for products like Perfect Pushup exercise equipment are among the least likely to be zapped. That kind of result will get a lot of scrutiny from all corners of the brand promotion business.

STUDY TOOLS CHAPTER 10

Located at back of the textbook
- **Rip out Chapter in Review Card.**

Located at www.cengagebrain.com
- **Review Key Terms Flashcards (Print or Online).**
- **Complete the Practice Quiz to prepare for tests.**
- **Play "Beat the Clock" and "Quizbowl" to master concepts.**
- **Complete "Crossword Puzzle" to review key terms.**
- **Watch videos on Pizza Hut and Pedigree UK for real company examples.**
- **For additional examples, go online to learn about Lester Wunderman and the invention of "direct marketing."**

LISTEN UP!

SHE DID

"Free" is a price few can resist. It also is a great sales promotion for McDonald's.

McDonald's credits free coffee giveaways with boosting breakfast revenues.

Photo Courtesy, OmniTerra Images.

Learning Outcomes

After studying this chapter, you should be able to:

LO 1   Explain the importance and growth of sales promotion.

LO 2   Describe the main sales promotion techniques used in the consumer market.

LO 3   Describe the main sales promotion techniques used in the trade channel and business markets.

LO 4   Identify the risks to the brand of using sales promotion.

LO 5   Understand the role and techniques of point-of-purchase advertising.

LO 6   Describe the role of support media in a comprehensive integrated marketing communication plan.

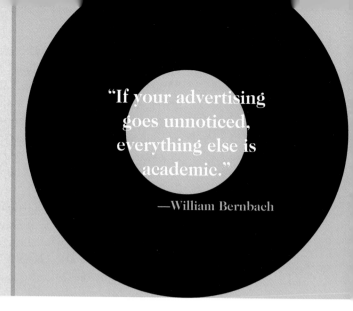

"If your advertising goes unnoticed, everything else is academic."

—William Bernbach

AFTER YOU
FINISH THIS
CHAPTER
GO TO
PAGE 243
FOR STUDY
TOOLS

Free Drinks!

As competition between fast-food chains continually intensifies, each brand is struggling to become consumers' favorite. Menus are tweaked, new stores are opened at convenient spots, ad campaigns are rolled out, and prices are slashed. So how can you persuade a jaded consumer to try *your* place? How about giving away the product?

Big, powerful fast-food operations like Wendy's, KFC, and McDonald's have found that price discounts sometimes can cheapen brand image and condition consumers to look for deals. In contrast, they can get positive attention and boost traffic by picking an item to give away for free. Wendy's launched a 25-city, six-month "taste tour" offering free hamburgers. KFC gave out free Colonel's Crispy Strips supported by a full-page ad in *USA Today*. During the first week of the sampling, the chain saw its highest sales for the strips. McDonald's launched Free Coffee Mondays as a way to lure consumers from Starbucks and demonstrate that its new premium coffee is just as good. McDonald's has credited coffee giveaways with boosting breakfast revenues.[1]

The Sonic Drive-In chain has drawn in new and repeat customers with a once-a-year Free Float Night. From 8 P.M. until midnight on Free Float Night, customers can order a root beer float at no charge. The first year Sonic tried the event, the chain of 3,500 drive-ins exceeded its goal of 3 million free floats, and in the second year, it gave away more than 5 million.[2] What's in it for Sonic? First, the company believes consumers will be charmed by its old-fashioned drive-in ambience. Second, customers who show up for a free float tend to order—and pay for—burgers and fries as well. The promotion also dovetails with the chain's effort to position itself

What do you think?

I'll try anything if it's free.

1   2   3   4   5   6   7

STRONGLY DISAGREE   STRONGLY AGREE

Find out what others think at CourseMate for PROMO.

as a place to purchase a wide variety of delicious drinks, using the slogan "Your Ultimate Drink Stop." And giving something away for a short time, rather than issuing coupons or announcing a sale, stimulates sales in a way that doesn't cause consumers to expect a price break the rest of the year.

Of course, freebies have their downside. One problem, of course, is that not everyone who shows up for something free also places a paid order or returns for another visit at full price. At the same time, the extra work of serving people for free requires plenty of employees, who may struggle to provide the restaurant's usual level of service. A Sonic vice president admitted that sales per customer and customer satisfaction levels suffer while the company is running one of these promotions.[3] Sonic tries to counter that challenge on Free Float Nights by getting employees in on the excitement. Employees have worn silly hats to keep up an atmosphere of fun as they hand out the free drinks.

Most likely, fast-food restaurants will keep the free trials coming. Although this kind of sampling always has been useful in attracting consumer attention and making consumers feel good about getting "something for free," sampling is valuable for building sales at existing units in the absence of opportunities to build new stores. Attractive real estate is getting scarcer, so new-unit growth has slowed considerably. Rather than building new stores, companies are trying to build traffic—and revenues—at existing stores by enticing old and new customers with free food and drink.

LO 1 Role of Sales Promotion

Sales promotion, such as the free trials offered by Sonic and other fast-food restaurants, often is a key component within an integrated marketing communication (IMC) campaign. Sales promotions can attract attention and give new energy to the overall marketing effort. Used properly, sales promotion is capable of almost instant demand stimulation, like the kind that contests and sweepstakes can create.

Formally defined, **sales promotion** is the use of incentive techniques that create a perception of greater brand value among consumers, the trade, and business buyers. The "message" in a sales promotion features price reduction, free samples, a prize, or some other incentive for consumers to try a brand or for a retailer to feature the brand in a store. The intent is to generate a short-term increase in sales by motivating trial use, encouraging larger purchases, or stimulating repeat purchases.

Based on the audience for the message, sales promotion falls into three categories:

1. **Consumer-market sales promotion** includes methods of inducing household consumers to purchase a firm's brand rather than a competitor's brand. Examples are coupons and samples. These incentives reduce price, offer a reward, or encourage a trip to the retailer.

2. **Trade-market sales promotion** is aimed at motivating distributors, wholesalers, and retailers to stock and feature a firm's brand in their store merchandising programs. Examples include allowances (a type of discount) and specially designed displays to feature the brand.

© iznogood/Shutterstock.

USED PROPERLY, SALES PROMOTION IS CAPABLE OF ALMOST INSTANT DEMAND STIMULATION.

3. **Business-market sales promotion** is designed to cultivate buyers in large corporations who are making purchase decisions about a wide range of products including computers, office supplies, and consulting services. Techniques used for business buyers are similar to the trade-market techniques.

Later in the chapter, we will identify and describe specific sales promotion techniques.

Importance of Sales Promotion

Sales promotion has proven to be a popular complement to mass-media advertising because it accomplishes things advertising cannot. Sales promotion is designed to affect demand differently than advertising does. Whereas most advertising is designed to build brand awareness, image, and preference over the long run, sales promotion primarily is aimed at eliciting an immediate purchase from a customer group. Samples, rebates, and similar techniques offer household consumers, trade buyers, or business buyers an immediate incentive to choose one brand over another. Even longer-term efforts, such as airline frequent-flier programs, not only provide an affiliation value for a brand but also offer practical benefits for repeat purchases, thus stimulating sales.

The goals for sales promotion and those of advertising are compared in Exhibit 11.1. While mass-media advertising is designed to build a brand image over time, sales promotion is conspicuous and designed to make things happen in a hurry. When a firm determines that a more immediate response is called for—whether the target customer is a household, business buyer, distributor, or retailer—sales promotions try to provide that incentive.

The importance of sales promotion in the United States should not be underestimated. Sales promotion may not seem as stylish and sophisticated as mass-media advertising, but expenditures on this tool are impressive. In recent years, sales promotion expenditures have grown at an annual rate of about 4 to 8 percent, compared with about a 3 to 5 percent rate for advertising. Spending on sales promotion efforts in the United States alone now exceed $300 billion annually. The rapid growth is occurring as big consumer products firms shift dollars out of media advertising and into promotions.[4]

It is important to realize that full-service advertising agencies specializing in advertising planning, creative preparation, and media placement typically do not prepare sales promotion materials for clients. These activities normally are assigned to sales promotion agencies that specialize in coupons, premiums, displays, or other forms of sales promotion and point-of-purchase techniques that require specific skills and creative preparation.

The development and management of an effective sales promotion program requires a major commitment by a firm. During any given year, it is typical that as much as 30 percent of brand management time is spent on designing, implementing, and overseeing sales promotions.

business-market sales promotion
promotion designed to cultivate buyers making purchase decisions in corporations

Exhibit 11.1
Complementary Roles

Sales Promotion
• Stimulates short-term demand
• Encourages brand switching
• Induces trial use
• Promotes price orientation
• Obtains immediate, often measurable results

Advertising
• Cultivates long-term demand
• Encourages brand loyalty
• Encourages repeat purchases
• Promotes images/ feature orientation
• Obtains long-term effects, often difficult to measure

Growing Use of Sales Promotion

Many marketers have shifted the emphasis of their promotional spending during the past decade. Much of the shift has been away from mass-media advertising. Some has made its way to the Internet, as we saw in Chapter 9, and more spending has found its way to consumer, trade, and business sales promotions. Currently, the budget allocation on average stands at about 17.5 percent for advertising, 54 percent for trade and business promotions, and 28.5 percent for consumer promotions.[5]

There are several reasons why many marketers have been shifting funds from mass-media advertising to sales promotions:

- *Demand for greater accountability:* In an era of cost cutting and shareholder scrutiny, companies are demanding greater accountability across all functions, including marketing. When activities are evaluated for their contribution to sales and profits, it often is difficult to draw specific conclusions regarding the effects of advertising. But the more immediate effects of sales promotions typically are easier to document. Various studies show that only 18 percent of TV advertising campaigns produced a short-term positive return on investment on promotional dollars.[6] Conversely, point-of-purchase in-store displays have been shown to positively affect sales by as much as 35 percent in some product categories.[7]

- *Short-term orientation:* Several factors have created a short-term orientation among managers. These include a bottom-line mentality and pressures from stockholders to increase quarter-by-quarter revenue and profit per share. Many organizations are developing marketing plans—with rewards and punishments for manager performance—based on short-term revenue generation. As a result, companies are seeking tactics that can have short-term effects. For example, McDonald's credits its "Play to Win" game with boosting store sales up to 15 percent during the game's promotion period.[8]

- *Consumer response to promotions:* Shoppers are demanding greater value across all purchase situations, and that trend is battering overpriced brands.[9] For shoppers who search for extra value in every purchase, coupons and other sales promotions increase the value of a brand. Historically, consumers report that coupons, price, and good value for their money influence 75 to 85 percent of their brand choices.[10]

(However, this does not necessarily mean consumers are choosing the *lowest*-priced item. The analysis suggests that sales promotion techniques act as an incentive to purchase the brand using a promotion, even if another brand has a lower basic price.)

- *Proliferation of brands:* Each year, thousands of new brands are introduced into the consumer market, creating a mind-dulling maze for consumers. Consider this case of brand proliferation: in one 12-month period, Coca-Cola's new head of marketing launched *1,000* new drinks or new variations of existing brands worldwide (has anybody tried Coca-Cola Blak?).[11] At any point in time, consumers are typically able to choose from about 60 spaghetti sauces, 100 snack chips, 50 laundry detergents, 90 cold remedies, and 60 disposable-diaper varieties. Gaining attention in this blizzard of brands is no easy task. Marketers turn to sales promotions to gain some attention.

- *Increased power of retailers:* Big retailers like Home Depot and Walmart now dominate retailing in the United States. These powerful retailers have responded quickly and accurately to the new environment for retailing, where consumers are demanding more and better products and services at lower prices. Because of these consumer demands, retailers are, in turn, demanding more deals from manufacturers. Many of the deals are delivered in terms of trade-oriented sales promotions,

Photo by Jeff Greenberg/Thomson Learning (now Cengage Learning).

When consumers are shopping for pasta sauce in today's supermarkets, they face a dizzying array of choices. Getting them to pay attention to any one brand is quite a challenge for marketers. Sales promotions like coupons in advertising or signs in the store are aimed at helping consumers choose the marketer's brand.

ETHICS   A NEW TOOL FOR BIG BROTHER?

In the battle to provide retailers with reasons to feature one brand over another, a new weapon is the successor to bar codes: radio frequency identification (RFID) tags, which provide an instant assessment of inventory in warehouses and on store shelves. RFID tags combine tiny information chips with an antenna. When a tag is placed on an item, it starts to radio its location. Receivers can be placed in offices, in storerooms, and on shopping carts. So when you get to the supermarket, you might grab a shopping cart with an RFID reader attached. After you swipe your frequent-buyer card, the store can offer you deals based on the items you put in your cart this day or in the past. The efficiency gained from improved inventory control would generate significant cost savings. But critics see another instance of "Big Brother" intruding on consumers' privacy.

Source: Gerry Khermouch and Heather Green, "Bar Codes Better Watch Their Backs," *BusinessWeek*, July 14, 2003, 42.

such as point-of-purchase displays and co-op advertising allowances. In the end, manufacturers use more and more sales promotions to gain and maintain good relations with the powerful retailers—a critical link to the consumer. And retailers use the tools of sales promotion as competitive strategies against each other. Manufacturers are coming up with clever ways to provide value to retailers and thus maintain the balance of power.

- *Media clutter:* A nagging and traditional problem in the advertising process is clutter. Many advertisers target the same customers because their research has led them to the same conclusion about whom to target. As a result, advertising media are cluttered with ads seeking the attention of the same people. When consumers encounter a barrage of ads, they tune out (remember the discussion in Chapter 5). And clutter is getting worse, not better, across all media—including the Internet, where pop-ups, pop-unders, and banners decorate nearly every website.[12] One way to break through the clutter effectively is to feature a sales promotion. In print ads, the featured deal often is a coupon. In television and radio advertising, sweepstakes, premium, and rebate offers can attract viewers' and listeners' attention.

LO 2 Consumer Sales Promotion

U.S. consumer product firms have made a tremendous commitment to sales promotion in their overall marketing plans. During the 1970s, consumer goods marketers allocated only about 30 percent of their budgets to sales promotion, with about 70 percent allocated to mass-media advertising. Now, at many consumer goods firms, the percentages are just the opposite, with nearly 75 percent of budgets spent on various forms of promotion and point-of-purchase materials. With this level of investment in mind, let's examine the objectives for sales promotion in the consumer market and the range of techniques available.

Objectives

To help ensure the proper application of sales promotion, specific strategic objectives should be set. As illustrated in Exhibit 11.2, several basic objectives can be pursued with sales promotion in the consumer market.

When a firm wants to attract new users, sales promotion can reduce the consumer's risk of trying something new. Offering a rebate or free sample may stimulate trial purchase. Peet's Coffee & Tea has attempted to stimulate trial use by creating a sampler pack available at a special price. This promotion tries to get consumers to try a brand, not a product category, because coffee is a mature product. As described in Chapter 1, promotion for mature products typically emphasizes selective demand stimulation—that

Exhibit 11.2
Objectives for Consumer-Market Sales Promotion

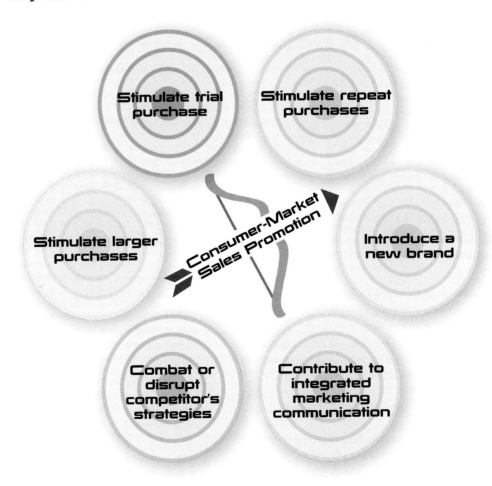

Exhibit 11.3
Allocation of Sales Promotion Spending

coupon sales promotion that entitles a buyer to a designated reduction in price for a product or service

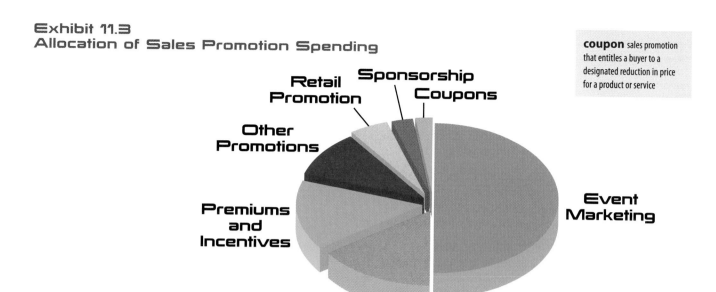

is, brand choice among people who already use the product category.

Sales promotion also seeks to stimulate repeat purchases. For example, a program in which consumers accumulate points with repeated purchases can keep them loyal to a particular brand. The most prominent frequency programs are found in the airline and hotel industries.

Besides stimulating more frequent purchases, sales promotion can stimulate larger purchases. Two-for-one sales can motivate consumers to stock up on a brand. Shampoo often is double-packaged to offer a value to consumers while reducing inventory or increasing cash flow.

Because sales promotion can attract attention and motivate trial purchase, it commonly is used for introducing a new brand. In one of the most successful uses of sales promotions to introduce a new brand, Curad introduced its kid-size bandage by distributing 7.5 million sample packs in McDonald's Happy Meal sacks. Initial sales of the bandages exceeded forecasts by 30 percent.

Because sales promotions often motivate consumers to buy in larger quantities or try new brands, they can be used to disrupt competitors' marketing strategies. If a firm knows that one of its competitors is launching a new brand or initiating a new advertising campaign, it can severely compromise competitors' efforts with a well-timed sales promotion. In an effort to address increasing competition from newspaper TV supplements and cable-guide magazines, *TV Guide* magazine ran a sweepstakes in several regional markets. Winners

won $200 shopping sprees in supermarkets—precisely where 65 percent of its sales are realized.

In conjunction with advertising, direct marketing, public relations, and other programs being carried out by a firm, sales promotion can add yet another type of communication to the promotional mix. Sales promotions suggest an additional value—a different message within the firm's IMC effort.

Techniques

A variety of techniques are used to stimulate demand and attract attention in the consumer market. Exhibit 11.3 shows how marketers allocate their spending among the alternatives.

Coupons

A **coupon** entitles a buyer to a designated reduction in price for a product or service. Coupons are the oldest and most widely used form of sales promotion. The first use of a coupon is traced to around 1895, when the C. W. Post Company used a penny-off coupon as a way to get people to try its Grape-Nuts cereal. Annually, about 350 billion coupons are distributed to American consumers, with redemption rates ranging from 2 percent for gum purchases to nearly 45 percent for disposable diaper purchases.

As a sales promotion tool, coupons offer several advantages:

- Marketers can give a discount to price-sensitive consumers while selling the product at full price to other consumers.

- Coupon-redeeming customers may use a competitive brand, so the coupon can induce brand switching.

- Marketers can control the timing and distribution of coupons, so retailers are not implementing price discounts in a way that might damage brand image.

- Coupons effectively stimulate repeat purchases. Once a consumer has purchased a brand, an in-package coupon can induce the consumer to buy it again.

- Coupons can get regular users to trade up within a brand array. For example, users of low-priced disposable diapers may be willing to try the premium version of a brand with a coupon.

On the downside, coupon use involves some administrative burdens and risks. Couponing entails careful administration and associated costs. There are costs for producing and distributing the coupons and for retailer and manufacturer handling. The total cost for handling, processing, and distributing coupons typically equals about two-thirds of the coupon's face value. Marketers must track these costs against the amount of product sold with and without coupon redemption.

Risks include uncertainty about timing, reduced profitability, and fraud. While the marketer controls when coupons are distributed, consumers control the timing of redemption. Some consumers redeem coupons immediately; depending on the expiration date, others may hold them for months. If the consumers who redeem coupons already are regular users of the brand, coupons merely reduce a firm's profitability.

Fraud is a chronic and serious problem with couponing. The problem relates directly to misredemption practices. Three types of misredemption cost firms money:

1. Redemption of coupons by consumers who do not purchase the couponed brand

2. Redemption of coupons by salesclerks and store managers without consumer purchases

3. Illegal collection or copying of coupons by individuals who sell them to unethical store merchants, who in turn redeem the coupons without the accompanying consumer purchases.

Price-Off Deals

Another straightforward sales promotion technique is the **price-off deal**, which offers consumers cents or even dollars off merchandise at the point of purchase through specially marked packages. The typical price-off deal is a 10 to 25 percent price reduction. The reduction is taken from the manufacturer's profit margin rather than the retailer's.

Manufacturers like the price-off technique because it is controllable. Also, when consumers at the point of purchase judge the offer, they may make a positive price comparison against competitors' products. Consumers like a price-off deal because it is straightforward and automatically increases the value of a known brand. Regular users tend to stock up on an item during a price-off deal.

Retailers are less enthusiastic about this technique. Price-off promotions can create inventory and pricing problems. Also, most price-off deals are snapped up by regular customers, so the retailer often doesn't benefit from new business.

© Jim Barber/Shutterstock.

Premiums and Advertising Specialties

Premiums are items offered free, or at a reduced price, with the purchase of another item. Many firms offer a related product, such as a free granola bar packed inside a box of granola cereal. Service firms, such as a car wash or dry cleaner, may use a two-for-one offer to persuade consumers to try the service.

Two options are available for the use of premiums.

1. A **free premium** gives consumers an item at no cost; the item either is included in the package of a purchased item or mailed to the consumer after proof of purchase is verified. The most frequently used free premium is an additional package of the original item or a free related item placed in the package (e.g., free conditioner with shampoo purchase).

2. A **self-liquidating premium** requires a consumer to pay most of the cost of the item received as a premium.

For example, Snapple can offer a "Snapple cooler" with the purchase of six bottles of Snapple for $6.99 (which equals the cost of the cooler to Snapple). Self-liquidating premiums are particularly effective with loyal customers. However, they must be used cautiously. Unless the premium is related to a value-building strategy for a brand, it can focus consumer attention on the premium rather than the benefits of the brand. If consumers buy a brand only to get a great-looking T-shirt at $4.99, then they won't purchase the brand again until another great premium becomes available.

Advertising specialties have three key elements: a *message* placed on a *useful item* that is *given to consumers* with no obligation. Popular advertising specialties are baseball caps, T-shirts, coffee mugs, computer mouse pads, pens, and calendars. Advertising specialties allow a firm to tout its company or brand name with a target customer in an ongoing fashion.

Contests and Sweepstakes

No other sales promotion technique can match contests and sweepstakes in drawing attention to a brand. Technically, there are important differences between contests and sweepstakes:

- In a **contest**, consumers compete for prizes based on skill or ability. Winners are determined by a panel of judges or based on which contestant comes closest to a predetermined criterion for winning, such as picking the total points scored in the Super Bowl. Contests tend to be somewhat expensive to administer because each entry must be judged.

> **advertising specialties** sales promotion consisting of a message placed on useful items given to consumers with no obligation
>
> **contest** sales promotion in which consumers compete for prizes based on skill or ability

Companies like Cook Advertising Specialties put logos on a wide variety of products. Marketers use these as specialties—giving them away to potential customers as a way to spread awareness of a brand and good feelings about it.

Photo Courtesy, Susan Van Etten.

- A **sweepstakes** is a promotion in which winners are determined purely by chance. Consumers need only to enter their names in the sweepstakes as a criterion for winning. Often consumers enter by filling out official entry forms, but instant-winner scratch-off cards are another method that tends to attract customers. Many retailers use scratch-off-card sweepstakes as a way of building and maintaining store traffic. Sweepstakes also can be designed so that repeated trips to the retail outlet are necessary to gather a complete set of winning cards.

Contests and sweepstakes create excitement and generate interest for a brand. For them to be effective, marketers must design them in such a way that consumers perceive value in the prizes and find playing the games intrinsically interesting. British Airways ran a contest with the theme "The World's Greatest Offer," in which it gave away thousands of free airline tickets to London and other European destinations. Besides increasing awareness, contests like these create a database of interested customers and potential customers. The company can send these people information on future programs and other premium offers.

Contests and sweepstakes also pose several challenges:

- They are subject to government regulations and restrictions. The design and administration of a contest or sweepstakes must comply with federal and state laws, and each state may have slightly different regulations. The legal problems are complex enough that most firms hire agencies specializing in contests and sweepstakes to administer the programs.

- Consumers may focus more on the game itself than on the brand being promoted. This technique thus fails to build long-term consumer affinity for a brand.

- In the context of a game, it is hard to get any meaningful message across. The consumer's interest is focused on the game, not on any feature of the brand.

- Administration of a contest or sweepstakes is complex enough that the risk of errors is fairly high and can create negative publicity.[13]

- For a firm trying to develop a quality or prestige image for a brand, contests and sweepstakes may contradict this goal.

Sampling and Trial Offers

Getting consumers to simply try a brand can have a powerful effect on future decision making. **Sampling** is a sales promotion technique designed to provide a consumer with an opportunity to use a brand on a trial basis with little or no risk. Most consumer product companies use sampling in some manner. Surveys have shown that consumers are very favorable toward sampling, with 43 percent indicating they would consider switching brands if they liked a free sample that was being offered.[14]

Sampling can involve any of six techniques:

1. **In-store sampling** takes place at the point of purchase, where consumers may be swayed by a direct encounter with the brand. It is popular for food products and cosmetics. In-store demonstrators often hand out coupons along with samples.

© GWImages/Shutterstock.

OFFERING SHOPPERS FREE SAMPLES GIVES THEM A WAY TO EXPERIENCE THE PRODUCT'S BENEFITS FIRSTHAND, WITH NO COST IF THEY ARE DISSATISFIED. OFTEN MARKETERS HAND OUT COUPONS ALONG WITH THE SAMPLES IN ORDER TO MAKE A PURCHASE EVEN MORE ATTRACTIVE.

2. **Door-to-door sampling** involves delivering samples to the homes of the target segment. This is extremely expensive because of labor costs, but it can be effective if the marketer has information that locates the target segment in a well-defined geographic area.

3. **Mail sampling** delivers samples through the postal service, which allows the marketer to target certain ZIP-code markets. A drawback is that the sample must be small enough that mailing it is economically feasible. Cox Target Media has developed a mailer that contains multiple samples related to a specific industry—like car-care products—and that can reach highly targeted market segments.[15]

4. **Newspaper sampling**—distributing samples in newspapers—has become very popular; 42 percent of consumers report having received samples of health and beauty products in this manner.[16] Much like mail sampling, newspaper samples allow specific geographic and geodemographic targeting.

5. **On-package sampling**, a technique in which the sample item is attached to another product package, is useful for brands targeted to current customers. Attaching a small bottle of Ivory conditioner to a regular-sized container of Ivory shampoo is a logical sampling strategy.

6. **Mobile sampling** is carried out by logo-emblazoned vehicles that dispense samples, coupons, and premiums to consumers at shopping centers, fairgrounds, and recreational areas.

Sampling is particularly useful for new products but should not be reserved for new products alone. It can be used successfully for established brands with weak market share in specific geographic areas. Ben & Jerry's "Stop & Taste the Ice Cream" tour gave away more than a million scoops of ice cream in high-traffic urban areas in order to reestablish a presence for the brand in weak markets.[17]

Sampling has its downside. Unless the brand has a clear value and benefit over the competition, a trial of the brand is unlikely to persuade consumers to switch brands. This is especially true for convenience goods because consumers perceive a high degree of similarity among brands, even after trying them. To develop a perception of benefit and superiority, marketers may have to combine sampling with advertising. In addition, sampling is expensive, especially if a significant quantity of a product, such as shampoo or laundry detergent, must be given away for consumers to appreciate a brand's value. Finally, sampling can be a very imprecise process. Even when using specialized agencies to handle sampling programs, marketers cannot completely ensure that the product is reaching the target audience.

Trial offers have the same goal as sampling—to induce trial use of a brand—but are used for more expensive items. Appliances and consumer electronics are typical of items offered on a trial basis. Trials offers can be free for low-priced products. The trial period can be as brief as a day to as long as 90 days for more expensive items like vacuum cleaners or computer software. The expense to the firm, of course, can be formidable. Segments chosen for this sales promotion technique must have high sales potential.

Phone and Gift Cards

A new and increasingly popular form of sales promotion is to offer phone and gift cards. This technique could be classified as a premium offer, but it has enough unique features to warrant separate classification as a sales promotion technique. The use of phone and gift cards is fairly straightforward. Manufacturers or retailers offer either free or for-purchase debit cards that provide the holder with a preset spending limit or minutes of phone time. The cards are designed to be colorful and memorable.

A wide range of marketers, including luxury car manufacturers like Lexus and retailers like the Gap, have made effective use of phone and gift cards. A significant benefit for marketers is that gift card holders tend to use them freely to pay the full retail price for items, so retailers and brand marketers earn higher profit margins from gift card purchases.[18]

Rebates

A **rebate** is a money-back offer requiring a buyer to mail in a form requesting the money back from the manufacturer, rather than from the retailer (as in couponing). The rebate technique has been refined throughout the years and now is used by a wide variety of marketers. More than 400 million rebates are offered each year for products as diverse as computers (Dell) and mouthwash (Warner-Lambert).[19] Rebates are well suited to increasing the quantity purchased, so they commonly are tied to multiple purchases. For

door-to-door sampling sampling in which samples are brought to the homes of the target segment in a well-defined geographic area

mail sampling sampling in which samples are delivered through the postal service

newspaper sampling sampling in which samples are distributed in newspapers to allow specific geographic and geodemographic targeting

on-package sampling sampling in which a sample item is attached to another product's package

mobile sampling sampling carried out using logo-emblazoned vehicles where samples are dispensed at malls or other high-traffic areas

trial offers sales promotion in which expensive items are offered on a trial basis to induce consumers to try a brand

rebate money-back offer requiring a buyer to mail in a form requesting the money back from the manufacturer

example, if you buy a 10-pack of Kodak film, you can mail in a rebate coupon worth $2.

Marketers like rebates because relatively few consumers take advantage of the rebate offer after buying a brand. By one estimate, only 60 percent of buyers ever bother to fill out and then mail in the rebate request—resulting in an extra $2 billion in revenue for manufacturers and retailers that offer rebates.[20]

Frequency (Continuity) Programs

One of the most popular consumer-market sales promotion techniques has been frequency programs. **Frequency programs**, also referred to as continuity programs, offer consumers discounts or free product rewards for repeat purchase or patronage of a brand or company. These programs were pioneered by airlines. Frequent-flyer programs such as Delta Air Lines' SkyMiles, frequent-stay programs such as Marriott's Honored Guest Award Rewards program, and frequent-renter programs such as Hertz's #1 Club are examples of such loyalty-building activities. But frequency programs are not reserved for the travel industry. Chart House Enterprises, a chain of 65 upscale restaurants, successfully launched a frequency program for diners, who earned points for every dollar spent. Frequent diners were issued "passports," which were stamped at each visit. Within two years, the program had more than 300,000 members.

"WHY IS OUR AWARD PROGRAM SO POPULAR WITH FREQUENT TRAVELERS? WE'RE IN EVERY CITY THEY FREQUENT."

Bill Marriott

As a business traveler you earn free vacations faster with Marriott's Honored Guest Award program. With over 250 locations worldwide, we're doing business wherever you're doing business. To join the program call 1-800-648-8024. For reservations, call your travel agent or 1-800-228-9290.

Marriott
HOTELS·RESORTS·SUITES
WE MAKE IT HAPPEN FOR YOU

© 1998 Marriott International, Inc.

Frequency (continuity) programs build customer loyalty and offer opportunities for building a large, targeted database for other promotions.

LO 3 Sales Promotion to the Trade and Business Buyers

Sales promotions also can be directed at members of the trade—wholesalers, distributors, and retailers—and business markets. For example, Hewlett-Packard designs sales promotion programs for its retailers, like Circuit City, to ensure that the HP line gets proper attention and display. HP also develops sales promotion campaigns aimed at business buyers like Accenture or IHC HealthCare. Firms spend big money to attract business to their brands with sales promotions. Recent estimates put business-to-business sales promotions at more than $44 billion annually.[21]

Objectives

The purpose of sales promotion as a tool does not change from the consumer market to the trade or business markets. It still is intended to stimulate demand in the short term and help push the product through the distribution channel or cause business buyers to act more immediately and positively toward the marketer's brand.

Effective trade and business market promotions can generate enthusiasm for a product and contribute positively to the loyalty distributors show for a brand. In the business market, sales promotions can mean the difference between landing a very large order and missing out entirely on a revenue opportunity. With the proliferation of new brands and brand extensions, manufacturers need to stimulate enthusiasm and loyalty among members of the trade and get the attention of business buyers suffering from information overload.

As in the consumer market, trade market sales promotions should be undertaken with specific objectives in mind. Generally speaking, when marketers devise incentives for the trade market, they are executing a **push strategy**: using sales promotions to help push a brand into the distribution channel until it ultimately reaches the consumer. These promotions have the four primary objectives shown in Exhibit 11.4.

Obtain Initial Distribution

The proliferation of brands in the consumer market generates fierce competition for shelf space. Sales promotion incentives can help a firm gain initial distribution and shelf placement. Like consumers deciding what to buy, members of the trade allocating shelf space need a reason to choose one brand over another. A well-conceived promotion may sway them.

Bob's Candies, a small family-owned business in Albany, Georgia, is the largest candy cane manufacturer in the United States. But Bob's old-fashioned candy was having trouble keeping distributors. To reverse the trend, Bob's designed a new name, logo, and packaging for the candy canes. It mailed each scheduled attendee at the All-Candy Expo trade show three strategically timed postcards with the teaser question "Wanna Be Striped?" The mailing got a 25 percent response rate, and booth visitations at the trade show were a huge success.[22]

Increase Order Size

One of the struggles in the channel of distribution is over the location of inventory. Manufacturers prefer that members of the trade maintain large inventories

> **push strategy** sales promotion strategy in which marketers devise incentives to encourage purchases by members of the trade, moving product into the distribution channel

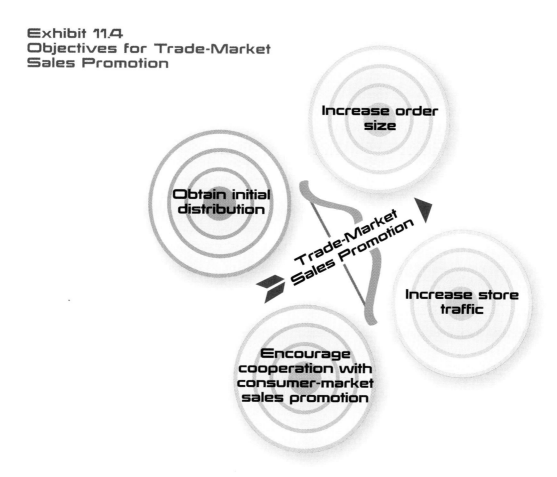

Exhibit 11.4
Objectives for Trade-Market Sales Promotion

push money trade incentive in which retail salespeople are offered monetary rewards for featuring a marketer's brand

so that the manufacturer can reduce inventory-carrying costs. Members of the trade would rather place frequent, small orders and carry little inventory. Sales promotion can encourage wholesalers and retailers to order in larger quantities, shifting the inventory burden to the trade channel.

Encourage Cooperation with Consumer-Market Sales Promotions

A sales promotion in the consumer market won't fly if there is little cooperation in the channel. Implementation of the promotion may require that wholesalers maintain larger inventories and retailers provide special displays or handling. When Toys "R" Us ran a "scan and win" promotion, the retailer ran out of several popular toys during the critical holiday buying season because distributors (and Toys "R" Us) were unprepared for the magnitude of consumers' response. To guard against such problems, marketers often run trade promotions simultaneously with consumer promotions.

Increase Store Traffic

Retailers can increase store traffic through special promotions or events. Door-prize drawings or live radio broadcasts from the store are common sales promotions aimed at increasing traffic. Burger King has become a leader in building traffic at its 6,500 outlets with special promotions tied to Disney movie debuts. Beginning in 1991 with a *Beauty and the Beast* tie-in promotion, Burger King has set records for generating store traffic with premium giveaways. The *Pocahontas* campaign distributed 55 million toys and glasses.

Manufacturers also can design sales promotions that increase store traffic for retailers. A promotion that generates a lot of interest within a target audience can drive consumers to retail outlets.

Techniques: Trade Market

The sales promotion techniques used with the trade emphasize financial incentives and support for the retailers' sales and advertising efforts.

Incentives

Incentives to members of the trade include tactics that resemble those used in the consumer market. Awards in the form of travel, gifts, or cash bonuses for reaching targeted sales levels can induce retailers and wholesalers to give a firm's brand added attention. The Volvo national sales manager put together an incentive program for dealerships, in which the leading U.S. dealership won a trip to the Super Bowl and dinner with Hall of Fame footballer Lynn Swann.[23] But the incentive does not have to be large or expensive to be effective. Weiser Lock offered its dealers a Swiss Army knife with every dozen cases of locks ordered. The program was a huge success. A follow-up promotion featuring a Swiss Army watch was an even bigger hit.

Another form of trade incentive is known as push money. **Push money** is carried out through a program in which retail salespeople are offered a monetary reward for featuring a marketer's brand with shoppers. The program is quite simple. If a salesperson sells a particular brand, the salesperson will be paid an extra $50 or $75 "bonus."

One risk with incentive programs for the trade is that salespeople can be so motivated to win an award or extra push money that they may try to sell the brand to every customer, whether it fits that customer's needs or not. Also, a firm must carefully manage such programs to minimize ethical dilemmas. An incentive technique can look like a bribe unless it is carried out in a highly structured and open fashion.

Allowances

Various forms of allowances are offered to retailers and wholesalers with the purpose of increasing the attention given to a firm's brands. Allowances typically are made available to wholesalers and retailers about every four weeks during a quarter. Several types of allowances are common:

- **Merchandise allowances**, in the form of free products packed with regular shipments, are payments to the trade for setting up and maintaining displays. The payments typically are far less than manufacturers would have to spend to maintain the displays themselves.

- **Slotting fees** are direct cash payments to induce food chains to stock an item. They are popular because of the high demand for shelf space in recent years, especially in supermarkets. The proliferation of new products has made shelf space so precious that these fees run in the hundreds of thousands of dollars per product.

- **Bill-back allowances** give retailers a monetary incentive for featuring a marketer's brand in advertising or in-store displays. If a retailer chooses to participate in an advertising campaign or a display bill-back program,

the marketer requires the retailer to verify the services performed and provide a bill for the services.

- **Off-invoice allowances** allow wholesalers and retailers to deduct a set amount from the invoice they receive for merchandise. This program really is only a price reduction offered to the trade on a particular marketer's brand. The price reduction increases the margin (and profits) a wholesaler or retailer realizes on the off-invoiced brand.

One risk with allowances is monitoring the extent to which retailers actually use the allowance to cover extra effort to feature a brand or else to reduce prices charged to consumers. Procter & Gamble, which spends more than $2 billion per year on trade promotions, has implemented controls to ensure that displays and other merchandising of the firm's brands are actually occurring.[24]

Photo courtesy of Omega Ltd.

James Bond's Choice

Seamaster Professional
Automatic chronometer.
Water-resistant to 300m/1000ft.
OMEGA — Swiss made since 1848.

Tomorrow Never Dies

Fine Jewelry & Jewel Gallery
LIBERTY HOUSE
Honolulu, HI

Ω
OMEGA

Here is a classic example of co-op advertising. Omega, the manufacturer, is being featured by Liberty House, a Hawaiian retailer, in this magazine ad. Notice that the James Bond and Omega watch components are national with the co-op sponsorship of the Hawaiian retailer highlighted in the lower left.

merchandise allowances trade-market sales promotion in which free products are packed with regular shipments as payment to the trade for setting up and maintaining displays

slotting fees trade-market sales promotion in which manufacturers make direct cash payments to retailers to ensure shelf space

bill-back allowances monetary incentive provided to retailers for featuring a marketer's brand in advertising or in-store displays

off-invoice allowance program allowing wholesalers and retailers to deduct a set amount from the invoice they receive for merchandise

cooperative advertising sharing of advertising expenses between national advertisers and local merchants

Sales Training

An increasingly popular trade promotion is to provide training for retail store personnel. This method is used for consumer durables and specialty goods, such as home theater systems and exercise equipment. The complexity of these products has made it important for manufacturers to ensure that the proper factual information and persuasive themes are reaching consumers at the point of purchase. For personnel at large stores, manufacturers can hold special classes that feature product information, demonstrations, and training about sales techniques.

Several training tools are available to marketers. They may provide training videos and brochures, or they may send sales trainers into stores to work side by side with store personnel. The use of trainers is costly but can be very effective because it offers one-on-one attention.

Co-op Advertising

Cooperative advertising as a trade promotion technique is referred to as vertical cooperative advertising and involves providing dollars directly to ret~~~ for featuring the company's brand in local adve~~~ Such efforts also are called vendor co-op progr~~~

Marketers try to control the content of this co-op advertising in two ways. They may set strict specifications for the size and content of the ad and then ask for verification that such specifications have been met. Or they may send retailers the template for an ad, into which retailers merely insert the names and locations of their stores.

Techniques: Business Market

The discussion of sales promotion often focuses only on consumer and trade techniques, but it is a major oversight to leave the business market out of the discussion. The Promotional Product Association estimates that several billion dollars a year in sales promotion is targeted to the business buyer.[25]

Trade Shows

Trade shows are events where several related products from many manufacturers are displayed and demonstrated to members of a trade. At a typical trade show, company representatives staff a booth that displays the company's products or service programs. The representatives are there to explain the products and services and perhaps make an important contact for the sales force. Literally every industry has trade shows. For example, Comdex, the annual trade show of the computer and electronics industry, is held in Las Vegas and attracts more than a quarter of a million business buyers.

Advertisers are finding that a trade show is an efficient way to reach interested current and potential buyers with the brand right at hand for discussion and actual use. The Promotional Products Association reports that, when trade show visitors receive a promotional item from a firm at a trade show booth, more than 70 percent of them remember the name of the company that gave them the item.[26] Trade shows can be critically important to a small firm that cannot afford advertising and has a sales staff too small to reach all its potential customers. At trade shows, salespeople can make far more contacts than they could with direct sales calls.

Trade shows also are an important route for reaching potential wholesalers and distributors. But the proliferation of trade shows has been so extensive in recent years that the technique really is more oriented to business buyers.

Business Gifts

By some estimates, nearly half of corporate America gives business gifts. These gifts are given as part of building and maintaining a close working relationship with suppliers. Business gifts that are part of a promotional program may include small items like logo golf balls, jackets, or small items of jewelry. Extravagant gifts or expensive trips that might be construed as "buying business" are not included in this category of business-market sales promotion.

Premiums and Advertising Specialties

As mentioned in the context of promoting to consumers, a key chain or mouse pad bearing a brand name and slogan can be an inexpensive but useful form of sales promotion. A significant portion of the $14 billion market for premiums and advertising specialties is directed to business buyers. Even though business buyers are professionals, they are not immune to the value perceptions created by an advertising specialty; getting something for nothing appeals to business buyers as much as it does to consumers. Will a business buyer choose one consulting firm over another to get a sleeve of golf balls? Probably not. But advertising specialties can create awareness and increase customer satisfaction.

Trial Offers

Trial offers are particularly well suited to the business market. Because many business products and services have a high cost and require a significant time commit-

GETTING SOMETHING FOR NOTHING APPEALS TO BUSINESS BUYERS AS MUCH AS IT DOES TO CONSUMERS.

ment to a brand (because these products and services have a long life), trial offers give buyers a way to lower the risk of making a commitment to a brand. A trial offer also can attract new customers who need a reason to try something new. An opportunity to try a new product for 30 days with no financial risk can be compelling.

Frequency Programs

The extensive travel associated with many business professions makes frequency programs an ideal form of sales promotion for the business market. Airline, hotel, and restaurant frequency programs are dominated by the business market traveler. In addition, retailers of business products—for example, Staples and OfficeMax—have programs designed to reward the loyalty of the business buyer. Costco has teamed with American Express to offer business buyers an exclusive Costco/American Express credit card. Among the card's benefits is a rebate at the end of the year based on the level of buying: the greater the dollar amount of purchases, the greater the percentage rebate.

LO 4 Risks of Sales Promotion

Although sales promotion can help marketers achieve important sales objectives, marketers must carefully consider some significant risks associated with sales promotion:

- *Creating a price orientation:* Because most sales promotions rely on some sort of price incentive or giveaway, the marketer risks having its brand perceived as cheap, with low price being its primary value or benefit. Creating this perception defeats the purpose of integrated marketing communication. If advertising messages highlighting the value of a brand are contradicted by a price emphasis in sales promotions, the market receives mixed signals.

- *Borrowing from future sales:* Sales promotions typically are short-term tactics designed to reduce inventories, increase cash flow, or show periodic boosts in market share. The downside is that a firm simply may be borrowing from future sales. Consumers or trade buyers who would have purchased the brand any way may be motivated to stock up at the lower price. Then, during the next few periods of measurement, sales will decline. This can play havoc

with the measurement and evaluation of the effect of advertising campaigns or other image-building communications. If consumers are responding to sales promotions, it may be impossible to tease out the effects of advertising.

- *Alienating customers:* When a firm relies heavily on sweepstakes or frequency programs to build loyalty among customers, particularly its best customers, any change in the program risks alienating these customers. Airlines suffered just such a fate when they tried to adjust the mileage levels needed for awards in their frequent-flier programs. Ultimately, many of the airlines had to give concessions to their most frequent fliers.

- *Time and expense:* Sales promotions are costly and time consuming. The marketer and retailer must handle promotional materials and protect against fraud and waste in the process. In recent years, funds allocated to sales promotions are taking dollars away from advertising. Advertising is a long-term, franchise-building process that should not be compromised for short-term gains.

- *Legal considerations:* As the popularity of sales promotions, particularly contests and premiums, has grown, legal scrutiny has intensified at the federal and state levels. Legal experts advise marketers planning promotions that use coupons, games, sweepstakes, and contests to check into lottery laws, copyright laws, state and federal trademark laws, prize notification laws, right-of-privacy laws, tax laws, and the regulations of the Federal Trade Commission and Federal Communications Commission. To stay out of legal trouble with sales promotions, marketers carefully and clearly should state the rules and conditions related to the program so that consumers are fully informed.

SHOPPERS OFTEN MAKE PRODUCT SELECTIONS BASED ON WHAT THEY SEE IN THE STORE.

© ifoto/Shutterstock.

LO 5 Point-of-Purchase Advertising

One of the fastest-growing categories of brand promotion in today's marketplace is **point-of-purchase (P-O-P) advertising:** materials used in the retail setting to attract shoppers' attention to a brand, convey primary brand benefits, or highlight pricing information. P-O-P displays also may feature price-off deals or other consumer sales promotions. A corrugated-cardboard dump bin and an attached header card featuring the brand logo or related brand information can be produced for pennies per unit. When the bin is filled with products and placed as a freestanding display at retail, sales gains usually follow.

Marketers clearly believe in the power of P-O-P. From 1981 to 2008, marketers' annual expenditures on point-of-purchase (P-O-P) advertising rose from $5.1 billion to more than $17 billion per year.[27] Why this dramatic growth? P-O-P is the only medium that places advertising, products, and a consumer together in the same place at the same time. According to research conducted by the trade association Point of Purchase Advertising International (http://www.popai.com), 70 percent of all product selections involve some final deliberation by consumers at the point of purchase.[28] Additionally, in an early study on the effects of P-O-P sponsored by Kmart and Procter & Gamble, P-O-P advertising boosted the sales of coffee, paper towels, and toothpaste by 567 percent, 773 percent, and 119 percent, respectively.[29]

Effective deployment of P-O-P advertising requires careful coordination with the marketer's sales force. Gillette found this out when it realized it was wasting money on a lot of P-O-P materials and displays that retailers simply ignored.[30] Gillette sales reps, who visit about 20,000 stores per month, are in a position to know what retailers will and will not use. Gillette's marketing executives finally woke up to this fact when their sales reps told them, for example, that 50 percent of the shelf signs being shipped to retailers from three separate suppliers were going directly to retailers' garbage bins. Reps helped redesign new display cards that mega-retailers such as Walmart approved for their stores and immediately put into use. Now, any time Gillette launches a new P-O-P program, it tracks its success carefully.[31] Having a sales force that can work with retailers to develop and deliver effective P-O-P programs is a critical element for achieving integrated marketing communication.

P-O-P Objectives

The objectives of point-of-purchase advertising are similar to those for sales promotion. The goal is to create a short-term impact on sales while preserving the long-term image of the brand being developed and maintained by advertising. Specifically, the objectives for sales promotion are as follows:

- Draw consumers' attention to a brand in the retail setting.
- Maintain purchase loyalty among brand-loyal users.
- Stimulate increased or varied usage of the brand.
- Stimulate trial use by users of competitive brands.

These objectives are self-explanatory. Key to the effective use of P-O-P is to maintain the brand image being developed by advertising.

P-O-P Advertising Formats

A myriad of displays and presentations are available to marketers. P-O-P materials generally fall into two categories:

1. **Short-term promotional displays** are used for six months or less.

2. **Permanent long-term displays** are intended to provide point-of-purchase presentation for more than six months.

Within these two categories, marketers have a wide range of choices, defined in Exhibit 11.5.[32] This array of in-store options gives marketers a way to attract shoppers' attention, induce purchase, and provide reinforcement for key messages being

Exhibit 11.5
Options for P-O-P Advertising

Window and door signage	Any sign that identifies and/or advertises a company or brand or gives directions to the consumer.
Counter/shelf unit	Smaller display designed to fit on counters or shelves.
Floor stand	Any P-O-P unit that stands independently on the floor.
Shelf talker	Printed card or sign designed to mount on or under a shelf.
Mobile/banner	Advertising sign suspended from the ceiling of a store or hung across a large wall area.
Cash register	P-O-P signage or small display mounted near a cash register and designed to sell impulse items such as lip balm or candy.
Full-line merchandiser	Unit that provides the only selling area for a manufacturer's line; often located as an end-of-aisle display.
End-of-aisle display/gondola	Usually large display of products placed at the end of an aisle.
Dump bin	Large bin with graphics or other signage attached.
Illuminated sign	Lighted signage used outside or in store to promote a brand or the store.
Motion display	Any P-O-P unit that has moving elements to attract attention.
Interactive unit	Computer-based kiosk where shoppers get information such as tips on recipes or how to use the brand; also can be a unit that flashes and dispenses coupons.
Overhead merchandiser	Display rack that stocks product and is placed above the cash register. The cashier can reach the product for the consumer. The front of an overhead merchandiser usually carries signage.
Cart advertising	Any advertising message adhered to a shopping cart.
Aisle directory	Sign delineating contents of a store aisle; also provides space for a brand message.
Retail digital signage	Video displays that typically have been ceiling- or wall-mounted and now are being moved to end-of-aisle caps or given strategic shelf placement to relay special pricing or new-product introductions; newest P-O-P device available.

Source: Information on retail digital signage from Dale Smith, "Coming Down to Eye Level," *Marketing at Retail*, June 2007, 28–31.

conveyed through other components of the promotional plan.

Retailers are increasingly looking to P-O-P displays as ways to differentiate and provide ambience for their individual stores. Therefore, the kind of displays valued by Whole Foods versus Walgreens versus Target (to name just a few) often will vary considerably. The marketer's field sales force will be critical in developing the right P-O-P alternative for each retailer stocking that marketer's products. Without retailers' cooperation, P-O-P advertising cannot work its magic.

P-O-P for Trade and Business Buyers

Even though we have focused on using point-of-purchase advertising as a technique to attract consumers, this promotional tool also is strategically valuable to marketers trying to secure the cooperation of the trade and appeal to business markets. Product displays and information sheets often encourage retailers to support one distributor or manufacturer's brand over another. P-O-P promotions can help win precious shelf space and exposure in a retail setting. From a retailer's perspective, a P-O-P display can enhance the atmosphere of the store and make the shopping experience easier for customers. Brand manufacturers and distributors obviously share that interest. When a retailer can move a particular brand off the shelf, that ability adds to the manufacturer's and distributor's sales.

Also, as store retailers combat the threat of losing business to online shopping, they are trying to enliven the retail environment. Point-of-purchase displays are part of the strategy. Distributors and retailers are trying to create a better and more satisfying shopping experience. The president of a large display company says, "We're trying to bring more of an entertainment factor to our P-O-P programs."[33]

LO 6 Support Media

Marketers use **support media** to reinforce or supplement a message being delivered via some other media vehicle. Support media are especially productive when used to deliver a message near the time or place where consumers are actually contemplating product selections—for example, a billboard ad on or near a store where the brand is sold. Because these media can be tailored to local markets, they can have value to any organization that wants to reach consumers in a particular venue, neighborhood, or metropolitan area.

Outdoor Signs and Billboards

Billboards, posters, and outdoor signs perhaps are the oldest advertising form. Posters first appeared in North America during the Revolutionary War, not as promotional pieces, but as a way to keep the civilian population informed about the war's status. In the 1800s, they became a promotional tool, with circuses and politicians among the first to adopt this new medium. Today, the creative challenge posed by outdoor advertising is as it always has been: to grab attention and communicate with minimal verbiage and striking imagery.

Total spending on outdoor advertising in the United States has been growing steadily since 2003 and now exceeds $7 billion per year.[34] The product categories that rely most heavily on outdoor advertising are local services (like gas stations), real estate and insurance companies, hotels, financial institutions, and automobile dealers and services.[35]

Pros and Cons

Outdoor advertising offers several distinct advantages:[36]

- It can achieve wide exposure of a message in specific local markets.
- Billboards are attention getting because of their size and features such as special lighting and moving elements. Billboards created for a store in Minneapolis even wafted a mint scent throughout the city as part of a candy promotion for Valentine's Day.[37]
- The medium offers around-the-clock exposure for the marketer's message.
- It is well suited to showing off a brand's distinctive packaging or logo.

Billboards and outdoor signs are especially effective when they reach viewers with a message that speaks to a need or desire that is immediately relevant. For instance, fast-food restaurants use billboards along major freeways to tell hungry travelers where to exit to enjoy a Whopper or Big Mac.

Billboards have obvious drawbacks. Long and complex messages simply make no sense on billboards; some experts suggest that billboard copy should be limited to no more than six words. Additionally, the impact of billboards can vary dramatically depending on their location, and assessing locations is tedious and time

riding the boards
assessing possible locations for
billboard advertising

Courtesy of Horst Salons.

Minimal verbiage is one key to success with billboard advertising. This example easily meets that standard.

consuming. To assess locations, companies may have to send individuals to the site to see if the location is desirable. This activity, known in the industry as **riding the boards**, can be a major investment of time and money. Moreover, the Institute of Outdoor Advertising has rated billboards as expensive relative to several other media alternatives.[38] Considering that billboards are constrained to short messages, often in the background, and not the primary focus of anyone's attention, their costs may be prohibitive for many marketers.

New Developments

Despite the cost issue and frequent criticism that billboards represent a form of visual pollution, advocates for this medium contend that important technological advances will make outdoor advertising an increasingly attractive alternative in the future. The first of these advances, which offers the prospect of changing what largely has been a static medium to a dynamic medium with previously unimagined possibilities, is that digital and wireless technologies have found their way to billboards. Google and Microsoft are experimenting with digital technology to make billboards a more targeted medium.[39] Digital billboard displays let advertisers rotate their messages on a board at different times during the day. This capability is especially appealing to local marketers—like television stations and food sellers—whose businesses are

time sensitive. For example, FreshDirect uses this technology to change the messaging for its food-delivery service—morning, noon, and night—on the billboard outside New York City's Queens Midtown Tunnel. Ultimately, billboard time may be sold in day-parts like radio or television, making them more appealing to time-sensitive advertisers.

Another key development entails a testing system to profile the people who see a billboard in any given day.[40] For the past 70 years, the only information available for assessing the impact of billboard advertising came from raw traffic counts. But recently, Nielsen Outdoor, part of the company known for rating television viewership, has developed a system using GPS satellites to track minute-by-minute movements in the "impact zone" of a billboard. Drivers in the Nielsen panel are paid a small stipend to have their latitude and longitude recorded by GPS every 20 seconds. Using demographic data provided by panel members, Nielsen can advise marketers about the characteristics of persons who viewed a billboard at any given time.

Finally, technology now allows for complete personalization of a billboard, thanks to radio frequency identification (RFID) tags. Mini USA has experimented with billboards in four U.S. cities. New Mini owners have volunteered to have RFID tags installed in their key fobs; when they drive by one of the Mini billboards, a personalized message will flash to the driver—for instance, "Have a Great Day, John!"[41]

Transit and Aerial Advertising

Billboards are closely related to and often are used in tandem with **transit advertising**—ads placed inside and on the outside of transit vehicles, at terminals, and on station platforms. Often, the combination of transit and billboard advertising is referred to as **out-of-home media**; this is a popular advertising form around the world. Out-of-home ads appear in many venues, including backs of buildings, subway tunnels, and sports stadiums. Transit ads may appear not only as signs on terminal and station platforms but may actually envelop mass-transit vehicles. One of the latest innovations in out-of-home media is taxi-top electronic billboards that deliver customized messages by neighborhood, using wireless Internet technology.[42]

Transit advertising is especially valuable when a marketer wishes to target adults who live and work in major metropolitan areas. The medium reaches people as they travel to and from work, week after week, so it offers an excellent means for repetitive message exposure. In large metro areas such as New York City, with its 200 miles of subways and 3 million sub-way riders, transit ads can reach many individuals in a cost-efficient manner. Even the once-utilitarian bus stop also has become big business.

When working with this medium, an advertiser may find it most appropriate to buy space on just those train or bus lines that consistently haul people belonging to the demographic segment being targeted. This type of demographic matching of vehicle with target audience derives more value from limited ad budgets. Transit advertising also can be appealing to local merchants because their messages may reach a passenger as he or she is traveling to a store to shop.

Transit advertising works best for building or maintaining brand awareness. But, as with billboards, it is not suitable for lengthy or complex messages. Also, transit ads can easily go unnoticed in the hustle and bustle of daily life. People traveling to and from work via a mass-transit system are one of the hardest audiences to engage with a brand message. They may be bored, exhausted, absorbed by their thoughts, or occupied by another medium. Given the static nature of a transit poster, its message may not be able to break through to a harried commuter.

When advertisers can't break through on the ground or under the ground, they always can look to the sky. **Aerial advertising** involves airplanes pulling signs or banners, skywriting, or those majestic blimps.

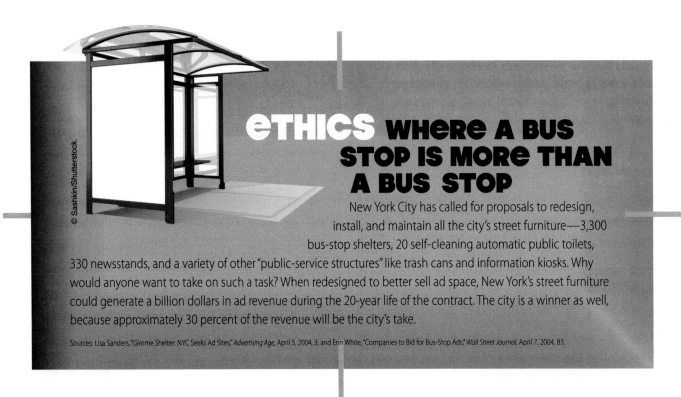

© Sashkin/Shutterstock.

ETHICS WHERE A BUS STOP IS MORE THAN A BUS STOP

New York City has called for proposals to redesign, install, and maintain all the city's street furniture—3,300 bus-stop shelters, 20 self-cleaning automatic public toilets, 330 newsstands, and a variety of other "public-service structures" like trash cans and information kiosks. Why would anyone want to take on such a task? When redesigned to better sell ad space, New York's street furniture could generate a billion dollars in ad revenue during the 20-year life of the contract. The city is a winner as well, because approximately 30 percent of the revenue will be the city's take.

Sources: Lisa Sanders, "Gimme Shelter: NYC Seeks Ad Sites," *Advertising Age*, April 5, 2004, 3; and Erin White, "Companies to Bid for Bus-Stop Ads," *Wall Street Journal*, April 7, 2004, B3.

© Chris T. Allen.

Happy Berliners enjoy their Cokes at three degrees Celsius while waiting for the U-bahn (subway).

replaced by scripted commentary that is written out in advance as part of the advertising contract.[45]

Directory Advertising

Yellow Pages advertising plays an important role in the media mix for many types of organizations, as evidenced by the $16 billion spent in this medium annually.[46] A wealth of current facts and figures about this media option are available from the Yellow Pages Association's website, http://www.buyyellow.com.

A phone directory can play a unique and important role in consumers' decision-making processes. While most support media keep the brand name or key product information in front of a consumer, Yellow Pages advertising helps people follow through on their decision to buy. By providing the information that consumers need to actually find a particular product or service, the Yellow Pages can serve as the final link in a buying decision. Because of their availability and consumers' familiarity with this advertising tool, Yellow Pages directories provide an excellent means to supplement awareness-building and interest-generating campaigns that a marketer might be pursuing through other media.

On the downside, the proliferation and fragmentation of phone directories can make this medium challenging. Many metropolitan areas are covered by multiple directories, some of which are specialty directories designed to serve specific neighborhoods, ethnic groups, or interest groups. Selecting the right set of directories to get full coverage of large sections of the country can be a daunting task. Thus, of the $16 billion spent in this medium annually, less than $2 billion is from advertisers looking for national coverage.[47] Additionally, working in this medium requires long lead times and ties the marketer into a yearlong message. Throughout the course of a year, information in a Yellow Pages ad can easily become dated. There also is limited flexibility for creative execution in the traditional paper format.

Growth of the Internet once was viewed as a major threat to providers of paper directories. Websites such as Switchboard (http://www.switchboard.com) and Superpages (http://www.superpages.com) provide online access to Yellow Pages–style databases that allow individualized searches at one's desktop. Other high-profile players such as Yahoo! and AOL

Aerial billboards, pulled by small planes or jet helicopters equipped with screeching loudspeakers also have proliferated in recent years, as advertisers look for new ways to connect with consumers.[43]

For several decades, Goodyear had blimps all to itself; now the availability of smaller, less-expensive blimps has made this medium more popular to advertisers. Virgin Lightships has created a fleet of small blimps that can be rented for advertising purposes for around $200,000 per month. The Family Channel has been a frequent user of Virgin Lightships' mini-blimps at sporting events such as the Daytona 500 NASCAR race. A recall study done after one such event showed that 70 percent of target consumers remembered the Family Channel as a result of the blimp flyovers.[44] Blimps carrying television cameras at sporting events also provide unique video that can result in the blimp's sponsor getting several on-air mentions. This brand-name exposure comes at a fraction of the cost of similar exposure through television advertising.

When a medium proves itself, more and more marketers will want it in their media mix. Of course, the irony is that, as a medium becomes more attractive and hence cluttered, its original appeal begins to be diluted. We already see this occurring with aerial advertising. With more and more blimps showing up at sporting events, networks can be choosy about which one gets the coveted on-air mention, even demanding that blimp sponsors carry an overhead camera for the network's benefit and purchase advertising time during the event in exchange for the mention. Additionally, the sportscasters' casual banter about the beautiful overhead shots from so-and-so's wonderful blimp now has been

also have developed online directories as components of their service offerings. But, as it turns out, consumers still want their old-style Yellow Pages; market research has established that people who spend the most time on the Internet searching for addresses and phone numbers are the same people who make heavy use of paper directories.[48] When people are in an information-gathering mode, they commonly use multiple media. So, thus far, the Internet has been more of an opportunity than a threat for Yellow Pages publishers.

Packaging

In the simplest terms, **packaging** is the container or wrapping for a product. Although the brand package is not a "medium" in the classic sense, we are treating it as an element of support media because it carries important brand information, and that information carries a message. Classic quotes from consultants describe packaging as "the last five seconds of marketing" and "the first moment of truth."[49]

Although the basic purpose of packaging seems fairly obvious, it also can make a strong positive contribution to the promotional effort. One of the best incidents demonstrating the power of packaging was Dean Foods' creation of the "Milk Chug," the first stylish, single-serving milk package. Officials of Dean Foods noted that "one thing milk didn't have was the 'cool' factor like Pepsi and Coke."[50] Twelve months after introduction of the new package, sales of white milk increased 25 percent, and chocolate and strawberry flavors saw increases of as much as 50 percent.

As we noted in the discussion of point-of-purchase advertising, more than two-thirds of supermarket purchases involve in-store decisions. For consumers in that important stage of their purchase decision, packaging adds another chance for a brand message. That gives packaging a role in promotional strategy and an important place in IMC.

Packaging provides several strategic benefits to the brand manufacturer. First, the package carries the brand name and logo and communicates the name and symbol to a consumer. In the myriad of products displayed at the retail level, a well-designed package can attract a buyer's attention and induce the shopper to more carefully examine the product. Several firms attribute renewed success of their brands to changes in package design. Kraft Dairy Group believes that significant package changes helped its Breyer's ice cream brand make inroads in markets west of the Mississippi. A package consulting firm came up with a package with a black background, a radically different look for an ice cream product.

Packaging helps create a perception of value for the product (and the "value" message is a key part of IMC). When consumers are buying image, the package must reflect the appropriate image. The color, design, and shape of a package have been found to affect

CRAYONS HAS DEVELOPED A PACKAGE FOR ITS ALL-NATURAL FRUIT JUICE DRINK THAT REFLECTS THE BRAND'S QUALITY AND EXCITEMENT.

© Crayons, Inc.

consumer perceptions of a brand's quality, value, and image.[51] Perrier, one of the most expensive bottled waters on the market, has an aesthetically pleasing bottle compared with the rigid plastic packages of its competitors.

More than Support

At times, the capabilities and economies of support media lead them to be featured in a company's media plan. In such instances, it would be a misnomer to label them merely "supportive." Out-of-home media used creatively and focused in major metropolitan markets are especially effective in this regard.

Altoids, "the curiously strong mints" made in England since 1780, used out-of-home media to invigorate its brand in 12 major U.S. cities. Altoids' target segment of young, socially active adults living in urban neighborhoods is hard to reach with traditional broadcast or print advertising. But geodemographic segmentation systems like those described in Chapter 4 enables marketers to identify the neighborhoods where these consumers live. Altoids and its ad agency, Leo Burnett, plastered those neighborhoods with quirky advertising signage on telephone kiosks, bus shelters, and the backs of buses. In each of the 12 tar-

geted metro areas, sales of Altoids increased by more than 50 percent.[52]

Edgy, often inexpensive promotional initiatives executed in major urban markets have become so popular that they now have their own name: **guerrilla marketing**. Many firms have adopted guerilla marketing as their primary promotional style, tailoring different executions market by market. A great exemplar of guerrilla marketing gone global is provided by IKEA, the Swedish furniture maker.[53] IKEA China, focusing on low-income customers in Beijing, transformed the elevators of 20 apartment buildings into furnished "rooms" with small cabinets, teapots, and an elevator operator handing out IKEA catalogs. The intent was to illustrate that IKEA offers many things for dressing up small spaces. IKEA Germany went a slightly different route, taking over train stations in Berlin. The walls of the dingy train stations were decorated with brightly colored fabrics and hanging lamps to make the point that any room can be brightened with a little help from IKEA. The IKEA philosophy is to use nontraditional approaches to make a big splash. That's the essence of guerilla marketing, and it raises out-of-home media from support to a central role in the media mix.

guerrilla marketing edgy, inexpensive promotional initiatives executed in major urban markets

STUDY TOOLS
CHAPTER 11

Located at back of the textbook

- **Rip out Chapter in Review Card.**

Located at www.cengagebrain.com

- **Review Key Terms Flashcards (Print or Online).**
- **Complete the Practice Quiz to prepare for tests.**
- **Play "Beat the Clock" and "Quizbowl" to master concepts.**
- **Complete "Crossword Puzzle" to review key terms.**
- **Watch videos on Gap and Nordstrom Rack for real company examples.**
- **For additional examples, go online to learn about Web-based incentive programs, the impact of P-O-P advertising, and the packaging of products.**

Sponsorship, Product Placements, and Branded Entertainment

P&G introduced consumers to Charmin toilet paper right where they needed it most.

P&G soon realized the kind of results it was looking for from this brand-building program. Various measures, including the Flush-O-Meter, indicated that the Restrooms program was a runaway success.

Learning Outcomes

After studying this chapter, you should be able to:

LO 1   Explain the popularity of event sponsorship as a means of brand promotion.

LO 2   Summarize the uses and appeal of product placements.

LO 3   Describe benefits and challenges of connecting with entertainment properties to build a brand.

LO 4   Discuss challenges presented by the ever-increasing variety of communication and branding tools.

"A brand is a living entity— and it is enriched or undermined cumulatively over time, the product of a thousand small gestures."

—Michael Eisner

AFTER YOU FINISH THIS CHAPTER GO TO PAGE 261 FOR STUDY TOOLS

When Promotion Was a Huge Relief

The number one question asked of New York City's finest as they patrol Times Square is "Where's the bathroom?" Sadly, in most instances, there's no good answer. But during one recent holiday season in New York, everyone had an exceptional answer that also just happened to be a robust brand-building tool, thanks to Procter & Gamble, maker of Charmin, Puffs, and many other brands.

From November 20 through December 31, 2006, Procter & Gamble (P&G) gave New York City and the 15 million visitors to the "Crossroads of the World" an irreplaceable bathroom experience, code-named Charmin Restrooms. On Broadway between West 45th and West 46th streets, the Charmin team built 20 plush restrooms complete with baby-changing stations, stroller parking, aromatherapy, and Charmin-logo city maps as take-home gifts. More than 10,000 "mega rolls" (four times the size of a regular roll) of Charmin toilet paper were stockpiled to get the party started. Flat-screen TVs showed a continuous loop of Charmin commercials, special messages, and something called the Potty Dance, for those waiting patiently for their turn on a perfect potty. Flush-O-Meters were installed to get an accurate count of usage, and for parents with kids in tow, there was a stage set on which the kids could be photographed with the playful bear that stars in all Charmin ads.

That's not all. Street teams roamed the Times Square area on custom-outfitted Charmin Segways looking to foster interest in a restroom break, which is really easy to do when you find people who "gotta go." Additionally, for such a grand undertaking, there had to be a celebrity spokesperson to cut the ribbon and execute the official "First Flush." For this high honor, the Charmin folks selected

What do you think?

I notice who sponsors the concerts or events I attend.

1	2	3	4	5	6	7
STRONGLY DISAGREE				STRONGLY AGREE		

Find out what others think at CourseMate for PROMO.

America's favorite mom, Doris Roberts from the sitcom *Everybody Loves Raymond*. Roberts, a mother and grandmother in real life, called the facility "a modern miracle" for families touring the Big Apple.[1] New York City mayor Michael Bloomberg said of the whole thing: "Whoever thought of this should come work for my team."

It did not take long for P&G, a results-oriented company, to realize the kind of results it was looking for from this brand-building program. Various measures, including the Flush-O-Meter, indicated that the Restrooms program was a runaway success. Using its proprietary system to calculate the numbers, P&G claimed that 191 million media impressions were generated for Charmin in only the first 24 hours. Every major network and newspaper in New York City covered the story of the Restrooms opening, with a *New York Times* editorial calling Time Square's newest attraction "the Disneyland" of restrooms. Families from all 50 states and more than 70 countries visited the Disneyland of restrooms, at a rate of more than 10,000 per day throughout the holiday season, spending on average 21 minutes inside the Charmin-branded experience. Indeed, the Charmin facility racked up more daily visits than popular tourist landmarks like the Statue of Liberty and Rockefeller Center, making this a true brand-building extravaganza for P&G.

Meet Me at Madison & Vine

The Charmin Restrooms exemplify the novel means that marketers are using to create meaningful connections with consumers because traditional mass media are no longer enough. Marketers are always on the lookout for new venues where they can advance their messages. Often these efforts are directed at hard-to-reach niche markets, particularly in urban locations, where market trends often originate. Likewise, every March, marketers seeking a youthful crowd head for the beaches of South Florida, where they make brands like Coke and Gillette a prominent sight during spring break festivities.[2]

The array of tools and tactics that marketers are using to create unique experiences with consumers is so wide that it not always is obvious what these innovations have in common. The dynamic nature of this subject matter also means that the rules for success are hard to pin down. But within this dynamic environment we find the central premise that the fields of advertising, branding, and entertainment are converging. More than ever, brand builders want to be embedded in the entertainment that their target consumers enjoy. They are pursuing this goal with integrated marketing communication (IMC) that includes event sponsorship, product placement in entertainment media, and branded entertainment.

As indicated by Charmin's Restrooms in the Big Apple, the Folgers Yellow People on YouTube (see Chapter 4), and many other examples we've provided in this book, marketers around the world are receptive to many possibilities for brand building, and the list continues to grow. Think about what these examples have in common. Whether it's touring New York City or scanning a few videos on YouTube, consumers are engaged with these brands as part of some entertainment activity. Advertising, branding, and entertainment are converging at an accelerating rate, and the resulting linkage now has its own catchphrase: **Madison & Vine**, which refers to two renowned avenues representing the advertising and entertainment industries, respectively.

Why the accelerating convergence? One reason is the erosion in the effectiveness of traditional broadcast media. Many forces have been undermining old-school media. People have an ever-expanding set of options to fill their leisure time, from playing video games to surfing the Web to watching DVDs. Among people who still do watch television, some are buying digital video recorders (DVRs) that can make watch-

BRAND BUILDERS
WANT TO BE EMBEDDED
IN THE ENTERTAINMENT THAT THEIR TARGET CONSUMERS ENJOY.

A TIVO DVR AUTOMATICALLY FINDS AND RECORDS TELEVISION SHOWS AND ALLOWS YOU TO PAUSE LIVE TV, WATCH IN SLOW MOTION, AND CREATE YOUR OWN INSTANT REPLAYS. YOU ALSO CAN FAST-FORWARD THROUGH ANY PRERECORDED CONTENT—INCLUDING THE ADS.

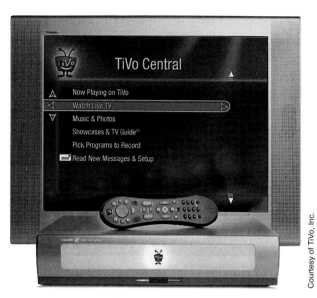

Courtesy of TiVo, Inc.

Chaos Scenario
exodus of ad revenue from traditional broadcast media in reaction to audience fragmentation and tools for ad avoidance; causes media cutbacks, followed by further reductions in audience size and even less advertising

event sponsorship
financial support for an event, given in exchange for the right to display a brand name, logo, or promotional message at the event

ing TV ads a thing of the past.[3] For example, TiVo Central offers an array of features, but in the minds of many, the best feature of this DVR is that it lets you skip commercials. The share of U.S. households with a DVR has passed the one-third mark, and about half of these consumers are skipping the ads when they watch recorded shows.[4]

In the "**Chaos Scenario**" predicted by *Advertising Age*'s Bob Garfield, a mass exodus from the traditional broadcast media is coming. According to Garfield, it will work something like this: Advertisers' dollars stop flowing to traditional media because audience fragmentation and ad-avoidance hardware are undermining their value. With reduced funds available, the networks will have less to invest in the quality of their programs, leading to further reductions in the size of their audiences. This then causes even faster advertiser defections, and on and on in what Garfield calls an "inexorable death spiral" for traditional media.[5] He predicts a brave new world where "marketing—and even branding—are conducted without much reliance on the 30-second [television] spot or the glossy [magazine] spread."[6]

As the old model collapses, billions of advertising dollars will be freed up to move to other brand-building tools. As discussed in Chapter 9, online advertising in its many forms will continue to surge because of this new money. But according to a 2007 Trendwatch survey, the brand-building options preferred by marketers as a replacement for old-school advertising involve sponsored events and experiential marketing (think Charmin Restrooms).[7]

Event sponsorship, product placements, and branded entertainment are surging in popularity not only because advertisers *must* find new ways to connect with their consumers. These tools and tactics also can work in numerous ways to assist with a brand-building agenda. In theory, they can foster brand awareness and even liking through a process known as mere exposure.[8] In addition, the meaning-transfer process discussed in Chapter 5 can change people's perceptions of the brand. That is, the fun and excitement of a Panama City beach at spring break can become part of your feelings about the brands that were there with you. The brand evokes that pleasant memory. Similarly, consumers' sense of self may be influenced by the events they attend (as in a NASCAR race or a sporting event), and brands associated with such venues may assist in embellishing and communicating that sense of self.[9]

LO 1 Event Sponsorship

One of the time-tested and increasingly popular means for reaching targeted groups of consumers on their terms is event sponsorship. **Event sponsorship** involves a marketer providing financial support to help fund an event, such as a rock concert, tennis tournament, or hot-dog-eating contest. In return, that marketer acquires the rights to display a brand name, logo, or advertising message on-site at the event. If the event is covered on TV, the marketer's brand and logo most likely will receive exposure with the television audience as well.

Event sponsorship can take varied forms. The events can be international in scope, as in the 2008 Summer Olympics in Beijing with big-name sponsors like Adidas and Visa. Or they may have a distinctive local flavor, like the Flying Pig Marathon. Events like the Summer Olympics or the Flying Pig Marathon provide a captive audience, may receive radio and television coverage, and often are reported in the print media. Hence, event sponsorship can yield face-to-face contact with real consumers and receive simultaneous and follow-up publicity—all good things for a brand.

Event sponsorship continues to produce impressive results, so it is receiving increases in funding from many marketers. Spending on event marketing and sponsorship has been growing at twice the rate of other advertising and branding tools. In 2006, marketers spent approximately $32 billion on events for which the sponsoring brand received top billing or, in essence, "owned" the event. At events that existed on their own (e.g., college football or basketball), marketers spent another $13 billion for rights to be a branded sponsor.[10]

Even though there are no gold medals at the Flying Pig Marathon in Cincinnati (a.k.a. Porkopolis), crossing the "finish swine" at the head of the pack still is cause for a bit of snorting. Events like this one provide sponsorship opportunities for Mercy Health Partners, a regional office of the accounting firm Ernst & Young, and other companies with a local presence.

Who Sponsors Events?

General Motors, one of the world's foremost old-school ad spenders, typifies the trend to events. GM has experimented with events that get consumers in direct contact with its vehicles or that associate the GM name with causes or activities of interest to its target customers. For example, GM has sponsored a scholarship program for the Future Farmers of America and a week of fashion shows in New York City. GM also has launched a movie theater on wheels that travels to state fairs, fishing contests, and auto races to show its 15-minute "movie" about the Silverado pickup truck. Like many marketers large and small, GM has been shifting more and more of its budget out of the "measured" media and into events and the Web.[11]

The list of companies participating in various forms of event sponsorships seems to grow every year. Jeep, Best Buy, and a host of other companies have sponsored tours and special appearances for recording artists such as Faith Hill and Tim McGraw. Soon after ESPN launched the X Games to attract younger viewers, a host of sponsors signed on, including Taco Bell, Levi Strauss, Kellogg's, Gatorade, and Activision. These brands were looking for benefits through association with something new and hip through a process that anthropologist Grant McCracken has labeled the movement of meaning (see Chapter 5).[12]

Professional soccer has become one of the darlings of the sports business because of the valuable marketing opportunities it supports. For example, Manchester United of the English Premier Soccer League surpasses the New York Yankees in its ability to generate revenues. In this world of big-time sports, global companies like Pepsi and Vodafone pay huge amounts to have their names linked to the top players and teams.[13]

Because sports sponsorships come in all shapes and sizes, including organizations like Professional Bull Riders and the World Hunting Association, marketers have diverse opportunities to associate their brands with the distinctive images of various participants, sports, and even nations (for example, in the case of Olympic teams).[14]

Choosing an Event

A major sweet spot in event sponsorship comes when an event's participants overlap significantly with the marketer's target audience. It's even better when the event also has big numbers of fans and/or participants.

Another consideration is the marketer's budget. Marketers stand to gain the most if they support an

It's hard to compete with the Nikes and Reeboks of the world when it comes to sports sponsorship. The dollars spent in this regard are prohibitive for some companies. But if sponsoring a team from a small country, such as track and field athletes in Jamaica, seems like a long shot, consider that Puma has sponsored Jamaican runner Usain Bolt, who set three world records at the most recent Summer Olympics.

event as its exclusive sponsor, but exclusivity can be extremely pricey. One solution is to sponsor smaller events. Sometimes marketers can find a small neighborhood event with passionate supporters just waiting to be noticed. Consider, for example, the World Bunco Association (WBA), chartered in 1996. Bunco is a dice game, usually played in groups of 8, 12, or 16. It's especially popular with middle-aged women. Bunco is a game of chance, so it leaves players with a lot of time for eating, drinking, and intimate conversation. Approximately 14 million women in the United States have played Bunco, and 4.6 million play regularly. Six out of 10 women say recommendations from their Bunco group influence their buying decisions.[15]

For marketers, the question is whether this group of women has a need that its products can meet. For the makers of Prilosec, the answer is a firm yes. About a third of regular Bunco players suffer from frequent heartburn, and 70 percent of frequent heartburn suffers are women. So in 2005, the makers of Prilosec OTC®, an over-the-counter heartburn medication, discovered Bunco and went to work learning about the women who play it regularly. Besides attending Bunco parties, they explored these consumers other interests by listening to country music, camping in RVs, and watching NASCAR races. Bunco seemed like a great fit. Prilosec's marketers entered into a partnership with the World Bunco Association to sponsor the first Bunco World Championship in 2006. With a $50,000 first prize, associated fund-raising for the National Breast Cancer Foundation, and a lot of favorable word-of-mouth from regional Bunco tournaments, the World Championships caught on fast. Before long, cable TV caught Bunco fever and began covering the championship matches, where the Prilosec OTC purple tablecloths made it a branded experience.

Prilosec OTC's sponsorship of the Bunco World Championship illustrates an ideal scenario. There is excellent overlap between the lifestyles of event enthusiasts and benefits of the sponsoring product. Supporting Bunco allows Prilosec OTC to connect with its core customer in a fun and meaningful way, and the unique connection between Prilosec OTC and Bunco fosters brand loyalty and favorable word-of-mouth. The marketing director for Prilosec OTC said business has responded "phenomenally" on all measures as a result of its Bunco sponsorships.

Assessing Results

In the early days of event sponsorship, it often wasn't clear what an organization was receiving in return for its sponsor's fee. Even today, many critics contend that sponsorships, especially those of the sporting kind, can be ego-driven and thus a waste of money.[16] Company presidents are human, and they like to associate with sports stars and celebrities. This is fine, but when sponsorship of a golf tournament is motivated mainly by a CEO's desire to play in the same foursome as Annika Sorenstam, the company is really just throwing money away.

More often today, however, companies have found ways to make a case for the effectiveness of their sponsorship dollars (see Exhibit 12.1). Boston-based financial-services company John Hancock has been a pioneer in developing detailed estimates of the advertising equivalencies of its sponsorships. John Hancock

media impressions instances in which a product or brand is exposed to consumers through media coverage, rather than paid advertising

began sponsoring a college football bowl game in 1986 and soon after had a means to judge the value of its sponsor's fee. Hancock employees scoured magazine and newspaper articles about their bowl game to determine name exposure in print media. Next, they factored in the exact number of times the John Hancock name was mentioned in pre-game promos and during the television broadcast. Early on, Hancock executives estimated they received the equivalent of $5.1 million in advertising exposure for their $1.6 million sponsorship fee. However, as the television audience for the John Hancock bowl dwindled in subsequent years, Hancock's estimates of the bowl's value also plunged. Hancock then moved its sports sponsorship dollars into other events, such as the Olympics, the Boston Marathon, and Major League Baseball.

Media Impressions

As marketers find better ways to gauge the effectiveness of marketing dollars spent, they generally are willing to spend more on any IMC tool.[17] In the realm of event sponsorship, Nielsen Media Research has developed a measurement it calls the Sponsorship Scorecard to give marketers a read on the impact of their signage in sports stadiums. Nielsen keeps track of when a sponsor's sign is shown on TV or the sponsor is mentioned on TV, and then it matches up those broadcast impressions with data it gathers on audience size for the broadcast to find the television audience for the sponsorship messages. In one assessment for Fleet Bank in Boston's Fenway Park, Nielsen calculated that Fleet signage received 84 impressions of at least five seconds each during a telecast of a Red Sox/Yankees baseball game. Based on the size of the TV audience for the game at the times when those impressions occurred, Nielsen determined that the images and mentions of Fleet's sponsorship generated a total of 418 million impressions among adults age 18 and over.[18]

In the John Hancock and Fleet Bank examples, marketers evaluated the effectiveness of their sponsorship spending by using a popular approach: **media impressions**, counting the number of instances in which a product or brand is exposed to consumers through media coverage, rather than paid advertising. (As described in the example at the beginning of the chapter, P&G also used media impressions to evaluate the marketing success of Charmin Restrooms.) Marketers use media impressions as a metric because it lets them directly compare sponsorship spending with spending in the traditional measured media.

Exhibit 12.1
When Event Sponsorship Is a Winner

Enough media impressions

Stronger brand loyalty

Targeted consumers in audience

Brand Loyalty

Adding to their appeal, sponsorships can furnish a unique opportunity to foster brand loyalty. When marketers connect their brand with the potent emotional experiences often found at rock concerts, in soccer stadiums, at the Bunco table, or on Fort Lauderdale beaches in March, positive feelings may attach to the sponsor's brand and linger well beyond the duration of the event. Therefore, judging whether your brand is receiving this loyalty dividend is another important aspect of sponsorship assessment.

Getting a good read on the return from one's sponsorship dollars requires a mix of qualitative and quantitative approaches.[19] On the quantitative side, marketers will need, at a minimum, good data on the number and types of consumers who are making direct contact with their brands at any given event. Technology provides useful tools like tablet-size wireless computers that allow data collection and input by those scouting the event. Also, as attendees exit, marketers can conduct a survey asking their impressions of the various brands sponsoring the event and the all-important question for predicting loyalty: Is this a brand you will recommend to a friend or family member?

Sponsorships yield their greatest benefit when they foster a relationship or deep connection between the target consumer and the sponsoring company or brand. This connection is created when the consumer's passion for the event in question (say, World Cup soccer) becomes associated with a sponsoring brand (such as Adidas or Heineken). Although traditional evaluation tools like exit surveys and media impressions are important in assessing the value of sponsorships, they cannot reveal deep connections. Careful listening is key to uncovering these connections.

Three areas of questioning can provide important insights for evaluating the relationship-building benefits of event sponsorship:

1. This qualitative research process should begin by exploring attendees' subjective experience of an event. Do they have strong feelings about the events they attend? What is it that ignites their passion for an event?

2. Next, it is critical to explore whether fans really understand the role of the sponsor. Most fans know little about the benefits that sponsors provide; research has shown that the more they know, the more the sponsor benefits. Auto-racing fans have the greatest understanding of the sponsor's role, which helps explain the eagerness of companies to get involved as sponsors of this sport.

3. Marketers need to probe the issue of connection: What specific brands do people connect with specific events, and how have their opinions of those brands been affected, if at all?

> **leveraging** using any collateral communication or activity to reinforce the link between a brand and an event

Tapping emotional connections requires sophisticated listening. Keen listening in these areas will help reveal whether sponsorships are deepening a brand's relevance and meaning in event goers' lives.

Audience Characteristics

Because various types of events attract well-defined target audiences, marketers also should monitor event participants to ensure the messages are reaching their desired target. Consider the marketing needs of JBL Electronics in reaching young consumers. JBL has teamed up with Trek Bikes to sponsor nationwide mountain-biking events. These so-called gravity sports are particularly attractive to skeptical teens, who reject traditional broadcast advertising and are starting to reject other forms of promotion. Their support of these sports at least puts JBL and Trek on the radar screen for this demanding audience.

Leveraging the Sponsorship

Marketers tend to justify event sponsorship by calculating the number of viewers who will be exposed to a brand either at the event or through media coverage of the event, and then assessing whether the sponsorship provides a cost-effective way of reaching the target segment. This approach assesses sponsorship benefits in direct comparison with traditional advertising media. However, some experts maintain that the benefits of sponsorship can be fundamentally different from anything that traditional media might provide.

In particular, marketers can benefit from finding ways to leverage the sponsorship. **Leveraging** or activating a sponsorship refers to any collateral communication or activity reinforcing the link between a brand and an event.[20]

Events can be leveraged as ways to entertain important clients, recruit new customers, motivate the firm's salespeople, and generally enhance employee morale. Events provide unique opportunities for face-to-face contact with key customers. Marketers commonly use this point of contact to distribute specialty-advertising items so that attendees will have a branded memento to remind them of the rock concert or their New York City holiday. Marketers also may use this opportunity to sell premiums such as T-shirts and hats, administer consumer surveys as part of their marketing research efforts, or distribute product samples. As you will see in the next chapter, a firm's event participation also may be the basis for public relations activities that then generate additional media coverage. Exhibit 12.2 provides a checklist of guidelines for selecting the right events and maximizing their benefits for the brand.

LO 2 Product Placements

As the fields of advertising, branding, and entertainment converge, marketers aspire to embed their brands in any form of entertainment that their target consumers enjoy. And while event sponsorship has been around for decades, brand builders also are looking elsewhere. Indeed, in today's world of integrated marketing communication, no show seems to be off limits. Brands now can be found whenever and wherever consumers are being entertained—whether at a sporting event, in a movie theater, on the Internet, or in front of a TV set or video game console.

This effort takes the form of **product placement**, the practice of placing any branded product into the content and execution of an established entertainment vehicle. These placements are purposeful and paid for by the marketer to expose and/or promote a brand. Product placement has come a long way since E.T. nibbled on Reese's Pieces in the movie *E.T. the Extra-Terrestrial*. But that product (or brand) placement foreshadowed much that has followed. Experts have estimated that spending for product placements around the world would approach $14 billion by 2010.[21]

Exhibit 12.2
Checklist for Event Sponsorship

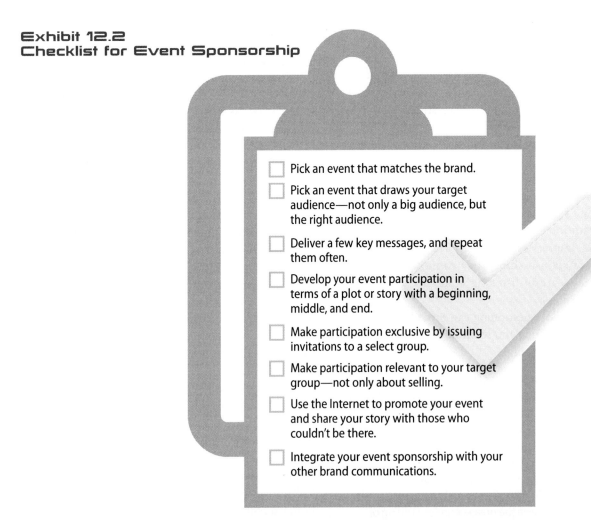

- Pick an event that matches the brand.
- Pick an event that draws your target audience—not only a big audience, but the right audience.
- Deliver a few key messages, and repeat them often.
- Develop your event participation in terms of a plot or story with a beginning, middle, and end.
- Make participation exclusive by issuing invitations to a select group.
- Make participation relevant to your target group—not only about selling.
- Use the Internet to promote your event and share your story with those who couldn't be there.
- Integrate your event sponsorship with your other brand communications.

Source: MARKETING NEWS: REPORTING ON MARKETING AND ITS ASSOCIATION by Laura Shuler. Copyright 1999 by AMERICAN MARKETING ASSOCIATION. Reproduced with permission of AMERICAN MARKETING ASSOCIATION in the format Textbook and in the format Other book via Copyright Clearance Center.

Product Placement Media

Product placement agencies work with marketers to build bridges to the entertainment industry. Working collaboratively, agents, marketers, producers, and writers find ways to incorporate the marketer's brand as part of the show. The show can be of almost any kind. Movies, short films on the Internet, and reality TV are great venues for product placements. Video games, novels, and magazines (or mag-a-logs) offer great potential.

Television

Television viewers have grown accustomed to product placements. Soap operas and reality shows have helped make product placements seem the norm on TV, and the tactic is spreading like wildfire. On Time Warner's WB network, a shiny orange Volkswagen Beetle convertible played an important role in the teen superhero drama *Smallville*. The final episode of NBC's long-running comedy *Frasier* included a special moment where Niles gave his brother a little gift to cheer him up. That gift? Pepperidge Farm Mint Milano cookies. The branded "special moment," like that one on *Frasier*, will only become more commonplace.[22]

There's even a school of thought contending that product placements can be television's savior.[23] Recall Bob Garfield's Chaos Scenario, discussed previously in this chapter, with its "inexorable death spiral" for the traditional media like TV. Concern that consumers won't watch ads on TV is a primary rationale for turning the programming itself into an ad vehicle. When contestants get rewarded with a Pringles snack on an episode of *Survivor*, that brand in effect is receiving an implicit endorsement. There were more than 100,000 product placements in TV shows in 2005, and that number continues to grow robustly.[24] There's no telling where this trend is headed, but maybe TV will be saved.

Movies

The car chase is a classic component of many action/adventure movies, and, in recent years, it has been seized as a platform for launching new automotive brands.[25] If you'd like to immerse yourself in a superb example of branded entertainment, rent the DVD of *The Italian Job*, a movie released in 2003 starring the lovable Mini Cooper. The Mini proves to be the perfect getaway car, as it deftly maneuvers in and out of tight spots throughout the movie. BMW has been a pioneer in the product-placement genre, starting with its Z3 placement in the 1995 James Bond thriller *Goldeneye*.

Of course, automakers aren't the only companies that have discovered product placements in movies and films. White Castle and the Weather Channel—to name just two—have joined the party as well. The 2006 movie *Talladega Nights: The Ballad of Ricky Bobby*, starring Will Ferrell, featured a cornucopia of product placements for everything from Applebee's to Wonder Bread.[26]

All this activity is supported by research indicating that persons under 25 years old are most likely to notice product placements in films and also are willing to try products they see in movies and films.[27] As we have emphasized, young consumers are increasingly difficult to reach via traditional broadcast media. Because they are likely to get their fill of product placements at the movies, in the near term, this looks like a good tactic for reaching an age cohort that can be hard to reach.

Video Games

According to Forrester Research, 100 million U.S. households have at least some gaming capability.[28] Moreover, most analysts conclude that around 40 percent of the hard-core players are in the 18-to-34 age cohort—highly sought after by advertisers because of their discretionary spending but expensive to reach via conventional media. For these consumers and media users, video games not only are an attractive entertainment option but also a form of entertainment where players rarely wander off during a commercial break. Nielsen research has established that the majority of players see brand placements as adding to the quality of play, and because brand exposures in games are repetitive, they affect purchase intent more than old-style media do.

With all those focused eyeballs in play, is it any wonder that marketers want to be involved? Indeed, Nielsen has forecast an increase in spending on product placements in video games from $75 million in 2005 to as much as $1 billion in 2010.[29] Billboard ads and virtual products have become standard fare in games like True Crime: Streets of L.A., starring Puma-wearing Nick Kang. And Tony Hawk must be a Jeep fan, because Wranglers, Grand Cherokees, and Liberties are always on the scene in his games.

The next big thing for marketers is Web-enabled consoles that allow more dynamic ad placements and precise tracking of where and how often players pause to take a closer look.[30] Whether you call these efforts "game-vertising" or "adver-gaming," you can expect to see more of brands as varied as LG Mobile, Ritz Bits, and Old Spice in the virtual world.

Requirements for Success

As the business of product placements has evolved, an activity that once was rare, haphazard, and opportunistic has become more systematic and, in many cases, even strategic. Even though product placement will never be as tidy as crafting and running a 30-second TV spot, numerous case histories help us identify factors that can improve the marketer's odds for success.[31]

First, product placements will add the greatest value when they are integrated with other elements of a promotional plan. As with event sponsorship, the idea is to leverage the placement of the brand message. Marketers should avoid isolated product placement opportunities and create connections to other elements of the IMC plan. For instance, a placement combined with a well-timed public relations campaign can yield synergy: novel product placements create great media buzz. In addition, a product placement can complement advertising initiatives that attend the launch of a new product.

Another factor affecting the value of any placement has to do with the elusive concept of **authenticity**—the quality of being perceived as genu-

One way video games differ from TV shows is that the players don't wander off to get a snack during commercial breaks. The product placements are an accepted part of the games, making the game environments appear more authentic.

ine and natural. As marketers and their agents look for more and more chances to write their brands into the script of shows, it is to be expected that some of these placements will come off as phony. For example, when Eva Longoria plugs a new Buick at a shopping mall during an episode of *Desperate Housewives,* the scene looks phony and contrived. No way would Longoria or her character in this TV show ever stoop to such an unflattering activity. Conversely, when Kramer argues with a homeless man in the show *Seinfeld* about returning his Tupperware containers, the spoof is perfect and adds to the comedic moment. Brands should be embedded in the entertainment, not detract from it. This often is a difficult goal to achieve.

Marketers foster success with product placements by developing deep relationships with the key players in this dynamic business. You need to have the right people looking for the right opportunities that fit with the strategic objectives established for the brand. This, too, is not a new idea. Advertising in particular, like marketing in general, is a team sport; the best team wins most of its games. You want to be part of a team where the various members understand each other's goals and are working to support one another. Good teams take time to develop. They also move product placement from an opportunistic and haphazard endeavor to one that supports integrated marketing communication.

Measuring Success

As with event sponsorship, a major challenge of product placements is how to measure the success or return on investment of the activity. The collective wisdom seems to be that calculating media impressions for placements does not tell the whole story regarding their value. Product placements can vary dramatically in the value they offer to the marketer.

One key item to look for is the celebrity connection in the placement.[32] When Tom Cruise puts on Wayfarer shades in one of his movies, the implied endorsement drives sales of the product.[33] Astute users of product placements are always looking for plot connections that could be interpreted by the audience as an implied brand endorsement from the star of the show.

LO 3 Branded Entertainment

Branded entertainment is a natural extension and outgrowth of product placement. It raises the stakes—and the potential payout. With product placement, the question is "What shows are in development that we might fit our brand into?" With branded entertainment, marketers create their own shows, so they don't have to find a place for their brand. This, of course, guarantees that the brand will be one of the stars in the show, as in the case of the Tide car on your TV at the Lowe's Motor Speedway.

For a stock-car racing fan, there is nothing quite like being at the Lowe's Motor Speedway on the evening of the Coca-Cola 600, NASCAR's longest night. Being there live is a rare treat, so the NASCAR Nextel Cup Series gets plenty of coverage on television, making it among the most popular televised sporting events in North America.[34] Although NASCAR is all about the drivers and the race, every race also is a colossal celebration of brands. The cars themselves carry the logos of something like 800 NASCAR sponsors. The announcers keep you informed throughout via the Old Spice Lap Leaders update and the Visa Race Break. We are told that Home Depot is the "Official Home Improvement Warehouse of NASCAR" and UPS is the "Official Delivery Service of NASCAR." At commercial breaks, Budweiser and Miller duel via advertisements, and we rejoin the race to follow the Budweiser or Miller Lite car around the track. None of this comes as any surprise because NASCAR openly and aggressively bills itself as the best marketing opportunity in sports. Said another way, a NASCAR race is a fantastic example of branded entertainment.

It's not hard to understand why NAPA Auto Parts or Budweiser, the King of Beers, would be willing to shell out millions of dollars to be a featured brand in the NASCAR Nextel Cup Series. But how does Procter & Gamble justify sponsorship of the Tide car? Well, first of all, a lot of women are NASCAR fans, and a lot of women buy Tide. Additionally, general industry research indicates that NASCAR fans are unusually loyal to the brands that sponsor cars and have no problem with marketers plastering their logos all over their cars and their drivers. Indeed, many NASCAR fans wear those logos proudly. Moreover, the data say race fans are three times more likely to purchase a product promoted by their favorite NASCAR driver, relative to the fans of all other sports.[35] One NASCAR marketing executive put it this way: "Our teams and drivers have done a wonderful job communicating to fans that the more Tide they buy, the faster Ricky Cravens is going to go."[36] Obviously, this entails impressing and connecting with consumers in a most

THE VALUE OF ANY PLACEMENT HAS TO DO WITH THE **ELUSIVE CONCEPT** OF AUTHENTICITY—THE QUALITY OF BEING PERCEIVED AS **GENUINE** AND **NATURAL.**

There's something special about the relationship between fans and their brands at a NASCAR event. Each race truly is a celebration, with brands as costars of the show. Fans are loyal to both NASCAR and its many sponsors.

© Roger Padgett/Reuters/Landov.

compelling way, making the Tide car or the Lowe's car a great symbol of branded entertainment.

NASCAR truly is a unique brand-building "vehicle," with numerous marketing opportunities for brands large and small.[37] But we use it here as an exemplar of something that is bigger, more pervasive, and growing in popularity as a way to support and build brands. Although it has been called many things, we have settled on the label **branded entertainment** to describe the development and support of any entertainment property (e.g., TV show, theme park, short film, movie, or video game) where a primary objective is to feature one's brand or brands in an effort to impress and connect with consumers in a unique and compelling way.

What distinguishes branded entertainment from product placement is that, in branded entertainment, the entertainment would not exist without the marketer's support, and in many instances, marketers themselves create the entertainment property. BMW's efforts in product placement versus branded entertainment provide a perfect example. The appearance of the Z3 in the 1995 James Bond thriller *Goldeneye* is a nice example of product placement. But BMW did not stop there. In 2001, BMW and its ad agency Fallon Minneapolis decided it was time to make their own movies with BMW vehicles as the star of the show. The result was a series of original, Web-distributed short films like *Beat the Devil*, starring Clive Owen, James Brown, Marilyn Manson, and most especially, the BMW Z4. The success of these custom-made BMW films helped launch the new era of branded entertainment.

Many have followed BMW's lead in developing their own forms of entertainment as a means to feature brands.[38] Goen Group has developed a reality show, the *Million Dollar Makeover Challenge*, starring its diet pill Trimspa. *The Fairway Gourmet*, featured on PBS stations, promoted images of the good life, courtesy of the Hawaii Visitors & Convention Bureau. By creating shows themselves (often with their ad agencies), marketers seek to attract a specific target audience with a carefully tailored story that shows their brands at their best. This is quite different from trying to find a special place for one's brand in an existing show. As others have suggested, "Clients often enter the (general) realm of entertainment marketing via small product placements that eventually develop into larger promotional programs."[39] On the path of brand building, it is natural to evolve from the simple product placement to the more elaborate enterprise of branded entertainment.

Returning to the NASCAR example, today's NASCAR racing circuit could not exist without big brands like Gillette and Tide sponsoring racing teams and their drivers. Without the brands, there would be no NASCAR. As exemplified by a NASCAR race, in today's world of brand building, it often is impossible to disentangle the brand building from the entertainment. That's a great scenario for brand builders because, among other things, it makes their efforts TiVo-proof.

Challenges of Product Placement and Branded Entertainment

The surging popularity of product placement and branded entertainment is understandable, considering how well they help marketers reach an otherwise unreachable audience with messages that stand out and connect with consumers. However, to make the most of these opportunities, marketers must be able to overcome some obstacles to success, collaborate with the entertainment industry, and coordinate product placements and branded entertainment with the rest of their promotional mix.

Obstacles Ahead

No one can really say how rapidly marketing dollars will flow into these options in the next decade because several complicating and countervailing forces could hinder that flow (see Exhibit 12.3).

One of the obvious countervailing forces is instant oversaturation. As when any promotional tactic becomes popular, especially if it becomes a fad, overuse by marketers can result in jaded consumers and a cluttered media environment. As stated by a former marketing vice president at General Motors, "Any reasonable observer today has to see most of the marketing world is chasing a handful of product-placement deals. This is problematic and limiting. There just aren't enough bona fide hits to go around."[40] Some will argue that creative collaboration can always yield new opportunities for branded entertainment, but you have to acknowledge at some point that yet another motion picture featuring another hot automobile will start to feel stale. Indeed, we already may be there.

A related problem involves the current processes and systems for matching brands with entertainment properties. Traditional media provide a well-established path for reaching consumers. Marketers like that predictability. Branded entertainment is a new and often

**Exhibit 12.3
Obstacles to Overcome**

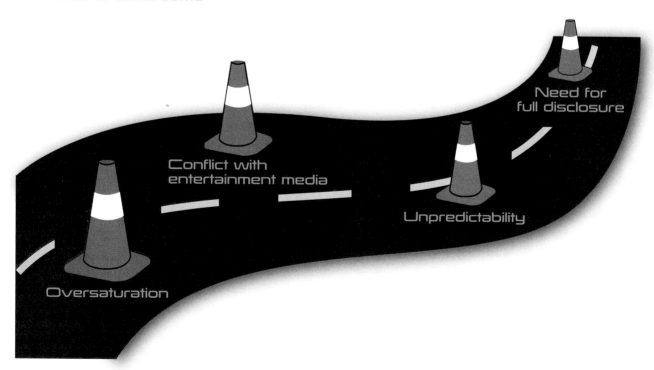

Need for full disclosure

Conflict with entertainment media

Unpredictability

Oversaturation

unpredictable path. As noted by a senior executive at Fallon Minneapolis, a pioneer in branded entertainment with BMW Films, "For every success you have several failures, because you're basically using a machete to cut through the jungle . . . with branded entertainment, every time out, it's new."[41] Lack of predictability causes the process to break down.

In some cases, marketers and filmmakers don't appreciate one another's needs. Consider the soured relationship between General Motors and Warner Bros.

© Monkey Business Images/Shutterstock.

GLOBAL CLUTTER VS. CONTROL IN EUROPEAN MARKETS

When it launched a cooking show called *Dinner Doctors* in the United Kingdom, H. J. Heinz intended to feature its products. But regulators don't allow products to be mentioned in any part of the programming—only sponsorship mentions as part of the credits. In a country that limits product placements, that may be enough to generate positive feedback from consumers.

In Spain, where commercial breaks on TV can last up to 15 minutes, the home improvement show *Deco-garden* sets the standard for product placements with 105 placements in only four episodes. There, a dramatic product placement is just about your only hope to be noticed amid the clutter.

Overall, the trend is toward the Spanish model, as new rules from the European Union are encouraging a more open advertising environment.

Sources: Erin White, "U.K. TV Can Pose Tricky Hurdles," *Wall Street Journal*, June 27, 2003, B7; Emma Hall, "Product Placement Faces a Wary Welcome in Britain," *Advertising Age*, January 8, 2007, 27; and Aaron Patrick and Keith Johnson, "Spanish Television Reigns as King of Product Plugs," *Wall Street Journal*, February 2, 2007, A1, A16.

over the promotion of the film *Matrix Reloaded*. GM's Cadillac division abandoned a big-budget TV campaign associated with the sequel when it couldn't get the talent cooperation or film footage it wanted. Samsung, Heineken, and Coke also complained in public about poor treatment from Warner Bros. These kinds of high-profile squabbles make big news and leave marketers wondering whether the branded-entertainment path is really worth all the aggravation.[42]

Finally, there is concern about playing it straight with consumers. Ralph Nader's Commercial Alert consumer advocacy group has filed a complaint with the Federal Trade Commission and the Federal Communication Commission alleging that TV networks deceive the public by failing to disclose the details of product-placement deals.[43] The group's basic argument seems to be that, because most product placements are in fact "paid advertisements," consumers should be advised as such. It is conceivable that a federal agency will call for some form of disclosure when fees have been paid to place brands in U.S. TV shows, although now that the practice has become prevalent, we expect that consumers already perceive there is money changing hands behind the scenes. Consumers generally are pretty savvy about this sort of thing. On the global front, opinions about this issue vary from country to country.

Collaborating with the Media

Marketers have much in common with media companies and entertainers: They do what they do for business reasons. And they have and will continue to do business together. Smart marketers recognize this as they go about their business of trying to reach consumers with a positive message on behalf of their brands. Thus, while branded entertainment is enjoying a huge surge of popularity recently, it has been around for decades.

No firm has managed this collaboration better throughout the years than Procter & Gamble. In 1923, P&G was on the cutting edge of branded entertainment in the then-new medium of radio. To promote its shortening product Crisco, the company helped create a new radio program called *Crisco Cooking Talks*. This 15-minute program featured recipes and advice to encourage cooks to find more uses for Crisco. Although it was a good start, P&G's market research soon indicated that listeners wanted something more entertaining than just a recipe show. So a new form of entertainment was created just for radio: the soap opera. These dramatic

IN THE 1920S, P&G WAS AN INNOVATOR IN THE MEDIUM OF RADIO, TRYING TO REACH CONSUMERS ON BEHALF OF BRANDS LIKE CRISCO SHORTENING AND IVORY SOAP.

series used a storyline that encouraged listeners to tune in day after day. *Guiding Light*, P&G's most enduring soap opera, started on the radio in 1937. In 1952, *Guiding Light* made a successful transition to television. It thus holds the distinction of being the longest-running show in the history of electronic media.[44] And, of course, P&G has become a dominant seller of soap—and many other products as well.

Today, P&G's consumer has changed, the soap opera has lost much of its traditional appeal, and new forms of integrated marketing communication are necessary. P&G works with partners like Viacom Plus and Starcom MediaVest Group to ensure that its brands are embedded in the entertainment venues preferred by its targeted consumers. A great example is the integration of P&G's CoverGirl brand in the CW network's *America's Next Top Model*, hosted by former CoverGirl model Tyra Banks. At the time of this writing, this relationship already had endured through several seasons, with plans to do several more. This CoverGirl/*Top Model* relationship exemplifies many best practices for branded entertainers.

An enduring relationship is clearly something to strive for. Long-term relationships beget trust, and when partners trust each other, they also look out for each other. So een though P&G does not have direct control over the content of *Top Model*, it is able to ask for brand inserts and sometimes influence the show's content because of the relationship. However, P&G has learned not to push too hard to get its brand featured. That can detract from the entertainment value of the programming, which wouldn't help anyone. To maintain the right balance, the CoverGirl brand receives strong integration into the plot in only three episodes per season. But online communication at the brand's website invites audience participation every week.

Authenticity of the brand integration is always desirable, and CoverGirl definitely gets that on *Top Model*. For example, each season, the three finalists must prepare to be photographed for a magazine ad. This is, after all, what models get paid to do: appear in ads. So it's perfectly natural that this is part of the show, and it's perfectly natural that the magazine ad will be for CoverGirl, a brand that stands for "enhancing your natural beauty." The content of

the show and the essence of the brand become intertwined, with an implied endorsement from *America's Next Top Model*. It doesn't get any better in the world of brand building.

LO 4 Coordinating IMC Efforts

As the choices for delivering messages to a target audience continue to evolve and as marketers constantly search for cost-effective ways to break through the clutter and connect with consumers, promotion portfolios are including everything from advertising in restrooms to sponsoring a marathon. Simply put, marketers have a vast and ever-expanding array of options for delivering messages to their potential customers. The keys to success for any promotional campaign are choosing the right set of options to engage a target segment and then coordinating the placement of messages to ensure coherent and timely communication.

Many factors work against coordination. As integrated marketing communication (IMC) has become more complex, organizations often become reliant on diverse functional specialists. For example, an organization might have separate managers for advertising, event sponsorship, branded entertainment, and Web development. Specialists, by definition, focus on their specialty and can lose sight of what others in the organization are doing.[45] Specialists also want their own budgets and typically argue for more funding for their particular area. This competition for budget dollars often yields rivalries and animosities that work against coordination. Never underestimate the power of competition for the budget. It is exceedingly rare to find anyone who will volunteer to take less of the budget so that someone else can have more.

Coordination is further complicated by the potential for a lack of agreement about who is responsible for achieving integration.[46] Should the client accept this responsibility, or should integration be the responsibility of a "lead" agency? Ad agencies often see themselves in this lead role but have not played it to anyone's satisfaction.[47] In one vision of the ideal arrangement, the lead agency plays the role of an architect and general contractor.[48] The campaign architect is charged with drawing up a plan that is media neutral and then hiring subcontractors to deliver aspects of the project that the agency itself is ill suited to handle. The plan also must be profit neutral—that is, the budget must go to the subcontractors who can deliver the work called for in the master plan. Here again, the question becomes, will the agency in the role of architect/general contractor really spread the wealth, even if doing so means the agency would forfeit wealth? Whether or not it will, one principle holds: When there is doubt about who is accountable for delivering an integrated campaign, the campaign is unlikely to be well integrated.

The objective underlying the need for coordination is to achieve a synergistic effect. Individual media can work in isolation, but advertisers get more for their dollars if various media and IMC tools build on one another and work together. Even savvy marketers like American Express are challenged by the need for coordination, especially as they cut back on their use of the 30-second TV spot and venture into diverse IMC tools. For instance, to launch its Blue card, AmEx employed an innovative mix, starting with Blue-labeled water bottles given away at health clubs and Blue ads printed on millions of popcorn bags. The company sponsored a Sheryl Crow concert in New York's Central Park and transformed L.A.'s House of Blues jazz club into the "House of Blue," with performances by Elvis Costello, Stevie Wonder, and Counting Crows. Print ads and TV also have been used to back the Blue, but AmEx's spending in these traditional media was down by more than 50 percent relative to previous campaigns. Making diverse components like these work together and speak to the targeted consumer with a single voice is the essence of IMC. AmEx appears to have found a good formula: The Blue card was the most successful new-product launch in the company's history.[49]

The coordination challenge does not end here. For example, added complexity—and opportunities—come from additional options, such as personal selling, public relations, and social media. These activities entail additional contacts with a target audience, and they should reinforce the other brand messages.

STUDY TOOLS
CHAPTER 12

Located at back of the textbook

- **Rip out Chapter in Review Card.**

Located at www.cengagebrain.com

- **Review Key Terms Flashcards (Print or Online).**
- **Complete the Practice Quiz to prepare for tests.**
- **Play "Beat the Clock" and "Quizbowl" to master concepts.**
- **Complete "Crossword Puzzle" to review key terms.**
- **Watch videos on Cannes Film Festival and BMW for real company examples.**
- **For additional examples, go online to learn about brand placement in TV shows, movies, and video games.**

Public Relations, Influencer Marketing, Social Media, and Corporate Advertising

Irresistible

P&G marketers place irresistible posters like this one in restrooms of popular night spots.

Does this ad create a reason for you to buzz about it to your friends?

Crest invites consumers who are out on the town to take the irresistibility IQ Quiz via their cell phones.

Resistible

Where do you fit in? Take the irresistibility i.q. quiz and enter for a chance to win prizes at **crestiq.com** or text "IQ" to CREST. **Crest** Healthy, beautiful smiles for life.

Learning Outcomes

After studying this chapter, you should be able to:

LO 1 Discuss the role of public relations as part of a strategy for integrated marketing communication (IMC).

LO 2 Identify the objectives and tools of public relations.

LO 3 Describe basic strategies for PR activities.

LO 4 Summarize how companies use influencer marketing programs.

LO 5 Describe how marketers use social media to promote brands.

LO 6 Discuss the applications and objectives of corporate advertising.

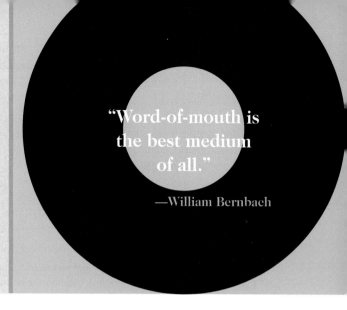

"Word-of-mouth is the best medium of all."

—William Bernbach

AFTER YOU FINISH THIS CHAPTER GO TO PAGE 281 FOR STUDY TOOLS

Making Crest Irresistible

With a hip or novel product like Red Bull or Mini Cooper, it's not so hard to get consumers and the media buzzing about your brand. But marketers often are working with familiar products and well-known brands. Their challenge is creating interest in and cultivating relationships with brands that are as familiar as the toothpaste in your medicine cabinet.

"Look Ma, No Cavities" was an ad slogan that created great buzz for the Crest brand—50 years ago. To revive its Crest brand by targeting young consumers, with their eclectic media habits and built-in skepticism about brands, Procter & Gamble introduced a line extension, Crest Whitening Plus Scope Extreme. P&G marketers focused on women age 18 to 34, with a primary emphasis on women 23 to 24 years old. These women are social, outgoing, and not married. They are heavy users of social networking sites and constantly converse with their friends and family via all forms of wireless communication. A key insight helped P&G in this campaign: While these women agree that an occasional "bad hair day" is unavoidable, a "bad breath day" is totally unacceptable. Additionally, making a good first impression is a high priority for these women; fresh breath and a big bright smile are definitely perceived as helpful in that regard.

So the big idea driving the Crest Extreme launch campaign was to help women make great first impressions in all social situations, add to their confidence, and enhance their irresistibility. The centerpiece of this initiative would be the Crest Extreme Irresistibility IQ Quiz. Interactive quizzes are common fare for this age group, and the Crest quiz would have to be a standout: diagnostic with a lot of expert and celebrity input, along with attractive prizes and other incentives for participation.

What do you think?

When my friends care about something, so do I.

1   2   3   4   5   6   7

STRONGLY DISAGREE   STRONGLY AGREE

Find out what others think at CourseMate for PROMO.

With the quiz as its centerpiece, P&G launched an integrated marketing communication (IMC) campaign to build buzz:

- The first people to take the Irresistibility Quiz were MTV personality Nick Cannon and members of the Hispanic boy band Reik, who gave interviews, resulting in local and national media coverage of Crest Extreme, which drove traffic to the English- and Spanish-language sites http://www.CrestIQ.com and http://www.AlientoCrest.com. Other celebrities also took the quiz and had their scores posted.

- Banner ads appeared on websites like Facebook, Evite, and AOL Instant Messenger. In addition, a member profile for a mythical "Miss Irresistibility" was created on MySpace, inviting more dialogue. To encourage MySpace users to friend Miss Irresistibility, P&G offered free Nick Cannon songs and other downloads. The company also hosted chats with Nick Cannon and Reik on MySpace.

- Crest Extreme partnered with Vibe.com to host a speed-dating event in Times Square. *Entertainment Tonight* and *The Insider* broadcast the event live, driving traffic to CrestIQ.com.

- Advertising included a print campaign that encouraged people to visit CrestIQ.com. Posters in restrooms of popular night spots invited consumers to take an abbreviated version of the quiz on the spot by mobile phone.

P&G has called this type of brand communication 360 degree/holistic marketing. Whatever you call it, it worked. At the close of the Extreme campaign, Crest boasted 401,902 quiz completions; 48,760 MySpace friends; 157 million media impressions; and 1,156,375 visitors to CrestIQ.com. The brand also enjoyed a dramatic increase in market share, especially among women aged 18 to 34.

The launch campaign for Crest Extreme is yet another example of how integrated marketing communication promotes brands through the use of multiple tools, selected for the target segment in question. Today, a popular approach is to combine paid messages such as advertising with public relations to build buzz so that consumers themselves are spreading the brand messages.

LO 1 Public Relations

The classic role of **public relations** is to foster goodwill between a firm and its many constituent groups. These constituent groups include customers, stockholders, suppliers, employees, government entities, citizen action groups, and the general public. The firm's public relations function seeks to highlight positive events like outstanding quarterly sales and profits (to stockholders) or noteworthy community service programs (to government entities and the general public). As well, PR is used strategically for "damage control" when adversity strikes.

Additionally, public relations has entered an exciting new era. New PR techniques have fostered a bolder, more aggressive role for public relations in brand promotion campaigns. The traditional functions of managing goodwill and engaging in damage control still are important, but societal forces support a growing role for PR activities as part of IMC campaigns:

- Increasingly sophisticated and connected consumers are talking to each other more and more about brands. Stephen Brown, a prolific and provocative writer on the subject of branding, says today's world is different from the heyday of mass marketing.[1] It is intensely commercial. TV shows feature stories about marketing and consumer psychology, stand-up comics perform skits about shopping routines and brand strategies, and documentaries like *Who Killed the Electric Car?* and *Wal-Mart: The High Cost of Low Price* make great anti-brand entertainment. Industry gossip, executive screw-ups, and product critiques are bloggers' standard fodder. It is a brand-obsessed world.

NEW PR TECHNIQUES HAVE FOSTERED A BOLDER, MORE AGGRESSIVE ROLE FOR PUBLIC RELATIONS.

COMPANY REPRESENTATIVES MAKE AN EFFORT TO COMMUNICATE EFFECTIVELY WITH THE NEWS MEDIA BECAUSE NEWS STORIES ARE AN IMPORTANT WAY TO SPREAD BELIEVABLE INFORMATION ABOUT THE COMPANY AND ITS BRANDS.

© R. Gino Santa Maria/Shutterstock.

- The consumer increasingly is in control, using tools like blogs, podcasts, YouTube, RSS feeds, and whatever will be invented next week to exert that control across the Internet.[2] Marketers must monitor the current buzz about their brands and become part of the dialogue in an effort to rescue or revive their brands. In contrast, mass-media advertising was never a dialogue.

- Although marketers have always believed that the most powerful influence in any consumer's decision is the recommendations of friends and family, they only are beginning to figure out what to do about it. In his bestseller *The Tipping Point,* Malcolm Gladwell makes the case that "mavens" and "connectors" are critically important in fostering social epidemics. If marketers locate these mavens and connectors, and give them useful information or interesting stories about a brand, these people may spread the news through their networks. The sharing is intensified online, where one connected person can spread the word to thousands of friends or followers with the simple click of a mouse.

Given that people talk about brands, the marketer's challenge then is to give them interesting things to talk about, bringing a brand into the conversation in a positive way. In that context, PR is about more than managing goodwill; it can involve many ways to get a brand into the day-to-day conversations of key consumers, as Crest Extreme did with the Irresistibility Quiz. Maytag is another company that has used PR expertise in a proactive way to build its brand. Its nationwide contest to select the next Maytag Repairman generated 2,000 candidates and a lot of buzz in the conventional media and across the Internet. Maytag's vice president of marketing described the effort as a $500,000 campaign that generated $10 million of value and attributed its success to integrating PR expertise into the planning process for the brand early and often.[3]

In today's dynamic marketplace, with multitudes of online and offline conversations about brands, a brand builder needs to influence at least some of those conversations. The necessary integration takes a strong team effort, and it is becoming increasingly clear that PR expertise must be well represented on any brand promotion team.[4]

Damage Control

As consumers become more informed and connected, bad news about companies and brands travels faster and lingers longer. And, of all the promotional tools, public relations is the only one that can provide damage control in response to bad publicity. Such public relations problems can arise either from a firm's own activities or from external forces outside the firm's control.

The bad news that turns into a need for damage control can take many forms. For Taco Bell, it was an Internet video of rats running amok at its Greenwich Village restaurant.[5] You can close the restaurant, but that video is out there still. Johnson & Johnson walked into a PR firestorm by suing the Red Cross for logo infringement.[6] That's a hard case to win in the court of public opinion, but it's definitely a self-inflicted wound for J&J.

Walmart seems to have developed a penchant for attracting negative news, like the ongoing controversy about how it treats its frontline employees. A group calling itself "Wake Up Walmart" has demonstrated PR prowess in trashing the Walmart brand.[7] Check out the group's approach at http://www.WakeUpWalmart .com. The Walmart example also shows what happens when bad publicity is handled poorly. According to a report by McKinsey & Company, a significant number of Walmart customers say they have stopped shopping there because of lingering negative news.[8]

Companies need to learn how to handle the bad news. No company is immune. But while many public relations episodes must be reactive, a firm can be prepared with public relations materials to conduct an orderly and positive relations-building campaign with its constituents.

LO 2 PR Objectives

Even though reacting to a crisis is a necessity, it is more desirable to be proactive. The key is to have a structured approach to public relations, including a clear understanding of objectives for PR. Public relations can address any combination of six primary objectives:

1. *Promoting goodwill:* This image-building function highlights industry events or community activities that reflect favorably on a firm. When Pepsi launched a program to support school music programs, the firm garnered widespread goodwill.

2. *Promoting a product or service:* Companies can spread "news" about its brands to increase public awareness of the brands. Large pharmaceutical firms such as Merck and GlaxoSmithKline issue press releases when they discover new drugs or achieve FDA approval.

3. *Preparing internal communications:* By disseminating information and correcting misinformation within a firm, public relations can reduce the impact of rumors and increase employee morale. Internal communications about major changes such as layoffs or mergers can dispel rumors circulating among employees.

4. *Counteracting negative publicity:* With PR's damage-control function, the attempt is not to cover up negative events but rather to prevent the negative publicity from damaging the image of a firm and its brands. When a lawsuit was filed against NEC alleging that one of its cell phones had caused cancer, McCaw Cellular Communications used PR activities to inform the public (especially cell phone users) of scientific knowledge that argued against the claims in the lawsuit.

5. *Lobbying:* The PR function can help a firm communicate with government officials and influence pending legislation. Microsoft reportedly spent $4.6 billion on lobbying efforts when antitrust violations were leveled at the company.

6. *Giving advice and counsel:* Helping management determine what (if any) position to take on public issues, preparing employees for public appearances, and helping management anticipate public reactions are ways that PR can deliver advice and counsel.

PR Tools

There are several means by which a firm can pursue its PR objectives. The goal is to gain as much control over the process as possible by integrating public relations with other brand communications.

Press Releases

Disseminating information that makes for good news stories puts the firm in a position to take advantage of free media coverage. To obtain that coverage, companies put that information in press releases sent to media outlets. In general, several kinds of topics are suitable for press releases:

- New products
- New scientific discoveries
- New personnel
- New corporate facilities
- Innovative corporate practices, such as energy-saving programs or employee benefit programs
- Annual shareholder meetings
- Charitable and community-service activities

Editors prefer information that focuses on technical or how-to features along with in-depth case studies about company successes and failures.

The drawback of press releases is that marketers don't control how the media use the message. A firm often doesn't know if or when the information will appear in the news. Also, journalists are free to edit or interpret a news release, which may alter its intended message. Marketers try to reduce these liabilities by cultivating relationships with editors at publications likely to have the most impact.

Feature Stories

Although a firm cannot write a feature story for a news medium, it can invite journalists to do an exclusive story on the firm when there is a particularly note-

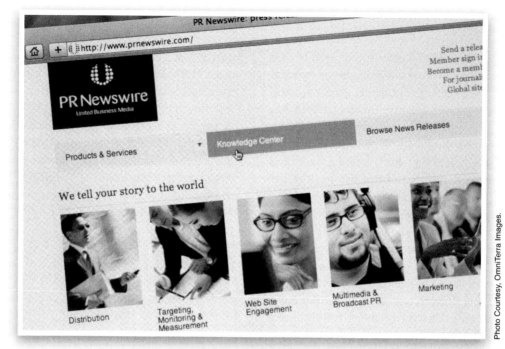

PR Newswire is the global leader in innovative communications and marketing services, enabling organizations to connect and engage with their target audiences worldwide. Pioneering the commercial news distribution industry over 56 years ago, PR Newswire's suite of services are used by many of the world's top organizations. From news dissemination to audience intelligence, engagement, measurement and compliance services, PR Newswire's offerings provide a comprehensive solution for communications success. For more information about PR Newswire, visit www.prnewswire.com.

worthy event. A feature story, as opposed to a news release, offers a single journalist the opportunity to do a fairly lengthy piece with exclusive rights to the information. Compared with a press release, a feature story is more controllable. Jupiter Communications, a research organization that tracks Internet usage and generates statistics about the Internet, has a simple philosophy about using feature stories as a public relations tool. Says Jupiter's CEO, "It is our goal to get every research project we do covered somewhere. We know this is the cheapest, and maybe most effective, way to market ourselves."[9]

Company Newsletters

In-house publications, such as newsletters, can disseminate positive information about a firm to its employees. As members of the community, employees are proud of their firm's achievements. The company also can distribute newsletters to important constituents in the community, such as government officials, the chamber of commerce, or the tourism bureau. Suppliers often enjoy reading about an important customer, so newsletters can be mailed to this group as well. These newsletters were traditionally printed and mailed or passed out, but firms increasingly are dis-

tributing company news online via email or posting newsletters on their websites.

Interviews and Press Conferences

Interviews with key executives or staged press conferences can be highly effective public relations tools. Often they are warranted in a crisis-management situation. Firms also call press conferences to announce important scientific breakthroughs or to explain the details of a corporate expansion or a new product launch. No one does this better than Steve Jobs each and every time Apple has big news about a new product. The press conference has an air of credibility because it uses a news format to present salient information.

Sponsored Events

As was discussed in Chapter 12, sponsoring events can be aimed at supporting public relations. Sponsorship opportunities can run the gamut from community events to mega-events such as the Olympics. At the local level, prominent display of the corporate name and logo shows residents that the organization is dedicated to supporting its community.

publicity unpaid-for media exposure about a firm's activities or its products and services

Many sponsored events are fund-raisers. Raising funds for non-profit organizations gives corporations a positive image. CIGNA has sponsored a basketball tournament to raise money for the Hope Network, which helps disabled people achieve greater independence and educates children about disabilities and healthy living. Supporting the Hope Network not only generates favorable news coverage for CIGNA, but it also is consistent with the insurance company's mission of helping people "improve their health, well-being, and security."[10] Small companies, too, can sponsor events on a local scale. Volkmann Diamonds, a jeweler in Kankakee, Illinois, staged a fund-raiser for a local animal shelter. The shelter bought 200 champagne glasses, and Volkmann provided a half-carat diamond and 200 cubic zirconia to place in the glass-

es, which were sold for $10 each. At the event, Volkmann provided a diamond expert to appraise the gems and identify the lucky purchaser whose glass held the diamond. Not only was Volkmann's name on the event's promotional materials, but in covering the fund-raiser, a local newspaper wrote about the featured diamond and a bridal event the store was planning. Owner Joyce Volkmann says customers often tell her they shop in the store because of its involvement with the community.[11]

Publicity

Essentially, **publicity** is "free" media exposure about a firm's activities or brands. The public relations function monitors and manages publicity, though it cannot control what journalists choose to say or report. Organizations must be prepared to take advantage of events

© Greg Kushmerek/Shutterstock.

ETHICS PUBLICITY GETS SCARY

To generate publicity for the Cartoon Network show *Aqua Teen Hunger Force*, Turner Broadcasting arranged for its street operatives Sean Stevens and Peter Berdovsky to place 40 blinking black boxes in public places around Boston. Unfortunately, while the campaign's creators saw the blinking lights as a humorous outline of a cartoon character making an obscene gesture, a few Bostonians saw possible bombs and alerted the police. Stevens and Berdovsky were arrested and charged with a felony: placing a hoax device with the intent to cause anxiety. For 48 hours, the Boston affair upstaged the Super Bowl. Was it great publicity for a cartoon show—or just irresponsible fear mongering?

Sources: Andrew Hampp, "Lite-Brites, Big City and a Whole Load of Trouble," *Advertising Age*, February 5, 2007, 1, 34; and Jennifer Levitz and Emily Steel, "Boston Stunt Draws Legal, Ethical Fire," *Wall Street Journal*, February 2, 2007, B3.

that generate good publicity and to counter events that are potentially damaging to their reputation.

The appeal of publicity—when the information is positive—is that it tends to carry heightened credibility. Publicity from stories on television and radio and in newspapers and magazines assumes an air of believability because of the credibility of the media context. Not-for-profit organizations often use publicity in the form of news and public-interest stories to gain widespread visibility at little or no cost.

Publicity is not always entirely out of the company's control. For instance, during the Academy Awards, a bracelet worn by actress Julia Roberts caused a stir. After Roberts won the award for best actress, she waved to the cameras, and suddenly the whole world wanted to know about the snowflake-design Van Cleef & Arpels bracelet adorning her right (waving) wrist. For the designers, that wasn't just a lucky break. The episode had been carefully planned by Van Cleef's PR agency, Ted, Inc., which lobbied hard to convince Roberts that the bracelet and matching earrings were stunning with her dress, knowing that if she won the Oscar, she would be highly photographed.[12]

Is there truth to the old saying "There's no such thing as bad publicity"? Stirring up a controversy is a sure way to get publicity, and many companies and their brands thrive on publicity. In most cases, a brand benefits from being in the news. But controversy can backfire if it generates ill will.

LO 3 PR Strategies

Although there are many ways to use public relations as part of a firm's overall IMC effort, the options fall into two basic categories of PR strategies:[13]

1. **Proactive public relations strategy** is guided by marketing objectives, seeks to publicize a company and its brands, and takes an offensive rather than defensive posture in the public relations process.

2. **Reactive public relations strategy** is dictated by influences outside the control of a company, focuses on problems to be solved rather than on opportunities, and requires a company to take defensive measures.

These two strategies involve different orientations to public relations.

Proactive Strategy

In developing a proactive PR strategy, a firm acknowledges opportunities to use public relations to accomplish something positive. Companies often rely heavily on their PR firms to help them put together a proactive strategy. Such a strategy aims to ensure that positive messages such as employee achievements, corporate contributions to the community, and the organization's social and environmental programs do not go unnoticed by important constituents.

Council for Biotechnology Information.

The biotechnology industry is subject to controversy regarding the use of genetically altered food and seed products. In this advertisement, the Council for Biotechnology Information, an industry group, attempts to take a proactive approach to dealing with the controversy by presenting a positive image and information.

public relations audit internal study that identifies aspects of the firm or its activities that are positive and newsworthy

public relations plan plan that identifies the objectives and activities of a firm's PR communications

To implement a proactive strategy, a firm needs to develop a comprehensive PR program. Such a program has two key components:

1. A **public relations audit** identifies the firm's characteristics or aspects of its activities that are positive and newsworthy. Those conducting the audit gather information much as they would for developing an advertising strategy: by questioning customers and collecting company information such as descriptions of company products and services, market performance of brands, profitability, goals for products, market trends, new product introductions, important suppliers, important customers, employee programs and facilities, community programs, and charitable activities.

2. Once the firm is armed with information from a public relations audit, it develops a structured **public relations plan**. This plan identifies the objectives and activities related to the firm's PR communications. The components of a public relations plan are described in Exhibit 13.1.

A proactive public relations strategy can make an important supportive contribution to a firm's IMC effort. Carefully placing positive information targeted to potentially influential constituents—such as members of the community or stockholders—supports the overall goal of enhancing the image, reputation, and perception of a firm and its brands.

Reactive Strategy

A reactive PR strategy may seem like a contradiction in terms, but as stated earlier, firms must implement a reactive strategy when events outside their control create negative publicity. Coca-Cola reined in negative publicity by acting swiftly after an unfortunate incident in Europe. Seven days after a bottling problem caused teens in Belgium and France to become sick after drinking Coke, the firm pulled all Coca-Cola products from the market and issued an apology from the CEO.[14] Coca-Cola's quick actions could not prevent a decline in product sales. That would call for new marketing programs tailored to meet the needs of consumers on a country-by-country basis. The programs relied heavily on IMC strategies including free samples, dealer incentive programs, and beach parties featuring sound and light shows, DJs, and cocktail bars with free Cokes to win back the critical teen segment.[15] In the end, this integrated effort restored trust and rebuilt the business across Europe.

It is difficult to organize for and provide structure around reactive PR. Because the events that trigger a reactive effort are unpredictable and uncontrollable, a firm simply must be prepared to act quickly and

Exhibit 13.1
Components of a PR Plan

Situation analysis	Summary of information obtained from the public relations audit, often broken down by category, such as product performance or community activity
Program objectives	Objectives stemming from the current situation and set for both short-term and long-term opportunities; generally focus on reputation, such as the credibility of product performance (e.g., placing products in verified, independent tests) or the stature of the firm's research and development efforts (article in a prestigious trade publication)
Program rationale	Identification of the PR program's role relative to the other brand promotion efforts; articulates an integrated marketing communication perspective
Communications vehicles	Specification of the tools (e.g., press releases, interviews, newsletters) to be used to implement the PR plan
Message content	Development of the PR message based on research such as focus groups and in-depth interviews

GLOBAL GUINNESS AS CULTURAL ICON

Guinness has attracted tourists to its St. James's Gate Brewery in Dublin, Ireland, for more than a century. But as visitor traffic grew to thousands per year, the reception area could no longer handle the volume. Goals for a new reception/visitor area included preserving the tradition of the brand, accommodating devotees who flocked to Dublin to connect with the brand's "spiritual home," and appealing to younger Irish consumers, who have been tempted by new beers and other drinks. The solution: a new seven-story structure called the Guinness Storehouse, which preserved and incorporated the five-story Market Street Storehouse, a Guinness storage facility in the early 1900s. It's now Ireland's number one fee-paying tourist spot.

Source: Arundhati Parmar, "Guinness Intoxicates," *Marketing News*, November 10, 2003, 4, 6.

thoughtfully. Two steps help firms implement a reactive public relations strategy:

1. *Public relations audit:* The public relations audit prepared for the proactive strategy helps a firm prepare its reactive strategy. The information in the audit helps the company issue public statements based on current and accurate data.

2. *Identification of vulnerabilities:* To be ready for a reactive strategy, companies need to recognize their *vulnerabilities*—areas of weakness in their operations or products that can damage relationships with important constituents. If aspects of a firm's operations are vulnerable to criticism, such as environmental issues related to manufacturing processes, then the PR function should be prepared to discuss the issues in a broad range of forums with various constituents.

When these steps don't uncover vulnerabilities, companies will be taken by surprise. Leaders at Quaker Oats and Philip Morris were in that situation when some of their shareholders forced a proxy vote on the issue of genetically modified foods.[16] Because that issue arose at their shareholders' meetings, these firms now understand that pursuing use of genetically modified foods will remain one of their vulnerabilities.

Keeping PR Integrated

Public relations, as much as every other method of brand promotion, must be part of an integrated and synergistic effort to communicate with diverse audiences. If a company fails to recognize PR activities as a component of the firm's overall communication effort, misinformation or disinformation may compromise the impact of advertising or other efforts at marketing communication. The coordination of public relations and other elements of an integrated program is a matter of recognizing and identifying the PR process as critical to the overall IMC effort and getting the right players on the team. At Guinness, for example, marketers understand that the historical nature of the 250-year-old brand of stout beer is essential to the brand's appeal. Therefore, preserving the brewery as a tourist attraction is as much a brand promotion effort as its advertising and sales promotions.

LO 4 Influencer Marketing

If public relations is the discipline devoted to monitoring and managing how people view us, then it also can be thought of as a discipline devoted to monitoring and managing what consumers are saying to one another about us. Moreover, because consumers have become increasingly predisposed to talk about our brands anyway, it seems prudent to follow the advice of Bonnie Raitt, who in her album *Luck of the Draw* sings in her 1990s blues-rock hit, "Let's give them something to talk about!"

The idea of giving people something to talk about underlies the evolution of influencer marketing. As defined by Northlich, a leader in influencer marketing programming, **influencer marketing** refers to a series of personalized marketing techniques directed at individuals or groups who have the credibility and capability to drive positive word-of-mouth in a broader and salient segment of the population. Whether these influential people are professionals or peers, marketing to them so that they influence others can provide one of the most valued assets for any brand builder—an advocacy message from a trusted source.[17] Think of influencer marketing as systematic seeding of conversations involving a consumer, an influencer, and a brand.

Professional Influencers

If you're a pet owner, you've probably made many visits to the vet. And perhaps you asked your vet about the best products to feed your puppy or kitten. If so,

you know what comes next. Not only is the vet ready to talk about proper feeding, he or she may offer you product samples or brochures describing the benefits of a particular brand of pet food. Coincidence? Not at all. The makers of IAMS, Eukanuba, and Hill's Science Diet know that vets are key influencers in the decision about what to feed one's pet, especially for devoted pet owners who don't mind paying a little extra to get the best. These brands target vets with influencer marketing programs aimed at earning their recommendation.

Many professionals are in a similar position. Your doctor, auto mechanic, and hair stylist all have the credibility to influence product choices in their specific areas of expertise. Sometimes the opportunity is obvious, as with vets recommending pet food. But more and more, creative programming takes influencer programming into new territory. An excellent example is how Select Comfort targets various types of healthcare professionals with an influencer program for its Sleep Number bed. For instance, Select Comfort targets occupational therapists (OTs), who provide therapy to individuals with serious physical challenges, helping them learn to carry out basic tasks of living. But are OTs experts on sleep? It doesn't matter. Many of their patients are likely to value their opinions, and all healthcare professionals commonly hear complaints from their patients about having trouble sleeping.

Obviously, if you're Select Comfort, you'd like the OT to encourage patients to have a look at the Sleep Number bed. Select Comfort starts by giving OTs firsthand experience with the product. Special promotions encourage OTs to purchase Sleep Number beds for their own bedrooms. Next, Sleep Comfort buys mailing lists from OT professional associations and journals in order to build a marketing database. When an OT expresses interest in the Sleep Number bed, Select Comfort sends the therapist an advocacy kit containing brochures and other helpful materials. Marketers at Select Comfort cannot control what the OT tells patients about the Sleep Number bed, but they can make available materials that will make

© David Davis/Shutterstock.

becoming an advocate easy if the OT believes it is justified.

Professionals in any field of endeavor take their role seriously, so influencer programs directed to them must be handled with great care. When developing programs for professionals, keep in mind that their time is money, so any program that wastes their time will be a waste of money. Valuable tactics include encouraging professionals to try the product themselves and delivering messages that are up-to-date and help the professional learn important benefits of the brand. For example, healthcare professionals' concerns will be better addressed through clinical studies than celebrity endorsements. Additionally, programs directed at professionals require a long-term commitment. Professionals will advocate only for brands they trust, and marketers needs patience and persistence to earn that trust.

Peer-to-Peer Programs

Peer-to-peer programs typically have a very different tone than programs for professionals. In peer-to-peer programs, the objective is to give influencers something fun or provocative to talk about. A great guiding principle for peer-to-peer programs is "Do something remarkable" to get people talking about your brand.[18] To promote Virgin Mobile's "Nothing to Hide" campaign, Richard Branson descended into Time Square on a giant cell phone while performing a striptease act. To launch its G6 model, Pontiac gave away 276 cars to the flabbergasted audience members of Oprah's season-opening show.[19]

But today's practice of influencer marketing amounts to more than publicity stunts. For one thing, peer-to-peer programs are shaped by the experience and sophistication of organizations like Northlich and Keller Fay Group, which assist clients with influencer programming. Keller Fay has developed a tracking system that can estimate the number of word-of-mouth conversations taking place daily. In 2006, the firm estimated that consumers shared opinions about brands on the order of 3.5 billion times per day. Of those

billions of word-of-mouth conversations, a majority were offline, but a growing percentage happened online.[20] And with billions of conversations every day, a lot of brand builders, from Beam to Baskin Robbins, want to be involved.

One area where we see dramatic advancements in influencer marketing on the peer-to-peer side involves identifying and cultivating connectors. Procter & Gamble has been building a connector database, focusing on women who have large social networks. P&G searches for them over the Internet at sites like iVillage.com and is always looking for referrals. (It seems connectors like the idea of being the first to receive new product samples and to feel that their voice is being heard by a big company.) One of P&G's connectors is Donna Wetherell, an outgoing mom who works at a customer-service call center, where she knows about 300 coworkers by name. She likes to talk about shopping and many different brands. She always seems to have a lot of extra coupons for the brands she likes—her coworkers call her the coupon lady. Donna is only one of 600,000 connectors that P&G has enrolled in its influencer program, called Vocalpoint.[21]

Once a company has developed a connector database, the influencer program gets back to basics: giving the connectors something to talk about. But it's not always simple to get consumers talking about a product like dishwashing detergent, so companies that sell such products have to start by finding a motivation to talk. P&G execs assert, "We do tremendous research behind it to give them a reason to care."[22] Just as with professional programs, you can't force someone to be an advocate for your brand. You can identify people who have big social networks, but they're not going to compromise their relationships with others by sharing dull stories or phony information. You must give them something interesting to talk about.

As marketers gain experience in influencer marketing, they are demystifying what once was mysterious: word-of-mouth marketing. A pioneer in this regard is Andy Sernovitz, who founded the Word of Mouth Marketing Association (WOMMA) in 2004.

PROFESSIONALS WILL ADVOCATE ONLY FOR **BRANDS THEY TRUST.**

social media websites where users create and share information about themselves, brands, and other mutual interests

The WOMMA website, http://www.womma.org, is a great resource for learning more about influencer marketing. In his book *Word of Mouth Marketing: How Smart Companies Get People Talking*, Sernovitz draws on numerous cases for a wide variety of brands to offer up success principles for those who desire favorable word-of-mouth. Turns out it's as simple as the Five *T*s, spelled out in Exhibit 13.2. And applying the Five *T*s nowadays tends to take marketers into the new realm of social media.

LO 5 Social Media

Today, more people are using community websites like Facebook and MySpace than are using email.[23] These social-networking sites have revolutionized the way marketers think about mediated communication. From the earliest work on brand communities, Muniz and O'Guinn noted that communication about brands in these communities has three nodes, rather than the traditional two (see Exhibit 13.3). In other words, not only do consumers interact with the brand, as they do when viewing an ad or entering a sweepstakes, but they also talk to each other about brands they care about. Thanks to the Internet, these brand-related interactions happen instantaneously, at almost no cost, and with huge numbers of participants.

These three-way online communications take place using what marketers call **social media**—websites where users create and share information about themselves, brands, and other mutual interests. The applications of social media continue to multiply, but the following are some of the most relevant to marketers:[24]

- Social networking on sites such as Facebook and MySpace
- Business networking on sites such as LinkedIn
- Works sharing on sites such as YouTube (for videos) and Flickr (for photos)
- Blogs, which may be sponsored by users (Cnet.com) or companies (Apple.com)
- Microblogging—sending short messages to subscribers (Twitter)

Exhibit 13.2
Five "T"s of Peer-to-Peer Influence

Talkers	Find and get to know the people who are predisposed to talk about brands in general and/or your brand in particular.
Topics	Give the talkers something to talk about—not a marketing message or mission statement but a mystery or engaging story or breaking news. For example, Apple's Steve Jobs creates interest with suspenseful product announcements and an implied promise that the next great thing is just around the corner.
Tools	Make good use of the tools that promote conversations. A story on a blog is more portable than a story on a corporate Web page.
Taking part	Instead of one-way communication, think in terms of dialogue. Listen to the conversations already taking place. You have to be tuned in if you ever want to join the conversation.
Tracking	Word-of-mouth on the Internet is very measurable. Keep track of what people are saying about your brand and why they are saying it.

Sources: Andy Sernovitz, *Word of Mouth Marketing: How Smart Companies Get People Talking* (Chicago: Kaplan Publishing, 2006); and Michael Krauss, "To Generate Buzz, Do Remarkable Things," *Marketing News*, December 15, 2006.

Exhibit 13.3
New Brand Relationships with Social Media

Traditional Relationship:
Brand to Customer

New Relationship:
Brand Community

BRAND

BRAND

Consumer

Consumer 1

Consumer 2

- Commerce communities, such as Amazon and Craigslist
- Social bookmarking—used for recommending content (for example, Digg and Reddit)
- Collaborative projects, such as Wikipedia

An important implication of social media is that marketers no longer generate all the important brand communications. Rather, consumers are making and distributing brand material—even ads—on the Internet. These may be celebrating beloved brands or mocking brands or brand messages that consumers find ridiculous. Consumer-generated content costs marketers nothing and offers them no control over the message. Several marketers have told of receiving a lot of great feedback for an Internet ad and calling their ad agency with congratulations, only to be told that the agency has no idea what the marketer is talking about. The ad turns out to have been made by some 14-year-old kid in Ohio.

Shaping the Message

Social media's impact on the marketing environment can be a little bit frightening: Nasty product reviews or satirical versions of the company's ads are only two of the possible new publicity nightmares. But for marketers who can shape the messages spread online, social media also present a tremendous opportunity.[25]

One way marketers can shape conversations about their brands is by creating venues online for consumers to gather around a brand-related in-

terest or value. Crest did this by setting up a Miss Irresistibility profile on MySpace, as described at the beginning of the chapter. Campbell Soup Company invites consumers to submit product ideas at its website (www.campbellsoupcompany.com/ideas).

Marketers also can invite consumer feedback via social media. Toyota invites drivers, automobile enthusiasts, and journalists to post replies to its Open Road Blog. The Red Robin restaurant chain invites customers to complete satisfaction surveys. Those who give the restaurant high ratings are asked to post a recommendation on their Facebook pages; about one out of five agree to do so.[26] Because the wording of the recommendations comes from the individual consumers, these brand messages come across as more natural and sincere than a company-generated message. Of course, you also have to be prepared for negative feedback. When someone complains, be ready to offer an apology, a coupon, or a way to fix problems.

Participants in social media want to feel like they are collaborating with others, not just being sold to. Marketers can become trusted participants in the conversation by sharing valuable information, such as tips for using its products, details about ingredients and prices, solutions to product-related problems, or general advice on brand-related topics, say, health or parenting. Videos and podcasts should be entertaining as well as informative; for example, instead of only saying your product is durable, make a video showing how it withstands tough conditions. Another way to

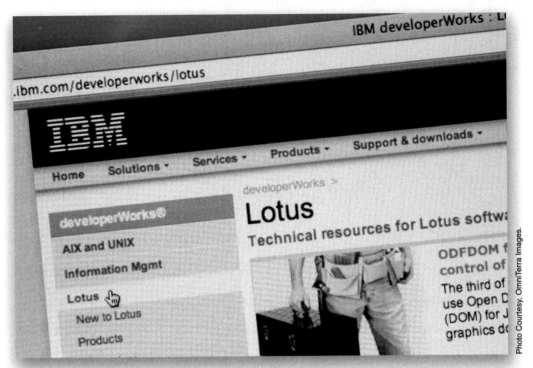

Following potential users' comments posted online helped IBM decide how to communicate its brand message for Lotus software. The company learned that people didn't talk about technology and features but about what they were trying to do with the software. IBM used the insights to develop its "Lotus Knows" theme.

talk about subjects consumers care about is to get involved in a social cause that matters to targeted consumers. Marketers also can personalize messages by taking advantage of the fact that many social-media venues provide information about participants—say, a profile on LinkedIn or a status message that tells where an individual is located or even what mood the person is in.[27]

Marketers using social media are to some extent relying on consumers to spread the word. Therefore, they should be careful to create messages that will be conveyed accurately. That means brand advantages should be clear, memorable, and easy to describe.

Buzz and Viral Marketing

Marketers often turn to social media to create buzz and stimulate viral marketing. Both of these objectives rely on word-of-mouth communication:

- **Buzz marketing** involves creating an event or experience that yields conversations that include the brand.

- **Viral marketing** is the process of consumers marketing to consumers via the Web (e.g., via blogs or forwarding YouTube links) or through personal contact stimulated by a firm marketing a brand.

Both buzz and viral marketing strategies target a handful of carefully chosen trendsetters or connectors as influencers, letting them spread the word.[28]

The offline components of buzz marketing programs often are fielded in major cities because places like New York and London are where you find the most trendsetters. Consider this scene at the cafés on Third Street Promenade in and around Los Angeles. A gang of sleek, impossibly attractive bikers pulls up, and guess what, they seem *genuinely* interested in getting to know you over an iced latte—their treat! Sooner or later, the conversation turns to their Vespa scooters glinting in the sun, and they eagerly pull out a pad and jot down an address and phone number—for the nearest Vespa dealer. The scooter-riding, latte-drinking models are on the Vespa payroll, and they're paid to create buzz about the scooters by engaging hip café dwellers in conversation.[29]

Generating buzz is important because it gets the brand noticed and sparks interest in trying the product. But for long-term success, marketers have to turn buzz into brand loyalty and sales. For that, they have to incorporate social-media messages into a broader IMC campaign. Threadless created buzz with its collaborative process for generating T-shirt designs: Anyone can post a design idea at the Threadless website, and then site visitors vote for their favorites, which are printed on shirts for sale. To sustain interest, Threadless has added sales promotion to its brand communications; the company sends gift codes and premiums to its followers on Twitter. Similarly, Batter Blaster generated a lot of buzz when it launched its innovative product, organic pancake batter sold in aerosol cans. Consumers fell in love with Batter Blaster, blogged about it, and posted videos about it on YouTube. To keep interest high, the company has added sampling and event sponsorship to its integrated marketing communication.[30]

Measuring Results

Maybe you're not in total control of your message on social media, but as a marketer, you still need to know whether the time and effort of social media are worthwhile. And in a sign that social media are firmly entrenched in the promotional mix, research services now are offering marketers performance metrics akin to those for other media. For example, Nielsen BuzzMetrics tracks more than a million blogs, social networks, and other consumer-generated online content to provide clients with information such as where conversations about the brand are taking place, what people are saying about the brand, and when threats to the brand's reputation are developing. Radian6 scans more than 100 million websites, including blogs, Twitter, and public Facebook groups to find messages, videos, and photos related to clients' brands. It delivers statistics such as the volume of comments, reach of messages, and type of consumer sentiment. Data also can be integrated with Web analytics software to measure how much traffic is being driven to the marketer's website from the social media—and even who is driving the most traffic and how much of that traffic leads to sales or subscriptions at the website.

One advantage of services like Radian6 and BuzzMetrics is that they offer real-time tracking and reporting. Online messages move fast—that's the thrill and terror of viral marketing—so if marketers don't like what's being said, they have to jump into the conversation immediately. Marketers also can watch social-media activity when they engage in other types of brand communication, such as an ad campaign or press release, to see whether those efforts are generating the desired buzz. If not, they can tweak their efforts right away.

This kind of immediate feedback rewards marketers for being flexible and responsive. Consider how data on social media helped Dell with its launch of the Mini 9 notebook computer. The buzz started almost immediately after a blogger spotted Michael Dell carrying a prototype at a technology conference four months before the product was to be released. As Dell marketers followed messages posted to technology blogs, forums, and social-networking sites, they selectively posted bits of information and corrected errors. They learned what consumers were expecting and used the information to adjust the product design and marketing messages. When the Mini 9 was released, Dell was ready with an on-target product and marketing campaign, and the buzz had reached a state of intense excitement that drove high demand. In addition, Dell's efforts to track social-media traffic helped the company identify key influencers, whom the company can target for roles in future brand communication.[31]

LO 6 Corporate Advertising

When social media are used to create buzz about the company as a whole, rather than a particular brand or product, the effort falls under the umbrella of corporate advertising. **Corporate advertising** is designed to establish a favorable attitude toward a company as a whole, rather than to promote the benefits of a specific brand. It typically uses major media to communicate a unique, broad-based message that is distinct from the company's product-specific brand building and contributes to the development of an overall image for a firm.

Corporate advertising often addresses the firm's trustworthiness and reputation. As consumers are becoming increasingly informed and sophisticated, they demand a higher standard of conduct from the companies they patronize. When a company has established trust and integrity, it has an easier time building productive relationships with consumers.

Scope of Corporate Advertising

Highly regarded and successful firms use corporate advertising to enhance the image of the firm and affect consumers' attitudes. The use of corporate advertising is gaining favor worldwide. Firms with the stature of General Electric and Toyota are investing in corporate ad campaigns. Billions of dollars are spent annually to buy media space and time for these campaigns.

Interestingly, most corporate campaigns run by consumer-goods manufacturers are undertaken by firms in the shopping-goods category, such as appliance and auto marketers. Studies also have found that larger firms are much more prevalent users of corporate advertising than smaller firms are. Presumably, these larger firms have broader communications programs and more money to invest in advertising, which allows the use of corporate campaigns.

In terms of media, magazines and television are well suited to corporate advertising.[32] Corporate ad-

vertising appearing in magazines has the advantage of being able to target particular constituent groups with image- or issue-related messages. Magazines also provide the space for lengthy copy, which often is needed to achieve corporate advertising objectives. Television is a popular choice for corporate campaigns because the creative opportunities provided by television can deliver a powerful, emotional message.

Objectives of Corporate Advertising

The objectives for corporate advertising should be focused. In fact, corporate advertising shares similar purposes with proactive public relations. Here are some of the possibilities for a corporate campaign:

- To build the image of the firm among customers, shareholders, the financial community, and/or the general public
- To boost employee morale or attract new employees
- To communicate an organization's views on social, political, or environmental issues
- To better position the firm's products against competition, particularly foreign competition
- To play a role in the company's overall advertising and IMC strategy, providing a platform for more brand-specific campaigns

Corporate advertising is not always targeted at consumers. Rather, the effort can target a broad range of constituents. For example, when Glaxo Wellcome and SmithKline Beecham merged to form a $73 billion pharmaceutical behemoth, the newly created firm, known as GlaxoSmithKline, launched an international print campaign aimed at investors who had doubts about the viability of the new corporate structure. The campaign was all about image and led with the theme "Disease does not wait. Neither will we."[33]

Types of Corporate Advertising

Corporate advertising campaigns are dominated by three basic types: image advertising, advocacy advertising, and cause-related advertising (see Exhibit 13.4). In addition, green marketing is an important special case of any of these.

Image Advertising

The majority of corporate advertising efforts focus on enhancing the overall image of a firm among important constituents—typically customers, em-

Delight in everyday perfection.

ELKAY.
elkay.com
specialty collection sinks. Style that endures.

Quality System ISO 9001 Certified ©2003 Elkay

© Elkay Manufacturing.

Firms often use corporate advertising as a way to generate name recognition and a positive image for the firm. Here Elkay, a high-end manufacturer of sinks and other plumbing fixtures, touts the company name, rather than any specific features of a brand.

Exhibit 13.4
Varieties of Corporate Advertising

ployees, and the general public. When IBM promotes itself as the firm providing "Solutions for a small planet" or when Toyota uses the slogan "Investing in the things we all care about" to promote its U.S. manufacturing plants, the goal is to enhance the overall image of the firm.

Bolstering a firm's image may not result in immediate effects on sales, but as we saw in Chapter 5, attitude can play an important directive force in consumer decision making. When a firm can enhance its overall image, it may well affect consumer predisposition in brand choice.[34]

Energy giant BP developed a series of television and print ads that featured real people out on the street candidly answering questions about the environment, pollution, and the use of natural resources and saying things like "I'd rather have a cleaner environment, but I can't imagine me without my car." One critic commented that the spots "don't convey a lot of information" but acknowledged that the campaign is likely to succeed in "getting the name equated in people's minds with a progressive, forward-thinking company"[35]—an appropriate and important goal for corporate image advertising.

Although image advertising intends to communicate a general, favorable image, the effects of such campaigns can be multifaceted. When PPG Industries undertook an image campaign to promote its public identity, the firm found that, throughout a five-year period, the number of consumers who said they had heard of PPG increased from 39.1 percent to 79.5 percent. Moreover, the perception of the firm's product quality, leadership in new products, and attention to environmental problems also increased greatly.[36]

Advocacy Advertising

Advocacy advertising attempts to establish an organization's position on important social or political issues. Advocacy advertising attempts to influence public opinion on issues of concern to a firm. For example, in a corporate advertising program begun in the 1990s, Phillips Petroleum (now ConocoPhillips) has linked its commitment to protect and restore bird populations and habitats to its efforts to reduce sulfur in gasoline. Typically, the issue featured in an advocacy campaign is directly relevant to the business operations of the organization.

Cause-Related Marketing

Cause-related marketing features a firm's affiliation with an important social or societal cause (for example, reducing poverty, increasing literacy, conserving energy, protecting the environment, and curbing drug

General Electric's Ecomagination program is based on the assumption that conserving the planet's resources also is good business. GE isn't shy about promoting that theme through corporate advertising, such as this message about its commitment to wind energy.

abuse). The goal of cause-related marketing can be to enhance the image of the firm by associating it with important social issues; this tends to work best when the firm confronts an issue that truly connects to its business. Anheuser-Busch's efforts to promote the control of teenage drinking, described in Chapter 6, are a good example. This campaign helps establish the firm as a responsible marketer of alcoholic beverages, while also helping society deal with an important problem.

Cause-related marketing often features philanthropic activities funded by a company. Each year, *Promo Magazine* publishes an extensive list of charitable, philanthropic, and environmental organizations that have formal programs in which corporations may participate. Most of the programs suggest a minimum donation for corporate sponsorship and specify how the organization's resources will be mobilized in conjunction with the sponsor's other resources.

Cause-related marketing is becoming increasingly common. In 2006, IEG forecast that spending on cause-related sponsorships would exceed $1.3 billion, a tenfold increase over spending levels in the 1990s.[37] One reason for the increase is that research supports the wisdom of such expenditures. In a 2004 consumer survey conducted by Cone, a Boston-based brand

strategy firm, 91 percent of respondents said they have a more favorable impression of companies that support good causes; respondents also said the causes a company supports can be a valid reason for switching brands.[38] Other studies indicate that support of good causes can translate into brand preference—and, importantly, that consumers will judge a firm's motives for the support.[39] If the firm's support is perceived as disingenuous, cause-related expenditures are largely wasted.

One also would like to think that the trend toward greater use of cause-related marketing is fueled by a desire to do the right thing. For instance, Whirlpool Corporation is a Habitat Cornerstone Partner and has assisted in the massive rebuilding effort needed in the wake of Hurricane Katrina. Jeff Terry, who manages the program of donations and volunteering on behalf of Whirlpool, says of the experience: "The first time you do this work, it will change your life."[40] Sure, Whirlpool's participation in this program brings the company a lot of favorable publicity, but its people's hearts also appear to be in the right place. That makes the program a win/win activity for everyone involved.

The range of firms participating in cause-related marketing programs continues to grow. Home Depot promotes water conservation in areas of desperate need through its "Use Water Wisely" campaign. To advance the cause of families spending more time together, Nick at Nite funds an initiative called "National Family Dinner Day," a day when Nick at Nite networks shut off for the dinner hour.[41]

Green Marketing

Among the many causes backed by companies, one area in particular seems to offer opportunities: concern for protecting and sustaining the natural environment. Corporate communication efforts that embrace a cause or a program in support of the environment are popularly known as **green marketing**. Such efforts include Timberland's use of shoe boxes made out of 100 percent recycled materials and the "Dawn Saves Wildlife" program sponsored by Procter & Gamble. General Electric's "Ecomagination" campaign is another high-profile exemplar of this movement. In funding this corporate campaign, GE has taken the stance that it simply is a good business strategy to seek real solutions to problems like air pollution and fossil-fuel dependency.[42]

The green marketing movement has been on again and off again, especially in the United States.

In the early 1990s, Jacquelyn Ottman's book *Green Marketing* predicted that going green would be a marketing revolution. It didn't come to pass, at least not in the United States. However, many signs now suggest that this time around, green marketing really will take hold as a major opportunity for businesses, maybe just in time to save our planet. Most informed people now accept the inconvenient truth that our addiction to fossil fuels is putting the planet at risk. Surveys show that environmental issues are of major concern to consumers, and a formidable segment is acting on this concern.[43] The green movement looks sustainable this time around.

In addition, the Internet again is changing the game. Companies no longer can pay lip service to environmental causes but hide their true motives. Websites like Green Seal and EnviroLink can assist in determining who really is doing what to protect the environment. Motivated, well-informed consumers are hard to fool, so it doesn't pay to make token gestures on behalf of the planet. When it comes to getting it right with green (or any other) marketing, firms just need to follow the one immutable law of branding: Underpromise and overdeliver.

> **green marketing**
> corporate communication efforts to promote a cause or program in support of the environment

STUDY TOOLS
CHAPTER 13

Located at back of the textbook

- **Rip out Chapter in Review Card.**

Located at www.cengagebrain.com

- **Review Key Terms Flashcards (Print or Online).**
- **Complete the Practice Quiz to prepare for tests.**
- **Play "Beat the Clock" and "Quizbowl" to master concepts.**
- **Complete "Crossword Puzzle" to review key terms.**
- **Watch videos on Red The Lazarus Effect and JCPenny for real company examples.**
- **For additional examples, go online to learn about green initiatives and buzz builders.**

and Sales Management

Sant's salespeople talk to its clients—other salespeople—in their language and about their goals.

Sant Corporation has developed software to help sales teams create more effective sales presentations.

282

Learning Outcomes

After studying this chapter, you should be able to:

LO 1 Explain why personal selling is important in brand promotion.

LO 2 Describe the activities besides selling performed by salespeople.

LO 3 Summarize the role of setting objectives for personal selling.

LO 4 Outline the steps involved in personal selling.

LO 5 Describe factors that contribute to a new environment for personal selling.

LO 6 Define the responsibilities of sales force management.

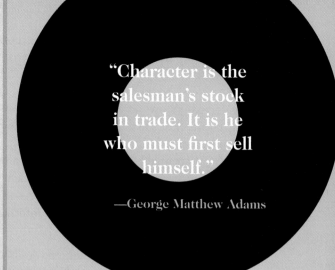

"Character is the salesman's stock in trade. It is he who must first sell himself."

—George Matthew Adams

Selling to Salespeople

AFTER YOU FINISH THIS CHAPTER GO TO PAGE 304 FOR STUDY TOOLS

If choosing a brand of jeans or a computer takes effort, consider the challenges faced by business managers. Their purchase decisions may be multiplied by thousands or even millions of units. Their choices affect the company's bottom line, its image, and its ability to satisfy customers. No wonder, then, that these customers want to talk to a human being—a salesperson—who can help them sort through their options.

That kind of marketing works great as long as salespeople speak their customers' language. But companies that sell highly technical products, such as software systems or manufacturing equipment, often rely on people with great technical expertise, who may not readily see situations from their business-oriented customers' point of view. Enter Sant Corporation. Founded by Tom Sant, a former English professor and writing consultant, the company has developed software that helps sales teams create more effective presentations.

A typical sales presentation starts with background about the salesperson's company. In contrast, Sant Corporation's products help salespeople analyze customers' needs and build each presentation around a desired outcome, such as cutting inventory costs, showing how the salesperson's products or services can help the customer reach the desired outcome.[1] The Sant software bases its guidance on academic research into communication persuasiveness. This frees technically oriented salespeople to focus on contributing their knowledge about their customers and their company's products. In addition, the software makes the creation of presentations more efficient by automatically producing standard data, graphs, and background information, such as prewritten statements of the selling company's strengths. Sant Corporation also provides consulting services to help its clients use the software effectively and improve their writing skills.

What do you think?

Salespeople succeed when they put the customer first.

1   2   3   4   5   6   7

STRONGLY DISAGREE   STRONGLY AGREE

Find out what others think at CourseMate for PROMO.

Of course, Sant Corporation needs its own sales force, too. Dozens of employees at the Cincinnati-based company contact leads, applying the company's own expertise to explain how Sant can help clients close sales. They also follow up to make sure clients are satisfied.

Sant's salespeople keep up with all this information by using customer relationship management software from Salesforce.com. The Salesforce software includes a database of easily retrievable information important to salespeople:

- Details about prospects, including tasks and deadlines for moving a prospect to a contract for software and services

- Data about customers, including products purchased, so that salespeople can identify additional services to offer

- Results from customer surveys so that salespeople can follow up with unhappy clients

- Types of problems and how they were resolved so that salespeople can quickly identify solutions that have worked in the past

- Reports and research sharing employees' knowledge so that salespeople can learn from one another and better inform their clients with the most up-to-date versions of documents

Since Sant Corporation began using the Salesforce.com software, it has shrunk the time needed to provide customer support and has enjoyed dramatic growth in revenues and customer satisfaction.[2]

LO 1 Personal Selling

Despite the conspicuousness of advertising, sales promotion, sponsorships, and other tools in the promotional mix, personal selling is the most important force for communication in many corporations. Along with the Sant Corporation, firms as diverse as Xerox and Nordstrom rely primarily on personal selling for contacting customers, communicating, and closing sales. Formally defined, **personal selling** is the face-to-face communication and persuasion process. It includes many activities such as the ones described in the example of the Sant Corporation: assessing customer needs, communicating with them about how the salesperson's company can address those needs, and following up to make sure they are satisfied. Effective salespeople are careful listeners, skilled problem solvers, and persuasive writers and speakers

© Simon van den Berg/Shutterstock.

who are knowledgeable about their products and their customers.

Personal selling is a key part of many firms' activities. Some companies spend hundreds of dollars for each face-to-face sales call. Compensation paid to these salespeople can range up to more than $100,000 a year for a top-notch sales engineer with in-depth knowledge of his or her customers' products and processes. Another measure of the importance of personal selling is the number of people employed in the profession. The most recent statistics from the U.S. Department of Labor put the number of people employed in sales jobs at roughly 11 percent of the civilian labor force in the United States. And, as Exhibit 14.1 shows, the various categories of salespeople (except travel agents) are expected to grow through 2018, with almost a million jobs added in sales occupations overall.[3]

There are good reasons why personal selling is the dominant component in the promotional mix for many firms. First, face-to-face communication is potent; it often generates action. And in many decision contexts, only a qualified and well-trained salesperson can address the questions and concerns of a potential buyer. Companies are especially dependent on personal selling if their products are higher priced, complicated to use, require demonstration, are tailored to

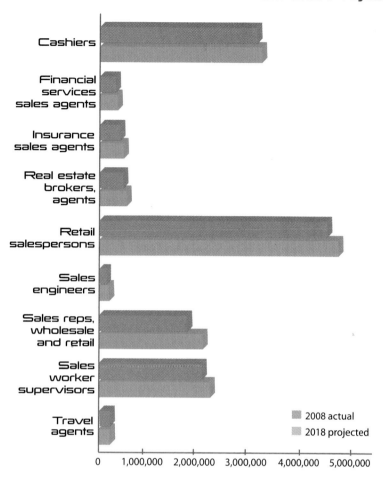

Exhibit 14.1
Number of Sales Jobs: Current and Projected

- Cashiers
- Financial services sales agents
- Insurance sales agents
- Real estate brokers, agents
- Retail salespersons
- Sales engineers
- Sales reps, wholesale and retail
- Sales worker supervisors
- Travel agents

■ 2008 actual
■ 2018 projected

0   1,000,000   2,000,000   3,000,000   4,000,000   5,000,000

Source: Bureau of Labor Statistics, *Occupational Outlook Handbook: 2010–11*, http://data.bls.gov.

users' needs, involve a trade-in, or are judged at the point of purchase. For these products, a salesperson helps consumers and business buyers make a decision and obtain value from their purchases.

LO 2 What Salespeople Do

Often, salespeople are responsible for more than the selling effort; they also may implement various aspects of marketing strategy. In a very real sense, the sales force is the embodiment of the firm's entire marketing program. The responsibilities of salespeople have expanded to include the following activities:

- *Market analysis:* Because of their direct contact with customers, salespeople can provide information related to trends in overall demand. Regular contact with buyers who also are buying competitors' products may help salespeople detect and report on competitors' activities.

- *Sales forecasting:* Salespeople can give marketing planners estimates of sales potential for the short and long term, based on the competitiveness of the firm's products and conditions in their customers' industries.

- *New product ideas:* Close contact with customers allows the sales force to detect unmet needs in the market and contribute ideas for new products.

- *Buyer behavior analysis:* The salesperson is in the best position to analyze buyer behavior. In negotiating sales with customers, the salesperson learns the criteria upon which buyers base their decisions. Salespeople feed this information to marketing strategists, who adjust the marketing and promotion mixes.

- *Communication:* To effectively inform and persuade customers, salespeople must be experts in communication methods. No matter how well the marketing mix is conceived, the sales force has to inform customers about the satisfaction to be gained from the brand.

- *Sales coordination:* The salesperson must coordinate the firm's many marketing and sales activities with the buyer.

- *Customer service:* When customers need service after a purchase, they turn first to the salesperson. Salespeople can coordinate product delivery, installation, training, and financing.

- *Customer relationship management:* Salespeople play an important role in building long-term relationships with customers—an effort referred to as **customer relationship management (CRM)**. For that reason, Merck spends 12 months training its sales representa-

tives, not only in knowledge of pharmaceuticals, but also in trust-building techniques. Its reps must take regular refresher courses as well. Similarly, General Electric stationed its own engineers full time at Praxair, a user of GE electrical equipment, to help the firm boost productivity.[4] Furthermore, CRM is a key strategy for gaining competitive advantage in foreign markets.[5]

Extending the idea of CRM, salespeople are instrumental in ensuring total customer satisfaction. Playing a role in marketing strategy, they do not simply approach customers with the intention of making a sale. Rather, they serve as problem solvers in partnership with customers. By accepting the role of analyzing customer needs and proposing solutions, the sales force

© Sean Prior/Shutterstock.

GLOBAL CRM WITHOUT BORDERS

CRM for a global sales team presents challenges beyond single-country programs. The first is to learn what sales reps need. When Information Systems Marketing developed a CRM for a German biotech company, it formed two teams—one made up of American and Australian reps with a European group leader, and the other consisting of European and Japanese reps with an American project leader—to identify the features needed. Also, companies must learn what kinds of sales relationships customers prefer in each foreign market. This reflects each country's political and social conditions, trade regulations, and business customs.

Sources: Erika Rasmusson, "Going Global with CRM," *Sales and Marketing Management,* May 2000, 96; and Lambeth Hochwald, "Are You Smart Enough to Sell Globally?" *Sales and Marketing Management,* July 1998, 53–56.

helps determine ways in which a firm can provide total customer satisfaction not only through the personal-selling process but with the entire marketing mix.

Types of Personal Selling

Although every salesperson is engaged in personal communication, there are quite different types of selling. As summarized in Exhibit 14.2, the communication requirements vary according to whether the salesperson is engaged in order taking, creative selling, or supportive communication.

Order Taking

The least complex type of personal selling is **order taking**, which involves accepting orders for merchandise or scheduling services either in written form or over the telephone. Order takers deal mostly with existing customers (who are lucrative because it costs less to generate revenue from this group). Order takers also deal with new customers, so they must be trained well enough to answer any questions a new customer might have about products or services. Order takers are responsible for communicating with buyers in a way that maintains a quality relationship. This type of selling rarely warrants in-depth analysis of the customer or involves communicating large amounts of information, but a careless approach to the job can turn off loyal customers, damaging their relationship with the company and the brand.

Order takers may work inside the company or call on customers:

1. A retail clerk who simply takes payment for products or services is an *inside order taker*. Examples are the person who runs the cash register at a supermarket and the people working the phones at an L.L.Bean catalog center. The buyer already has chosen the product or service and merely uses the salesperson to make payment.

2. An *outside order taker* typically calls on business buyers or members of the trade channel and performs relatively routine tasks related to orders for inventory replenishment or catalog orders. The customer accounts have been established, and the salesperson merely services them on a regular basis.

Although order takers do not engage in many of the marketing activities discussed earlier, they are an important link between the firm and the market. They help bring about customer satisfaction through their courteous, timely, and attentive service.

Creative Selling

To conduct **creative selling**—the type of selling where customers rely heavily on the salesperson for technical information, advice, and service—salespeople need considerable effort and expertise. Situations where creative selling takes place include retail stores,

> **order taking** practice of accepting and processing customer information for prearranged purchase or scheduling services a customer will purchase
>
> **creative selling** assisting and persuading customers regarding purchase decisions (typically for specialty goods or high-priced items)

Exhibit 14.2
Three Types of Selling

Order taking
- Answering questions
- Being courteous

Creative selling
- Providing technical information and advice
- Analyzing and solving problems

Supportive communications
- Providing background information
- Monitoring satisfaction

presentations aimed at selling services to business clients, and the sale of large industrial installations and component parts. At the retail level, stores that sell higher-priced items and specialty goods have a fully trained sales staff and emphasize customer and product knowledge. The services of an insurance agent, stockbroker, media representative, or real estate agent represent another type of creative selling. These salespeople provide services customized to the unique needs and circumstances of each buyer.

The most complex and demanding creative-selling positions serve the business-to-business market. Many of these salespeople have advanced degrees in technical areas like chemical engineering, computer science, or mechanical engineering. Business salespeople who deal in large-dollar purchases and complex corporate decisions for capital equipment, specialized component parts, or raw materials often are called on to analyze the customer's product and production needs and carry this information back to the firm so that product design and supply schedules can be tailored for each customer. At MCI, sales representatives can spend weeks inside a customer's organization determining the precise mix of hardware and communications services needed to solve customer problems.

Three types of creative selling in the business market are worth particular attention:

1. In **team selling**, a group of people from different functional areas within the organization call on a particular customer. A sales engineer might analyze the customer's operations and design a product; a financial expert could work out a purchase or lease agreement that fits the customer's financial situation; and a service representative could participate to ensure that delivery, installation, and training are carried out. Sales teams often are used to sell communications equipment, computer installations, and manufacturing equipment. At IBM, a marketing strategist, salespeople, and financial experts operated as a team that consulted with customers such as G. Heilemann Brewing and Gulfstream Aerospace. After interviewing clients, touring facilities, analyzing operations, and studying the customer's information systems, the team modeled the client's company to show its financial performance with and without investments in IBM software. The effort greatly simplified purchase decisions for IBM's clients.[6]

2. **Seminar selling** is designed to reach a group of customers, rather than an individual customer, with information about the firm's products or services. The focus of seminar selling is not an immediate sale. Rather, the intent is to educate customers and potential customers about various aspects of a company's market offerings. Seminar selling is a good way to begin developing relationships with potential customers without the pressures of trying to close a sale.

3. **System selling** entails selling a set of interrelated components that fulfill all or a majority of a customer's needs in a product or service area. System selling has emerged in response to customers' desire for "system buying." In particular, large industrial and government buyers often seek out one or a few suppliers that can provide a full range of products and services needed in an area. System selling offers the convenience of buying from one source. Systems selling reflects the CRM aspects of selling discussed earlier. Large government purchases in China and Eastern Europe for huge infrastructure projects like sea ports, airports, and communications systems demand that project engineering firms like Bechtel employ just such a system-selling approach.

Creative-selling tasks call for high levels of preparation, expertise, and close contact with the customer and are primary to the process of relationship building. This sort of personal selling assumes that the sales function is part of a comprehensive marketing strategy. Some widely used creative-selling positions include *account representatives,* who sell to large, established accounts (typically wholesalers and retailers), and *sales engineers,* who use their technical training to help customers identify needs for products such as software systems and manufacturing equipment.

Supportive Communications

When a sales force is deployed with the purpose of supportive communications, it is not charged directly with generating sales. Rather, people in this sales area aim to give customers information, offer services, and generally create goodwill. Salespeople involved in supportive communications try to ensure that buyers are satisfied with the firm's products and services. Supportive communications takes place with two types of salespeople:

1. A **missionary salesperson** calls on accounts to monitor buyers' satisfaction and update their needs. They may provide some product information after a purchase. Many firms carry out missionary sales through telemarketing techniques, which use telephone and computer (voicemail and email) communications.

As an account executive for Gateway Computers, David Jahan handles telephone sales for small and midsized businesses and sees himself as "the key person between marketing and the customer." Each of his sales calls is a little different because every customer has unique needs. His role is to listen to customers' needs so that he can uncover how Gateway computers can meet those needs. Describing obstacles he must overcome, Jahan says, "One of my biggest challenges is speaking to a client who is already dealing with another company." He uses those conversations as an "opportunity to turn that conversation around and ask where the current vendor may be lacking so we can come in and prove ourselves." Gateway supports its salespeople by informing them about its new products and how they compare with competitors' offerings.

2. A **detail salesperson** introduces new products and provides product information to potential buyers without trying to make an immediate sale. Detail salespeople are widely used by large pharmaceutical firms to introduce new prescription drugs to physicians and provide information about the drugs' application and efficacy.

LO 3 Personal-Selling Objectives

The appropriate overall objective for any element of the promotional mix, including personal selling, is to communicate. In general, the message conveys the brand's value and benefits. Also, because several of the types of personal selling involve culminating a sale, reaching a sales objective is primary. Because a salesperson is typically present when a contract is signed or an order is placed, the direct effect of personal selling on sales is more identifiable than the effect of other elements of the promotional mix. Besides these basics, every encounter with potential buyers may be approached with specific objectives in mind.

Note that these objectives are external in their orientation: each focuses on the buyer. The emphasis is to understand the buyer's needs and use that understanding to provide information on how the firm can satisfy those needs. If these objectives are accomplished, the probability of a sale increases greatly.

Create a Competitive Advantage

Buyers ultimately will choose the product they perceive as best suited to their needs. It is up to the salesperson to quickly understand what is best from the buyer's perspective. Different buyers value different attributes of a product—functional, emotional, or self-expressive. Further, their assessment of value will factor in the services offered—delivery, installation, and repair services, for example. The salesperson must identify what is valued and then pursue the objective of demonstrating to the buyer that the firm's products and services match the buyer's needs more closely than what competitors offer. In this way, the salesperson conveys a competitive advantage that differentiates the firm's products and services from the competition.

Treat Each Buyer as Unique

The salesperson also may grant the potential buyer unique status. To do this, the salesperson manages the communication process to ensure that a buyer does not feel like he or she is being "sold." Rather, the buyer comes away from the contact feeling as if he or she made a voluntary decision to buy.

An important part of accomplishing this objective is to listen attentively. Good listening skills allow the salesperson to grant a buyer unique status by actually learning the buyer's individual needs and desires. Also, the salesperson can shape the communication specifically to each buyer's unique desire for information, thus making full use of personal communication's primary advantage: tailoring the message to each receiver.

Manage Relationships for Mutual Benefit

One of the greatest challenges facing a salesperson is determining how his or her firm is uniquely capable of satisfying customer needs. Matching what the firm is capable of doing with what a buyer desires allows both parties to enter a buying–selling relationship that is mutually beneficial.

To achieve this objective, the salesperson must determine the basis on which the firm can satisfy the buyers:

- Product superiority
- Service superiority
- Price superiority
- Source (company) superiority
- People superiority

The buyer's expression of his or her needs can reveal which of these is most highly valued in the purchase decision. Then the salesperson can emphasize the firm's unique capabilities in terms of satisfying the customer.

Over time, loyalty develops between organizations as firms rely on each other and fulfill promises. Several firms offer specialized sales force training designed to prepare salespeople for the task of managing the buying–selling relationship for mutual benefit.

Control the Communication

Both buyer and seller benefit if the communication process is managed efficiently. The salesperson is in the best position to bring about effective and efficient information exchange by controlling the communication. If a salesperson can control the content and direction of the encounter, the potential buyer will be able to learn quickly and accurately what a firm has to offer.

One way firms are learning to communicate effectively and efficiently and to control the communication is by using "virtual presentations."[7] Virtual

One of the key objectives of personal selling is to manage the buying–selling relationship so well that buyers develop loyalty to the seller's brand. Firms like Cambient train clients' sales forces in managing that relationship for mutual benefit.

presentations rely on a variety of technologies that let sellers send buyers information via the Internet. One firm that has saved time and money with Web presentations is Sterling Software. Company executives turned to the Internet when they realized they couldn't afford to have people away from the office as much as they had been. More importantly, Sterling's customers were unwilling to give a day or a portion of a day for the kind of presentation salespeople needed to deliver. Web communications can enhance the quality of presentations, as well. Running seminars from remote locations has increased Sterling's ability to attract keynote speakers who otherwise would not have participated. In some situations, only a face-to-face environment will accomplish the objectives of a presentation. But if Web-based communication can accomplish the desired result, then the savings and potential quality enhancements are worth the loss of personal contact.

LO 4 The Selling Process

Objectives for personal selling are achievable only in the context of a well-conceived and well-executed sales effort. Therefore, the selling effort must be organized into a sequence of well-defined activities. Every organization has its own perspective on the steps required for effective personal selling. Generally, a well-conceived process involves the activities depicted in Exhibit 14.3.

Preparation

Preparation for personal selling involves gathering relevant information about current customers, potential customers, product characteristics and applications, product choice criteria, corporate support activities (such as advertising and trade channel support), and competitors' products and activities. Further, the salesperson analyzes economic and demographic trends that affect customers. A firm can greatly aid its salespeople in preparing for sales calls by maintaining an effective marketing information system (MkIS). This contains data about purchasing behavior in the market as well as records relating to past behavior of current customers.

For example, a well-prepared salesperson may recognize that potential business buyers of drilling equipment have a general dissatisfaction with suppliers' ability to deliver on a dependable schedule. In general, dependable delivery is a primary motive in business buyer behavior. Armed with such knowledge, the salesperson can approach a prospect with a sales presentation that highlights the reliability and dependability of the firm's distribution and delivery program.

Exhibit 14.3
How to Sell: Steps in the Process

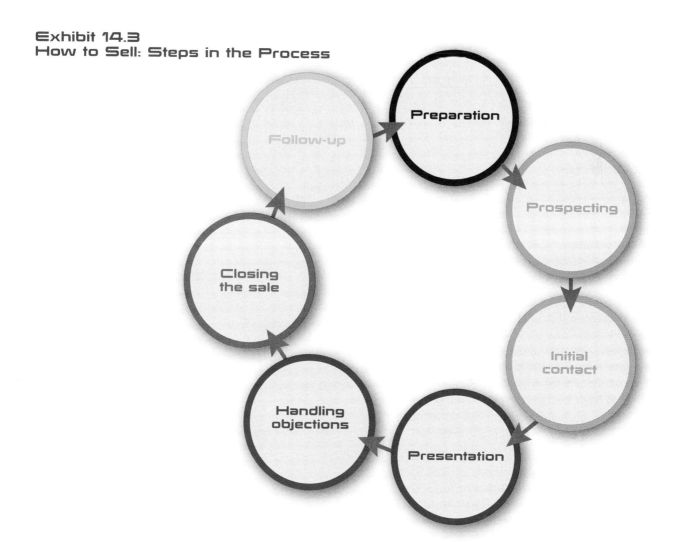

Another important aspect of preparation is to recognize the extent to which the buying decision will be an individual decision versus a group buying decision. With individual buyers, the salesperson can tailor a very specific sales presentation to that person. Group buying decisions may involve representatives from several different functional areas in the firm as well as pure administrators (like purchasing agents). Communication at the group level must recognize the information needs of a wide range of constituents. Some experts recommend that salespeople encourage multiple decision makers within their customer firms. If the salesperson relies on one contact to champion a specific brand or project, the sale will die if that person leaves the firm or team making the buying decision.[8]

Overall, well-prepared salespeople know their firm's capabilities in all areas of the marketing mix, competitors' strengths and weaknesses, effects of the external environment, and customer choice criteria. With this information, they can deliver a relevant and persuasive message. This preparation phase is so important that Ken Morse, director of MIT's Entrepreneurship Center and a former salesman, used to spend up to eight hours preparing for a 15-minute sales call.[9]

Prospecting

Growth in a company's revenues depends partly on the sales force cultivating new customers. Therefore, salespeople must prospect for new accounts. Successful prospecting depends on generating leads—names of new potential buyers. Current customers are an excellent source of leads because the salesperson benefits from a personal "introduction" to a potential customer. Advertising can create leads—for example, from mail-in coupons placed in trade magazines. Mail-in coupons can be a particularly valuable source of leads because the person filling out the coupon normally provides the name of the proper contact, including a current address and phone number. In addition, the firm may purchase leads from companies that specialize in creating databases of firms in different industries. These lists can help the firm identify potential customers in well-defined target areas, and existing lists offer time and cost savings. Of course, these same lists are readily available to competitors.[10]

Telemarketing has increased the efficiency of the use of leads. Some firms maintain a full staff or outsource a call center operation to qualify sales leads. Leads then can be classified as either high or low potential, and salespeople can avoid unproductive, expensive in-person sales calls for leads that seem to hold little promise.

Leads are the most valuable and effective source of prospecting, but salespeople also use cold calls as a prospecting method. Here, the salesperson either telephones or visits a potential customer with whom there has been no previous contact. Compared with the use of leads, cold calling is inefficient and rarely profitable.

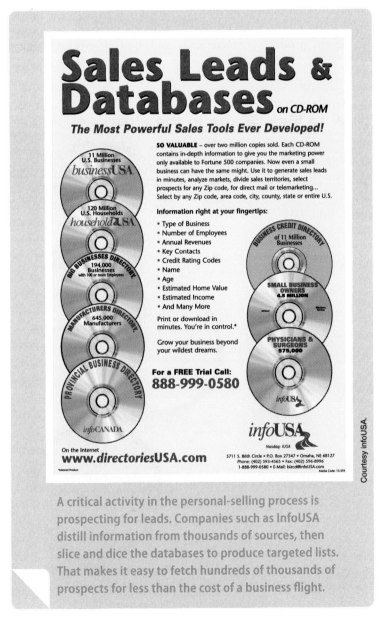

Courtesy infoUSA.

A critical activity in the personal-selling process is prospecting for leads. Companies such as InfoUSA distill information from thousands of sources, then slice and dice the databases to produce targeted lists. That makes it easy to fetch hundreds of thousands of prospects for less than the cost of a business flight.

Initial Contact

During the initial contact with a potential customer, the salesperson must begin to address the objectives of creating a profitable competitive advantage, according uniqueness to each buyer, and developing the buyer–seller relationship. Merely "stopping by" to call on a potential customer with vague notions of what might be accomplished is wasteful. The potential customer is likely to view such a call as an intrusion. A professional, well-planned, purposeful, and brief initial contact can establish the salesperson as a new and important source.

Reasonable activities in an initial contact can include leaving comprehensive information about the firm and its products, introducing the buyer to corporate selling programs, and gathering information about the buyer's organization and product needs.

Presentation

The presentation is an important focal point of the personal-selling process. On rare occasions, it will occur during the initial contact. Normally, it is a separately scheduled phase in the process. Presentations require great skill and preparation.

There are several ways in which a presentation can be carried out. Some firms will require a **canned presentation**, meaning the salesperson recites, nearly verbatim, a prepared sales pitch. The canned-presentation approach ensures that important selling points are covered and also can enhance the performance of marginally skilled salespeople. However, the canned presentation undermines fundamental advantages of personal communication: tailoring the message to the buyer's unique needs and being able to respond to buyer feedback. Further, such an approach presumes (often incorrectly) that every buyer faces a similar buying situation.

An often implemented but marginally useful approach is **attention-interest-desire-action (AIDA)**. In this form of presentation, the salesperson carefully structures the selling contact so that the presentation first gains the buyer's attention and then stimulates interest in the firm's offering by touting product and service attributes. Next, in an effort to stimulate the buyer's desire, the salesperson demonstrates how the firm's offering fulfills the buyer's needs. Finally, the salesperson attempts to close the sale (the buyer's action). This approach is considered marginally effective because it grants the buyer very little participation in the process. The salesperson dominates (not only controls) the communication, leading the buyer through the various stages of the AIDA system. Experienced buyers, after years of being subjected to this technique, find it tiresome and obvious.

A far more sophisticated and informed approach to the presentation is referred to as **need satisfaction**.[11] With this customer-oriented approach, the salesperson assesses each buyer's need state during every sales encounter and then adjusts the selling effort to that need state. The approach considers the following possible need states:

- *Need development:* Potential customers are beginning to recognize the types of problems that exist in their organizations. The salesperson does very little talking and almost exclusively monitors feedback during the presentation. The salesperson concentrates on according uniqueness to the buyer.

- *Need awareness:* The buyer can articulate specific needs in his or her organization. The salesperson can help define the buyer's needs relative to which of the firm's products and services address those needs.

- *Need fulfillment:* The buyer is fully aware of what products and services are needed, and the salesperson assumes a dominant communication role by demonstrating how the firm and its products can fulfill the needs. With this sort of buyer, the salesperson concentrates on creating a differential competitive advantage.

The superiority of the need satisfaction approach is that it explicitly recognizes that a sales presentation will emphasize different information depending on how developed the buyer's need recognition is. Occasionally, a salesperson can lead a buyer through all the need stages in a single presentation, but, more often, buyers are already at different levels, and the salesperson has to adjust the presentation accordingly. Besides emphasizing the buyer's needs and state of mind, this approach takes full advantage of direct feedback and tailoring the message according to that feedback.

Besides choosing presentation content, salespeople can use either of two basic presentation formats:

1. *Face-to-face presentations* take place when the salesperson and the prospect(s) are together, in person. This format allows the salesperson to present materials or product examples and to demonstrate the product. Analysts suggest that face-to-face presentations are critical for recruiting new customers and maintaining good relationships with existing customers.[12] Often referred

canned presentation recitation of a prepared sales pitch

attention-interest-desire-action (AIDA) structured presentation aimed at capturing attention, identifying features of interest, defining desirable benefits, and requesting action in the form of a purchase

need satisfaction sales presentation that begins with assessment of each buyer's need state and then adjusts the selling effort to that need state

to as **consultive selling**, face-to-face sales presentations can be used by the sales force to create significant value for customers by helping them define their problems and design unique solutions.

2. *Telemarketing* is a process whereby salespeople make their sales and information presentations over the telephone. With telemarketing, companies can reach many more customers and more often than they can with consultive selling. For small accounts that wouldn't warrant a face-to-face presentation because of expense, telemarketing offers a way to maintain relationships. An efficient way to develop and maintain a global presence is to establish call centers that can reach a worldwide customer base regularly and efficiently.[13]

Handling Objections

During a presentation, especially with buyers in the need fulfillment stage, objections are likely to surface. The most serious objections relate to the buyer's perception that the firm's product is not well suited to the need being discussed.

The salesperson must be prepared to deal with objections. This is a highly sensitive situation that requires great skill. The salesperson must counter objections without seeming argumentative. Objections cannot be met with defensiveness or brushed aside as insignificant or irrational. Again, the buyer must be accorded uniqueness, so *every* objection is legitimate and reasonable. The best method for handling objections is to probe for the exact nature of the obstacle and then try to lead the buyer to proposing a solution. This effort creates an alliance with the buyer so that seller and buyer can work in partnership to solve the customer's problem.

Closing the Sale

After the presentation, or perhaps several presentations, the salesperson must try to close the sale. Closing the sale is generally regarded as the most difficult part of the personal-selling process—for good reason. The salesperson is asking a buyer to incur costs—monetary, time, risk, opportunity, and, potentially, anxiety costs. The salesperson must ensure that the buyer perceives an opportunity to obtain satisfaction that will exceed the costs. This is another reason why the need-satisfaction approach to the presentation can be so effective.

A variety of techniques have been recommended for closing a sale. Critical to the process is that the salesperson actually ask for the order! Amazingly, according to surveys, about 60 percent of the time, salespeople never ask for the order.[14] There are several ways to ask, but the best approach is a straight-forward close. The salesperson senses when to ask for

© Sean Prior/Shutterstock.

CRITICAL TO [CLOSING A SALE]
IS THAT THE SALESPERSON ACTUALLY ASK FOR THE ORDER.

© /Shutterstock.

an order in a straightforward, courteous manner—no tricks, no presumptions, no innuendo. If a salesperson has successfully achieved the objective of developing a buying–selling relationship for mutual profit, then a buyer will find this method most acceptable. This is the technique used by Ken Libman, founder of the architecture, engineering, and construction firm Libman Wolf Couples. Libman closes an astonishing 80 percent of all the new business he competes for. He explains his success by saying, "I understand people; I put myself in their shoes."[15]

Follow-Up

Two distinct and important activities occur after a sale has been made. First, the salesperson must ensure that all commitments of the negotiated sale are fulfilled. The salesperson can monitor shipping dates, installation, financing, and any training required.

In addition, the salesperson should prepare to deal with buyer post-purchase behavior. The salesperson makes the purchase more satisfying and lays the foundation for future sales when he or she relieves any regrets, doubts, or second thoughts the buyer may be experiencing. Salespeople can help buyers release these concerns through direct communication, either written or oral. Salespeople at Nordstrom department stores send customers a handwritten and personalized note expressing appreciation for the purchase and encouraging them to contact the salesperson for any future clothing needs. Dealing with post-purchase also includes inquiring about needs for related items. Many consumers, out of enthusiasm or newly recognized needs, will purchase items that complement an initial purchase.

LO 5 Selling in a New Environment

Changes in the broad business environment have created a significantly new environment for personal selling.

Better Planning

First, the increased sophistication of marketing planning has greatly altered activities of salespeople. More precise segmentation of markets means the efforts of the sales force are more tightly focused on specific types of customers. Enhanced marketing planning also enables salespeople to respond more quickly to customer requests because the marketing effort is more narrowly defined on a customer-by-customer basis. Also, promotional campaigns rely more on telemarketing to help qualify leads and to relieve the sales force of repeated calls on existing customers.

Sales Force Automation

A second major change is new technology that enables **sales force automation (SFA)**, which is the incorporation of computers, cell phones, personal digital assistants (PDAs), the Internet, and other technologies to improve the efficiency and effectiveness of personal selling. Firms like Salesforce.com provide sales automation software to help integrate the various technologies for communication among the sales force, the firm, and customers.[16]

SFA has made the personal-selling process database driven. Salespeople now rely on marketing information systems to store and help them find knowledge about customers, markets, and company products. They can prepare for sales calls by entering prices and forecasts, update their forecasts as orders are booked, and retrieve product data or presentations during meetings with customers. Salespeople can connect to these databases at their home office or on the road via their laptop, cell phone, or PDA. In this way, salespeople can stay connected to their company's data sources on a global basis.[17]

Communication technology provides salespeople with an arsenal of tools that greatly enhance the ability to manage information. Judicious use of such devices is paramount, however. If the only contacts a customer has with a sales representative are voicemail and email messages, the lack of personal attention can strain an otherwise healthy relationship. These tools aid efficiency but are not substitutes for personal contact and customer service.

Many of these tools are more useful and more efficient because of Internet technology. Experts see the Internet bringing value to personal selling in several areas:[18]

- Building customer loyalty
- Saving customers money
- Increasing the speed of the sales process
- Improving customer relationships with more frequent communication
- Lowering the sales cost

But using the Internet also introduces a major threat to the selling process if firms fail to consider the impact of their Web strategies on compensation and incentive plans. If salespeople see the company's website as competing with them, they will discourage customers from using it. To avoid this problem, compensation arrangements should balance the desired efficiency of Internet promotion against the need to motivate salespeople. This issue was part of the reasoning behind Dell Computer's decision to give sales reps full commission on sales generated through the Internet.[19]

One of the best ways for salespeople to flourish in the Internet-based world of sales is to be completely knowledgeable about what the Internet can and cannot do in the personal-selling process. This means knowing when face-to-face communication is needed and what to focus on during those communications.[20]

© Ewa Walicka/Shutterstock.

Exhibit 14.4
What Sales Managers Do

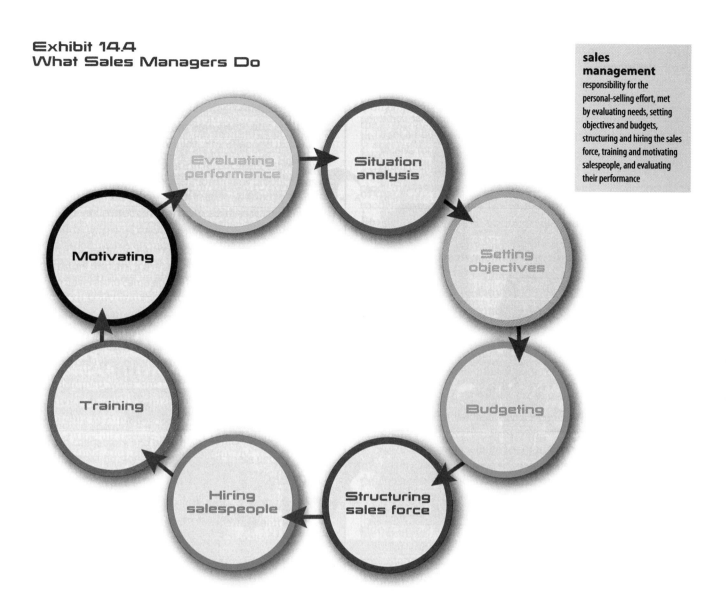

More-Demanding Buyers

Salespeople now deal with more-demanding buyers. While salespeople have benefited from readily available and larger amounts of information, so have buyers. Customers can easily look up and compare product reviews and prices for many kinds of products before they talk to a salesperson.

Along with more information, today's buyers have higher expectations of products and the firms that provide them. Competitive pressures to satisfy customers have escalated the average level of product performance and service, so sellers have to perform to higher standards. Household and business customers will expect the salesperson to provide timely and high-quality service and respond to specific requests.

LO 6 Sales Management

Whereas salespeople are responsible for managing their own individual efforts, the sales management team is responsible for the overall performance of the entire sales force. **Sales management** involves responsibility for the many activities related to the personal-selling effort, from analyzing needs, through hiring and motivating salespeople, to evaluating their work. Exhibit 14.4 identifies the manager's areas of responsibility for ensuring that the sales force is effectively designed and efficiently deployed to carry out its role in the organization. Notice that these areas of responsibility are depicted in a circular fashion. No phase of the management process takes priority over the others.

Notice also that the activities in Exhibit 14.4 are different from actually selling. As obvious as it sounds, sales managers are charged with managing; in practice, research suggests that they often see themselves more as superstar salespeople who lead by example. Interviews with salespeople and sales managers have suggested that managers can best fulfill their responsibility by communicating expectations, building salespeople's confidence, developing their abilities, and motivating them to excel.[21] These activities fit well with the manager's areas of responsibility.

Situation Analysis

Managers of the sales process must engage in a comprehensive situation analysis of the conditions in which the sales effort will take place. This analysis has two parts:

1. An *external situation analysis* identifies trends in the industry, technological advances in product categories, economic conditions that may affect the firm's customers, competitors' activities, and the choice criteria emphasized by buyers. It also includes an evaluation of the markets within which the firm has a significant competitive advantage, as well as the potential for new products and markets. For example, when Apple Computer and IBM were competing to sell personal computers in schools and colleges—a target market emphasized by Apple—Apple conducted surveys of these customers to see what they wanted in new software and hardware. Teams of employees visited universities on "camping trips" to pick the brains of students and faculty."[22] Apple's sales management incorporated that information into planning for the sales effort.

2. An *internal situation analysis* entails assessing the strengths and weaknesses of the sales force and corporate support for the selling effort. The manager evaluates sales force performance in the context of the firm's overall marketing mix. (Note that, in Exhibit 14.4, performance evaluation feeds directly into situation analysis.) The manager also examines sales force knowledge and training relative to the competition. Corporate support for the sales force includes product development and positioning activities that give the product an advantage, pricing incentives that help salespeople make attractive offers, inventory levels and delivery schedules that enable the company to keep promises, and integrated marketing communication that stimulates demand.

Sales Objectives

Sales managers must set objectives at various levels. At the broadest level, the objective is the total sales for the company. This type of sales objective is determined by sales forecasts that draw on projections of total industry sales and the firm's estimate of its share of those sales.

The next level of specificity is the desired level of sales by territory or product category. Here, different geographic territories or product groups are evaluated for conditions that may affect the firm's ability to generate sales during a given time period. Quarterly and annual sales objectives are set for territories and product categories.

The most specific level of objectives is the amount of sales to be generated by each salesperson, typically expressed as sales quotas. The most common way of specifying a sales quota is to state it as a percentage of the prior year's sales (usually greater than 100 percent). In setting sales quotas, the manager considers the effects of new products, competitors' activities, economic conditions, and nonselling tasks that the salesperson is expected to carry out.[23]

Budgets

Establishing a budget for the personal-selling effort requires painstaking effort. The budget includes a variety of expenses:

- Salaries and benefits
- Incentive programs—bonuses, awards
- Recruiting costs
- Training costs
- Travel expenses
- Promotional materials—samples, catalogs, product brochures

Salaries, benefits, recruiting, training, and travel expenses are self-explanatory. Promotional materials are materials from the promotional mix used by salespeople to support the selling effort. For example, an auto parts sales rep may have a catalog of several thousand items to give customers so that they can easily place orders. The coordination of marketing communications materials is managed in consultation with the marketing manager. In the best spirit of integrated marketing communication (IMC), any promotional program that might affect the salesperson's job must be carefully coordinated with the sales effort.

Exhibit 14.5
Ways to Budget Selling Expenses

Method	Description	Pros and Cons
Percentage-of-sales approach	Multiply a product line's sales volume by a predetermined percentage; the result is the sales budget for that product line	Easy to use; fails to recognize unique challenges or opportunities facing the sales force
Competitive-parity approach	Base the size of the budget (particularly salary, benefit, and bonus programs) on what other firms in the industry are doing	Attempts to avoid falling behind competitors; fails to account for differences in companies' objectives; can easily result in over- or underpaying salespeople
Objective-and-task method	Assess the objectives established for the overall selling effort, specify tasks for the sales force, define the required compensation and incentive programs, and then match the budget to the costs associated with these requirements	Most effective method because it relates activities to costs; the only rational and reasonable basis for establishing a budget

The methods of establishing a budget for personnel are defined and compared in Exhibit 14.5.

Sales Force Structure

The sales management must determine how the sales force will be structured to achieve the sales goals. The structure uses some form of three basic options:

1. *Structured by product lines:* Salespeople are assigned to handle specific products. Structuring the sales force around product lines is helpful when products are technologically complex because salespeople will need special training and experience to sell the products. Pharmaceutical firms that manufacture both prescription and over-the-counter drug items often have a separate sales force for each product line based on the complexity of the product.

2. *Structured by type of customer:* Customer groups can be segmented based on order size, position in the channel, or product use characteristics. For example, some salespeople might call on wholesalers, whereas others call on retailers, or salespeople might be assigned to particular industry groups so that they can specialize in how their products meet different needs.

3. *Structured by geographic territory:* When salespeople are assigned to geographic territories, each salesperson

calls on all types of customers in the area and is prepared to sell the firm's entire product line. This structure is most appropriate for standardized items that are sold to a variety of customers. Stanley Tools, for example, can have its sales force call on hardware stores, home improvement centers, and discount retailers with the firm's entire line of hammers, screwdrivers, wrenches, and the like.

The choice or combination of these structures depends on the nature of the product and the nature of the market.

Hiring Salespeople

Decisions about sales force structure help managers determine how many and what kinds of salespeople to hire. The hiring process includes defining job requirements, recruiting candidates, and making selections.

Job Requirements

Sales managers must prepare complete job descriptions and identify the qualifications an individual must have for each sales job. A *job description* identifies all the selling and nonselling tasks to be performed by the salesperson. Nonselling tasks include

RESEARCH SUGGESTS THAT A **SUCCESSFUL SALESPERSON** IS A GOOD LISTENER, ENJOYS SOCIAL EVENTS, FEELS SOCIALLY SATISFIED, AND IS RELATIVELY INDIVIDUALISTIC.

paperwork and service activities such as maintaining point-of-purchase displays, coordinating and monitoring delivery, and arranging financing or training for the customer.

The tasks included in a job description translate directly into the *qualifications* of the individuals needed to fill positions—the combination of skills and training that relate to effective performance. Highly technical selling jobs require people with relevant technical training. When job descriptions include significant nonselling tasks, salespeople need skills in those kinds of activities.

In determining what qualifications are most directly related to success, many firms draw on their experience with current sales personnel, including personal characteristics of successful salespeople. Research suggests that a successful salesperson is a good listener, enjoys social events, feels socially satisfied, and is relatively individualistic. Top salespeople also tend to be more disciplined, aggressive, and creative than unsuccessful salespeople.[24]

Recruiting

A firm with well-written job descriptions and statements of qualifications can begin to recruit people to meet staffing needs. The recruiting effort should be a continuous process. A manager who begins to recruit only when a need arises may feel so pressed for time that he or she is tempted to accept unqualified or inappropriate people.

Managers can turn to various sources to generate a pool of qualified applicants. These include college and university campuses, employment agencies, and advertisements in newspapers, trade journals, and online. Many companies recruit internally by moving salespeople among products or divisions. Procter & Gamble regularly moves salespeople among its Noxell, Revlon, and Richardson-Vicks divisions.[25]

Effective recruiting understands the value that applicants bring to the recruiting process. In tight labor markets, firms need to battle for top recruits. Winning the recruiting war will depend largely on offering top candidates what they want. According to Development Dimensions International, a recruiting research firm, employers say that successful recruiting depends on corporate reputation, benefits package, potential for advancement, corporate culture, salary scale, and stock options, in that order.[26] Notice that corporate culture and reputation rank higher than salary in the minds of modern recruits.

Screening and Evaluation

When recruiting efforts produce job applicants, the firm must screen and evaluate them. Typical methods include reviewing résumés, administering psychological tests designed to identify personality and motivation characteristics related to job success, and conducting personal interviews. At Capital One Financial, managers have applied the company's data-driven approach to its hiring process. The Capital One system relies on a battery of tests that measure everything from data analysis skills to reliability.[27]

Interviews should aim to identify traits, such as personal appearance and verbal skills, that are not evident from résumés and test results. To economize, more and more firms screen candidates through telephone or videoconference interviews. Videoconferencing is playing a part in the interview process because firms can get feedback about candidates faster and from more parts of the organization. People in different departments or offices can tune in to the videoconference or view a video posted on a secure website.[28]

Training

Training is a critical sales management responsibility, whether salespeople are new or experienced. Because the selling effort is integral to achieving corporate revenue objectives, the firm must have a well-planned training program.

Content and Methods

The content of the training program will depend on the sales force structure, type of product, tasks involved, and sales objectives. Every salesperson needs adequate knowledge about the products and the choice criteria used by customers. Beyond these basics, popular topics for training include industry trends and economic conditions affecting the firm's market. Companies that use team selling need to provide training in team building, team managing, and team membership skills. Seminar selling, which requires the ability to communicate to a diverse group of participants, also requires the development of unique skills. And companies that use sales force automation tools must train the sales force in the use of those tools, including the hardware and software used.[29]

Plans for training include the techniques to use. Options include role playing, classroom lectures, videotaping of presentations, computer simulations, tours of corporate facilities, and other possibilities.

Duration

Plans for training should identify how long it will take to properly train salespeople. At Procter & Gamble, the training period lasts 12 to 18 months; at State Farm, training is a two-year stint. The duration of training depends on the complexity of the selling task and the company's product line, as well as the trainees' background and experience.

Personnel

Many firms rely on experts outside the firm to conduct some or all of their training programs. Universities and colleges of business often have corporate training programs, many of which concentrate on selling tasks. Outsourcing the training program to specialized firms can be a much more effective way of achieving training goals than trying to do all the training in-house.

At some firms, sales managers and highly successful members of the current sales staff act as trainers. Occasionally, upper-level management will participate as well. Home Depot founder Bernie Marcus helped prepare the sales training program for his home improvement products chain and often participates in training sessions. Besides giving the sales staff extensive technical training (how to lay tile and do electrical installations, for example), Home Depot trains the staff in effective selling techniques like listening to customers' needs and walking customers through the store to find the materials they require.[30]

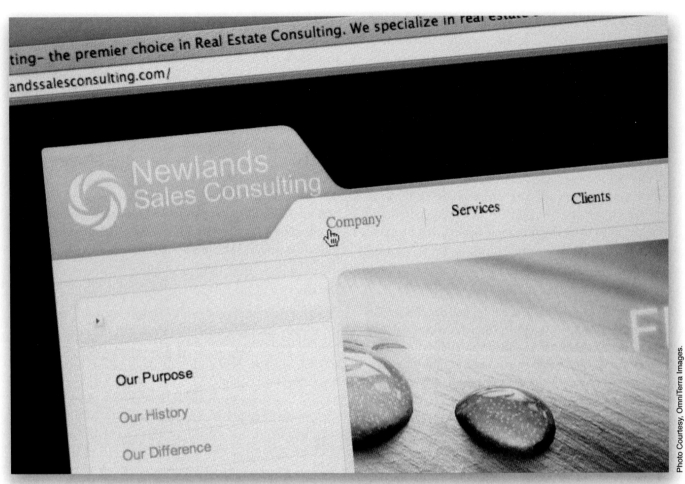

COMPANIES THAT NEED SALES TRAINING OFTEN TURN TO TRAINING SPECIALISTS. NEWLANDS SALES CONSULTING SPECIALIZES IN TRAINING REAL ESTATE BROKERS AND AGENTS. ITS SERVICES INCLUDE GROUP SEMINARS IN SELLING SKILLS, CLASSES IN AN AGENCY'S OFFICES, AND EVEN ONE-ON-ONE COACHING.

Location

The broad choice with regard to training location is whether the trainees will learn in a classroom setting or go out into the field to learn. Classrooms offer a low-pressure environment where there are few consequences for mistakes. Training in the field allows salespeople to encounter actual selling situations under the tutelage of an experienced salesperson. The drawbacks of training in the field are the mistakes a trainee might make with customers and the time drain on the salespeople who conduct the training.

Nowadays, classroom training isn't confined to actual classrooms, as a growing number of firms post training materials on the Web. For example, Fisher Scientific, a New Hampshire–based chemical company, uses the Internet to teach the majority of its salespeople in the privacy of their homes, cars, hotel rooms, or wherever else they bring their laptops. To get updates on pricing or to refresh themselves on a technical product feature, salespeople log on to the Web and select from a lengthy list of subjects in which they might need training or support. They can get information on a new product, take an exam, or post messages for product experts.[31]

Sales training should not be reserved for new salespeople. As the external environment changes, as the firm develops new products and customer knowledge, and as experts develop new selling techniques, members of the existing sales staff can benefit enormously from regular training sessions.

Motivation

Perhaps the most challenging responsibility of sales management is to motivate salespeople to do their best. The motivation effort includes decisions about how to compensate salespeople, but money is far from the only motivator that matters. The amount of satisfaction and sense of personal achievement individuals feel from performing tasks also are important to motivation.

Compensation

For paying salespeople, three basic compensation alternatives are available: straight salary, straight commission, and some combination of the two. Exhibit 14.6 indicates the factors influencing the use of salary and commission alternatives. Straight salary is most effective when the sales staff is highly skilled, the selling effort is drawn out over a long period, salespeople are expected to carry out time-consuming nonselling tasks, or a team selling approach is being used. As the selling task becomes less complex and requires fewer service activities, then the commission approach is more feasible. Many firms use a combination plan because many selling efforts include features from both ends of the spectrum.

If a firm relies on a commission compensation program but the selling task strongly warrants a salary arrangement, salespeople work so hard to generate sales and, therefore, income for themselves that they do not attend to important nonselling activities. Such a conflict of interest usually spells disaster for the firm. Customers are dissatisfied and will seek alternative suppliers. Because customer satisfaction is so important to long-term success and profitability, firms like General Electric and AT&T are tying sales force compensation to customer satisfaction surveys.[32]

Task Clarity

Salespeople will be more motivated when their realm of responsibility is well defined. Further, they will engage in more goal-oriented behavior when they clearly know the criteria upon which they will be evaluated. Clear criteria show salespeople that they have attainable goals to pursue. This motivational approach seems to work especially well with today's employees, who expect a more cooperative relationship with managers.

JCPenney learned that managers had complaints about the firm's brightest and most talented salespeople. The managers struggled to relate to the "twentysomethings" effectively. Task clarity and a more cooperative relationship turned out to be the key to the managers' new approach to these valued employees.[33]

Recognition of Goal Attainment

The organization also should recognize goal achievement by its salespeople. Short-term goal attainment, such as exceeding sales quotas, should be rewarded with incentive pay, such as bonuses or stock options.

**Exhibit 14.6
Salaries or Commissions?
How to Choose**

Salary for . . .
- High-cost products
- Long planning intervals
- Technical selling
- Well-structured tasks
- Many service functions

Commissions for . . .
- Low-cost products
- Few service functions
- Need for motivation
- Little supervision
- Financially weak firm

Photo: © Jules Studio/Shutterstock.

Attainment of longer-term goals, such as market or customer development, should be rewarded with status-enhancing recognition, such as promotions or job titles. Recognition also comes in the form of feedback. By launching a website where its 9,000 salespeople could check on their goal attainment, IBM found it could effectively keep its sales force focused on the company's goals. The site also gave the sales reps immediate feedback on how their performance was matching up against objectives. Brad Brown from the sales consulting firm Reward Strategies says that such systems are "important in terms of keeping salespeople motivated and focused on selling. These tools give reps instantaneous access to where they are versus their goals—it's like knowing the score of a ball game."[34]

Job Enrichment

Managers also can motivate salespeople with job-enriching experiences. Many firms send salespeople to professional conferences. Paid attendance at sales training programs is a similar reward. The firm also can consider allowing salespeople to participate in corporate planning sessions with management personnel. This can give the sales force a sense of "ownership" in the corporate strategies they will be asked to support. Of course, the most job-enriching experience is to offer people new tasks, responsibilities, and projects. When employees feel as if they are constantly being challenged, they will be more motivated and likely to stay with a firm.[35]

Perquisites

Along with money, sales professionals often appreciate being rewarded with "perks." A new car every year or so, membership at a health club, dinner at fine restaurants, or season tickets to sporting events are all legitimate business expenses that salespeople can enjoy while doing business.

Flexibility is another kind of perk. Compensation experts have been advising firms to try to let people, as much as is legally and organizationally possible, design their own compensation packages. Whereas one person may be very focused on salary, another may be far more motivated by a flexible work schedule.

Evaluation

Evaluating the performance of salespeople draws directly on the objectives set for the personal-selling process and the sales objectives. Managers can judge performance based on several objective and subjective criteria described in the next chapter. The criteria used should be consistent with the way the firm conducts the overall assessment of the IMC effort.

STUDY TOOLS CHAPTER 14

Located at back of the textbook
- **Rip out Chapter in Review Card.**

Located at www.cengagebrain.com
- **Review Key Terms Flashcards (Print or Online).**
- **Complete the Practice Quiz to prepare for tests.**
- **Play "Beat the Clock" and "Quizbowl" to master concepts.**
- **Complete "Crossword Puzzle" to review key terms.**
- **Watch videos on Porsche and Bogusky On Creativity for real company examples.**
- **For additional examples, go online to learn about Internet-based sales management, Dell's support system, and setting sales quotas.**

REVIEW

HE DID

PROMO puts a multitude of study aids at your fingertips. After reading the chapters, check out these resources for further help:

- **Chapter in Review cards**, found in the back of your book, include all learning outcomes, definitions, and visual summaries for each chapter.

- **Online printable flashcards** give you three additional ways to check your comprehension of key concepts.

Other great ways to help you study include **interactive games and online tutorial quizzes with feedback**.

You can find it all at **ww.cengagebrain.com**.

CHAPTER 15

Measuring the Effectiveness of Brand Promotions

Read further to find out how Unilever measured the effectiveness of their Dove promotional efforts.

The Campaign for Real Beauty enhanced Dove's visibility. They made it their mission to "make women feel more beautiful every day."

discover the beauty treatment for your underarms.
Dove deodorant has a unique combination of ingredients found in a face cream: Omega 6, hydrating glycerol and 1/4 moisturising cream. The result? Soft, smooth and evenly toned underarms and of course 24 hour protection. Dove Deodorant.

Courtesy, Advertising Archives.

Learning Outcomes

After studying this chapter, you should be able to:

LO 1 Discuss issues that shape the evaluation of brand promotion.

LO 2 Describe how marketers measure the effectiveness of advertising.

LO 3 Identify measures of effectiveness for Internet advertising, direct marketing, sales promotion, point of purchase, sponsorships, public relations, and corporate advertising.

LO 4 Explain how sales managers evaluate salespeople and the personal-selling effort.

LO 5 Describe the process of evaluating the effectiveness of IMC campaigns.

"The idea that business is just a numbers affair has always struck me as preposterous."

—Richard Branson

Research and the Campaign for Real Beauty

AFTER YOU FINISH THIS CHAPTER GO TO PAGE 325 FOR STUDY TOOLS

The Campaign for Real Beauty was one of the most successful and controversial advertising campaigns of all time. The effort enhanced Dove's visibility and contributed to record profits for Unilever, Dove's parent company. Unilever's managers attributed much of the increased sales of Dove to the innovative advertising campaign, which featured the theme "Real Beauty."

The Dove Campaign for Real Beauty (CFRB) began in the United Kingdom in 2004 to respond to Dove's declining sales as a result of a crowded market. Unilever approached Edelman, its PR agency, for a solution. Together, they conceived a campaign that focused not on the product but on a way to make women feel beautiful regardless of their age and size. According to Unilever, sales of the products featured in the ads increased by 600 percent in the first two months of the campaign.

In 2005, the CFRB was brought to the United States and Canada. CFRB aimed not only to increase sales of Dove beauty products but also to target women of all ages and shapes. According to the CFRB website (www.dove.us/#/cfrb/), "The Dove Campaign for Real Beauty is a global effort that is intended to serve as a starting point for societal change and act as a catalyst for widening the definition and discussion of beauty. The campaign supports the Dove mission: To make women feel more beautiful every day by challenging today's stereotypical view of beauty and inspiring women to take great care of themselves."

What do you think?

You know brand promotion is working if sales are strong.

1	2	3	4	5	6	7
STRONGLY DISAGREE				STRONGLY AGREE		

Dove commissioned The Real Truth About Beauty study as a way to explore what beauty means to women. The following statistics are a sampling of results from the study:

- Only 2 percent of these women describe themselves as "beautiful"

- About three-quarters of them rate their beauty as "average"

- Almost half of them think their weight is "too high"

Larry Koffler, the senior vice president of consumer brands at Edelman, maintained that the research was vital to the campaign: "Without having a foundation in the global research study, which showed that the image of beauty was unattainable, we wouldn't have had the credibility in creating the materials, in pitching stories and being able to answer some of the folks that didn't agree with the campaign."

After the initial study, Dove commissioned two more studies, one in 2005 and one in 2006. The additional information furthered Dove's research about women's perceptions of beauty across several cultures.[1]

Unilever's experience highlights the importance of measuring the effectiveness of a promotional effort. Managers may be tempted to make decisions based on their experience in a product category and marketing discipline. But applying this experience to a particular target segment often cannot fully meet the challenge of judging how best to craft a message and assess its effectiveness. By drawing on research, marketers can better identify which tools are working best. In a world of multimillion-dollar (or even billion-dollar) promotional budgets, managers are held responsible for verifying the effectiveness of all that spending. As you will see in this chapter, many issues are involved in measuring the effectiveness of the whole array of promotional options, and many measurement tools are available for meeting the challenge.

LO 1 Issues in Measuring Effectiveness

Several issues must be addressed regarding the process of measuring the effectiveness of the promotional tools and the overall integrated marketing communication (IMC) effort. The most basic of these is the scope of promotion research. **Promotion research** is a specialized form of marketing research that focuses on the development and performance of promotional materials.

Research comes into the promotional process at several points. It helps strategists understand who will be the audience members for the promotional message and which buttons to push. It also provides information for making go or no-go decisions, determining when to pull a promotion that is worn out (as Goodyear did), and evaluating the performance of an advertising or promotion agency.

Another issue is how to decide whether the promotion research itself is doing its job. Research is not magic or truth, although it sometimes seems to be confused with such. When research is used to make important promotional decisions, marketers need to consider whether that research meets some basic criteria:

- **Reliability**: Does the method generate consistent findings over time?

- **Validity**: Is the information generated relevant to the research questions being investigated? In other words, does the research investigate what it seeks to investigate?

- **Trustworthiness**: Knowing how the data were collected, can the marketer trust the data, and to what extent? This term usually is applied to qualitative data.

- **Meaningfulness**: Just what does a piece of research really mean (if anything)? This can be the hardest question to answer.

It is important for marketing professionals to take a moment (or several) to consider the limitations inherent in their data and in their interpretations.

In the research method illustrated here, consumers in a theater watch an advertisement frame by frame and turn dials to indicate electronically how much they like each part of the advertisement. The researcher graphs average responses of the audience and superimposes these results over the ad so that marketers can see which parts of the ad generated the most interest (the highest points on the graph). Such results are interesting to marketers, but they don't measure how consumers normally see advertising or tell what qualities of the ad consumers liked or disliked.

account planning system in which an agency assigns a coequal account planner to work alongside the account executive and analyze research data, staying with projects on a continuous basis

naturalistic inquiry broad-based research method that relies on qualitative data collection, including video and audio recordings and photography

Research can result from logic and adaptive decision making, or it may be driven by custom and history. In the best case, reliable, valid, trustworthy, and meaningful tests are appropriately applied. In the worst case, tests in which few still believe continue to thrive because they represent "the way we have always done things." More typically, industry practice falls somewhere in between. The pressure of history and the felt need for normative data (allowing comparisons with the past) partially obscure questions of appropriateness and validity. In this environment, the best test is not always done, and the right questions are not always asked.

Research Systems

Jon Steel, director of Account Planning and vice chairman of Goodby, Silverstein, and Partners, has called account planning "the biggest thing to hit American advertising since Doyle Dane Bernbach's Volkswagen campaign."[2] That may be stretching it a bit (it is), but account planning is a big story in the industry, so it's important to compare its role with traditional promotion research.

Account planning is a system in which an agency assigns a coequal account planner to work with the brand's account executive and analyze research data

for projects on an ongoing basis. It differs from traditional promotion research mostly in three ways:

1. In terms of organization, the assignment of an account planner to work as coequal with the account executive on a given client's business contrasts with the traditional approach of depending on a separate research department's occasional involvement. The planner is assigned to a single client and stays with the project on a continuous basis. In the traditional system, the research department gets involved from time to time as needed, and members of the research department work on several clients' materials.

2. This organizational structure puts research and measurement in a different, more prominent role. Researchers (or "planners") seem to be more actively involved throughout the entire promotional process and seem to have a bigger impact on it as well. Advertising and promotion agencies that practice account planning tend to do more developmental research and less evaluative or measurement research.

3. "Planning agencies" tend to do more qualitative and naturalistic research than their more traditional counterparts, which use quantitative techniques and models to measure effectiveness. **Naturalistic inquiry** is a broad-based research approach that relies on data collection methods that are more qualitative than quantitative and that use video and audio recordings and photography in an effort to investigate an issue more holistically.

Issues in Message Evaluation

At the heart of any successful promotional campaign is the message that will be used to engage a target audience and give audience members a reason to believe in the brand. The various types of advertising have the most elaborate message development and execution. But direct-marketing materials, sales promotion appeals, and public relations have message content, too. Even sponsorships send a message about the brand's image projected by the firm's affiliation with the event. For example, what sort of message does it send to an audience if a firm is a sponsor of a World Wrestling Federation event as opposed to being the sponsor of a fund-raiser for a children's hospital?

Given the image effects and the meaning consumers take from messages, it should come as no surprise that much of the research conducted by promotion agencies and their clients involves testing messages. Message-testing research may be conducted before a promotional campaign is executed (a pretest) or after a promotional campaign is placed (a post-test). There is no one right way to test messages used in a campaign, so experts offer conflicting advice about how to execute this type of measure of effectiveness. This di-

versity of opinion stems from multiple and sometimes competing testing criteria or outright confusion about what a promotion must do to be considered effective.

Motives and Expectations

What do marketers and agencies want out of their message tests? The answer, of course, depends on who you ask. Generally speaking, the account team wants some assurance that the promotional message does essentially what it's supposed to do. Many times, the team simply wants whatever the client wants. The client typically wants to see some numbers, generally meaning **normative test scores**; in other words, the client wants to see how well a particular advertisement or promotion scored against average campaigns of its type that were tested previously.

Whenever people begin looking at the numbers, there is a danger that trivial statistical differences can be made monumental. Other times, the required measure is simply inappropriate. Still other times, managers wishing to keep their jobs simply give clients whatever they ask for. If clients want to see that consumers can recall an ad for the brand, then the ad will mention the brand more often, even to the point of silliness. If the client craves sales, this can be achieved with a big package of short-term sales promotions, even if these erode the brand's image and long-term profitability.

Based on the content of this advertisement, which of the assessment criteria do you think the marketer was most interested in?

Courtesy, Nissan North America, Inc.; Advertising: Team One; Photographer: Scott Downing.

These tactics may not make good campaigns, but they boost scores and, presumably, make the client happy for a while.

Despite the politics involved, message-testing research probably is helpful most of the time. Properly conducted, such research can yield important data that management can use to determine the suitability of a promotional effort. It's far better to shelve an expensive direct-mail piece or proposed sponsorship than to execute a campaign that will produce little good and may even do harm.

Dimensions of Message Assessment

Marketers judge the effectiveness of promotional messages against many standards. In fact, they need to avoid using only sales as the single measure for judging messages. Certainly, inquiries or sales are a valid measure of a direct-action message that implores receivers to call in and order today. But especially in other situations, an immediate uptick in sales may not be an appropriate measure of success.

Picking the right criteria is not always easy, but it is the essence of effective message evaluation. A message can be judged along many dimensions and with several criteria. Four possibilities are widely used:

1. *Imparting knowledge:* It commonly is assumed that a promotional message generates thoughts, some of which are later retrieved and then influence a purchase. Some messages are judged to be effective if they leave this knowledge about the brand, whether in the form of a jingle, a product symbol, or merely brand-name recognition at the point of purchase. When McDonald's launched the "Two all-beef patties, special sauce, lettuce, cheese, pickles, onions on a sesame seed bun" Big Mac campaign, people had the jingle stuck in their heads for weeks! Generally, when knowledge generation is the marketer's primary concern, marketers use tests of recall and recognition.

2. *Shaping attitudes:* Attitudes can tell us a lot about where a brand stands in the consumer's eyes. Attitudes can be influenced by what people both know and feel about a brand, so they are a summary evaluation that ties together the influence of many different factors. Marketers thus may view shaping or changing attitudes as a key dimension of advertising effectiveness. Message-testing research frequently is structured around questions related to attitudes. If a researcher asks how much you like or dislike Tide versus Bold versus Wisk laundry detergent, the research is focusing on a summary evaluation of attitude toward the brands.

3. *Attaching emotions.* Marketers always have had a special interest in emotions. Ever since the 1920s, there has been a belief that feelings may be more important than thoughts as a reaction to certain messages, and this belief has spurred interest in developing better measures of the feelings generated by promotional messages.[3] Measures of emotions include paper-and-pencil assessments and dial-turning devices where those receiving a message turn a dial in either a positive or negative direction to indicate their emotional response to the message. Participants' responses are tracked by computer and can be aggregated and superimposed over the message during playback to allow brand managers to see the pattern of emotional reactions generated.

4. *Legitimizing the brand.* Legitimizing a brand within its target audience means receivers embrace the message as meaningful and relevant to their view of the world. Thus, in a **resonance test**, the goal is to determine to what extent the message resonates or rings true with target-audience members.[4] The questions become, Does this message match consumers' own experiences? Does it produce an affinity reaction? Do consumers who view it say, "'Yeah, that's right; I feel just like that"? Do consumers receive the message and make it their own?[5]

> **resonance test**
> message assessment aimed at determining the extent to which a message rings true with target audience members

LO 2 Effectiveness of Advertisements

Maybe because advertising is so conspicuous, or because of the billions of dollars spent on production, or because it relies so much on creative execution, advertising has been and continues to be the subject of more measurement effort than any other promotional tool, even on a global scale.

Throughout many years, many different methods to measure the effectiveness of advertising have been developed. In general, these methods take the form of pretest evaluations of advertising effectiveness, pilot testing of ads in the marketplace, and post-test evaluations of advertising effectiveness in the marketplace during or after a campaign.

Pretest Evaluations

Because so much time, effort, and expense are involved in the development of advertising messages, most organizations pretest their messages to gauge consumer reaction *before* advertisements are placed. The goal is to save the firm the expense (or embarrassment) of running ads that will not achieve the desired objectives. A variety of tools may be used in pretesting.

Communication Tests

A **communication test** simply investigates whether a message is communicating something close to what is desired. Communication tests usually are done in a group setting, with data coming from a combination of pencil-and-paper questionnaires and group discussion.

Communication tests are done with one major goal in mind: to avoid a major disaster from communicating something the creators of the ad are too close to see even if it is obvious to consumers seeing the ad—for example, an unintended double entendre or unexpected interpretation of the visual imagery in an ad in different parts of the world. Cadillac embarrassed itself with an unfortunate bit of film introducing the Cadillac Catera. In an effort to show consumers the handling capability of the "Cadillac that Zigs," one ad demonstrated the car's ability to pass on a curvy road—right over a double yellow line. A communication test might have caught this unfortunate oversight.

Marketers should balance the risk of an error in an ad against the possibility of nitpicking. Test respondents tend to feel responsible for being helpful, so they may try too hard to see things. Well-trained and experienced researchers must be counted on to draw a proper conclusion from the testing.

© Ronen/Shutterstock.

GLOBAL NIELSEN'S GLOBAL VIEW

ACNielsen Corporation has expanded services for international marketers through its Nielsen Media International division in order to give global marketers a method for measuring the results of multicountry programs. The company's offerings include measurement of international television audiences and global Internet advertising and sales. Nielsen can provide marketers with data from dozens of international markets.

Source: Juliana Koranteng, "ACNielsen Shoots for Global Growth," *Ad Age International,* December 1999, 29.

Courtesy, The Coca-Cola Company.

GOOD MORNING

In this ad, Diet Coke is relying on only one picture and two words to get its point across. Do readers get it, or is Coke too clever? A communication test can answer that question.

Magazine Dummies

Dummy advertising vehicles are mock-ups of magazines that contain editorial content and advertisements, as a real magazine would. Inserted in the dummy vehicle are one or more test advertisements. Consumers representing the target audience are asked to read through the magazine as they normally would. The test usually is administered in consumers' homes, so it has some sense of realism. Once the reading is completed, the consumers are asked questions about the content of *both* the magazine and the advertisements as a way to divert heightened attention away from only the ads. Questions typically relate to recall of the test ads and feelings toward the ad and the featured brand. This method is most valuable for comparing alternative messages.

Theater Tests

Advertisements also are tested in small theaters, usually set up in or near shopping malls. Members of the theater audience have an electronic device through which they can express how much they like or dislike the advertisements shown. Simulated shopping trips also can be a part of these **theater tests**.

The problem with theater tests is that it is difficult to determine whether the respondent is re-ally expressing feelings toward the ad or the brand being advertised. Given the artificial and demanding conditions of the test, experienced researchers again are needed to interpret the results.

This form of message pretesting has become quite common in the United States, so considerable data are available for judging the validity of this approach. Analyses of these data by John Philip Jones, a professor of communications at Syracuse University, are very supportive.[6] According to Jones, even if this form of message pretesting yields some incorrect predictions about ads' potential effectiveness (as it occasionally will), a marketer's success rate will improve relative to what would be realized without this sort of testing.

Thought Listings

Advertising generates thoughts (cognitions) during and after exposure. Message research that tries to identify specific thoughts that may be generated by an ad is referred to as **thought listing** or cognitive response analysis. Typically, researchers have groups of individuals watch the commercial and, as soon as it is over, ask these audience members to write down all the thoughts that were in their minds while watching the commercial. The hope is that this will capture what the ad meant to the audience members and how they reacted to it.

The usual way to analyze these responses is to compile simple percentages or box scores of word counts. Marketers might find the ratio of favorable to unfavorable thoughts or count the number of times subjects' reactions to an ad included a self-relevant connection, such as "That would be good for me" or "That looks like something I'd like."

Attitude Change Studies

The typical **attitude change study** uses a before-and-after ad exposure design, frequently in a theater test setting. Researchers recruit people from the target market and ask about their preexposure attitudes toward the advertised brand and competitors' brands. Then the subjects are exposed to the test ad and some dummy ads. Following this exposure, subjects' attitudes are

dummy advertising vehicles mock-ups of magazines that contain editorial content and advertisements, including ads being tested

theater tests pretest message research in which subjects view ads played in small theaters and record their reactions

thought listing pretest message research that tries to identify specific thoughts that may be generated by an ad

attitude change study message research that uses a before-and-after ad exposure design

measured again. The goal, of course, is to gauge the potential of specific ad versions to change brand attitudes.

To test attitude change with print ads, test ads contained in test magazines can be dropped off at the participants' homes. Inserting the test ads into the magazines makes the competitive environment for communication more realistic. To measure attitudes before and after exposure, the researchers ask subjects to choose from a variety of potential prizes being offered in a drawing. The subjects select from the same alternatives when the magazines are dropped off and again the next day. Attitude change studies in radio are rare, perhaps because most people consider radio to be most useful for building awareness and recall, not for attitude change.

The reliability of these procedures is fairly high, but questions remain about meaningfulness. The change is measured after only one or two ad exposures in an unnatural viewing environment. Many marketers believe that commercials don't register their impact until after three or four exposures. Still, a significant swing in before-and-after scores with a single exposure suggests that something is going on, and some of this effect might be expected when the ad reaches the target audience.

Physiological Measures

Several message pretests use physiological measurement devices. **Physiological measures** detect how consumers react to messages, based on their physical responses:

- **Eye-tracking systems** monitor eye movements across print ads. With one such system, respondents wear a gogglelike device that records (on a computer system) pupil dilations, eye movements, and length of view by sectors within a print advertisement.

- A **psychogalvanometer** measures galvanic skin response (GSR)—minute changes in perspiration, which suggest arousal related to some stimulus (in this case, an advertisement).

- A new physiological measurement, borrowed from NASA research, employs brain wave tracking technology. This research is being applied to measure how effective banner ads are in causing an emotional response in Web users and how that response might translate into click-throughs and brand recall.[7]

- **Voice response analysis** measures inflections in the voice when consumers are discussing an ad and identifies patterns that indicate excitement and other physiological states. Deviations from a flat response are claimed to be meaningful.

Other, less frequently used physiological measures record heart rate, blood pressure, and muscle contraction.

All physiological measures suffer from the same drawbacks. Even though we may be able to detect a physiological response to an advertisement, there is no way to determine whether the response is to the ad or the brand, or which part of the advertisement was responsible for the response. In some sense, even the positive–negative dimension is obscured. Is excitement, increased heart rate, a change in blood pres-

MARKETERS OFTEN BELIEVE THAT HARD SCIENCE TECHNIQUES, SUCH AS MEASURING PHYSIOLOGICAL RESPONSES, LEND LEGITIMACY TO EFFORTS AT MESSAGE EVALUATION.

sure, or muscle contraction the result of a positive or negative reaction? Without being able to correlate specific effects with other dimensions of an ad, physiological measures are of minimal benefit. Thus, these measures tell us little beyond the simple degree of arousal attributable to an ad. For most marketers, this minimal benefit usually doesn't justify the expense and intrusion involved.

Pilot Testing

Before committing to the expense of a major campaign, marketers often take their message-testing programs into the field. Pursuing message evaluation with experimentation in the marketplace is known as **pilot testing**.

The fundamental options for pilot testing fall into one of three classes:

1. **Split-cable transmission** allows testing of two versions of an advertisement through direct transmission to two separate samples of similar households within a single, well-defined market area. This method heightens realism by providing exposure in a natural setting. The frequency and timing of transmission can be carefully controlled. The advertisements then are compared in terms of exposure, recall, and persuasion.

2. **Split-run distribution** applies similar principles to the print medium. One version of an advertisement is placed in every other copy of a magazine, and a second version is placed in the other magazines. To use direct response as a test measure, researchers can design ads with a reply card, coupons, or a toll-free number. The realism of this method is a great advantage in the testing process. Expense is, of course, a major drawback.

3. **Split-list experiments** test the effectiveness of various aspects of direct-mail advertising pieces. Multiple versions of a direct-mail piece are prepared and sent to various segments of a mailing list. The version that produces the most sales is deemed superior.

The advantage of all the pilot-testing methods is the natural setting within which the test takes place. A major disadvantage is that competitive or other environmental influences in the market cannot be controlled and may affect the performance of an advertisement without being detected by the researcher.

Post-Testing

Post-test message tracking assesses the performance of advertisements during or after the launch of an advertising campaign. Common measures of an ad's perfor-

mance are recall, recognition, awareness and attitude, and behavior-based measures.

Overall, post-testing is appealing because of the strong desire to track the continuing effectiveness of advertising in a real-world setting. However, the problems of expense, delay of feedback, and inability to separate sources of effect are compromises that need to be understood and evaluated when using this form of message testing.

Recall Testing

Building on the basic idea that, if an ad is to work, it has to be remembered, the most common method of advertising research is the **recall test**, which aims to see how much, if anything, the viewer of an ad remembers of the message. Recall is used in the testing of print, television and radio, and some supportive communications like billboard advertising.

In television, the basic procedure is to recruit a group of individuals from the target market who will be watching a certain channel during a certain time on a test date. They simply are asked to watch the show. A day after exposure, the testing company phones the individuals, identifies which ones actually saw the ad, and asks those subjects what they can recall. In analyzing the transcribed interview, researchers code responses into various categories representing levels of recall. For radio advertising, recall testing follows similar procedures.

In a typical print recall test, consumers are recruited from the target market and given a magazine containing the ads to be tested. The participants are told that they should look at the magazine and will be telephoned the following day and asked some questions. During the telephone interview, the participants answer questions about ads they remember seeing. The analysis determines the percentage that showed evidence of actually remembering the ad. Other tests go into more detail by actually bringing the ad back to the respondent and asking about various components of the ad, such as the headline and body copy.

Some research indicates there is little relation between recall scores and sales effectiveness.[8]

pilot testing message evaluation that consists of experimentation in the marketplace

split-cable transmission pilot testing of two versions of an advertisement through direct transmission to separate sample households

split-run distribution pilot testing in which different versions of an advertisement are placed in magazines and direct responses to each advertisement are compared

split-list experiments pilot testing in which multiple versions of a direct-mail piece are sent to segments of a mailing list and responses to each version are compared

post-test message tracking assessment of an ad's performance during or after the launch of an ad campaign

recall test test of how much the viewer of an ad remembers of the message

Remembering an ad does not necessarily make you want to buy a particular brand. For example, although the "Got Milk?" ad campaign is hugely popular and widely familiar, milk consumption in the United States continued to decline throughout the campaign.

Recognition Testing

Recognition tests ask subjects whether they remember having seen particular advertisements and whether they can name the company sponsoring each of those ads. For print advertising, the actual advertisement is shown to respondents, and for television advertising, a script with accompanying photos is shown. Recognition is a much easier task than recall because respondents are cued by the very stimulus they are supposed to remember, and they aren't asked to do anything more than say yes or no.

In a typical recognition test, subscribers to a relevant magazine are contacted and asked if an interview can be set up in their home. The readers must have at least glanced at the issue to qualify. The readers are shown each target ad and asked if they remember seeing the ad, if they read or saw enough of the ad to notice the brand name, and if they claim to have read at least 50 percent of the copy. This testing usually is conducted only a few days after the current issue becomes available.

The history of recognition scores is longer than that of any other testing method, so there are normative data on many types of ads. The biggest problem with this test is that of a yeah-saying bias; many people say they recognize an ad that in truth they haven't actually seen. Respondents probably believe they are telling the truth, but marketers whose brands have similar features tend to prepare ads that are astonishingly similar.

Recognition tests suffer from two other problems. First, because direct interviewing is involved, the test is expensive. Second, because respondents are given visual aids, the risk of overestimation threatens the meaningfulness of the collected data.

Awareness and Attitude Tracking

Tracking studies measure the change in an audience's brand awareness and attitude before and after an advertising campaign. This common type of advertising research is almost always conducted as a survey. Members of the target market are surveyed on a fairly regular basis to detect any changes. Any change in awareness or attitude usually is attributed (rightly or wrongly) to the advertising effort.

The problem with this type of test is the inability to isolate the effect of advertising on awareness and attitude amid a myriad of other influences—media reports, observation, friends, competitive advertising, and so forth.

Behavior-Based Measures

Other post-testing tries to get beyond what is in the heads of audience members and see how they respond in the marketplace. The usual assumption in planning these behavior-based post-test measures is that the sole "behavior" to measure is sales. Even though measuring sales often is reasonable, other measures of behavior may be relevant to an advertising campaign's effectiveness. For example, the goal of an ad campaign may be to drive traffic to the firm's website—certainly a meaningful and obtainable behavioral measure of advertising effectiveness. It's a measure that must have given pause to E*Trade after it ran well-liked ads during Super Bowl 2000. In the week following ad exposure, unique visitors to the E*Trade site *fell 5.5 percent.*[9] More positively, the Census Bureau ran an ad campaign with the

CONSUMERS DON'T WATCH NEW TELEVISION COMMERCIALS THE WAY THEY WATCH NEW, EAGERLY AWAITED FEATURE FILMS.

theme "It's Your Future. Don't Leave It Blank" to stem the tide of steadily declining response rates for mailing back census forms. Following the campaign, a 66 percent mail-in rate was an improvement over previous censuses and 5 percentage points higher than the Census Bureau had expected.[10]

So, even though sales may be the most obvious behavioral measure of the effectiveness of advertising, there certainly are other behaviors that would suggest advertising has had an intended effect. Marketers need to be sensitive to behavioral measures other than sales that are related to the effectiveness of advertising.

Practical Limitations

None of the methods for measuring the effectiveness of advertising is perfect. All of them pose challenges to reliability, validity, trustworthiness, and meaningfulness. One reason is that consumers don't watch new television commercials the way they watch new, eagerly awaited feature films, nor do they listen to radio spots the way they listen to a symphony, or read magazine ads as carefully as a Steinbeck novel. Rather, we watch TV while we eat and study, we use radio as a background noise, and we skim through magazines looking for content.[11] Although the traditional methods of advertising evaluation have their strengths, more naturalistic methods—where researchers observe consumers observing advertising—are clearly recommended.

LO 3 Identifying Measures of Effectiveness

Internet Advertising

Unlike advertising in traditional media, Internet ads are evaluated by measuring individuals' Web-surfing activity. The information a website typically gets when a user connects with a site is the Internet Protocol (IP) address identifying the site requesting the page, the IP address for the page requested, and the time of the request. If a registered user signs in at the site, then additional information provided by the user (for example, email address or age) also is identifiable. The challenge with gathering information from registrations is that consumers may be wary of registering because they want to protect their privacy or limit email from marketers.

Common Measurements

Chapter 9 introduced widely used measures of Web audience size and activity:

- *Hits*—the number of times a given element is requested from a given page—provide almost no indication of actual Web traffic. For instance, a user's request for a page containing four graphical images counts as five hits. Thus, by inflating the number of images, a site can pull up its hit count quickly.

- A *click-through*—the number of page elements (hyperlinks) that have been requested—typically is equal to 1 to 2 percent of hits. The click-through number (and percentage) is the best measure of the effectiveness of banner advertising. Clicks on a link in an ad suggest that the ad was viewed and was motivating.

- *Page views*—the pages (actually the number of HTML files) sent to the requesting site—indicate what information was requested but not whether the requester examined the entire page. Also, this measure doesn't reveal the number of visitors: "100,000 page views in a week could be ten people reading 10,000 pages, or 100,000 people reading one page, or any variation in between."[12]

- *Visits*—the number of occasions in which a user interacted with a site in a given time period (say, 30 minutes)—is a rough count of website traffic. If a user interacts with the site at 8:30 p.m., then takes a phone call, and interacts with the site again at 9:45 p.m., this counts as two visits.

- *Unique visitors*—the number of different people visiting a site during a specified time period—is the most reasonable measure of visits to a site. A new user is determined from the user's registration with the site. Besides the address, page, and time, a website can find out the referring link address, which provides insight into which links people are taking to the site. Knowing which links bring people to the site can be helpful in planning online advertising. However, this method identifies visitors by their IP numbers, and many Internet service providers use a dynamic IP number, which is different every time a given user logs in through the service.

Web Measurement Tools

Marketers continue to seek new measurement systems that verify and justify their Web advertising investments. One such tool is **log analysis software**, measurement software that not only provides information on hits, pages, visits, and users, but it also lets a website track audience traffic within the site. A site could determine which pages are popular and expand on them. It also is possible to track the behavior of people as they go through the site, thus providing inferential information on what people find appealing and unappealing. A marketer then can modify the content and structure accordingly, as well as gain a deeper understanding of how buyers make purchase decisions.[13] However, these tools still can't identify what people actually do with website information.

There is no industry standard for measuring the effectiveness of one interactive ad placement over another. There also is no standard for comparing Internet with traditional media placements. Moreover, demographic information on who is using the Web is limited to consumers who have signed up for opt-in programs and, for example, allow targeted emails to be sent to them. Until these limitations are overcome, many marketers will remain hesitant to spend substantial dollars for advertising on the Web.

Nielsen NetRatings and comScore Media Metrix have invoked older technology to develop measures of Web ad effectiveness. They use sampling to draw a representative set of families, install tracking software on the computers of households that agree to participate in a panel, and then use the software to collect data about the households' online activities. These data are projected to the universe of Internet users. The figure that has become the standard is the *reach*, which here represents the percentage of users who visit a site in any one-month period. Of course, this method has some systematic biases, such as undercounting of workplace surfing.

As a measure of Web use, reach is weighted toward the superficial: It favors sprawling sites with vast collections of largely unrelated pages (for instance, About.com) over well-focused sites that collect specific groups of users with shared interests. For marketers, then, the more valuable sites may not be the ones with the largest reach but the ones that attract individuals who are in the marketer's target audience and have a very great interest in the website's subject matter.

Measurement and Payment

Internet marketers pay for ads in several ways, but they all, in one way or another, depend on the measurement of activity related to website visits where banner ads appear. Many pay in terms of impressions, a measure intended to represent the number of times a page with the ad on it is viewed. In reality, impressions are roughly equivalent to hits, which are opportunities to view.

Prices may be stated as flat fees (so many dollars for so many impressions) or as pay-per-click, which in effect is the same as impressions. Others pay a price per click-through. Other advertisers will buy on cost per lead (documented business leads) or cost per actual sale (a rare arrangement).

Direct Marketing

Direct marketing (including e-commerce) is by far the easiest promotional technique to measure for effectiveness. By its very nature, direct marketing is designed to stimulate action. In some cases, the action is a request for information. In many cases, direct-marketing promotions offer an opportunity to place an inquiry or respond directly through a website, reply card, or

With direct marketing, the basic measure of success is the number of the desired responses obtained. How would JCPenney measure the success of this direct-marketing message?

toll-free phone number. An appeal that implores a behavioral response on the part of receivers allows for **inquiry/direct-response measures**. These measures are quite straightforward. Promotions that generate a high number of inquiries, such as orders or website visits, are deemed effective. Additional analyses may compare the number of inquiries or responses with the number of sales generated.

Aside from measuring only the number of inquiries or sales, direct marketing allows for a more refined evaluation. Because these tools primarily are database driven for targeting audiences, the responses similarly can be partitioned with respect to the nature of respondents. That is, marketers can compare one promotional campaign against another based on who responded, what region of the country the responses came from, and how quickly the responses occurred. For example, in telemarketing, various scripts can be tested to see if any one particular message helps phone solicitors exceed the historical average. Marketers can tailor different types of messages to different target markets depending on historical response data.

Finally, the data-rich nature of direct marketing also allows for a profitability analysis of these tools. Because of the fairly direct correlation with sales, a return on investment is quite easily calculated for direct-marketing campaigns.

Sales Promotion and Point of Purchase

The approach to measuring the effectiveness of sales promotion is similar to measuring the effectiveness of advertising. Marketers can evaluate sales promotion through pretesting and post-testing using techniques similar to those used for advertising.

Pretesting Sales Promotion

The options for pretesting sales promotion vary somewhat depending on whether the efforts are aimed at consumers or the trade channel.

Consumer Sales Promotion When a sales promotion is aimed at consumers, marketers pretest it by measuring consumers' perception of the value of a promotion. They test the perceived value of different levels of cents-off coupons, premiums, giveaways, frequency programs, or contests. For example, researchers might ask consumers to compare the perceived value of a 50-cents-off coupon for a brand they never

use versus paying 50 cents more for a brand they have been using regularly and find satisfying. Similarly, they might ask them whether they would consider switching brands to enter a contest or sweepstakes. When it comes to premiums or bonus packs, it's relatively easy to predict a brand-loyal customer's perception of value: more of a preferred brand at less cost. But for a consumer contemplating trial use, getting an additional quantity of an unknown brand may be perceived as a liability because there is the risk the brand will not offer sufficient satisfaction.

Marketers can pretest each of the possibilities by using standard and fairly simple research methods like focus groups or a ballot method. A **ballot method** consists of mailing target consumers a list of promotional options and asking them to rank their preferences; the consumer then mails the ballot back to the firm.

Sales Promotion in the Trade Channel Two issues arise with respect to pretesting sales promotion in the trade channel. First, the effectiveness of consumer-oriented sales promotions is greatly compromised if members of the trade channel are not excited about the promotion and do not support it. If trade partners don't maintain sweepstakes entries, coupons, or premium packs, the effectiveness of a sales promotion effort will be undermined. The best approach for pretesting consumer promotions with the trade channel is to meet with trade channel managers and work out the details of the execution with them.

The second issue in pretesting sales promotion in the channel has to do with trade-oriented sales promotions—that is, promotions directed at the channel members themselves. Here, the techniques used to pretest sales promotions with consumers are valuable as well. A survey of key retail partners, asking what they would perceive as an energizing and high-value promotion, will provide important feedback. Getting a read on the channel's perceptions of value can mean the difference between motivating channel members and creating a program they will totally ignore.

Post-Testing Sales Promotion

Post-testing sales promotion is largely a matter of generating a quantified measure of the performance of a sales promotion device. In the broadest sense, for

inquiry/direct-response measures post-test message tracking in which an advertisement calls for a direct response and the number of responses is counted

ballot method pretest of sales promotion in which consumers are given a list of promotional options and asked to rank their preferences

any sales promotion tool, changes in sales can be used as a measure of effectiveness. Other measures will be suitable for certain promotional tools (see Exhibit 15.1). For example, Nestlé distributed coupon inserts for its Ortega salsa in Sunday papers slated to reach 50 million consumers. A reasonable measure of effectiveness would be tracking the redemption rate of that particular coupon.[14]

In terms of working with trade channel partners, relying on sales measures time period by time period will allow a comparison of the effects of any sales promotion program. And you can be sure that the trade itself is focused on sales as a measure of a promotion's success. When Procter & Gamble introduced the Swiffer sweeper/duster, some retailers resisted carrying the brand because of the high price: $18 for the mop. But one supermarket buyer who had decided against carrying the product because of the high price said he might have to bow to consumer demand if P&G promotions were successful.[15] Some retailers are fairly aggressive at devising sales promotion programs and having ways of measuring their effectiveness.

As program manager for J. Rice Communications in Santa Ana, California, Nicole Del Prato has spent most of her marketing career helping business clients ensure that their trade show marketing supports their entire communications plan. Before each show, questionnaires and surveys are used to benchmark the awareness of each client's target audience. Preshow mailings sent to conference attendees, encouraging them to visit the client's booth, often contain offers that can be redeemed at the trade show, providing a way to track their effectiveness at drawing customers. During the show, in-booth profiling questionnaires and drawings help determine visitor interest levels and planned buying activity. After the show, Del Prato and her staff conduct surveys to see how much actual buying activity resulted from the show.

Point of Purchase

The success of point-of-purchase (P-O-P) materials is measured almost exclusively on the basis of sales effects. Because the context for P-O-P materials offers little opportunity for "message" execution per se, changes in sales are a legitimate and appropriate measure of effectiveness. Also, because this promotional communication takes place at the point of behavior, the display material should play a role in catalyzing a sale.

Sponsorship and Supportive Communications

Sponsorship probably shouldn't even be measured. Sponsoring an event or community activity is meant to enhance the image of a brand and ultimately create a more positive attitude—which, in the long term, may have an effect on sales. But in an era of accountability, managers usually are pressed to come up with some measure of effectiveness for their sponsorship spending. Some simple quantitative measures are available:

- If the sponsorship is an event, the number of people attending the event is easily obtained.

- If the event is televised, the number of viewers of the event gives a proxy measure of exposure to the brand.

Managers at John Hancock Insurance counted the number of times the company logo appeared on the television screen and the number of times the company name was mentioned during the telecast of a sponsored college football game. They then came up with a fairly elaborate model to translate those exposures into the equivalent of advertising dollars.[16]

Several research firms offer services to calculate the effects of sponsorship. Some specialize in performing sales audits in event areas, conduct exit in-

Exhibit 15.1
Measures for Post-Testing Sales Promotion

Type of Promotion	Suitable Measures
Contests and sweepstakes	Changes in sales; number of entries
Coupons	Changes in sales; number of coupons redeemed
Rebates	Changes in sales; number of rebate forms submitted
Trade promotions	Changes in sales

Nicole Del Prato, program manager at J. Rice Communications, a trade show marketing communications firm, helps clients plan how they will communicate their marketing messages to potential customers before, during, and after a trade show. She gathers data to measure brand awareness of her clients' customers before and after a visit to the clients' exhibits, as well as any impact on sales. She uses the results of the measurements to advise her clients about which events and communication media are delivering the most value.

terviews with attendees, and offer economic-impact studies.[17] Others try to identify the impact of an event on the firm's image, and some have tried to calculate the effects on sales—but with fairly strained methodologies.[18]

Testing the effectiveness of supportive communications should rely on recall of the messages that appear in the major support media, including billboards, transit, and aerial ads. A basic approach for testing recall is to conduct a survey before and after a message has run. For example, researchers might make random phone calls in an area and ask, "Who was the 22nd and 24th president of the United States?" Researchers then would place a test message on a billboard or bus board or blimp stating simply, "Grover Cleveland was the 22nd and 24th president of the United States." After the message has run for some designated time— usually two to four weeks—another random sample of households is surveyed. The difference in knowledge then is attributed to recall of the message. Although that may seem to be a simple enough test of effective-

ness, it does have a significant flaw: The message in this example is so strange to passersby that it may be an artificial measure of effectiveness.

There are, however, some supportive communication tools that can be tracked directly for effectiveness. John Deere relies heavily on a wide range of promotional tools to communicate with both its commercial and consumer target audiences. In one recent consumer promotion, the firm mailed videotapes to a select consumer target group. The promotion not only doubled the response rate of previous campaigns (measured by inquiries), but it also was credited with doubling sales—an obviously measurable result.[19]

PR and Corporate Advertising

One attitude about measuring the effects of public relations and corporate advertising is that it really shouldn't even be tried. Because the primary objectives of public relations and corporate advertising are long-term image effects, trying to measure the effect

© 2000 Deloitte Consulting.

The effects of corporate advertising campaigns like this one for Deloitte Consulting are extremely hard to measure. Why?

exposures created by the PR program. Public relations firms often present clients with a "clippings" book showing all the media that carried stories about the company, its employees, its products, or its events. But equating placement with exposure is a tenuous link at best.

Another measure of the effects of either public relations or corporate advertising would be to measure changes in awareness or attitude. This would require original research that measures awareness and attitude before and then after a campaign has been carried out. Of course, it is likely that a firm will be running a wide range of promotional activities along with the PR and corporate campaign. This being the case, it would be almost impossible to separately measure the effects of public relations or corporate advertising from the other elements of the promotional mix.

Given the broad and subtle effects of public relations and corporate advertising, it may be advisable to save the expense of the measurement process and have faith that these are important and useful forms of promotion and are doing their behind-the-scenes job. Should such a perspective meet with resistance from managers, the best recommendation is to carry out pre- and postcampaign attitude and opinion tests and regularly monitor the image of the firm and each brand.

of such programs at any one time seems pointless. For example, just what would you be measuring if you attempted to measure the effectiveness of the Deloitte Consulting campaign featuring the ad shown here? This ad doesn't focus on the features of the service or distinctive characteristics of Deloitte as consulting firm—easy fodder for measurement. Rather, this beautifully creative piece evokes feeling and more than likely will have a positive effect on brand image. But how does it affect brand image? And when? After a week, a month, five years? Just what would the measurement criteria be? Herein lies the problem with measuring the effects of public relations and corporate advertising.

But in an environment where promotional budgets are subject to heavy scrutiny, attempts are made to measure the effects of these types of subtle promotional efforts. One easy measure of the effects of public relations merely is to count the number of media

LO 4 Effectiveness of Personal Selling

Measuring the performance of salespeople draws directly on the objectives set for the personal-selling process and sales objectives discussed in Chapter 14. There are several objective and subjective criteria upon which sales staff members can be judged.[20] Exhibit 15.2 identifies these criteria.

The objective criteria need to be carefully applied. For example, the total dollar volume of sales must be judged against the order size and expenses generated.

Exhibit 15.2
Performance Criteria for Salespeople

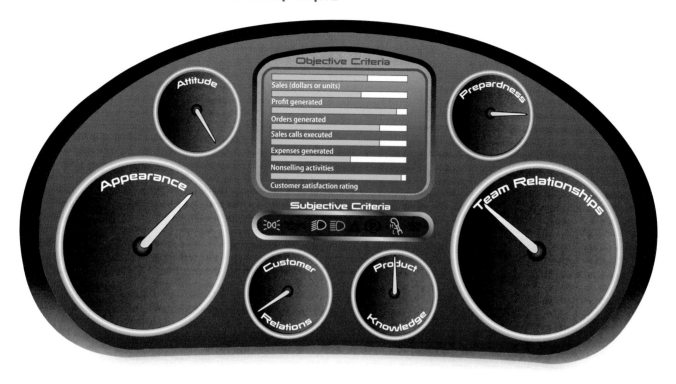

A salesperson or an entire sales force might be rated highly on total dollar volume at the expense of many, repeated small orders at great cost to the firm. Also, depending on the specific objectives and the selling tasks involved, the nonselling tasks may be critical to long-range plans even if they slow short-term growth in sales. Customer satisfaction also is critical. As part of the process of relationship building, quantifiable customer satisfaction criteria can be of value to both management and the salesperson.

Subjective criteria can be difficult to define and measure accurately. Sales managers must be flexible and allow individual styles to manifest themselves. The strength of any particular salesperson may lie in his or her unique style. Suppression of individual differences may be inefficient and demoralizing.

Measuring the effectiveness of sales personnel is important for two reasons. First, salespeople need feedback on which they can base future efforts. An evaluation exercise itself can motivate the sales staff. The evaluation also is the basis on which management will make annual salary and bonus decisions. Second, the measurement of effectiveness is a primary source of information for an internal situation analysis. It helps managers determine strengths and weaknesses in the sales staff, changes that need to be made in the nature of the selling task, and the level of corporate support needed for the sales staff.

LO 5 Effectiveness of the IMC Program

Marketers attempting to measure the effectiveness of the overall IMC program have tried several approaches. One merely is to measure each of the promotional tools used in a campaign, weighing each one independently. This fragmented process makes no attempt to account for the synergies that are the hallmark of IMC in the first place. The purpose of creating and executing an integrated campaign is to enhance the impact of the communication. Logically, then, marketers would want to measure the full impact of that effort. But the limitations of measurement methodologies make that task difficult.

Consider the complexity of measuring the overall effect of IBM's $30 million campaign called "Business Intelligence." The goal was to establish IBM as a leader in developing solutions to gather, analyze, and manage data about a company's customers. The campaign had many dimensions:[21]

- Print ads ran in high-profile publications, including *Business Week* and *Forbes,* to build widespread awareness.

- Print ads also were placed in "vertical market" magazines that specifically targeted decision makers in the banking, retail, and insurance industries.

- Radio ads were run in the top 10 North American markets.

- Television commercials were run during prime-time programs to build awareness.

- Direct-mail pieces were sent to 250,000 executives in three target industries. A week after the initial mailing, an additional 10,000 special mailers were sent to key companies in the targeted industries.

- Public relations initiatives included using IBM employees and local PR agencies to target analysts and industry publications.

- Banner ads were run on approximately 40 websites, including several vertical industry sites and IT-related sites.

This campaign targeted a broad market, a narrow market, executives, IT managers, and more. The methodologies available pale in comparison to IMC campaigns like IBM's.

Despite the methodological challenges, there are some recommendations on how to proceed. One of these is to use **single-source tracking measures**, which identify the extent to which a sample of consumers potentially has been exposed to multiple promotional messages and the effect those messages have had on their behaviors. Researchers create a respondent pool of households with known demographics. They use devices attached to the households' televisions to monitor viewing behavior. Checkout scanners read the universal product codes (UPCs) on product packages and coupons. Data about shoppers' viewing behavior and data about coupon use and brand purchases are combined so that marketers can gauge the impact of brand promotion on consumers' actual purchases.

The main problem with these measures is that it is impossible to determine what aspects of advertising had positive effects on consumers. And although such a system is sophisticated, it really focuses on only two promotional tools: television advertising and couponing. Researchers are developing methods that try to integrate more forms of research in a final assessment. Some of these approaches synthesize tracking data with mall-intercept and consumer survey research.[22]

Another approach is offered by industry practitioners Helen Katz and Jacques Lendrevie.[23] Katz and Lendrevie offer a measurement program that segments total exposures of an integrated program. Their orientation is that, regardless of the promotional tools used in the promotional mix, communication will occur in up to three ways:

THE PURPOSE OF . . . AN INTEGRATED CAMPAIGN IS TO **ENHANCE THE IMPACT** OF THE COMMUNICATION. LOGICALLY, THEN, MARKETERS WOULD WANT TO **MEASURE** THE FULL IMPACT.

1. *Media exposure:* Consumers may be exposed to the brand through traditional media, including advertising in all media, public relations and publicity that appear in mass media, and media exposure from any sales promotion announced through placement in major media (for example, free-standing inserts in the Sunday paper).

2. *Product (brand) impressions:* The target audience receives information and forms impressions based on exposure to the brand itself.[24] This includes in-store and in-home contact with the product, as well as contact with the product on the street, while visiting friends and acquaintances, or in the workplace. Incidental exposure such as passing by a McDonald's and seeing the store sign and logo also would be counted as a brand impression. Although the authors do not mention event sponsorship, personal exposure to a brand message as a result of a sponsorship presumably would be included as well.

3. *Personal contacts:* A variety of personal contacts create brand impressions. Examples include interactions with salespeople at dealerships, conversations with friends, contact with opinion leaders, or the professional advice of a doctor, pharmacist, or hairstylist. These can affect brand knowledge and awareness.

For the evaluation program to be worthwhile, marketers must somehow measure each kind of communication. The developers of this model offer some tenuous and hypothetical approaches to measuring brand impressions and personal contacts.[25]

© Kristian Sekulic/Shutterstock.

Overall, the challenge of measuring the effectiveness of the total IMC effort is extremely difficult. Communication is a complex process that varies across times and places and from individual to individual. Testimony to the difficulty in measuring the effectiveness of the IMC effort is the almost total lack of literature devoted to the discussion.[26] Consider this lack of literature a sign of just how complex and fascinating the topic of integrated marketing communication is and will continue to be.

STUDY TOOLS

CHAPTER 15

Located at back of the textbook

- **Rip out Chapter in Review Card.**

Located at www.cengagebrain.com

- **Review Key Terms Flashcards (Print or Online).**
- **Complete the Practice Quiz to prepare for tests.**
- **Play "Beat the Clock" and "Quizbowl" to master concepts.**
- **Complete "Crossword Puzzle" to review key terms.**
- **Watch videos on Starling, SXSW, and Wolfram Alpha for real company examples.**
- **For additional examples, go online to learn about Internet audience tracking and measuring the effects of IMC programs.**

Endnotes

Chapter 1

1. Jessi Hempel, "The MySpace Generation," *Business Week*, December 15, 2005, 86–94.
2. Robert Levine, "Reaching the Unreachables," *Business 2.0*, October 2005, 109–116.
3. Question of the Week, Ad Infinitum, *Business Week*, November 20, 2006, 18.
4. To see current "Madison and Vine" campaign strategies, go to http://www.adage.com/madisonandvine.
5. Emily Bryson York, "How Heinz Satisfies Moms' Hunger for Comfort Food," *Advertising Age*, September 7, 2009, Business & Company Resource Center, http://galenet.galegroup.com (interview with Brian Hansberry).
6. A special issue of the *Journal of Advertising*, Vol. 34, No. 4, Winter 2005, featuring research and perspectives on IMC; contains several articles that focus on the integrated brand promotion aspects of IMC.
7. John Gaffney, "Most Innovative Campaign," *Business 2.0*, May 2002, 98–99.
8. "2005 Survey of Buying Power," *Sales and Marketing Management*, 2005, 8, 13.
9. Ibid., 17.
10. This definition of marketing was approved in 1995 by the American Marketing Association (http://www.marketingpower.com) and remains the official definition offered by the organization.
11. Peter D. Bennett, *Dictionary of Marketing Terms*, 2nd ed. (Chicago: American Marketing Association, 1995), 4.
12. "Top 100 Global Brands Scoreboard," *Business Week*, August 6, 2007, 59–64.
13. Michael Myser, "Marketing Made Easy," *Business 2.0*, June 2006, 43–45.
14. Alice Z. Cuneo, "Cell Giants Plot $1.5B Ad Bonanza," *Advertising Age*, October 6, 2003, 1, 44.
15. Douglas W. Vorhies, "Brand Extension Helps Parent Gain Influence," *Marketing News*, January 20, 2003, 25. This concept was verified in academic research as well. See Franziska Volckner and Henrik Sattler, "Drivers of Brand Extension Success," *Journal of Marketing* 70, April 2006, 18–34.
16. Stephanie Thompson, "The Bowl Is Where It's at for New Frozen Meal Lines," *Advertising Age*, August 14, 2000, 4.
17. Kevin L. Keller, *Strategic Brand Management: Building, Measuring, and Managing Brand Equity*, Upper Saddle River, NJ: Prentice Hall, 1998, 2.
18. Kevin L. Keller, "Conceptualizing, Measuring, and Managing Customer-Based Brand Equity," *Journal of Marketing*, 57, January 1993, 4.
19. Stephanie Thompson, "Kraft Counters Unilever Launch," *Advertising Age*, August 25, 2003, 4.
20. Franziska Volckner and Henrik Sattler, "Drivers of Brand Extension Success," *Journal of Marketing*, 70, April 2006, 18–34.
21. Peter F. Drucker, *People and Performance: The Best of Peter Drucker*, New York: HarperCollins, 1997, 90.
22. The research study is reported in Robert G. Docters, Michael R. Reopel, Jeanne-Mey Sun, and Stephen M. Tanney, *Winning the Profit Game: Smarter Pricing, Smarter Branding*, New York: McGraw-Hill, 2004; the information on Louis Vuitton was taken from Carol Matlack et al., "The Vuitton Machine," *Business Week*, March 22, 2004, 98–102.
23. U.S. Bureau of the Census, *Statistical Abstract of the United States: 1995*, 115th ed., Washington, D.: U.S. Government Printing Office, 1995; "Got Results?" *Marketing News*, March 2, 1998, 1.
24. For an excellent summary of decades of research on the topic, see Mark S. Abion and Paul W. Farris, *The Advertising Controversy: Evidence of the Economic Effects of Advertising*, Boston: Auburn House, 1981; and J. C. Luik and M. S. Waterson, *Advertising and Markets*, Oxfordshire, England: NTC Publications, 1996.
25. Kerry Capell, "How Philips Got Brand Buzz," *Business Week*, July 31, 2006, accessed at http://www.businessweek.com on August 1, 2006.
26. There are several historical treatments of how advertising is related to demand. See, for example, Neil H. Borden, *The Economic Effects of Advertising* (Chicago: Richard D. Irwin, 1942), 187–189; and John Kenneth Galbraith, *The New Industrial State*, Boston: Houghton Mifflin, 1967, 203–207.
27. This fundamental argument about the effect of advertising on competition was identified and well articulated many years ago by Colston E. Warn, "Advertising: A Critic's View," *Journal of Marketing*, 26(4), October 1962, 12.
28. "100 Leading National Advertisers," *Advertising Age*, June 25, 2007, 5–14.
29. For a historical perspective on culture, consumers, and the meaning of goods, see Ernest Ditcher, *Handbook of Consumer Motivations*, New York: McGraw-Hill, 1964, 6. For a contemporary view, see David Glen Mick and Claus Buhl, "A Meaning-Based Model of Advertising Experiences," *Journal of Consumer Research*, 19 December 1992, 312–338.

Chapter 2

1. Matthew Creamer, "Caught in the Clutter Crossfire: Your Brand," *Advertising Age*, April 2, 2007, 1, 35.
2. Teressa Iezzi, "You Got All the Recognition, but Agencies Did Great Work in 2006," *Advertising Age*, January 15, 2007, 15.
3. Robert D. Hof, "The Power of Us," *Business Week*, June 20, 2005, 74–82.
4. Tom Lowry, "A Whole New View at Hearst," *Business Week*, June 6, 2006, 87–88.
5. Bob Garfield, "The Chaos Scenario 2.0: The Post Advertising Age," *Advertising Age*, March 26, 2007, 1, 12–14.
6. Erick Schonfeld, "Tuning Up Big Media," *Business 2.0*, April 6, 2006, 61–63.
7. Dean Foust and Brian Grow, "Coke: Wooing the TiVo Generation," *Business Week*, March 1, 2004, 77–78.
8. Beth Snyder Bulik, "Ad Dollars Flow into Online Games," *Advertising Age*, March 26, 2007, 10.
9. Jon Fine, "Now, an Ad from Our Network," *Business Week*, November 27, 2006, 26.
10. Tom Lowry, "The Dilemma Vexing Big Media," *Business Week*, July 3, 2006, 94–98.
11. Catherine Holahan, "Advertising Goes Off the Radio," *Business Week*, December 7, 2006 (accessed at http://www.businessweek.com on December 7, 2006).
12. Peter Henderson, "Internet Ad Growth Pressures TV to Change," *Reuters*, December 2, 2005 (accessed at http://www.news.yahoo.com on December 2, 2005).
13. Matthew Creamer, "Stars Align for Big Bang, the Sequel," *Advertising Age*, December 4, 2006, 1, 37.
14. Hillary Chura, "Marketers: One-Stop Shops Could Compromise Creative," *Advertising Age*, June 16, 2003, 6.
15. David Ho, "FCC Votes to Ease Media Ownership Rules," *Washington Post*, available at http://news.yahoo.com, accessed on June 2, 2003.
16. Nat Ives, "Special Report: More Than Magazines," *Advertising Age*, March 12, 2007, S1–S6.
17. Matthew Boyle, "Brand Killers," *Fortune*, April 11, 2003, 89–100.
18. Betsy Spethmann, "Pre-Game Warmups," *Promo*, December 2000, 33–34; Bruce Horovitz, "Gee-Whiz Effects Make Super Bowl Ads Super Special," *USA Today*, January 30, 2004, B1–B2.
19. Jack Neff, "J&J Jolts 'Old Media' with $250M Spend Shift," *Advertising Age*, March 19, 2007, 1, 29.
20. Betsy Streisand, "Why Great American Brands Are Doing Lunch," *Business 2.0*, September 2003, 146–150.

21. David Kiley, "Learning to Love the Dreaded TiVo," *Business Week*, April 17, 2006, 88.

22. Ibid.

23. Lev Grossman, "Invention of the Year," *Time*, November 13, 2006, 61–65.

24. Tom Lowry and Robert D. Hof, "Smart Move or Silly Money 2.0?" *Business Week*, October 23, 2006, 34–37; Maggie Rauch, "Virtual Reality," *Sales & Marketing Management*, January/February 2007, 18–23.

25. "100 Leading National Advertisers," *Advertising Age*, June 25, 2007, S-4.

26. Ibid.

27. Bradley Johnson, "Top 100 Spending Up 3.1% to $105 Billion," *Advertising Age*, June 25, 2007, S-2.

28. The 2006 ranking for the U.S. government was 29th at $1.13 billion annual spending on advertising. "100 Leading National Advertisers," *Advertising Age*, June 25, 2007, S-4.

29. Bob Garfield, "Army Ad Strong—If You Totally Forget We're at War," *Advertising Age*, November 13, 2006, 57.

30. "63rd Annual Agency Report," *Advertising Age*, April 30, 2007, S-4.

31. Bradley Johnson, "Diller Leads Top Execs in 2005 Pay," *Advertising Age*, December 4, 2006, S-2.

32. David Kiley, "The Craziest Ad Guys in America," *Business Week*, May 22, 2006, 72–80.

33. Hillary Chura and Kate MacArthur, "Cramer-Krasselt Thinks Small," *Advertising Age*, September 11, 2000, 32.

34. Martin Sorell, "Agencies Face New Battle Grounds," *Advertising Age*, April 13, 1998, 22.

35. Jonah Bloom, "Zimmerman's Virtual Agency Marks the Rise of Machines," *Advertising Age*, January 15, 2007, 15.

36. Jack Neff, "P&G Boosts Design's Role in Marketing," *Advertising Age*, February 9, 2004, 1, 52.

37. Betsy Streisand, "Why Great American Brands Are Doing Lunch," *Business 2.0*, September 2003, 146–150.

38. Jon Steel, *Truth, Lies & Advertising: The Art of Account Planning*, New York: John Wiley & Sons, 1998, 42.

39. Tobi Elkin, "Motorola Tenders Brand Challenge," *Advertising Age*, August 14, 2000, 14.

40. Allen Winneker, "Avoiding Bonus Envy," *Promo*, November 1999, 35–37.

41. Patricia Sellers, "Do You Need Your Ad Agency?" *Fortune*, November 15, 1993, 148.

42. Lisa Sanders and Alice Z. Cuneo, "Fed-Up Agencies Quit Punching the Clock," *Advertising Age*, January 27, 2007.

43. Matthew Creamer, "March of the Management Consultants," *Advertising Age*, June 5, 2006, 1, 53.

44. Clair Atkinson, "AOL Sees Future in Ad Networks," *Advertising Age*, December 11, 2006, 4.

Chapter 3

1. Julian Simon, *Issues in the Economics of Advertising* (Urbana: University of Illinois Press, 1970), 41–51.

2. Vincent P. Norris, "Advertising History— According to the Textbooks," *Journal of Advertising* 9(3) (1980): 3–12.

3. James W. Carey, *Communication as Culture: Essays on Media and Society* (Winchester, MA: Unwin Hyman, 1989).

4. Christopher P. Wilson, "The Rhetoric of Consumption: Mass-Market Magazines and the Demise of the Gentle Reader, 1880–1920," in *The Culture of Consumption: Critical Essays in American History, 1880–1980*, ed. Richard Weightman Fox and T. J. Jackson Lears (New York: Pantheon, 1983), 39–65.

5. Frank Presbrey, *The History and Development of Advertising* (Garden City, NY: Doubleday, Doran & Co., 1929), 7.

6. Ibid., 11.

7. Ibid., 40.

8. James P. Wood, *The Story of Advertising* (New York: Ronald, 1958), 45–46.

9. Daniel Pope, *The Making of Modern Advertising and Its Creators* (New York: William Morrow, 1984), 14.

10. Cited in Stephen Fox, *The Mirror Makers: A History of American Advertising and Its Creators* (New York: William Morrow, 1984), 14.

11. Ibid., 14.

12. Presbrey, *The History and Development of Advertising*, 16.

13. Bruce Barton, *The Man Nobody Knows* (New York: Bobbs-Merrill, 1924).

14. James Lincoln Collier, *The Rise of Selfishness in America* (New York: Oxford University Press, 1991), 162.

15. Ibid., 303–304.

16. Fox, *The Mirror Makers*, 168.

17. Mark Pendergrast, *For God, Country & Coca-Cola: The Definitive History of the Great American Soft Drink and the Company That Makes It* (New York: Basic Books, 2003).

18. Wini Breines, *Young, White and Miserable: Growing Up Female in the Fifties* (Boston: Beacon, 1992).

19. Vance Packard, *The Hidden Persuaders* (New York: D. McKay, 1957). With respect to the effects of "subliminal advertising," researchers have shown that, while subliminal communication is possible, subliminal persuasion, in the typical real-world environment, remains all but impossible. As it was discussed, as mind control, in the 1950s, it remains a joke. See Timothy E. Moore, "Subliminal Advertising: What You See Is What You Get," *Journal of Marketing* 46 (Spring 1982), 38–47.

20. Stuart Rogers, "How a Publicity Blitz Created the Myth of Subliminal Advertising," *Public Relations Quarterly* (Winter 1992–1993), 12–17.

21. Fox, *The Mirror Makers*, 218.

22. Thomas Frank, *The Conquest of Cool: Business Culture, Counterculture, and the Rise of Hip Consumerism* (Chicago: University of Chicago Press, 1997).

23. Ibid., 235.

24. Tom Engelhardt, "The Shortcake Strategy," in *Watching Television*, ed. Todd Gitlin (New York: Pantheon, 1986), 68–110.

25. Marty Westerman, "Death of the Frito Bandito," *American Demographics*, March 1989, Business & Company Resource Center, http://galenet.galegroup.com.

26. Collier, *The Rise of Selfishness in America*, 230.

27. This quote and information from this section can be found in Steve Yahn, "Advertising's Grave New World," *Advertising Age*, May 16, 1994, 53.

28. Kevin Goodman, "Sprint Chief Lectures Agencies on Future," *Wall Street Journal*, April 28, 1995, B6.

29. Stuart Elliot, "Procter and Gamble Calls Internet Marketing Executives to Cincinnati for a Summit Meeting," *New York Times*, August 19, 1998, D3; available at http://www.nytimes.com.

30. Frank Ahrens, "$2 Million Airtime, $13 Ad," *Washington Post*, January 31, 2007, D1.

31. Beth Snyder Bulik, "Procter & Gamble's Great Web Experiment," *Business 2.0*, November 28, 2000, 48–54.

32. Claire Atkinson, "Ad Distraction Up, Say Consumers," *Advertising Age*, January 6, 2003, 19.

33. "100 Leading National Advertisers," *Advertising Age*, June 28, 2004, S4.

Chapter 4

1. Christie L. Nordhielm, *Marketing Management: The Big Picture* (Hoboken, NJ: John Wiley & Sons, Inc. 2006).

2. For more on STP marketing, see Philip Kotler, *Marketing Management* (Upper Saddle River, NJ: Prentice Hall, 2003), Chs. 10, 11.

3. Nina Munk, "Why Women Find Lauder Mesmerizing," *Fortune*, May 25, 1998, 96–106.

4. See, for example, Stephanie Thompson, "Gager Mixes Art, Commerce to Boost M.A.C. Sales, Image," *Advertising Age*, April 12, 2004, 60.

5. Steve Hughes, "Small Segments, Big Payoff," *Advertising Age*, January 15, 2007, 17.

6. Deborah Ball, "Toll-Free Tips: Nestle Hotlines Yield Big Ideas," *Wall Street Journal*, September 3, 2004, A7.

7. This four-way scheme is detailed in David W. Stewart, "Advertising in Slow-Growth Economies," *American Demographics* (September 1994), 40–46.

8. Allanna Sullivan, "Mobil Bets Drivers Pick Cappuccino over Low Prices," *Wall Street Journal*, January 30, 1995, B1.

9. Sally Beatty, "Nickelodeon Sets $30 Million Ad Deal with the Bahamas," *Wall Street Journal*, March 14, 2001, B6.

10. Kelly Greene, "Marketing Surprise: Older Consumers Buy Stuff, Too," *Wall Street Journal*, April 6, 2004, A1, A12.

11. Amy Merrick, "Counting on the Census," *Wall Street Journal*, February 14, 2001, B1.

12. Michael R. Solomon, *Consumer Behavior* (Upper Saddle River, NJ: Pearson Prentice Hall, 2007), 215–219.

13. Rebecca Piirto, *Beyond Mind Games: The Marketing Power of Psychographics* (Ithaca, NY: American Demographics Books, 1991), 222–223.

14. Ibid.; see Chs. 3, 5, and 8 for an extensive discussion of the VALS system.

15. Kotler, *Marketing Management*, 296–298.

16. Thomas S. Robertson and Howard Barich, "A Successful Approach to Segmenting Industrial Markets," *Planning Forum* (Nov/Dec 1992), 5–11.

17. Kotler, *Marketing Management*, 280–281.

18. Timothy Aeppel, "For Parker Hannifin, Cable Is Best," *Wall Street Journal*, August 7, 2003, B3.

19. Scott McCartney, "Profit for Southwest Air Is Industry Rarity," *Wall Street Journal*, October 18, 2002, B4.

20. Darren Garnick, "The Working Stiff: There Really Is a 'Verizon Guy,'" *Boston Herald*, October 29, 2008, Business & Company Resource Center, http://galenet.galegroup.com; and Richard Mullins, "Goodbye Chad, Hello Verizon Test Guy," *Tampa Tribune*, January 8, 2009, Business & Company Resource Center, http://galenet.galegroup.com.

21. A more elaborate case for the importance of a single, consistent positioning premise is provided in Ries and Trout's classic, *Positioning: The Battle for Your Mind* (New York: Warner Books, 1982).

22. Other positioning options are discussed in Philip Kotler and Kevin Lane Keller, *A Framework for Marketing Management* (Upper Saddle River, NJ: Pearson Prentice Hall, 2007), Ch. 9.

23. Geoffrey Smith and Ron Stodghill, "Are Good Causes Good Marketing?" *BusinessWeek*, March 21, 1994, 64–65.

24. Stephanie Thompson, "Good Humor's Good Deeds," *Advertising Age*, January 8, 2001, 6.

25. Albert M. Muniz Jr. and Thomas C. O'Guinn, "Brand Community," *Journal of Consumer Research* 27 (2001), 412–432.

26. Vanessa O'Connell and Joe White, "After Decades of Brand Bodywork, GM Parks Oldsmobile—for Good," *Wall Street Journal*, December 13, 2000, B1, B4. 27. Jean Halliday, "Mazda Repositioning Begins to Show Results," *Advertising Age*, January 6, 2003, 4.

28. This definition is adapted from David Aaker, *Building Strong Brands* (New York: Free Press, 1996), Ch. 3.

29. These examples are adapted from Aaker, *Building Strong Brands*, Ch. 3.

30. Esther Thorson and Jeri Moore, *Integrated Communication: Synergy of Persuasive Voices* (Mahwah, NJ: Erlbaum, 1996).

Chapter 5

1. Martin Davidson, "Objects of Desire: How Advertising Works," in Martin Davidson, *The Consumerist Manifesto: Advertising in Postmodern Times*, London: Routledge, 1992, 23–60.

2. Kate MacArthur, "Marriage of Convenience: 7-Eleven, 'Simpsons,'" *Advertising Age*, July 16, 2007.

3. Terry G. Vavra, *Aftermarketing: How to Keep Customers for Life through Relationship Marketing*, Homewood, IL: Business One Irwin, 1992, 13.

4. Michael R. Solomon, *Consumer Behavior*, Upper Saddle River, NJ: Prentice Hall, 2004, Ch. 4.

5. Shirley Leung, "Fast-Food Firms' Big Budgets Don't Buy Consumer Loyalty," *Wall Street Journal*, July 24, 2003, B4.

6. Icek Ajzen and Martin Fishbein, *Understanding Attitudes and Predicting Social Behavior*, Englewood Cliffs, NJ: Prentice Hall, 1980, 63.

7. Clutter creates a variety of problems that compromise the effectiveness of advertising. For instance, research has shown that clutter interferes with basic memory functions, inhibiting a person's ability to keep straight which brands are making what claims. For more details, see Anand Kumar and Shanker Krishnan, "Memory Interference in Advertis-

ing: A Replication and Extension," *Journal of Consumer Research*, 30, March 2004, 602–612.

8. Joel Schwarz, "Bugs at Disney? Not on Your Life, Doc," *University Week* (University of Washington), July 5, 2001, http://depts.washington.edu/uweek/archives/2001.07.JUL_05/_article5.html; Kathryn A. Braun-LaTour, Michael S. LaTour, Jacqueline E. Pickrell, and Elizabeth F. Loftus, "How and When Advertising Can Influence Memory for Consumer Experience," *Journal of Advertising*, 33, Winter 2004, 7–25.

9. For an expanded discussion of these issues, see Richard E. Petty, John T. Cacioppo, Alan J. Strathman, and Joseph R. Priester, "To Think or Not to Think: Exploring Two Routes to Persuasion," in *Persuasion: Psychological Insights and Perspectives,* eds. Sharon Shavitt and Timothy C. Brock, Boston: Allyn & Bacon, 1994, 113–147.

10. For additional discussion of this issue, see Frances K. McSweeney and Calvin Bierley, "Recent Developments in Classical Conditioning," *Journal of Consumer Research,* 11, September 1984, 619–631.

11. Associations like Jay-Z with Heineken, Missy Elliott with Gap, and Queen Latifah with Cover Girl illustrate the influence of Russell Simmons in bringing hip-hop into the advertising mainstream. (See "The CEO of Hip Hop," *BusinessWeek,* October 27, 2003, 91–98.) It is fair to say that Simmons found great success by lining up hip-hop icons as peripheral cues for all sorts of big-name advertisers.

12. The rationale for cultivating brand interest for mature brands is discussed more fully in Karen A. Machleit, Chris T. Allen, and Thomas J. Madden, "The Mature Brand and Brand Interest: An Alternative Consequence of Ad-Evoked Affect," *Journal of Marketing,* 57, October 1993, 72–82.

13. Davidson, "Objects of Desire."

14. Gordon Marshall, ed., *The Concise Oxford Dictionary of Sociology,* New York: Oxford University Press, 1994, 104–105.

15. Ibid., 452.

16. Melanie Wallendorf and Eric J. Arnould, "We Gather Together: Consumption Rituals of Thanksgiving Day," *Journal of Consumer Research*, 18, no. 1, June 1991, 13–31.

17. For a great review, see Cele C. Otnes and Tina M. Lowrey, eds., *Contemporary Consumption Rituals: A Research Anthology*, Mahwah, NJ: Lawrence Erlbraun, 2004.

18. Alvin W. Gouldner, "The Future of Intellectuals and the Rise of the New Class," in *Social Stratification in Sociological Perspective: Class, Race, and Gender,* ed. David B. Grusky, San Francisco: Westview Press, 1994, 711–729.

19. John Seabrook, "Sunday in Soho," in *Nobrow: The Culture of Marketing—The Marketing of Culture*, New York: Knopf, 2000, 161–175, available at http://www.booknoise.net/johnseabrook/stories/culture/nobrow/index.html. See also Jennifer Steinhauer, "When the Joneses Wear Jeans: Signs of Status Are Harder to Spot, but Look Again," in *Class Matters,* ed. Correspondents of the *New York Times,* New York: Times Books, 2005, 134–145.

20. C. Whan Park, "Joint Decisions in Home Purchasing: A Muddling-Through Process,"

Journal of Consumer Research, 9, September 1982, 151–162.

21. Jannette L. Dates, "Advertising," in *Split Image: African Americans in the Mass Media,* ed. Jannette L. Dates and William Barlow, Washington, DC: Howard University Press, 1990, 421–454.

22. Roland Marchand, *Advertising: The American Dream,* Berkeley: University of California Press, 1984, 25.

23. Laura Koss-Feder, "Out and About: Firms Introduce Gay-Specific Ads for Mainstream Products, Services," *Marketing News,* May 25, 1998, 1, 20.

24. Wally Snyder, "Advertising's Ethical and Economic Imperative," *American Advertising,* Fall 1992, 28.

25. Albert Muniz Jr. and Thomas O'Guinn, "Brand Community," *Journal of Consumer Research,* 27, 2001, 412–432.

26. Mark Weingarten, "Designed to Grow," *Business 2.0,* June 2007, p. 35; Rob Walker, "Consumed: Mass Appeal," *New York Times Magazine,* July 8, 2007, p. 16.

27. Davidson, "Objects of Desire."

Chapter 6

1. Teena Massingill, "Buyer Beware: Retailers Sharing Data," Knight Ridder News Service, September 17, 1999.

2. Jack Neff, "Spam Research Reveals Disgust with Pop-Up Ads," *Advertising Age,* August 23, 2003, 1, 21.

3. Erika Rasmusson, "What Price Knowledge?" *Sales and Marketing Management,* December 1998, 56.

4. Stephen Baker, "Where Danger Lurks," *BusinessWeek,* August 25, 2003, 114–118.

5. George J. Stigler, "The Economics of Information," *Journal of Political Economy,* June 1961, 213–220.

6. Anheuser-Busch, "Responsibility Matters," corporate social responsibility Web page, http://www.beeresponsible.com, accessed May 26, 2007.

7. Clair Atkinson, "Ad Intrusion Up, Say Consumers," *Advertising Age,* January 6, 2003, 1, 19.

8. Hank Kim, "Just Risk It," *Advertising Age,* February 9, 2004, 1, 51.

9. Matthew Creamer, "Caught in the Clutter Crossfire: Your Brand," *Advertising Age,* April 2, 2007, 1, 35.

10. Ibid., 35.

11. Richard Caves, *American Industry: Structure, Conduct, Performance,* Englewood Cliffs, NJ: Prentice-Hall, 1964, 102.

12. A. H. Maslow, *Motivation and Personality,* New York: Harper & Row, 1970.

13. Vance Packard, *The Status Seekers,* New York: David McKay, 1959.

14. This argument was first offered by authors George Katona, *The Mass Consumption Society,* New York: McGraw-Hill, 1964, 54–61; and John Kenneth Galbraith, *The Affluent Society,* Boston: Houghton Mifflin, 1958.

15. Fox, *The Mirror Makers: A History of American Advertising and Its Creators,* New York: William Morrow, 1984, 330.

16. Normandy Madden, "Honda Pulls Suicide Car Ad from Australian TV Market," *Advertising Age,* September 22, 2003, 3.

17. Kevin Goldman, "From Witches to Anorexics, Critical Eyes Scrutinize Ads for Political Correctness," *Wall Street Journal,* May 19, 1994, B1, B10.

18. Georgia Flight, "Hits and Misses," *Business 2.0,* April 2006, 140.

19. Don E. Schultz, "Subliminal Ad Notions Still Resonate Today," *Marketing News,* March 15, 2007, 5, 9.

20. Murphy, Monahan, and Zajonc, "Additivity of Nonconscious Affect: Combined Effects of Priming and Exposure," *Journal of Personality and Social Psychology,* 69, 1995, 589–602.

21. Timothy E. Moore, "Subliminal Advertising: What You See Is What You Get," *Journal of Marketing,* 46, Spring 1982, 38–47; Timothy E. Moore, "The Case against Subliminal Manipulation," *Psychology and Marketing,* 5, no. 4, Winter 1988, 297–317.

22. Andy Warhol, *The Philosophy of Andy Warhol: From A to B and Back Again,* New York: Harcourt Brace Jovanovich, 1975, 101.

23. "100 Leading National Advertisers," *Advertising Age,* June 25, 2007, S1.

24. B. G. Gregg, "Tax Funds Bankroll New Anti-Drug Ads," *Cincinnati Enquirer,* July 10, 1998, A1, A17.

25. Jay Reeves, "Scrushy Said to Pay for Positive Stories," *Associated Press,* January 19, 2006, accessed at www.news.yahoo.com on January 20, 2006.

26. Eamon Javers, "This Opinion Brought to You by . . . ," *BusinessWeek,* January 30, 2006, 35.

27. Claire Atkinson, "Watchdog Group Hits TV Product Placement," *Advertising Age,* October 6, 2003, 12.

28. Richard Linnett, "Psychologists Protest Kids' Ads," *Advertising Age,* September 11, 2000, 4.

29. Patrick J. Sheridan, "FCC Sets Children's Ad Limits," *1990 Information Access Company,* 119, No. 20, 1990, 33.

30. Laura Bird, "NBC Special Is One Long Prime-Time Ad," *Wall Street Journal,* January 21, 1994, B1, B4.

31. Stephanie Thompson and Ira Teinowitz, "Big Food's Big Deal Not Such a Big Concession," *Advertising Age,* November 20, 2006, 1, 29.

32. Kathleen Deveny, "Joe Camel Ads Reach Children, Research Finds," *Wall Street Journal,* December 11, 1991, B1, B6.

33. See, for example, Joseph R. DiFranza et al., "RJR Nabisco's Cartoon Camel Promotes Camel Cigarettes to Children," *Journal of the American Medical Association,* 266, No. 22, 1991, 3168–3153.

34. For a summary of more than 60 articles that address the issue of alcohol and cigarette advertising and the lack of a relationship between advertising and cigarette and alcohol industry demand, see Mark Frankena et al., "Alcohol, Consumption, and Abuse," Bureau of Economics, Federal Trade Commission, March 5, 1985. For a similar listing of research articles where the same conclusions were drawn during congressional hearings on the topic, see "Advertising of Tobacco Products," hearings before the Subcommittee on Health and the Environment, Committee on Energy and Commerce, and House of Representatives, 99th Congress, July 18 and August 1, 1986, No. 99–167.

35. For examples of the more recent studies that reaffirm peers and family rather than advertis- ing as the basis for smoking initiation see Charles R. Taylor and P. Greg Bonner, "Comment on 'American Media and the Smoking-Related Behaviors of Asian Adolescents,'" *Journal of Advertising Research,* December 2003, 419–430; Bruce Simons Morton, "Peer and Parent Influences on Smoking and Drinking among Early Adolescents," *Journal of Health Education and Behavior* (February 2000); and Karen H. Smith and Mary Ann Stutz, "Factors That Influence Adolescents to Smoke," *Journal of Consumer Affairs,* 33, No. 2, Winter 1999, 321–357.

36. With regard to cartoon characters, see, for example, Lucy L. Henke, "Young Children's Perceptions of Cigarette Brand Advertising: Awareness, Affect and Target Market Identi- fication," *Journal of Advertising,* 24, No. 4, Winter 1995, 13–27; and Richard Mizerski, "The Relationship between Cartoon Trade Character Recognition and Attitude toward the Product Category," *Journal of Market- ing,* 59, October 1995, 58–70. The evidence in Europe is provided by Jeffrey Goldstein, "Children and Advertising—the Research," *Commercial Communications,* July 1998, 4–8.

37. For research on this topic across several de- cades, see Richard Schmalensee, *The Econom- ics of Advertising,* Amsterdam and London: North-Holland, 1972; Mark S. Albion and Paul W. Farris, *The Advertising Controversy,* Boston: Auburn House, 1981; and Michael J. Waterson, "Advertising and Tobacco Con- sumption: An Analysis of the Two Major Aspects of the Debate," *International Journal of Advertising,* 9, 1990, 59–72.

38. Ira Singer et al., "The Underground Web," *BusinessWeek,* September 2, 2002, 67–74.

39. Bloomberg News, "Frank Eyes Restoring Web Gaming," *Boston Globe,* March 17, 2007, accessed at www.boston.com/news.

40. Mercedes M. Cardona, "Marketers Bite Back as Fat Fight Flares Up," *Advertising Age,* March 1, 2004, 3, 35.

41. Rep. Ric Keller (R-Fla.), quoted in Joanne Kenen, "U.S. House Backs Ban on Obe- sity Lawsuits," *Yahoo Finance,* March 10, 2004, http://biz.yahoo.com/rc/040310/ congress_obesity_3.html.

42. Stephanie Thompson and Kate MacArthur, "Obesity Fear Frenzy Grips Food Industry," *Advertising Age,* April 23, 2007, 1, 46.

43. One of the best discussions of the FTC's definition of deception was offered many years ago by Gary T. Ford and John E. Calfee, "Recent Developments in FTC Policy on De- ception," *Journal of Marketing,* 50, July 1986, 82–103.

44. Ivan Preston, *The Great American Blow Up,* Madison: University of Wisconsin Press, 1975, 4.

45. Christy Fisher, "How Congress Broke Unfair Ad Impasse," *Advertising Age,* August 22, 1994, 34. For additional discussion of the FTC's definition of unfairness see Ivan Preston, "Unfairness Developments in FTC Advertising Cases," *Journal of Public Policy and Marketing,* 14, No. 2, 1995, 318–321.

46. Daniel Golden and Suzanne Vranica, "Dura- cell's Duck Will Carry Disclaimer," *Wall Street Journal,* February 7, 2002, B2.

47. "Children Not Seeing More Food Ads on Television," *Federal Trade Commission Re- port,* June 1, 2007, accessed at http://www.ftc .gov on June 4, 2007.

48. The full text and specifications of the Chil- dren's Online Privacy Protection Act can be found at http://www.ftc.gov/ogc/coppa1.htm.

49. For a discussion of the origins and intent of the FTC's advertising substantiation program and its extension to require reasonable basis, see Debra L. Scammon and Richard J. Semenik, "The FTC's 'Reasonable Basis' for Substantiation of Advertising: Expanded Standards and Implications," *Journal of Advertising,* 12(1), 1983, 4–11.

50. The history and intent of the corrective-advertising concept and several of its applica- tions are provided by Debra L. Scammon and Richard J. Semenik, "Corrective Advertising: Evolution of the Legal Theory and Applica- tion of the Remedy," *Journal of Advertising,* 11(1), 1982, 10–20.

51. Steven W. Colford and Raymond Serafin, "Scali Pays for Volvo Ad: FTC," *Advertising Age,* August 26, 1991, 4.

52. Neal Boudette, "Internet Self-Regulation Seen Lacking Punch," *Yahoo Finance,* September 14, 1999, http://biz.yahoo.com.

53. "Upstaged Advertisers Riled by Bowl Stunt," *Advertising Age* (*Advertising Age* Roundup), February 9, 2004, 1.

54. This statement of purpose can be found inside the cover of any issue of *Consumer Reports.*

55. Marcia Stepanek, "Protecting E-Privacy: Washington Must Step In," *BusinessWeek E.Biz,* July 26, 1999, EB30; and Michael Krauss, "Get a Handle on the Privacy Wild Card," *Marketing News,* February 28, 2000, 12.

56. G. Beato, "Big Data's Big Business," *Business 2.0,* February 2001, 62.

57. Peter Kaplan, "FTC Wants More Data on Google-DoubleClick Deal" *Reuters News Service,* May 29, 2007, http://www.reuters. com.

58. "Image Spam: The E-Mail Epidemic of 2006," *Security Trends Overview,* Special Report, IronPort Systems, Inc., September 2006.

59. "Senate Approves Antispam Bill," *Reuters News Service,* October 22, 2003, http://news. reuters.com.

60. Elaine Porterfield, "First Arrest under Spam Law Could Dent E-Mail Flood," *Reuters News Service,* May 31, 2007.

61. Ira Teinowitz, "Congress Nears Accord on Sweepstakes Limits," *Advertising Age,* August 9, 1999, 33.

62. James Heckman, "Online, but Not on Trial, though Privacy Looms Large," *Marketing News,* December 6, 1999, 8.

63. Jack Neff, "Package-Goods Players Just Can't Quit Coupons," *Advertising Age,* May 14, 2007, 8.

64. Melissa Allison, "Starbucks Coupon Gets out of Hand," *Seattle Times,* August 31, 2006, available at http://archives.seattletimes. nwsource.com/web.

65. Ibid.

66. Lorraine Woellert, "The Do-Not-Call Law Won't Stop the Calls," *BusinessWeek,* September 29, 2003, 89.

67. Atkinson, "Watchdog Group Hits TV Product Placement," 12.

68. Rich Thomaselli, "Philip Morris: No Smoking in Movies," *Advertising Age,* November 20, 2006, 3, 27.

Chapter 7

1. Monee Fields-White, "Expanding Her Turf," *Crain's Chicago Business,* October 19, 2009, Business & Company Resource Center, http://galenet.galegroup.com.
2. "Global Marketers: Top 10 Global Marketers by Country," *Advertising Age,* December 8, 2008.
3. Matthew Karnitschnig, "Comedy Central Export Aims for Local Laughs," *Wall Street Journal,* March 2, 2007, B1.
4. Gregory Fowler, "Mac and PC's Overseas Adventures," *Wall Street Journal,* March 1, 2007, B1.
5. Antonio Regalado, "Marketers Pursue the Shallow-Pocketed," *Wall Street Journal,* January 26, 2007, B3.
6. Clay Chandler, "Changing Places," *Fortune,* September 18, 2006, 61–64.
7. Gautam Naik, "Leveraging the Age Gap," *Wall Street Journal,* February 27, 2003, B1, B4.
8. Johny Johansson, "The Sense of Nonsense: Japanese TV Advertising," *Journal of Advertising,* March 1994, 17–26.
9. S. Han and S. Shavitt, "Persuasion and Culture: Advertising Appeals in Individualistic and Collectivistic Societies," *Journal of Experimental Social Psychology,* 30, 1994: 326–350.
10. Spencer Ante, "The Science of Desire," *BusinessWeek,* June 5, 2006, 98–106.
11. Louise Lee, "Depicting Men Doing Housework Can Be Risky for Marketers in Asia," *Wall Street Journal,* August 14, 1998, B6.
12. Robert Kirby, "Kirby: Advertising Translates into Laughs," *Salt Lake Tribune,* http://www.sltrib.com, accessed February 24, 1998.
13. Charles Goldsmith, "MTV Seeks Global Appeal," *Wall Street Journal,* July 21, 2003, B1, B3.
14. STAR website, http://www.startv.com, accessed April 6, 2007.
15. Nandini Lakshman, "The Great Indian Beer Rush," *BusinessWeek,* April 23, 2007, 50.
16. David Scheer, "Europe's New High-Tech Role: Playing Privacy Cop to the World," *Wall Street Journal,* October 10, 2003, A1, A16.
17. Normandy Madden, "Culture Clash Thwarts Shops from Enjoying China's Boom," *Advertising Age,* May 3, 2004, 20.
18. For contrasting points of view, compare Douglas B. Holt, John A. Quelch, and Earl L. Taylor, "How Global Brands Compete," *Harvard Business Review,* September 2004, 68–75; with Darrell K. Rigby and Vijay Vishwanath, "Localization: The Revolution in Consumer Markets," *Harvard Business Review,* April 2006, 82–92.
19. Arundhati Parmar, "Global Youth United," *Marketing News,* October 28, 2002, 1, 49.
20. Lisa Bannon, "One-Toy-Fits-All: How Industry Learned to Love the Global Kid," *Wall Street Journal,* April 29, 2003, A1, A12.
21. Michael Fielding, "Walk the Line," *Marketing News,* September 1, 2006, 8–10.

Chapter 8

1. Carl G. Jung, cited in Astrid Fitzgerald, *An Artist's Book of Inspiration: A Collection of Thoughts on Art, Artists, and Creativity,* New York: Lindisfarne, 1996, 58.
2. Warren Berger, "Dare-Devils," *Business 2.0,* April 2004, 111–116.
3. Matthew Creamer, "Crispin Ups Ante," *Advertising Age,* January 10, 2005, S-1, S-2.
4. Ibid.
5. Eloy Trevino and Scott Davis, "There's Nothing New in Desperate Marketing," *Advertising Age,* April 23, 2007, 22.
6. Kate MacArthur, "BK Sets High Score with Its Adver-games," *Advertising Age,* January 8, 2007, 3, 31.
7. Jonah Bloom, "Savaging Crispin May Be Fun, but the Agency Is Not the Enemy," *Advertising Age,* January 29, 2007, 11.
8. Matthew Creamer, "Caught in the Clutter Crossfire: Your Brand," *Advertising Age,* April 2, 2007, 1, 35.
9. Brian Till and Daniel Baack, "Recall and Persuasion: Does Creative Advertising Matter?" *Journal of Advertising,* Fall 2005: 47–57.
10. Karen Machleit, Chris Allen, and Thomas Madden, "The Mature Brand and Brand Interest," *Journal of Marketing,* October 1993: 72–82.
11. Marc Gobe, *Emotional Branding: The New Paradigm for Connecting Brands to People,* New York: Allworth, 2001.
12. Cris Prystay, "When Being First Doesn't Make You No. 1," *Wall Street Journal,* August 12, 2004, B1, B2.
13. Socrates, quoted in Plato, *Phaedrus and the Seventh and Eighth Letters,* trans. Walter Hamilton, Middlesex, England: Penguin, 1970, 46–47, cited in Kay Redfield Jamison, *Touched with Fire: Manic-Depressive Illness and the Artistic Temperament,* New York: Free Press, 1993, 51.
14. Howard Gardner, *Creating Minds: An Anatomy of Creativity Seen through the Lives of Freud, Einstein, Picasso, Stravinsky, Eliot, Graham, and Gandhi,* New York: Basic Books, 1993.
15. Ibid., 364.
16. Ibid.
17. Ibid., 145; Sigmund Freud, *The Interpretation of Dreams,* in *The Basic Writings of Sigmund Freud,* ed. A. A. Brill, New York: Modern Library, 1900/1938.
18. Gardner, *Creating Minds,* 369.
19. Ibid.
20. Alice Cuneo, "The Dude Who Thought Different," *Advertising Age,* July 31, 2006, 1, 25.
21. Ibid.
22. Berger, "Dare-Devils."
23. Luke Sullivan, "Staring at Your Partner's Shoes," in *Hey Whipple, Squeeze This: A Guide to Creating Great Ads,* New York: Wiley, 1998, 20–22.
24. William Bernbach, quoted in Thomas Frank, *The Conquest of Cool: Business Culture, Consumer Culture, and the Rise of Hip Consumerism,* Chicago: University of Chicago Press, 1997.
25. D. West, "Restricted Creativity: Advertising Agency Work Practices in the U.S., Canada, and the U.K.," *Journal of Creative Behavior,* 27, No. 3, 1993, 200–213; D. C. West, "Cross-National Creative Personalities, Processes, and Agency Philosophies," *Journal of Advertising Research,* 33, No. 5, 1993: 53–62.
26. P. C. Michell, "Accord and Discord in Agency-Client Perceptions of Creativity," *Journal of Advertising Research,* 24, No. 5, 1984: 9–24.
27. Elizabeth Hirschman, "The Effect of Verbal and Pictorial Advertising Stimuli on Aesthetic, Utilitarian, and Familiarity Perceptions," *Journal of Advertising* (1985): 27–34.
28. B. G. Vanden Berg, S. J. Smith, and J. W. Wickes, "Internal Agency Relationships: Account Service and Creative Personnel," *Journal of Advertising,* 15, No. 2, 1986: 55–60.
29. A. J. Kover and S. M. Goldberg, "The Games Copywriters Play: Conflict, Quasi-Control, a New Proposal," *Journal of Advertising Research,* 25, No. 4, 1995: 52–62.
30. R. L. Vaughn, "Point of View: Creatives versus Researchers—Must They Be Adversaries?" *Journal of Advertising Research,* 22, No. 6, 1983: 45–48.
31. Kover and Goldberg, "The Games Copywriters Play."
32. John Sweeney, "Assuring Poor Creative," in Thomas C. O'Guinn, Chris T. Allen, and Richard J. Semenik, *Advertising and Integrated Brand Promotion,* Mason, OH: South-Western Cengage Learning, 2009, 325–326.
33. Cuneo, "The Dude Who Thought Different," 25.
34. Jon R. Katzenbach and Douglas K. Smith, *The Wisdom of Teams: Creating the High-Performance Organization,* Boston: Harvard Business School Press, 1993.
35. Dorothy Leonard and Susaan Straus, "Putting Your Company's Whole Brain to Work," *Harvard Business Review,* July–August 1997: 111–121.
36. Katzenbach and Smith, *The Wisdom of Teams,* Ch. 7.
37. Katzenbach and Smith, *The Wisdom of Teams,* 144.
38. Teresa Amabile, "How to Kill Creativity," *Harvard Business Review,* Fall 1998: 77–87. See also Jaafar El-Murad and Douglas C. West, "The Definition and Measurement of Creativity: What Do We Know?" *Journal of Advertising Research,* June 2004: 188–201.
39. Brooke Capps, "Playtime, Events, Perks Go Long Way in Team Building," *Advertising Age,* January 15, 2007, 30.
40. Jacob Goldenberg, David Mazursky, and Sorin Solomon, "The Fundamental Templates of Quality Ads," *Marketing Science,* 18, No. 3, 1999: 333–351.
41. Dale Buss, "Bridging the Great Divide in Marketing Thinking," *Advertising Age,* March 26, 2007, 18–19.
42. Dorothy Leonard and Walter Swap, *When Sparks Fly: Igniting Creativity in Groups,* Boston: Harvard Business School Press, 1999.
43. Ibid.
44. Robert J. Sternberg, "Creativity as a Decision," *American Psychologist,* May 2002, 376; and Robert J. Sternberg, "Identifying and Developing Creative Giftedness," *Roeper Review,* 23, No. 2, 2000: 60–65.

Chapter 9

1. Steve Hamm, "Children of the Web," *BusinessWeek,* July 2, 2007, 51–58.
2. Ibid., 56.
3. U.S. Census Bureau, "E-Stats," May 25, 2007, http://www.census.gov/eos/www/2005/2005reportfinal.pdf.
4. Digital Marketing & Media Fact Pack, *Advertising Age,* April 23, 2007, 6.

5. Tobi Elkin, "Record Labels Turning to Web to Boost Sales," *Advertising Age,* June 9, 2003, 16.
6. "Stats—Web Worldwide," *ClickZ,* http://www.clickz.com/showPage.html?page=stats/web_worldwide, accessed July 13, 2007.
7. Digital Marketing & Media Fact Pack, *Advertising Age,* April 23, 2007, 6.
8. "Stats—Web Worldwide," *ClickZ,* http://www.clickz.com/showPage.html?page=stats/web_worldwide, accessed December 1, 2009.
9. Allison Enright, "Guerrilla-Style Spam Wars," *Marketing News,* November 1, 2006, 13–14.
10. Tobi Elkin, "Spam: Annoying but Effective," *Advertising Age,* September 22, 2003, 40.
11. Digital Marketing & Media Fact Pack, *Advertising Age,* April 23, 2007, 32.
12. Om Malik, "Growing in the Shadow of Google," *Business 2.0,* December 2006, 40.
13. Robert D. Hof, "Mix, Match, and Mutate," *BusinessWeek,* July 25, 2005, 72–74
14. Digital Marketing & Media Fact Pack, *Advertising Age,* April 23, 2007, 21.
15. Nancy Einhart, "Clean Sweep of the Market," *Business 2.0,* March 2003, 56.
16. PricewaterhouseCoopers, "IAB Internet Advertising Report," April 2004, 5; 2003 Marketing Fact Book, *Advertising Age,* July 7, 2003, 21; and Digital Marketing & Media Fact Pack, *Advertising Age,* April 23, 2007, 6.
17. Jessica E. Vascellaro, "Google Says Internet Advertising Picked Up Steam in Third Quarter," *Wall Street Journal,* October 16, 2009, http://online.wsj.com; and Peter Kafka, "Yes, We Know, Online Ads Are Down," *All Things Digital,* June 5, 2009, http://mediamemo.allthingsd.com.
18. Kris Oser, "Targeting Web Behavior Pays, American Airlines Study Finds," *Advertising Age,* May 17, 2004, 8.
19. Kelli S. Burns and Richard J. Lutz, "The Function of Format," *Journal of Advertising,* 35, No. 1, Spring 2006, 53–63.
20. Bob Parks, "Let's Remake a Dealership," *Business 2.0,* June 2004, 65–67.
21. Ibid.
22. Fuyuan Shen, "Banner Advertisement Pricing, Measurement, and Pretesting Practices: Perspectives from Interactive Agencies," *Journal of Advertising,* 31, No. 3, Fall 2002, 59–68.
23. Search Marketing Fact Pack 2006, *Advertising Age,* November 6, 2006, 6.
24. Ibid., 33.
25. Ibid., 36.
26. Satya Menon and Dilip Soman, "Managing the Power of Curiosity for Effective Web Advertising Strategies," *Journal of Advertising,* 31, No. 3, Fall 2002, 1–14.
27. Ibid., 6.
28. The statistics referenced here were from a Forrester Research survey cited in Digital Marketing & Media Fact Pack, *Advertising Age,* April 23, 2007, 45.
29. Stephen Baker, "Pop-Up Ads Had Better Start Pleasing," *BusinessWeek,* December 8, 2003, 40.
30. Kathryn Kranhold, "Internet Advertisers Use Humor in Effort to Entice Web Surfers," *Wall Street Journal,* August 17, 1999, B9.
31. Steve Jurvetson, "Turning Customers into a Sales Force," *Business 2.0,* March 2000, 231.
32. Heather Green and Ben Elgin, "Do E-Ads Have a Future?" *BusinessWeek e.biz,* January 22, 2001, 46–49; and S. Shyam Sundar and Sriram Kalyanaraman, "Arousal, Memory,

and Impression Formation Effects of Animation Speed in Web Advertising," *Journal of Advertising,* 33, No.1, Spring 2004, 7–17.
33. Emily Steel, "Sprucing Up Online Display Ads," *Wall Street Journal,* May 6, 2009, http://online.wsj.com.
34. Spencer E. Ante, Heather Green, and Catherine Holahan, "The Next Small Thing," *BusinessWeek,* July 23, 2007, 58–62.
35. Robert D. Hof, "My Virtual Life," *BusinessWeek,* May 1, 2006, 72–80. A visit to Second Life on July 23, 2007, showed 8,310,736 total residents; 1,548,131 logged in within the last 60 days; 33,940 online at the moment; and $1,761,092 spent in the past 24 hours.
36. Peter Valdes-Dapena, "Real Cars Drive into Second Life," CNNMoney.com, November 18, 2006, accessed at http://www.cnn.com.
37. Frank Rose, "Lonely Planet," *Wired,* August 2007, 140–145.
38. Ibid., 142.
39. Frank Rose, "Blind Spots," *Wired,* August 2007, 144–145.
40. Lynn Ward, "Hidden Costs of Building an E-Commerce Site," *E-Commerce Times,* April 28, 2003, http://www.ecommercetimes.com.
41. Duff McDonald, "A Website as Big (and Cheap) as the Great Outdoors," *Business 2.0,* October 2003, 70–71.
42. Gary L. Geissler, George M. Zinkhan, and Richard T. Watson, "The Influence of Home Page Complexity on Consumer Attention, Attitudes, and Purchase Intent," *Journal of Advertising,* 35, No. 2, Summer 2006, 69–80.
43. Thomas Mucha, "Operation Sign 'Em Up," *Business 2.0,* April 2003, 44.
44. Vicki Powers, "Flour Power," *Business 2.0,* June 2004, 80–81.
45. Hanjun Ko, Chang-Hoan Cho, and Marilyn S. Roberts, "Internet Uses and Gratifications," *Journal of Advertising,* 34, No. 2, Summer 2005, 57–70.
46. Laurie Freeman, "Domain-Name Dilemma Worsens," *Advertising Age,* November 8, 1999, 100.
47. Paul Sloan, "Masters of Their Domain," *Business 2.0,* December 2005, 138–144.
48. Adam Goldman, "Domain Names: 21st Century Real Estate," Associated Press, July 22, 2007, accessed at http://biz.yahoo.com.
49. Ann Harrison, "Privacy? Who Cares," *Business 2.0,* June 12, 2001, 48–49.
50. Jan-Benedict E. M. Steenkamp and Inge Geyskens, "How Country Characteristics Affect the Perceived Value of Web Sites," *Journal of Marketing,* 70, No. 3, July 2006, 136–150.
51. Definitions in this section adapted from Brian Getting, "Web Analytics: Understanding Visitor Behavior," *Practical eCommerce,* January 2006, 8.
52. Stephen Baker, "Wiser about the Web," *BusinessWeek,* March 27, 2006, 55.
53. Sundar and Kalyanaraman, "Arousal, Memory, and Impression Formation Effects."
54. Brian Grow and Ben Elgin, "Click Fraud," *BusinessWeek,* October 2, 2006, 46–57.
55. Burt Helm, "How Do You Clock the Clicks?" *BusinessWeek,* March 13, 2006, 44; and Reuters News Service, "Yahoo Taps Click Fraud Watchdog," March 22, 2007, accessed at http://www.cnnmoney.com.

56. Digital Marketing & Media Fact Pack, *Advertising Age,* April 23, 2007, 46.
57. Ibid., 43, 50.
58. Yukari Iwatani Kane, "iPhone Gets Bigger as Ad Medium," *Wall Street Journal,* May 12, 2009, http://online.wsj.com.
59. John Kuczala, "Online Video Ads Get Ready to Grab You," *Business 2.0,* May 2005, 42; and Peter Kafka, "Media Memo," *All Things Digital,* November 20, 2009, http://mediamemo.allthingsd.com.
60. Digital Marketing & Media Fact Pack, *Advertising Age,* 30.
61. Kuczala, "Online Video Ads Get Ready to Grab You," 25.
62. Robert D. Hof and Catherine Holahan, *BusinessWeek,* May 21, 2007, 46.
63. Robert D. Hof, "Google Launches Double-Click Ad Exchange," *BusinessWeek,* September 18, 2009, http://www.businessweek.com; and Abbey Klaassen, "Yahoo Rebrands Its Right Media Exchange as Premium," *Advertising Age,* November 16, 2009, http://adage.com/digital/.
64. Parks, "Let's Remake a Dealership."

Chapter 10

1. Interactive Promotions Brand Marketing by ePrize, http://eprize.com/portfolio, accessed February 16, 2010. CarMax's Tweet Yourself to a New Ride Sweepstakes, http://www.carmax.com/enUS/tweetstakes/default.html, accessed February 16, 2010.
2. Kris Oser, "Speedway Effort Decodes NASCAR Fans," *Advertising Age,* May 17, 2004, 150.
3. Ibid.
4. Anthony Malakian, "Ad Beat: Scratch and Win Customers," *Banking Wire,* November 26, 2008, Business & Company Resource Center, http://galenet.galegroup.com.
5. Amy Johannes, "Jelly Belly Names Illinois Man Winner of Flavor Contest," *Promo,* September 16, 2008, Business & Company Resource Center, http://galenet.galegroup.com.
6. Bob Stone, *Successful Direct Marketing Methods,* Lincolnwood, IL: NTC Business Books, 1994.
7. The discussion to follow builds on that of Stone, *Successful Direct Marketing Methods.*
8. Louise Lee, "Catalogs, Catalogs, Everywhere," *BusinessWeek,* December 4, 2006, 32–34.
9. Allanna Sullivan, "From a Call to a Click," *Wall Street Journal,* July 17, 2000, R30.
10. See Edward Nash, "The Roots of Direct Marketing," *Direct Marketing Magazine,* February 1995, 38–40; Cara Beardi, "Lillian Vernon Sets Sights on Second Half-Century," *Advertising Age,* March 19, 2001, 22.
11. Allison Cosmedy, *A History of Direct Marketing,* New York: Direct Marketing Association, 1992, 6.
12. Ibid.
13. Daniel Klein, "Disintegrated Marketing," *Harvard Business Review,* March 2003, 18, 19; Michael Fielding, "Spread the Word," *Marketing News,* February 15, 2005, 19, 20; and Michael Fielding, "Direct Mail Still Has Its Place," *Marketing News,* November 1, 2006, 31, 33.
14. Nash, "The Roots of Direct Marketing."

15. Anthony Bianco, "The Vanishing Mass Market," *Business Week,* July 12, 2004, 61–68.

16. Gary Levin, "AT&T Exec: Customer Access Goal of Integration," *Advertising Age,* October 10, 1994, S1.

17. Like many authors, Winer contends that direct marketing starts with the creation of a database. See Russell Winer, "A Framework for Customer Relationship Management," *California Management Review,* Summer 2001: 89–105.

18. Ibid.

19. *The 2001 Mailing List Catalog,* New York: Hugo Dunhill Mailing Lists, 2001.

20. Murray Raphel, "What's the Scoop on Ben & Jerry?" *Direct Marketing Magazine,* August 1994, 23, 24.

21. Ibid.

22. Christina Binkley, "Harrah's Is Revamping Rewards Plan," *Wall Street Journal,* June 17, 2003, D4.

23. Ira Teinowitz and Ken Wheaton, "Do Not Market," *Advertising Age,* March 12, 2007, 1, 44.

24. Stone, *Successful Direct Marketing Methods.*

25. Sally Beatty, "Drug Companies Are Minding Your Business," *Wall Street Journal,* April 17, 1998, B1, B3.

26. Michael Edmondson, "Postcards from the Edge," *Marketing Tools,* May 1995, 14.

27. Allison Enright, "Guerrilla-Style Spam Wars," *Marketing News,* November 1, 2006, 13, 14.

28. Ibid.

29. Cara Beardi, "Opt-In Taken to Great Heights," *Advertising Age,* November 6, 2000, S54; and Michael Battisto, "Preparation Yields Spam-Free E-Mail Lists," *Marketing News,* February 17, 2003, 17.

30. Jodi Mardesich, "Too Much of a Good Thing," *Industry Standard,* March 19, 2001, 85.

31. Thomas Mucha, "Stronger Sales in Just 28 Minutes," *Business 2.0,* June 2005, 56–60; and Elizabeth Holmes, "Golf-Club Designer Hopes to Repeat TV Success," *Wall Street Journal,* January 30, 2007, B4.

32. Evantheia Schibsted, "Ab Rockers, Ginsu Knives, E320s," *Business 2.0,* May 29, 2001, 46–49; and Jean Halliday, "Pontiac Models Get Infomercial Push," *Advertising Age,* April 19, 2004, 12.

33. Brian Steinberg, "How to Stop Them from Skipping: TiVo Tells All," *Advertising Age,* July 16, 2007, 1, 33.

Chapter 11

1. Kate MacArthur, "Give It Away: Fast Feeders Favor Freebies," *Advertising Age,* June 18, 2007, 10.

2. "Float Night Surpasses Oklahoma City-Based Sonic's Expectations," *Daily Oklahoman (Oklahoma City),* June 5, 2009, Business & Company Resource Center, http://galenet.galegroup.com; and Sonic Corp., "Summer at Sonic Starts with Free Root Beer Floats," News Release, May 29, 2009, http://www.sonicdrivein.com.

3. Pamela Parseghian, "Panel: Unique Promotions Add Value to Guest Experience," *Nation's Restaurant News,* October 26, 2009, 44.

4. Bradley Johnson, "Leading National Advertisers Report: Spending up 3.1% to $105

Billion," *Advertising Age,* June 25, 2007, S-2.

5. 2004 Industry Trends Report, *Promo Magazine.*

6. Jack Neff, "TV Doesn't Sell Packaged Goods," *Advertising Age,* May 24, 2004, 1, 30.

7. Cara Beardi, "POP Ups Sales Results," *Advertising Age,* July 23, 2001, 27.

8. Kate MacArthur, "McD's Sees Growth, but Are Ads a Factor?" *Advertising Age,* November 24, 2003, 3, 24.

9. Jack Neff, "Black Eye in Store for Big Brands," *Advertising Age,* April 30, 2001, 1, 34.

10. *Cox Direct 20th Annual Survey of Promotional Practices,* Chart 22, 1998, 37.

11. Dean Foust, "Queen of Pop," *Business Week,* August 7, 2006, 44–45.

12. Matthew Creamer, "Caught in the Clutter Crossfire: Your Brand," *Advertising Age,* April 2, 2007, 1, 35.

13. Barry M. Benjamin, "Plan Ahead to Limit Potential Disasters," *Marketing News,* November 10, 2003, 15.

14. *Cox Direct 20th Annual Survey of Promotional Practices,* 1998, 28.

15. Cara Beardi, "Cox's Introz Mailer Bundles Samples in Industry," *Advertising Age,* November 2000, 88.

16. *Cox Direct 20th Annual Survey of Promotional Practices,* 1998, 27.

17. Betsy Spethmann, "Branded Moments," *Promo Magazine,* September 2000, 84.

18. Louise Lee, "What's Roiling the Selling Season," *Business Week,* January 10, 2005, 38.

19. Brian Grow, "The Great Rebate Runaround," *Business Week,* December 5, 2005, 34–38.

20 Ibid., 34.

21. 2007 Marketing Fact Book, *Marketing News,* July 15, 2007, 32.

22. Lee Duffey, "Sweet Talk: Promotions Position Candy Company," *Marketing News,* March 30, 1998, 11.

23. Ron Donoho, "It's Up! It's Good!" *Sales and Marketing Management,* April 2003, 43–47.

24. Jack Neff, "P&G Trims Fat off Its $2B Trade-Promotion System," *Advertising Age,* June 5, 2006, 8.

25. Data available at Promotional Products Association International website at http://www.ppa.org, accessed on August 5, 2007.

26. Ibid.

27. Ibid.

28. Data on point-of-purchase decision making cited in Kate Fitzgerald, "In-Store Media Ring Cash Register," *Advertising Age,* February 9, 2004, 43–45.

29. Data cited in Lisa Z. Eccles, "P-O-P Scores with Marketers," *Advertising Age,* September 26, 1994.

30. Nicole Crawford, "Keeping P-O-P Sharp," *Promo Magazine,* January 1998, 52, 53.

31. Neff, "P&G Trims Fat off Its $2B Trade-Promotion System."

32. Retailer Guide to Maximizing In-Store Advertising Effectiveness, Washington, DC: Point of Purchase Advertising International, 1999, 5–7.

33. 2004 Industry Trends Report, *Promo Magazine.*

34. 2007 Marketing Fact Book, *Marketing News,* July 15, 2007, 29.

35. Data on outdoor advertising categories obtained from Outdoor Advertising Association of America website, http://www.oaaa.org, accessed on August 4, 2007.

36. Jack Z. Sissors and Lincoln Bumba, *Advertising Media Planning,* Lincolnwood, IL: NTC Business Books, 1996.

37. Ronald Grover, "Billboards Aren't Boring Anymore," *Business Week,* September 21, 1998, 88–89.

38. Sissors and Bumba, *Advertising Media Planning.*

39. Andrew Hampp, "What Are Online Giants Doing in Out-of-Home?" *Advertising Age,* January 29, 2007, 30.

40. Lisa Sanders, "Nielsen Outdoor Tracks Demo Data," *Advertising Age,* May 31, 2004, 14.

41. Jonathan Mummolo, "Ads Made for You," *Business Week,* March 5, 2007.

42. Stephen Freitas, "Evolutionary Changes in the Great Outdoors," *Advertising Age,* June 9, 2003, C4.

43. Barry Newman, "Sky-Borne Signs Are on the Rise as Most Ad Budgets Take a Dive," *Wall Street Journal,* August 27, 2002, B3.

44. Fara Warner, "More Companies Turn to Skies as Medium to Promote Products," *Wall Street Journal,* January 5, 1995, B6.

45. Bill Richards, "Bright Idea Has Business Looking Up for Ad Blimps," *Wall Street Journal,* October 14, 1997, B1.

46. 2007 Marketing Fact Book, *Marketing News,* July 15, 2007, 29.

47. Lisa Sanders, "Major Marketers Turn to Yellow Pages," *Advertising Age,* March 8, 2004, 4, 52.

48. Bradley Johnson, "Yellow Pages Deals Red Hot as Telecom Industry Regroups," *Advertising Age,* January 6, 2003, 4, 20.

49. Don Hootstein, "Standing Out in the Aisles," *Marketing at Retail,* June 2007, 22–24.

50. Catherine Arnold, "Way Outside the Box," *Marketing News,* June 23, 2003, 13–14.

51. Robert L. Underwood and Julie L. Ozanne, "Is Your Package an Effective Communicator? A Normative Framework for Increasing the Communicative Competence of Packaging," *Journal of Marketing Communications,* December 1998, 207–219.

52. Brad Edmondson, "The Drive/Buy Equation," *Marketing Tools,* May 1998, 28–31.

53. Emma Hall, "IKEA Courts Buyers with Offbeat Ideas," *Advertising Age,* April 12, 2004, 10.

Chapter 12

1. Kathryn Holl and Dewayne Guy, "Charmin Restrooms Offer the Plushest Flush in Times Square," P&G Press Release, November 20, 2006.

2. "Special Report: 10 Leading Brand Events," *Advertising Age,* March 19, 2007, S-1.

3. Jack Neff and Lisa Sanders, "It's Broken," *Advertising Age,* February, 16, 2004, 1, 30; Julia Angwin, "In Embracing Digital Recorders, Cable Companies Take Big Risk," *Wall Street Journal,* April 26, 2004, A1, A11; and Ronald Grover, "Can Mad Ave. Make Zap-Proof Ads?" *Business Week,* February 2, 2004, 36–37.

4. Bill Carter, "DVR, Once TV's Mortal Foe, Helps Ratings," *New York Times,* November 2, 2009, http://www.nytimes.com; and Brooke Gladstone, "TV's Unlikely Ally," *On the Media,* November 6, 2009, http://www.onthemedia.org (interview of Bill Carter).

5. Bob Garfield, "The Post Advertising Age," *Advertising Age,* March 26, 2007, 1, 12–14.

6. Ibid.

7. Dan Lippe, "Events Trail Only Ads in Alignment with Brands," *Advertising Age,* March 19, 2007, S-2.

8. Bettina Cornwell, Clinton Weeks, and Donald Roy, "Sponsor-Linked Marketing: Opening the Black Box," *Journal of Advertising* (Summer 2005): 21–42.

9. Chris Allen, Susan Fournier, and Felicia Miller, "Brands and Their Meaning Makers," in *Handbook of Consumer Psychology* (Hillsdale, NJ: LEA Publishing, 2007), Chapter 31.

10. Jack Neff, "Specialists Thrive in Fast-Growing Events Segment," *Advertising Age,* March 19, 2007, S-2, S-4; and "Event & Sponsorship Spending," *AMA Marketing Fact Book,* July 15, 2007, 31.

11. Emily Steel, "Measured Media Lose in Spending Cuts," *Wall Street Journal,* March 14, 2007, B3; and Mike Spector and Gina Chon, "The Great Texas Truck Fair," *Wall Street Journal,* October 20, 2006, B1, B10.

12. Grant McCracken, "Culture and Consumption: A Theoretical Account of the Structure and Movement of the Cultural Meaning of Consumer Goods," *Journal of Consumer Research,* June 1986: 71–84.

13. Charles Goldsmith, "Join the Club: Thai Wants In on U.K. Soccer," *Wall Street Journal,* May 12, 2004, B1, B2.

14. Jim Hanas, "Going Pro: What's with All These Second-Tier Sports?" *Advertising Age,* January 29, 2007, S-3.

15. Ellen Byron, "An Old Dice Game Catches On Again, Pushed by P&G," *Wall Street Journal,* January 30, 2007, A1, A13.

16. Amy Hernandez, "Research Studies Gauge Sponsorship ROI," *Marketing News,* May 12, 2003, 16; and Ian Mount, "Exploding the Myths of Stadium Naming," *Business 2.0,* April 2004, 82, 83.

17. Kate Fitzgerald, "Events No Longer Immune to Marketer Demand for ROI," *Advertising Age,* March 19, 2007, S-3.

18. Rich Thomaselli, "Nielsen to Measure Sports Sponsorship," *Advertising Age,* May 3, 2004, 14.

19. The ideas in this section are drawn from Julie Zdziarski, "Evaluating Sponsorships," *Promo Magazine,* March 2001, 92, 93; and Fitzgerald, "Events No Longer Immune."

20. Cornwell, Weeks, and Roy, "Sponsor-Linked Marketing."

21. Marc Graser and T. L. Stanley, "Study: Placements to Surge 25% in '06," *Advertising Age,* August 28, 2006, 6.

22. Brian Steinberg and Suzanne Vranica, "Prime-Time TV's New Guest Stars: Products," *Wall Street Journal,* January 12, 2004, B1, B4; Brian Steinberg, "Frasier Finale: Amid Nostalgia, A Product Plug," *Wall Street Journal,* May 12, 2004, B1, B2; and Grover, "Can Mad Ave. Make Zap-Proof Ads?"

23. Marc Graser, "TV's Savior?" *Advertising Age,* February 6, 2006, S-1, S-2.

24. Ibid.

25. Marc Graser, "Automakers: Every Car Needs a Movie," *Advertising Age,* December 11, 2006, 8.

26. Kate Kelly and Brian Steinberg, "Sony's 'Talladega Nights' Comedy Is Product-Plug

Rally," *Wall Street Journal,* July 28, 2006, A9, A12.

27. Emma Hall, "Young Consumers Receptive to Movie Product Placements," *Advertising Age,* March 29, 2004, 8.

28. David Kiley, "Rated M for Mad Ave," *Business Week,* February 27, 2006, 76, 77.

29. Ibid.

30. John Gaudiosi, "In-Game Ads Reach the Next Level," *Business 2.0,* July 2007, 36, 37.

31. See also Cristel Russell and Michael Belch, "A Managerial Investigation into the Product Placement Industry," *Journal of Advertising Research,* March 2005: 73–92.

32. James Karrah, Kathy McKee, and Carol Pardun, "Practitioners' Evolving Views on Product Placement Effectiveness," *Journal of Advertising Research,* June 2003: 138–149.

33. Christina Passariello, "Ray-Ban Hopes to Party Like It's 1983 by Re-launching Its Wayfarer Shades," *Wall Street Journal,* October 27, 2006, B1, B4.

34. Tom Lowry, "The Prince of NASCAR," *Business Week,* February 23, 2004, 91–98; and Rich Thomaselli, "How NASCAR Plans to Get Back on the Fast Track," *Advertising Age,* February 12, 2007, 3, 26.

35. Rich Thomaselli, "Nextel Link Takes NASCAR to New Level," *Advertising Age,* October 27, 2003, S-7.

36. Lisa Napoli, "A New Era in Stock-Car Racing," *New York Times,* July 14, 2003, available at http://www.nytimes.com.

37. Rich Thomaselli, "Hitch a Ride with NASCAR for Under $5M," *Advertising Age,* November 6, 2006, 4, 80.

38. Burt Helm, "Bet You Can't TiVo Past This," *Business Week,* April 24, 2006, 38, 40; and Louise Story, "Brands Produce Their Own Shows," *New York Times,* November 10, 2006, available at http://www.nytimes.com.

39. Cristel Russell and Michael Belch, "A Managerial Investigation into the Product Placement Industry," *Journal of Advertising Research,* March 2005: 82, 83.

40. Phil Guarascio, "Decision Time at Mad + Vine," *Advertising Age,* September 1, 2003, 15.

41. Kate MacArthur, "Branded Entertainment, Marketing Tradition Tussle," *Advertising Age,* May 10, 2004, 6.

42. T. L. Stanley, "Sponsors Flee Matrix Sequel," *Advertising Age,* October 13, 2003, 1, 71.

43. Claire Atkinson, "Watchdog Group Hits TV Product Placements," *Advertising Age,* October 6, 2003, 12.

44. Davis Dyer, Frederick Dalzell, and Rowena Olegario, *Rising Tide: Lessons from 165 Years of Brand Building at Procter & Gamble,* Boston: Harvard Business School Publishing, 2004.

45. Don E. Schultz, Stanley I. Tannenbaum, and Robert F. Lauterborn, *Integrated Marketing Communications,* Lincolnwood, IL: NTC Business Books, 1993; and Daniel Klein, "Disintegrated Marketing," *Harvard Business Review,* March 2003: 18–19.

46. Laura Q. Hughes and Kate MacArthur, "Soft Boiled: Clients Want Integrated Marketing at Their Disposal, but Agencies Are (Still) Struggling to Put the Structure Together," *Advertising Age,* May 28, 2001, 3, 54; Claire Atkinson, "Integration Still a Pipe Dream for

Many," *Advertising Age,* March 10, 2003, 1, 47; and Burt Helm, "Struggles of a Mad Man: Saatchi & Saatchi CEO Kevin Roberts," *Business Week,* December 3, 2007, 44–50.

47. Joe Cappo, *The Future of Advertising,* Chicago: McGraw-Hill, 2003, Chapter 8.

48. Ibid., 153, 154.

49. Suzanne Vranica, "For Big Marketers Like AmEx, TV Ads Lose Starring Role," *Wall Street Journal,* May 17, 2004, B1, B3.

Chapter 13

1. Stephen Brown, "Ambi-brand Culture," in *Brand Culture,* New York: Routledge, 2006, pp. 50–66.

2. Frank Rose, "Let the Seller Beware," *Wall Street Journal,* December 20, 2006, D10.

3. Jeffrey Davidoff, "Want Great PR? Get Your Agencies to Share the Load," *Advertising Age,* August 13, 2007, 12–13.

4. Claire Stammerjohan, Charles M. Wood, Yuhmiin Chang, and Esther Thorson, "An Empirical Investigation of the Interaction Between Publicity, Advertising, and Previous Brand Attitudes and Knowledge," *Journal of Advertising,* Winter 2005, 55–67; and Jonah Bloom, "Marketing, PR Departments Must Bridge the Cultural Gulf," *Advertising Age,* March 12, 2007, 18.

5. Kate MacArthur, "Taco Hell: Rodent Video Signals New Era in PR Crises," *Advertising Age,* February 26, 2007, 1, 46.

6. Jack Neff, "J&J Targets Red Cross, Blunders into PR Firestorm," *Advertising Age,* August 13, 2007, 1, 22.

7. Barney Gimbel, "Attack of the Wal-Martyrs," *Fortune,* December 11, 2006, 125–130.

8. Jon Birger, "The Unending Woes of Lee Scott," *Fortune,* January 22, 2007, 118–122.

9. Andy Cohen, "The Jupiter Mission," *Sales and Marketing Management,* April 2000, 56.

10. "CIGNA Funds Hoops Tournament to Help People with Disabilities Stay Healthy Through Sports, Hobbies," *Leisure & Travel Business,* July 5, 2009, Business & Company Resource Center, http://galenet.galegroup.com.

11. William George Shuster, "Thriving in Troubled Times," *New York Diamonds,* July 2009, 52–58.

12. Beth Snyder Bulik, "Well-Heeled Heed the Need for PR," *Advertising Age,* June 11, 2001, S2.

13. These definitions were developed from discussions offered by Jordan Goldman, *Public Relations in the Marketing Mix,* Lincolnwood, IL: NTC Business Books, 1992, pp. xi–xii.

14. Kathleen V. Schmidt, "Coke's Crisis," *Marketing News,* September 27, 1999, 1, 11.

15. Amie Smith, "Coke's European Resurgence," *Promo Magazine,* December 1999, 91.

16. James Cox, "Shareholders Get to Put Bio-Engineered Foods to Vote," *USA Today,* June 6, 2000, 1B.

17. Robert Berner, "I Sold It Through the Grapevine," *Business Week,* May 29, 2006, 32–34.

18. Michael Krauss, "To Generate Buzz, Do Remarkable Things," *Marketing News,* December 15, 2006, 6.

19. Matthew Creamer and Jean Halliday, "Dead Giveaways," *Advertising Age,* March 14, 2005, 3.

20. Ed Keller and Jon Berry, "Word-of-Mouth: The Real Action Is Offline," *Advertising Age,* December 4, 2006, 20.

21. Berner, "I Sold It Through the Grapevine."

22. Ibid., 34.

23. Jessica E. Vascellaro, "Why Email No Longer Rules," *Wall Street Journal,* October 12, 2009, http://online.wsj.com.

24. W. Glynn Mangold and David J. Faulds, "Social Media: The New Hybrid Element of the Promotion Mix," *Business Horizons,* 52, 2009, 357–365.

25. Ibid., 361–364; and Diana Ransom, "How to Channel Your Twitter Voice," *Wall Street Journal*, October 29, 2009, http://online.wsj .com.

26. Emily Bryson York, "Red Robin Calls in a Facebook Favor from 1,500 Fans," *Advertising Age*, September 28, 2009, Business & Company Resource Center, http://galenet .galegroup.com.

27. Vascellaro, "Why Email No Longer Rules."

28. Gerry Khermouch and Jeff Green, "Buzz-z-z Marketing," *BusinessWeek,* July 30, 2001, 50–56.

29. Ibid.

30. Raymund Flandez, "Entrepreneurs Strive to Turn Buzz into Loyalty," *Wall Street Journal,* July 21, 2009, http://online.wsj.com.

31. Radian6, "Dell: Free Range Marketing," Case Studies, Radian6 website, accessed December 31, 2009.

32. David W. Schumann, Jan M. Hathcote, and Susan West, "Corporate Advertising in America: A Review of Published Studies on Use, Measurement and Effectiveness," *Journal of Advertising,* September 1991, 40–53.

33. David Goetzl, "GlaxoSmithKline Launches Print Ads," *Advertising Age,* January 8, 2001, 30.

34. For an exhaustive assessment of the benefits of corporate advertising, see David M. Bender, Peter H. Farquhar, and Sanford C. Schulert, "Growing from the Top," *Marketing Management,* Winter–Spring 1996, 10–19, 24.

35. "Campaign Close-up—BP," *Sales and Marketing Management,* February 2004, 13.

36. Schumann, Hathcote, and West, "Corporate Advertising in America," 43, 49.

37. James Tenser, "The New Samaritans," *Advertising Age,* June 12, 2006, S-1, S-6.

38. Stephanie Thompson, "Raising Awareness, Doubling Sales," *Advertising Age,* October 2, 2006, 4.

39. Michael J. Barone, Anthony D. Miyazaki, and Kimberly A. Taylor, "The Influence of Cause-Related Marketing on Consumer Choice," *Journal of the Academy of Marketing Science,* 28(2), 2000, 248–262.

40. Tenser, "The New Samaritans," S-1.

41. Tenser, "The New Samaritans."

42. Kathryn Kranhold, "GE's Environment Push Hits Business Realities," *Wall Street Journal,* September 14, 2007, A1, A10.

43. Mya Frazier, "Going Green? Plant Deep Roots," *Advertising Age,* April 30, 2007, 1, 54–55.

Chapter 14

1. Jenny Callison, "Firm Refines Sales Pitches," *Cincinnati Enquirer,* February 10, 2006, http://cincinnati.com; and R. Dennis Green,

"Professor of Persuasion—Dr. Tom Sant," *APMP Journal,* Fall/Winter 2003, 8–14.

2. Jessica Tsai, "Selling to the Sales Experts," *Customer Relationship Management,* November 2009, 46–47; and "The Sant Corporation Runs Its Entire Business in the Cloud with Salesforce.com," *Marketing Weekly News,* August 29, 2009, Business & Company Resource Center, http://galenet.galegroup.com.

3. Bureau of Labor Statistics, "Occupational Employment," *Occupational Outlook Quarterly,* Winter 2009–10, 6–10; and Bureau of Labor Statistics, *Occupational Outlook Handbook: 2010–11,* http://data.bls.gov.

4. Michele Marchetti, "What a Sales Call Costs," *Sales and Marketing Management,* September 2000, 80.

5. Erika Rasmusson, "Going Global with CRM," *Sales and Marketing Management,* May 2000, 96.

6. Patricia Sellers, "How IBM Teaches Techies to Sell," *Fortune,* June 6, 1988, 146.

7. Erika Rasmusson, "The Value of Virtual Presentations," *Sales and Marketing Management,* November 1999, 113.

8. William Weeks, "Buying Decisions a Group Effort," *Marketing News,* December 6, 1999, 22.

9. Ann Harrington, "I'll Take That Pitch with a Dash of Politesse," *Fortune,* June 12, 2000, 334.

10. Jamie Teschner, "Skill Workshop: Prospecting," *Selling Power,* March 2000, 34.

11. This section is based on an excellent discussion in Gary M. Grikscheit, Harold C. Cash, and Cliff E. Young, *Handbook of Personal Selling,* New York: John Wiley & Sons, 1993, Chapter 1.

12. Neil Rackham, "The Other Revolution in Sales," *Sales and Marketing Management,* March 2000, 34–36.

13. Erika Rasmusson, "Global Sales on the Line," *Sales and Marketing Management,* March 2000, 76–81.

14. Joseph P. Vaccaro, "Best Salespeople Know Their ABCs (Always Be Closing)," *Marketing News,* March 28, 1998, 10.

15. Erika Rasmusson, "Image Is Everything," *Sales and Marketing Management,* December 1999, 25.

16. Tim R. Furey, "Sales Rep Not Dead, Just Redefined," *Marketing News,* December 6, 1999, 16.

17. Janet Guyon, "The World Is Your Office," *Fortune,* June 12, 2000, 227–234.

18. Rochelle Garner, "The E-Commerce Connection," *Sales and Marketing Management,* January 1999, 40–46.

19. Dana James, "Hit the Bricks," *Marketing News,* September 13, 1999, 1, 15.

20. Garner, "The E-Commerce Connection."

21. Jason Jordan, "From Sales Star to Sales Supporter," *Sales and Marketing Management,* February 26, 2009, Business & Company Resource Center, http://galenet.galegroup.com.

22. Barbara Buell et al., "Apple: New Team, New Strategy," *BusinessWeek,* October 15, 1991, 93.

23. Michele Marchetti, "How High Can Your Reps Go?" *Sales and Marketing Management,* September 1998, 101.

24. Bradley D. Lockman and John H. Hallaq, "Who Are Your Successful Salespeople?"

Journal of the Academy of Marketing Science (Fall 1982), 463–468; and Timothy J. Trow, "The Secret of a Good Hire: Profiling," *Sales and Marketing Management,* May 1990, 44.

25. Patricia Sellers, "How to Remake Your Sales Force," *Fortune,* May 4, 1992; and Erin Strout, "Finding Your Company's Top Talent," *Sales and Marketing Management,* May 2000, 113.

26. Geoffrey Brewer, "How to Win Today's Recruiting Wars," *Sales and Marketing Management,* March 2000, 85.

27. Mike McNamee, "We Try to Minimize Face-to-Face Interviews," *BusinessWeek,* November 22, 1999, 176.

28. Dan Hanover, "Hiring Gets Cheaper and Faster," *Sales and Marketing Management,* March 2000, 87.

29. Jack Retterer, "Successful Sales Automation Calls for Incorporating People," *Marketing News,* November 8, 1999, 12.

30. Walecia Konrad, "Cheerleading, and Clerks Who Know Awls from Augers," *BusinessWeek,* August 3, 1992, 51.

31. Melinda Ligos, "Point, Click, and Sell," *Sales and Marketing Management,* May 1999, 51–56.

32. Christopher Power, Lisa Driscoll, and Earl Bohn, "Smart Selling," *BusinessWeek,* August 3, 1992, 48.

33. Slade Sohmer, "Retention Getter," *Sales and Marketing Management,* May 2000, 80.

34. Michele Marchetti, "Helping Reps Count Every Penny," *Sales and Marketing Management,* July 1998.

35. Ibid.

Chapter 15

1. Information on Unilever's development of the Campaign for Real Beauty is adapted from Melinda Brodbeck and Erin Evans "Public Relations Problems and Cases: 'Dove Campaign for Real Beauty' Case Study," March 5, 2007; Jack Neff, "Study: Stick to Skinny Models for Fat Profits" *Advertising Age,* August 4, 2008; and The Campaign for Real Beauty website (www.dove.us/#/cfrb/), accessed February 15, 2010.

2. Jon Steel, *Truth, Lies & Advertising: The Art of Account Planning,* New York: John Wiley & Sons, 1998, Jacket.

3. Stuart J. Agres, Julie A. Edell, and Tony M. Dubitsky (eds.), *Emotion in Advertising* (Westport, CT: Quorum Books, 1990); see especially Chapters 7 and 8.

4. David Glenn Mick and Claus Buhl, "A Meaning-Based Model of Advertising Experiences," *Journal of Consumer Research,* 19, December 1992, 317–338.

5. Linda Scott, "The Bridge from Text to Mind: Adapting Reader Response Theory for Consumer Research," *Journal of Consumer Research,* 21, December 1994, 461–486.

6. John Philip Jones, "Advertising Pre-Testing: Will Europe Follow America's Lead?" *Commercial Communications,* June 1997, 21–26.

7. Jennifer Gilbert, "Capita Taps Brain Waves to Study Web Ads' Potency," *Advertising Age,* February 14, 2000, 55.

8. Rajeev Batra, John G. Meyers, and David A. Aaker, *Advertising Management,* 5th ed.,

Upper Saddle River, NJ: Prentice Hall, 1996, p. 469.

9. Jennifer Gilbert, "Top 10 Ads Score Raves, Not Hits Post-Super Bowl," *Advertising Age,* February 7, 2000, 63.

10. Ira Teinowitz, "Census Bureau Counts Ad Effort a Success," *Advertising Age,* May 22, 2000, 8.

11. James Lull, "How Families Select Television Programs: A Mass Observational Study," *Journal of Broadcasting* 26, No. 4, 1982, 801–811.

12. For an article that focuses exclusively on the measurement issue, see Scott Rosenberg, "Let's Get This Straight: Reach for the Hits," at http://www.salon.com/21st/rose/1999/02/05straight.html; see also Allan L. Baldinger, "Integrated Communication and Measurement: The Case for Multiple Measures," in Esther Thorson and Jeri Moore (eds.), *Integrated Communications* (Mahwah, NJ: Lawrence Erlbaum Associates, 1996), pp. 271–283.

13. Eric Johnson, "Microsoft Developing Oscar's Website," *Marketing Doctoral Consortium,* Wharton Business School, August 1995.

14. Stephanie Thompson, "Nestlé Tries Fresh Approach for Premium Ortega Salsa," *Advertising Age,* February 21, 2000, 16.

15. Jack Neff, "P&G Introduces Trio of Products in DMB&B Boon," *Advertising Age,* May 22, 2000, 77.

16. Michael J. McCarthy, "Keeping Close Score on Sports Tie-ins," *Wall Street Journal,* April 24, 1991, B1.

17. B. Spethmann, "Sponsorships Sing a Profitable Tune in Concert with Event Promotions," *Brandweek,* January 1, 1994, 20.

18. Scott Hume, "Sports Sponsorship Value Measured," *Advertising Age,* June 3, 1996, 46.

19. Amanda Beeler, "Deere Goes Beyond Famed Brand to Cultivate Ties with Customers," *Advertising Age,* May 22, 2000.

20. For an extensive discussion of sales force evaluation procedures and criteria, see Gilbert A. Churchill Jr., Neil M. Ford, Orville C. Walker Jr., Mark W. Johnson, and John F. Tanner, *Sales Force Management,* 5th ed., Burr Ridge, IL: Irwin Publishing, 2000, Chapter 16.

21. Chad Kaydo, "Big Blue's Media Blitz," *Sales and Marketing Management,* December 1999, 80.

22. Michael Hess and Robert Mayer, "Integrate Behavioral and Survey Data," *Marketing News,* January 3, 2000, 22.

23. Helen Katz and Jacques Lendrevie, "In Search of the Holy Grail: First Steps in Measuring Total Exposures of an Integrated Communications Program," in Thorson and Moore (eds.), *Integrated Communications,* pp. 259–270.

24. We presume the authors really mean "brand" rather than "product" impressions. It does Honda or Adidas little good if consumers encounter automobiles or sport shoes as a product category. The intent of the authors here would clearly seem to be that consumers encounter the "brand" in question not the broad product category.

25. Katz and Lendrevie, "In Search of the Holy Grail," pp. 266–268.

26. Although there is extensive literature on measuring the effectiveness of *individual* elements of the promotional mix, aside from the Katz and Lendrevie article discussed here, the author was able to locate only *one* other article that focuses exclusively on the measurement issue: Allan L. Baldinger, "Integrated Communication and Measurement: The Case for Multiple Measures," in Thorson and Moore (eds.), *Integrated Communications,* pp. 271–283.

Glossary

account executive liaison between an advertising agency and its clients

account planner person in an advertising agency who synthesizes all relevant consumer research and uses it to design an advertising strategy

account planning system in which an agency assigns a coequal account planner to work alongside the account executive and analyze research data, staying with projects on a continuous basis

account services team of managers that identifies the benefits a brand offers its target audiences and the best competitive position, and then develops a promotion plan

account team group of people comprising different facets of the promotion industry who work together under a team leader

Action for Children's Television group formed during the 1970s to lobby the government to limit the amount and content of advertising to children

advertisement a specific message that an organization has placed to persuade an audience

advertising a paid, mass-mediated attempt to persuade

advertising agency organization of professionals who provide creative and business services related to planning, preparing, and placing advertisements

advertising campaign a series of coordinated promotional efforts, including advertisements, that communicate a single theme or idea

advertising clutter volume of similar ads for products or services that presents an obstacle to brand promotion

advertising specialties sales promotion consisting of a message placed on useful items given to consumers with no obligation

advertising substantiation program FTC program that ensures advertisers make available to consumers supporting evidence for advertising claims

advocacy advertising advertising that attempts to influence public opinion about social, political, or environmental issues of concern to the advertiser

aerial advertising advertising that involves airplanes pulling signs or banners, as well as skywriting and blimps

affirmative disclosure FTC action requiring that important material determined to be absent from prior ads be included in future ads

appropriation use of pictures or images owned by someone else without permission

attention-interest-desire-action (AIDA) structured presentation aimed at capturing attention, identifying features of interest, defining desirable benefits, and requesting action in the form of a purchase

attitude overall evaluation of any object, person, or issue; varies along a continuum, such as favorable to unfavorable or positive to negative

attitude change study message research that uses a before-and-after ad exposure design

audience a group of individuals who may receive and interpret promotional messages

authenticity quality of genuineness or naturalness

ballot method pretest of sales promotion in which consumers are given a list of promotional options and asked to rank their preferences

beliefs a person's knowledge and feelings about an object or issue

benefit positioning a positioning option that features a distinctive customer benefit

benefit segmentation market segmentation that identifies the various benefit packages consumers want from a product category

bill-back allowances monetary incentive provided to retailers for featuring a marketer's brand in advertising or in-store displays

blog personal journal on a website that is frequently updated and intended for public access

blogger author of a blog

brainstorming organized approach to idea generation in groups

brand a name, term, sign, symbol, or any other feature that identifies one seller's good or service as distinct from those of other sellers

brand advertising advertising that communicates a brand's features, values, and benefits

brand attitudes summary evaluations that reflect preferences for various products or brands

brand community group of consumers who feel a commonality and shared purpose grounded in or attached to a consumer good or service

brand equity positive associations with a brand in the minds of consumers

brand extension an adaptation of an existing brand to a new product area

brand loyalty decision-making mode in which consumers repeatedly choose to buy the same brand of a product to fulfill a specific need

brand-loyal users a market segment made up of consumers who repeatedly buy the same brand of a product

branded entertainment embedding brands or brand icons as part of an entertainment property in an effort to connect with consumers in a unique and compelling way

branding strategy of developing brand names so manufacturers can focus consumer attention on a clearly identified item

business markets the institutional buyers who purchase items to be used in other products and services or to be resold to other businesses or households

business-market sales promotion promotion designed to cultivate buyers making purchase decisions in corporations

buzz marketing creation of events or experiences that yield conversations that include the brand or product

canned presentation recitation of a prepared sales pitch

cause-related marketing marketing messages that identify corporate sponsorship of philanthropic activities

cease-and-desist order FTC action requiring an advertiser to stop running an ad so a hearing can be held to determine whether the ad is deceptive or unfair

celebrity sociological category of famous individuals who shape identity for others

celebrity endorsements advertisements that use an expert or celebrity as spokesperson to endorse the use of a product or service

Chaos Scenario exodus of ad revenue from traditional broadcast media in reaction to audience fragmentation and tools for ad avoidance; causes media cutbacks, followed by further reductions in audience size and even less advertising

click fraud act of clicking on Internet ads solely to generate revenue for the website carrying the ads

click-through measure of the number of hyperlinks that users click on, especially links from advertisements to the advertiser's website

client or **sponsor** the organization that pays for advertising

cognitive consistency maintenance of a system of beliefs and attitudes over time

cognitive dissonance anxiety or regret that lingers after a difficult decision

cognitive responses thoughts that occur at the exact moment when beliefs and attitudes are being challenged by a message

cognitive style an individual's preference for thinking about and solving a problem

commission system method of agency compensation based on the amount of money the advertiser spends on the media

communication test pretest message research aimed at measuring whether a message is communicating something close to what is desired

community group of people loosely joined by a common characteristic or interest

comparison advertisements ads that compare the advertiser's brand with competitors' brands

competitive field the companies that compete for a segment's business

competitive positioning a positioning option that uses an explicit reference to an existing competitor to help define precisely what a brand can do

consent order FTC action asking an advertiser to stop running deceptive or unfair advertising without admitting guilt

consideration set subset of brands from a product category that becomes the focal point of a consumer's evaluation

consultant individual who specializes in areas related to the promotional process

consultive selling face-to-face selling in which salespeople help customers define problems and design solutions

consumer behavior activities and decision processes directly involved in obtaining, consuming, and disposing of products and services

consumer culture a way of life centered around consumption

consumer markets the markets for products and services purchased by individuals or households to satisfy their specific needs

consumer sales promotion sales promotion that is aimed at consumers and focuses on price-off deals, coupons, sampling, rebates, and premiums

consumer-generated content (CGC) advertisements made partly or completely by the product's end users, typically with the aid of Internet tools

consumer-market sales promotion sales promotions designed to induce consumers to purchase a firm's brand rather than a competitor's

consumerism actions of individual consumers to exert power over the marketplace activities of organizations

contest sales promotion in which consumers compete for prizes based on skill or ability

cookies online tracking markers that advertisers place on a web surfer's hard drive to track that person's online behavior

cooperative advertising sharing of advertising expenses between national advertisers and local merchants

cooperative promotion (co-op promotion) sharing of promotion expenses between national advertisers and local merchants

corporate advertising advertising intended to establish a favorable attitude toward a company

corporate home page website that focuses on a corporation and its products

corrective advertising FTC action requiring an advertiser to run additional ads to dispel false beliefs created by deceptive advertising

cost per inquiry (CPI) number of inquiries generated by a direct-marketing program divided by the program's cost

cost per order (CPO) number of orders generated by a direct-marketing program divided by that program's cost

cost per thousand (CPM) dollar cost of reaching 1,000 members of an audience

coupon sales promotion that entitles a buyer to a designated reduction in price for a product or service

creative abrasion clash of ideas, abstracted from the people who propose them, from which new ideas can evolve

creative boutique advertising agency that emphasizes copywriting and artistic services

creative brief document that outlines and channels an essential creative idea and objective

creative revolution shift toward greater influence of "creatives" in advertising agencies during the 1960s

creative selling assisting and persuading customers regarding purchase decisions (typically for specialty goods or high-priced items)

creative services group in an advertising agency that develops the message to be delivered through advertising, sales promotion, direct marketing, event sponsorship, or public relations

creativity ability to consider and hold together seemingly inconsistent elements and forces, making a new connection

cross-selling marketing programs aimed at selling additional products to existing customers

culture a group's characteristic ways of behaving

customer relationship management (CRM) continual effort to cultivate and maintain long-term relationships with customers by emphasizing customer needs

customer satisfaction good feelings that come from a favorable postpurchase experience

dailies newspapers published every weekday

database agency agency that helps customers construct databases of target customers, merge databases, develop promotional materials, and execute direct-marketing campaigns

deception making false or misleading statements in a promotional message

defamation untrue communication that damages the reputation of an individual

delayed-response promotion promotion that relies on imagery and message themes to emphasize a brand's benefits and positive qualities to encourage customers to purchase the product at a later date

demographic dividend favorable climate for economic expansion in developing nations as a result of falling labor costs, a younger and healthier population, and entry of women into the workforce

demographic segmentation market segmentation that divides consumers according to basic descriptors such as age, gender, race, marital status, income, education, and occupation

designer specialist involved in execution of creative ideas and efforts by designing logos and other visual promotional pieces

detail salesperson salesperson who introduces new products and provides product information without aiming for an immediate sale

differentiation creation of a perceived difference, in the consumer's mind, between an organization's brand and the competition's

direct mail direct-marketing medium that uses the postal service to deliver marketing materials

direct marketing interactive marketing system that uses multiple media to generate a transaction or other measurable response at any location

direct-marketing agency or **direct-response agency** agency that maintains large databases of mailing lists and may design direct-marketing campaigns

direct-response advertising advertising that asks the receiver of the message to act immediately

direct-response promotion promotion that asks the receiver of the message to act immediately

display or banner ads advertisements placed on websites that contain editorial material

domain name unique URL that establishes a Web location

door-to-door sampling sampling in which samples are brought to the homes of the target segment in a well-defined geographic area

dummy advertising vehicles mock-ups of magazines that contain editorial content and advertisements, including ads being tested

e-business promotion in which companies selling to business customers rely on the Internet to send messages and close sales

e-commerce agency agency that handles planning and execution of activities related to promotions using electronic commerce

economies of scale lower per-unit production costs resulting from larger volume

elaboration likelihood model (ELM) social psychological model of the response to a persuasive communication, expressing the response in terms of motivation and ability

emergent consumers a market segment made up of the gradual but constant influx of first-time buyers

emotional benefits benefits not typically found in a product's tangible features or objective characteristics

ethics moral standards and principles against which behavior is judged

ethnocentrism tendency to view and value things from the perspective of one's own culture

evaluative criteria product attributes or performance characteristics on which consumers base their product evaluations

event sponsorship financial support for an event, given in exchange for the right to display a brand name, logo, or promotional message at the event

event-planning agency agency that finds locations, secures dates, and assembles a team of people to pull off a promotional event

extended problem solving decision-making mode in which inexperienced but highly involved consumers go through a deliberate decision-making process

external facilitator organization or individual that provides specialized services to advertisers and agencies

external lists mailing lists purchased from a list compiler or rented from a list broker; used for cultivating new business

external position competitive niche pursued by a brand

external search gathering product information by visiting retail stores to examine alternatives, seeking input from friends and relatives, or perusing professional product evaluations

eye-tracking systems physiological measure that monitors eye movements across advertisements

Federal Trade Commission (FTC) government regulatory agency most directly involved in overseeing the advertising industry

fee system method of agency compensation whereby the advertiser and agency agree on an hourly rate for services provided

free premium sales promotion that gives consumers an item at no cost by including the item in the package or mailing it after proof of purchase is verified

frequency programs sales promotion that offers consumers discounts or rewards for repeat purchases

frequency-marketing programs direct-marketing programs that provide concrete rewards to frequent customers

fulfillment center operation that ensures consumers receive products ordered in response to direct marketing

full-service agency advertising agency that includes an array of advertising professionals to meet all the promotional needs of clients

functional benefits benefits that come from a product's objective performance characteristics

gender social expression of sexual biology or sexual choice

geodemographic segmentation market segmentation that identifies neighborhoods sharing common demographic characteristics

global agencies advertising agencies with a worldwide presence

global promotion developing and placing messages with a common theme and presentation in all markets around the world where the brand is sold

globalized campaigns promotional campaigns that use the same message and creative execution across all or most international markets

government officials and employees advertising audience that includes employees of government organizations at the federal, state, and local levels

Great Depression a period (1929–1941 in the United States) of a severe economic decline affecting the vast majority of people in many countries

green marketing corporate communication efforts to promote a cause or program in support of the environment

gross domestic product (GDP) the total value of goods and services produced within an economic system

guerrilla marketing edgy, inexpensive promotional initiatives executed in major urban markets

habit decision-making mode in which consumers buy a single brand repeatedly as a solution to a simple consumption problem

heavy users consumers who purchase a product or service much more frequently than others

highly industrialized countries countries with a high GDP and a high standard of living

hits number of pages and graphical images requested from a website

household consumers the most conspicuous audience for advertising

in-house agency advertising department of a marketer's own firm

in-store sampling sampling that occurs at the point of purchase

Industrial Revolution a rapid shift in Western society from an agricultural to an industrial economy, beginning in the mid-eighteenth century

inelasticity of demand low sensitivity to price increases; may result from brand loyalty

influencer marketing series of personalized marketing techniques directed at individuals or groups with the credibility and capability to drive positive word of mouth in a market segment

infomercial long advertisement that looks like a talk show or product demonstration

inquiry/direct-response measures post-test message tracking in which an advertisement calls for a direct response and the number of responses is counted

integrated marketing communication (IMC) the use of a wide range of promotional tools working together to create widespread brand exposure

interactive agency advertising agency that helps clients prepare communications for new media (for example, the Internet and interactive kiosks)

interactive media media that allow consumers to call up games, entertainment, shopping, and educational programs on a subscription or pay-per-view basis

intergenerational effect choice of products based on what was used in the consumer's childhood household

internal lists organization's records of its customers and inquirers; used for developing better customer relationships

internal position niche a brand occupies with regard to the company's other, similar brands

internal search search for product information that draws on personal experience and prior knowledge

international affiliates foreign-market advertising agencies with which a local agency has established a relationship to handle international advertising needs

international brand promotion the preparation and placement of brand communication in different national and cultural markets

international promotion preparation and placement of messages in different national and cultural markets

Internet global collection of computer networks linking public and private computer systems to connect more than a billion users

interpersonal abrasion clash of people, often resulting from an inability to regard

idea feedback as separate from personal feedback, causing communication to shut down

interstitial Internet ad that appears briefly on a website after a page has been requested but before it has loaded

involvement degree of perceived relevance and personal importance accompanying the choice of a product or service in a particular context

less-developed countries countries whose economies lack most resources necessary for development: capital, infrastructure, political stability, and trained workers

leveraging using any collateral communication or activity to reinforce the link between a brand and an event

libel defamation that occurs in print (for example, in a magazine story)

life stage circumstance that changes a family's consumption patterns

lifestyle segmentation market segmentation that identifies consumers sharing similar activities, interests, and opinions

limited problem solving decision-making mode in which relatively inexperienced and uninvolved consumers are not systematic about decisions

local agency advertising agency in a foreign market hired because of its knowledge of the culture and local market conditions

local promotion promotion directed to an audience in a single trading area (a city or state)

localized campaigns promotional campaigns that involve different messages and creative executions for each foreign market served

log analysis software measurement software that provides data about online consumer behavior, including hits, pages, visits, and users, as well as audience traffic within a website

logo graphic mark that identifies a company

Madison & Vine convergence of advertising and entertainment; reference to the names of streets that represent each industry

mail sampling sampling in which samples are delivered through the postal service

mailing list file of names and addresses used for contacting prospects or customers

market niche a relatively small group of consumers with a unique set of needs and the willingness to pay a premium price to a firm that meets those needs

market segmentation breaking down a large, heterogeneous market into submarkets that are more homogeneous

marketer business, not-for-profit, or government organization that uses advertising and other promotional techniques to communicate with target markets to stimulate awareness of and demand for its brands

marketing the process of conceiving, pricing, promoting, and distributing ideas, goods, and services to create exchanges that benefit customers

marketing database mailing list with added information collected directly from individual customers

marketing mix the blend of the four responsibilities of marketing (conception, pricing, promotion, and distribution) used for a particular idea, product, or service

markup charge method of agency compensation based on adding a percentage charge to a variety of services the agency purchases from outside suppliers

mash-up combination of websites into a single site for analyzing or comparing information

meaning what a brand message intends or conveys

meaningfulness in promotion research, practical applicability of conclusions to the promotional effort

media impressions instances in which a product or brand is exposed to consumers through media coverage, rather than paid advertising

media planning and buying services services that are related to media planning or buying and are provided by advertising agencies or specialized media-buying organizations

media specialist organization that specializes in buying media time and space and that offers media strategy consulting to agencies and advertisers

members of a trade channel advertising audience that includes retailers, wholesalers, and distributors

members of business organizations advertising audience that buys business and industrial goods and services

merchandise allowances trade-market sales promotion in which free products are packed with regular shipments as payment to the trade for setting up and maintaining displays

missionary salesperson salesperson who calls on accounts to monitor buyers' satisfaction and update their needs

mobile sampling sampling carried out using logo-emblazoned vehicles where samples are dispensed at malls or other high-traffic areas

Mobile-Fi wireless Internet technology with multi-mile access and ability to access the Internet while the user is moving in a car or train

monopoly power a company's ability, either through advertising or in some other way, to prevent rivals from competing

multi-attribute attitude models (MAAMs) framework and set of procedures for collecting information from consumers to assess their salient beliefs and attitudes about competing brands

National Advertising Review Board body formed by the advertising industry to oversee its practices

national promotion promotion directed to all geographic areas of one nation

naturalistic inquiry broad-based research method that relies on qualitative data collection, including video and audio recordings and photography

need satisfaction sales presentation that begins with assessment of each buyer's need state and then adjusts the selling effort to that need state

need state psychological state arising when one's desired state of affairs differs from one's actual state of affairs

newly industrialized countries countries where traditional ways of life are changing into modern consumer cultures

newspaper sampling sampling in which samples are distributed in newspapers to allow specific geographic and geodemographic targeting

nonusers a market segment made up of consumers who do not use a particular product or service

normative test scores scores determined by testing an ad and then comparing the scores with those of previously tested campaigns of the same type

off-invoice allowance program allowing wholesalers and retailers to deduct a set amount from the invoice they receive for merchandise

on-package sampling sampling in which a sample item is attached to another product's package

opt-in email messages sent to website visitors who have given permission to receive commercial email about particular topics or products

order taking practice of accepting and processing customer information for prearranged purchase or scheduling services a customer will purchase

out-of-home media transit and billboard advertising

packaging a product's container or wrapping, which conveys product information and user appeal

page views record of the pages that have been sent to a user's computer; multiscreen pages are counted as one page

paid search the practice of paying search engines and portals to place ads near relevant search results

pay-for-results compensation plan based on an agreement in which fee amounts are tied to a set of results criteria

peripheral cues features of an advertisement other than the actual arguments about the brand's performance

permanent long-term displays P-O-P materials intended for presentation for more than six months

permission marketing sending commercial email only to Web users who have agreed to receive it

personal selling process of face-to-face communication and persuasion

physiological measures interpretation of biological feedback from subjects exposed to an ad

picturing creating representations of things

pilot testing message evaluation that consists of experimentation in the marketplace

point-of-entry marketing advertising strategy designed to win the loyalty of consumers whose brand preferences are under development

point-of-purchase (P-O-P) advertising advertising that appears in the retail setting

pop-under ad Internet ad that is displayed "under" the active window, so it appears only after that window is closed

pop-up ad Internet advertisement that opens a separate window while a Web page is loading

portal website that serves as a starting point for Web access and search

positioning the process of designing and representing a product or service to occupy a distinct and valued place in the target customer's mind

positioning strategy the key themes or concepts that an organization features when communicating a product's or service's distinctiveness to a target segment

post-test message tracking assessment of an ad's performance during or after the launch of an ad campaign

premiums items that feature a sponsor's logo and are offered free or at a reduced price with the purchase of another item

price-off deal type of sales promotion that offers consumers money off merchandise at the point of purchase through specially marked packages

primary demand demand for an entire product category

primary demand stimulation promotion aimed at creating demand for a product category

principle of limited liability limitation of an investor's risk in a corporation to his or her investment in the company's shares

proactive public relations strategy PR strategy that is dictated by marketing objectives, seeks publicity, and takes the offense

product placement sales promotion technique of getting a marketer's product featured in movies and television shows

production facilitator organization that offers essential services during and after the production process

production services team in an agency that takes creative ideas and turns them into advertisements, direct-mail pieces, or events materials

professionals advertising audience that includes workers with special training or certification

promotion the communications process in marketing that is used to create a favorable predisposition toward a brand of product or service

promotion agency specialized agency that handles promotional efforts

promotion research marketing research focused on the development and performance of promotional materials

promotional mix a blend of communications tools used to carry out the promotion process and communicate directly with an audience

psychogalvanometer device that measures galvanic skin response, or minute changes in perspiration that may suggest arousal

psychographics a form of market research that emphasizes the understanding of consumers' activities, interests, and opinions

public relations function that provides communications to foster goodwill between a firm and its constituent groups

public relations audit internal study that identifies aspects of the firm or its activities that are positive and newsworthy

public relations firm firm that handles an organization's needs regarding relationships with the local community, competitors, industry associations, and government organizations

public relations plan plan that identifies the objectives and activities of a firm's PR communications

publicity unpaid-for media exposure about a firm's activities or its products and services

puffery use of superlatives like "number one" and "best in the world" in promotional messages

Pure Food and Drug Act 1906 U.S. law requiring manufacturers to list the active ingredients of their products on their labels

push money trade incentive in which retail salespeople are offered monetary rewards for featuring a marketer's brand

push strategy sales promotion strategy in which marketers devise incentives to encourage purchases by members of the trade, moving product into the distribution channel

reactive public relations strategy PR strategy that is dictated by influences outside the company's control, focuses on solving problems, and requires defensive measures

rebate money-back offer requiring a buyer to mail in a form requesting the money back from the manufacturer

recall test test of how much the viewer of an ad remembers of the message

recognition tests tests in which audience members are asked whether they recognize an ad or something in an ad

regional promotion promotion concentrated on a large, but not national, region

reliability tendency to generate consistent findings over time

repositioning returning to the STP marketing process to arrive at a revised positioning strategy

resonance test message assessment aimed at determining the extent to which a message rings true with target audience members

RFM analysis analysis of how recently and frequently a customer bought from an organization, and how much the customer spent

rich media, video, and audio use of streaming video and audio that plays when the user's mouse passes over an Internet ad

riding the boards assessing possible locations for billboard advertising

rituals repeated behaviors that affirm, express, and maintain cultural values

sales force automation (SFA) integration of computers, communication technology, and the Internet to improve the efficiency and effectiveness of personal selling

sales management responsibility for the personal-selling effort, met by evaluating needs, setting objectives and budgets, structuring and hiring the sales force, training and motivating salespeople, and evaluating their performance

sales promotion use of innovative techniques that create a perception of greater brand value among consumers or distributors

salient beliefs the few beliefs that are the critical determinants of an attitude

sampling sales promotion technique that offers consumers a trial opportunity

search engine software tool for finding websites by entering keywords

search engine optimization (SEO) process for improving the volume and quality of traffic to a website from a search engine's results pages

Second Life online virtual world where participants can roam landscapes and interact, simulating real-world activities, including (often real) business transactions

selective attention processing of only a few messages among many encountered

selective demand stimulation promotion aimed at stimulating demand for a specific brand

self-liquidating premium sales promotion that requires a consumer to pay most of the cost of the item received as a premium

self-reference criterion (SRC) unconscious reference to one's own cultural values, experiences, and knowledge as a basis for decisions

self-regulation the advertising industry's attempt to police itself

seminar selling education of customer or prospect groups to inform them about the firm's products or services

short-term promotional displays P-O-P materials used for six months or less

single-source tracking measures post-test message tracking that uses a combination of scanner data and devices that monitor television-viewing behavior to collect information about brand purchases, coupon use, and television ad exposure

slander oral defamation (for example, during a radio broadcast)

slotting fees trade-market sales promotion in which manufacturers make direct cash payments to retailers to ensure shelf space

social media websites where users create and share information about themselves, brands, and other mutual interests

spam uninvited commercial messages sent to electronic mailing lists or online discussion groups

split-cable transmission pilot testing of two versions of an advertisement through direct transmission to separate sample households

split-list experiments pilot testing in which multiple versions of a direct-mail piece are sent to segments of a mailing list and responses to each version are compared

split-run distribution pilot testing in which different versions of an advertisement are placed in magazines and direct responses to each advertisement are compared

sponsorship payment to maintain a section of a website and perhaps provide content for the site in exchange for being mentioned on the site

sticky site website that attracts visitors again and again and keeps them for a long time

STP marketing developing a strategy through segmenting, targeting, and positioning

stratification (social class) individuals' relative standing in a social system as produced by systematic inequalities

subliminal advertising advertisements alleged to work on a subconscious level

support media media used to reinforce a message being delivered via some other media vehicle

surfing gliding from website to website, guided by hyperlinks, a search engine, or word of mouth

sweepstakes sales promotion in which winners are awarded prizes based on chance

switchers or variety seekers a market segment made up of consumers who often buy what is on sale or choose brands that offer price incentives

symbolic value nonliteral meaning of a product or service, as perceived by consumers

system selling selling a set of interrelated components that fulfill a majority of a customer's needs in a product or service area

target audience a particular group of consumers singled out for an advertising or promotion campaign

target segment the subgroup (of the larger market) chosen as the focal point for a marketing program and advertising campaign

taste a generalized set or orientation to consumer preferences

team selling sales effort by a team of salespeople representing different functions

telemarketing direct-marketing medium that involves using the telephone to deliver a spoken appeal

theater tests pretest message research in which subjects view ads played in small theaters and record their reactions

thought listing pretest message research that tries to identify specific thoughts that may be generated by an ad

TiVo service that automatically records a consumer's selected television shows when they air and allows consumers to skip commercials

top-level domain (TLD) suffix that follows a website name

trade journals magazines that publish technical articles for members of a trade

trade reseller organization in the marketing channel of distribution that buys products to resell to customers

trade shows events where several related products from many manufacturers are displayed and demonstrated to members of the trade

trade-market sales promotion sales promotion that is designed to motivate distributors, wholesalers, and retailers to stock and feature a firm's brand in their merchandising programs

transit advertising advertising that appears as interior and exterior displays on mass-transit vehicles and at terminal and station platforms

trial offers sales promotion in which expensive items are offered on a trial basis to induce consumers to try a brand

trustworthiness quality of deserving confidence

ultrabroadband wireless Internet technology allowing users to move extremely large files quickly over short distances

unfair advertising acts by advertisers that cause or are likely to cause substantial injury that is not reasonably avoidable or outweighed by other benefits

unique visitors number of people (identified using registration information) who visit a site during a given time period

Usenet collection of more than 13,000 discussion groups on the Internet

user positioning a positioning option that focuses on a specific profile of the target user

validity relevance in terms of actually answering the questions being investigated

value perception that a product or service provides satisfaction beyond the cost incurred to acquire it

value proposition a statement of the functional, emotional, and self-expressive benefits that are delivered by the brand and provide value to customers in the target segment

values defining expressions of what is important to a culture

variety seeking decision-making mode in which consumers switch their selection among various brands in a category in a random pattern

vertical cooperative advertising sharing of advertising expense by a manufacturer and dealer (wholesaler or retailer)

viral marketing process of consumers marketing to consumers over the Internet through word of mouth

viral marketing process of consumers spreading brand messages through email

virtual mall gateway to a group of Internet storefronts where the user gains access to a retailer by clicking on a storefront

visits number of occasions on which a particular user looks up a particular website during a given time period

voice response analysis physiological assessment in which computers measure inflections in subjects' voices

Web analytic software software that measures hits, pages, visits, and users, and allows a website to track audience traffic on the site

website collection of Web pages, images, videos, and other content hosted on a Web server

widget software module that people can add to their blog or their personal page on a social network; may feature a brand or direct the user to an e-commerce site

WiFi wireless technology allowing Internet access connections to reach out about 300 feet

WiMax wireless Internet technology capable of a range of 25 to 30 miles

World Wide Web (WWW) database of information available online in a graphical environment that simplifies navigation

Company Index

Subject Index

E

E-business, 62–63
E-commerce, 133–137
E-commerce agencies, 34
E-communities, 193–194
Economic development, 143–144, 146
Economies of scale, 17, 153
Educational attainment, 104
Einstein, Albert, 160, 161
Elaboration likelihood model (ELM), 99–100
Eliot, T.S., 160, 161
Email
    from direct marketers, 212–215
    explanation of, 178–179
    promotional use of, 184–185
Emergent consumers, 72
Emotional benefits, 89, 95
Emotions, 311
Entertainment, branded, 63–64
E promotion revolution, 61
E-revolution, 59–61
Esteem needs, 117
Ethical issues
    controversial products as, 123–124
    database marketing and, 113–114
    deception and unfairness as, 124–125
    privacy as, 127, 133, 137, 189–190, 209–210
    targeting children as, 122
    truth and, 121–122
Ethics, 121
Ethnicity, 106–107
Ethnocentrism, 142, 143
European Union, 149
Evaluative criteria, 91
Event-planning agencies, 35
Event sponsorships
    effectiveness of, 320
    event choice and, 248–249
    explanation of, 247–248
    leveraging of, 251–252
    results of, 249–251
Extended problem solving, 93
External facilitators
    explanation of, 40
    types of, 41–42

External lists, 205
External position, 16–17
External search, 91
External situation analysis, 298
Eye-tracking systems, 314

F

Face-to-face presentations, 293–294
Fair Credit Reporting Act of 1970, 127
Fair Packaging and Labeling Act of 1966, 127
Families, consumer behavior and, 105–106
Feature stories, 266–267
Federal Communications Commission (FCC), 25, 58, 123, 124, 126
Federal government regulation, 126–128
Federal Trade Commission Act of 1914, 127
Federal Trade Commission (FTC), 58, 123, 127–128, 133, 135, 136, 259
Fee system, 39
Feminist movement, 57
Food and Drug Administration (FDA), 126–127
Fox, Stephen, 118
Frank, Thomas, 59
Free premiums, 226
Frequency programs
    in business market, 235
    in consumer market, 230
    explanation of, 208–209
Freud, Sigmund, 160, 161
Frost, Geoffrey, 37–38
FTC Improvement Act of 1975, 127
Fulfillment centers, 34
Full-service agencies, 32
Functional benefits, 89
Functional feeders, 74
Fur Products Labeling Act of 1951, 127

G

Gambling, promotion of, 123
Gandhi, Mahatma, 160, 161

Gardner, Howard, 160, 161
Garfield, Bob, 247
Gates, Bill, 104
Gays/lesbians, 56, 108
Gender, 108
Gender roles, 146
Geodemographic segmentation, 74, 243
Geography, segmenting by, 73–74
Geopolitics, 107
Gift cards, 229
Gladwell, Malcolm, 265
Global agencies, 151
Global Business Dialog on electronic Commerce (GDBe), 131–132
Globalized campaigns, 152–154
Global marketplace, 153–154
Godin, Seth, 214
Government agency advertising expenditures, 31
Government officials and employees, 11
Graham, Martha, 160, 161
Great Depression, 45–46, 52–53
Green marketing, 281
Gross domestic product (GDP), 19
Guerrilla marketing, 243

H

Habit, 94
Hansberry, Brian, 4
Happy cookers, 75
Heavy users, 71
Highly industrialized countries, 144
Hispanics, brand loyalty and, 107
Hits, 190, 317
Hopkins, Claude, 49
Household consumers, 10
Humor, 143

I

Image advertising, 278–279
IMC. See Integrated marketing communication (IMC)
Incentives, 232
Income, 104
Individualism, 145
Industrialization period, 49

Industrial Revolution, 47
Industry associations, 131
Inelasticity of demand, 17
Influencer marketing
    explanation of, 272
        peer-to-peer programs and, 273–274
        professional influencers and, 272–273
Infomercials
    explanation of, 34, 59
    function of, 215–216
Information
    from brand promotion, 114–116, 311
    consumer acquisition of, 89–91
Information processing, 97–98
In-house agencies, 33–34
In-house publications, 267
Inquiry/direct-response measures, 319
Institutional advertising, 19
In-store sampling, 228
Integrated marketing communication (IMC)
    advertising during, 7
    coordination of, 260–261
    creativity and, 166–172
    explanation of, 6–7
    in marketing, 12–17
    measuring effectiveness of, 323–325
    overview of, 4
    promotional objectives and, 17–21, 46
    role of marketers in, 31
Interactive agencies, 32–33
Interactive media, 43, 60
Intergenerational effect, 105
Internal lists, 205
Internal position, 17
Internal search, 90, 91
Internal situation analysis, 298
International affiliates, 152
International audiences. See Cross-cultural audiences
International brand promotion. See also Cross-cultural audiences
    advertising agencies and, 151–152
    challenges of, 147–150

exposure to, 325
interactive, 43, 60
in international markets, 148–149
Internet, 178–180
print, 43, 148, 278, 292
social, 274–277
support, 43, 238–243
Media buyers, 38
Media conglomerates, 43
Media impressions, 250
Media organizations
collaboration with, 259–260
consolidation of, 25–26
function of, 42–43
growth in, 26–27
self-regulation by, 131
target audience and, 43
types of, 42
Media planners, 38
Media planning and buying services, 38
Media researchers, 38
Media specialists, 34
Members of business organizations, 10
Members of trade channels, 10
Merchandise allowances, 233
Message-testing research, 310–311. See also Advertising messages
Microblogging, 274
Missionary salespeople, 288
Mobile-Fi, 195, 196
Mobile sampling, 229
Monopoly power, 126
Moore, Jeri, 84
Morse, Ken, 292
Motivation, sales force, 303–304
Movies, 253
Multi-attribute attitude models (MAAMs), 96–97

N

Nader, Ralph, 132
National Advertising Division (NAD) (Council of Better Business Bureaus), 130–131
National Advertising Review Board (NARB), 58, 130–131

National Association of Broadcasters (NAB), 131
National promotion, 12
Naturalistic inquiry, 309
Need creation, 117
Needs, recognition of, 89–90
Need satisfaction
brand promotion and, 117–118
explanation of, 293
Need states, 88–89
Negotiation, in mass-media communication, 9
New Class, 104
Newly industrialized countries, 144
Newsletters, in-house, 267
Newspaper advertisements, 48–49
Newspaper sampling, 229
Niche marketing, 78
Nonusers, 72
Normative test scores, 310
Not-for-profit organizations, 31
Nutrition Labeling and Education Act (NLEA) of 1990, 127

O

Occupation, 104
Offensive advertisements, 119–120
Off-invoice allowances, 233
Ogilvy, David, 23, 56, 113
Older individuals
diversity among, 77–78
stereotypes of, 119
Online promotion. See Internet promotion
On-package sampling, 229
Opt-in email, 178
Order taking, 287
Organizations, 31, 162
Ottman, Jacquelyn, 281
Outdoor advertising, 238–239

P

Packaging, 242–243
Page views, 191, 317
Paid search, 183
Palmer, Volney, 49
Pay-for-results, 39–40

Peer-to-peer programs, 273–274
Peripheral cues, 99–100
Permanent long-term displays, 237
Permission marketing, 114, 184
Perquisites, 304
Personal-care products, 146–147
Personal selling. See also Sales management; Salespeople
explanation of, 284–285
measuring effectiveness of, 322–323
in new environment, 295–297
objectives of, 289–290
process of, 291–295
role of salespeople in, 285–287
types of, 287–289
Phone cards, 229
Physiological measures, 314
Picasso, Pablo, 160, 161
Picturing, 147–148
Pilot testing, 315
Podcasts, 275
Point-of-entry marketing, 72
Point-of-purchase (P-O-P) advertising
explanation of, 236
formats for, 237–238
measuring effectiveness of, 320
objectives of, 236–237
for trade and business buyers, 238
Pop-under ads, 184
Pop-up ads, 184
Portals, 180, 188
Positioning
benefit of, 80–81
competitive, 81–82
decisions related to, 16–17
explanation of, 16, 69
user, 81
Positioning strategy
consistency in, 79–80
elements of, 79
explanation of, 69, 78, 79
repositioning, 82
themes in, 80–82
Postpurchase satisfaction, 92

Post-testing
advertising, 315–317
sales promotion, 319–320
Post-test message tracking, 315
Powers, John E., 49
Preindustrialization period, 48–49
Premiums
in business market, 234
in consumer market, 226–227
explanation of, 136
Presentations, sales, 293–294
Press conferences, 267
Press releases, 266, 267
Pretest evaluations, 311–315
Price, 20
Price-off deals, 226
Primary demand, 123
Primary demand stimulation, 18
Principle of limited liability, 47
Print media
corporate advertising in, 278
explanation of, 43
in international markets, 148
mail-in coupons in, 292
Privacy
appropriation and, 137
database marketing and, 209–210
Internet and, 127, 133, 189–190
Proactive public relations strategy, 269–270
Problem solving, 93–94. See also Decision making
Production facilitators, 41–42
Production services, 38
Product placement
branded entertainment vs., 256
challenges of, 257–260
explanation of, 63, 252
measuring success of, 255
movies and, 253
television and, 253
in television programs and films, 136
value of, 254

GLOSSARY TERMS

promotion the communications process in marketing that is used to create a favorable predisposition toward a brand of product or service

promotional mix a blend of communications tools used to carry out the promotion process and to communicate directly with an audience

advertising a paid, mass-mediated attempt to persuade

client or **sponsor** the organization that pays for advertising

integrated marketing communication (IMC) the use of a wide range of promotional tools working together to create widespread brand exposure

advertisement a specific message that an organization has placed to persuade an audience

advertising campaign a series of coordinated promotional efforts, including advertisements, that communicate a single theme or idea

audience a group of individuals who may receive and interpret promotional messages

target audience a particular group of consumers singled out for an advertising or promotion campaign

household consumers the most conspicuous audience for advertising

members of business organizations advertising audience that buys business and industrial goods and services

members of a trade channel advertising audience that includes retailers, wholesalers, and distributors

professionals advertising audience that includes workers with special training or certification

trade journals magazines that publish technical articles for members of a trade

government officials and employees advertising audience that includes employees of government organizations at the federal, state, and local levels

CHAPTER SUMMARY

LO 1

Define promotion and integrated marketing communication (IMC).

Promotion is the communications process in marketing that is used to create a favorable predisposition toward a brand of product or service, an idea, or even a person. Promotional efforts are combined into a promotional mix that includes tools such as advertising, direct marketing, public relations, and personal selling. One of the most widely used tools is advertising, which is distinguished by its three essential elements: paid sponsorship, use of mass media, and the intent to persuade. The promotional mix will be most effective if the elements are integrated to achieve particular goals, and the realities of promotion in the 21st century demand that these goals be centered on brand. As a result, marketers have been turning toward the use of integrated marketing communication (IMC). IMC is the process of using a wide range of promotional tools working together to build and maintain brand awareness, identity, and preference.

LO 2

Discuss a basic model of communication.

Promotion occurs through various forms of communication, and advertising involves a particular type: mass-mediated communication. A model of mass-mediated communication that helps explain how advertising works show this type of communication as a process where people, institutions, and messages interact. This model has two major components—production and reception—each of which is a quasi-independent process. Between these are the mediating (interpretation) processes of accommodation and negotiation. According to this model, consumers create their own meanings when they interpret advertisements.

[Exhibit 1.2]
Mass-Mediated Communication

LO 3

Describe the different ways of classifying audiences for promotion and IMC.

In the language of promotion, an audience is a group of individuals who receive and interpret advertisements and other promotional messages sent from companies. Broad audience categories are household consumers, members of business organizations, members of a trade channel, professionals, and government officials and employees. Audiences also may be defined by the scope of their location as global, international, national, regional, or local. Besides directing advertisements to audience groups at these levels, marketers may engage in cooperative advertising, a team effort in which producers and retailers work together on messages about a brand and where it is available for sale.

global promotion developing and placing messages with a common theme and presentation in all markets around the world where the brand is sold

international promotion preparation and placement of messages in different national and cultural markets

national promotion promotion directed to all geographic areas of one nation

regional promotion promotion concentrated on a large, but not national, region

local promotion promotion directed to an audience in a single trading area (a city or state)

cooperative promotion (co-op promotion) sharing of promotion expenses between national advertisers and local merchants

marketing the process of conceiving, pricing, promoting, and distributing ideas, goods, and services to create exchanges that benefit customers

marketing mix the blend of the four responsibilities of marketing (conception, pricing, promotion, and distribution) used for a particular idea, product, or service

brand a name, term, sign, symbol, or any other feature that identifies one seller's good or service as distinct from those of other sellers

brand extension an adaptation of an existing brand to a new product area

brand loyalty decision-making mode in which consumers repeatedly buy the same brand to fulfill a specific need

brand equity positive associations with a brand in the minds of consumers

market segmentation breaking down a large, heterogeneous market into submarkets that are more homogeneous

differentiation creation of a perceived difference, in the consumer's mind, between an organization's brand and the competition's

positioning designing a product or service to occupy a distinct and valued place in the target consumer's mind and then communicating this distinctiveness

external position competitive niche pursued by a brand

LO 4 — Explain the key role of IMC as a business process.

As organizations carry out marketing activities, IMC helps them do so in a way that achieves profitability and other goals. It provides a way to coordinate promotional activities, which are a key part of the marketing mix—the blend of strategic emphasis on product, pricing, promotion, and distribution. In IMC, the role of promotional tools is to communicate a brand's value, including product features, convenience, and emotional benefits through information and persuasion, introduction of new offerings, cultivation of brand loyalty among consumers and the trade, and creation of a brand's image and meaning. In these ways, IMC contributes to building brand awareness and brand equity. IMC also helps marketers implement market segmentation, differentiation, and positioning. All these efforts enhance revenues and profits. In addition, IMC involves selection of options such as primary versus selective demand stimulation, direct- versus delayed-response advertising, and promotion of the company or the brand.

[Exhibit 1.3]
The Marketing Mix

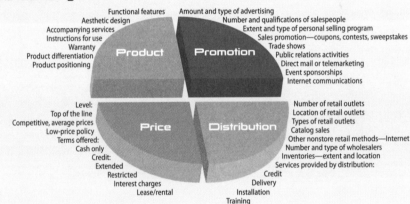

Use the skills you've learned in this chapter to get started on the brand campaign card at the end of the book.

internal position niche a brand occupies with regard to the company's other, similar brands

economies of scale lower per-unit production costs resulting from larger volume

inelasticity of demand low sensitivity to price increases; may result from brand loyalty

primary demand stimulation promotion aimed at creating demand for a product category

selective demand stimulation promotion aimed at stimulating demand for a specific brand

direct-response promotion promotion that asks the receiver of the message to act immediately

delayed-response promotion promotion that relies on

imagery and message themes to emphasize a brand's benefits and positive qualities to encourage customers to purchase the product at a later date

brand advertising advertising that communicates a brand's features, values, and benefits

corporate advertising advertising intended to establish a favorable attitude toward a company

gross domestic product (GDP) the total value of goods and services produced within an economic system

value perception that a product or service provides satisfaction beyond the cost incurred to acquire it

symbolic value nonliteral meaning of a product or service, as perceived by consumers

Visit CourseMate for PROMO at www.cengagebrain.com for additional study tools.

CHAPTER 1

GLOSSARY TERMS

blog personal journal on a website that is frequently updated and intended for public access

marketer business, not-for-profit, or government organization that uses advertising and other promotional techniques to communicate with target markets to stimulate awareness of and demand for its brands

client organization that pays for advertising

trade reseller organization in the marketing channel of distribution that buys products to resell to customers

advertising agency organization of professionals who provide creative and business services related to planning, preparing, and placing advertisements

full-service agency advertising agency that includes an array of advertising professionals to meet all the promotional needs of clients

creative boutique advertising agency that emphasizes copywriting and artistic services

interactive agency advertising agency that helps clients prepare communications for new media (for example, the Internet and interactive kiosks)

in-house agency advertising department of a marketer's own firm

media specialist organization that specializes in buying media time and space and that offers media strategy consulting to agencies and advertisers

promotion agency specialized agency that handles promotional efforts

direct-marketing agency or **direct-response agency** agency that maintains large databases of mailing lists and may design direct-marketing campaigns

database agency agency that helps customers construct databases of target customers, merge databases, develop promotional materials, and execute direct-marketing campaigns

CHAPTER SUMMARY

LO 1 Discuss important trends transforming the promotion industry.

Recent years have seen dramatic changes in the promotion industry. The late-1990s trend toward agency consolidation has reversed as numerous industry acquisitions and mergers failed to impress clients or produce greater profitability. The proliferation of media from cable television to the Internet has created new advertising options, and giant media conglomerates are expected to control a majority of these television, radio, and Internet properties. Media proliferation has led to increasing media clutter and fragmentation, reducing the effectiveness of advertisements. As a result, marketers are using sales promotions, event sponsorships, and public relations to enhance the advertising effort. Finally, today's consumers have greater control over the information they receive about brands. New technology applications from blogs to TiVo empower consumers and diminish the role of promotion.

LO 2 Describe the promotion industry's size, structure, and participants.

Spending on promotional efforts exceeds a trillion dollars a year. The industry serves marketers, which are organizations that have a message they wish to communicate to a target audience. Typically, a marketer hires advertising and promotion agencies to launch and manage a campaign. Often, other external facilitators are brought in to perform specialized functions, such as assisting in the production of promotional materials or managing databases for efficient direct-marketing campaigns. These external facilitators also include consultants with whom advertisers and their agencies may confer regarding advertising and IMC strategy decisions. Promotional campaigns use some type of media to reach target markets, so marketers and their agencies work with media companies that have time or space to sell.

[Exhibit 2.1]
Structure of the Promotion Industry

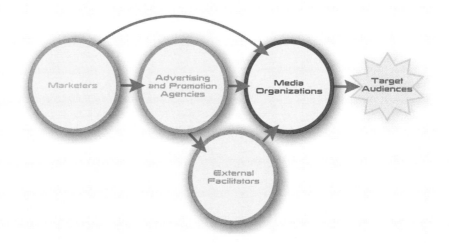

fulfillment center operation that ensures consumers receive products ordered in response to direct marketing

infomercial long advertisement that resembles a talk show or product demonstration

e-commerce agency agency that handles planning and execution of activities related to promotions using electronic commerce

consumer sales promotion sales promotion that is aimed at consumers and focuses on price-off deals, coupons, sampling, rebates, and premiums

trade-market sales promotion sales promotion that is designed to motivate distributors, wholesalers, and retailers to stock and feature a firm's brand in their merchandising programs

event-planning agency agency that finds locations, secures dates, and assembles a team of people to pull off a promotional event

designer specialist involved in execution of creative ideas and efforts by designing logos and other visual promotional pieces

logo graphic mark that identifies a company

public relations firm firm that handles an organization's needs regarding relationships with the local community, competitors, industry associations, and government organizations

account services team of managers that identifies the benefits a brand offers its target audiences and the best competitive position, and then develops a promotion plan

account planner person in an advertising agency who synthesizes all relevant consumer research and uses it to design an advertising strategy

creative services group in an advertising agency that develops the message to be delivered through advertising, sales promotion, direct marketing, event sponsorship, or public relations

production services team in an agency that takes creative ideas and turns them into advertisements, direct-mail pieces, or events materials

LO 3 Summarize what advertising and promotion agencies do and how they are compensated.

Advertising and promotion agencies offer diverse services with respect to planning, preparing, and executing advertising and IMC campaigns. These services include market research and marketing planning, the creation and production of ad materials, the buying of media time or space for ad placement, and traffic management to keep production on schedule. Some advertising agencies offer a full array of services under one roof; others such as creative boutiques develop a particular expertise and win clients with their specialized skills. Promotion agencies specialize in one or more of the other forms of promotion beyond advertising. New-media agencies serve the Internet and other new-media needs of marketers. Clients pay agencies for services rendered based on commissions, markups, fee systems, and pay-for-results programs.

LO 4 Identify experts who help plan and execute integrated marketing communication campaigns.

Marketing and advertising research firms help advertisers and their agencies understand the market environment. Other external facilitators consult on marketing strategy, event planning, or retail display. Perhaps the most widely used facilitators specialize in production of promotional materials. In advertising, outside facilitators are used for the production of broadcast and print advertising. In promotions, designers and planners assist in creation and execution of promotional mix tools. Software firms fill a new role in the industry by providing expertise in tracking and analyzing consumer usage of new media technology.

LO 5 Discuss the role played by media organizations in IMC campaigns.

Media organizations are the essential link in delivering advertising and IMC messages to target audiences. Traditional media organizations include television, radio, newspaper, and magazines. Interactive media include the Internet, CD-ROMs, electronic kiosks, and less widely known communications companies. Media conglomerates control several different aspects of the communications system, such as cable broadcasting and Internet connections.

Use the skills you've learned in this chapter to get started on the brand campaign card at the end of the book.

media planning and buying services services that are related to media planning or buying and are provided by advertising agencies or specialized media-buying organizations

commission system method of agency compensation based on the amount of money the advertiser spends on the media

markup charge method of agency compensation based on adding a percentage charge to a variety of services the agency purchases from outside suppliers

fee system method of agency compensation whereby the advertiser and agency agree on an hourly rate for services provided

pay-for-results compensation plan based on an agreement in which fee amounts are tied to a set of results criteria

external facilitator organization or individual that provides specialized services to advertisers and agencies

consultant individual who specializes in areas related to the promotional process

production facilitator organization that offers essential services during and after the production process

Visit CourseMate for PROMO at www.cengagebrain.com for additional study tools.

CHAPTER 2

GLOSSARY TERMS

Industrial Revolution a rapid shift in Western society from an agricultural to an industrial economy, beginning in the mid-18th century

principle of limited liability limitation of an investor's risk in a corporation to his or her investment in the company's shares

branding strategy of developing brand names so that manufacturers can focus consumer attention on a clearly identified item

dailies newspapers published every weekday

consumer culture a way of life centered around consumption

Pure Food and Drug Act 1906 U.S. law requiring manufacturers to list the active ingredients of their products on their labels

Great Depression a period (1929–1941 in the United States) of a severe economic decline affecting the vast majority of people in many countries

subliminal advertising advertisements alleged to work on a subconscious level

creative revolution shift toward greater influence of "creatives" in advertising agencies during the 1960s

Action for Children's Television group formed during the 1970s to lobby the government to limit the amount and content of advertising to children

Federal Trade Commission (FTC) government regulatory agency most directly involved in overseeing the advertising industry

National Advertising Review Board body formed by the advertising industry to oversee its practices

infomercial long advertisement that looks like a talk show or product demonstration

interactive media media that allow consumers to call up games, entertainment, shopping, and educational programs on a subscription or pay-per-view basis

CHAPTER SUMMARY

LO 1   **Identify economic changes that gave rise to advertising.**

Advertising as we know it today is connected with the emergence of capitalistic economic systems. In such systems, business organizations must compete for survival in a free market setting. In this setting, it is natural that a firm would embrace a tool that assists it in persuading potential customers to choose its products over those offered by others. The explosion in production capacity that marked the Industrial Revolution added to the importance of demand stimulation tools. Mass moves of consumers to cities and modern times helped create, along with advertising, consumer culture.

[Exhibit 3.1]
A Foundation for Advertising

LO 2   **Discuss how the relationship between marketers and retailers has changed over time.**

Marketing and branding play a key role in the ongoing power struggle between manufacturers and their retailers. Retailers have power in the marketplace deriving from the fact that they are closer to the customer. To assert more power in distribution channels, U.S. manufacturers began branding their products in the late 1800s. They used advertising to build awareness of and desire for their brands. Customers who are loyal to brands demand that retailers carry those brands and will pay a premium price for those brands. Lately, big retailers have been reclaiming some of the power by negotiating large purchases from manufacturers at lower prices.

LO 3   **Describe significant eras of promotion in the United States, including the impact of social change on promotion.**

Social and economic trends, along with technological developments, are major determinants of the marketing messages used in advertising and other forms of promotion. Before the Industrial Revolution, advertising's presence in the United States was barely noticeable. With an explosion in economic growth around the turn of the century, modern advertising was born: The "P. T. Barnum era" and the 1920s established advertising as a major force in the U.S. economic system. With the Great Depression and World War II, cynicism and paranoia regarding advertising began to grow. This concern led to refinements in practice and more careful regulation of advertising in the 1960s

consumer-generated content (CGC) advertisements made partly or completely by the product's end users, typically with the aid of Internet tools

e-business promotion in which companies selling to business customers rely on the Internet to send messages and close sales

branded entertainment embedding brands or brand icons as part of an entertainment property in an effort to connect with consumers in a unique and compelling way

TiVo service that automatically records a consumer's selected television shows when they air and allows consumers to skip commercials

and 1970s. Consumption was again in vogue during the designer era of the 1980s. The new communication technologies that emerged in the 1990s era seem certain to affect significant changes in future practice. Finally, the interactive, wireless, and broadband technologies that are leading advertising in the 21st century hold great promise.

[Exhibit 3.2]
Periods of Promotion

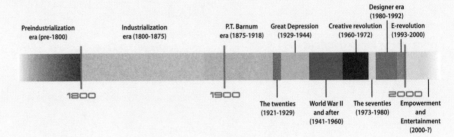

[Exhibit 3.3]
Better Data Online?

LO 4 Define consumer empowerment and branded entertainment.

Integrated, interactive, and wireless technologies recently have been reshaping marketing practices. The technologies present new options like videos that highlight brands. In this Web 2.0 era, consumers are joining in the creation of brand-related messages. This consumer-generated content can build excitement for brands but also requires that marketers cede some control to their customers. Interactive media not only allow marketers to reach consumers in the digital realm but also let them gauge consumers' attitudes. While the use of services like TiVo demonstrates a consumer backlash against the ubiquity of advertising, marketers can still grab attention and interest with branded entertainment, which blends marketing messages with entertainment in movies, music, and television programming. Communicating about brands through branded entertainment gives marketers freedom to work outside the constraints of traditional advertising.

LO 5 Identify forces that will continue to affect the evolution of integrated marketing communication.

History is practical. Consumers will always be affected by social and cultural change, and marketers will always convey messages about how they can help people cope with life's challenges. Learning how marketers addressed societal changes effectively in the past offers useful lessons for IMC opportunities in the future.

Use the skills you've learned in this chapter to get started on the brand campaign card at the end of the book.

Visit CourseMate for PROMO at www.cengagebrain.com for additional study tools.

GLOSSARY TERMS

target segment the subgroup (of the larger market) chosen as the focal point for a marketing program and advertising campaign

positioning the process of designing and representing a product or service to occupy a distinct and valued place in the target customer's mind

positioning strategy the key themes or concepts that an organization features when communicating a product's or service's distinctiveness to a target segment

STP marketing developing a strategy through segmenting, targeting, and positioning

market segmentation the breaking down of a large, heterogeneous market into more homogeneous submarkets or segments

heavy users consumers who purchase a product or service much more frequently than others

nonusers a market segment made up of consumers who do not use a particular product or service

brand-loyal users a market segment made up of consumers who repeatedly buy the same brand of a product

switchers or **variety seekers** a market segment made up of consumers who often buy what is on sale or choose brands that offer price incentives

emergent consumers a market segment made up of the gradual but constant influx of first-time buyers

point-of-entry marketing advertising strategy designed to win the loyalty of consumers whose brand preferences are under development

demographic segmentation market segmentation that divides consumers according to basic descriptors such as age, gender, race, marital status, income, education, and occupation

CHAPTER SUMMARY

LO 1 Explain the process of STP marketing.

STP marketing is the process of segmenting, targeting, and positioning. Marketers pursue this set of activities to formulate marketing strategies for their brands. STP marketing also provides a strong foundation for the development of advertising campaigns. While no single approach can guarantee success in marketing and advertising, STP marketing should be considered when customers in a category have heterogeneous wants and needs.

[Exhibit 4.1]
STP Marketing

LO 2 Describe bases for identifying target segments.

In market segmentation, the goal is to break down a heterogeneous market into more manageable subgroups or segments. Markets can be segmented on the basis of usage patterns and commitment levels, demographics, geography, psychographics, lifestyles, benefits sought, SIC codes, or stages in the purchasing process. Different bases are typically applied for segmenting consumer versus business-to-business markets.

LO 3 Discuss criteria for choosing a target segment.

In STP marketing, after segment identification, an organization must settle on one or more segments as a target for its marketing and advertising efforts. Several criteria are useful in establishing a target segment: the organization's ability to serve the segment in question, the size of the

Targeting children raises ethical concerns. Disney met the challenge by setting standards for healthful food options in its parks.

© Monkey Business Images/Shutterstock.

geodemographic segmentation market segmentation that identifies neighborhoods sharing common demographic characteristics

psychographics a form of market research that emphasizes the understanding of consumers' activities, interests, and opinions

lifestyle segmentation market segmentation that identifies consumers sharing similar activities, interests, and opinions

benefit segmentation market segmentation that identifies the various benefit packages consumers want from a product category

consumer markets the markets for products and services purchased by individuals or households to satisfy their specific needs

business markets the institutional buyers who purchase items to be used in other products and services or to be resold to other businesses or households

competitive field the companies that compete for a segment's business

market niche a relatively small group of consumers with a unique set of needs and the willingness to pay a premium price to a firm that meets those needs

benefit positioning a positioning option that features a distinctive customer benefit

user positioning a positioning option that focuses on a specific profile of the target user

competitive positioning a positioning option that uses an explicit reference to an existing competitor to help define precisely what a brand can do

repositioning returning to the STP marketing process to arrive at a revised positioning strategy

value proposition a statement of the functional, emotional, and self-expressive benefits that are delivered by the brand and provide value to customers in the target segment

segment and its growth potential, and the intensity of the competition the firm is likely to face in the segment. Often, small segments known as market niches can be quite attractive because they will not be hotly contested by numerous competitors.

LO 4 Identify the essentials of a positioning strategy.

The P in STP marketing refers to the positioning strategy, which should guide all marketing and advertising activities undertaken in pursuit of the target segment. Effective positioning strategies should be linked to the substantive benefits offered by the brand. They are also consistent internally and over time, and they feature simple and distinctive themes. Options for positioning strategies include benefit positioning, user positioning, and competitive positioning.

LO 5 Review the necessary ingredients for creating a brand's value proposition.

Many complex considerations underlie marketing and advertising strategies, so it is useful to summarize the essence of one's strategy with a device such as a value proposition. A value proposition is a statement of the brand's various benefits (functional, emotional, and self-expressive) that create value for the customer. These benefits as a set justify the price of the product or service. Clear expression of the value proposition is critical for developing advertising that sells.

[Exhibit 4.4]
Value Propositions for Two Popular Brands

McDonald's

Functional benefits	Good-tasting hamburgers, fries, and drinks served fast; extras such as playgrounds, prizes, premiums, and games.
Emotional benefits	Kids—fun via excitement at birthday parties; relationship with Ronald McDonald and other characters; a feeling of special family times. Adults—warmth via time spent enjoying a meal with the kids; admiration of McDonald's social involvement such as McDonald's Charities and Ronald McDonald Houses.

Nike

Functional benefits	High-technology shoe that will improve performance and provide comfort.
Emotional benefits	The exhilaration of athletic performance excellence, feeling engaged, active, and healthy; exhilaration from admiring professional and college athletes as they perform wearing "your brand"—when they win, you win too.
Self-expressive benefits	Using the brand endorsed by high-profile athletes lets your peers know your desire to compete and excel.

Use the skills you've learned in this chapter to get started on the brand campaign card at the end of the book.

GLOSSARY TERMS

consumer behavior activities and decision processes directly involved in obtaining, consuming, and disposing of products and services

need state psychological state arising when one's desired state of affairs differs from one's actual state of affairs

functional benefits benefits that come from a product's objective performance characteristics

emotional benefits benefits not typically found in a product's tangible features or objective characteristics

internal search search for product information that draws on personal experience and prior knowledge

consideration set subset of brands from a product category that becomes the focal point of a consumer's evaluation

external search gathering product information by visiting retail stores to examine alternatives, seeking input from friends and relatives, or perusing professional product evaluations

evaluative criteria product attributes or performance characteristics on which consumers base their product evaluations

customer satisfaction good feelings that come from a favorable postpurchase experience

cognitive dissonance anxiety or regret that lingers after a difficult decision

involvement degree of perceived relevance and personal importance accompanying the choice of a product or service in a particular context

extended problem solving decision-making mode in which inexperienced but highly involved consumers go through a deliberate decision-making process

limited problem solving decision-making mode in which relatively inexperienced and uninvolved consumers are not systematic about decisions

habit decision-making mode in which consumers buy a single brand repeatedly as a solution to a simple consumption problem

CHAPTER SUMMARY

LO 1 **Describe the four stages of consumer decision making.**

Marketers need a keen understanding of their consumers as a basis for effective brand communication. This understanding begins with a view of consumers as systematic decision makers who follow a predictable process in making choices among products and brands. The process begins when consumers perceive a need, and it proceeds with a search for information that will help in making an informed choice. The search-and-evaluation stage is followed by purchase. Then, in postpurchase use and evaluation, customer satisfaction is ultimately determined.

[Exhibit 5.1]
Consumer Decision Making

LO 2 **Explain how consumers adapt their decision-making processes based on involvement and experience.**

Some purchases are more important to people than others, a fact that adds complexity to consumer behavior. To accommodate this complexity, marketers think about the level of involvement that attends any given purchase. High or low involvement and experience with a product or service category determine the mode of consumer decision making: extended problem solving, limited problem solving, habit or variety seeking, or brand loyalty.

LO 3 **Discuss how brand communication influences consumers' psychological states and behavior.**

Brand messages are developed to influence the way people think about products and brands, specifically their beliefs and brand attitudes. Marketers use multi-attribute attitude models (MAAMs) to help them ascertain the beliefs and attitudes of target consumers. However, consumers employ perceptual defenses to ignore or distort most of the commercial messages to which they are exposed. When consumers are not motivated to process an advertiser's message thoughtfully, the marketer may need to feature peripheral cues as part of the message.

LO 4 **Describe the interaction of culture and advertising.**

Advertisements are cultural products, and culture provides the context in which an ad will be interpreted. Marketers who overlook the influence of culture are bound to struggle in their attempt to communicate with the target audience. Culture is based on values, which are enduring beliefs that shape more-transitory psychological states, such as brand attitudes. Within a culture, individuals share patterns of behavior, or rituals. Violating cultural values and rituals is a sure way to squander advertising dollars.

variety seeking decision-making mode in which consumers switch their selection among various brands in a category in a random pattern

brand loyalty decision-making mode in which consumers repeatedly choose to buy the same brand of a product to fulfill a specific need

attitude overall evaluation of any object, person, or issue; varies along a continuum, such as favorable to unfavorable or positive to negative

brand attitudes summary evaluations that reflect preferences for various products or brands

beliefs a person's knowledge and feelings about an object or issue

salient beliefs the few beliefs that are the critical determinants of an attitude

multi-attribute attitude models (MAAMs) framework and set of procedures for collecting information from consumers to assess their salient beliefs and attitudes about competing brands

cognitive consistency maintenance of a system of beliefs and attitudes over time

advertising clutter volume of similar ads for products or services that presents an obstacle to brand promotion

selective attention processing of only a few messages among many encountered

cognitive responses thoughts that occur at the exact moment when beliefs and attitudes are being challenged by a message

elaboration likelihood model (ELM) social psychological model of the response to a persuasive communication, expressing the response in terms of motivation and ability

peripheral cues features of an advertisement other than the actual arguments about the brand's performance

meaning what a brand message intends or conveys

culture a group's characteristic ways of behaving

values defining expressions of what is important to a culture

rituals repeated behaviors that affirm, express, and maintain cultural values

Advertising and other elements of the promotional mix turn products into brands when they wrap brands with cultural meaning. Brands with high cultural capital are worth more. In these ways, brands are co-created by consumers and marketers.

LO 5 Explain how sociological factors affect consumer behavior.

Consumer behavior is an activity each person undertakes before a broad audience of other consumers. Brand promotion helps the transfer of meaning. Gender, ethnicity, and race are important influences on consumption. Who consumers are—their identity—is changeable; through what they buy and use, consumers rapidly and frequently change aspects of who they are. Celebrities are particularly important in this regard.

LO 6 Discuss how advertising transmits sociocultural meaning in order to sell things.

Advertising transfers a desired meaning to the brand by placing the brand within a carefully constructed social world represented in an ad, or "slice of life." Marketers paint a picture of the ideal social world, with all the meanings they want to impart to their brand. The brand is placed carefully in that picture, and the two (the constructed social world and the brand) rub off on each other, becoming a part of each other. Meaning thus is transferred from the ad's constructed social world to the brand.

[Exhibit 5.8]
The Movement of Meaning

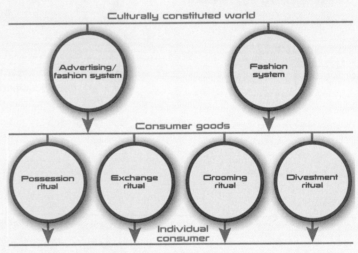

Use the skills you've learned in this chapter to get started on the brand campaign card at the end of the book.

stratification (social class) individuals' relative standing in a social system as produced by systematic inequalities

taste a generalized set or orientation to consumer preferences

intergenerational effect choice of products based on what was used in the consumer's childhood household

life stage circumstance that changes a family's consumption patterns

celebrity sociological category of famous individuals who shape identity for others

gender social expression of sexual biology or sexual choice

community group of people loosely joined by a common characteristic or interest

brand community group of consumers who feel a commonality and shared purpose grounded in or attached to a consumer good or service

Visit CourseMate for PROMO at www.cengagebrain.com **for additional study tools.**

6   The Regulatory and Ethical Environment of Promotions

GLOSSARY TERMS

ethics moral standards and principles against which behavior is judged

deception making false or misleading statements in a promotional message

puffery use of superlatives like "number one" and "best in the world" in promotional messages

primary demand demand for an entire product category

unfair advertising acts by advertisers that cause or are likely to cause substantial injury that is not reasonably avoidable or outweighed by other benefits

vertical cooperative advertising sharing of advertising expense by a manufacturer and dealer (wholesaler or retailer)

comparison advertisements ads that compare the advertiser's brand with competitors' brands

monopoly power a company's ability, either through advertising or in some other way, to prevent rivals from competing

advertising substantiation program FTC program that ensures advertisers make available to consumers supporting evidence for advertising claims

consent order FTC action asking an advertiser to stop running deceptive or unfair advertising without admitting guilt

cease-and-desist order FTC action requiring an advertiser to stop running an ad so that a hearing can be held to determine whether the ad is deceptive or unfair

affirmative disclosure FTC action requiring that important material determined to be absent from prior ads be included in future ads

corrective advertising FTC action requiring an advertiser to run additional ads to dispel false beliefs created by deceptive advertising

CHAPTER SUMMARY

LO 1   **Discuss the impact of promotion on society's well-being.**

On the positive side, promotional efforts are said to benefit society by lowering costs to increase the standard of living, fostering innovation, providing revenues to mass media, delivering a constant flow of information valued by consumers, and informing about political and social issues. At the same time, critics have said promotional expenditures are wasteful and intrusive, messages often are offensive to society and frustrating to those who can't afford a lavish lifestyle, and advertisements rarely furnish useful information but instead perpetuate superficial stereotypes. For many years, some critics have been concerned that advertisers are controlling consumers with subliminal advertising messages—a claim that is not well supported.

LO 2   **Summarize ethical considerations related to brand promotion campaigns.**

Ethical considerations that frequently arise involve truthfulness, concern for the impact of promotional messages on children, and the promotion of controversial products and practices such as firearms, gambling, alcohol, and cigarettes. Ethical standards are a matter for personal reflection; for example, there are many shades of gray between purely fact-based ads and intentional efforts to deceive by withholding information or lying. However, it certainly is the case that unethical people can create unethical advertising. But there also are many safeguards against such behavior, including the corporate and personal integrity of advertisers.

LO 3   **Describe aspects of advertising regulated by the U.S. government.**

In the United States, advertisers may not engage in deceptive or unfair practices, including bogus cooperative advertising allowances, unfair comparison advertising, and the exercise of monopoly power. The government places limits on the amount of advertising aimed at children on television, and industry groups have developed guidelines for the content of ads targeting children.

[Exhibit 6.2]
Don't Go There . . .

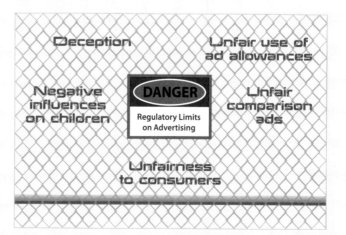

celebrity endorsements advertisements that use an expert or celebrity as spokesperson to endorse the use of a product or service

self-regulation the advertising industry's attempt to police itself

consumerism actions of individual consumers to exert power over the marketplace activities of organizations

cookies online tracking markers that advertisers place on a Web surfer's hard drive to track that person's online behavior

spam unsolicited commercial messages sent through email

premiums items that feature a sponsor's logo and are offered free or at a reduced price with the purchase of another item

appropriation use of pictures or images owned by someone else without permission

defamation untrue communication that damages the reputation of an individual

slander oral defamation (for example, during a radio broadcast)

libel defamation that occurs in print (for example, in a magazine story)

LO 4 Summarize the regulatory role of the Federal Trade Commission.

In the United States, the Federal Trade Commission (FTC) was established in 1914 and has been especially active in trying to deter deception and unfairness in advertising. The FTC has developed regulatory remedies, such as the advertising substantiation program. When the FTC determines that advertising is unfair or deceptive, it may issue a consent or cease-and-desist order, or require affirmative disclosure or corrective advertising. The FTC also has issued guidelines for the use of celebrity endorsements.

[Exhibit 6.3]
Remedies Sought
by the FTC

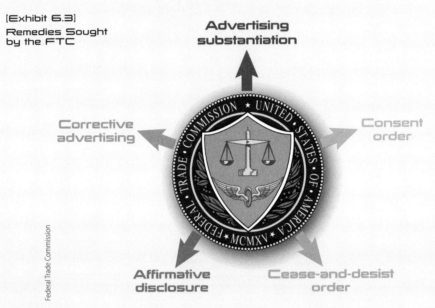

Federal Trade Commission

Advertising substantiation

Corrective advertising

Consent order

Affirmative disclosure

Cease-and-desist order

LO 5 Explain the meaning and importance of self-regulation by marketers.

Some of the most important controls on advertising involve voluntary self-regulation by marketing professionals. For example, the American Association of Advertising Agencies has issued guidelines for promoting fairness and accuracy when using comparative advertisements. Many other organizations, such as the Better Business Bureau, the National Association of Broadcasters, and the Direct Marketing Association, participate in the process to help ensure fairness and assess consumer complaints about advertising and promotion.

LO 6 Discuss the regulation of direct marketing, sales promotion, and public relations.

In direct marketing and e-commerce, the primary concern has to do with consumer privacy. Laws and regulations, including the Do Not Call Registry and the CAN SPAM Act, restrict the ways in which companies can contact consumers with a sales offer. Other restrictions are aimed at ensuring that contests and sweepstakes do not amount to gambling opportunities. In sales promotions, premium offers, trade allowances, and offline contests and sweepstakes are subject to regulation. Firms must state the fair value of "free" premiums, trade allowances must follow the guidelines of fair competition, and contests and sweepstakes must follow strict rules specified by the FTC. The regulation of public relations efforts requires that privacy be protected and that firms avoid copyright infringement and defamation.

Use the skills you've learned in this chapter to get started on the brand campaign card at the end of the book.

Visit CourseMate for PROMO at www.cengagebrain.com for additional study tools.

GLOSSARY TERMS

international brand promotion the preparation and placement of brand communication in different national and cultural markets

ethnocentrism tendency to view and value things from the perspective of one's own culture

self-reference criterion (SRC) unconscious reference to one's own cultural values, experiences, and knowledge as a basis for decisions

less-developed countries countries whose economies lack most resources necessary for development: capital, infrastructure, political stability, and trained workers

newly industrialized countries countries where traditional ways of life are changing into modern consumer cultures

highly industrialized countries countries with a high GDP and a high standard of living

demographic dividend favorable climate for economic expansion in developing nations as a result of falling labor costs, a younger and healthier population, and entry of women into the workforce

picturing creating representations of things

global agencies advertising agencies with a worldwide presence

international affiliates foreign-market advertising agencies with which a local agency has established a relationship to handle international advertising needs

local agency advertising agency in a foreign market hired because of its knowledge of the culture and local market conditions

globalized campaigns promotional campaigns that use the same message and creative execution across all or most international markets

CHAPTER SUMMARY

LO 1 **Identify types of audience research that contribute to understanding cultural barriers to effective communication.**

All of us wear cultural blinders, so we must overcome substantial barriers in trying to communicate with people from other countries. This is a major problem for international marketers as they seek to promote their brands around the world. To overcome this problem and avoid errors in advertising planning, marketers need to conduct cross-cultural audience analysis. Such analyses involve evaluation of economic conditions, demographic characteristics, customs, values, rituals, and product use and preferences in the target countries.

[Exhibit 7.1]
Wide Differences in Wealth

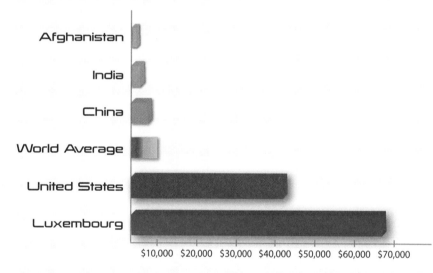

Per capita GDP

LO 2 **Describe challenges that complicate integrated marketing communication in international settings.**

Worldwide marketers face three distinctive challenges in executing their campaigns. The first is a creative challenge that derives from differences in experience and meaning among cultures. Even the pictures featured in an ad may be translated differently from one country to the next. Media availability, media coverage, and media costs vary dramatically around the world, adding a second complication to international brand promotion. Finally, the amount and nature of advertising regulations vary dramatically from country to country, sometimes forcing a complete reformulation of a promotional campaign.

Courtesy, SkyPort T.V. of Japan.

localized campaigns promotional campaigns that involve different messages and creative executions for each foreign market served

LO 3 Compare the basic types of agencies that can assist in brand promotion around the world.

Advertising agencies offer marketers the expertise needed to develop and execute brand promotion campaigns in international markets. Marketers can choose to work with global agencies, an international affiliate of the agency they use in their home country, or local agencies in the targeted market. Each of these agency types brings different advantages and disadvantages on evaluative dimensions such as geographic proximity, economies of scale, political leverage, awareness of the client's strategy, and knowledge of the local culture.

[Exhibit 7.2]
Take Your Pick

LO 4 Discuss the advantages and disadvantages of globalized versus localized promotional campaigns.

A final concern for international brand promotion entails the degree of customization a marketer should attempt in campaigns designed to cross national boundaries. Globalized campaigns involve little customization among countries, whereas localized campaigns feature heavy customization for each market. Standardized messages bring cost savings and create a common brand image worldwide, but they may miss the mark with consumers in different nations. As consumers around the world become more similar, globalized campaigns may become more prevalent. Teenagers in many countries share similar values and lifestyles and thus make a natural target for globalized campaigns.

Use the skills you've learned in this chapter to get started on the brand campaign card at the end of the book.

GLOSSARY TERMS

creativity ability to consider and hold together seemingly inconsistent elements and forces, making a new connection

account executive liaison between an advertising agency and its clients

account team group of people comprising different facets of the promotion industry who work together under a team leader

creative brief document that outlines and channels an essential creative idea and objective

cognitive style an individual's preference for thinking about and solving a problem

creative abrasion clash of ideas, abstracted from the people who propose them, from which new ideas can evolve

interpersonal abrasion clash of people, often resulting from an inability to regard idea feedback as separate from personal feedback, causing communication to shut down

brainstorming organized approach to idea generation in groups

CHAPTER SUMMARY

LO 1 — Describe characteristics of great creative minds.

How we recognize and define creativity in marketing rests on our understanding of the achievements of acknowledged creative geniuses from the worlds of art, literature, music, science, and politics. A look at great creative minds—such as Picasso, Gandhi, Freud, Eliot, Stravinsky, Graham, and Einstein—reveals shared sensibilities including a strikingly exuberant self-confidence, (childlike) alertness, unconventionality, and an obsessive commitment to their work. However, self-confidence at some point becomes crass self-promotion, and an unconstrained childlike ability to see the world as forever new eventually devolves into childish self-indulgence. In spite of creativity's downside, it is essential. Without creativity, there can be no brand promotion.

[Exhibit 8.1]
Seven Creative Geniuses

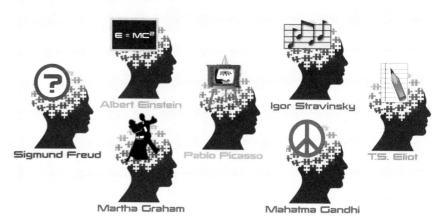

Albert Einstein

Igor Stravinsky

Sigmund Freud

Pablo Picasso

T.S. Eliot

Martha Graham

Mahatma Gandhi

LO 2 — Contrast the roles of an agency's creative department and its business managers/account executives.

The significant effort required to get the right idea, coupled with the client's apparent ease in dismissing that idea, underlies the contentiousness between an agency's creative staff and its account executives and clients. Creatives provoke. Managers restrain. Ads that win awards for creative excellence don't necessarily fulfill a client's business goals. All organizations deal with the competing agendas of one department versus another, but in advertising agencies, this competition plays out at an amplified level. The difficulty of assessing the effectiveness of brand promotion only adds to the problem. Advertising researchers are in the unenviable position of judging the creatives, pitting "science" against art. In spite of these tensions, creativity is essential to the vitality of brands. Creativity makes a brand, and creativity reinvents established brands in new and desired ways.

LO 3 Discuss how teams manage tensions and promote creativity in integrated marketing communication.

There are many sources of conflict and tension in the creation of a promotional mix. Many organizations attempt to address this challenging issue through systematic utilization of teams. Teams, when effectively managed, will produce outputs that are greater than the sum of their individual parts. Teams need to be managed to promote creative abrasion but limit interpersonal abrasion. They need guidance from a maestro (like a Lee Clow or Alex Bogusky). Use of a creative brief can get teams headed in the right direction and preempt many forms of conflict.

[Exhibit 8.3]
Keys to Creativity

LO 4 Evaluate your own passion for creativity.

Self-assessment is an important part of learning and growing. Now is the perfect time to be thinking about yourself and your passion for creativity. If marketing, especially brand promotion, interests you, then improving your own creative abilities should be a lifelong quest. Now is the time to decide to become more creative.

[Exhibit 8.4]
Eight Rules for Brainstorming

1. Build off each other.	Don't just generate ideas: build off them.
2. Fear drives out creativity.	Be sure no one is teased or embarrassed.
3. Prime individuals before and after.	Give everyone a chance to prepare and learn.
4. Make it happen.	Put ideas into action.
5. It's a skill.	Use a skilled facilitator.
6. Embrace creative abrasion.	Welcome conflicting ideas and viewpoints.
7. Listen and learn.	Focus on learning and building trust.
8. Follow the rules.	If you don't, you're not really brainstorming.

Source: Based on Robert L. Sutton, "The Truth about Brainstorming," *Inside Business Week*, September 25, 2006, 17–21.

Use the skills you've learned in this chapter to get started on the brand campaign card at the end of the book.

Visit CourseMate for PROMO at www.cengagebrain.com for additional study tools.

CHAPTER 8

GLOSSARY TERMS

Internet global collection of computer networks linking public and private computer systems to connect more than a billion users

opt-in email messages sent to website visitors who have given permission to receive commercial email about particular topics or products

spam uninvited commercial messages sent to electronic mailing lists or online discussion groups

Usenet collection of more than 13,000 discussion groups on the Internet

World Wide Web (WWW) database of information available online in a graphical environment that simplifies navigation

surfing gliding from website to website, guided by hyperlinks, a search engine, or word-of-mouth

search engine software tool for finding websites by entering keywords

portal website that serves as a starting point for Web access and search

website collection of Web pages, images, videos, and other content hosted on a Web server

mash-up combination of websites into a single site for analyzing or comparing information

blog personal journal that is published on a website, frequently updated, and intended for public access

blogger author of a blog

click-through measure of the number of hyperlinks that users click on, especially links from advertisements to the advertiser's website

cost per thousand (CPM) dollar cost of reaching 1,000 members of an audience

paid search the practice of paying search engines and portals to place ads near relevant search results

search engine optimization (SEO) process for improving the volume and quality of traffic to a website from a search engine's results pages

CHAPTER SUMMARY

LO 1 **Summarize the Internet's role in integrated marketing communication (IMC).**

The Internet will be important but is unlikely to replace other forms of brand promotion or even to become the main method of communicating with target audiences. Internet technologies and opportunities are changing dramatically. For example, small businesses are selling through auction sites, social networking provides a new way of delivering promotional messages, and new venues like Second Life offer communication opportunities very different from traditional message delivery. Finally, the Internet's structure and potential as an advertising medium offer ways for marketers to create and deliver messages that are significantly different from those in traditional mass media.

LO 2 **Describe the nature of the Internet as a medium for communicating promotional messages.**

The Web offers target market selectivity—targeting that is more finely tuned than traditional segmentation schemes such as demographics, geographics, and psychographics. Marketers can focus on very specific interest areas or geographic regions, time of day, or computer platform. The Internet also allows advertisers to track how users interact with their brands and learn what interests current and potential customers. In addition, online content is delivered 24 hours a day, seven days a week, at the convenience of the receiver. A campaign can be tracked on a daily basis and updated, changed, or replaced almost immediately. Furthermore, the Internet is immediately a global medium unlike any traditional media option. Another benefit is interactivity: A marketer can engage a prospective customer to a degree that just cannot be accomplished in traditional media. Finally, Web promotion is the most easily integrated and coordinated with other forms of promotion.

[Exhibit 9.2]
What Americans Are Doing Online

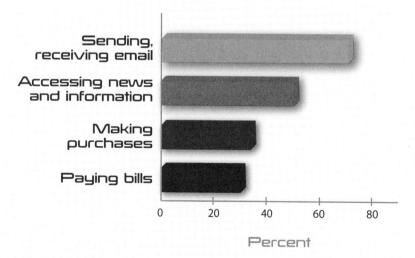

Source: Based on Digital Marketing & Media Fact Pack, *Advertising Age*, April 23, 2007, 32.

display or banner ads advertisements placed on websites that contain editorial material

sponsorship payment to maintain a section of a website and perhaps provide content for the site in exchange for being mentioned on the site

pop-up ad Internet advertisement that opens a separate window while a Web page is loading

interstitial Internet ad that appears briefly on a website after a page has been requested but before it has loaded

pop-under ad Internet ad that is displayed "under" the active window, so it appears only after that window is closed

permission marketing sending commercial email only to Web users who have agreed to receive it

viral marketing process of consumers spreading brand messages through email

rich media, video, and audio use of streaming video and audio that plays when the user's mouse passes over an Internet ad

corporate home page website that focuses on a corporation and its products

virtual mall gateway to a group of Internet storefronts where the user gains access to a retailer by clicking on a storefront

widget software module that people can add to their blog or their personal page on a social network; may feature a brand or direct the user to an e-commerce site

Second Life online virtual world where participants can roam landscapes and interact, simulating real-world activities, including (often real) business transactions

sticky site website that attracts visitors again and again and keeps them for a long time

domain name unique URL that establishes a Web location

top-level domain (TLD) suffix that follows a website name

hits number of pages and graphical images requested from a website

page views record of the pages that have been sent to a user's computer; multiscreen pages are counted as one page

LO 3 **Define options for promotion on the Web.**

Web advertising includes paid search (placement of ads in or near relevant search results), display or banner ads (placed on sites containing editorial material), and pop-up or pop-under ads (which appear as a Web page is loading or after a page has loaded). Internet ads can use rich media, video, and audio (which include music and video clips) and widgets (software that people can drag and drop onto their personal Web page or blog). Marketers also can engage users with their brands through website sponsorship, email messages, and their corporate home pages. They can offer brand information and purchase opportunities in a virtual mall (a gateway to a group of Internet storefronts). And they can place billboards or branded business opportunities in a virtual world such as Second Life.

LO 4 **Identify the issues involved in establishing a website.**

Three issues are key to successfully establishing and maintaining a site on the World Wide Web: getting surfers to come back by creating a "sticky" site, purchasing keywords and developing a domain name, and promoting the website.

LO 5 **List developments likely to shape the future of IMC on the Web.**

The future of IMC on the Web will be guided by technological developments and marketers' strategic focus. Two important trends in technology are the emergence of faster, more widespread wireless delivery systems and greater use of Web-launched video as high-speed connections become more widely available. The strategic approach to IMC is evident in mergers of powerful media companies. Marketers are combining expertise in techniques used on and off the Web to match marketing goals with new communication opportunities that engage today's Web-savvy consumers.

Use the skills you've learned in this chapter to get started on the brand campaign card at the end of the book.

visits number of occasions on which a particular user looks up a particular website during a given time period

unique visitors number of people (identified using registration information) who visit a site during a given time period

Web analytic software software that measures hits, pages, visits, and users, and allows a website to track audience traffic on the site

click fraud act of clicking on Internet ads solely to generate revenue for the website carrying the ads

WiFi wireless technology allowing Internet access connections to reach out about 300 feet

WiMax wireless Internet technology capable of a range of 25 to 30 miles

Mobile-Fi wireless Internet technology with multi-mile access and ability to access the Internet while the user is moving in a car or train

ultrabroadband wireless Internet technology allowing users to move extremely large files quickly over short distances

GLOSSARY TERMS

direct marketing interactive marketing system that uses multiple media to generate a transaction or other measurable response at any location

cost per inquiry (CPI) number of inquiries generated by a direct-marketing program divided by the program's cost

cost per order (CPO) number of orders generated by a direct-marketing program divided by that program's cost

mailing list file of names and addresses used for contacting prospects or customers

internal lists organization's records of its customers and inquirers; used for developing better customer relationships

external lists mailing lists purchased from a list compiler or rented from a list broker; used for cultivating new business

marketing database mailing list with added information collected directly from individual customers

RFM analysis analysis of how recently and frequently a customer bought from an organization, and how much the customer spent

frequency-marketing programs direct-marketing programs that provide concrete rewards to frequent customers

cross-selling marketing programs aimed at selling additional products to existing customers

direct-response advertising advertising that asks the receiver of the message to act immediately

direct mail direct-marketing medium that uses the postal service to deliver marketing materials

telemarketing direct-marketing medium that involves using the telephone to deliver a spoken appeal

infomercial long advertisement that looks like a talk show or product demonstration

CHAPTER SUMMARY

LO 1 **Identify purposes served by direct marketing.**

Many types of organizations are increasing their expenditures on direct marketing. These expenditures serve three primary purposes: direct marketing offers potent tools for closing sales with customers, identifying prospects for future contacts, and offering information and incentives that help foster brand loyalty.

[Exhibit 10.1]
Some Direct-Marketing Milestones

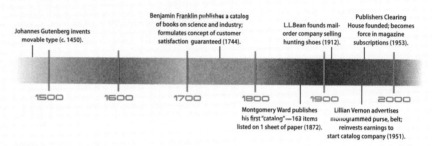

Source: Based on Direct Marketing Association, "Grassroots Advocacy Guide for Direct Marketers" (1993).

LO 2 **Explain the popularity of direct marketing.**

The growing popularity of direct marketing can be attributed to several factors. Direct marketers make consumption convenient: Credit cards, 800 numbers, and the Internet take the hassle out of shopping. Additionally, today's computing power, which allows marketers to build and mine large customer information files, has enhanced direct marketing's impact. The emphasis on producing and tracking measurable outcomes also is well received by marketers in an era when everyone is trying to do more with less.

LO 3 **Distinguish a mailing list from a marketing database, and review the applications of each.**

A mailing list is a file of names and addresses of current or potential customers, such as lists that might be generated by a credit card company or a catalog retailer. Internal lists are valuable for creating relationships with current customers, and external lists are useful in generating new customers. A marketing database is a natural extension of the internal list, but it also includes information about individual customers and their specific preferences and purchasing patterns. A marketing database allows organizations to identify and focus their efforts on their best customers. Recognizing and reinforcing preferred customers can be a potent strategy for building loyalty. Cross-selling opportunities also emerge once a database is in place. In addition, as one gains keener information about the motivations of current best customers, insights usually emerge about how to attract new customers.

[Exhibit 10.2]
What Makes a Marketing Database

List Enhancements
(demographic, geodemographic, psychographic, and/or behavioral data)

Mailing List
(names and addresses)

Consumer Provided Information
(e.g., preferences, behavior patterns)

Marketing Database

LO 4 **Describe the media used by direct marketers in delivering messages to consumers.**

Direct-marketing programs emanate from mailing lists and databases, but there still is a need to deliver a message to the customer. Direct mail and telemarketing are the most common means used in executing direct marketing programs. Email has emerged as a low-cost alternative. Because the advertising done as part of direct-marketing programs typically requests an immediate response from the customer, it is known as direct-response advertising. Conventional media such as television, newspapers, magazines, and radio also can be used to request a direct response by offering an 800 number or a Web address to facilitate customer contact.

Use the skills you've learned in this chapter to get started on the brand campaign card at the end of the book.

Visit CourseMate for PROMO at www.cengagebrain.com for additional study tools.

CHAPTER 10

GLOSSARY TERMS

sales promotion use of innovative techniques that create a perception of greater brand value among consumers or distributors

consumer-market sales promotion sales promotions designed to induce consumers to purchase a firm's brand rather than a competitor's

trade-market sales promotion sales promotion designed to motivate distributors, wholesalers, and retailers to stock and feature a firm's brand

business-market sales promotion promotion designed to cultivate buyers making purchase decisions in corporations

coupon sales promotion that entitles a buyer to a designated reduction in price for a product or service

price-off deal type of sales promotion that offers consumers money off merchandise at the point of purchase through specially marked packages

premiums items that feature a sponsor's logo and are offered free or at a reduced price with the purchase of another item

free premium sales promotion that gives consumers an item at no cost by including the item in the package or mailing it after proof of purchase is verified

self-liquidating premium sales promotion that requires a consumer to pay most of the cost of the item received as a premium

advertising specialties sales promotion consisting of a message placed on useful items given to consumers with no obligation

contest sales promotion in which consumers compete for prizes based on skill or ability

sweepstakes sales promotion in which winners are awarded prizes based on chance

sampling sales promotion technique that offers consumers a trial opportunity

in-store sampling sampling that occurs at the point of purchase

CHAPTER SUMMARY

LO 1

Explain the importance and growth of sales promotion.

Sales promotions use incentives to motivate action by consumers, members of the trade channel, and business buyers. They serve different purposes than mass-media advertising does, and many companies spend more on sales promotions than on advertising. Reasons for greater reliance on promotions include pressure on marketing managers to account for their spending and meet sales objectives in short time frames, along with deal-prone shoppers, brand proliferation, the increasing power of large retailers, and media clutter.

LO 2

Describe the main sales promotion techniques used in the consumer market.

Coupons, price-off deals, phone and gift cards, and premiums provide obvious incentives for purchase. Contests, sweepstakes, and product placements can be excellent devices for stimulating brand interest. A variety of sampling techniques are available to get a product into the hands of the target audience. Rebates and frequency programs provide rewards for repeat purchase.

[Exhibit 11.2]
Objectives for Consumer-Market Sales Promotion

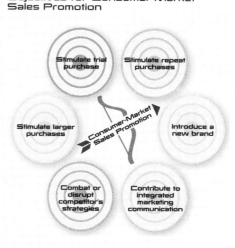

LO 3

Describe the main sales promotion techniques used in the trade channel and business markets.

Sales promotions directed at the trade are a necessity in obtaining initial distribution of a new brand. For established brands, they can be a means to increase distributors' order quantities or obtain retailers' cooperation in implementing a consumer-directed promotion. Incentives, allowances, sales training programs, and cooperative advertising programs can motivate distributors' support for a brand. In the business market, professional buyers are attracted by various sales promotion techniques. Frequency (continuity) programs are very valuable in the travel industry and have spread to business-product advertisers. Trade shows efficiently reach a large number of highly targeted business buyers. Other tools that have proven successful include gifts, premiums, advertising specialties, and trial offers.

[Exhibit 11.4]
Objectives for Trade-Market Sales Promotion

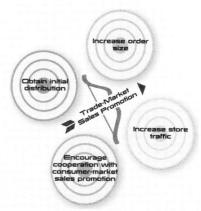

door-to-door sampling sampling in which samples are brought to the homes of the target segment in a well-defined geographic area

mail sampling sampling in which samples are delivered through the postal service

newspaper sampling sampling in which samples are distributed in newspapers to allow specific geographic and geodemographic targeting

on-package sampling sampling in which a sample item is attached to another product's package

mobile sampling sampling carried out using logo-emblazoned vehicles where samples are dispensed at malls or other high-traffic areas

trial offers sales promotion in which expensive items are offered on a trial basis to induce consumers to try a brand

rebate money-back offer requiring a buyer to mail in a form requesting the money back from the manufacturer

frequency programs sales promotion that offers consumers discounts or rewards for repeat purchases

push strategy sales promotion strategy in which marketers devise incentives to encourage purchases by members of the trade, moving product into the distribution channel

push money trade incentive in which retail salespeople are offered monetary rewards for featuring a marketer's brand

merchandise allowances trade-market sales promotion in which free products are packed with regular shipments as payment to the trade for setting up and maintaining displays

slotting fees trade-market sales promotion in which manufacturers make direct cash payments to retailers to ensure shelf space

bill-back allowances monetary incentive provided to retailers for featuring a marketer's brand in advertising or in-store displays

off-invoice allowance program allowing wholesalers and retailers to deduct a set amount from the invoice they receive for merchandise

cooperative advertising sharing of advertising expenses between national advertisers and local merchants

trade shows events where several related products from many manufacturers are displayed and demonstrated to members of the trade

point-of-purchase (P-O-P) advertising advertising that appears in the retail setting

short-term promotional displays P-O-P materials used for six months or less

permanent long-term displays P-O-P materials intended for presentation for more than six months

support media media used to reinforce a message being delivered via some other media vehicle

riding the boards assessing possible locations for billboard advertising

transit advertising advertising that appears as interior and exterior displays on mass-transit vehicles and at terminal and station platforms

out-of-home media transit and billboard advertising

aerial advertising advertising that involves airplanes pulling signs or banners, as well as skywriting and blimps

packaging a product's container or wrapping, which conveys product information and user appeal

guerrilla marketing edgy, inexpensive promotional initiatives executed in major urban markets

---

LO 4 Identify the risks to the brand of using sales promotion.

Offering constant deals for a brand can erode brand equity, and sales resulting from a promotion simply may be borrowing from future sales. Constant deals also can create a customer mind-set that leads consumers to abandon a brand as soon as a deal is retracted. Sales promotions are expensive to administer and fraught with legal complications. Sales promotions yield their most positive results when carefully integrated with the overall advertising plan.

LO 5 Understand the role and techniques of point-of-purchase advertising.

Point-of-purchase (P-O-P) advertising refers to materials used in the retail setting to attract shoppers' attention to a firm's brand, convey primary brand benefits, or highlight pricing information. P-O-P can reinforce a consumer's brand preference or change a consumer's brand choice in the retail setting. P-O-P displays may feature price-off deals or other consumer and business sales promotions. A myriad of displays and presentations are available in two categories: short-term promotional displays (used for six months or less) and permanent long-term displays (used for more than six months). In trade and business markets, P-O-P displays encourage retailers to support one manufacturer's brand over another; they also can be used to gain preferred shelf space and exposure in a retail setting.

LO 6 Describe the role of support media in a comprehensive integrated marketing communication plan.

The traditional support media include billboard, transit, aerial, and directory advertising. Billboards and transit advertising are excellent means for carrying simple messages into specific metropolitan markets. Street furniture is becoming increasingly popular as a placard for brand builders around the world. Aerial advertising also can be a great way to break through the clutter and target specific geographic markets in a timely manner. Directory advertising, primarily the Yellow Pages directories, can be a sound investment because it helps a committed customer locate an advertiser's product. Finally, packaging can be considered in the support media category because the brand's package carries important information for consumer choice at the point of purchase, including the brand logo and "look and feel" of the brand.

Use the skills you've learned in this chapter to get started on the brand campaign card at the end of the book.

Visit CourseMate for PROMO at www.cengagebrain.com for additional study tools.

GLOSSARY TERMS

Madison & Vine convergence of advertising and entertainment; reference to the names of streets that represent each industry

Chaos Scenario exodus of ad revenue from traditional broadcast media in reaction to audience fragmentation and tools for ad avoidance; causes media cutbacks, followed by further reductions in audience size and even less advertising

event sponsorship financial support for an event, given in exchange for the right to display a brand name, logo, or promotional message at the event

media impressions instances in which a product or brand is exposed to consumers through media coverage, rather than paid advertising

leveraging using any collateral communication or activity to reinforce the link between a brand and an event

product placement sales promotion technique of getting a marketer's product featured in movies and television shows

authenticity quality of genuineness or naturalness

branded entertainment embedding a brand in any entertainment property to impress and connect with consumers

CHAPTER SUMMARY

LO 1 **Explain the popularity of event sponsorship as a means of brand promotion.**

The list of companies sponsoring events grows with each passing year, and the events include a wide variety of activities. Of these activities, sports attract the most sponsorship dollars. Sponsorship can help build brand familiarity, can promote brand loyalty by connecting a brand with powerful emotional experiences, and in most instances allows a marketer to reach a well-defined target audience. Events also can facilitate face-to-face contacts with key customers, and they present opportunities to distribute product samples, sell premiums, and conduct consumer surveys.

[Exhibit 12.1]
When Event Sponsorship Is a Winner

Enough media impressions

Stronger brand loyalty

Targeted consumers in audience

[Exhibit 12.2]
Checklist for Event Sponsorship

☐ Pick an event that matches the brand.

☐ Pick an event that draws your target audience—not only a big audience, but the right audience.

☐ Deliver a few key messages, and repeat them often.

☐ Develop your event participation in terms of a plot or story with a beginning, middle, and end.

☐ Make participation exclusive by issuing invitations to a select group.

☐ Make participation relevant to your target group—not only about selling.

☐ Use the Internet to promote your event and share your story with those who couldn't be there.

☐ Integrate your event sponsorship with your other brand communications.

Source: Based on Laura Shuler, "Make Sure to Deliver When Staging Events," *Marketing News*, September 13, 1999, 12.

LO 2 **Summarize the uses and appeal of product placements.**

Product placements have surged in popularity, and there are many reasons to believe that marketers will continue to commit more resources to this activity. Like any other brand promotion tactic, product placements offer the most value when they are connected to other elements of the promotional plan. One common use of the placement is to help create excitement for the launch of a new product. Implicit celebrity endorsements and authenticity are key issues to consider when judging placement opportunities. High-quality placements are most likely to result from great collaboration among marketers, agents, producers, and writers.

LO 3 **Describe benefits and challenges of connecting with entertainment properties to build a brand.**

Brand builders want to connect with consumers, and to do so, they are connecting with the entertainment business. Although not everyone can afford a NASCAR sponsorship, in many ways, NASCAR sets the standard for celebrating brands in an entertaining setting. Many marketers, such as BMW and Unilever, are developing their own entertainment properties to feature their brands. However, the rush to participate in branded-entertainment ventures raises the risk of oversaturation and consumer backlash, or at least consumer apathy. As with any tool, while it is new and fresh, good things happen. When it gets old and stale, advertisers will turn to the next big thing.

[Exhibit 12.3]
Obstacles to Overcome

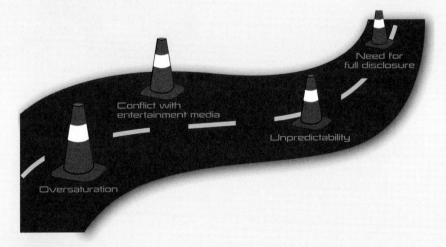

Conflict with entertainment media

Need for full disclosure

Unpredictability

Oversaturation

LO 4 **Discuss challenges presented by the ever-increasing variety of communication and branding tools.**

The tremendous variety of media options represents a monumental challenge for a marketer wishing to speak to customers with a single voice. Achieving this single voice is critical for breaking through the clutter of the modern marketing environment. However, the functional specialists required for working in the various media have their own biases and subgoals, which can get in the way of integration.

Use the skills you've learned in this chapter to get started on the brand campaign card at the end of the book.

Visit CourseMate for PROMO at www.cengagebrain.com for additional study tools.

CHAPTER 12

GLOSSARY TERMS

personal selling process of face-to-face communication and persuasion

customer relationship management (CRM) continual effort to cultivate and maintain long-term relationships with customers by emphasizing customer needs

order taking practice of accepting and processing customer information for prearranged purchase or scheduling services a customer will purchase

creative selling assisting and persuading customers regarding purchase decisions (typically for specialty goods or high-priced items)

team selling sales effort by a team of salespeople representing different functions

seminar selling education of customer or prospect groups to inform them about the firm's products or services

system selling selling a set of interrelated components that fulfill a majority of a customer's needs in a product or service area

missionary salesperson salesperson who calls on accounts to monitor buyers' satisfaction and update their needs

detail salesperson salesperson who introduces new products and provides product information without aiming for an immediate sale

canned presentation recitation of a prepared sales pitch

attention-interest-desire-action (AIDA) structured presentation aimed at capturing attention, identifying features of interest, defining desirable benefits, and requesting action in the form of a purchase

need satisfaction sales presentation that begins with assessment of each buyer's need state and then adjusts the selling effort to that need state

consultive selling face-to-face selling in which salespeople help customers define problems and design solutions

CHAPTER SUMMARY

LO 1 **Explain why personal selling is important in brand promotion.**

Household consumers and business buyers frequently are confronted with purchase decisions that are facilitated by interaction with a salesperson. This especially is true for products that are higher priced and complicated to use, require demonstration, are tailored to users' needs, involve a trade-in, or are judged at the point of purchase. In many decision contexts, only a qualified and well-trained salesperson can address a potential buyer's questions and concerns.

LO 2 **Describe the activities besides selling performed by salespeople.**

The modern salesperson resembles a one-person marketing strategy program. Aside from the direct tasks of personal selling, salespeople contribute to the overall marketing effort by providing information relevant to market analysis, sales forecasting, ideas for new product development, and analysis of buyer behavior. Salespeople also participate in brand communications, sales coordination, customer service, and customer relationship management (CRM).

LO 3 **Summarize the role of setting objectives for personal selling.**

A salesperson in a contemporary selling environment doesn't only sell but rather manages a set of buying–selling relationships between the buyer and seller for mutual benefit. One of the greatest challenges facing a salesperson is determining how his or her firm is uniquely capable of satisfying customer needs. Matching what the firm is capable of doing with what a buyer desires allows both parties to enter a buying–selling relationship that is mutually beneficial. The salesperson must determine which features of a firm's products and services are most attractive and potentially satisfying.

[Exhibit 14.3]
How to Sell: Steps in the Process

sales force automation (SFA) integration of computers, communication technology, and the Internet to improve the efficiency and effectiveness of personal selling

sales management responsibility for the personal-selling effort, met by evaluating needs, setting objectives and budgets, structuring and hiring the sales force, training and motivating salespeople, and evaluating their performance

Based on the buyer's expression of needs, a salesperson can determine what is most highly valued in the purchase decision. Through such a determination, the salesperson can emphasize the firm's unique capabilities in satisfying the customer. Negotiations can emphasize the firm's ability to provide superior satisfaction on the desired factors.

LO 4 Outline the steps involved in personal selling.

A well-conceived personal-selling process involves seven distinct steps: preparation, prospecting, initial contact, presentation, handling objections, closing the sale, and follow-up.

LO 5 Describe factors that contribute to a new environment for personal selling.

The key factors that have contributed to a new environment for personal selling are more sophisticated marketing planning techniques, information technologies (both hardware and software), communication technologies, the Internet, and a trend for customers to be more demanding and knowledgeable. The technological changes have enabled companies to benefit from greater use of sales force automation (SFA).

LO 6 Define the responsibilities of sales force management.

Sales force management includes the following areas of responsibility: conducting a situation analysis, setting sales objectives, establishing a budget for selling activities, identifying the proper sales force structure based on the situation analysis and budget, hiring salespeople (identifying job requirements and recruiting, screening, and evaluating candidates), training salespeople, motivating the sales force (including the use of compensation and recognition programs), and evaluating the performance of salespeople.

[Exhibit 14.4]
What Sales Managers Do

Use the skills you've learned in this chapter to get started on the brand campaign card at the end of the book.

Visit CourseMate for PROMO at www.cengagebrain.com for additional study tools.

15 | Measuring the Effectiveness of Brand Promotions

GLOSSARY TERMS

promotion research marketing research focused on the development and performance of promotional materials

reliability tendency to generate consistent findings over time

validity relevance in terms of actually answering the questions being investigated

trustworthiness quality of deserving confidence

meaningfulness in promotion research, practical applicability of conclusions to the promotional effort

account planning system in which an agency assigns a coequal account planner to work alongside the account executive and analyze research data, staying with projects on a continuous basis

naturalistic inquiry broad-based research method that relies on qualitative data collection, including video and audio recordings and photography

normative test scores scores determined by testing an ad and then comparing the scores with those of previously tested campaigns of the same type

resonance test message assessment aimed at determining the extent to which a message rings true with target audience members

communication test pretest message research aimed at measuring whether a message is communicating something close to what is desired

dummy advertising vehicles mock-ups of magazines that contain editorial content and advertisements, including ads being tested

theater tests pretest message research in which subjects view ads played in small theaters and record their reactions

thought listing pretest message research that tries to identify specific thoughts that may be generated by an ad

CHAPTER SUMMARY

Discuss issues that shape the evaluation of brand promotion.

First among the issues to consider when exploring the measurement of promotion's effectiveness is the scope of promotion research. It is a specialized form of marketing research that helps marketers learn who audience members are and which messages will work most effectively. A second issue is that marketers must determine whether research meets the criteria of reliability, validity, trustworthiness, and meaningfulness. In addition, the research effort may be carried out piecemeal by experts in particular tasks or managed through an ongoing process of account planning. Finally, marketers must assess marketers' motives and expectations and define criteria for the assessment—that is, whether the message imparts knowledge, shapes attitudes, attaches feelings and emotions, or legitimizes the brand.

Describe how marketers measure the effectiveness of advertising.

Advertising is measured more than other promotional tools because it is conspicuous and expensive to prepare. It is measured in three main ways: (1) Pretest evaluations use communication tests, magazine dummies, theater tests, thought listings, attitude change studies, and physiological measures to measure the effectiveness of advertising before a campaign launches, (2) Marketplace pilot testing uses split-cable transmission for TV ads, split-run distribution for print ads, and split-list distribution for direct mail to measure effectiveness in real market conditions, and (3) Post-testing, which occurs after a campaign is running, tests recall and recognition and tracks awareness and attitude.

[Exhibit 15.1]
Measures for Post-Testing Sales Promotion

Type of Promotion	Suitable Measures
Contests and sweepstakes	Changes in sales; number of entries
Coupons	Changes in sales; number of coupons redeemed
Rebates	Changes in sales; number of rebate forms submitted
Trade promotions	Changes in sales

Identify measures of effectiveness for Internet advertising, direct marketing, sales promotion, point of purchase, sponsorships, public relations, and corporate advertising.

Internet advertising is judged by counting visits to websites, hits on banner ads, unique visitors, and impressions formed. Direct marketing is relatively easy to evaluate by measuring the responses (sales or inquiries) that are the primary intention for the campaign. Sales promotions can be pretested by asking customers to rate alternative promotions and post-tested by measuring changes in sales or number or responses. Point-of-purchase promotion also is judged mainly by changes in sales. Sponsorships can be measured by the number of people attending an event or viewing a televised event sponsored by the firm. Rough measures for public relations and corporate advertising are surveys of attitude changes and counts of the number of exposures.

attitude change study message research that uses a before-and-after ad exposure design

physiological measures interpretation of biological feedback from subjects exposed to an ad

eye-tracking systems physiological measure that monitors eye movements across advertisements

psychogalvanometer device that measures galvanic skin response, or minute changes in perspiration that may suggest arousal

voice response analysis physiological assessment in which computers measure inflections in subjects' voices

pilot testing message evaluation that consists of experimentation in the marketplace

split-cable transmission pilot testing of two versions of an advertisement through direct transmission to separate sample households

split-run distribution pilot testing in which different versions of an advertisement are placed in magazines and direct responses to each advertisement are compared

split-list experiments pilot testing in which multiple versions of a direct-mail piece are sent to segments of a mailing list and responses to each version are compared

post-test message tracking assessment of an ad's performance during or after the launch of an ad campaign

recall test test of how much the viewer of an ad remembers of the message

recognition tests tests in which audience members are asked whether they recognize an ad or something in an ad

log analysis software measurement software that provides data about online consumer behavior, including hits, pages, visits, and users, as well as audience traffic within a website

inquiry/direct-response measures post-test message tracking in which an advertisement calls for a direct response and the number of responses is counted

ballot method pretest of sales promotion in which consumers are given

a list of promotional options and asked to rank their preferences

single-source tracking measures post-test message tracking that uses a combination of scanner data

and devices that monitor television-viewing behavior to collect information about brand purchases, coupon use, and television ad exposure

---

LO 4 Explain how sales managers evaluate salespeople and the personal-selling effort.

Measuring the performance of salespeople draws directly on the objectives set for the personal-selling process and sales objectives. Sales staff can be judged on several objective and subjective criteria. The objective criteria include quantifiable variables such as sales volume, profits or orders generated, and activities including sales calls and nonselling activities. Subjective criteria describe how a salesperson manages time and account relationships—for example, preparedness, product knowledge, and team relationships. Measurement of salespeople's performance provides a basis for evaluating the success of the overall personal-selling effort.

[Exhibit 15.2]
Performance Criteria for Salespeople

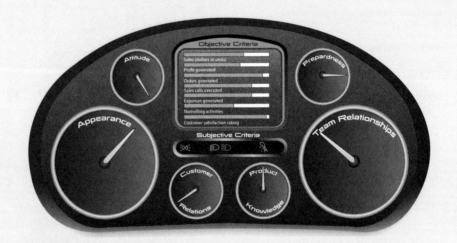

LO 5 Describe the process of evaluating the effectiveness of IMC campaigns.

One approach to measuring the effectiveness of the overall IMC program is to measure each of the promotional tools used in a campaign as if it were independent of the others. This fragmented approach fails to account for the synergies that are the hallmark of IMC campaigns. Another approach is to use single-source tracking measures, which identify the extent to which a sample of consumers potentially has been exposed to multiple promotional messages. A third alternative proposed by practitioners suggests measuring media exposures, product (brand) impressions, and personal contacts as a basis for determining the overall effect of an IMC program. However, measuring the interaction of all elements of the promotional mix elements is extremely complicated and may be beyond the methodological tools available at this time.

Use the skills you've learned in this chapter to complete the brand campaign card at the end of the book.

Visit CourseMate for PROMO at www.cengagebrain.com for additional study tools.

GLOSSARY TERMS

SWOT analysis assessment of the strengths, weaknesses, opportunities, and threats facing a firm and its brand, so that a strategy will capitalize on strengths and opportunities while avoiding or overcoming weaknesses and threats

brand promotion plan document that specifies the thinking, tasks, and timetable needed to conceive and implement the brand promotion effort

PLANNING A BRAND CAMPAIGN

Marketers and their agencies (see Chapters 2 and 8) engage in many activities to plan a successful brand campaign:

- Studying the firm's marketing plan to identify objectives and activities that will affect decisions about brand promotion

- Conducting SWOT analyses (see next page) to evaluate what promotional activities and messages are possible and desirable, given the resources and needs at hand

- Researching the target audience to identify messages that might be well received (see Chapters 5 and 7)

- Defining objectives for the campaign—for example, a desired level of sales, trial use, or awareness of the brand

- Identifying appropriate media for reaching the target audience in an integrated marketing campaign (see Chapters 1 and 9 through 14)

- Preparing a brand promotion plan (see next page), including objectives, budgets, activities, and schedules

- Creating brand promotion messages for each medium

- Testing messages and revising them as necessary to achieve promotional objectives (see Chapter 15)

- Measuring the effectiveness of the campaign (see Chapter 15) and adjusting media and messages if needed

To build a brand campaign, use a calendar to schedule the activities.

[Exhibit CIR16.1]
Brand Campaign Calendar

Time Period	Activities Scheduled
Month 1	
Month 2	
Month 3	
Month 4	
Month 5	
Month 6	
Month 7	
Month 8	
Month 9	
Month 10	
Month 11	
Month 12	

© Sean Prior/Shutterstock.

KEY QUESTIONS

- What message will best convey the brand's value proposition (see Chapter 4)?

- Who is in the brand's target audience (see Chapter 4)? What do we know about those potential and current customers?

- What media do people in our target audience use? Where do they encounter our brand or competitors' brands?

- Will the message we want to send be most effective in a particular format—for example, conveyed creatively on television or easily shared on the Internet?

- Are our brand message and brand promotion strategy legal and ethical (see Chapter 6)?

- Will customers in different geographic areas respond differently to our message (see Chapter 7)?

- How many times will the target audience need to be exposed to our message for us to meet our objectives? To reach that level of exposure, how should we schedule our message delivery?

- Will our sales force need training to present the new campaign message? If so, how much training?

- If our firm can't afford our original marketing plan, how can we achieve objectives on a tighter budget?

SWOT ANALYSIS

A **SWOT analysis** assesses four types of information:

1. *Strengths:* What advantages do the firm and its brand already possess, relative to other companies and brands?

2. *Weaknesses:* In what areas are the firm and its brand at a disadvantage, relative to other companies and brands?

3. *Opportunities:* What developments and needs in the market might be addressed by the firm's product line and brand? Opportunities may arise from changes in technology, laws, social norms, customer needs, or any other source of a new demand in the marketplace.

4. *Threats:* What changes in the market might make it harder for the firm and its brand to meet customer needs? The same areas of change that produce opportunities may also create threats.

After identifying and describing the strengths, weaknesses, opportunities, and threats facing the firm and its brand, planners develop objectives aimed at building on the strengths and opportunities while overcoming or avoiding the weaknesses and threats.

Applying SWOT analysis to brand promotion, marketers generally develop messages that emphasize the brand's strengths and downplay its weaknesses (although, as described in the opening story in Chapter 8, a creative message can sometimes have fun with weaknesses such as the high fat content of a company's sandwiches or the creepiness of its mascot). Also, marketers generally examine the target audience to find opportunities and threats that will help them define a relevant and convincing message.

BRAND PROMOTION PLAN

The **brand promotion plan** specifies the thinking, tasks, and timetable needed to conceive and implement the brand promotion effort. It describes the decisions made in planning the brand campaign. A complete plan contains all the elements shown in the following table.

[Exhibit CIR16.2]
Elements of a Brand Promotion Plan

Introduction	Summary of objectives and tactics for executing the plan
Situation analysis	Historical background and description of the industry, market, and competition
Objectives	Goals of the plan, stated specifically enough to indicate how to tell when the plan succeeded
Budget	Amount that each part of the plan is expected to cost
Strategy	Type of media and promotional tools to be used in achieving the objectives
Execution	Details about how the firm will carry out the plan, including responsibilities and deadlines
Evaluation	Methods to be used in measuring the outcome of the brand campaign and determining whether it succeeded or must be revised

GLOSSARY TERMS

public relations function that provides communications to foster goodwill between a firm and its constituent groups

publicity unpaid-for media exposure about a firm's activities or its products and services

proactive public relations strategy PR strategy that is dictated by marketing objectives, seeks publicity, and takes the offense

reactive public relations strategy PR strategy that is dictated by influences outside the company's control, focuses on solving problems, and requires defensive measures

public relations audit internal study that identifies aspects of the firm or its activities that are positive and newsworthy

public relations plan plan that identifies the objectives and activities of a firm's PR communications

influencer marketing series of personalized marketing techniques directed at individuals or groups with the credibility and capability to drive positive word-of-mouth in a market segment

social media websites where users create and share information about themselves, brands, and other mutual interests

buzz marketing creation of events or experiences that yield conversations that include the brand or product

viral marketing process of consumers marketing to consumers over the Internet through word-of-mouth

corporate advertising advertising intended to establish a favorable attitude toward a company as a whole

advocacy advertising advertising that attempts to influence public opinion about social, political, or environmental issues of concern to the advertiser

cause-related marketing marketing messages that identify corporate sponsorship of philanthropic activities

CHAPTER SUMMARY

LO 1

Discuss the role of public relations as part of a strategy for integrated marketing communication (IMC).

Public relations focuses on communications that can foster goodwill between a firm and constituent groups such as customers, stockholders, employees, government entities, and the general public. Businesses use PR activities to highlight positive events associated with the organization and to engage in damage control when adversity strikes. Public relations has entered a new era, as changing corporate demands and new techniques have fostered a bolder, more aggressive role for PR in IMC campaigns.

LO 2

Identify the objectives and tools of public relations.

An active PR effort can serve many objectives, such as building goodwill and counteracting negative publicity. Public relations activities also may be orchestrated to support the launch of new products or communicate with employees on matters of interest to them. The PR function also may be instrumental to the firm's lobbying efforts and in preparing executives to meet with the press. The primary tools of public relations are press releases, feature stories, company newsletters, interviews and press conferences, and participation in the firm's event sponsorship decisions and programs.

LO 3

Describe basic strategies for PR activities.

When companies perceive public relations as a source of opportunity for shaping public opinion, they are likely to pursue a proactive PR strategy. With a proactive strategy, a firm strives to build goodwill with key constituents via aggressive programs. The foundation for these proactive programs is a rigorous public relations audit and a comprehensive public relations plan. The plan should include an explicit statement of objectives to guide the overall effort. In many instances, however, PR activities take the form of damage control, which places the firm in a reactive mode. Although a reactive strategy may seem a contradiction in terms, organizations can be prepared to react to bad news. Organizations that understand their inherent vulnerabilities can prepare themselves to react quickly and effectively in the face of hostile publicity.

[Exhibit 13.1]
Components of a PR Plan

Situation analysis	Summary of information obtained from the public relations audit, often broken down by category, such as product performance or community activity
Program objectives	Objectives stemming from the current situation and set for both short-term and long-term opportunities; generally focus on reputation, such as the credibility of product performance (e.g., placing products in verified, independent tests) or the stature of the firm's research and development efforts (article in a prestigious trade publication)
Program rationale	Identification of the PR program's role relative to the other brand promotion efforts; articulates an integrated marketing communication perspective
Communications vehicles	Specification of the tools (e.g., press releases, interviews, newsletters) to be used to implement the PR plan
Message content	Development of the PR message based on research such as focus groups and in-depth interviews

green marketing corporate communication efforts to promote a cause or program in support of the environment

LO 4 **Summarize how companies use influencer marketing programs.**

Given that consumers are predisposed to talk about brands and what they say is vital to the well-being of those brands, it is no surprise that marketers are pursuing strategies to influence the conversation. Influencer marketing refers to tools and techniques directed at driving positive word-of-mouth about a brand. In professional programs, important gatekeepers may be a focal point. Peer-to-peer programs look for the connectors who spread influential messages. In both types of program, the marketer is challenged to give the influencers a meaningful or provocative topic that they will want to talk about.

LO 5 **Describe how marketers use social media to promote brands.**

Social media are websites where users create and share information. Examples include social-networking sites, works-sharing sites, blogs, and microblogging (Twitter). To engage in brand communication via social media, marketers need to enter a community conversation that includes listening as well as transmitting messages. They can shape conversations by creating venues, seeking feedback, providing valued information, and crafting messages that are simple enough to convey accurately. Often, marketers' use of social media is aimed at creating buzz and stimulating viral marketing.

[Exhibit 13.3]
New Brand Relationships with Social Media

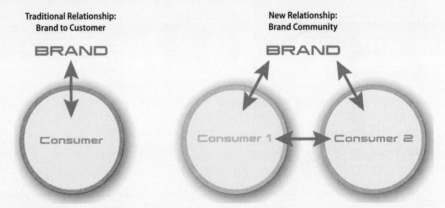

LO 6 **Discuss the applications and objectives of corporate advertising.**

Corporate advertising, rather than supporting an organization's specific brands, aims to build the general reputation of the organization in the eyes of key constituents. This form of advertising serves goals such as enhancing the firm's image and building credibility for its line of products. Corporate advertising also may serve the objectives of improving employee morale, building shareholder confidence, or denouncing competitors. Corporate ad campaigns may take the form of image advertising, advocacy advertising, or cause-related advertising. Corporate advertising may be orchestrated in such a way as to be newsworthy, so it must be carefully coordinated with the organization's PR programs.

Use the skills you've learned in this chapter to get started on the brand campaign card at the end of the book.

Visit CourseMate for PROMO at www.cengagebrain.com for additional study tools.